CHRISTIANITY
AND THE
RENAISSANCE

Entrance to the fifteenth-century cloister of San Lorenzo, Florence, from the public square, showing Medici coats of arms. Photo Alinari/Art Resource, N.Y.

CHRISTIANITY
AND THE
RENAISSANCE

Image and Religious Imagination
in the Quattrocento

Edited by
TIMOTHY VERDON
and JOHN HENDERSON

SYRACUSE UNIVERSITY PRESS

Copyright © 1990 by SYRACUSE UNIVERSITY PRESS
Syracuse, New York 13244-5160
All Rights Reserved

First Edition 1990

94   93   92   91   90   6   5   4   3   2   1

Published with the assistance of the Getty Grant Program.

This book has been supported by a grant from the National Endowment for the Humanities, an independent federal agency.

This book is published with the assistance of a grant from the Samuel H. Kress Foundation.

The paper used in this publication meets the minimum requirements of American National Standard for Information Sciences — Permanence of Paper for Printed Library Materials, ANSI Z39.48-1984. ∞™

Library of Congress Cataloging-in-Publication Data

Christianity and the Renaissance : image and religious imagination in
        the Quattrocento / edited by Timothy Verdon and John Henderson. —
        1st ed.
                p.   cm.
        Includes bibliographies and index.
        ISBN 0-8156-2414-X (alk. paper). — ISBN 0-8156-2456-5 (pbk. :
alk. paper)
                1. Christian art and symbolism—Renaissance, 1450-1600—Italy.
        2. Catholic Church and Art.   I. Verdon, Timothy.   II. Henderson,
        John, 1949–
        N7952.A1C47   1990
        704.9′482′0945—dc19   89-30918
                                                                                    CIP

Manufactured in the United States of America

CONTENTS

Part Three: **THE WORLD OF THE CHRISTIAN HUMANIST**

Part Four: **CODA ON METHOD**

ILLUSTRATIONS

TABLES

FIGURES

PREFACE

THE STUDIES PRESENTED in this volume are intended for students of Italian Renaissance history and art. They explore, from a range of viewpoints, the relationship between religious belief, as manifest in various institutional and private forms in fifteenth-century Italy, and the expressive means by which Renaissance Italians articulated what they believed. It is the editors' and authors' hope that these studies may contribute to the ongoing process of redefinition of the civilization of the Renaissance and offer insights into the more fundamental issue of the role of religious faith in the evolution of Western culture.

The essays that comprise this volume, together with others already published in *Arte lombarda* and elsewhere (see the bibliographical note at the end of this preface), grew out of a symposium held in America and Italy in the spring and summer of 1985, which in turn may be said to have developed in four stages. In the immediate background were the 1980 symposium "Monasticism and the Arts" and its related exhibition, "Monastic Themes in Renaissance Art," at Yale and in Washington, D.C. Parallel to their examination of the art and life of religious orders was new research into lay spirituality and confraternities by historians associated with the Harvard Center in Florence and by others. A third aspect of the project developed out of the documentation of Lombard monuments, which offered a particularly coherent illustration of the connection between monastic reform and the art and architecture in one major center of Renaissance culture — Milan and its environs. Finally, the Cattedra di Storia della Miniatura e delle Arti Minori (Dipartimento di Studi sul Medioevo e Rinascimento) of the Università di Firenze, in cataloguing and interpreting objects of liturgical and "popular" religious art, provided an ideal accompaniment to the themes discussed in *Christianity and the Renaissance:* an exhibit at the Biblioteca Nazionale Centrale di Firenze of woodcut illustrations of the writings of Fra Girolamo Savonarola. Several of these woodcuts have been reproduced in the present volume.

The eight days of the 1985 symposium involved presentations by more than forty scholars, the participation of fifteen invited commentators, three exhibits, liturgical celebrations, the performance of Renaissance music and drama, and *in situ* study. In light of this formal and thematic diversity, it has not been practical or desirable to combine the many aspects of the symposium into a single publication. Several of the papers presented have now appeared in learned journals, usually to fulfill previous commitments made by the authors, and are not included here. A list of these and other publications connected with the project is given in the bibliographical note following.

In the same spirit, it seemed best to present the Lombard portion of the symposium in a separate publication. Like the exhibits, the papers on monastic history and art in Lombardy were conceived with the audience's direct experience of the "originals" in mind; during the symposium, they were given in conjunction with a weekend tour of five of the sites studied. And although no printed text can recapture the immediacy of those discussions amid the beauty of lakeside cloisters, their presentation in *Arte Lombarda* has the advantage of situating them in a proper frame.

An undertaking of the breadth of *Christianity and the Renaissance* is the work of many people; it would be difficult to name all who have provided help and encouragement. Special acknowledgment is clearly due, however, to the late archbishop Giovanni Fallani, President of the Pontifical Commission for Religious Art in Italy, who brought the symposium the greetings of Pope John Paul II; his death three years ago was deeply felt by all who knew him. Special thanks are due also to several other key individuals and institutions, among them Bishop Keith J. Symons, of the Diocese of Pensacola–Tallahassee; the Honorable George Firestone, Secretary of State of Florida; H. E. Rinaldo Petrignani, Ambassador of Italy to the United States; the Honorable Frederick Hassett, Consul-General of the United States to Florence at the time of the symposium; the late Honorable Lando Conti, tragically assassinated in 1986, who was Mayor of Florence at the time of the symposium; Professor Eugenio Garin, President of the Istituto Nazionale di Studi sul Rinascimento; Professor Craig Hugh Smyth, then Director

of Villa I Tatti; Dr. Giorgio Bonsanti, Director of the Museo di San
Marco; Dr. Anna Lenzuni, Director of the Biblioteca Nazionale Cen-
trale di Firenze; Dr. Anthony Janson, Curator of the European Art
Collection at the Ringling Museum in Sarasota; Mr. A. C. Viebranz,
Assistant Director of the National Gallery of Art, Washington, D.C.;
and Allys Palladino Craig, Director of the Florida State University Art
Gallery.

TIMOTHY VERDON
The Florida State University
Department of Art History

JOHN HENDERSON
Wolfson College, Cambridge

MARIA LUISA GATTI PERER
Dipartimento di Studi Medioevali e Umanistici
Università Cattolica, Milano

MARIA GRAZIA CIARDI DUPRÉ DAL POGGETTO
Dipartimento di Studi sul Medioevo e Rinascimento
Università di Firenze

BIBLIOGRAPHICAL NOTE

Papers given at the symposium, either in Florida or in Florence, and
not published in this volume include Piero Morselli, "Immagini di cera
votive in Sta. Maria delle Carceri di Prato nella prima metà del '500,"
in A. Morrogh, F. Superbi Gioffredi, P. Morselli, E. Borsook, eds.,
Renaissance Studies in Honor of Craig Hugh Smyth, 2 vols. (Florence: Giunti
Barbera, 1985), 2:327–40; John Henderson, "Society and Religion in
Renaissance Florence," in *Historical Journal* 29 (1986): 213–25; Diane Cole
Ahl, "Benozzo Gozzoli's Frescoes of the Life of St. Augustine in S.
Gimignano: Their Meaning in Context," in *Artibus et Historiae* 13 (VII)
(1986): 35–53; Rona Goffen, "S. Giobbe and Altar Egos," in *Artibus et
Historiae* 14 (VII) (1986): 57–70; Charles Trinkaus, "Italian Humanism
and Scholastic Theology," in Albert Rabil, ed., *Renaissance Humanism:
Foundation, Forms, and Legacy*, 3 vols. (Philadelphia: University of Penn-
sylvania Press, 1988), 3:327–48; and five articles in *Arte lombarda* 76/77
(1986): Patrizia Barbara, "Un'Adorazione quattrocentesca nella chiesa

milanese di Sta. Maria Bianca in Casoretto," 57–61; Alessandra Galizzi, "La riforma amadeita e Sta. Maria in Bressanoro: Un'episodio all'interno dell'Osservanza francescana," 62–67; Adriano Frattini, "La Congregazione di Sta. Giustina in S. Pietro in Gessate di Milano: la cappella di Sant'Antonio Abate," 68–78; Marco Rossi, "L'Osservanza domenicana a Milano: Vincenzo Bandello e l'iconografia della beatitudine nella cupola di Sta. Maria delle Grazie," 79–88; Alessandro Rovetta, "Sta. Maria delle Grazie a Gravedona e la cultura osservante nell'Alto Lario," 89–99.

PERMISSION ACKNOWLEDGMENTS

Permission to use the following illustrations is gratefully acknowledged:

Alinari/Art Resource, N.Y.: Frontispiece; Figures 10–11, 1.2, 2.1, 3.1, 3.2, 5.1, 5.2, 5.3, 5.4, 5.5, 5.6, 5.7, 5.8, 5.11, 5.12, 5.13, 5.14, 7.1, 10.1, 10.2, 11.1, 12.2, 12.3, 13.3, 13.4, 13.6, 16.1, 18.1, 19.1, 20.2, 20.3, 20.5, 22.3, 22.4, 22.5, 22.6, 22.8, 22.9, 22.11, 22.12, 22.13, 23.1

Amministrazione Provinciale della Toscana: Figure 14.1

Archivio di Stato, Florence: Figure 13.5

Biblioteca Apostolica Vaticana: Figures 4.4, 4.7, 4.10, 4.11, 13.7

Biblioteca Capitolare, Lucca: Figure 13.2

Bowes Museum, Barnard Castle, County Durham, U.K.: Figure 6.12

The British Library: Figure 15.5

Budapest Museum of Fine Arts: Figure 6.10

Florence, Biblioteca Medicea Laurenziana: Figure 8.1

Florence, Biblioteca Nazionale Centrale: Cover; Figures 1.1, 2.2, 9.1, 15.1, 15.2, 15.4, 15.6, 15.7, 20.1, 20.4, 20.6, 21.1, 21.2

Frick Art Reference Library: Figure 6.8

Gabinetto fotografico, Soprintendenza Beni artistici e storici di Firenze: Figures 4.2, 4.3, 4.5, 4.6, 4.8, 4.9, 6.14, 6.15, 6.16, 6.17, 13.1, 13.8

National Gallery of Art, Washington, DC, Rosenwald Collection: Figure 15.3

National Gallery of Victoria, Melbourne: Figure 6.13

Paris, Louvre: Figure 22.7

Pasadena, Norton Simon Foundation: Figure 6.2

Pisa, Museo Nazionale di San Matteo: Figures 4.1, 13.9

San Sepolcro, Pinacoteca: Figure 11.2

Siena, Pinacoteca. Foto Soprintendenza B.A.S.: Figures 6.1, 6.3, 6.4, 6.5, 6.6, 6.7, 6.11

Soprintendenza Beni Ambientali del Friuli, Venezia Guilia, Trieste: Figure 22.10

Vatican, Pinacoteca: Figures 6.9, 22.2

TIMOTHY VERDON is professor of art history at Florida State University, assigned to Florida's Study Center in Florence. He is the author of *The Art of Guido Mazzoni* (1978) and of articles on Masaccio, Donatello, Leonardo da Vinci, and Bramante. He is also the editor of *Monasticism and the Arts* (Syracuse University Press, 1985) and of *L'Arte e la Bibbia: immagine come esegesi biblica* (Milan: A. Pizzi, forthcoming).

JOHN HENDERSON is Fellow of Wolfson College, Cambridge, and director of a research project at the University of London examining plague in early modern Europe. He is the author of a forthcoming monograph on lay piety and charity in Renaissance Florence, has edited a volume of essays on charity and the poor in Italy and England, and is the author of a series of articles on religion, welfare provision for the poor, and plague in Renaissance Italy.

CHRISTIANITY
AND THE
RENAISSANCE

CHRISTIANITY, THE RENAISSANCE, AND THE STUDY OF HISTORY

Environments of Experience and Imagination

TIMOTHY VERDON

F OR MOST OF THE LAST 130 years, any close association of the terms *Christianity* and *the Renaissance* would have seemed contradictory, a pairing of opposites. Jacob Burckhardt, the writer who more than any other shaped our concept of Renaissance life, put religion last; his *Civilisation of the Renaissance in Italy,* written in the 1850s, discussed "the State," "the Individual," "the Revival of Antiquity," "the Discovery of the World and Man," and "Society and Festivals" before exploring "Morality and Religion," and that chapter in turn ended with reflections on "ancient and modern superstition" and "the general disintegration of belief." Nor are such views surprising from a man of Burckhardt's time and circumstances. Born in the same year as Karl Marx — 1818, exactly forty years after the death of Voltaire — Burckhardt had turned to historical research from preparation for the ministry. Like Marx, he witnessed the social and political upheavals of Europe in 1848. Indeed, Burckhardt's vision of the past, like Marx's vision of the future, appealed precisely because of its revolutionary modernity. His portrait of Italian Renaissance Catholicism as subjective, tolerant, and skeptical — "an affair of the individual and of his own personal feeling" — pointed beyond the liberal Protestantism of Burckhardt's time to the "post-Christian" spirit of ours. Down to the final sentence of his book, Jacob Burckhardt insisted that "the Italian Renaissance must be called the mother of our modern age."[1]

It has been the particular merit of recent scholarship to qualify such attitudes, especially those regarding the revival of antiquity and the vitality of traditional Christian practices. Where Burckhardt, for example, read Lorenzo de' Medici's assertion that "without Plato it would be hard to be a good Christian or a good citizen" as the manifesto of a humanist counterculture,[2] modern historians give more weight to the stated objects of the phrase "to be a good Christian" and "a good citizen." "Christian humanism" and "civic humanism" are recent and important additions to the area of Renaissance study.[3] So, too, in the history of art; where "Renaissance iconography" once meant almost exclusively analysis of antique literary and visual sources, scholars are now exploring the meaning of those religious works that in quantity alone continued to constitute the bulk of what Renaissance artists made and the public saw.[4]

The present volume came into being in this changed climate and takes Christianity and the Renaissance as equal coefficients. Indeed, the phrasing of our title is significant; to have called this collection "Christianity *in* the Renaissance," or "Renaissance Christianity," would have suggested subordination — of the ancient religious system to an intellectual and artistic movement in the first case, or of the astonishing vitality of this movement to established religion in the second. It was a question here, as in all areas of historical interpretation, of weighing tradition against innovation: of evaluating the respective influence of things that had always been and things that were new. For Renaissance studies the issue is critical, since imbalance in either direction not only distorts but tends to negate the object of study. Burckhardt's Renaissance, isolated in modernity from its medieval Christian past, risks turning into caricature, but an entirely medievalist reading of the data can raise doubts that there was ever a distinctive "Renaissance" at all. This book sees the historical reality as more subtle: an equilibrium of stimuli — precarious, but at the same time dynamic in its tension between continuity and change. "To be a good Christian" remained a central existential goal of the Renaissance, but Plato could help achieve it.

The breadth of interests suggested by our title also requires explanation. *Christianity* as used here means more than *Christendom,* the old term for the politico-social unit comprised by believing Western peoples, and much more than *the Church,* or *Christian theology.* The narrow concerns of ecclesiastical history and the history of dogma do not

coincide with the scope of this volume, which aims at a more panoramic view of Renaissance religious experience. For within such special-
ized categories of research it is impossible to assess the force of the
"official" statements of polity and belief which are their subject; a more
fluid and variegated picture emerges, albeit imperfectly, from a wider
range of sources. One object of *Christianity and the Renaissance,* therefore, is to sketch the existential context—to propose a coherent notion
of what Lorenzo de' Medici and his contemporaries understood when
they aspired to be good Christians. The term *Christianity,* that is to say,
is used anthropologically; it denotes a total systemic reality: what students of comparative religion call *le spirituel vécu* ("spiritual experience
as it was really lived"), and what Annales historians call a *mentalité* (that
is, the reconstruction of a specific sensibility as the context for social
and artistic expression).

This approach arises from a conviction that the historical study
of religious culture in any age is more than a subcategory of the history of ideas—just as religious belief in individuals is more than a function of intellect. In individuals and in societies, deep religious faith is
a matter of practice rather than theory, even though in successive stages
it may come to be articulated in theoretical language. Christianity in
particular has always stressed the preeminence of experience. The early
Church presented Christ as "something . . . that we have heard, and
we have seen with our own eyes, that we have watched and touched
with our own hands: the Word, who is life . . . made visible" (1 John
1:1–2). The early Christian development of signs and rites incarnated
this belief, for sacraments and liturgy involve the whole person: "they
are not purely religious or merely rational or intellectual exercises, but
also human experiences calling on all human faculties: body, mind, senses,
imagination, emotions, memory."[5]

Because of this experiential model of church life, a crucial task
of organized religion in every age has been the creation of settings in
which believers may "hear" and "see" and "touch" the object of faith—
settings that have been called "symbolic environments." The rise of
monasticism in the patristic era and earlier Middle Ages, for example,
furnished devout Christians with an efficacious "environment" in which
to symbolize religious commitment—one that would endure in influence
through the later Middle Ages and early Renaissance, in the revitalized

monastic life of the mendicant orders.[6] In late medieval Europe, however, new contexts of religious experience were taking shape: the pious confraternities and *compagnie* that flourished under the impetus of Franciscan and Dominican spirituality from the trecento to the Council of Trent. These privileged devotional environments allowed their members to touch sacred realities through liturgical, penitential, and charitable activities formerly reserved for the clergy. There is a parallel in fifteenth-century Italian painting, where devices such as linear perspective and correct anatomical rendering made sacred history a credible extension of the viewer's individual experience.

The absolute novelty in the Renaissance—the mutant gene in the organism, as it were—was the love of classical learning. Yet it would be simplistic to "oppose" this antiquarian revival to traditional religion, and modern scholarship in fact has affirmed the shared goals of quattrocento humanists and religious thinkers. Monastic reform movements such as the Dominican Osservanza are now seen as having arisen from an interest in early Christian ascetical texts comparable to the humanists' fascination with pagan philosophy and literature: two aspects of a common taste for antiquity. The emphasis, it appears, was on a reciprocity of experience, in which Christians used the ancient classics not as an alternative to traditional religion but as a powerful formal vehicle through which to express their faith.[7] A similar pattern can be seen in Renaissance art, where Greco-Roman form was used to deepen the emotional resonance of Christian subject matter. Leonardo da Vinci's eloquent use of gesture in the *Last Supper*, for example, may reflect a knowledge of humanist drama (Figure I). The obscure plots and Latin texts of classicizing plays would have called on Renaissance actors to develop a repertory of mimed reactions more expressive than those in conventional religious drama, in order to communicate unfamiliar content. Artists could then reapply these insights to traditional religious themes with revolutionary effect.[8]

It was traditional Christianity, however, with its ingrained patterns of thought and emotional response, that furnished the raw material upon which the impress of the new could be received. When Leonardo painted his *Last Supper* in a Dominican monastery in Milan, Catholic Christianity had been the official religion of Italy for almost

FIGURE I. Leonardo Da Vinci, *Last Supper*, Milan, Santa Maria delle Grazie, refectory. Detail. Photo Alinari/Art Resource, N.Y.

twelve centuries, since the emperor Constantine recognized it in an edict issued from the same city. Humanist ideas were perhaps "in the air," much as existentialism may be said to color later twentieth-century thought, but the weight of ancient religious tradition was in the blood: bred into the bones of men and women who from cradle to grave heard Scripture readings and interpretive sermons, took part in prescribed rites, and daily saw paintings and statues of Christ, Mary, and the saints. Ineluctably, traditional Christianity was the matrix of experience, the prism in which Renaissance man would seek a focus for his feelings. And this was probably the case irrespective of personal piety, for in cultures permeated by religious tradition individuals need not be fully conscious of the meaning of the symbols of faith around them. Symbols deliver their message and fulfil their function even when their meaning escapes awareness.[9]

FAITH AND KNOWLEDGE

The topics treated in this volume, and their arrangement, seek to re-capture that world of experience — to reassemble its scaffolding of interlocking social and individual reaction. Implicit in this effort are ideas about the function and possibilities of cultural history as an activity, ideas that have enjoyed a distinguished career in our century. Foremost among them is what might be called the *visualizational principle:* the concept articulated by Johan Huizinga, of history writing as "morphology," in which past events are rendered comprehensible less through causal connections than by arrangement of the facts in a meaningful pattern. The heart of this approach is a student's capacity for "historical contact," a kind of presentiment (*Ahnung*) of the internal dynamics of events. Writing in the 1920s, Huizinga said:

> This not completely reduceable contact with the past is entry into an atmosphere, it is one of the many forms of reaching beyond oneself, of experiencing truth, which are given to man. It is not an esthetic enjoyment, a religious emotion, an awe of nature, a metaphysical recognition — and yet it is a figure in this series. . . . This contact with the past, which is accompanied by an utter conviction of genuineness and truth, can be evoked by a line from a document or a chronicle, by a print, by a few notes of an old song. It is not an element that the writer infuses in his work by using certain words. It lies beyond the book of history, not in it. The reader brings it to the writer, it is his response to the writer's call.[10]

In the 1940s, Henri Focillon advanced a related idea with regard to the history of art. To explain formal correspondences between objects made centuries apart, Focillon predicated the existence of "spiritual families" unbound by time. In his view, natural predilections can align themselves along "axes of affinity": an artist is necessarily a member of his own generation, but "he is also a contemporary of the spiritual group to which he belongs," dwelling among ancestors of his own choosing. Focillon was chiefly concerned with the Middle Ages, but his ideas have obvious appeal for students of the Italian Renaissance.[11]

Perhaps the most persuasive statement of this approach is the metaphor elaborated by Focillon's former student George Kubler, of historical knowledge as comprised of "signals" from "senders" to "receivers," often across such vast expanses of time and space as to put the historian in the posture of an astronomer, who experiences in a given present the "light" generated by events from the distant past. For Kubler, the historian is one who can see patterns, who can discern a shape in constellations and with a name reveal them to his fellows. Or again, the historian is a portraitist of time: "he transposes, reduces, composes and colors a facsimile, like a painter, who in his search for the identity of the subject must discover a patterned set of properties that will elicit recognition all while conveying a new perception of the subject." And Kubler's historian proceeds by a kind of faith: "these processes of [historical] change are all mysterious, uncharted regions. . . . The clues to guide us are very few indeed: perhaps the jottings and sketches of architects and artists, put down in the heat of imagining a form, or the manuscript *brouillons* of poets and musicians, crisscrossed with erasures and corrections, are the hazy coastlines of this dark continent of the 'now.'"[12]

The cognitive phenomenon described in these passages depends less upon quantity of information than on the mode of knowing brought to bear. It is analogous to what contemporary epistemologists call 'personal' or 'participatory knowledge': a vision of the "whole" capable of giving organic meaning to the "parts," a vision arising from direct or sympathetic immersion in the process or phenomenon in question. This is a preliminary vision of meaning similar to Platonic 'remembering' or Augustinian 'infused knowledge', into which fragmentary factual data can be fitted as they become available, like stones in a structure whose general shape the builder already imagines. It seems at the furthest remove from modern "scientific method." Yet, as Michael Polanyi has argued, scientific discovery itself normally depends upon just such a preliminary "act of faith" to direct experimentation and integrate data toward the intermittently glimpsed result.[13]

This noetic mechanism has special relevance for studies of religion and culture. In religious consciousness generally, and in the Judeo-Christian tradition in particular, preliminary "knowledge" of spiritual realities arising from faith is at once the end of and means toward perfect understanding. "Nisi credideritis, non intelligetis" is how the Vulgate translated Isaiah 7:9: "Unless you believe, you will not [be able to] understand." It is the most basic principle of Christian epistemology; Augustine explicitly invoked it to make the point that, in matters pertaining to divinity, one comes to know first by believing the testimonies of trustworthy witnesses, only afterward arriving at a measure of intellectual understanding.[14] In the same way, Anselm of Canterbury opened his *Proslogion* with the assurance that "I do not seek to understand so that I may believe, but I believe in order to understand"; elsewhere he argued that right order requires us to believe the deep things of the Christian faith before we undertake to discuss them by reason.[15] Even the empiricism of fifteenth-century humanists could serve this "fiduciary" principle: in his beautiful sermon on the mystery of the Eucharist, Lorenzo Valla affirmed that the sacrament is not a matter of knowledge but one of faith. He reasoned that we believe God by faith in the same way as we believe a friend whose truthfulness we have previously experienced; Valla found that faith in God and faith in friends have a common basis, inasmuch as they both rest on experience and trust rather than on "objective" knowledge.[16]

The point is simple: if as historians we seek to understand *what* the past knew or thought or felt, we must make the effort to understand it *as* the past knew it and thought it and felt it. This is not magical—a kind of intellectual time machine—since obviously we also necessarily know past events from the viewpoint of our own particular present. But to try at least to establish something like Huizinga's "historical contact" does seem an essential task of cultural history. If we "process" medieval and early Renaissance data through twentieth-century "systems," a future generation of historians will find that—like Burckhardt—we have merely refashioned the Renaissance in our own image. We need a Renaissance "system" or mentalité; or, to adapt New Testament language, we must "put on the mind" of the Christian age we want to study if we wish to understand its cultural products.[17]

That this is theoretically possible is the premise of modern comparative religion studies, which focus on the structures informing historical myth-systems and organized religions. And that Christianity as a specific system can be understood in this way is affirmed by the same writers who insist on the primacy of faith. Anselm gave his *Proslogion* a title intended to describe the typical Christian approach to religious knowledge: *fides quaerens intellectum* ("faith seeking understanding"), and offered another of his writings as a "an example of meditating on the logic of faith."[18] While possible, however, it is not easy to "put on the mind" of a past religious culture; the "logic of faith" is neither linear nor Aristotelian—neither what the modern mind considers logical nor what ancient thought could readily accommodate. "Jews call for miracles, Greeks look for wisdom," Paul told the believers in Corinth, "but we proclaim Christ—yes, Christ nailed to the cross; and this is a stumbling block to Jews and folly to Greeks, yet to those who have heard his call . . . he is the power of God and the wisdom of God" (1 Cor. 1:22–24).

The most basic challenge to historians of religious culture is to articulate for those who may not have "heard the call" the patterned set of properties which made it seem wise to those who did. In the context of their particular expertise, historians must plausibly reconstruct the believer's "grammar of assent," so that the enormous vocabulary of facts accumulated by archival and archeological research can be arranged in configurations that would be recognizable to the people whose lives furnished the data. The importance of this integrative approach is especially clear for the history of art, since religious artifacts are concrete expressions of the beliefs that shape lives. But where a Renaissance artist could take lived faith-experience for granted—his creative process presupposing a correlative re-creative process in his public—modern historians have to feel their way back into that way of "seeing things," cautiously reassembling the apparatus of imagination which first gave plastic and pictorial images their power to stir feeling and elicit response. Nevertheless, only such a grasp of the specific emotional gravity of their subject allows scholars to analyze the relationship between form and content central to the creative process.

Taken together, the studies that comprise this volume elucidate the "logic" of early Renaissance faith—the "foolish wisdom" of Christian life in fourteenth-, fifteenth-, and early sixteenth-century Italy. They illustrate the changing role of conventual life, the spirituality of lay men and women, and the Christian character of Renaissance humanism. In no sense, however, are these essays put forward as a comprehensive survey of the subject. Rather, as in an artist's working sketch, certain aspects are developed, others barely suggested; the resulting picture is uneven. Thus, before discussing the individual chapters and their organization in the book, it will be helpful to "work up" the background of the environments or "worlds" in which the style of Renaissance Christianity took shape; such is the task of the following sections of this introduction.

FAITH AND HUMAN FEELINGS

The Christian life and art of the Italian Renaissance arose from a fundamental shift in European religious consciousness first apparent in the twelfth century. This was a movement away from the theologized, "objective" piety of the patristic era and earlier Middle Ages toward increasingly interior expressions of religious sentiment—the "affective" or emotional pietism we associate with the thirteenth, fourteenth, and fifteenth centuries. This transformation, marked by the desire for a felt rather than a reasoned faith, gave rise to a spiritual climate of tender inwardness. At the same time, drawing on currents in medieval Byzantine spirituality, it inclined toward violent, even lurid, religious sensations. These contradictory but inseparable tendencies constituted the dual tradition on which preachers and artists would rely for reactions of empathy among their public.[19]

Two illustrations from religious literature will suggest the distance between the older mode of knowing and the new sensibility. Both are classic texts on the Passion by major writers: the hymn *Vexilla regis* by the patristic poet Venantius Fortunatus (c. 530–609) and the sermon on Mary at Calvary by Bernard of Clairvaux (1090–1153). The patristic hymn develops the paradox of crucifixion as exaltation: Christ's being "lifted up" on the cross adumbrates his future "rising in glory." The opening words introduce the metaphor: the cross is a "royal standard" (*vexilla regis*), advancing in triumph over human mortality. Venantius Fortunatus's language and style are rhetorical, to a degree, and rich in classical and biblical allusions. He never passes up an opportunity to spell out the doctrinal meaning of the event: "Life [i.e., Christ] endured death," he tells us, and hastens to add, "and by his death procured us life." Narrative is theologized: "From the wound opened by a cruel lance poured forth water and blood, *to cleanse us from the stain of our sins.*" Even when he passes from his "royal standard" metaphor to an earthier image, the poet is unwilling to treat it naturalistically. "O beauteous tree and radiant," he exclaims, "adorned with royal purple; precious wood, found worthy to touch [Christ's] sacred limbs. Blessed tree, on whose branches hung the ransom of the world—happy beam, that weighed the sacred body, cheating Tartarus of its prey."[20]

By contrast, the twelfth-century writer eschews both theology and metaphor, carrying his listener straight to the human core of the Passion. Bernard acknowledges and goes beyond the "cruel lance which opened Christ's side and would not spare him death," to ponder how Mary, the mother of Jesus, must have *felt* as she watched him die. In a remarkably modern way, the saint interprets the enigmatic prophecy that a sword would pierce Mary's heart as foretelling psychological anguish. He does not offer the standard doctrinal readings of Christ's last words from the cross but, addressing Mary directly, calls them "a sword thrust that pierced your soul and touched the quick." And then, as if to explain how he arrived at this interpretation, Bernard insists that "these words *must* have pierced your loving soul, since just to recall them breaks our hearts, hard and stony though they be." That is, he projects back onto a scriptural personage his own spontaneous emotional reaction, locking Mary, himself, and his listeners in an identity of human feeling.[21]

Then, in what is surely one of the most amazing passages in medieval literature, Bernard faces the question raised by his own emotionalism, the question on which the new religious sensibility will in fact hinge. If Mary (and by extension any Christian) truly believes Christ's promise to rise from the dead, should she not be able to transcend suffering? Are not fear and desire incompatible with perfect faith? As if concerned that some in his monastic audience may hold this "anesthetic" view, Bernard interrupts his dialogue with Mary in order to address his hearers:

> Do not marvel, brethren, that Mary is said to have endured martyrdom in her soul. Only he will marvel who forgets what Paul said of the Gentiles, that among their worst vices was that they were without compassion. Not so with Mary! May it never be so with those who venerate her. Someone will say: "Did she not know in advance that her son would die?" Without a doubt. "Did she not have sure hope in his immediate resurrection?" Full confidence indeed. "Did she then grieve when he was crucified?" Intensely. Who are you, brother, and what sort of judge-

ment is yours, that you marvel at the grief of Mary any more than that
the Son of Mary should suffer? Could he die bodily and she not share
his death in her heart? Love it was that moved him to suffer death, love
greater than that of any man before or since: love too moved Mary, the
like of which no mother has ever known.[22]

Thus Bernard of Clairvaux, often portrayed as an enemy of
the sensory side of religious experience, stands at the head of a tradition in Western spirituality which would have incalculable influence
upon the visual arts. The charmingly human Madonnas with their jo-
cund or solemn infants, the bleeding Christs and plangent Pietàs that
make up so great a part of fourteenth- and fifteenth-century sculpture
and painting all owe a debt to Bernard and to the wider Cistercian
influence.[23]

There is a figure still more important, however, whose name
has always and properly been linked to the beginnings of Italian Renaissance art: St. Francis of Assisi (1182–1226). It was Francis who took
the new sensibility to the people. Where Bernard had written and
preached chiefly for other monks, Francis acted out his embarrassing
feelings in country roads and city squares: poignant empathy with the
sufferings of Christ, lyrical veneration for Mary, and a rhapsodic joy
in the beauty of nature. More than any other man or woman in Christian history, he captured the imagination of his age. The thousands who
followed him as friars in his lifetime, and the tens of thousands who
in successive generations embraced Franciscan ideals as layfolk— in the
Third Order and later in confraternities and pious sodalities— spread
the religious consciousness of which Francis himself was both product
and promoter, in song and sermon, liturgy and play.[24]

The impact of the Franciscan movement upon early Italian painting is especially striking. Again, examples will help make the point:
two monumental Tuscan crosses that originally hung over altars and
now are exhibited in museums in Florence and San Gimignano. The
older cross (Figure 2), painted about the time of Francis's birth, might
be taken to illustrate the religious attitude we noted in Venantius Fortunatus's hymn: objective, impassive, avoiding naturalistic rendering of
the event in favor of symbolism. It belongs to an iconographical type
known as the *Christus triumphans;* crosses of this kind sometimes showed

Figure 2. Unknown artist, painted cross. Florence, Uffizi Gallery. Photo Alinari/Art Resource, N.Y.

Christ draped in royal robes and wearing a kingly diadem in place of the crown of thorns. The emotionless, floating Christ-figure embodies a theological assertion about the glory achieved through suffering, rather than suffering itself.[25]

In the second cross, painted by Coppo di Marcovaldo in the decades following Francis's death, serenity gives way to an immediacy of feeling awful to behold (Figures 3 and 4). Coppo's use of hyperbole has been described by Frederick Hartt: "the closed eyes are treated as two fierce, dark, hooked slashes, the pale mouth quivers against the sweat-soaked locks of the beard, the hair writhes like snakes against the tormented body."[26] Clearly, this is no timeless symbol but the raw wound of physical pain held up to our gaze. Like Mary in Bernard's sermon, the viewer here is expected to "grieve . . . intensely." Indeed, this dramatic involvement in the human dynamics of sacred history is the principal Franciscan contribution to late medieval religious sensibility. "Heed all these things as though you were present," urged the author of the great Franciscan devotional tract, *Meditations on the Life of Christ,* written about the time of Coppo's painted cross.[27] Another of the early Franciscan writers, the poet and playwright Jacopone da Todi, supplied the response: in Jacopone's *lauda drammatica* of the Passion, the actor playing Mary at the foot of the cross keens, "Figlio, figlio, figlio, figlio amoroso giglio" — "O Son, Son, Son, My Son, lovesome lily, who will counsel my heart in anguish?"[28]

These developments in the arts, and the new importance of monumental plastic and pictorial art in general in the fourteenth and fifteenth centuries, were more than by-products of later medieval spirituality. The vivid communication of spiritual insights was, on the contrary, central to the new consciousness for which Francis was so eloquent a spokesman. One might say that the saint himself was the first Franciscan artist: Francis's vocation had been given when Christ spoke to him from a painted cross, telling the young saint to "Go, rebuild my Church" (Figure 5).[29] This "speaking cross," which can still be seen in Assisi, is very similar to the pre-Franciscan cross discussed above, although less fine in execution. Standing before the artistically inferior relic with its stiff figure of Christ, one cannot help wondering how Francis got a message out of such a painting. Clearly he had great faith. And that is the point: what the saint was privileged to "see" in spite

Figure 3. Coppo di Marcovaldo, painted cross. San Gimignano, Museo Civico. Photo Alinari/Art Resource, N.Y.

Figure 4. Detail of Figure 3. Photo Alinari/Art Resource, N.Y.

Figure 5. Giotto(?), *St. Francis Praying before the Cross of San Damiano*. Assisi, Basilica di San Francesco, upper church. Photo Alinari/Art Resource, N.Y.

of the rigid conventions of twelfth-century art and ecclesiastical life, he translated into forms that others could see and feel with ease. This "translation" happened in life before it reached art, for Francis acted out in his own body, tortured by fasting and marked with the stigmata, the intense identification with Christ's sufferings which we later observe in Coppo di Marcovaldo's cross. But in the whole process—in life and in art—a mystical vision, fruit of a holy man's heightened spiritual awareness, was freely passed on to others. And this was to be the function of the new religious orders that emerged along with the Franciscans from the thirteenth to the fifteenth centuries: *contemplata aliis tradere* ("to hand on to the many what had been seen in contemplation by the privileged few").[30]

This new goal in religious life called for a new style in art, better suited to convey human feelings than was Coppo di Marcovaldo's post-Byzantine expressionism. In the last decades of the dugento, Italian artists drew upon ancient sources and direct observation to evolve a more natural style, characterized by spatial depth and fullness of form. One of the masterpieces of this style, in the fresco cycle in the upper church at Assisi traditionally associated with Giotto, allows us to sum up the essential marks of this shift in Christian sensibility.[31] It is the scene immediately to the viewer's right upon entering, *St. Francis Celebrates Christmas at Greccio* (Figure 6). The event shown took place in 1223, in the town of Greccio, not far north of Rome. Forced by bad weather to spend Christmas there rather than joining his followers in Assisi, Francis brought the meaning of Christ's birth alive for the townsfolk by miming the events of the first Christmas; in the process he invented the *crèche* or Christmas crib. The early Franciscan literature touchingly captures the spirit of the event; it recounts how for the midnight Mass between 24 and 25 December the saint built a manger and outdoor altar in a wood near town:

> The friars were all invited and the people came in crowds. The forest reechoed with their voices, and the night was lit up with a multitude of bright lights, while the beautiful music of God's praises added to the solemnity. The saint stood before the crib and his heart overflowed with tender compassion; he was bathed in tears but overcome with joy. The Mass was sung there, and Francis, who was a deacon, sang the Gospel.

Figure 6. Giotto(?), *St. Francis Celebrates Christmas at Greccio.* Assisi, Basilica di San Francesco, upper church. Photo Alinari/Art Resource, N.Y.

Then he preached to the people about the birth of the poor king, whom
he called the Babe of Bethlehem in his tender love.[32]

The fresco shows it all: Francis, in his deacon's vestments, kneeling before the crib, and the "bright lights" on a high lectern behind
him illuminating a musical text from which four friars sing with gusto.
In the foreground are those laypeople whom the saint so loved; they
look dubious, as if Francis's little drama strikes them as irreverent. In
contrast to the rather riotous friars, these burghers of Greccio are dis-
tinctly uncomfortable at being brought inside the rood screen, the physical wall that normally separated laity from clergy. Their wives hesitate
at the entrance, uncertain how near they dare come to the manger and
altar (Figure 7). It would not be sentimental to see an epochal moment
here: the crossing of a religious Rubicon from the ritual "separation"
of the older piety to new human intimacy. St. Francis embodies the
transition, singing the Gospel in Latin (in his institutional role as deacon)
and then preaching to the people in vernacular Italian—both, presumably, from the candle-lit pulpit in the upper left. The sermon itself
must have been a kind of interlinear translation of formal theological
concepts into everyday language: "he preached . . . about the birth of
the poor king, *whom he called the Babe of Bethlehem.*"

It should be stressed that both sides of the late medieval religious reality, symbolic and experiential, are fully present here. The
charismatic popular preacher, vernacular language, paraliturgical representation, and layfolk in the sanctuary do not—either at this time or
later in Italy—imply a rejection of traditional ritual or of the theological apparatus of meaning. "The saint stood before the crib . . ." but
then, as always, "the Mass was sung." The painter here in fact has replaced the forest described in the text with a permanent-looking church
chancel, presumably to stress liturgical aspects. His placement of the
manger right next to the altar is the clearest hint of this intention. As
a twelfth-century Cistercian writer tells us, "the manger at Bethlehem
is the altar of the church; it is there that Christ's creatures are fed . . .
in this manger is Jesus, wrapped in the swaddling bands which are the
outward form of the sacraments."[33] Francis, and this artist after him, used
nature to render visible the supernatural: the fragile body of a newborn
child to communicate the mystery of the Eucharist. This approach does

Figure 7. Detail of Figure 6. Photo Alinari/Art Resource, N.Y.

not so much "explain" the Incarnation as reactivate it! So, too, the monumental cross seen from behind above the rood screen is simultaneously "slice-of-life" realism and profound theological symbol. For as Leo the Great had explained centuries earlier, "the sole purpose of God's Son in being born was to make the crucifixion possible . . . in the Virgin's womb he assumed mortal flesh, and in this mortal flesh the unfolding of his Passion was accomplished."[34]

Our book begins with this incarnational tension between earth and heaven characteristic of trecento and quattrocento monasticism. Opening chapters by Gene Adam Brucker and Nicolai Rubinstein sketch the demographic and social realities of cloistered life in early Renaissance Florence, suggesting the complex mix of motives that led some to become monks and nuns and others to promote monasticism as laypeople. Rab Hatfield and William Hood illustrate how distinctively Franciscan and Dominican spiritual ideals found expression in painting, while several papers touch upon the internal reform of spiritual life in fifteenth-century religious orders. This movement, called the Osservanza (Observant reform), aimed at a return to the simplicity and fervor of early Christian monasticism through strict observance of the particular order's rule and traditions. Like the twelfth-century Cistercian reform of Benedictine life articulated by St. Bernard and his companions, the fifteenth-century Osservanza gave enormous impetus to the visual arts — in both cases owing to the support of wealthy lay patrons attracted by the reformers' energy and obvious sincerity. And like the early Franciscans, fifteenth-century monks utilized art and history to forge a new self-image — mystical, quietly emotional, and above all rooted in Christian antiquity. Typically, quattrocento painting paired St. Francis, St. Dominic, and other "moderns" with the ancient founders of Christian ascetical life: John the Baptist, St. Jerome, St. Benedict; in their essays, Creighton Gilbert and Kaspar Elm discuss this "antiquarian" redefinition of identity in the Carmelites and Augustinians.[35] Finally, Daniel R. Lesnick and Marcia B. Hall suggest how such concerns in "professional" religious life influenced the laity particularly through the main apostolic activity of the mendicant orders, preaching.

At the heart of this collection are the chapters dealing exclusively with laypeople; their preoccupation with penitence and mortality (John Henderson, Neri Capponi, James R. Banker); their organization of devotional and philanthropic activity (Brian Pullan); and their religious creativity in liturgy, preaching, art, and elaborate dramatic productions incarnating the mysteries of faith (Ronald F. E. Weissman, Kathleen Giles Arthur, George Kubler, Nerida Newbigin, Cyrilla Barr, Paola Ventrone). These chapters take their character from dynamic recent research by social historians into the structures of private and public association in late medieval and Renaissance Europe.[36] John Henderson's opening essay, like Gene Brucker's in the section preceding, serves to introduce the other papers in Part Two. It provides an overview of the motivation, composition, and growth of lay confraternities in Florence. John Henderson organized the sessions of the symposium which corresponded to this section of the book.

CHRISTIAN SOCIAL VISION AND THE RENAISSANCE

Our emphasis on confraternities as a principal environment of lay religious experience in the Renaissance calls for some explanation. We have already suggested the relation of lay piety to the monastic world with the image of St. Francis at Greccio: ordinary men and women enter "through the narrow gate" beneath the cross, and, amidst lights and music provided by professional religious, learn to translate theological and ritual information into vernacular experience. This tutelary bond between religious orders and confraternities remained typical throughout the fifteenth century. A monastery or convent often furnished both the meeting place where the brothers or sisters of a confraternity could gather, and a chaplain or spiritual adviser to help design the liturgical and devotional activities of these layfolk, usually on a monastic model. To a greater extent than can be shown for parish life, therefore, or for more private phenomena such as the veneration of particular saints and of "miraculous" images, confraternal life rendered the unique spiritual experience of the age in lay terms.

A still deeper aspect of Christian life transpires in the prominence of lay brotherhoods, however. Far from being "an affair of the individual and of his personal feeling," as Burckhardt believed, Italian Renaissance Christianity put new emphasis on the social dimension of the entire Judeo-Christian tradition. From the early Christian era through what David Knowles called the "Benedictine centuries," it had been the monastery that served as a paradigm for Christian living: communal life grounded in love and trust, seasoned by ascesis, expressing itself in art, music, and ritual. Those who joined a monastery could live out the New Testament communitarian vision of men and women "united heart and soul," praying and worshiping together under constituted authority (Acts 2:42–47 and 4:32–35). They had—and we must assume it was one of the things they sought—a feeling of touching the very essence of what they believed: of sacramentalizing Christian fellowship in their everyday lives.[37]

The lay man or woman who joined a confraternity entered upon a similar pattern of experience. Through the exercise of social options ingrained in the Christian imagination—symbolic separation from the world, public religious consecration, and sacramental "miming" of their commitment—confraternity members took part in that ecclesial fellowship believed to go back to Christ and the apostles. By sharing experience, strength, and hope with one another through lay preaching and counsel, by mutual aid within the group and outward-directed philanthropy, and through the challenging creative effort of staging religious plays and festivals, these people must have attained a vivid sense of corporate Christian life. And the structural framework of a confraternity must have provided the same satisfying consciousness of order and definition that linear perspective gave in quattrocento painting: a rational and experiential "credibility."

Corporate Christian life is in fact the larger subject of the first masterpiece of pictorial perspective, Masaccio's *Holy Trinity with Mary, St. John and donors,* executed circa 1427 (Figure 8). This fresco was made for the main church of the Dominicans in Florence, Santa Maria Novella, which housed an unusually high percentage of the ninety-six or more lay confraternities active in that city in the mid-quattrocento.[38] Although not commissioned by a confraternity, the *Holy Trinity* was painted on the wall of the southern aisle directly opposite the monumental entrance from the church's cemetery; since a principal function of lay confraternities was to intercede for the souls of deceased members, this image of Jesus' death—on axis with the cemetery door and showing a skeleton in its lower zone—must have been a focus of confraternal piety. At the very least, Masaccio's striking rendering of the body on the cross in believable pictorial space must have dominated the attention of laypeople entering from the cemetery.[39]

Yet Masaccio depicts more than the crucifixion here. In a setting of nobly projected architecture he shows three interrelated social groupings. First, in the upper zone, is the Trinity: God the Father, Son, and Holy Spirit. The Father stands on a raised platform with his arms outstretched to support the cross on which Jesus hangs. Between them — between the Father's beard and Jesus' head—is the white, dovelike form of the Holy Spirit, the *vinculum caritatis* ("bond of love") uniting Father and Son, the very essence of their relationship. The Father "breathes the Spirit" upon his tortured Son as he once breathed life into Adam, imparting the new life of resurrection. This is the first "corporate" or social grouping, and it is familial in character.

Figure 8. Masaccio, *Holy Trinity with Mary, St. John, and Donors*. Florence, Santa Maria Novella. Photo Alinari/Art Resource, N.Y.

At the foot of the cross stand Mary, the mother of Jesus, and John, his friend. From the cross Jesus spoke to both of them: asking Mary to accept his young friend as a second son, and asking John to treat Mary as if she were his mother. "And from that moment the disciple made a place for her in his home" (John 19:25–27). Thus this second social grouping is also a kind of family, brought into being by Christ on the cross, who arbitrarily redefined John as Mary's son and Mary as John's mother. In traditional patristic and medieval exegesis this event was of crucial importance for the history of the Church: in John were seen all future Christians, and in Mary the Christian community as a whole (as Mary is the mother of Christ, so the Church—which she symbolizes—is the mother of Christians).[40] The authoritative posture that Masaccio gave Mary in the fresco alludes to this official role, and her gesture, directing our attention to the cross, underlines the origin of the viewer's filial relationship to Mother Church in the will of the crucified Savior.

Finally, the two donors kneeling at left and right of the illusionistic architecture form a third group, also familial in that they are husband and wife. Indeed, as Masaccio has positioned them, apparently nearer the viewer than any of the figures from sacred history, this Renaissance couple perfectly embodies the Christian concept of human association—what are sometimes called "horizontal" social relationships: that is, relationships formed among equals. The husband and wife are joined here through or against the background of a higher social grouping—the Church (in the fresco, Mary and John)—which in turn pivots on the self-sacrifice of Christ. But the cross introduces another kind of relationship, "vertical" rather than horizontal, the association with a superior rather than with peers: the upright of the cross in the center of Masaccio's composition balances the left-right horizontal of husband and wife, lifting our gaze to Christ, the Spirit, and the Father.

Thus Masaccio used perspective and composition to express a theology of relationships in which the ultimate paradigm or model of "social groupings" is found in God himself, who is three Persons, not one, coexisting in perfect harmony.[41] That supernal "family" intersects with human history in Christ, who became man even to the point of dying in agony. The cross is a "ladder . . . standing on the ground with its top reaching to heaven" (Gen. 28:12; John 1:51), just as in the fresco the vertical beam connects the upper and lower zones of the composition. And from that "ladder," as he returns to God, Jesus extends the family love subsisting between himself and his Father to include not only Mary (who is already "family" in that she is his physical mother) but also John, unrelated to them by consanguinity. That is, the model of a new type of human relationship is found in the inner life of the Trinity: the self-emptying, reciprocal love that circulates without beginning or end among Father, Son, and Spirit, expressed tangibly in history in Christ's willingness to die for the sins of many. The church, as the ideal environment of Christian society—and within the church, ecclesial subgroups such as monastic communities and confraternities— are nothing else but the "extended family" of God, stretching from eternity, through Calvary, to the present.

CHRISTIAN HUMANISM

It is not surprising to find so profound a statement in a Dominican setting: the Dominicans were the unrivaled intellectual leaders in the medieval church, renowned especially as theologians. A cycle of fourteenth-century frescoes in the chapter house adjacent to Santa Maria Novella in fact offers an analogous *summa* of ideas, with scenes depicting Christ's Passion, the mission of the Dominican Order, and a schematic diagram of the history of human learning, showing Thomas Aquinas in the place of honor (Figure 9). Yet if Masaccio knew these earlier examples of doctrinal illustration, their visual prolixity must not have appealed to him. The *Trinity* is distinguished precisely by economy of means and clarity of synthesis—an ability to organize complex ideas pictorially as if the image had taken shape through a natural process allowing no other solution—that are fundamentally new. These stylistic qualities, like the classical architecture with which Masaccio surrounds his scene and the statuesque dignity of his figures, belong to the third "environment" of Renaissance Christianity which our book considers, the humanist movement.

Much has been written of this intellectual movement, which occasionally has been seen as the distinguishing mark of Renaissance thought and life. In this collection we have positioned the chapters on

Figure 9. Andrea da Firenze, *St. Thomas Aquinas Enthroned.* Florence, Santa Maria Novella, chapter house in the Chiostro Verde. Photo Alinari/Art Resource, N.Y.

humanism toward the end of the book, not in order to minimize the importance of the revival of ancient philosophy and letters, but to insist upon an obvious order of events. Before reading Plato, Renaissance thinkers had read Augustine; many of them were monks and priests, and their familiarity with Scholastic thought was at least as great as their familiarity with the ancient peripatetics; even where there is no evidence of special Christian erudition or piety, their entire cultural surroundings spoke to them in the religious terms described above.

The attempt of Italian Renaissance humanists to wed Greco-Roman learning with the truths revealed in Christ was perhaps the most optimistic venture in Western intellectual history. For although extensive areas of affinity did exist between ancient philosophy and the body of medieval theological and speculative thought, there were also fundamental conflicts which would raise critical and ultimately unanswerable questions for the Christian humanists, both as thinkers and as men. The chapters by Salvatore Camporeale, O.P., Melissa Meriam Bullard, and Eugenio Garin illustrate specific instances of this "crisis"—case studies, as it were. Again, however, it will be useful to sketch in broad strokes what is treated in detail in Part Three: in this case, the portrait of a troubled marriage.

Among the philosophical ideas derived from antiquity which most moved Renaissance thinkers was a belief in the godlike dignity of the human being: "man the measure of all things," as the Greek teacher Protagoras called him in the fifth century before Christ. Leonardo da Vinci's well-known drawing of a nude man seen simultaneously in two poses suggests the Renaissance rediscovery of this notion (Figure 10). Following the Roman architect Vitruvius, Leonardo shows man literally measuring the limits of the real world: with arms and legs akimbo, the figure touches the circumference of a circle; standing upright, with head straight and arms extended in a cross, he defines the perimeter of a square. Square and circle, perfect forms in plane geometry: the idea is that the inherent perfection of the universe—its mathematical symmetry—is found in the human body, a microcosm of all creation.[42]

But there is an obvious contradiction between this lofty concept and the New Testament view of man as sinful and needing a "savior." Paul's description of men and women in the Epistle to Titus, for example, is anything but optimistic: he says we are "ignorant, disobedient and misled and enslaved by different passions . . . [living] in wickedness and ill-will, hating each other and hateful to ourselves" (Titus 3:3). In the next sentence of the same passage, however, Paul says a curious thing. He asserts that this dreadful condition was corrected "when the kindness and humanity of God appeared"—in the Latin version of the text which the Renaissance knew, "cum autem benignitas et humanitas apparuit Salvatoris nostri Dei" (Titus 3:4). This is a paradox. Paul ascribes "humanity" to God, whom we normally think of as not human but divine. The association of ideas is crucial for an understanding of the role of humanism in the Renaissance.

As Paul defines human beings, they—we—are "steeped in all sorts of depravity, rottenness, greed and malice, and addicted to envy, murder, wrangling, treachery and spite . . . without brains, honor, love

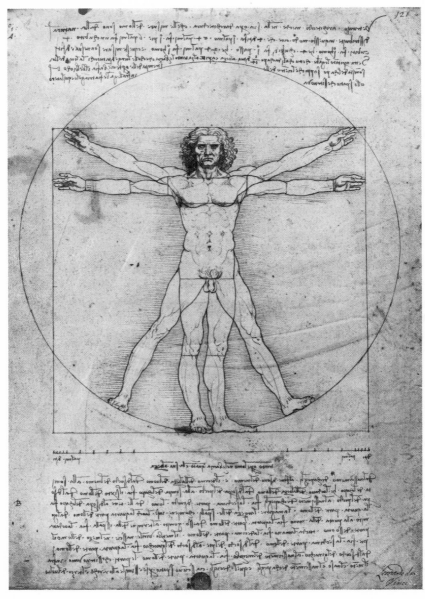

Figure 10. Leonardo da Vinci, *Man of Perfect Proportions,* drawing. Venice, Accademia. Photo Alinari/Art Resource, N.Y.

or pity" (Rom. 1:29–31). That is to say, left to ourselves we are hardly human at all, incapable of those very qualities which Western tradition has always considered the essence of both humanity and the "humane" — honor, love, and pity. Paul believed that God had "appeared" in the world, in the person of Jesus Christ, precisely to teach men and women what true humanity is, through the lessons of compassion and self-sacrifice explicit in Jesus' life and death. (A thousand years later Bernard of Clairvaux invoked this same idea, urging his listeners to emulate not the pagans who were without compassion, but Mary, who could feel grief at the foot of the cross.)

The Italian Renaissance inherited both these visions of human nature: the pagan view, in which the source of humankind's greatness is intrinsic, instinct in our being; and the Christian understanding, in which our dignity derives from an external source — from God, who came himself to show us what it means to be human. The achievement of the Christian humanists, their genius actually, was to reconcile these opposing concepts. The "humanity of God" visible in Christ was understood not as a lesson dictated from above, separate from God himself, but as the perfect reflection of his own divinity, the "icon of the unseen God" (Col. 1:15); to learn humanity in this school was to become like God himself. As Giovanni Pico della Mirandola put it, "no one can doubt that from the man, Christ, the perfection of all goodness in all men is derived; that is to say, the Spirit has been given to him alone without measure, so that we all receive it from his plenitude."[43] It was humankind's oldest and most basic desire, often depicted by Renaissance artists — what Adam and Eve wanted at the dawn of human history: to be like God, to enjoy the plenitude of God himself. And God had come down from heaven to satisfy human aspiration.

If we turn again to Masaccio's *Holy Trinity,* the equilibrium of these ideas is clear. Masaccio shows us the God who has "come down": Jesus, who "did not cling to his equality with God, but emptied himself . . . and became as men are; and being as all men are . . . was humbler yet, even to accepting death . . . on a cross" (Phil. 2:6–8). But the artist situates this Christian lesson in humility beneath a magnificent coffered vault, what Renaissance viewers would have identified as a Roman triumphal arch (Figure 11). Death visibly is swallowed up in victory, as God "raises" the cross and its burden into this zone of antique glory.

Figure 11. Masaccio, *Holy Trinity,* detail showing Christ lifted into the classical architectural structure inhabited by the Father. Florence, Santa Maria Novella. Photo Alinari/Art Resource, N.Y.

Both visions of human nature are implied: the classical splendor of the arch is worthy of a conquering hero, but the "hero" held up for our veneration is "humbler yet" than the common run of men. What is remarkable is not the age-old mystery of a God who suffers, but the Renaissance artist's ability to express both sides of the paradox without doing violence to either. Masaccio has combined the Christian sign of abnegation with a classical symbol of human greatness in such a way that these seemingly irreconcilable views enrich and expand one another, as if in illustration of another Pauline text, where the Apostle to the Gentiles claims that God "wanted all things to be reconciled through [Christ] and for him, everything in heaven and everything on earth, when he made peace by his death on the cross" (Col. 1:19–20).

THE ORGANIZATION OF THE BOOK

These reflections suggest the vision of our subject which led to the organization of the material in broad sections devoted to "The Monastic World," "The Religious World of the Laity," and "The World of the Christian Humanist." These categories are fluid, however: some papers might have fit as well into one part of the book as another. Lesnick's study of Giovanni Dominici's sermons, for example, which we located in "The Monastic World," could have gone equally well into the section on the laity: the Dominican friar's preaching was directed, after all, to the lay men and women of Florence. Similarly, Ronald Weissman's analysis of humanist involvement in lay confraternities would fit into Part Three, on Christian humanism, almost as well as where we have put it, among the papers on lay confraternities. In the last analysis, the overall structure of the book and the arrangement of individual papers within each section have involved decisions as to emphasis. It seemed particularly significant that Dominici's message came out of a monastic context, in the first case, and in the second, the specifically humanist content of the sermons discussed by Weissman appeared less important than the fact that they were delivered by and to laypeople. To assist the reader, a short prefatory paragraph has been provided for each chapter, in which we suggest what we see as its "place" within the larger whole. Nonetheless the book remains a collection, and the reader is free to rearrange the components.

Finally, while unified in overarching concept, this book is richly diverse in the points of view and methodological presuppositions of the contributing scholars. The two concluding studies in fact, by Charles Hope and Eugenio Marino, O.P., constitute a *coda* or excursus on method. They represent quite different approaches to the fundamental question of how to "read" religious images, corresponding to what might be called "the limits of conscious awareness" and the "limitless polyvalence of religious symbols." Hope's view represents a revisionist current in the interpretation of Renaissance imagery argued especially well by British scholars. Father Marino, like Salvatore Camporeale a Dominican and member of the Santa Maria Novella community, has drawn upon structuralist thought in a challenging effort to articulate "from within" how members of a living tradition understand artifacts molded by that tradition.

NOTES

1. Jacob Burckhardt, *The Civilization of the Renaissance in Italy,* trans. S. G. C. Middlemore, rev. and ed. Irene Gordon (New York: New American Library, 1960), 356–83 in particular. As Irene Gordon notes on page viii, Burckhardt was fully conscious of the contemporary bias of his historical view: writing to King Maximilian II of Bavaria, he explained that "the Renaissance was to have been portrayed in so far as she was the mother and the source of modern man, in thought and sensibility as well as in the shaping of form."

2. Ibid., 172.

3. See, for example, Myron P. Gilmore, "The Program of Christian Humanism," in *The World of Humanism, 1453–1517* (New York: Harper and Row, 1952); and Hans Baron, *The Crisis of the Early Italian Renaissance: Humanism and Republican Liberty in an Age of Classicism and Tyranny,* rev. ed. (Princeton, N.J.: Princeton University Press, 1966).

4. I analyze this development in *"Le spirituel vécu:* La Maddalena e l'epistemologia dell'arte cristiana," *Arte cristiana* 74 (1986): 409–14.

5. Bishops' Committee on the Liturgy, *Environment and Art in Catholic Worship* (Washington, D.C.: National Conference of Catholic Bishops, 1978), 8.

6. This development is discussed at length in my "Monasticism and Christian Culture," which forms the introduction to *Monasticism and the Arts,* ed. Timothy Verdon with John Dally (Syracuse; N.Y.: Syracuse University Press, 1984), 1–27. See also Avery Dulles, S.J., *Models of the Church* (Garden City, N.Y.: Doubleday, 1974); idem, "The Symbolic Structure of Revelation," *Theological Studies* 41 (1980): 61; and Nathan Mitchell, "Symbols Are Actions, Not Objects," *Living Worship* 13, no. 2 (February 1977): 1–2.

7. See, for example, the essays comprising part 3 of *The Pursuit of Holiness in Late Medieval and Renaissance Religion,* ed. Charles Trinkaus with Heiko A. Oberman (Leiden: E. J. Brill, 1974), and Charles Trinkaus, *In Our Image and Likeness: Humanity and Divinity in Italian Humanist Thought,* 2 vols. (Chicago: University of Chicago Press, 1970), 2: pt. 4.

8. Cf. Eva Tea, "Leonardo e il costume," *Raccolta vinciana* 17 (1954): 63–79.

9. See Mircea Eliade, "Methodological Remarks on the Study of Religious Symbolism," in *The History of Religions: Essays in Methodology,* ed. M. Eliade and J. M. Katagawa, 6th ed. (Chicago: University of Chicago Press, 1973), 95.

10. "The Task of Cultural History," in *Men and Ideas: Essays by Johan Huizinga,* trans. and ed. James S. Holmes and Hans van Marle (1959; reprint, New York: Harper and Row, Torchbooks, 1970), 53–54.

11. A concise summary of Focillon's historical thinking may be found in Jean Bony's preface to Henri Focillon, *The Art of the West in the Middle Ages*, ed. Jean Bony, 2d ed. (London: Phaidon, 1969), xxii ff. Focillon's chief theoretical work is the short *Vie des formes*, first published in 1934 and translated into English by his students at Yale C. B. Hogan and George Kubler as *The Life of Forms in Art* (1942), rev. ed. (New York: Wittenborn, Schultz, 1948).

12. George Kubler, *The Shape of Time* (New Haven, Conn.: University Press, 1962), 12–13 and 16–18.

13. See Michael Polanyi, "Faith and Reason," *Journal of Religion* 41 (1961): 237–47; and Dulles, "Symbolic Structure," 63.

14. See Robert Cushman, "Faith and Reason in the Thought of St. Augustine," *Church History* 19 (1950): 271–94, who cites examples. I am indebted to Father Avery Dulles for calling my attention to this thrust in Augustine's epistemology and for direction in reading.

15. The first citation is from the end of chapter 1 of the *Proslogion* where, in the next sentence, Anselm quotes the passage from Isaiah mentioned above, naming Augustine as his interpretive source. The second citation here is from the *Cur Deus homo*, where Anselm puts it into the mouth of Abbot Boso of Bec as a point of departure for his discourse. See Eugene R. Fairweather, ed. and trans., *A Scholastic Miscellany: Anselm to Ockham*, Library of Christian Classics, no. 10 (Philadelphia: Westminster, 1956), 73 and 102; see also Anselm's analysis of the roles of faith and understanding in his letter to Pope Urban II, 97–99.

16. *Sermo Laurentii Vallae de mysterio Eucharistiae* in *Lactanii opera* (Venice, 1521), paraphrased in English and quoted in Latin in Trinkaus, *Image and Likeness*, 2:634–35 and 838.

17. Cf. Phil. 2:6. Of interest in this connection is the stimulating essay by Natalie Zemon Davis, "Some Tasks and Themes in the Study of Popular Religion," in Trinkaus and Oberman, *Pursuit of Holiness*, 307–36.

18. Anselm uses the latter expression to describe his *Monologium*. For both, see his preface to the *Proslogion* in Fairweather, *Scholastic Miscellany*, 69–70.

19. I traced this development in relation to the arts in *The Art of Guido Mazzoni* (New York: Garland Publishing, 1978), 17–18.

20. See A. S. Walpole, *Early Latin Hymns* (Cambridge: Cambridge University Press, 1922), 174–77.

21. From the sermon given on the Sunday within the octave of the Assumption. See *Sancti Bernardi opera omnia*, ed. Jean Leclercq, O.S.B. (Rome: Editiones cistercienses, 1957–72), 5:273–74. The English translation here is taken from *The Divine Office, The Liturgy of the Hours According to the Roman Rite*, 3 vols. (London: Collins, 1974), 3:263.

22. Ibid.

23. See Otto von Simson, "The Cistercian Contribution," in Verdon and Dally, *Monasticism and the Arts*, 115–38.

24. For the influence of St. Francis and the Franciscan movement upon art, the older, classic source is Henry von Thode, *Franz von Assisi und die Anfänge der Kunst der Renaissance in Italien* (Berlin, 1885). Recent essays in this spirit include John V. Fleming, *From Bonaventure to Bellini: An Essay in Franciscan Exegesis* (Princeton, N.J.: Princeton University Press, 1982); and Rona Goffen, *Piety and Patronage in Renaissance Venice: Bellini, Titian, and the Franciscans* (New Haven, Conn.: Yale University Press, 1986). Also helpful are Caroline Bynum's "Franciscan Spirituality: Two Approaches," *Medievalia et Humanistica*, n.s. 7 (1976): 195–97, and *Jesus as Mother: Studies in the Spirituality of the High Middle Ages* (Berkeley and Los Angeles: University

of California Press, 1982). See also Ewert H. Cousins, "Francis of Assisi: Christian Mysticism at the Crossroads," in *Mysticism and Religious Traditions,* ed. Steven T. Katz (New York: Oxford University Press, 1983), 163–90.

25. This kind of Romanesque cross is found throughout Europe. See Erich Pattis and Eduard Syndicus, S.J., *Christus Dominator: Vorgotische Grosskreuze* (Innsbruck: Tyrolia, 1964).

26. Frederick Hartt, *History of Italian Renaissance Art,* 3d ed. (New York: Harry N. Abrams, 1987), 43.

27. The Pseudo-Bonaventure [pseud.], *Meditationes vitae Christi.* See *Meditations on the Life of Christ,* trans. E. Green and ed. Isa Ragusa (Princeton, N.J.: Princeton University Press, 1961), 320.

28. The Italian and English texts here are taken from *The Penguin Book of Italian Verse,* ed. George R. Kay (1958; reprint, Baltimore: Penguin Books, 1966), 10, (but see following note).

29. Recounted in Bonaventure's *Legenda maior,* 2:1 (Quaracchi: Collegio di S. Bonaventura, 1941). For an up-to-date English translation, see Marion Habig, ed., *St. Francis of Assisi, Writings and Early Biographies: English Omnibus of Sources* (Chicago: Franciscan Herald Press, 1979), 640.

30. This phrase, one of the two mottos of the Dominican order, (see the chapter by William Hood in this book), derives from Thomas Aquinas: "Sicut enim maius est illuminare quam lucere solum, ita maius est contemplata aliis tradere quam solum contemplari" (*Summa theologica,* ed. Jacques Paul Migne, 4 vols. [Paris, 1841], 3:1373 [Secunda secundae, Quaest. 188, art. 6»).

31. For a helpful review of the problems of attribution connected with the frescoes in the upper church at Assisi, see Alistair Smart, *The Assisi Problem and the Art of Giotto* (New York: Oxford University Press, 1971); for a consideration of the program as well as a detailed discussion of the art historical issues throughout the basilica, see Hans Belting, *Die Oberkirche von S. Francesco in Assisi* (Berlin: Mann, 1977).

32. *Legenda maior,* 10:7; Habig, *St. Francis of Assisi,* 711.

33. St. Aelred of Rievaulx, *Sermo 2 in Natale Domini,* in *Patrologia cursus completus, series latina,* ed. Jacques Paul Migne, 221 vols. (Paris, 1844–64), 195:226–27. An English translation of parts of this sermon may be found in Henry Ashworth, O.S.B., ed., *A Word in Season,* 2 vols. (Dublin: Talbot, 1973–74), 1:73–74.

34. Tractatus 48, 1, in *Sancti Leonis Magni Romani pontifici tractatus septem et nonaginta,* ed. A. Chavasse, Corpus Christianorum, series latina, no. 138 A (Turnhout: Brepols, 1973), 279–80. An English translation is found in Ashworth, *Word in Season,* 2:156.

35. See also Timothy Verdon, *Monastic Themes in Renaissance Art* (Washington: D.C.: National Gallery of Art, 1980), 1 and 11–12, where I discuss related ideas.

36. See John Henderson's article in which he reviews five books on this subject: "Society and Religion in Renaissance Florence," *Historical Journal* 29 (1986): 213–25.

37. Verdon, "Monasticism and Christian Culture," 7–15.

38. "As many as eleven per cent of all fraternities in the city were housed in this church" (Henderson, "Society and Religion," 223).

39. The reading of the *Trinity* advanced here is new in its emphasis on social and relational meanings in the context of Sta. Maria Novella; I develop this interpretation in "Chris-

tian Mysteries in Renaissance art," now in preparation. For other aspects of meaning in this work, see Ursula Schlegel, "Observations on Masaccio's Trinity Fresco in Sta. Maria Novella," *Art Bulletin* 45 (1963): 19–33; John Coolidge, "Further Observations of Masaccio's Trinity," *Art Bulletin* 48 (1966): 382–84; Michael Mallory, "An Early Quattrocento Trinity," Art Bulletin 48 (1966): 85–89; Otto von Simson, "Uber die Bedeutung von Masaccios Trinitätsfresko in Sta. Maria Novella," *Jahrbuch der Berliner Museen* 8 (1966): 119–59; Charles Dempsey, "Masaccio's Trinity: Altarpiece or Tomb," *Art Bulletin* 54 (1972): 279–81; Carlo Del Bravo, "Nicchia con crocefisso e statue," in *Essays Presented to Myron P. Gilmore,* ed. Sergio Bertelli and Gloria Ramakus, 2 vols. (Florence: Nuova Italia, 1978), 2:131–32; E. Hertlein, *Masaccios Trinität: Kunst, Geschichte und Politik der Frürenaissance in Florenz* (Florence: Biblioteca Tascabile, Studi d'Arte, 1979); Rona Goffen, "Masaccio's Trinity and the Letter to the Hebrews," *Memorie domenicane,* n.s. 11 (1980): 489–504; Ralph Lieberman, "Brunelleschi and Massaccio in Sta. Maria Novella," *Memorie domenicane,* n.s. 12 (1981): 127–39; Philipp Fehl, "The Naked Christ in Sta. Maria Novella in Florence," *Storia dell'arte* 45 (1982): 161–64. More generally, for the *Trinity* and for Masaccio's oeuvre, see Luciano Berti, *Masaccio* (Milan: Istituto editoriale italiano, 1964).

40. See, for example, Blessed Guerric of Igny: "She who glories in having borne the only begotton of the Father, embraces that same only-begotten of hers in all his members . . . she herself, like the Church of which she is the type, is a mother of all who are reborn to life" (Sermo 47:2–4, in Migne, *Patrologia latina,* 185:188–89; English from *The Divine Office,* 1:254*).

41. This "social" reading of the mystery of the Trinity is clear in the thought of Richard of St. Victor, the twelfth-century theologian who posited love as the perfection of the divine nature and—by analogy with human love—concluded that there must necessarily be three in the Godhead: one to love, a second to be loved and to return love, and a third to share the love of these two. For, he argues, the love of two persons for one another would not yet be perfect, unless each was ready to share his or her love with still a third person. That is to say, the lover's love for the beloved is so secure that he or she can tolerate without fear or jealousy a "rival" for the love of the beloved. See Joseph A. Bracken, S.J., *What Are They Saying About the Trinity* (Youngstown, Ohio: Paulist Press, 1979), 18.

42. For the original text, see Vitruvius, *The Ten Books on Architecture,* trans. Morris H. Morgan (New York: Dover, 1960), 72–75 (bk. 3, chap. 1). Leonardo da Vinci's adaptation of this text is found in Jean Paul Richter, *The Literary Works of Leonardo da Vinci* (London, 1883), no. 343. On the significance of these ideas for the Renaissance generally, see Rudolph Wittkower, *Architectural Principles in the Age of Humanism* (London: Tiranti, 1952). See also Henry Millon, "The Architectural Theory of Francesco di Giorgio," in *Renaissance Art,* ed. Creighton Gilbert (New York: Harper and Row, 1970), 146–47.

43. Giovanni Pico della Mirandola, *Heptaplus;* see Eugenio Garin, ed., *Opere di Pico della Mirandola,* 3 vols. (Florence: Vallecchi, 1942, 1946, 1952), 1:220. The English translation is from Trinkaus, *Image and Likeness,* 2:508–9.

Part One

THE MONASTIC WORLD

I ❧

MONASTERIES, FRIARIES, AND NUNNERIES IN QUATTROCENTO FLORENCE

GENE ADAM BRUCKER

F ROM EARLY CHRISTIAN TIMES, the monastery has been understood as an ideal microcosm of Christian life and commitment: an *ecclesiola* or small scale but intense example to the wider church community of what "Church" means. In this opening chapter of Part One, Gene Adam Brucker provides a detailed introductory sketch of the demographic, economic and human components of the monastic environment in fifteenth-century Florence: the kinds of religious communities in and near the city; the numbers of members and nonmembers directly dependent upon the life of these institutions; the overlapping interests of lay society and this monastic world; and the concern shared by ecclesiastical and lay authorities for proper maintenance of order and high standards in these "exemplary" communities. This chapter also introduces the reader to some of the principal sources of our knowledge of Florentine Renaissance conventual life: tax records (the *catasto*); "efficiency reports" in the form of questionnaires filled out during visits to monasteries by Church authorities; and death notices contained in the necrologies of monastic communities. From Professor Brucker's essay emerges a richly diverse picture of these "cities of God" existing in and alongside the city of man: of their internal politics, of the external social pressures influencing their lives, and of the social and economic factors that allowed the members of some communities to live comfortably on accumulated income while those of others had to engage in manual labor.

GENE ADAM BRUCKER is professor of history at the University of California, Berkeley, and visiting professor at the Harvard University Center for Italian Renaissance Studies, Villa I Tatti, Florence. His numerous publications include *Florentine Politics and Society, 1343–1378* (1962), *Renaissance Florence* (1969), and *The Civic World of Early Renaissance Florence* (1977).

HIS ESSAY IS AN ATTEMPT to describe, in general and schematic terms, conventual experience in fifteenth-century Florence. I shall pose some basic questions concerning the city's religious communities, as a prelude to a more intensive analysis of this complex phenomenon. My account relies in part upon the work of Walter and Elisabeth Paatz, David Herlihy and Christiane Klapisch-Zuber, Richard Trexler, and Stefano Orlandi, and in part upon my own preliminary researches in the Florentine state archives.[1] My chapter embraces the whole spectrum of conventual life in Florence and its environs: urban and suburban, male and female, cloistered and uncloistered, unreformed and Observant. It concerns large, wealthy monasteries and convents, and small, poor houses struggling for survival. There is, inevitably, the risk of superficiality in treating so large and varied a subject in such a sketchy fashion. But there are compensating advantages in looking at these religious communities from this global perspective. One can discern filiations and relationships among these orders and their individual units. One can detect changes—in size, in wealth, in vitality—of particular communities, and one can make comparisons: concerning their organization, their *esprit,* their adherence to their rule, and their relations with the secular world (Figure 1.1).

How many monasteries, friaries, and nunneries existed within Florence's walls, and in the peripheral zones outside the walls in the fifteenth century? Basing one's calculations upon the careful researches of Walter and Elisabeth Paatz, it would seem to be a simple matter to count these foundations. In fact, the numbers were constantly changing, as a result of the supression of some and the creation of others throughout the century. While Pope Eugenius IV resided in Florence in the 1430s, he suppressed a cluster of small and undisciplined convents, particularly in the Via San Gallo area, and distributed their personnel to other nunneries *di buon governo.*[2] In its *catasto* report of 1478, the Benedictine nunnery of Sant'Agata reported that it had been united with the convents of San Francesco a Vichio, Santa Margherita a Mon-

C Operetta molto diuota composta da frate Hieronymo da
Ferrara dellordine de frati predicatori sopra edieci coman
damenti di Dio: diricta alla Madona / o uero Badessa del
monasterio delle Murate diFirenze: nella quale sicotiene
la examina de peccati dogni & qualunque peccatore: che e
utile & perfecta confessione.

LA Charita di Christo mistringe dilectissime mie
no dare repulsa alla uostra honestissima & sancta
domanda: per laquale ho chiaramete inteso quan
to zelo sia in uoi dello honor di Dio & della salute

Figure 1.1. Two friars visiting a convent of nuns. Woodcut illustration for Fra Girolamo Savonarola's *Operetta molto divota . . . directa alla Badessa del monasterio delle Murate
di Firenze*. Published 24 October 1495 in Florence by Bartolomeo de' Libri. Florence,
Biblioteca Nazionale Centrale. Photo Artini.

tici, Santa Maria delle Neve, San Silvestro, San Gherardo, and San Clemente.[3] But these suppressions and incorporations were counterbalanced
by new foundations; for example, the Observant Franciscan house of
San Salvatore near San Miniato in 1418, the Benedictine nunnery of the
Murate in the 1420s, and the Franciscan tertiaries of Annalena in the
1450s.[4] The number of masculine communities was more stable than
that of nunneries. Excluding the houses of military orders and the hospitals, the total in the late fifteenth century was nineteen within the
city walls and eleven more in the peripheral zone. (See Tables 1.1 and
1.2.) Herlihy and Klapisch-Zuber have counted, in the 1427 catasto records, twenty-seven nunneries within the city, and twenty-one in the
suburbs, for a total of forty-eight.[5] According to my calculations, the
number of houses within the walls had increased to thirty-seven by
the end of the century, while seventeen convents were located outside
the walls within a four-mile radius of the city center. (See Tables 1.3
and 1.4.)

The thirty male communities of monks and friars embraced a
broad range of orders. The Benedictine, Vallombrosan, and Camaldoli
houses together comprised ten foundations, or one-third of the total.
Among the new houses established during the fifteenth century were
the Observant communities of San Marco and San Domenico di Fiesole
(Dominican), San Salvatore near San Miniato al Monte (Franciscan), and
Santa Maria a San Gallo (Augustinian), the last subsidized by Lorenzo
de' Medici. Catasto and notarial records provide information about the
size of these communities. The numbers of members were quite stable
throughout the century, suggesting that those houses were able to recruit new blood, unlike their counterparts in the rural areas of Tuscany,
which experienced a significant decline in membership. Santa Croce
housed some 50 friars throughout the century; Santo Spirito and Santa
Maria degli Angeli, 30 each; Santa Maria del Carmine, 25. There were
exceptions to this pattern of stability, however. The Cistercian monastery of Certosa declined from 20 monks in 1427 to 9 in 1475; San Felice
in Piazza, a Camaldolese house, dwindled from 11 members to 4 between 1427 and 1490. The most dramatic increase was registered by
the Observant Dominican community of San Marco, which expanded
from 25 friars in 1474 to 120 during Savonarola's tenure as prior in the
1490s.[6] From catasto evidence of 1427, Herlihy and Klapisch-Zuber have

TABLE 1.1

MASCULINE RELIGIOUS HOUSES WITHIN CITY WALLS

Name(s)	Order	Modern location	Gross property value in gold florins, 1427–38
Badia Fiorentina	Benedictines	Via Proconsolo	19,614
Sta. Brigida del Paradiso	S. Salvatore	Via Roma	5,372
S. Barnaba	Augustinians	Via Guelfa	515
S. Basilio	S. Basil	Via S. Gallo	672
Sta. Croce	Franciscans	Piazza Sta. Croce	2,370
S. Felice in Piazza	Camaldolese	Piazza S. Felice	2,572
S. Giorgio	Sylvestrines (after 1437)	Costa S. Giorgio	3,714
S. Marco	Sylestrines (after 1436, Observant Dominicans)	Piazza S. Marco	2,270
Sta. Maria degli Angeli	Camaldolese	Via Alfani	6,370
Sta. Maria del Carmine	Carmelites	Piazza Sta. Maria del Carmine	3,472
Sta. Maria Maddellena di Cestello	Cistercians (1440)	Borgo Pinti	—
Sta. Maria Novella	Dominicans	Piazza Sta. Maria Novella	7,345
Sta. Maria de' Servi (SS. Annunziata)	Servites	Piazza SS. Annunziata	5,000
Ogni Santi	Humiliati	Piazza Ogni Santi	13,028
S. Pancrazio	Vallombrosans	Via della Spada	6,315
S. Piero de Morone	Celestines	Via Cavour	1,057
S. Salvatore	Camaldolese	near Viale Petrarca	2,857
Sto. Spirito	Augustinian Hermits	Piazza Sta. Spirito	6,100
Sta. Trinita	Vallombrosans	Piazza Sta. Trinita	6,000

SOURCES: Modern location data from Paatz; gross property value data from ASF, Catasto, 195.
NOTE: The omitted property value figure is the result of lacunae in the records.

calculated a total of 750 monks and friars in Florence and its environs.[7] Counting the significant increase in the size of Observant houses, particularly San Marco, that figure probably exceeded 800 by the end of the century.

Estimating the number of women housed in nunneries is a more hazardous enterprise. The evidence from tax declarations, notarial protocols, and the records of the Conventi Soppressi is incomplete. The

TABLE 1.2

MASCULINE RELIGIOUS HOUSES OUTSIDE CITY WALLS
(WITHIN FIVE-MILE RADIUS OF CENTER)

Name(s)	Order	Modern location	Gross property value in gold florins, 1427–38
Badia Fiesolana voc. "S. Bartolomeo"	Benedictines	S. Domenico di Fiesole	—
S. Bartolomeo de Monte Oliveto	Benedictines	outside Porta S. Frediano	2,757
S. Benedetto	Camaldolese	outside Porta a Pinta	3,709
S. Domenico de Fiesole	Observant Dominicans	S. Domenico di Fiesole	—
S. Donato de Scopeto	Augustinian Canons	outside Porta Romana	—
Ingesuati	Gesuati	outside Porta a Pinti	—
S. Lorenzo de Certosa	Cistercians	Galluzzo	20,670
S. Miniato al Monte	Olivetans	S. Miniato	7,652
Sta. Maria a San Gallo	— (1488)	outside Porta S. Gallo	—
SS. Salvatore e Francesco	Franciscan Observants	S. Miniato	—
S. Salvi	Vallombrosans	outside Porta a Giustizia	12,857

SOURCES: Modern location data from Paatz; gross property value data from ASF, Catasto, 195.
NOTE: The omitted property value figures are the result of lacunae in the records.

problem is further complicated by the heterogeneous composition of this convent population, which included not only professed nuns and novices, but *conversi,* adolescent girls and widows who were boarded in these houses but did not take religious vows.[8] Herlihy and Klapisch-Zuber have proposed these figures, based on the 1427 catasto: 553 female religious within the city walls and 353 in the outlying areas, totalling 906. Although that figure may be too high for the 1420s, it was certainly surpassed by mid-century, and by 1500, the number of female religious in the city and its environs had grown to over 2,000. By 1515 the fifteen largest convents housed 1,467 professed nuns, and the total almost certainly exceeded 2,500.[9] Figures for specific convents illustrate the pattern of this growth. Some of the most dramatic increases were registered by the newly established convents: membership in the Bene-

TABLE 1.3

<small>NUNNERIES WITHIN CITY WALLS</small>

Name(s)	Order	Modern location	Gross property value in gold florins, 1427–38
Sant'Agata voc. "donne di Bibbiena"	Benedictines	Via S. Gallo	3,290
S. Ambrogio	Benedictines	Piazza S. Ambrogio	4,200
Ammantelate voc. "Sta. Maria delle sette dolori"	Servites, Third Order	Via Laura	—
Sant'Apollonia	Benedictines	Via S. Gallo	2,400
Sta. Caterina a Mugnone	Augustinians	Via Sta. Caterina	3,536
S. Caterina de Cafaggio	Augustinians	Piazza S. Marco	—
S. Domenico de Cafaggio	Dominicans	Via Michele	5,143
Sta. Elisabetta voc. "Convertite"	Augustinians	Via Serragli	515
Sta. Felicita	Benedictines	Piazza Sta. Felicita	9,185
S. Francesco voc. "donne di Foligno"	Franciscans, Third Order	near Piazza Sta. Croce	2,251
S. Giovanni Laterano voc. "le Santuccie"	Sto. Spirito de Roma	near S. Piero Maggiore	—
S. Girolamo voc. "le Donne di S. Giorgio"	Franciscans, Third Order	Via della Costa S. Giorgio	—
S. Girolamo voc. "le Poverine"	Gesuate	Corso dei Tintori	—
S. Giuliano a Montaione	Dominicans	near Porta Faenza	3,086
S. Jacopo de Ripoli	Observant Dominicans	Via della Scala	5,360
SS. Jacopo e Lorenzo	Franciscans	Via Ghibellina	1,570
S. Luca	Augustinians	Via S. Gallo	950
Sta. Lucia	Carmelites until 1440; then Dominicans, Third Order	Via S. Gallo	839
Sta. Maria a Candeli voc. "Sta. Maria di Monteloro"	Augustinians	Via Pilastri	2,314
Sta. Maria della Neve voc. "Sta. Maria degli Scalzi"	Vallombrosans (suppressed, 1442)	Via S. Gallo	1,215
Sta. Maria di Querceto	Vallombrosans	Via S. Gallo	1,429
Sta. Maria delle Murate voc. "Santissima Annunziata" voc. "le donne di suora Agata"	Benedictines (1424)	Via Ghibellina	—
Sta. Maria sul Prato voc. "Sta. Maria del Pinto"	Augustinians	near Porta al Prato	989
Sta. Maria Magdalena de Cestello	Cisterians (suppressed, 1443)	Borgo Pinti	2,857
S. Martino ad Mugnone	Camaldolese	near Porta a Prato	1,693
Sta. Monaca	Augustinians	near Piazza del Carmine	—
S. Niccolò de Cafaggio	Benedictines	Via Ricasoli	3,015
Nunziatina	Carmelites (1453)	near Piazza del Carmine	—

TABLE 1.3 *(continued)*

Name(s)	Order	Modern location	Gross property value in gold florins, 1427–38
S. Onofrio voc. "de Foligno"	Benedictines until 1429; then Franciscans, Third Order	Via Nazionale	—
S. Orsola	Vallombrosans until 1429; then Observant Franciscans, Third Order	Via Guelfa	1,761
S. Piero Maggiore	Benedictines	Piazza S. Piero Maggiore	9,800
S. Piero Martire	Observant Dominicans	Via Romana	4,615
Pinzochere voc. "convento delle vestite di Sta. Croce" voc. "suore della Penitenza"	Franciscans, Third Order	near Piazza Sta. Croce	3,336
S. Salvatore voc. "di Chiarito" voc. "Sta. Maria Regina Coelorum" voc. "S. Bartolomeo a Gignoro"	Augustinians	Via S. Gallo	1,543

SOURCES: Modern location data from Paatz; gross property value data from ASF, Catasto, 195.
NOTE: The omitted property value figures are the result of lacunae in the records.

dictine foundation of the Murate, for example, rose from 11 nuns in 1426 to 124 in 1458 and to over 200 in 1515; that in the Dominican Observant convents of St. Peter Martyr rose from 22 in 1427 to 60 in 1493; and that in the Annalena rose from 32 in 1474, to 68 in 1494. The population of the Dominican tertiary convent of Santa Lucia, with its close ties to San Marco and Savonarola, expanded from 7 in 1458 to 130 by 1515. San Onofrio, a Franciscan Observant house, enclosed 18 nuns in 1439 and 79 in 1515. The Benedictine convent of Sant'Agata on the Via San Gallo doubled its population, from 50 to 100, between 1469 and 1515.[10]

Richard Trexler, the first scholar to chart this demographic explosion in the nunneries, also provided an explanation of it which was essentially fiscal: parents from upper- and middle-class families were unable to provide adequate dowries for their daughters to marry respectably.[11] During the middle decades of the fifteenth century, the problem was alleviated by the *monte delle doti*,[12] but by the age of Lorenzo de' Medici—from 1470 onward—the dowry fund could no longer be relied upon to supply these investments in marriage. A cursory scrutiny of the 1480 catasto records reveals a very large number of teenage girls without dowries, many of whom were destined for the conventual life.

TABLE 1.4

NUNNERIES OUTSIDE CITY WALLS
(WITHIN FIVE-MILE RADIUS OF CENTER)

Name(s)	Order	Modern location	Gross property value in gold florins, 1427–38
Sant'Anna in Verzaia voc. "Sta. Maria in Verzaia"	Benedictines	near Porta S. Frediano	1,940
S. Baldassare de Coverciano	Augustinians	Coverciano	1,362
S. Bartolomeo a Mugnone voc. "Sta. Maria a Mugnone"	Camaldolese	near Porta a Prato	–
Sta. Caterina a Monte voc. "S. Gaggio"	Augustinians	near Via Senese	8,743
Sta. Chiara Novella voc. "di Monna Scotta" voc. "S. Giovanni Battista" voc. "S. Johannino"	Augustinians until 1452; then Observant Franciscans	Via delle Fornace	592
S. Donato in Polverosa	Benedictines	[?]	5,615
S. Giovanni Evangelista voc. "de Faenza" voc. "Boldrone"	Vallombrosans	near Porta a Faenza	2,529
S. Giusto fuori le mure	Gesuati	near Porta a Pinti	1,356
Sta. Maria del Fiore voc. "le donne di Lapo"	Augustinians	near Badia di Fiesole	1,366
Sta. Maria della Disciplina voc. "de Portico"	[?]	near Porta Romana	3,588
Sta. Maria a Monte Domini voc. "de Simone Baroncelli"	Franciscans	near S. Miniato al Monte	4,286
Sta. Maria a Monticelli	Franciscans	Bellosguardo	8,286
Sta. Marta a Montughi	Humiliati	near Porta a Faenza	3,200
S. Martino a Maiano	Benedictines	Maiano	869
S. Martino a Mensola	Benedictines (suppressed, 1451)	Ponte a Mensola	1,629
S. Matteo de' Arcetri voc. "Sta. Maria de' Arcetri"	Franciscans	Arcetri	2,572
S. Piero a Monticelli	Benedictines	near Porta S. Frediano	2,257
S. Silvestro	S. Silvestro	Via S. Gallo	286
Sta. Verdiana	Vallombrosans	Via dell'Agnolo	3,186
S. Vincenzo de Annalena	Observant Dominicans (1459)	Via Romana	–

SOURCES: Modern location data from Paatz; gross property value data from ASF, Catasto, 195.
NOTE: The omitted property value figures are the result of lacunae in the records.

Consider the plight of Giovanni di Domenico d'Andrea di Giovanni: the father of one son, Domenico, age twelve, and of six daughters — Bartolomea, Piera, Dianora, Sandra, Caterina, and Lorenza — who ranged in age from nineteen to one year and not one of whom had a dowry.[13] In the period after 1494 the difficulties of arranging marriages for daughters of good family were exacerbated. These years of warfare, political instability, and economic and social vicissitudes persuaded many Florentine fathers that a convent was the most secure place for a daughter. Even after the return of order and stability under Grand Duke Cosimo de' Medici, this pattern of aristocratic marriage was perpetuated. In a sample of twenty-one aristocratic lineages during the Granducato, Burr Litchfield found that one-half of the daughters entered convents. By 1552 the number of Florentine religious, male and female, had risen to 6.5 percent of the total population, compared with only 2.8 percent in 1427.[14]

The catasto records, which provide such valuable information on conventual demography, also contain important data on the property owned by these religious communities. The yield from that property was only one part, but probably the most important, of the total revenues accruing to these foundations and their inmates. Most nuns, and many monks and friars, were sustained partially by their patrimonies, which they brought with them to their convents. Suora Lena di Bartolomeo Barbadori, living in the convent of San Niccolò on the Via Cocomero, reported in her catasto declaration (1430) that the income from her dowry supplemented her diet, beyond that provided by the convent, and provided her with special care during illness.[15] Other sources of conventual income included gifts from the laity, income from dependent parishes and convents, communal subsidies, fees from burials, and the coins collected from the sale of candles, from the alms boxes at altars, and by mendicants on their begging rounds (*questue*) through the city. The revenue from these sources varied significantly. At one extreme was the rich yield from offerings in the Servite church of SS. Annunziata which, for the year 1434, amounted to 780 florins.[16] At the other was the money collected in Santa Maria del Carmine during Lent of 1448; it amounted to only 7 lire, 10 soldi, which did not pay the salary of the preacher hired for the season. The Carmelite friars who begged for alms on Saturdays in the convent's neighborhood collected just 3 soldi during their rounds.[17] In 1496 the friars of Santa Maria Novella collected, on average, only 2 lire per week during Lent, though the amount did increase to 15 lire during Holy Week. Two years later, in

1498, the collections had fallen to less than 1 lire each week, though 10 lire were given by the faithful during Holy Week which, incidentally, coincided with the beginning of Savonarola's martyrdom.[18]

The property owned by these religious communities is thus only a rough guide to their income and their economic condition. The catasto records identify a small number of ancient and rich monasteries: for example, the Badia in Florence and the Certosa of Galluzzo, each with assets in excess of 20,000 florins in 1427; and the Vallombrosan convent of San Salvi and the Humiliati house of Ogni Santi, each with an endowment of 13,000 florins. San Salvi's property could support very comfortably its abbot, seven monks, one converso, and five servants; its annual revenue of 900 florins would provide 65 florins for each member of the community, including the salaried employees. These very rich houses were exceptional; most urban monasteries were less well endowed. In 1427 the Dominicans of Santa Maria Novella owned property valued at 8,500 florins; Santa Trinita and Santo Spirito, property valued at 7,200 florins; Santa Maria degli Angeli, property valued at 6,300 florins, and Santa Maria de' Servi, 5,600. Among the less well endowed monasteries were Santa Croce and San Pancrazio (3,300 florins in 1438), San Felice in Piazza (1,500 florins), and, at the bottom of the spectrum, San Barnaba, whose holdings worth 500 florins provided few amenities for its complement of six Augustinian friars.[19]

The extant evidence does suggest that most male monasteries and friaries were in moderately good economic condition throughout the fifteenth century. Their population and resources were relatively stable; they were the beneficiaries of both private and civic largesse, in the form of endowments, tax exemptions, and communal assistance in obtaining legacies from lay donors. Santa Trinita, Santo Spirito, Santa Maria Novella, and Santa Croce benefitted from the appointment of lay commissions of *operai* (building committees), who funded the organized rebuilding programs. Escaping the fate of many rural monasteries, those within the city walls were never subjected, in the fifteenth century, to systematic looting of their resources by absentee abbots holding their office *in commendam*. But even affluent houses might experience a fiscal crisis, as a result of levies owed to the commune or the pope or because of debts to creditors. In his catasto declaration of 1427, the abbot of the Badia, the city's wealthiest monastery, calculated the foundation's annual income at 237 florins, its expenditure at 1,100 florins, and its debts at 2,148 florins.[20] The Camaldolese monastery of Santa Maria degli Angeli and the Vallombrosan house of San Pancrazio both prospered under the leadership of their prudent abbots, Ambrogio Traversari and Benedetto Toschi. But in the second half of the century, both houses experienced severe financial difficulties, possibly linked to ambitious building programs undertaken by each. These problems were of such gravity that civic authorities appealed to Rome to reform both houses and to restore them to a decent condition.[21]

The Observant foundations of the Dominican and Franciscan orders were the most favored, the most generously subsidized, of all religious houses in Florence and its dominion in the fifteenth century. Their ability to attract this support was due in large part to their being able to create, or re-create, a conventual experience—austere, spiritually intense—that appealed powerfully to the upper echelons of Florentine society. Cosimo de' Medici's largesse to San Marco and San Francesco al Bosco in the Mugello is well known (Figure 1.2), but other Observant communities received similar subsidies from private citizens and from the commune. I will cite some examples of civic benefits to the Franciscan Observants by the Florentine government in the 1430s and 1440s: in June 1431 wood valued at 100 florins was given to the Observant convent of San Salvatore to complete a building project; in June 1432 the convent of La Verna in the Apennines was placed under the protection of the consuls of the Lana guild, who were charged with promoting the well-being of that community; in December 1439, the Florentine Signoria appointed a group of syndics for the Observant houses of San Salvatore and of San Francesco al Monte in Castel San Giovanni, with responsibility for gaining possession for all property that had been bequeathed to those houses; in October 1440, a subsidy was authorized for the Observant house of San Francesco de Sorgiano near Arezzo, to subsidize the construction of that convent; in March 1451 the Observant community of San Salvatore received a communal grant of ten *staiora* of salt per year; and in February 1451 the Florentine Signoria instructed its ambassador in Rome to support a petition of the *frati* of La Verna that they be allowed to hear confessions of the pilgrims who came to their shrine in the Apennines.[22]

During the fifteenth century there may have been some decline

Figure 1.2. Michelozzo, Cloister of San Marco donated by Cosimo de' Medici. Florence. Photo Alinari/Art Resource, N.Y.

in the level of support by the city's residents for the older monastic foundations in favor of hospitals and orphanages and of the newly established Observant houses. But with the sole exception of the Silvestrines of San Giorgio, these communities all survived, and some, for example San Marco, grew rapidly. Florence's nunneries, by contrast, were much less stable, as the rapid expansion of their numbers severely taxed their facilities and resources. These houses were, in 1427, quite well endowed, possessing on average property valued at 3,760 florins (fl.). The richest foundations were the Benedictines of San Pier Maggiore and Santa Felicita (9,800 and 9,200 fl.), the Augustinians of Santa Caterina a Monte (8,743 fl.), and the Franciscans of Santa Maria a Monticelli (8,286 fl.). At the other end of the economic spectrum were the poor Benedictine nunnery of Sant'Anna in Verzaia (759 fl.), the Jerusalemites of San Giovanni Battista (592fl.), and San Silvestro in the Via San Gallo (286fl.).[23]

San Pier Maggiore and Santa Felicita were atypical in their affluence, and in their demographic patterns. San Pier Maggiore's complement of Benedictine nuns actually declined from seventeen in 1427 to eleven in 1485. The Benedictine convents of Santa Felicita and Sant'Ambrogio maintained their numbers, at thirty and twenty-four *suore* respectively, throughout the century.[24] This policy of restricting growth was doubtless motivated by the desire of these nuns and their kinfolk to maintain a genteel standard of living for those well-born suore. Santa Felicita's twenty-four nuns in 1478 were supported by ten servants, five priests, three acolytes (*chierici*), and a factor who, with three female boarders (*commesse*) formed a community of forty-six *bocche* (mouths), who lived quite comfortably on the yield from eighteen farms, and the revenues from fifteen houses and four shops in the city. The majority of Florentine convents, however, succumbed to social pressure from parents seeking havens for their unmarried daughters. We know very little about the building programs of these convents — such as Sant'Agata, Santa Chiara Novella, the Convertite — that must have been inaugurated to house this flood of professed nuns in these years. In the archival records there are references to communal subsidies to the Franciscan nuns of Santa Chiara and the Augustinians of Santa Monaca, for expanding their convents, to the construction of a new dormitory in San Niccolò's de Cafaggio, and to the appointment of a group of operai for the Convertite to enlarge their establishment.[25] This is a rich and almost totally unexplored subject awaiting students of ecclesiastical architecture in fifteenth-century Florence.

The well-born women in rich houses such as San Pier Maggiore and Sant'Ambrogio lived comfortably on their convent revenues and private endowments; their lives were not troubled by economic anxieties. Not so the inhabitants of poor and crowded nunneries, who were dependent upon alms from the community and on the earnings of their own labor. In their petitions to the commune for subsidies, several of these convents revealed that their members engaged in manual labor to survive. In June 1449 the Franciscan tertiaries of San Onofrio noted that their income from alms and from spinning and weaving had declined as a result of adverse economic conditions. Among the other convents whose inmates worked "day and night" to earn their bread were the Augustinian nuns of Santa Maria a Candeli and the Convertite, the Benedictines of Santa Maria delle Murate, the Clares of San Francesco, and the nuns of San Donato in Polverosa, Santa Maria della Disciplina, and San Giorgio. The fifty Benedictine nuns of San Piero a Monticelli complained in December 1495 that since the French invasion the year before, they were unable to earn any money spinning thread and embroidering cloth.[26] In good times, these convents made a significant contribution to the Florentine economy, but when the cloth industry was depressed, they became a burden on the community.

Catasto reports, notarial protocols, and the records of the Conventi Soppressi are valuable sources for investigating the material conditions of Florence's religious houses; they are much less informative about the tenor of their social and religious life. The ideals and aspirations of those communities were defined by their rules, which governed the collective life and individual behavior of their members. These members were judged, by their ecclesiastical superiors and by lay society, in terms of their observance of their rule. The questions addressed to these religious by visitors summarize the standards. Typical is the questionnaire used by the Vallombrosan general, Francesco Altovita, in his 1463 visitation to the monasteries of his province.[27] Did the monks celebrate divine office night and day? Was the church well illuminated and furnished with books, chalices, and vestments? Did the monks live and eat together; sleep in a dormitory in single beds? Were they well fed, and did they wear the habit of their order? Did the monastery give alms to the poor, in accordance with its resources? Were any monks suspected of fornication, gambling, carrying arms, or participating in mercantile activity. Were any guilty of disobeying the abbot? Was the monastery's property in good condition, properly inventoried, and not too heavily mortgaged? In their inspection of the city's nunneries, visitors were particularly concerned with the security of the cloistered women, who (supposedly being weak and vulnerable by nature) were in constant peril of losing their virginity. Florence's secular government established a special magistracy in 1421 to maintain surveillance of these convents, and in particular to restrict access by unauthorized males to these cloistered communities.[28]

Though they must be used with caution, visitation records are the most informative source for evaluating the condition of religious communities. Only a few fragments of those documents have survived for fifteenth-century Florence, however. The Camaldoli general, Ambrogio Traversari, wrote about his visits in the 1430s to the monasteries and convents under his jurisdiction. He found the convent of Santa Verdiana to be in good condition, while the nuns of Santa Maria de Querceto lived in such disorder that he threatened to suppress their convent.[29] Thirty years later (1463), the Vallombrosan general Francesco Altoviti reported that his order's major houses in Florence (San Pancrazio, Santa Trinita, San Salvi) were economically sound, well disciplined, and spiritually vital. Archbishop Antoninus was an assiduous inspector of the churches and convents of his diocese, but only the record of his visit to the Benedictine house of Sant'Agata in 1450 has survived.[30] Antoninus listened to the complaints of several nuns that the abbess, Francesca Micucci, had mismanaged the convent's property, had allowed her male relatives to visit the cloister, and had been lax in maintaining discipline. Antoninus persuaded Francesca to resign her office and selected Suor Appollonia di Cambio Francesci to replace her. Other sources — papal letters, penitentiary records, archiepiscopal acts, civic documents — describe cases of aberrant behavior by members of the city's religious communities: the dissolute abbot with his concubine; the wandering monk who rejected the cloistered life; the nun who succumbed to the blandishments of her seducer. Such incidents are too random to permit any meaningful generalizations about the moral condition of the city's religious communities, together or singly. The records do suggest, however, that the scrutiny and disciplining of convents became less rigorous during the second half of the century. In the later quattrocento, popes and archbishops were not so scrupulous in their surveillance as Pope Eugenius IV and Archbishop Antoninus had been, and Lorenzo de' Medici's commitment to exacting standards of monastic discipline was probably not so strong as that of his grandfather Cosimo.

Owing to the survival of its famous *Necrologio,* and the thorough researches of Padre Orlandi and his Dominican colleagues, we are better informed about the convent of Santa Maria Novella and its members than about any other Florentine religious house. The biographies in the *Necrologio* describe these friars, often in detail: their social background, character, education, and conventual careers. In an order so

renowned for learning, the emphasis on the intellectual training and
achievement of the friars was naturally stressed both in these biographies and in the *Vite fratrum* of Giovanni Caroli, the learned historian
of the convent. The ability to write and deliver effective sermons and
to draw crowds to their preaching was also emphasized in these obituaries. Not all of the friars who entered Santa Maria Novella, however,
achieved distinction as scholars, teachers, and preachers, though these
were the most highly regarded talents. Exceptional skills and dedication in other spheres of conventual life were noted by the authors of
the *Necrologio;* for example, the craftsmanship of the converso carpenter
and painter Fra Giannino from the Mugello. A friar of modest attain-
ments, Fra Bonfantino Bonfantini, was praised for "fleeing from idle-
ness, constantly occupying himself in useful activities, rejecting all vanities, curiosities and distractions." Fra Gratia di Bardo was lauded for
his meticulous observance of the rule and for regular attendance at divine services. Fra Giovanni Masi was noted to be very active as a con-
fessor and as a visitor of the sick within and outside the convent. Fra
Jacopo da Pontormo was described as "an outstanding solicitor of alms
[*questuarius*], thus gaining much wealth for the convent." Similarly, Fra
Matteo de Campi was praised as "an excellent procurer of *temporalia*
[material goods], making his rounds in search of alms and seeking bequests from the laity." A member of a prominent Florentine family,
Fra Giovanni Sigoli, was cited for his social talents in cultivating relationships with the laity.[31]

Since its foundation in the 1220s, Santa Maria Novella had attracted friars of unusual talent and dedication, whose lives and labor
had contributed significantly to its reputation. But in the middle years
of the fifteenth century, the convent experienced a severe crisis, whose
origins are not fully understood. Giovanni Caroli, a prominent Dominican theologian and historian, was personally involved in these troubles,
and alluded to them in his writings.[32] He explained the crisis as a consequence of the decline in the quality of the convent's personnel, who
were not so committed to the order and its rules, and particularly to
learning and scholarship, as previous generations of friars had been. As
prior to the convent in 1459–60, Caroli could observe the decay of conventual discipline, the lack of commitment to the *vita comune* and the
growth of an anarchic spirit of individualism and particularism. The

novices were not properly supervised or disciplined by their superiors, he wrote: "each was concerned only for himself."[33] The evidence from the *Necrologio* suggests that the crisis was directly linked to the heavy plague losses in the convent in those years before 1460, and particularly to the deaths of five masters of theology in the 1430s. These scholars would have been the teachers of the new generation of friars, and would also have been candidates for leadership roles in the convent and in the Dominican order. Seventeen friars died in the 1430s and another twenty-four in the 1440s, including eleven in the plague year of 1449. By the 1450s the community of Santa Maria Novella had been much reduced in size: there were thirty-six friars in 1457 compared with seventy-one in 1427. The friars who replaced the plague victims were young and indifferently educated, and some may have lacked a strong sense of religious vocation.[34]

In the period around 1460 the friars of Santa Maria Novella were sharply divided over the issue of reform. One faction agitated for a more rigorous discipline in the Observant mode while their conservative opponents favored the continuation of the old conventions and standards. The reformers appealed to Rome for support; the conservatives, many from Florentine families, sought help from their relatives and the civic authorities. What had begun as an internal dispute among Dominicans eventually involved the Florentine laity and the Medicean state in a controversy with Pope Pius II. The pope, who had visited Florence and thus had firsthand knowledge of the situation, sent the master general of the Dominican order, Marziale Auribelli, to the convent to supervise its reform. But this campaign foundered on the obdurate resistance of the traditionalists, who skillfully used their connections in the city, and particularly in the Palazzo della Signoria, to sabotage Auribelli's position. The *signoria* wrote letters to the pope, to cardinals, and to other contacts in Rome, denouncing Auribelli and those "rebellious" friars who supported him. In a letter to the Signoria dated 1 September 1460, Pius II sharply criticized these obstructionist tactics and warned that magistracy to desist from such intervention in the convent's affairs. Auribelli had deposed Giovanni Caroli as prior, and as the head of the Roman province. But the new leadership could not prevail against the stubborn opposition of the antireform friars and their lay supporters in the city. So frustrated was Pius over the failure of his project that in 1462 he took the extraordinary step of deposing Auribelli from the generalship of the order. In Santa Maria Novella, those friars who had been expelled from the convent for their disobedience to Auribelli were readmitted to their cells, on orders from the provincial, Giuliano Nardi, and the cardinal protector of the order.[35]

After the crisis of the 1460s, Santa Maria Novella entered a more stable phase. It was able to recruit new members, some from prominent Florentine families, others from more obscure backgrounds and places. By 1478 it had recouped some of its personnel losses, with ninety-two bocche (including boarders and servants) being counted in the catasto declaration of that year. But in 1479 the convent lost sixteen friars to another plague epidemic.[36] Among the dead were several theologians who taught in the convent and also in the Florentine *Studio*. With the exception of Giovanni Caroli, these theologians were not scholars of the first rank, certainly not comparable to the great intellectual figures of the fourteenth and early fifteenth centuries. Florentine patrons continued to support the convent by endowing chapels and by commissioning such works as Alberti's façade and Ghirlandaio's cycle of frescoes in the Cappella Maggiore. Still, the convent was in some financial difficulty in the 1490s, when both the republic and the papacy imposed very heavy burdens on the Florentine church. Santa Maria Novella's total tax obligation in 1496 exceeded two hundred florins; the convent's *camerlingo* (treasurer) twice had to pawn silver vessels from the sacristy to raise the money for its tax payments.[37]

The issue of reform in Santa Maria Novella, and in other Florentine convents, was not simply, or exclusively, a matter of strict versus lax adherence to the rule; it was much more complex. Inextricably involved in these disputes were the personalities and ambitions of the protagonists; the convent's (and often the order's) administrative structure and autonomy; and the relations of its members to the wider world, both ecclesiastical and secular. These complexities are well illustrated by the crisis in the Vallombrosan order in the 1490s, recently analyzed by Rodolfo De Maio in his *Savonarola e la curia romana*. The crisis ostensibly arose over the efforts of a group of Vallombrosan monks to reform the convent of San Salvi, inspired (so they alleged) by the example of Savonarola and San Marco. The controversy, which erupted in 1495, spread through the entire order, involving the general, Don Biagio

Milanesi, the abbots and monks of the Tuscan monasteries, and the protector of the Vallombrosans, Cardinal Oliviero Caraffa. Savonarola and his clerical and lay supporters in Florence were ardent supporters of the reform party. They persuaded the Signoria to send an official messenger (*mazzerius*) to take possession of San Salvi, pending the outcome of the dispute, and they wrote to Caraffa in Rome, urging him to decide in favor of the reform faction. But Caraffa gave his firm support to the general and the antireform party; Savonarola, perhaps realizing that he had been manipulated by the reform faction for their less than holy purposes, withdrew from the controversy.[38] The episode did not redound to the friar's credit and reputation, and it illustrates, once again, the ambiguities that surround such concepts as "reform" and "renovation" in the history of the Church.

NOTES

All archival sources are in the Archivio di Stato di Firenze (hereafter ASF). All dates are New Style.

1. W. Paatz and E. Paatz, *Die Kirchen von Florenz,* 6 vols. (Frankfurt am Main: Klostermann, 1940–54); D. Herlihy and C. Klapisch-Zuber, *Les Toscans et leurs familles* (Paris: Presses de la fondation nationale des sciences politiques, 1978), available in English as *Tuscans and Their Families: A Study of the Florentine Catasto of 1427* (New Haven, Conn.: Yale University Press, 1985); R. Trexler, "Le célibat à la fin du Moyen Age: Les religieuses de Florence," *Annales: Economies, sociétés, civilisations* 27 (1972): 1329–50; S. Orlandi, *"Necrologio" di Sta. Maria Novella,* 2 vols. (Florence: Leo S. Olschki, 1955).

2. G. Richa, *Notizie istoriche delle chiese fiorentine divise ne' suoi quartieri* (Florence, 1754–62), 5:219–24, 271–74; ASF, Notarile Antecosimiano (hereafter NA), I 33 (1440–44): unpaginated, 11 July 1443; NA, M 347, no. 131, 17 Oct. 1435; Trexler, "Le célibat," 1346 n. 93.

3. ASF, Catasto, 989: fol. 27r.

4. D. Buoninsegni, *Storia della città di Firenze dall'anno 1410 al 1460* (Florence, 1637), 52; Richa, *Notizie* 2:79–85; ASF, Provvisioni Registri (hereafter Provv., Reg.), 95: fols. 81v–82r, 21 June 1406; 145: fols. 97v–100r, 20 July 1454; 154: fols. 246v–247v, 24 November 1463.

5. Herlihy and Klapisch-Zuber, *Les Toscans,* 151–58.

6. This demographic data is culled from ASF, Catasto, 184; fols. 116v–120v, 125v–135r, 138r–148v, 236r–237v; 192: fols. 343v–347r; 194: fols. 164r–167r, 170r–174r, 368v–369v; 989: fols. 6r–8r, 262r–267v, 495r–503r, 515r–517v, 790r–793r; and Provv. Reg. 187: fol. 139r–v.

7. Herlihy and Klapisch-Zuber, *Les Toscans,* 157. This table also contains data on nuns.

8. Trexler, "Le célibat," 1334–36.

9. ASF, Balìe, 4: fols. 75r–77r.

10. For numbers of nuns in 1515, see ibid. For figures on Murate, see ASF, NA, 507 (1418–26): unpaginated, 6 Jan. 1426; on St. Peter Martyr, see ASF, Provv. Reg. 120: fol. 22v, and 184: fol. 127v; on Annalena, see ASF, NA, G 570 (1467–74): fol. 347r; on Sta. Lucia, See ASF, NA, A 279: fol. 212v, and G 591 (1490–94): fol. 591v; on S. Onofrio, see ASF, NA, M 568 (1434–43): fol. 174r; and on Sant'Agata, see ASF, Provv. Reg. 159: fols. 270v–271r.

11. Trexler, "Le célibat," 1338–40.

12. J. Kirshner and A. Molho, "The Dowry Fund and the Marriage Market in Early Quattrocento Florence," *Journal of Modern History* 50 (1978): 403–38.

13. ASF, Catasto, 1016: fol. 229r.

14. Cited in Trexler, "Le célibat," 1338.

15. ASF, Catasto, 421: fol. 23r.

16. ASF, Conventi Soppressi, no. 119 (SS. Annunziata), 48: fols. 3r–6v.

17. Ibid., no. 113 (Sta. Maria del Carmine), 81: fols. 426v–427v.

18. Ibid., no. 102 (Sta. Maria Novella), 88: fol. 75r.

19. ASF, Catasto, 195: fols. 43v, 45r, 116r, 245r, 245v, 247r, 255r, 261v, 268r, 273v, 285r.

20. Ibid., 192: fol. 289r.

21. On Traversari, see A. Dini Traversari, *Ambrogio Traversari e i suoi tempi* (Florence: B. Seeber, 1912); on Toschi, see F. W. Kent and D. V. Kent, *Neighbours and Neighbourhoods in Renaissance Florence: The District of the Red Lion in the Fifteenth Century* (Locust Valley, N.Y.: J. J. Augustin, 1982), 141–72. On the difficulties of the two monasteries, see ASF, Provv. Reg., 140: fols. 76r–77v; ASF, NA, G 591 (1485–89): fol. 300r (S. Pancrazio); Provv. Reg. 178: fol. 101r–v; ASF, NA, A 279: fol. 73r; ASF, Signori e Collegi, Carteggi, Legazioni e Commissarie, 18: fol. 16r–v (Sta. Maria degli Angeli).

22. ASF, Provv. Reg. 122: fol. 129r–v; 123: fol. 136r–v; 131: fols. 227v–228v; 142: fol. 18r–v; ASF, Signori e Collegi, Deliberazioni (ordinaria autorità), 51: fol. 30r.

23. Catasto, 195: fols. 41r, 42r, 43r, 248v, 273r.

24. Ibid., 194: fols. 130v, 134v, 139v, and 989: fols. 58r, 253v; ASF, NA, G 591 (1485–89): fol. 10r.

25. ASF, NA, D 89 (1466–69): fol. 266r–v (S. Niccolò); ASF, Provv. Reg., 137: fols. 317v–318v and 138, fols. 23v–25r (Convertite), 151: fols. 88v–89r, and 159: fols. 8v–9r (Sta. Chiara), 148: fols. 423v–424r (Sta. Monaca).

26. ASF, Provv. Reg., 151: fols. 13v–14r (S. Onofrio), 160: fol. 61r–v (Sta. Maria Candeli), 165: fols. 103v–104r and 169: fol. 129r–v (Murate), 137: fols. 317v–318v and 172, fol. 19r–v (Convertite), 139: fol. 101r–v (S. Giorgio), 186: fol. 179r (S. Piero a Monticelli), 151: fols. 88v–89r (Sta. Chiara), 175: fol. 59r–v (S. Donato Polverosa).

27. ASF, Conventi Soppressi, no. 260 (Vallombrosa), 217: fols. 3v–4v.

28. ASF, Provv. Reg. 111: fol. 45r–v.

29. Dini Traversari, *Ambrogio Traversari*, 15–16, 49–50.

30. ASF, NA, M 342 (1432–39): fols. 166r–168r and B 384: fol. 231r.

31. Orlandi, *"Necrologio,"* 1:46, 50, 51, 62, 67, 103.

32. S. Camporeale, "Giovanni Caroli e le 'Vitae Fratrum S. M. Novellae'; umanesimo e crisi religiosa (1460–80)," *Memorie Domenicane*, n.s. 12 (1981): 141–52.

33. Orlandi, *"Necrologio,"* 2:355.

34. Ibid., 1:152–205; ASF, Catasto, 184: fol. 133r; ASF, NA, U 57: unpaginated, 6 August 1457, and B 382: fol. 458r.

35. R. Creytens, "La déposition de maître Martial Auribelli O.P.," *Archivum Fratrum Praedicatorum* 45 (1975): 152–53, 184–85; ASF, Signori e Collegi, Carteggi, Missive, 43: fols. 61v–69r, 78v–79r, 99v–100r; ASF, NA, D 88 (1458–61): fol. 228r–v.

36. ASF, Catasto, 989: fol. 501v; Orlandi, *"Necrologio,"* 1:18–86.

37. ASF, Conventi Soppressi, no. 102 (Sta. Maria Novella), 88: fols. 1r, 14r, 24v.

38. R. De Maio, *Savonarola e la curia romana* (Rome: Edizioni di storia e letteratura 1969), 79–98, 184–223.

2

LAY PATRONAGE
AND OBSERVANT REFORM
IN FIFTEENTH-CENTURY FLORENCE

NICOLAI RUBINSTEIN

A CENTRAL CONCERN of late medieval and Renaissance Christians was with the "authenticity" of religious life—its conformity to the animating spirit of the early Church and of the sainted founders of religious orders. The normal consequence of this preoccupation was internal reform in religious orders, the call for stricter observance of the rule handed down within each institution. In this chapter, Nicolai Rubinstein analyzes the interest of laypeople in this process of reform in Florence: their financial contributions to the building or enlargement and embellishment of Observant religious houses and their influence on the character of Observant life. Like Gene Brucker, Professor Rubinstein introduces a number of the main personalities and themes of *Christianity and the Renaissance:* Cosimo and Lorenzo de' Medici and his grandson, Lorenzo; their exemplary initiative in providing lay support on a lavish scale; the role of learned lay patrons in promoting humanistic studies in monasteries; and the sometimes conflicting tastes of lay patrons concerned with personal aggrandizement and friars looking for simplicity of life.

NICOLAI RUBINSTEIN is Emeritus Professor of History of the University of London. He is the author of *The Government of Florence under the Medici (1434–1494),* published in 1966, and of many essays on Italian, particularly Florentine, medieval, and Renaissance history. He is general editor of the letters of Lorenzo de' Medici.

ROM AN EARLY DATE the movement of reform within the religious orders, which aimed at the strict observance of the rule and which gathered strength toward the end of the fourteenth century, involved the laity as well as the religious. Just as in the thirteenth century the new orders of friars had immediately attracted widespread support from the laity, so now the Observants obtained the allegiance of citizens, civic governments, and princes. Such allegiance could take the form of material aid to existing Observant communities, but it could also extend to the foundation of new ones at the expense of the Conventuals. In either case, support could be private or official or both. The distinction, however, between private and official patronage was far less relevant in princely states such as those of the Gonzaga, the Este, and the Sforza, than in republics such as Florence and Siena. And also in the case of the republics, it is not always easy to draw the line between the actions of private individuals and those of the government, which in turn might have been influenced by leading citizens, perhaps reflecting their preferences in the matter of ecclesiastical patronage. Insofar as these preferences affected the building of new convents or the rebuilding of existing ones, they were liable to lead to conflicts between the architectural objectives of the patrons and the strict observance of the rule of poverty which was one of the principal aims of the reformers. Moreover, the growth in the size of religious communities made possible by such building projects could aggravate the economic problems of the religious, unless patrons were also prepared to help meet the ongoing expenses of reformed convents that were not allowed to own landed property and receive annual rents.

In Florence, lay support of Observants gained momentum around 1400 and reached its highest point under Cosimo de' Medici, to culminate again — for a brief spell and in a rather different form — under Savonarola. From the very beginning, the Observance attracted the patronage of wealthy and influential citizens: Guido del Palagio, who settled the first Observant Franciscan house in Tuscany in a monastery near Fiesole of which he was the patron;[1] Barnaba degli Agli, whose will made possible, in 1418, the completion of the Dominican Observant convent of San Domenico di Fiesole,[2] was a member of an old Magnate family; the family of Niccolò Guasconi, abbot *in commendam* of the Badia of Florence, who on the advice of Ludovico Barbo (the reformer of the Paduan convent of Santa Giustina) handed over his monastery to the Benedictine Observant Gomes Ferreira da Silva.[3]

It was Cosimo de' Medici, however, who provided the outstanding example of patrician patronage of the Observants. His principal beneficiaries were the Franciscan Observants, for whom in the 1420s he began construction of the convent and church of San Francesco al Bosco;[4] the Dominican Observants of San Domenico di Fiesole, for whom he rebuilt on a magnificent scale the convent and church of San Marco after helping them acquire it from the Silvestrines in 1436;[5] and the reformed Augustinian canons of the Lateran Congregation, who in 1440 had taken possession of the Badia of Fiesole and whose church and convent he began to rebuild, late in life, in 1456.[6]

According to Vespasiano da Bisticci, it was Eugenius IV who, having transferred San Marco, during his residence in Florence, to the friars of San Domenico, persuaded Cosimo to undertake the rebuilding of their new convent.[7] In view of Cosimo's prior patronage of the Observants of Bosco ai Frati, this statement has to be taken with a grain of salt,[8] but it is highly probable that the presence of the pope in Florence contributed to Cosimo's allegiance to the Observance. Eugenius IV was dedicated to the reform of the orders. During his long residence in Florence he actively promoted, as "a most zealous supporter of the religious manner of life" monastic reform in the city and its territory.[9] Vespasiano da Bisticci later writes how Eugenius "saw to it most diligently that the religious kept within their bounds, and, as far as he could, made Conventuals accept the Observance."[10] Cosimo's sympathies for the Observance may also have been enhanced by his exile in Venice. As Gabriel Condulmer, Eugenius IV had been a leading member of the group of young Venetian patricians who at the beginning of the century had founded the congregation of the secular canons of San Giorgio in Alga. The congregation became the focal point for the reform of monasteries in the Veneto, foremost among them the Benedictine convent of Santa Giustina in Padua, reformed by Ludovico Barbo from

1408.[11] Cosimo, who spent a year in Padua and Venice, must have become familiar with the reform ideals of men whose social background was similar to his own, even before he met Eugenius IV in Florence on his return from exile at the end of 1434.

According to Giuliano Lapaccini, author of the chronicle of San Marco (written at mid-century), Eugenius IV transferred the convent in 1436 from the Silvestrines to the Dominican Observants at the request of the Signoria but "out of respect for" Cosimo and his brother Lorenzo de' Medici.[12] This initiative reflects yet another dimension of Cosimo's patronage, reminding one of the interventions in favor of Observants on the part of *signori* such as the Gonzaga and the Este[13] — although owing to the nature of Cosimo's political ascendancy in the Florentine republic, an initiative of this kind would likely be officially effected by the Signoria. Similarly, the exemption from indirect taxes which the friars of San Marco, "whom the people call Observants," received in the following year from the Signoria was probably due to Cosimo's influence,[14] as was the increase in that exemption which the councils granted them in 1445 on the grounds that in the meantime their numbers had increased.[15] In fact, the register of the *professi* of San Marco lists seventeen names between 1436 and 1439 and seventeen between 1439 and 1444.[16]

It was normal practice for the commune to make refunds to religious houses of payments of gabelles for goods imported into the city; the Statutes of 1415 list the houses that enjoyed this concession and specify the amount of the refunds.[17] The Commune also gave annual subsidies, based on the size of the communities, to a number of convents.[18] For convents such as Santa Maria Novella, exemptions of this kind can hardly have been of vital importance. Matters stood differently with communities that insisted on the strict observance of the rule of poverty, did not possess landed property and fixed annual revenues, and relied entirely on alms. Insofar as lay patronage of Observant houses covered buildings and furnishings, it was not concerned with assistance to the friars and may indeed have rendered their lives more difficult by providing space for the increase in their numbers.

Antoninus's complaint in the 1450s that laymen "are mean in giving alms and prefer to spend on chapels, superfluous ornaments, and ecclesiastical pomp rather than on the support of the poor"[19] had a special relevance for Observant communities.

Cosimo's help in meeting the living expenses of the friars of San Marco constitutes, therefore, a departure from the normal pattern of patronage in favor of Observant houses. From the time they took possession of the convent, the friars received from him for "spese minute" (minor expenses) 6 pounds weekly; this amount was raised in 1444 to 10 pounds, no doubt as a result of the increase in their numbers.[20] These alms, later raised to 12 pounds, which the friars believed to have been given "in perpetuo,"[21] were supplemented by all manner of recurrent gifts, so that Giuliano Lapaccini calculated in 1453 that Cosimo had been spending, during the preceding ten years, about one gold ducat a day for the friars.[22] But, either because these gifts and the weekly subsidies were not considered sufficient to meet the expenses of the convent or because Cosimo wished to place its economic future on a more permanent foundation, he obtained two years later, in 1455, from Calixtus III a bull permitting the friars of San Marco to accept and retain property and annual revenues, with the somewhat inconsistent proviso (in the words of the *Cronaca* of San Marco) that "the convent remains Observant."[23]

One of the two Florentine ambassadors to the pope — the other was Cosimo's son Giovanni — through whose offices the bull was obtained, was none other than Archbishop Antoninus, a leading figure in the Observant reform of the Dominican order who had been prior of San Marco from 1439 to 1444.[24] The bull, which anticipates by seventeen years the general dispensation from the vow of poverty accorded by Sixtus IV to the Franciscans[25] and by twenty years that granted to the Dominicans,[26] reflects the fact that the financial support Cosimo gave to the friars could hardly be expected to continue ad infinitum. In fact, Cosimo made no bequests to the convent in his will: its *Ricordanze* comment on his death: "he did not leave us anything."[27] Cosimo's son and grandson did raise the weekly alms to the convent from 10 to 12 pounds,[28] but there is no evidence to suggest that they continued supplementing them in the same generous fashion as Cosimo, and gifts from other donors were very small in comparison with those that Cosimo had lavished on the convent.[29]

Antoninus himself may provide an explanation for the convent's departure from strict observance of the rule of poverty (which, according to the chronicle of San Marco, had the full consent of the friars), as well as his own apparent volte-face.[30] A chapter of his *Chronicae* written shortly after this event,[31] begins with a sharp attack on the comfort and sumptuous display indulged in by Dominican houses: what would the holy founder, St. Dominic, say if he considered their "houses and cells enlarged, vaulted, raised to the sky, and most frivolously adorned with superfluous sculptures and paintings"?[32] But he goes on to point out that changed conditions, "mutatis conditionibus," require different responses, and concedes that it might be necessary to dispense with the rule of poverty, "since otherwise it would not appear to be possible [for the friars] to maintain themselves."[33] For while the numbers of mendicants had multiplied, charity had declined, the laity preferring to spend on sumptuous building rather than on the relief of the poor.[34]

Antoninus's criticism of the magnificence of Dominican houses bears on yet another problem of lay patronage of the Observance: patrons and Observants were liable to hold different views on the size and form of the building projects for convents and churches. Biondo reports that people considered Cosimo's expenses for the buildings of the "famous convent of San Marco" insane.[35] And Cosimo's friend, the Augustinian canon Timoteo Maffei, for whom he rebuilt the Badia of Fiesole,[36] while praising the size and decoration of San Marco, the richness of its library, and the splendor of its furnishings (Figure 2.1), observes that these were such as "the profession of poor religious would hardly appear to require."[37] He adds, moreover, that some people might condemn Cosimo for having spent so much—Vespasiano says more than 40,000 florins—on its building and furnishing. Maybe some of the friars of San Marco shared these misgivings about Cosimo's building program; if so, their qualms are not recorded in the chronicle of the convent. Other Observants certainly did resent, and indeed oppose, ambitious building projects of their patrons. According to the sixteenth-century historian of the Tuscan Franciscans, the Franciscan Observants of San Salvatore al Monte protested against the excessive magnificence of Castello Quaratesi's project for their new church, giving in only after his death in 1465. Castello had replied to their protests "that they did not intend to build it according to the status of the friars, but according to what was suitable to the city.[39] As for the "status of the friars," the limitations it was meant to impose on the buildings of their convents and churches were explicitly defined, in 1474, for the Franciscan Observants of San Salvatore, by a commission "on the buildings," set up that

Figure 2.1. Michelozzo, Library of San Marco, donated by Cosimo de' Medici. Florence. Photo Alinari/Art Resource, N.Y.

year by the congregation of the Tuscan province: thus the nave of their new church was to be 20 *braccia* wide and 60 long, its choir chapel 13 braccia wide and 13 long and vaulted, with "the roof simple."[40]

Criticism of lay patronage that appeared to conflict with the ideal of poverty professed by the Observants may have contributed to the antireform stance of the Conventuals and their friends and relatives; but the chief causes of their opposition must be sought in the Observant reforms themselves, which were bound to affect profoundly the material conditions and the lifestyle of the religious houses into which they were introduced. Roberto Bizzocchi has analyzed the many and varied kinds of involvement of the Florentine patriciate in the organization of the Florentine church during the fifteenth century;[41] the relations between that class and the religious houses also well merit a systematic inquiry. Such an inquiry would have not only to identify the members of patrician families who embraced the profession of religious orders but also to investigate the links that, as "representatives" of their families or class, they provided between these orders and the laity. These links form yet another aspect of the laity's attitude to, and patronage of, the Observants.

During the general chapter of the Dominican order held at Santa Maria Novella in 1414, at which Leonardo Dati was elected master general of the order,[42] Simone da Cascina singled out, in his eulogy of that convent, its aristocratic membership: "there is no great family in the city of which we have not had members among our brethren."[43] About sixty-five years later, Giovanni Caroli enlarged upon the same theme in his *laudatio* of his convent: "No family of the nobility has ever scorned having its sons in our house."[44] Similar observations could well have been made about other prestigious convents of fourteenth- and fifteenth-century Florence. It would have been surprising if the personal relations between Florence's aristocracy and its religious houses had not affected the former's views on the latter's reform. In 1460 Santa Maria Novella was the object of an attempt by Pope Pius II, who actively supported Observant reform,[45] to introduce such reform in that convent.[46] He had, he wrote from Siena to the Signoria of Florence at the beginning of June, learned daily "innumerable things about the depraved life and customs of the friars." Consequently, he had ordered the archbishop of Florence, Orlando Bonarli, and the master general of the order, Martial Auribelli, "that they reform this convent" and restore it "to the observance of the rule"[48] and that they expel from it those friars who refused to live according to the rule.

It emerges from Pius's letter, as well as from a letter he wrote to the Signoria three months later, that his attempt at reform was meeting with opposition not only from the friars but also from their relatives in the Signoria. For the pope requests in his first letter that its members, "ignoring all family predilection and love," assist an initiative that was bound to bring the Florentine people "great comfort and edification"[49]; then he drives home his point by assuring the members of the Signoria of his conviction that they value the "honorem religionis et honestatis" more highly than the "friendship or familial relationship" of the friars. It was not uncommon at that time for communal magistracies to take the initiative in introducing the Observant reform in convents of their cities;[50] but if Pius II was still hoping to obtain the backing of the Florentine government for his reform scheme, he was sorely disappointed. The Signoria replied to his request by rejecting all the accusations he had leveled against the friars of Santa Maria Novella; in that convent, they wrote, "there are a great many citizens of ours who, owing to their learning and to the integrity of their life, have received the highest praise." These excellent men ("optimi viri") had been living for many years in a place frequently visited by all citizens; had they been guilty of the vices and dissolute life of which they were accused, "this would not have escaped those of our citizens who could observe them closely every day, and who enjoyed no little familiarity with them." Indeed, their "religio, integritas, fides et excellens doctrina" were so obvious that Florence's citizens loved the friars "like relatives," and the Signoria found it unbearable that such "optimi viri" should be slandered in this way.[51] Their successors in the two-month office were not more cooperative. On 1 September the pope sent a letter to the new Signoria contending that their predecessors had given active support to the resistance the friars had put up to his reform measures. "We know for certain," he wrote from Siena, that the rebellion of these friars arose from the favor the Signoria of July–August had shown them.[52] In fact, the situation was more complex than represented by Pius II: Giovanni Caroli, for one, who was prior of Santa Maria Novella until he was removed from this office by Martial Auribelli in September 1460, was strongly in favor of reform but wanted it effected from within the convent, not imposed from above.[53] As for the Signoria of July–August, its head, the Gonfalonier of Justice, had been one of the leading Mediceans, Tommaso Soderini, and it had also included two other prominent members of the regime, Bernardo del Nero and Ruberto Lioni.[54] The example set by Cosimo de' Medici in supporting Observant reform had evidently not been followed by some of his closest collaborators, in a situation in which the pursuit of reforming ideals clashed with the conservatism and the vested interests of friars who were connected with them by links of friendship or of parentage.

According to the sixteenth-century Franciscan historian Pulinari, it was Cosimo who had persuaded the wealthy Castello Quaratesi to rebuild the church of the Observant convent of San Salvatore al Monte.[55]

One may, in fact, ask oneself to what extent Cosimo's patronage altogether set an example for other members of the patriciate (Figure 2.2). The extent and scope of his magnificence, as well as his action in helping to introduce Observant reform in San Marco, reminds one of princely rather than of private support of the Observants. His grandson Lorenzo, who proudly records the vast amount spent by his family on charity,[56] continued to subsidize the friars of San Marco as his father had done, and his wife made a bequest to them in her will;[57] but Lorenzo's building patronage lagged far behind that of his grandfather: he failed to complete even the construction of the Badia of Fiesole and of its church, which had been continued by his father.[58] It was the more significant, then, that his only substantial building project for a church or convent was for an Observant community, the Augustinian Hermits of Santa Maria, outside Porta San Gallo. The construction, or rather reconstruction, of the convent was begun in 1488 and appears to have been practically completed by the time of Lorenzo's death in 1492;[59] a visitor to Florence in that year described it as "exquisite and sumptuous,"[60] and less than a year later, an official document stated that the new house of the friars, which had been built at the Porta San Gallo "entirely at the expense of . . . Lorenzo de' Medici," was "almost completed."[61] Lorenzo's admiration for the learned Augustinian friar and famous preacher Fra Mariano da Genazzano, who in 1484 and 1488 was vicar general of the Observant congregation of Lecceto, may have contributed to his decision to undertake this project;[62] Poliziano writes that he was building the "insigne coenobium" for Fra Mariano,[63] and according to Lorenzo's biographer, Niccolò Valori, Lorenzo built the "large and magnificent convent" for Fra Mariano and his brethren "in order to keep him in Florence."[64] Lorenzo also appears to have backed (but without subsidizing it) another building project for an Observant convent, the long delayed completion of the new church of the Franciscans of San Salvatore al Monte, which was financed by Castello Quaratesi's large bequest.[65]

Like his grandfather, Lorenzo also intervened in the internal affairs of the Dominican order in introducing the Observant reform in one of its convents.[66] In August of the same year in which the construction of the new convent and church of Porta San Gallo was taken in hand, Innocent VIII, "moved by the prayers of our beloved son Lo-

¶ Frate Hieronymo da Ferrara feruo iutile di
Iefu Xpo a tutti li electi di Dio & figluoli del
padre eterno defidera gratia pace & confola,
tione del fpirito fancto.

Olendo noi dilectiffimi imitare el noftro
faluator: Elquale molte uolte credette al
la grande ira & acceſo furore delli fcribi & pha
rifei habbiamo laffato il predicare ifino a tanto
che allui piacera : Ma fapendo che il demonio
non fi cura de corpi: ma defidera leanime & chi

Figure 2.2. Layman at prayer in a private palace domestic chapel. Woodcut illustration to Fra Girolamo Savonarola's *Epistola a tutti gli eletti di Dio,* published in Florence in 1497 by Bartolomeo de' Libri. Florence, Biblioteca Nazionale Centrale. Photo Artini.

renzo de' Medici," transferred the Dominican convent of Santa Caterina at Pisa to the Lombard Observant Congregation.[67] This was the final result of a diplomatic operation mounted by Lorenzo and aimed at obtaining from the pope the reform of a convent of which its sixteenth-century historian writes that for many years its members had possessed and freely disposed of properties: "the rest I pass under silence," he adds, "as it would offend chaste ears."[68] In July 1487 Lorenzo wrote to the Florentine ambassador in Rome, Giovanni Lanfredini, that he had recently "made strong representations to His Holiness that he reform the convent of Santa Caterina at Pisa," which was in the hands of Conventuals, by transferring it to the friars of San Marco.[69] He had been advised to await the election of the new master general of the order; and since it had now taken place — Gioacchino Torriani had been elected master general in the preceding month — he could ask Lanfredini to request "this reform, which I greatly desire for the honor of God, and for my own and the city's satisfaction."[70] Lanfredini should employ all available means ("ogni arte") to stop delays, which would be open to exploitation by "these Conventuals" of Santa Caterina.[71] Three months later, he wrote to Lanfredini on the matter of the convent of the Carmine in Florence: since the convent "is now reduced to such a state that it has become a shelter of fools and knaves," the master general has, to prevent its complete ruin, decided "that it be reformed and that Observants of the same Order be introduced into it."[72] In his letter of 27 July, Lorenzo had advised Lanfredini that he intended San Marco to be the convent that should carry out the reform of Santa Caterina in Pisa: the ambassador knew "what kind of community that of San Marco is, which today consists entirely of worthy men [uomini da bene], and most of them are dedicated to studies."[73] As in the days of Cosimo, patronage of the Observants could have its humanist connotations. Lorenzo may well have been trying, by providing the convent of Porta San Gallo with "a most delightful place for a library,"[74] to follow the example of his grandfather's magnificent endowment of San Marco with its great library. Indeed, his choice, for his only major building project other than his villa at Poggio a Caiano, of a convent belonging to the Augustinian order, may also have been owing to the share of the Augustinian Hermits in humanist studies and to their status among the humanists.[75]

Savonarola's views of Observant reform were different from those of the Medici. Two years after he had become prior of San Marco, after the convent was, in 1493, separated from the Lombard Congregation to which (apart from an interruption of five years) it had been affiliated since 1451. After this separation he revived the strict observance of the rule of poverty—barely forty years after it had been relaxed with the help of Cosimo.[76] "About the same time," records the *Vita* of Savonarola, whose author used to go under the name of Burlamacchi, "the friars of San Marco sold their possessions in order to serve God in truth and in strict poverty."[77] The *Vita* also describes Savonarola's model of an ideal monastery, which conforms to the principles the Observants had been trying to impose on their convents throughout the century: "And he wanted that the monastery should be famous for its simplicity and not for its precious stones . . . he wanted it to be simple and low-built . . . with small cells . . . and the rooms whitewashed . . . the cloisters and the church simple, without vaults, the columns of wood or bricks, in the church no frivolous figures but only simple and devout ones, devoid of any vanity."[78] Written about three decades after the event, the *Vita* gives an idealized picture of Savonarola's reforms;[79] in fact, the greatly increased number of friars who entered the convent under his priorate, many of them from the city's aristocracy, necessitated first of all the provision of additional space for their living quarters.[80] We know little about the extent of Savonarola's success in carrying out his reforms at San Marco, yet it is hard to escape the conclusion that he too had to face the predicament of the Observance in a city where its very success could militate against the achievement of its aims.

NOTES

1. Fra Dionisio Pulinari da Firenze, O.F.M., *Cronache dei Frati Minori della provincia di Toscana,* ed. Saturnino Mencherini (Arezzo: Cooperativa tipografica, 1913), 318–19. On Guido del Palagio, see Gene Brucker, *The Civic World of Early Renaissance Florence* (Princeton, N.J.: Princeton University Press, 1977), 133.

2. Raoul Morçay, *Saint Antonin Fondateur du couvent de St.-Marc. Archevêque de Florence: 1389–1459* (Tours/Paris: A. Mame et Fils-Gabalda, [1914]), 43. On the Agli, see Lauro Martines, *The Social World of the Florentine Humanists, 1390–1460* (London: Routledge and Kegan Paul, 1963), 337.

3. Rudolf Blum, *La biblioteca della Badia fiorentina e i codici di Antonio Corbinelli*

(Città del Vaticano: Biblioteca Apostolica Vaticana, 1951), 15ff; Maurilio Adriani, "La Badia fiorentina: Appunti storico-religiosi," in *La Badia fiorentina* (Florence: Cassa di Risparmio di Firenze 1982), 27–28. On Gomez, see Guido Battelli, "Due celebri monaci portoghesi in Firenze nella prima metà del quattrocento: L'Abate Gomes e Velasco di Portogallo," *Archivio storico italiano* 96, 2 (1938): 218–23; on the Guasconi, see Brucker, *Civic World,* 268.

4. Herbert Siebenhüner and Ludwig Heydenreich, "Die Klosterkirche San Francesco al Bosco im Mugello," *Mitteilungen des Kunsthistorischen Institutes in Florenz* 5 (1937–40): 194–96; Crispin C. Robinson," Cosimo de' Medici's Patronage of the Observantist Movement" (M.Phil. thesis, Courtauld Institute, University of London, 1984), chap. 2; Miranda Ferrara and Francesco Quinterio, *Michelozzo di Bartolomeo* (Florence: Salimbeni, 1984), 164–67.

5. Walter and Elisabeth Paatz, *Die Kirchen von Florenz* (Frankfurt am Main: Klostermann, 1940–54), 3:9–10; Evelyn Curtis, "The Convent of San Marco in Florence, 1436–94" (M.A. thesis, University of London, 1956); Hans Teubner, "San Marco in Florenz: Umbauten vor 1500: Ein Beitrag zum Werk des Michelozzo," *Mitteilungen des Kunsthistorischen Institutes in Florenz* 23 (1979): 239–72; Ferrara and Quinterio, *Michelozzo,* 185ff.

6. Vincenzo Viti, *La Badia fiesolana* (Florence: Tipografia Giuntina, 1926), 19, 23; Ugo Procacci, "Cosimo de' Medici e la costruzione della Badia fiesolana," *Commentari* 29 (1982): 80–97. See Ernst H. Gombrich, "Alberto Avogadro's Descriptions of the Badia of Fiesole and of the Villa of Careggi," *Italia medioevale e umanistica* 5 (1962): 217–29, for a panegyrical and mostly fictitious account of the rebuilding of the Badia by Cosimo.

7. Aulo Greco, ed., *Le Vite* (Florence: Istituto Nazionale di Studi sul Rinascimento, 1970–76), 2:177–78. For the bull of 21 January 1436, see T. Ripoll and A. Bremond, eds., *Bullarium Ordinis Fratrum Praedicatorum* (Rome, 1729–40), 3:65.

8. See note 4 above.

9. Antoninus, *Chronicae,* pt. 3, tit. 22, chap. 10, sec. 5 (Lyons, 1586), vol. 3:526: "zelator praecipuus religiose conversationis."

10. Greco, *Le Vite,* 1:11: "Atendeva con ogni diligentia a riformare la Chiesa, et fare che religiosi istessino a' termini loro, et di conventuali fargli oservanti, giusto alla possa sua."

11. Silvio Tramontin, "La cultura monastica del quattrocento dal primo patriarca Lorenzo Giustiniani ai Camaldolesi Paolo Giustiniani e Pietro Quirini," *Storia della cultura veneta* 3, pt. 1 (Vicenza: Neri Pozza, 1980), 431ff.

12. Raoul Morçay, ed., "La Cronaca del Convento fiorentino di San Marco: La parte più antica, dettata da Giuliano Lapaccini," *Archivio Storico Italiano* 71, pt. 1 (1913): 8. According to the *Cronaca,* the convent was transferred to the Dominican Observants by the pope "procurantibus civibus et praecipue Magnificis viris Cosma et Laurentio germanis . . . postulante hoc Dominio civitatis Florentie ob intuitum et contemplationem praedictorum Cosme et Laurentii de Medicis."

13. See my "'Reformatio' und Ordensreform in italienischen Stadtrepubliken und Signorien," in Kaspar Elm, ed., *Reform- und Observanzbewegungen im spätmittelalterlichen Ordenswesen,* forthcoming.

14. Archivio di Stato di Firenze [hereafter ASF], Provvisioni Registri [hereafter Provv. Reg.], 136: fols. 170v–171r, 22–24 September 1445. The friars had, in October 1437, received permission to import into the city each year "absque aliqua solutione gabelle tot res necessarias pro victu et vestitu ipsorum," for which they would otherwise have had to pay up to 60 lire "in totum et pro anno." This exemption had been granted to them by the Signoria and the

Colleges jointly with the *Regolatori delle entrate e delle uscite del Comune.* The Signoria was by statute authorized to grant such exemptions; see *Statuta Populi et Communis Florentiae,* bk. 5, tract. 3, rub. 22, Freiburg, 1778–83, 3:408–9.

15. The upper limit of the exemption was raised to 100 lire: ASF, Provv. Reg., 136: fols. 170v–71r. The exemption was this time granted by the Councils of the People and of the Commune. See also Morçay, "Cronaca del convento," 25. The friars point out in their petition, as recorded in the *provvisione,* that the original exemption had at the time been "quasi sufficiens," but that it was no longer so, since their numbers had increased "per dimidium," and were bound to increase further, "propter devotionem que habetur ad dictam ecclesiam" of S. Marco.

16. "Ricordanze," Biblioteca Laurenziana, Florence, Cod. S. Marco 370: fol. 91r–v; Curtis, "Convent of San Marco," app., xviii–xix.

17. *Statuta Populi et Communis,* bk. 5, tract. 3, rub. 21, 3:402–8.

18. Ibid.

19. Antoninus, *Chronicae,* pt. 3, tit. 23, chap. 4, sec. 13, vol. 3:629: "parci sunt in eleemosynis dandis, et libentius expendunt in capellis vel ornamentis superfluis et pompis ecclesiarum, quam in subventione pauperum."

20. "Ricordanze," Biblioteca Laurenziana, Florence, Cod. S. Marco 902, fol. 9r.

21. Ibid. See below, n. 28.

22. Morçay, "Cronaca del convento," 23–24. After enumerating Cosimo's recurrent gifts, Lapaccini adds, "et plura alia faciebat ad requisitionem fratrum."

23. Ibid., 28–29; "quatenus conventus iste recipere ac retinere posset possessiones et reditus annuales . . . cum hac tamen conditione procurata fuit [scil. the bull], durante videlicet in hoc conventu observantia." Cf. *Bullarium Ordinis Fratrum Praedicatorum,* 3:340, 7 June 1455: "Cum itaque, sicut . . . petitio continebat . . . Cosmas de Medicis . . . super modum desideret, quod in ea [scil. domo] observantia perpetua vigeat . . . et quod vos et . . . successores vestri commode sustentare ac bona immobilia recipere et retinere possitis," the pope grants the friars and their successors the petition, "cupientes ut dicta observantia in praefata domo semper vigeat . . . , observantiam praedictam tenentibus et secundum illam viventibus." Giuliano Lapaccini, by paraphrasing the text of the bull in a conditional clause, may have wished to counter any objection to the exemption granted by the bull, on the grounds that it was contrary to the ideals of the observance.

24. Morçay, "Cronaca del Convento," 23–24. Cf. Morçay, *Saint Antonin,* 68, 95.

25. John Moorman, *A History of the Franciscan Order from Its Origins to the Year 1517* (Oxford: Clarendon Press, 1968), 487–88.

26. Daniel Antonin Mortier, *Histoire des Maîtres Généraux de l'Ordre des Frères Prêcheurs* (Paris: Alphonse Picard, 1903–20), 4:496–98.

27. "Non lasciò che avessimo nulla," "Ricordanze," fol. 9r. This entry was written before December 1469, as Piero de' Medici is subsequently recorded as alive.

28. Ibid.: "Ricordo chome Piero di Cosimo cominciò adì 29 di marzo 1465 . . . a dare al convento libre dodici la septimana, et cosi intende fare tutttavia . . . Ricordo come Lorenzo e Giuliano di Piero de' Medici sequitano la limosina delle dodici lire la septimana; credesi si ordinava che lla abbiamo in perpetuo."

29. Curtis, "Convent of San Marco," 106–11.

30. Morçay, "Cronaca del Convento," 28–29: "ad quod etiam accessit consensus fratrum."

31. See James Bernard Walker, *The "Chronicles" of Saint Antoninus. A Study in Historiography* (Washington, D.C.: Catholic University of America, 1933), 24.

32. Antoninus, *Chronicae*, pt. 3, tit. 23, chap. 4, sec. 13, vol. 3:628. "Quid diceret pater sanctus, si nunc attenderet ad ecclesiam et domos et cellas fratrum ampliatas, testudinatas, in coelum elevatas, in sculpturis et picturis curiosissime ornatas." On the concept of *curiositas*, cf. his *Summa theologica* (Venice, 1503), pt. 2, tit. 3, chap. 7, fols. 127r–130v; vol. 2, fol. 129r: "De curiositate et aspectu vano oculorum quantum est periculosus plus quam aliorum sensuum abusus. Committi potest peccatum per visum magis quam per alium sensum multipliciter, incessanter et faciliter."

33. Antoninus, *Chronicae*, pt. 3, tit. 23, chap. 4, sec. 13, vol. 3:628–29: "si mutatis conditionibus illius temporis, mutetur seu dispensetur illa constitutio, cum aliter apparet sustentari non posse." On the question of papal dispensation from the rule of poverty, see idem, *Summa theologica*, pt. 3, tit. 16, chap. 1, sec. 12, vol. 3, fols. 256r–257v.

34. See note 19 above.

35. *Italia illustrata*, in *De Roma triumphante* . . . (Basle, 1559), 304: "in quo quum superbae sunt et, ut aiunt, insanae extructiones."

36. Greco, *Le Vite*, 1:282: "Per l'autorità sua Cosimo de' Medici fu cagione s'edificasse la badia di Fiesole." See Viti, *La Badia fiesolana*, and Gombrich, "Alberto Avogadro's descriptions," 224.

37. ". . . quantum religiosorum pauperum professio non videtur exposcere,"*In Magnificentiae Cosmi Medicei Florentini detractores libellus*, in Giovanni Lami, *Deliciae eruditorum* (Florence, 1736–54), 12:155.

38. Greco, *Le Vite*, 2:178. According to Giuliano Lapaccini, Cosimo had spent, by 1453, about 36,000 ducats for the buildings and furnishings of S. Marco and for its library: Morçay, "Cronaca del Convento," 23.

39. Pulinari, *Cronache dei Frati Minori*, 188: "che non erano per fabbricarla secondo lo stato de' frati, ma secondo che si conveniva alla città." Pulinari, writing circa 1580, followed the lost chronicle of Fra Mariano Ughi, who died in S. Salvatore in 1523.

40. Ibid., 187 n. 1: "con tecto simplice."

41. Roberto Bizocchi, "Chiesa e aristocrazia nella Firenze del Quattrocento," *Archivio Storico Italiano* 142 (1984): 191–282.

42. Mortier, *Histoire des Maîtres Généraux*, 4:86–87.

43. Tommaso Käppelli, ed., "La raccolta di discorsi e di atti scolastici di Simone da Cascina O.P. (died c. 1420)," *Archivum Fratrum Praedicatorum* 12 (1942): 201–2: "non est domus aliqua famosa in civitate de qua non habuerimus aliquem nostrum fratrem." Cf. Kaspar Elm, "Mendikanten und Humanisten im Florenz des Tre- und Quattrocento . . . ," in *Die Humanisten in ihrer politischen und sozialen Umwelt*, Kommission für Humanismusforschung, Mitteilung 3, ed. O. Herding and R. Stupperich (Boppard: Boldt, 1976), 56–67.

44. Salvatore Camporeale, "Giovanni Caroli e le 'Vitae fratrum S. M. Novellae.' Umanesimo e crisi religiosa (1460–1480)," *Memorie domenicane*, n.s. 12 (1981): 241–42: "Nulla enim nobilitatis familia fuit, que earum in domo suos habere natos fuerit dedignata. . . . Enumerarem certe earum familiarum viros, quos in omni statu ac genere sumus consecuti, nisi

me temporis et orationis arceret angustia." On the date of the composition of the *Vitae fratrum* (1479/80), 161.

45. Ludwig Pastor, *The History of the Popes,* English trans., 2d ed. (London: Kegan Paul, Trench, Trübner, 1900), 3:277–81; Mortier, *Histoire des Maîtres Généraux,* 4:393.

46. Raymond Creytens, "La déposition de maître Martial Auribelli O.P. par Pie II (1462)," *Archivum Fratrum Praedicatorum* 45 (1975): 166–70; Camporeale, "Giovanni Caroli," 150–52.

47. ". . . infinita . . . de impudica vita et moribus fratrum" (letter of 2 June 1460, Creytens, "La déposition," 187). Cf. Camporeale, "Giovanni Caroli," 156 ff., on Caroli's views on the decline of the convent in the fifteenth century.

48. ". . . ad observationem illum redigant regularem" (Creytens, "La déposition," 187).

49. ". . . seposita omni affectione et caritate parentum" (Creytens, "La déposition," 187). On Pius II's letter of 1 September, see note 52 below.

50. See, for example, Mortier, *Histoire des Maîtres Généraux,* 4:369, and my forthcoming paper, "'Reformatio.'"

51. ASF, Signori, Missive, 1a Cancelleria (hereafter Miss. 1a Canc.) 43: fols. 64v–65r, 7 August 1460: "in quo [conventu] plerique sunt cives nostri, qui sibi doctrina, vite integritate, laudem eximiam pepererunt. . . . Hi enim, Beate Pater, multos iam annos in urbe nostra versati ea in sede, quam frequenter cives omnes adire solent, si avare, libidinose, petulanter egissent vitam . . . non incogniti essent nostris, quorum in oculis quotidie versabantur, qui cum illis non parvam consuetudinem habebant." The letter must also have been in reply to a brief Pius II had sent Orlando Bonarli and Martial Auribelli on 20 July (Creytens, "La déposition," 188–89), in which he had accused the friars of Sta. Maria Novella that "norma pie vite, studio et suavi contemplationis iugo sepositis prosilientes ad vetita, diversa excessus et crimina committere detestabiliter non pavescunt."

52. Creytens, "La déposition," 190: "Quod tum ex favore illis per eos vestros predecessores provenisse certo scimus." The Signoria replied on 6 September (Miss. 1a Canc. 43: fols. 78v–79r) that the trouble had originated in the "discordia" between Martial Auribelli "et plurimos fratres," which "plures iam menses fuit." The master general expelled a number of friars from the convent, but they were reinstated later in the year, as the Signoria writes on 23 October to Cardinal Niccolò Forteguerri (Miss. 1a Canc. 43: fol. 184r). On the conflict between Martial Auribelli and the friars of Sta. Maria Novella, see Creytens, "La déposition," 168–69.

53. Camporeale, "Giovanni Caroli," 143–44.

54. See Francesco Guicciardini, *Storie fiorentine,* ed. Roberto Palmarocchi (Bari: Laterza, 1931), 17, 21.

55. Pulinari, *Cronache dei Frati Minori,* 187. On his source, see note 39 above.

56. Angelo Fabroni, *Laurentii Medicis Magnifici vita* (Pisa, 1784), 2:47: "Somma incredibile [di danari . . . abbiamo spesi] . . . tra lemosine, muraglie e gravezze."

57. See above, page 000; Curtis, "Convent of San Marco," 149.

58. Procacci, "Cosimo de' Medici." Cf. Guicciardini, *Storie fiorentine,* 81: "Rispetto alle tante e tali muraglie di Cosimo, si può dire murassi nulla."

59. F. W. Kent, "New Light on Lorenzo de' Medici's Convent at Porta San Gallo," *Burlington Magazine* 124 (1982): 292–94.

60. Francesco Castelli to Eleonora d'Este, 4 April 1492 in Cornelius von Fabriczy, "Giuliano da San Gallo," *Jahrbuch der preussischen Kunstsammlungen* 23, Beiheft (1902): 16–17: "mai vidi il più polito et somptuoso [locho]."

61. ASF, Provv. Reg., 183: fols. 68r–69r, 8–12 March 1493: "ubi domus nova in habitationem dictorum fratrum constructa est et quasi absoluta omnibus sumptibus . . . Laurentii Medicis." Bartolomeo Dei writes in 1488, however, that Lorenzo "in buona parte fa la spesa e è auctore della muragla, insieme col nostro ser Giovanni" (Kent, "New Light"). Bartolomeo Dei was a member of the Florentine chancery, as was Giovanni Guidi, notary of the Riformagioni. On Giovanni Guidi and his prominent role in Lorenzo's entourage, see Guicciardini, *Storie fiorentine, 79.*

62. See David A. Perini, *Un emulo di Fr. Girolomo Savonarola. Fr. Mariano da Genazzano* (Rome: Tipografia dell'Unione Editrice, 1917), 20, 22–23.

63. To Tristano Calchi, XI Kal. Aprilis 1489 (22 March 1489); *Opera* (Basle, 1553), 52–53. If, as is probable, the date is according to the Florentine calendar, the year is 1490; but see Kent, "New Light," 292.

64. Lorenzo Mehus, ed., *Laurentii Medicei vita* (Florence, 1749), 47–48: "ut Florentie detineret, coenobium illi et fratribus eius amplum ac magnificum prope urbem faciendum curavit." Cf. also Iacopo Nardi, *Istorie della città di Firenze,* ed. Lelio Arbib (Florence, 1838–41), 1:126: "a sua contemplazione aveva restaurato quasi tutto il convento di San Gallo." Both Valori and Nardi must have known the convent well before it was destroyed by the Florentines during the siege in 1529.

65. Pulinari, *Cronache dei Frati Minori,* 189. "Finalmente i frati . . . acconsentirono al magnifico Lorenzo . . . che egli fabbricasse la chiesa, come che lui voleva, e così fu incominciata l'anno del Signore 1490 e finita per insino all'ultimo."

66. He also intervened in the internal affairs of San Marco by vigorously supporting, in 1471, the appointment, against the wishes of the general of the Order, of Santi Schiattesi as vicar of the convent and its separation from the Observants of Ferrara to whom it had been recently joined. Cf. Lorenzo's letters to Marziale Auribelli and to the Florentine ambassador in Rome, Donato Acciaiuoli, in Lorenzo de' Medici, *Lettere,* I, ed. R. Fubini (Florence: Giunti-Barbèra, 1977): 298–302). He justifies his action by telling Auribelli that he had inherited [the concern for] "the peace and welfare of our convent of San Marco" from his father and grandfather (ibid., 299).

67. *Bullarium Ordinis Fratrum Praedicatorum,* 4:38, to the master general of the Dominican order, 24 July 1488. "Intelligentes Monasterium S. Catherinae Pisis necessaria indigere reformatione, tibi . . . committimus per praesentes, ut ad ipsum monasterium te conferas, illudque tam in capite quam in membris reformes et reducas ad Observantiam Ordinis Praedicatorum Congregationis Lombardiae." Cf. Innocent's letter to the vicar general of the Lombard congregation of 18 August 1488 *Bullarium Ordinis,* 4:38: "Dudum precibus delecti filii Laurentii Medicis inclinati commisimus dilecto filio Generali Ordinis tui per alias nostras litteras in forma brevis, ut Conventum Sanctae Catherinae de Pisis reformaret, ad instar aliorum conventuum Lombardiae reformatorum."

68. Francesco Bonaini, ed., *Annali del Convento di S. Caterina,* in *Archivio Storico Italiano* 6, pt. 2 (1845): 604: "a multis annis, singulis quod facere magis libuisset licebat, propria possidendo, expendendo, donando, et caetera quae veri domini faciunt pro arbitrio faciendo: caetera taceo, quae castas aures offensura, certo certius scio."

69. ASF, Mediceo avanti il Principato (hereafter MAP), 57:70, 27 July 1487: "Mentre era costì Pier Filippo [Pandolfini] et poi la partita sua Francesco Gaddi, feci grandissima instantia con la Santità di Nostro Signore per riformare el convento di Santa Caterina di Pisa de' frati di San Marcho nostro, sendo quelli di Pisa conventuali." Gaddi had been Florentine ambassador to the pope in April and May of that year: cf. his "Ricordanze," in Biblioteca Laurenziana, Florence, MS Acquisti e doni, 213: fol. 93v.

70. "Fummi decto era bene aspectare che il Capitolo Generale de l'Ordine, che s'avea ad fare de proximo, si facesi, perché s'avea ad provedere di nuovo Generale. Sendo facto el Capitolo, sendo facta la electione di decto Generale, vi mando la supplicatione . . . acciò che possiate sollicitare questa reformatione, la quale io desidero grandemente per honore di Dio et satisfactione di quella città et mia." On Gioacchino Torriani's election on 2 June 1487, see Mortier, Histoire des Maîtres Généraux, 5:4.

71. "Et essendovi data dilatione alchuna, harò caro usiate ogni arte per tagliarle, perché come si dà tempo a simili cose, sono poi più difficili per le arti usano questi conventuali." Innocent VIII's letter of 18 August to the vicar general of the Lombard Congregation (see note 67 above) may have been partly the result of Lanfredini's efforts to prevent delays in carrying out the reform: the pope orders that it be undertaken within ten days of the receipt of his letter, "sive per te, sive per alium idoneum et probatum religiosum tui Ordinis."

72. ASF, MAP, 57:130, 27 October 1487: "Questo nostro convento del Carmine è hoggi ridocto a termini che è una sentina di pazzi et di tristi. . . . In forma che per ultimo remedio, perché quello convento et chiesa . . . non ruini interamente, al Generale è paruto che si riformi et mettavisi observanti dello Ordine medesimo, in che si sono conformati tucti questi huomini da bene."

73. ASF, MAP, 57, 70: "Sapete che famiglia sia questa di San Marcho, che hoggi è ridocta in tucti huomini da bene, ché la maggiore parte si dà alli studii; però havevo disegnato questo luogo per honore di quella città et honore di Dio." The two letters to Giovanni Lanfredini will be edited by Melissa Bullard in vol. 9 of the edition of the letters of Lorenzo de' Medici (Lettere [Florence: Giunti-Barbèra, 1977–]).

74. Francesco Castelli to Beatrice d'Este, in von Fabriczy, "Giuliano da San Gallo," 16–17: "uno locho de una libreria amenissimo."

75. See Katherine Walsh, "Papal policy and local reform. Congregatio Ilicetana: the Augustinian Observant movement in Tuscany and the humanist ideal," Römische Historische Mitteilungen 22 (1980): 141ff.; Elm, "Die Mendikanten," 71ff.

76. See Joseph Schnitzer, Savonarola im Streite mit seinem Orden und seinem Kloster (Munich: J. F. Lehrmann, 1914), 56ff.

77. Piero Ginori Conti, ed., La Vita del Beato Ieronimo Savonarola (Florence: Leo S. Olschki, 1937), 60: "e' frati di Santo Marco venderono le loro possessioni per poter servire a Dio in verità e in strecta povertà."

78. Ibid., 51: "Et voleva che detto monasterio fussi famoso in ogni semplicità et non in pietre pretiose, perché e' non voleva che vi fussi marmi o macinghi, e altre simile pietre dal mondo stimate, ma humile e basso a terra, acciochè non si estendessi molto in alto, et piccole celle . . . et le camere intonicate . . . e' chiostri e chiesa semplici, sanza volte; le colonne di legno, o mattoni cotti; in chiesa non figure curiose, ma semplice et devote, senza alcuna vanità."

79. That is the "Vita latina." On the relation between this work and its Italian

version, see Roberto Ridolfi, "Soluzione di un fondamentale problema savonaroliano: dipendenza dello Pseudo-Burlamacchi dalla 'Vita latina,'" *Bibliofilia* 37 (1935): 401–18.

80. See Armando F. Verde, "La Congregazione di San Marco dell'ordine dei frati Predicatori: Il 'reale' della predicazione savonaroliana," *Memorie domenicane,* n.s. 14 (1983): 152–54.

3 ❧

AUGUSTINUS CANONICUS–AUGUSTINUS EREMITA

A Quattrocento *Cause Célèbre*

KASPAR ELM

A T THE HEART OF THE FIFTEENTH-CENTURY quest for religious authenticity lay fundamental historical and historiographic questions that would shape the religious reform of the next century: What had the "glorious" past really been like? What "models" from early Christian experience should be allowed to determine present and future Church development? In this chapter, Kaspar Elm studies the case of those religious communities which followed the "Rule" of St. Augustine, and their heated disagreement as to the kind of Christian life intended by the great fourth-century church father. Did Augustine want his followers to live in close interaction with lay society, or to withdraw into eremitical seclusion? From Elm's analysis of this cause célèbre emerge two distinct ideals of Christian life which in the early sixteenth century would become crucial issues of interpretation, polarized as "protestant" and "catholic" views by another Augustinian, Martin Luther.

KASPAR ELM is Professor of Medieval History at the Freie Universität Berlin, and was a visiting scholar of the Harvard University Center for Byzantine Studies, Dumbarton Oaks, in Washington, D.C., 1984/85. He has published widely on the history and historiography of the Augustinians and other medieval religious orders.

HE MEMBERS of the Fabbrica del Duomo of Milan did not envisage the problems that would ensue from their decision in 1474 to erect a statue of St. Augustine on the roof of their still unfinished cathedral (Figure 3.1) These problems were not, as might be expected, of a financial nature; neither was there a lack of artistic ability. The difficulties centered around the question: In what habit should the church father be dressed? Initially they seemed to have agreed on the proposition advanced by the Hermits of St. Augustine — also known as the Austin Friars — that the saint should appear as a Hermit dressed in the habit of their order: *cum scapulari et corrigia* (with scapular and belt).[1] The Canons Regular, who also followed the Rule of St. Augustine, were enraged by this suggestion, insisting instead that the saint should not be represented in any garment but the tunic of their order. Perturbed by these conflicting arguments, the Milanese submitted the case to Gian Galeazzo Visconti, the duke of Milan, who decided in favor of the Hermits.

The Canons, however, would not accept the decision that Augustine should be vested in the habit of the Austin Friars. They prepared themselves for a renewed and more vigorous attack and drew upon the most learned of their Lombard and Venetian brothers: Domenico da Treviso, Agostino da Pavia, Celso Maffei, and Eusebio Corradi, all famous authors, who were thought of as highly competent in literary and legal matters. The Hermits, for their part, called upon Paolo Olmi da Bergamo, Bartolomeo da Padova, Giacomo Filippo Foresti da Bergamo, and Ambrogio Massari da Cora, all of whom had been trained in scholastic argumentation and theological disputation. Within a short time both orders had come forward with a multiplicity of *Tractatus, Defensiones, Apologia, Chronica,* and *Libelli* dedicated to the pope and their respective cardinal protectors. These works were printed by the leading printers of Rome, Milan, and Venice and were distributed both within

Figure 3.1. Renaissance statues of saints on the upper pinnacles of Milan Cathedral.
Photo Alinari/Art Resource, N.Y.

and outside the orders involved.[2] In the case of the Hermits, this was done through the chapter general, which decided in 1482 that every convent and every capitular member of the order should acquire at least one copy of the prior general's writings,[3] a demand that met with widespread obedience, as the catalogues of incunabula and early printed books testify.[4]

This dispute, which had originated in 1474 at a local level, soon became an issue affecting Hermits and Canons not only in Italy, but also beyond the Alps. In France, England, and Germany, numerous learned members of the Order of the Hermits supported the case of their Italian brethren,[5] while many Canons Regular, particularly members of the Windesheim Congregation, united themselves with the Venetian and Lombard Canons in defending St. Augustine as "form and norm of canonical life" against the unfounded claims of the Hermits.[6] Furthermore, such personalities as Jacob Wimpfeling and Johannes Reuchlin, Johannes Trithemius and Erasmus, Johannes von Paltz and Martin Luther became involved in the *causa augustiniana*.[7] While most of them reacted cautiously, the Alsatian Wimpfeling, one of the most distinguished members of the older generation of German humanists, risked excommunication for being so injudicious as to accede to a request of the chancellor Konrad Stürzel, who asked him to arbitrate between Hermits and Williamites at Freiburg im Breisgau.[8] Wimpfeling declared that Augustine neither dressed in a cowl nor was a monk by profession; arguing not only against the Hermits, but also against the Canons, he insisted that the church father was simply a member of the secular clergy.[9]

Although both orders repeatedly appealed to the Holy See, Pope Sixtus IV refrained from taking a definite stance. On 13 May 1484, he prohibited all further discussion, simply excommunicating all infractors.[10] One year after Sixtus's death, however, the indefatigable and indomitable spokesman for the Hermits, Prior General Ambrogio da Cori, renewed the attack against the Canons Regular with such harshness that some authors believed it was the reason for his dismissal by Innocent VIII and his imprisonment in Castel San Angelo in Rome.[11] When the statue erected in Milan in 1476–77 was replaced thirteen years later by a smaller one, the spokeman for the Canons Regular, Eusebio Corradi, repeated the proposal that the saint should be dressed in the garment of their order.[12] But neither Innocent nor his successor, Pope

Alexander VIII, was able to settle the dispute, and in 1487 the pressure from both orders was so strong that the Curia had to give way. The Austin Friars' cardinal protector managed to interpret Alexander VIII's prohibition upon further dispute in such a way that it ceased to be an obstacle.[13] When discussion was renewed in the seventeenth and eighteenth centuries, it assumed a new and even broader dimension. Only today does the matter seem to have been settled. In 1969, the Austin Friars convinced the Congregazione per i Religiosi that they should have the exclusive right to the title Ordo S. Augustini, whereas before they had merely been the Ordo S. Augustini Fratrum Eremitarum S. Augustini.[14]

II

Ostensibly, the Milanese fifteenth-century dispute was about whether Augustine should be dressed in the habit of an Austin Canon or of an Austin Hermit, but in reality the treatises published during the quarrel suggest that it was the saint himself who presented the main problem. The Hermits claimed him as the founder of their order and argued that they were therefore his true and proper sons. The Canons, on the other hand, were adamant that their order, the *ordo canonicus,* was the true successor of the religious life established by Augustine in the monasteries of Thagaste and Hippo. They based their argument mainly on the collection of the Pseudo-Augustinian texts, *Sermones ad fratres in eremo,* to which the German friar Jordan of Saxony had already drawn attention in the fourteenth century.[15] They declared that Augustine, before being baptized at Milan in 386, had lived as a hermit in the seclusion of Cassiciacum, a villa between Milan and Bergamo. Later, they asserted, he had organized the eremetical life in Tuscany, and finally had transferred this type of religious life to northern Africa. According to their interpretation, it was taken overseas to Spain, southern France, and Italy when Vandals and Moslems put an end to the flourishing church of Africa. Only in the thirteenth century, the Canons declared, were the dispersed hermits united into the Order of the Hermits of St. Augustine.

   Those who wrote in favor of the Austin Friars denied any relationship between the church father and the Canons. Based on a brief statement by Joachim of Fiore, they believed that the institution of the ordo canonicus was to be dated not to the early but to the high Middle Ages and that Rufus, the alleged initiator of the French Congregation of St. Ruf, was its father and founder. It goes without saying that the Canons advanced a quite different view: the bishop of Hippo had given them his rule, thus organizing their traditional way of life, the "truly apostolic life" or *vita vere apostolica,* which had been introduced to the primitive church by Christ and the Apostles. According to them, the Order of the Hermits was a more recent foundation dating to William of Malavalle, a French hermit of the twelfth century. In fact, this dispute touches on an even deeper split, which went far beyond the argument about the habit of St. Augustine and the history of his orders. The discussion between the Hermits and the Canons was really concerned with the question of how to interpret and achieve the "perfect" Christian life. The Canons and the Hermits, and those monks and friars, humanists and laymen who later participated in the dispute, discussed the hierarchy of the orders, the relations among the state of the secular clergy, the monks, and the laity. They evaluated the qualities of the various kinds of spirituality—the active life, the contemplative life, and the combination of both, the *vita mixta*—and finally searched for a justification of their way of life in Holy Scripture as well as in the tradition stemming from the Apostles and church fathers.

The same issues had been raised in the eleventh and twelfth centuries, when Hugh of St. Victor, Gerhoch of Reichersberg, Anselm of Havelberg, and other learned Canons defended the preeminence of the ordo canonicus against the claims of the *ordo monasticus.*[16] They were eager to establish the correct and legitimate way of canonical life by discussing which of the texts commonly supposed to be the "Rule" of St. Augustine should be taken as authentic: the *Praeceptum,* which was more adapted to clerical life, or the *Ordo monasterii,* the more ascetic or eremitical variant, what we call the Rule of St. Augustine.[17] In fact, the Pseudo-Augustinian sermons on which the Hermits of the fourteenth and fifteenth century mainly relied were not simply an ad hoc falsification intended to document their particular claim on Augustine as founder, but partly an adaption of letters addressed originally to secular canons of the twelfth century to exhort them to abandon their life and to adopt the Rule of St. Augustine.[18] This process, moreover, suggests the close connection between the claims on Augustine the hermit and the idea of reform within the order during the fifteenth century.

The canons Domenico da Treviso, Celso Maffei, Agostino da Pavia, and Eusebio Corradi were leading figures in the Lateran Congregation of Canons, which originated in 1401–2 at the famous chapter of S. Frediano in Lucca and was introduced in 1444 by Eugenius IV at S. Giovanni in Laterano.[19] The Austin Friars Paolo Olmi da Bergamo, Philippo da Bergamo, and Ambrogio da Cora, on the other hand, held leading offices in the Lombard Observant Congregation, which had spread all over North and Central Italy.[20] S. Maria Bianco di Casoretto, the Milanese base of the Canons, had just been incorporated into the Lateran Congregation when the trouble arose. In S. Maria Incoronata, the main stronghold of the Hermits at Milan, the Observance had already been introduced in 1445. When the dispute began, a spacious convent and a marvelous church were under construction.[21]

The most famous cradle of the Augustinian Observance was the small hermitage of S. Salvatore di Lecceto, near Siena.[22] Gregory IX had already taken it under papal protection in 1228, and there is good reason to believe that the eremitical way of life had been practiced there and elsewhere near Siena since the early Middle Ages, if not since late antiquity.[23] However, it was not only its age that made Lecceto one of the nuclei of the Augustinian Observance. The Austin Friars had been convinced since the early fourteenth century that it was in Centocelle near Civitavecchia, on the Monte Pisano, and in Lecceto that Augustine had assembled the early Tuscan hermits to give them his rule. This story was repeated by a series of important writers, including Paolo da Venezia, Maffeo Vegio da Lodi, Filippo Leonardo Agazzari, and Egidio da Viterbo.[24] The selection of Lecceto also helped to make it the nucleus of the Observant movement and the head of the Congregatio Ilicetana. The isolated position was also much appreciated by St. Catherine of Siena and her circle.[25] This underlines the fact that in the Order of the Austin Friars, as in other orders, the initial tendency of the Observants was to withdraw to an eremitical life of simplicity and contemplation and place less emphasis on pastoral and academic activities.[26]

The stubborn vigor of the Hermits of St. Augustine, which was suppressed by neither arguments nor excommunication, calls for further explanation beyond the search for reform and the inclination to lead an eremitical life. Having a founder like Augustine was essential to the very existence of the Austin Hermits, as can be gathered from their origins and early history.

In March 1256, the representatives of a series of groups of Italian hermits assembled in S. Maria del Popolo in Rome. They had been summoned by Pope Alexander IV and Cardinal Richard Annibaldi to complete a union, the Magna Unio Augustiniana, that had already been preceded by smaller-scale unions of Tuscan hermits. The papal bull *Licet ecclesiae catholicae,* which was promulgated on 9 April 1256, commemorates the outcome of this gathering. It led to the creation of a new order, the Order of the Austin Friars, not by negotiation among the representatives of the assembled hermits, or even, as usual, by the inspiration of a holy person, but by a decision of the Roman Curia. The pope and his influential cardinals intended to unite the large number of individual hermits and eremitical communities, which were threatened frequently by disorder and decay. The main purpose, however, was to create an order able to cope with the spiritual needs of the rapidly expanding population of the Italian cities. To this end they modeled the order on the Franciscans and Dominicans, who had already successfully met the demands of a changing society. The united hermits, the Austin Friars, were eager to carry out this task. They abandoned their rural hermitages, settled in the cities, offered pastoral care and social services, and extended the scope of their religious life to preaching and study.[27] I need mention only the most distinguished members of the Schola Augustiniana — Giles of Viterbo, James of Viterbo, William of Cremona, Augustine of Ancona, and Gregory of Rimini — to prove how swiftly the friars fulfilled their task.[28]

The metamorphosis from hermits to friars was not achieved without considerable difficulty and conflict. Faced with the growing influence of the Minorites and Preachers and confronted with the systematic propagation of the fame of St. Francis and St. Dominic, attacked by the less than benevolent secular clergy, always in danger of being taken for heretics, the united groups found their origin a heavy burden. If they wanted to survive amid the increasing number of regular and semiregular institutions, of orders, congregations, and confraternities, if they wanted to gain acceptance and even prominence, they had to display more than papal privileges and descent from unknown ascetics and hermits. To claim that their origins dated back to St. Augustine provided a prestige not evoked by the names of Giovanni Buono, William of Malavalle, and Prete Rustico, who were the real initiators of some of the united groups, or of William of Settala and Guido of Staggia, who were the first priors general of the order formed in 1256.

Until the last decades of the thirteenth century, the claim of Augustine as founder was merely a matter of status and legitimation, but after the Second Council of Lyon in 1275, it became essential to the existence of the Austin Hermits. In Canon 23, the council fathers at Lyon had demanded the abolition of all mendicant orders founded after the Fourth Lateran Council of 1215, exempting only the Franciscans and Dominicans.[29] The dating of the origin of the Austin Friars before 1215 was thus essential to their survival. The manipulation of their own history became a vital duty not only for the Austin Friars, Carmelites, and Servites, but also for the Friars of the Sack and the other smaller mendicant orders that had come into existence since 1215.

It is well known that the Austin Friars and Carmelites did survive.[29] The fact, however, that in the first quarter of the fourteenth century the Austin Friars still had to struggle against those who questioned their legitimacy and right to existence is often ignored. In 1327 Pope John XXII conferred upon them the ultimate recognition, entrusting them with the task of guarding S. Pietro in Ciel d'Oro at Pavia, where the relics of St. Augustine had been deposited in the eighth century.[30] It was within this context that the first systematic steps were taken for writing the history of the order. The first historians of the Hermits were in fact the anonymous Italian author of the tract titled *Initium sive progressus ordinis heremitarum S. Augustini,* the Parisian Master Gerardo da Bergamo, the *lector in curia* Nicolaus de Alessandria, and the Thuringian theologian Henry of Friemar. They had all been asked by the order to investigate whether or not Augustine had founded this order, and to convince the pope and cardinals that the custody of the tomb of the saint should be bestowed on the Hermits.[31]

Henry of Friemar and his confrères claimed St. Augustine, bishop and church father, teacher and preacher, as the founder of their order. They also insisted on its eremitical character, which had been prefigured by Elias and John the Baptist and derived from Paul of Thebes, the first of the hermits, and Anthony of Alexandria, the ancient exempla of eremitical life. This combination made reassessment of the order's origins and early history more difficult than for the Carmelites and Servites. They overcame the problem by combining the Pseudo-Augustinian texts, the *Sermones ad fratres in eremo,* with local tradition. Thus they attributed the status of hermit to Simplicianus of Milan. During his youth in Rome, Simplicianus had apparently served God most devoutly, following the example of Paul the first hermit and of Anthony; then he went to Milan, where he led a solitary and eremitical life and was later joined by a large number of followers. It was he who had hosted Augustine after his arrival in Milan at Cassiciacum (an alleged *lavra* or grouping of hermit dwellings) and who had familiarized Augustine with the eremitical life, even before his baptism in 387: "Which shows quite evidently that St. Augustine, who was at last converted to the Christian faith by St. Simplicianus, was the model of all the hermits who were the founders of our Order." It was after his baptism that Augustine, on the way from Milan to Rome, met with adherents of the *vita eremitica* in Tuscany, whom he provided with "a rule and form." When in the sixth and seventh centuries his disciples had to withdraw from North Africa, they joined the communities of Augustinian hermits in southern Europe. Provided by the church father with "rule and form," the ancient Augustinian eremitical life had thus never ceased to be vital. The foundation of the Order of the Augustinian Hermits in the thirteenth century, therefore, was not anything new, but simply unified the ancient Augustinian hermits, formerly dispersed by migration and Islamic expansion. The unification was not brought about by either cardinal or pope, but was based on the will of St. Augustine himself and transmitted to the pope in a vision.

This concept of the Augustinian order as essentially eremitical was reiterated constantly. In 1330 William Flete, who had renounced Oxford for the alleged Augustinian foundation Lecceto near Siena,[32] alluded to it in an address to his English brethren: "Brothers, grasp the true sense of your name, because you are not called hermits in vain, ensure that nothing with you is false because your name stands above all other names."[33] Between 1338 and 1347, Simone da Cascia, the famous Florentine preacher, dedicated his monumental *Opus de gestis domini Salvatoris* to praising the vita eremitica, emphasizing its advantages and the necessity of returning to the eremitical past so that the order should survive and prosper.[34] The impact of both these propositions can only be grasped fully if one remembers that both Simone da Cascia and William Flete were in contact with the Franciscan Spirituals. This link explains their conviction that only the maintenance of the eremitical character of their own order would lead to the fulfillment of Joachim of Fiore's prophecy: "An order appears which seems to be new, but is not; dressed in black robes and girded with a belt they appear and their fame will spread. This will be the order of the hermits who strive to equal the life of the angels."[35]

Similarly, the Augustinian friar-humanists, beginning with Luigi Marsili in Florence and Andrea Biglia in Siena and Lecceto, looked to the example of Augustine the hermit, for he legitimized their way of life.[36] The vita mixta combined ascetic monasticism with learned scholarship. This way of life was highly favored by Leon Battista Alberti, Niccolò Niccoli, and Leonardo Bruni, as it had been earlier by Petrarch, who had admired Augustine and was a friend of the Austin Friars, whom he believed to be the true sons and followers — *proprii filii et discipuli* — of the church father.[37]

Yet despite their efforts, these writers did not succeed in imposing on the entire order the tradition of the vita eremitica and the stylized picture of Augustine as anchorite. The emphasis on the *vita activa* in the treatises, sermons, and letters of such men as Jordan of Saxony, Geoffrey Hardeby, and Hermann von Schildesche militated against the general acceptance of the eremitical way of life. In contrast to the propagators of the eremitical tradition, Jordan of Saxony, member of the Erfurt convent, did not view the history of the order as a homogeneous process.[38] Rather he interpreted the order's development as a succession of two conditions or states of life — the old state, or "state of the fathers," and the modern state, or "state of the brethren." Both were initiated by Augustine himself as a unifier of dispersed hermits: the *status antiquus* in person, the *status modernus* via a vision. In both cases, Augustine meant the hermits to serve the Church and exhorted them to abandon ascetic seclusion and to take part in service to the community. Thus Augustine became what he truly was, a priest and shepherd, a teacher and a missionary among the heathen, a protagonist of the true faith and a defender of orthodoxy against heresy. The father of the Hermits was transformed into the model for all religious and clerics.[39] Guided by such a concept, the Austin Friars could be active as well as contemplative, secluded and in the world, engaged in preaching and in persecuting heretics.

The wide range of options now open to the order soon became obvious. In the controversy of the 1380s surrounding the question of mendicant property, Geoffrey Hardeby argued against the secular clergy, asserting that not Francis and Dominic but Augustine was the first to practice poverty and furthermore provided the theological background for that particular way of life.[40] According to him, the circle at Cassiciacum was in essence a mendicant religious order, its eremitical origins being completely irrelevant. The only important feature was the fact that the Augustinians were founded as a mendicant order centuries before Francis and Dominic were born.

As early as 1334, on the occasion of the feast of St. Augustine, the Westphalian friar Hermann von Schildesche preached on the theme of the Samaritan leper, who had been healed by Jesus.[41] This episode serves to explain the history and character of the order, which left behind all worldly curiosity and false science to achieve cleansing and enlightenment. As Augustine himself had turned away from curiosity and heresy to the true faith, the order had become a School of God where the true knowledge of the faith was guaranteed by the teacher, who was himself the founder of the order. Thus the masters and doctors of the Augustinian order never failed to point to Augustine as their father and teacher and to build the theology of their order on the foundations he had laid.

The theme of the order as a school of St. Augustine frequently reappears. From early humanism to Renaissance philosophy, from Luigi Marsili to Girolamo Seripando, from Lecceto and Florence to Prague, Nuremberg, and Hungary, the Austin Friars took part in the rediscovery of antiquity.[42] The motives for this involvement become most apparent in a letter written by Andrea Biglia to a young scholar who was hesitating about which order to join. Andrea not only recommends Augustine as the prototype of the vita mixta, but also describes his order as a community where religion and science, contemplation and action, are equally appreciated.[43] He enlarged on this concept some years later when preaching at the chapter general of his order at Bologna.[44] He declared that the order had become a school of philosophers equal to the school of Socrates and Pythagoras. Indeed, it even exceeded them in the qualities of its master, who combined the fame of Pythagoras with the seriousness of Socrates. Another most revealing variation on the theme emerged in Westphalia in the early sixteenth century. When the Austin Friars' convent in Lippstadt was transformed into a public school by the reformed magistrates, the remaining friars consented to this change as being in accordance with the history of their order.[45] One convent member explained that the circle of Cassiciacum was essentially a school and that therefore the magistrates had only restored the original character of the order. In this instance, the adaptability of the role of the founder-figure was carried to an extreme. Even the dissolution of the order might be justified and explained by the authority of Augustine.[45]

III

The claims of the friars were not easily defended. It was not sufficient to propose a founder; the proposition had also to be maintained and authenticated in constant battles against competing orders, as well as against sceptical clerics and the laity. The Benedictines, especially the learned members of the Congregation of Sta. Giustina, reacted sharply against the allegation that the church father Augustine and not their patriarch St. Benedict was the first to found an order.[46] The canonical orders as well as the many noncanonical orders following the rule of St. Augustine — among them the Crutched Friars — claimed him exclusively as their father and patron.[47] The Carmelites and the Hungarian Hermits of St. Paul insisted that their respective orders had been founded by Elias and Paul of Thebes long before the Augustinian Hermits had come into being.[48] The Dominicians pointed to the fact that they, too, continued the tradition of the Augustinian *vita religiosa*.[49] The Franciscans reacted angrily against the allegation that the Augustinian order, rather than their own, should be considered as the first one to be founded on poverty. They could not bear the idea that St. Francis would therefore be seen as simply a disciple of Augustine, as was claimed by the Austin Friars at the beginning of the fourteenth century.[50]

The Austin Friars' concept of their origins had to be defended in pulpits and classrooms, in the churches of Rome, Pavia, Bologna, and Milan, in the universities of Paris, Oxford, and Cologne, and in the streets and the marketplaces of Siena, Reims, Pavia, and Freiburg. These disputes all focused on whether Augustine had been a canon or a hermit. All available resources were mobilized against this onslaught. A flow of tracts was produced from the early fourteenth century, whose authors used methods ranging from blatant fraud to the most refined philological and historical argument.[51] Art performed the same task for all those who could or did not want to listen or read. In earlier centuries Augustine was represented as bishop, scholar, and teacher. Then from the twelfth and thirteenth centuries, he appears as a father of religious communities and author of a rule. This enrichment of the traditional iconographic program stemmed from the canonical reform, during which Augustine as the *norma et forma canonicorum* became a key figure. The fact that from the beginning of the fourteenth century the saint is shown not only as a canon but also as a hermit is the direct result of the claims of the Austin Friars. Since then, nearly the entire iconography of Augustine has been dominated by the confrontation of these two opinions. These two different historical concepts were expressed not in single works of art but in the great cycles representing the saint's life, which from the beginning had accompanied the literary controversies.[52] At the same time as the Thuringian friar Heinrich of Friemar elaborated his concept of his order's origin and development, the church of his convent, the Augustinerkirche at Erfurt, was decorated with scenes of Augustine's early life in a cycle of stained-glass panels illustrating the Hermits' and not the Canons' view.[53]

When Pope John XXII entrusted the order with the guardianship of the tomb of St. Augustine in S. Pietro in Ciel d'Oro at Pavia, the famous *Arca S. Augustini* was commissioned, and it became a kind of arch of triumph for the Austin Friars.[54] At the time of the Milanese dispute, a spacious convent had been begun, together with a church that has been characterized as a masterpiece of late fifteenth-century architecture.[55] The church should also be considered as a monument erected in honor of St. Augustine the hermit, as the true and legitimate founder of the Order of the Austin Friars. It cannot be coincidental that during the last decades of the fifteenth century, when the dispute was at its most virulent, famous cycles were being created at Crema,

Cremona, San Gimignano, Constance Neustift, Bruges, and Carlisle. All of them had been commissioned by either the Hermits or the Canons. In each case, the artists were instructed by reforming members of the order, who themselves were involved in the discussions.[56] At San Gimignano, for example, it was Fra Domenico Strambi, the learned doctor from Paris and reformer of the local convent, who instructed Benozzo Gozzoli and made him familiar with the discussion between the Hermits and canons (Figure 3.2).[57] Neither side was content to propagate its view of the origins of the order just through iconography; each also collected and classified earlier representations according to the extent to which they confirmed its particular point of view. A rudimentary form of art historical research was established in this way.[58] Thus to understand medieval Augustinian iconography, a familiarity with the status of the dispute at any particular moment is indispensable. This is a problem that has not always been taken into consideration. As Fabio Bisogni has observed in another context, "iconographic material . . . must in future be analyzed with greater care and undertaken with more stringent methods, allied to the precise historical facts."[59] These observations on the fifteenth-century causa augustiniani are neither exceptional nor unique. Instead of St. Augustine, I could have made John the Baptist and Anthony, Ambrose[60] and Jerome,[61] or the Holy Virgin Mary Magdalene and Helena the subjects of this essay. In almost exactly the same way, they were made founders and patrons respectively of the Servites, of the Hermits of St. John, of the Antonites, Ambrosians, and Jeronomites, of the Friars of the Holy Cross, and of the Sisters of the Order of Penance.[62] Instead of concentrating on the conflicts between Hermits and Canons, I could have substituted those between the military and hospital orders, which indiscriminately claimed the Maccabaens as their predecessors and insisted that the house of Zachary and Ann, which sheltered Jesus, Mary, and Joseph, was one of their order's earliest hospitals.[63]

The comparison that would have yielded the most conclusive evidence would have been among the Austin Friars, the Carmelites, and the Hungarian Hermits of St. Paul, but I have discussed it elsewhere.[64] These orders were of eremitical origin and had been transformed almost simultaneously into mendicant orders. They confronted the same challenge with the same remedy, looking to Elias and Paul of Thebes as

Figure 3.2. Benozzo Gozzoli, *St. Augustine Robed as an Austin Friar Visits the Brethren at Monte Pisano.* San Gimignano, Sant'Agostino. Photo Alinari/Art Resource, N.Y.

their founders and patrons. The dependence on Elias caused a problem, however, for since early Christianity the Old Testament prophet had been considered the prototype of asceticism, in the same way St. Paul of Thebes had been traditionally venerated as the prince of the hermits. These traditions make it difficult to justify the dismissal of seclusion in favor of pastoral activity. Although numerous learned Carmelites struggled to propagate the idea of their founder Elias as the prototype of prophet and preacher, their campaign was without the success they had expected. The view of Elias as hermit and monk formulated by the church fathers remained the focal point of Carmelite spirituality and of all reform movements within the Carmelite order, particularly those of Theresa of Avila and John of the Cross. Similarly, whenever attempts were made in the order of the Hermits of St. Paul to abandon the vita eremitica in favor of the vita activa, they were dismissed on the basis of the teachings of St. Paul the leader and father, the *Dux* and *Pater:* teachings at best fragmentarily contained in St. Jerome's *Vita pauli.*[64]

One could take this argument further, beyond religious orders and their founders. Cities and nations, bishops, patriarchs, and popes had recourse to eminent ancestral and founding figures to legitimate their authority.[65] This apparent need to define one's own status by reference to an eminent predecessor, be it a historical or a mythical figure, is ever present. Yet, as I hope I have demonstrated, the reference to ancestors did not have to result in conservatism, unthinking preservation of the past, or stagnation. Provided that the founder-figure symbolized a sufficient variety of characteristics, he or she could promote versatility, innovation, and a high degree of adaptability. This was not always so; in the case of the Hermits of St. Paul, recourse to a traditional image of holiness resulted in stagnation. But for the Austin Friars the same process was a highly dynamic force, which enabled them not only to develop a great variety of iconographical motifs, but also to adapt to the changing demands of Church and society.

NOTES

1. Ambrogio da Cora. *Defensorium ordinis fratrum heremitarum S. Augustini responsivum ad maledicta canonicorum assertorum regularium congregationis Frisonariae* (Rome, Georg Herolt, 1481), 521; C. Cantú, ed., *Annali della Fabbrica del Duomo di Milano* (Milan: G. Brigola, 1877–85), 8:480. *Storia di Milano, VII: L'età sforzesca dal 1400 al 1500* (Milan: Treccani degli Alfieri, 1956); M. L. Gatti Perer, ed., *Il duomo di Milano. Atti del congresso internazionale. Museo Nazionale della Scienza e della Tecnica, 8–12 settembre 1968* (*Arte Lombarda*, Monografie: Monumenti 3) (Milan, 1969) mention neither the statue nor the circumstances of its erection. For further information: E. Verga, *L'Archivio della Fabbrica del Duomo di Milano* (Milan: U. Allegretti, 1908); A. Ciceri, "L'Archivio della Veneranda Fabbrica del Duomo di Milano," in *Studi storici in memoria di Mons. Angelo Mercati Prefetto dell'Archivio Vaticano* (Fontes Ambrosiani XXX) (Milan: Giuffré-Editori, 1956), 164–83.

2. D. da Treviso, *Defensio canonicorum regularium contra heremitas* (1475), mentioned in P. Ulmeus, *Apologia religionis fratrum heremitarum ordinis S. Augustini contra falso impugnantes* (Rome: Fr. de Cinquinis, 1479); Venice, Biblioteca Marciana, MS lat. cl. 4, n. 72, segn. 2216: A. da Pavia, *Libellus contra fratres heremitas pro canonicis regularibus* (n.p., n.d.); C. Maffeus, *Defensiones Canonicorum regularium contra Monachos. Responsiones ad rationes monasticas* (Venice: Pietro Quarengi, 1487); idem, *Defensiones in Monachos pro vero Canonicorum regularium gradu ac dignitate* (Venice, 1491); idem, *Defensiones Canonicorum regularium contra Monachos* (Venice: An-

drea Torresani, 1499); idem, *Ad Rev. Dom. Cardinalem Sancti Marci: Quomodo Apostoli et clerici primitivae ecclesiae erant regulares vivebantque in communi et vota perfectioris vitae emittebant* (Rome: E. Silber alias Franck; 1491); idem, *Apologia adversus libros Ambrosii de Chora* (Brescia, 1502); A. de Novis, *Vita S. Augustini et b. matris Monicae* (Brescia, 1506); idem, *De antiquitate et dignitate Ordinis Canonicorum Regularium S. Augustini* (Milan; 1503); E. Corradi, *Responsio adversus quendam fratrem eremitam* (Milan: Leonhard Pachel, Ulrich Schinzenzeller, 1479); idem, *Brevis annotatio in errores scribentium Augustinum fuisse eremitam* (Rome: Johannes Schoemberger, 1483); idem, *De dignitate canonicorum regularium deque ipsorum et monachorum differentia* (Rome: Johannes Franscigena, 1489); idem, *Tractatus secundus . . . de praestantia et dignitate clericorum regularium prae monachis* (Milan: Ulrich Schinzenzeller, 1500); P. Ulmeus, *Apologia religionis fratrum heremitarum ordinis S. Augustini contra falso impugnantes* (Rome: Fr. de Cinquinis, 1479); A. da Cremona, *Contra Augustiniani nominis hostes apologia ordinis,* is mentioned by J. F. Ossinger, *Bibliotheca Augustiniana historica, critica et chronologica* (Ingolstadt: J. F. X. Graetz, 1768), 273, and D. A. Perini, *Bibliographia Augustiniana cum notis bibliographicis: Scriptores Itali* (Florence: Sordomuti, 1929–37), I: 269; G. F. da Bergamo, *Supplementum Chronicarum vulgo appellatum in omnimoda Historia novissime congesta* (Venice: Bernardinus de Bonaliis, 1483); A. da Cora, *Defensorium ordinis Sancti Augustini* (Rome: Georg Herolt, n.d.); idem, *Vita Sancti Augustini. Commentarii super regulam Sancti Augustini. Oratio de laudibus Sancti Augustini. Chronica sacratissimi ordinis fratrum Heremitarum Sancti Augustini* (Rome: Georg Herolt, 1481).

3. "Acta capituli generalis Ord. Erem. S. Augustini Perusii anno 1482 celebrati," *Analecta Augustiniana* 19 (1943): 279.

4. L. Hain, *Repertorium Bibliographicum* (Stuttgart-Tübingen: J. G. Cotta, 1826–38), nos. 962, 2805–14, 5634–40, 5683–85, 10328, 10441–42, 16086; W. A. Copinger, *Supplement to Hain's Repertorium Bibliographicum* (London: H. Southeran, 1895–1902), nos. 150, 1767, 16086; D. Reichling, *Appendices ad Hainii-Copingerii Repertorium Bibliographicum* (Munich: J. Rosenthal, 1905–14), I: 203; 3: 96; *Catalogue of Books Printed in the XVth Century now in the British Museum IV* (London: Trustees of the British Museum, 1916), 76, 126–27; *Gesamtkatalog der Wiegendrucke* (Leipzig: K. W. Hiersemann, 1925–40), nos. 3052, 7414–17; F. R. Goff, *Incunabula in American Libraries* (New York: The Bibliographical Society of America, 1964), no. 1365; M. Pellechet and L. Polain, *Catalogue général des Incunables des Bibliothèques Publiques de France* (reprint, Nedeln, Lichtenstein: Kraus-Thomson, 1970), nos. 3609, 3938–39, 3970–71; T. M. Guarnaschelli and E. Valenziani, *Indice generale degli incunaboli delle biblioteche d'Italia* (Rome: Libreria dello Stato, 1943–81), nos. 437–39, 1063, 3170–73, 5030–37, 10020–22; M. L. Polain, *Supplément au catalogue des livres imprimés au quinzième siècle des bibliothèques de Belgique* (Brussels: Fl. Tulkens, 1978), no. 4369; D. E. Rhodes, *A Catalogue of Incunabula in all the Libraries of Oxford University outside the Bodleian* (Oxford: Clarendon Press, 1982), no. 233; P. Casciano, "Indice delle edizioni romane a stampa (1467-1500)," in *Scrittura, biblioteche e stampe a Roma nel Quattrocento. Aspetti e problemi. Atti del seminario 1-2 giugno 1979* (Vatican City: Scuola di Paleografia, Diplomatica e Archivistica, 1980), nos., 598–91, 660, 673, 795.

5. München, Bayrische Staatsbibliothek (= BayStB), Clm 18223, fols. 239r-41r: *Disputatio canonicorum regularium et Augustiniensium mendicantium sive heremitarum et propositio monachorum scribentium ad canonicos regulares;* BayStB, Clm 8340, fols. 141r–41v: *Tractatus de vita et habitu S. Augustini;* Wolfenbüttel, Herzog-August-Bibliothek 1055 (Cod. Helmstedt 953), fols. 154v-157r: *Disputatio canonicorum regularium et fratrum heremitarum beati Augustini;* BayStB, Clm 14053, fols. 165r-74v: *Chronica Sacri Ordinis Fratrum Heremitarum S. Augustini;* Colmar, Bibliothèque Municipale, MS 349, fol. 184v: *De Origine Ordinis Eremitarum S. Augustini.* Cf. A. Zum-

keller, *Manuskripte von Werken der Autoren des Augustiner-Eremitenordens in mitteleuropäischen Bibliotheken* (Würzburg: Augustinus-Verlag, 1966); G. Dotti, "Manoscritti Agostiani in Biblioteche Spagnole," *Augustiniana* 34 (1984): 331–48; E. Ypma, "Liste d'auteurs augustins français," *Augustiniana* 19 (1969): 487–531; 20 (1970): 347–96; 21 (1971): 594–636; 22 (1972): 611–42.

      6. Brussels, Bibliothèque Royale (= Bibl.Roy.), MS 2342–51, fols. 1r–52v: *Vita S. Augustini,* fols. 75–78: *Legenda de beato Augustino;* fols. 78v–79v: *Quando et qualiter incepit ordo Augustinensium mendicantium;* Bibl. Roy., MS 858–61, fols. 377v–79v: J. Mombaert, *Responsiones ad tria, que ordini canonicorum regularium obiciuntur;* Würzburg, Universitätsbibliothek, M. ch. 63, fols. 78–88v, 97–106v: Petrus Hilgerius, *Armariolum veritatis contra errorem scribencium Augustinum fuisse heremitam et nunquam canonicum regularem* (1508). British Library, MS Add. 38665, fols. 6–13v: *Cronica cuiusdam amici veritatis in argumentum fundatoris Canonicorum Regularium Ordinis S. Augustini Doctoris et Episcopi* (15. sec.).

      7. E. Böcking, ed., *Ulrichi Hutteni equitis operum supplementum: Epistolae obscurorum virorum* (Leipzig: Teubner, 1864), 267; K. Arnold, *Johannes Trithemius 1462–1516* (Quellen und Forschungen zur Geschichte des Bistums und Hochstiftes Würzburg 23) (Würzburg: Schöningh, 1971), 140–43; P. S. Allen and H. M. Allen, eds., *Opus epistolarum Des. Erasmi Roterodami* (Oxford: Clarendon Press, 1906–65), 2:73; 3:442; 8:19–20; C. H. Miller, ed., *Moriae Encomium, id est Stultitiae Laus* (Opera omnia Desiderii Erasmi Roterodami IV, 3) (Amsterdam-Oxford: North-Holland Publishing Co., 1979), 160–62; Buchwald, ed., "Randbemerkungen Luthers zu Augustini Opuscula," in *D. Martin Luthers Werke Kritische Gesamtausgabe* 9 (Weimar: H. Böhlau, 1893), 12; O. Scheel, *Martin Luther. Vom Katholizismus zur Reformation* (Tübingen: J. C. B. Mohr, 1930), 2:188–90, 410–14; A. Hamel, *Der junge Luther und Augustin* (Gütersloh: C. Bertelsmann, 1934) 2–3; B. Hamm, Ch. Burger and V. Marcolino, eds., *Johannes von Paltz. Werke 2: Supplementum Coelifodinae* (Spätmittelalter und Reformation. Texte und Untersuchungen 3) (Berlin, New York: de Gruyter, 1903): 272–78.

      8. J. Knepper, *Jakob Wimpfeling (1450–1528). Sein Leben und seine Werke nach den Quellen dargestellt* (Erläuterungen und Ergänzungen zu Janssens Geschichte des deutschen Volkes 3, 2–4) (Freiburg: Herder, 1902), 187–91.

      9. J. Wimpfeling, *De integritate libellus: Cum epistolis praestantissimorum virorum hunc libellum approbantium et confirmantium* (Strasbourg: *Johannes Knoblauch,* 1506); idem, *Appologetica declaratio in libellum suum de integritate, de eo: an sanctus Augustinus fuerit monachus. Cum epistolis Thome Volphii iunioris. Keyserspergii epistola elegantissima de modo praedicandi passionem Domini* (n.p., n.d.); idem, *Contra quendam, qui se Franciscum Schatzer appellat complicesque suos. Expurgatio Ja. Wimphelingi. Epistola ad Julium II. summum pontificem. Epistola ad Albertum episcopum Argentinensem* (n.p. 1506); idem; *Ad Julium secundum pont. max. contra indignam Fratrum Augustinensium accusationem* (n.p., n.d.).

      10. L. Empoli, *Bullarium Ordinis Eremitarum S. Augustini* (Rome: Typographia Rev. Camerae Apostolicae, 1628), 321–24.

      11. Empoli, *Bullarium Ordinis Eremitarum,* 40–41; A. Palmieri, "Ambroise de Cora," in *Dictionnaire d'histoire et de géographie ecclésiastique* (Paris: Letouzey et Ané, Editeurs, 1914), 2:1116–19.

      12. A. Bzovius, *Annalium ecclesiasticorum post illustriss. et reverendiss. D. D. Caesarem Baronium . . . continuatio* (Cologne: A. Boetzerus, 1618–40), 18:250ff.; K. Walsh, "Corrado, Eusebio (Eusebius Conradus)," in *Dizionario Biografico degli Italiani* (Rome: Istituto della Enciclopedia Italiana, 1983), 29:412–13.

102   KASPAR ELM

13. Empoli, *Bullarium Ordinis Eremitarum,* 324–26.

14. G. Cuypers, "De S. Aurelio Augustino illustri ecclesiae doctore et Hipponensi episcopo . . . commentarius praevius," in *Acta Sanctorum, Aug. VI* (Paris/Rome: Palme, 1868), 248–52; P. M. Vélez, *Leyendo nuestras cronicas. Notas sobre nuestros cronistas y otros historiadores. Studio critico y reconstructivo de la historia antiqua de la Orden de san Agustín* (Escorial: Impr. des Monasterio, 1932); C. D. Fonseca, "Il formarsi di una coscienza storica canonicale attraverso polemiche giurisdizionali e storiografiche," in *Medioevo canonicale* (Pubblicazioni dell'Università Cattolica del Sacro Cuore. Contributi III, Scienze Storiche 12 (Milan: Vita e pensiero, 1970), 5–56. B. Rano, "Agostiniani II: Il posto di S. Agostino nell' Ordine," in *Dizionario degli Istituti di Perfezione* (Rome: Edizione Paoline, 1973), 1:292–302; K. Elm, "Elias, Paulus von Theben und Augustinus als Ordensgründer. Ein Beitrag zur Geschichtsschreibung und Geschichtsdeutung der Eremiten- und Bettelorden des 13. Jahrhunderts," in H. Patze, ed., *Geschichtsdeutung und Geschichtsschreibung im Spätmittelalter* (Vorträge und Forschungen 35 (Sigmaringen: Thorbecke, 1987), 371–97.

15. J. P. Migne, ed., *Patrologiae cursus completus. Series Latina 40* (Paris: J. P. Migne, 1841), ca. 1255–358; P. Glorieux, "Pour révaloriser Migne. Tables rectificatives. Cahier supplémentaire," *Mélanges de Science Religieuse* 9 (1952): 31; A. Hamann, *Patrologiae cursus completus. Series Latina. Supplementum II* (Paris: Garnier, 1960), ca. 876; E. Dekkers and E. Gaar, "Clavis Patrum Latinorum," *Sacris Erudiri* 3 (1981): 93.

16. Ch. Dereine, "L'élaboration du statut canonique des chanoines réguliers spécialement sous Urban II," *Revue d'histoire ecclésiastique* 46 (1951): 534–65; *La vita comune del clero nei secoli XI e XII, Atti della Settimana di Studio, Mendola, Settembre 1959.* 2 vols. (Pubblicazioni dell'Università Cattolica del Sacro Cuore III, Scienze storiche 2–3) (Milan: Vita e pensiero, 1962); L. Milis, *Erémites et chanoines réguliers au XII siècle (Ghent, 1979); C. W. Bynum, Docere verbo et exemplo. An aspect of twelfth century spirituality* (Missoula: Scholars Press, 1979); Fonseca, "Il formarsi di una coscienza storica" (cf. n. 14).

17. L. Verheijen, *La Règle de Saint Augustin I. Tradition manuscrite 2. Recherches historiques* (Paris: Etudes Augustiniennes, 1967); idem, *Nouvelle approche de la Règle de St. Augustin* (Bégrolles-en-Mauges: Abbaye de Bellefontaine, 1980); idem, La Règle de Saint Augustin. Complément bibliographique, *Augustiniana* 36 (1986): 297–303.

18. Recently: B. Rano, "San Augustín y los orígenes de su Orden. Regla, Monasterio de Tagaste y «Sermones ad fratres in eremo»," *La Ciudad de Dios* 200 (1987): 649–727. K. Walsh, "Wie ein Bettelorden zu (s)einem Gründer kam. Fingierte Traditionen um die Entstehung der Augustiner-Eremiten," in *Fälschungen im Mittelalter. Teil V: Fingierte Briefe, Frömmigkeit und Fälschung, Realienfälschung* (Monumenta Germaniae Historica Schriften 33, V) (Hannover 1988): 585–610.

19. N. Widlöcher, *La Congregazione dei Canonici regolari Lateranensi* (Gubbio: Oderisi, 1929); E. Coturri, "La canonica di S. Frediano di Lucca dalla prima istituzione (metà del sec. XI) all' unione alla Congregazione riformata di Fregionaia (1517)," *Actum* 3 (1974): 47–88; W. Gehrt, *Die Verbände der Regularkanonikerstifte S. Frediano in Lucca, S. Maria in Reno bei Bologna, S. Maria in Porto bei Ravenna und die cura animarum im 12. Jahrhundert* (Europäische Hochschulschriften III, 224) (Frankfurt a.M., Bern, New York, Nancy: P. Lang, 1984).

20. B. van Luijk, "Sources italiennes pour l'histoire générale de l'Ordre des Augustins," *Augustiniana* 3 (1953): 128–39, 314–27; 4 (1954): 98–106, 185–95; 8 (1958): 397–424; 9 (1959): 183–202; idem, "Les Archives de la Congrégation de Lombardie et du couvent de S.

Maria del Popolo à Rome," *Augustiniana* 18 (1968): 100–101; idem, *L'Ordine Agostiniano e la riforma monastica dal Cinquecento alla vigilia della Rivoluzione Francese. Un sommario cronologico-storico* (Heverlee-Louvain: Institutum Historicum Augustinianum, 1973).

21. M. L. Gatti Perer, ed., *Umanesimo a Milano: L'Osservanza agostiniana all' Incoronata (Arte Lombarda*, N.S. 53–54) (Milan, 1980).

22. M. B. Hackett, "The Medieval Archives of Lecceto," *Analecta Augustiniana 40* (1977): 14–45. K. Walsh, "Papal Policy and Local Reform: A) The Beginning of the Augustinian Observance in Tuscany; B) Congregatio Ilicetana. The Augustinian Observant Movement in Tuscany and the Humanist Ideal," *Römische Historische Mitteilungen* 21 (1979): 35–57; 22 (1980): 105–45.

23. G. T. Radan and A. Lengyel, "The Eremo di S. Lucia di Rosia: Archaeological Documentation of an Augustinian Hermitage," *Etruscans* 3 (1974): 5–33. G. T. Radan, "Out of the Cave: Excavations at San Leonardo al Lago in Tuscany," *Protocol of the PMR Conference 5* (Villanova, 1980): 83–107.

24. Cf. F. X. Martin, "Giles of Viterbo and the Monastery of Lecceto. The Making of a Reformer," *Analecta Augustiniana* 25 (1962): 225–53; A. M. Voci, *Petrarca e la vita religiosa: Il mito umanista della vita eremitica* (Studi di Storia Moderna e Contemporanea 13) (Rome: Istituto Storico Italiano per l'Età Moderna e Contemporanea, 1983); M. B. Hackett, "A Lost Work of Giles of Viterbo. Critical Edition of his Treatise on Lecceto," in *Egidio da Viterbo O.S.A. e il suo tempo. Atti del V Convegno dell'Istituto storico Agostiniano, Roma-Viterbo, 20–23 Ottobre 1982* (Rome: Analecta Augustiniana, 1983): 117–36.

25. M. B. Hackett, "Un profilo del pensiero agostiniano di Caterina nel suo periodo formativo," in *Accademia Senese degli Intronati. Atti del Simposio Internazionale Cateriniano-Bernardiniano, Siena 17–20 Aprile 1980* (Siena: Accademia, 1982), 137–41; K. Walsh, "The Augustinian Observance in Siena in the Age of S. Caterina and S. Bernardino," in *Atti del Simposio Internazionale Cateriniano-Bernardiniano*, 939–50.

26. K. Elm, "Verfall und Erneuerung des Ordenswesens im Spätmittelalter," in J. Fleckenstein, ed., *Untersuchungen zu Kloster und Stift* (Veröffentlichungen des Max-Planck-Instituts für Geschichte. 14. Schriften der Germania Sacra) (Göttingen: Vandenhoeck u. Ruprecht, 1980), 188–238.

27. F. Roth, "Cardinal Richard Annibaldi. First Protector of the Augustinian Order (1243–76)," *Augustiniana* 2 (1952): 26–60, 108–49, 230–47; K. Elm, "Italienische Eremitengemeinschaften des 12. und 13. Jahrhunderts," in *L'eremitismo in Occidente nei secoli XI e XII. Atti della seconda Settimana internazionale di Studio, Mendola, 30 agosto–6 settembre 1962* (Pubblicazioni dell'Università Cattolica del Sacro Cuore III, Varia 4) (Milan: Vita e pensiero, 1965), 491–559; B. van Luijk, *Gli eremiti neri nel Dugento con particolare riguardo al territorio Pisano e Toscano* (Pisa: Il Telegrafo, 1968); K. Elm, "Gli eremiti neri nel dugento," *Quellen und Forschungen aus italienischen Archiven und Bibliotheken* 50 (1971): 58–79; D. Gutiérrez, *Los Agustinos en la edad media 1256–1356* (Historia de la Orden de San Agustín I, 1), (Rome: Institutum Historicum Ordinis Fratrum S. Augustini, 1980).

28. A. Zumkeller, "Die Augustinerschule des Mittelalters. Vertreter und philosophisch-theologische Lehre (Übersicht nach dem heutigen Stand der Forschung)," *Analecta Augustiniana* 27 (1964): 174–76; idem, "Die Rezeption Augustins in unserem Orden," *Cor Unum* 38 (1980): 154–69.

29. R. W. Emery, "The Second Council of Lyons and the Mendicant Orders," *The*

Catholic Historical Review 39 (1953): 257–71; St. Kuttner, "Conciliar Law in the Making. The Lyonese Constitutions (1274) of Gregory X in a Manuscript at Washington," in *Miscellanea Pio Paschini. Studi di storia ecclesiastica* (Lateranum NS 15), (Rome, 1949), 2:39–47; M. de Fontette, "Les Mendiants supprimés au 2me Concile de Lyon (1274). Frères Sachets et frères Pies" in *Les Mendiants en pays d'oc au 13ᵉ siècle* (Cahiers de Fanjeaux 8) (Toulouse: Privat, 1976), 193–216; K. Elm, "Ausbreitung, Wirksamkeit und Ende der provençalischen Sackbrüder (Fratres de Poenitentia Jesu Christi) in Deutschland und den Niederlanden. Ein Beitrag zur kurialen und konziliaren Ordenspolitik des 13. Jahrhunderts," *Francia* 1 (1972): 257–324.

30. R. Maiocchi and N. Casacca, *Codex Diplomaticus Ordinis Eremitarum S. Augustini Papiae* (Pavia: C. Rossetti, 1905), 1:13–38. G. Romano, "Eremitani e Canonici Regolari in Pavia nel secolo XIV," *Archivio Storico Lombardo* 22 (1895): 1–42; idem, "Una protesta di Giacomo dal Verme a favore degli Agostiniani di S. Pietro in Ciel d'Oro," *Bolletino della Società Pavese di storia Patria 1 (1901):* 377–87.

31. R. Arbesmann, "Henry of Friemar's Treatise on the Origin and Development of the Order of the Hermit Friars and Its True and Real Title," *Augustiniana* 6 (1956): 37–145; idem, "The Vita Aurelii Augustini Hipponensis Episcopi in Cod. Laurent, Plut. 90 Sup. 48," *Traditio* 18 (1962): 319–55; idem, "A Legendary of Early Augustinian Saints," *Analecta Augustiniana* 29 (1966): 5–58; B. Rano, "Las dos primeras obras conocidas sobre el origen de la Orden Agustiniana," *Analecta Augustiniana* 45 (1982): 329–76.

32. A. Gwynn, *The English Austin Friars in the Time of Wyclif* (London: Oxford University Press, 1940), 139–210; M. B. Hackett, "William Flete and his De remediis contra temptaciones," in *Medieval Studies presented to Aubrey Gwynn S.J.* (Dublin: Colm o Lochain, 1961), 331–48; A. C. de Romanis, "Santa Caterina da Siena e gli Eremitani di Sant'Agostino," *Bolletino Storico Agostiniano* 24 (1948): 3–12, 48–55; 25 (1949): 10–15; 26 (1950): 17–19.

33. M. H. Laurent, "De litteris ineditis Fr. Willelmi de Fleete cc. 1368–1380," *Analecta Augustiniana* 18 (1941): 303–27.

34. *B. Simonis Fidati de Cascia Gesta Salvatoris Domini nostri Jesu Christi* (Ratisbon: 1734). N. Mattiolo, *Il beato Simone da Cascia dell Ordine Eremitano di S. Agostino e i suoi scritti editi ed inediti* (Rome: Campidoglio, 1898); M. G. Mc Neil, *Simone Fidati and his De Gestis domini Salvatoris* (Studies in Medieval and Renaissance Latin Language and Literature 21) (Washington D.C.: The Catholic University of America, 1950).

35. S. Meuccius, ed., *Expositio magni prophetae Abbatis Joachim in Apocalypsim* (Venice, 1527), fol. 176; M. Reeves, "Joachimist Expectations in the Order of Augustinian Hermits," *Recherches de théologie ancienne et médiévale* 25 (1958): 111–41; A. Zumkeller, "Joachim von Fiore und sein angeblicher Einfluss auf den Augustiner-Eremitenorden," *Augustinianum* 3 (1963): 382–88.

36. F. del Secolo, *Un teologo dell' ultimo Trecento: Luigi Marsili* (Trani: V. Vecchi, 1898); S. Bellandi, *Luigi Marsili degli Agostiniani, apostolo ed anima del rinascimento letterario in Firenze, an. 1342–1394:* (Florence: Tipografia Arcivescovile, 1911); R. Arbesmann, "Andrea Biglia. Augustinian friar and humanist (+ 1435)," *Analecta Augustiniana* 28 (1965): 167–70; D. M. Webb, "Andrea Biglia at Bologna 1424–7: a humanist friar and the troubles of the Church," *Bulletin of the Institute of Historical Research* 49 (1976): 41–59.

37. R. Arbesmann, *Die Augustiner-Eremitenorden und der Beginn der humanistischen Bewegung* (Cassiciacum 19) (Würzburg: Augustinus-Verlag, 1965); K. Elm, "Mendikanten und Humanisten im Florenz des Tre- und Quattrocento. Zum Problem der Legitimierung hu-

manistischer Studien in den Bettelorden," in O. Herding and R. Stupperich, eds., *Die Humanisten in ihrer politischen und sozialen Umwelt* (DFG. Kom. für Humanismusforschung. Mitteilung III) (Boppard: Boldt, 1976), 53–85.

38. R. Arbesmann and W. Hümpfner, eds., *Jordani de Saxonia Ordinis Eremitarum S. Augustini Liber Vitasfratrum* (Cassiciacum. Studies in St. Augustine and the Augustinian Order. Vol. I. American Series) (New York: Cosmopolitan Science and Art Service, 1943). Cf. also: R. Arbesmann, "Jordanus of Saxony's Vita S. Augustini the Source for John Capgrave's Life of St. Augustine," *Traditio* 1 (1943): 341–52; A. Zumkeller, "Jordan von Quedlinburg," in *Die deutsche Literatur des Mittelalters. Verfasserlexikon* (Berlin–New York: de Gruyter, 1983) 4:855–61.

39. J. Munroe, ed., *John Capgrave's Lives of St. Augustine and St. Gilbert of Sempringham and a Sermon* (London: Kegan Paul, Trench, Trübner, 1910), 146; G. Sanderlin, "John Capgrave speaks up for the Hermits," *Speculum* 17 (1943): 358–62; A. de Meijer, "John Capgrave, O.E.S.A. (Lynn, 21 April 1393–Lynn, 12 August 1464)" *Augustiniana* 7 (1957): 118–48, 531–37; E. Colledge, "John Capgrave's Literary Vocation," *Analecta Augustiniana* 40 (1977): 185–95.

40. K. Walsh, *The «Liber de Vita Evangelica» of Geoffrey Hardeby OESA (1320–c. 1385). A Study in the Mendicant Controversies of the Fourteenth Century* (Bibliotheca Augustiniana. NS Sectio Historica 4) (Rome: Institutum Historicum Ordinis Fratrum S. Augustini, 1973).

41. A. Zumkeller, *Hermann von Schildesche O.E.S.A. (+ 8 Juli 1357). Zur 600. Wiederkehr seines Todestages* (Cassiciacum 15) (Würzburg: Augustinus-Verlag, 1957), 8–13.

42. Arbesmann, *Der Augustiner-Eremitenorden und der Beginn der humanistischen Bewegung* (Cf. n. 37).

43. R. Arbesmann, ed., "Fratris Andree Mediolanensis ad Fratrem Ludovicum de ordinis nostri forms et propagatione," *Analecta Augustiniana* 28 (1965): 186–218. A. M. Voci, "La suggestione umanista dell' eremo in Andrea Biglia," *Critica Storica* 18 (1981): 661–81.

44. A. Biglia, *De disciplina ordinis admonitio habita in capitulo Bononiensi,* Biblioteca Ambrosiana, Milan, H 117 Inf., fol. 42. J. C. Schnaubelt, "Prolegomena to the Edition of the Extant Works of Andrea Biglia, O.S.A. (+ 1435)," *Analecta Augustiniana* 40 (1977): 141–84 (cf. n. 36).

45. W. Ehbrecht, *Lippstadt. Beiträge zur Stadtgeschichte* (Lippstadt: Stadt Lippstadt, 1985), 1:295.

46. C. D. Fonseca, "La polemica tra i canonici lateranensi e i monaci di Santa Giustina nel Quattrocento," in *Medioevo Canonicale,* 5–26; idem, "I canonici e la riforma di S. Giustina," in *Riforma della chiesa, cultura e spiritualità nel Quattrocento Veneto. Atti del convegno per il VI centenario della nascita di Ludovico Barbo (1382–1443). Padova, Venezia, Treviso 19–24 settembre 1982* (Cesena: Badia di Santa Maria del Monte, 1984), 293–307.

47. P. Damon, "The Preconium Augustini of Godfrey of St. Victor," *Mediaeval Studies* 22 (1960): 93–107; C. de Clercq, "La «De vita canonica» de Raimbaud de Liège," *Archivum Latinitatis Medii Aevi* 32 (1962): 57–85; A. K. Huber, "Das Fortleben des hl. Augustinus bei den Prämonstratensern," in *Augustinus. Bij het sestiende eeuwfest van zijn geborte, 355–1954* (Averbode: Abdij, 1954), 58–76; U. E. Geniets, "Het augustinisme in de ordre von prémontré," in *gedenkboek orde van prémontré 1121–1971* (Averbode: Abdij, 1971), 79–84; C. P. H. van Dal, "De Regel van Sint-Augustinus in de Geschiedenis van de Reguliere Kanunniken van de Orde van het H. Kruis," *Clairlieu* 38 (1980): 39–70; 39 (1981): 13–28; J. Stiennon, "L'iconographie de saint Augustin d'après Benozzo Gozzoli et les Croisiers de Huy. Deux interprétations contemporaines et divergentes," *Bulletin de l'Institut historique belge de Rome* 27 (1952): 235–48.

48. Elm, "Elias, Paulus von Theben und Augustinus" (cf. n. 14).

49. Th. Kaeppeli, ed., *Stephanus de Salaniaco et Bernardus Guidonis De quatuor in quibus Deus Praedicatorum Ordinem insignavit* (Monumenta Ordinis Fratrum Praedicatorum Historica XXII) (Rome: Institutum Historicum Fratrum Praedicatorum Romae ad S. Sabinae, 1949); A. Walz, "Magne pater Augustine. Dominikanisches zur Regel des hl. Augustinus," *Angelicum* 31 (1954): 211–31; J. B. Schneyer, "Albert des Grossen Augsburger Predigtzyklus über den hl. Augustinus," *Recherches de theologie ancienne et médiévale* 36 (1969): 100–147.

50. Nicolaus Barianus de Placentia, *Causa Vitaliana de precedentia heremitarum et minorum* (Cremona, 1508); A. Daca, *Chronica general de nuestro padre San Francisco y su apostolica orden* (Valladolid, 1611); Th. de Herrera, *Responsio pacifica ad Apologeticum de praetenso monachato Augustiniano S. Francisci* (Bologna 1635); L. Wadding, "Apologeticus de praetenso monachatu Augustiniano S. Francisci," in *Annales Minorum* (Quaracchi: Institutum Franciscanum Historicum, 1931), 2:501–668; G. Cannarozzi, "Il Defensorium veritatis," *Studi Francescani* 2 (1930): 266–72; D. Crese, "L'opuscolo defensiorio della verità di Mariano da Firenze," *Studi Francescani* 61 (1964): 169–230.

51. R. J. Halliburton, "Fact and Fiction in the Life of St. Augustine. An Essay in Mediaeval Monastic History and Seventeenth Century Exegesis," *Recherches augustiniennes* 5 (1968): 15–40; D. Webb, "Eloquence and Education. A Humanist Approach to Hagiography," *The Journal of Ecclesiastical History* 31 (1980): 19–39; Elm, "Elias, Paulus von Theben und Augustinus" (cf. n. 14).

52. J. Courcelle and P. Courcelle, *Iconographie de Saint Augustin: Les Cycles du XIVe siècle* (Paris: Etudes Augustiniennes, 1965); idem, *Iconographie de Saint Augustin: Les Cycles du XVe siècle* (Paris: Etudes Augustiniennes, 1969); idem, *Iconographie de Saint Augustin: Les Cycles du XVIe et XVIIe siècles* (Paris: Etudes Augustiniennes, 1972).

53. E. Drachenberg, K. J. Maercker and C. Schmidt, *Die mittelalterliche Glasmalerei in den Ordenskirchen und im Angermuseum zu Erfurt* (Vienna, Cologne, Graz: Böhlau, 1976), 213–46.

54. R. Maiocchi, *L'arca di San Agostino in S. Pietro in Ciel d'Oro* (Pavia: C. Rossetti, 1900); C. Bonjour, "De loco obitus S. Augustini. De sepultura et translatione eiusdem prima et secunda," *Analecta Augustiniana* 2 (1907–8): 376–80, 401–5, 440–46, 487–92; A. Addeo, *Pavia e S. Agostino. Gli splendori di S. Pietro in Ciel d'Oro* (Pavia, 1951). On the early history of S. Pietro in Ciel d'Oro: Ch. Schroth-Köhler, *Die Fälscherwerkstatt von S. Pietro in Ciel d'Oro zu Pavia* (Münchener Historische Studien. Abt. Geschichtl. Hilfswissenschaften XVIII) Kallmünz: M. Lassleben 1982), 1–10.

55. Gatti Perer, "Umanesimo a Milano" (cf. n. 21).

56. Cf. n. 52 and E. Pfeiffer, "Der Augustiner-Hochaltar und vier weitere Nürnberger Altäre des ausgehenden 15. Jahrhunderts," *Mitteilungen des Vereins für Geschichte der Stadt Nürnberg* 52 (1963–64): 305–98; Christian Altgraf zu Salm, "Die Wandgemälde der Augustinerkirche zu Konstanz," *Studien zur Kunstgeschichte des Oberrheins. Festschrift für Werner Noack* (Constance-Freiburg: Thorbecke/Rombach, 1968); E. Colledge, "The Augustine Screen in Carlisle Cathedral," *Augustiniana* 36 (1986): 65–99.

57. D. Cole Ahl, "Benozzo Gozzoli's Frescoes of the Life of Saint Augustine in San Gimignano: Their Meaning in Context," *Artibus et historiae* 13 (1986): 35–53.

58. On similar intentions in the Franciscan order, see: D. Blume, *Wandmalerei als Ordenspropaganda. Bildprogramme im Chorbereich franziskanischer Konvente Italiens bis zur Mitte des 14. Jahrhunderts* (Worms: Wernersche Verlagsgesellschaft, 1983). Cf. n. 5, above, particularly: Ulmeus, *Libellus de apologia*.

59. F. Bisogni, "Iconografia dei predicatori dell'Osservanza nella pittura dell'Italia del Nord fino agli inizi del Cinquecento," in *Il Rinnovamento del Francescanesimo: L'Osservanza. Atti dell'XI Convegno Internazionale. Assisi, 20, 21, 22 ottobre 1983* (Assisi: Università di Perugia, Centro di Studi Francescani, 1985), 235 n. 5.

60. G. Penco, "S. Giovanni Battista nel ricordo del monachesimo medievale," *Studia Monastica* 3 (1961); 8–31; E. Lupieri, "Felices sunt qui imitantur Johannem (Hier., Hom. in Jo.). La figura di S. Giovanni Battista come modello di santità," *Augustinianum* 24 (1984): 33–71; J. Leclercq, "Saint Antoine dans la tradition monastique médiévale," in *Antonius Magnus Eremita 356–1956. Studia ad antiquum monachismum spectantia* (Rome: Pia Società S. Paolo, 1956), 229–47; A. Mischlewski, *Grundzüge der Geschichte des Antoniterordens bis zum Ausgang des 15. Jahrhunderts* (Cologne-Vienna: Böhlau, 1976), 18–21, 45–57.

61. P. Courcelle, *Recherches sur Saint Ambroise. Vies anciennes, culture, iconographie* (Paris: Etudes Augustiniennes 1973); G. Turazza, *Sant'Ambrogio ad nemus in Milano. Notizie storiche dal 357 al 1912* (Milan: Istituto S. Gaetano 1914); R. Jungblut, *Hieronymus. Darstellung und Verehrung eines Kirchenvaters* (Ph.D. diss. University of Tübingen, 1968); E. F. Rice, Jr., *Saint Jerome in the Renaissance* (The Johns Hopkins Symposia in Comparative History) (Baltimore, London 1985); J. de Sigüenza, *Historia de la Orden de San Jeronimo* (Madrid: 1907–9); J. R. L. Highfield, "The Jeronomites in Spain, their patrons and success, 1373–1516," *The Journal of Ecclesiastical History* 34 (1983): 513–33. D. Russo, *Saint Jérôme en Italie. Étude d'iconographie et de spiritualité XIIe–XIVe siècle* (Images à l'appui 2) (Paris-Rome: Ed. La Découverte — École Française de Rome 1988).

62. F. A. Dal Pino, *I frati Servi di S. Maria dalle origini all'approvazione (1233 ca.– 1304)*, I–II (Louvain: Bibliothèque de l'Université and Publications Universitaires, 1972); V. Saxer, *Le culte de Marie-Madeleine en Occident des origines à la fin du moyen-âge* (Paris: Clavreuil, 1959); M. Janssen, *Maria Magdalena in der abendländischen Kunst. Ikonographie der Heiligen von den Anfängen bis ins 16 Jhdt.* (Ph.D. diss., University of Freiburg, 1962); A. Simon, *L'Ordre des Penitentes de Ste. Marie-Madeleine en Allemagne au XIIIe siècle* (Fribourg: L'Oeuvre de Saint Paul, 1918); J. Maurice, *Sainte Hélène* (Paris: H. Laurens, 1930); J. Vogt, "Helena Augusta das Kreuz und die Juden. Fragen um die Mutter Constantins des Grossen," *Saeculum* 27 (1976): 211–22; P. van den Bosch, "Sancta Helena, nobilissima femina," *Clair-Lieu*, 39 (1981), 71–88.

63. J. Delaville Le Roulx, *De prima origine hospitalariorum Hierosolymitanorum* (Paris: E. Thorin, 1885); idem, *Les Hospitaliers en Terre Sainte et à Chypre (1100–1310)* (Paris: E. Leroux, 1904), 15–19; M. Schatkin, "The Makkabean Martyrs," *Vigiliae Christianae* 28 (1974): 97–113.

64. Elm, Elias, "Paulus von Theben und Augustinus" (cf. n. 14).

65. C. Peyer, *Stadt und Stadtpatron im mittelalterlichen Italien* (Zürich: Europa Verlag, 1955); A. M. Orselli, "Il Santo Patrono cittadino fra Tardo Antico e Alto Medioevo," *Bullettino dell'Istituto Storico Italiano* 89 (1980–81): 349–67; H. Seton-Watson, "Nationalbewusstsein als historisches Phänomen," *Südost-Forschungen* 43 (1984): 271–85; A. Borst, *Der Turmbau von Babel. Geschichte und Meinungen über Ursprung und Vielfalt der Sprachen und Völker 1–4* (Stuttgart: Hiersemann, 1957–63); E. Ewig, "Die Kathedralpatrozinien im römischen und fränkischen Gallien," *Historisches Jahrbuch* 79 (1960): 1–61; E. Morini, "Richiami alle tradizioni di apostolicità ed organizzazione ecclesiastica nelle sedi patriarcali d'Oriente," *Bullettino dell' Istituto Storico Italiano* 89 (1980–81): 1–69; M. Maccarone, *Apostolicità, episcopato e primato di Pietro. Ricerche e testimonianze dal II al V secolo* (Lateranum 1976, N.S. 42, 2) (Rome: Lateranum, 1976).

4 ❧

FRA ANGELICO AT SAN MARCO
Art and the Liturgy of Cloistered Life

WILLIAM HOOD

T HE APPEAL of all forms of monastic life down the ages is best summed up in its character as a life of prayer. In this chapter, William Hood analyzes the role of images in forming monastic prayerfulness, through a study of Fra Angelico's cycle of frescoes at the Observant Dominican convent of San Marco, Florence. Hood reconstructs the functions of key images in the "ritual topography" of the monastic enclosure, and reflects upon their intended messages for distinct social groups in the monastic community: the preaching friars, the novices still in formation, and the lay brothers whose work was restricted to the cloister. His picture of Dominican "habits of prayer" illustrates how the basic ideals of monastic spirituality were transmitted from one generation of friars to the next, and suggests how images were used programatically to shape the religious imagination of those "professionals" whose task it was to preach to the laity.

WILLIAM HOOD is associate professor of art history at Oberlin College. Among his publications is an essay on Renaissance art and popular religion in *Monasticism and the Arts,* the companion volume to *Christianity and the Renaissance.* He is currently finishing a book on Fra Angelico at San Marco.

ETWEEN ABOUT 1440 AND 1453, Fra Angelico and his shop executed the pictorial decoration in the Observant Dominican convent of San Marco.[1] When Fra Angelico began to work there, San Marco was almost entirely new. It had been established in 1436 by the friars from San Domenico in Fiesole; and in fact the two communities formed a canonical entity governed by a single, common prior and two subpriors, one at San Domenico and the other at San Marco. From the very beginning, however, San Marco developed in ways that seem to have strained familial bonds between the houses, and in 1445 the two convents separated, each electing its own prior. The greatest single factor in San Marco's development was, of course, the virtually unlimited financial and political support of Cosimo de' Medici.

Between 1437 and 1444, Cosimo's architect Michelozzo supervised the remodelling and new construction of the church and the convent, which we know today as the Museo di San Marco.[2] Michelozzo built a new roof and added a polygonal apse to the cardinal north end of the church, which he then enclosed with the friars' choir; he also erected another wall about halfway down the nave, thus dividing the church into three sections, one for women, one for men, and the choir for the Dominicans. Otherwise, the church seems to have remained structurally unaltered and to have retained its mostly trecento fresco decoration. Of the dilapidated conventual buildings still standing in 1436, only the refectory could be saved intact. It continued its original function and provided the foundation on which the east dormitory rests. This was built in 1437. The other two wings on the north and south followed. The north wing, housing among other things the sacristy and chapter room below and another dormitory above, went up in 1440–41. The south wing, which contained the entrance, porter's lodge, and guest rooms on the ground floor and the novitiate above, followed later in 1441. The famous library was added on the north side, almost as an afterthought, in 1443/44.

For these spaces, Fra Angelico and his assistants provided an altarpiece in the choir, frescoes in standard locations for conventual buildings, such as the chapter room and refectory, scenes in each cell of the dormitory, and three other scenes in the dormitory corridors. When completed, the ensemble constituted the most extensive program of convent decoration ever carried out, as far as we know.

Fra Angelico and the other friars responsible for deciding on the decoration seem to have wanted a series of images that would continue the venerable traditions of Dominican art, some of which had emerged in Bologna around the middle of the thirteenth century and others in Pisa and Siena a generation or two later. Dominican scholars such as Fathers Stefano Orlandi, Venturino Alce, and Eugenio Marino have been among the leaders in placing Fra Angelico's work within the general outlines of Dominican traditions.[3] As my own work on San Marco progresses, moreover, it becomes increasingly clear to me that the artistic conventions were themselves equally as valuable as the order's other traditions in the treasury of Dominican corporate identity, in no way subordinate or even subsequent to the ones better expressed in words.

Students of the period have often remarked on the sharply different characters of Dominican and Franciscan institutional history. As is well known, the Franciscans found it impossible to remain united as an order. The sons and daughters of St. Francis had begun to separate into various splinter groups and even rival families practically before their father in religion was cold in his grave. The Dominicans, by contrast, however strongly they may have disagreed among themselves from time to time, were able to maintain their unity; their order remained intact, as it does to this day. It is worth pausing a moment to consider the sources of this extraordinary corporate unit, because I believe that a major purpose of Dominican art, whether altarpieces or conventual frescoes, was to help preserve the common bonds that guaranteed the unity of such highly individualistic, and thus potentially factious, people.

The corporate strength of the Order of Preachers seems to rest on several interconnected foundations, not the least of which is the charitable, yet nonmystical, clear-headedness of St. Dominic himself. St. Francis had a tendency toward a kind of literalistic affective piety, and he set lofty but unspecific ideals for the Friars Minor. These could

hardly be further removed from what we know of Dominic's more contemplative, even cerebral and abstract, prayer life and his unambiguous
insistence that the single purpose of the Order of Preachers was preaching.

All Dominican legislation was therefore designed to support
and strengthen the mission to preach. The early Dominicans fully understood that an immutable system of governance, based, like the Benedictine rule, on unquestioning obedience to the will of a single person,
might discourage interesting and speculative minds from developing their
unique gifts to the fullest. Thus the most original piece of Dominican
legislation is the Constitutions, which form a flexible document that
interprets the Augustinian rule according to the needs of the order at
the moment. The Constitutions are susceptible to constant change by
a fully representational and frequently meeting general chapter. The friar
thus owes obedience not to a superior but to the order at large, as the
order expresses its will through this mutable, and therefore historically
responsive, form of legislation. Among other things, this means that
there is no such thing as a "typical" Dominican; that a "Dominican"
point of view must always represent a consensus and may never be arbitrarily claimed for an individual friar; and that everything connected
with the lives of friars in community—including their art—is infinitely
flexible in regard to interpretation and is oriented at once toward two
goals. The first of these is the obligation to preach, and this obligation
unites the group; the second is the goal of guaranteeing the individual
within the group the maximum freedom possible to seek his own path.
As we shall see, the first goal is found in the themes of Fra Angelico's
frescoes in the chapter room, refectory, and so on; the second and more
personal one is reflected in the cell frescoes.

Painted images performed the task of maintaining unity in three
major ways. First, Dominican convents and churches contained pictures
that explained the ideals of the activities being conducted before them.
Thus we may say that the primary function of Dominican art was to
parallel and reinforce the common life, that is to say, the liturgy of the
Dominican Constitutions. Second, the painted portrait had a vital, though
little studied, place in Dominican lore because the order's origins and
historical mission were understood to have been vested in and lived out
by radically different individuals, each of whom nonetheless embodied
the Dominican vocation. Collectively, these effigies represented a pic-

torial history of the order, and commemorating the brethren by means of their likenesses in the church and convent is a custom whose beginnings, as best I can tell, are exactly contemporary with the beginnings of the order's written history.[4] Third, Dominican art provided the friars with images of models or exemplars of the preaching life. These images may be distinguished from the portraits because they do not preserve facial likenesses so much as bodily gestures. And their purpose was to stimulate imitation in the friar who beheld them, rather than to symbolize the order's corporate history.

Common dedication to the vocation to preach, and the meaning of that vocation in the economy of salvation, found visual expression in a number of ways. Most important were the two images before which every community of friars gathered every day, namely, the altarpiece in the choir and the fresco in the chapter room. Joanna Cannon's work has led me to the discovery that Dominican altarpieces in choirs invariably showed two related themes, the first being the special role of Mary in sacred history, in particular the history of the Dominican order, and the second, the order's authority to preach, given by Christ to the successors of the apostolic preachers, the Dominicans. The altarpiece for Santa Caterina in Pisa by Simone Martini, dating from 1320, clearly illustrates both themes; its iconography has been fully explained by Cannon (Figure 4.1).[5] These two ideas had appeared even earlier than on Simone Martini's polyptych, however, and developed steadily throughout the rest of the fourteenth century; by Fra Angelico's day, they were found on every altarpiece in Dominican choirs throughout Central Italy.

Fra Angelico's altarpiece for San Marco follows one of these traditions and breaks with the other (Figure 4.2). Its symbols are exclusively Marian, but the theme of Dominican preaching authority has almost disappeared, except for the long quotation from St. Mark's Gospel, which the saint holds exposed in his arms.[6] Fra Angelico, however, gave this displaced emphasis on the order's authority and on the exemplars who embodied the order's ideals fuller development in the convent. In fact, the function of SS. Dominic, Peter Martyr, and Thomas Aquinas as the models of Dominican life in all its varying expressions is the major conceptual principle that organizes the disparate parts of the San Marco decoration into an ensemble.

We know that part of this ensemble was a fresco that Fra An-

Figure 4.1. Simone Martini, Polyptych from Santa Caterina. Pisa, Museo Nazionale di San Matteo. Photo Villa I Tatti.

gelico painted on the end wall of the refectory. It has disappeared, but Creighton Gilbert has made some altogether plausible suggestions regarding its subject, which is probably reflected in the 1536 fresco by Andrea Sogliani now on the end wall.[7] Fra Angelico's painting seems to have joined the theme of the Crucifixion with a scene from Dominican history. Unfortunately, we shall probably never know with any greater accuracy what this fresco showed, because it does not, as is often claimed, lie beneath Sogliani's fresco. That is because the wall on which Fra Angelico painted his composition was destroyed when the refectory was enlarged to its present size in 1526.[8] However, the conjunction of the Crucifixion and Dominican history is still fully—and, one may say, magnificently—visible in the chapter room.

The great scene of the Crucifixion, which Gail Geiger has rightly related to the frescoes in the Spanish Chapel at Santa Maria Novella,[9] is organized on compositional principles and with a rhetorical tone that

Figure 4.2. Fra Angelico, San Marco Altarpiece. Florence, Museo di San Marco. Gabinetto fotografico, Soprintendenza Beni Artistici e Storici di Firenze.

seems to me to come very late in Fra Angelico's career, certainly after 1450. The characters from sacred history occupy only the left half of the composition; these are the biblical witnesses and the patron saints of the convent. The right half (in other words, equal space) is given to an array of more recent saints, each of whom is associated with the reform of religious life. Their responses to the crucified Christ are just as charged as those of the figures on the left. It seems clear that the visual equivalence of the two groups to the left and right of center is a statement about their functional equivalence relative to the community of friars assembled daily before this image. That is to say, the cloistered life in general is held up as a model by which both the community and the individual friars in it may conform themselves to the companions of Christ shown in the fresco. The frieze of portraits in roundels extending across the bottom of the composition is an example of the widespread and ancient Dominican custom, mentioned above, of preserving the likenesses of the order's more important members. Such portraits are found in Dominican chapter rooms from Treviso to Florence, but Fra Angelico has used them to locate the more general theme of exemplars in the Crucifixion scene in the specific history of the Dominican Observance.[10] As far as one can tell, many of the portrait medallions represent friars, chiefly of Santa Maria Novella, who were particular models of the austerity and holiness the Dominican Observance sought to recover.

Like the monastic reformers in the Crucifixion scene itself, the Dominican effigies appear in the chapter room primarily as embodiments of San Marco's historical ideals. By contrast, the exhortation for the single friar to imitate an exemplar in his own personal life as a Dominican is the theme of the huge fresco, *St. Dominic with the Crucifix,* on axis with the entrance to the cloister (Figure 4.3). Unlike similar arrangements in which St. Francis is shown adoring the crucified Christ, the appearance of St. Dominic in the same place is extremely rare. The only examples I know outside Fra Angelico's oeuvre, in fact, are small-scale panels.[11] It was certainly Fra Angelico who expanded the image into the monumental one found twice at San Marco—once here and again in the corridor upstairs—and he seems to have developed it for San Domenico in Fiesole in the 1420s or 1430s.[12] Therefore, although there is the precedent on a small scale, one seems justified in saying that St. Dominic and the crucifix makes its first appearance in monumental art in the work of Fra Angelico for two Dominican convents.

The panels and Fra Angelico's frescoes probably had a common source in an even smaller group of paintings. These are the miniatures of an illustrated Dominican prayer treatise dating from the mid-thirteenth century, called *De modo orandi.*[13] Often copied and widely dispersed throughout the order, *De modo orandi* is of interest to us for a variety

Figure 4.3. Fra Angelico, *St. Dominic with the Crucifix*. Florence, Museo di San Marco. Gabinetto fotografico, Soprintendenza Beni Artistici e Storici di Firenze.

of reasons. Not the least of these is that its text presupposes that an illustration would accompany the description of each of the nine modes of prayer the treatise explains. That is because the treatise rests on the fundamental assumption that one can precipitate a psychological state by assuming the gesture appropriate to it. Thus the gesture that stimulates a state of humility, for example, is said to be a deep bow from the waist. And the deep bow illustrated here appropriately accompanies the text describing the virtue of humility in prayer (Figure 4.4).

The author of *De modo orandi* claims that his text is an eyewitness report of St. Dominic at prayer. He purports to describe nine ways in which the saint himself was observed to pray, and eight of these were silent. That is to say, the only indication of what was in Dominic's mind was what his body was doing. These modes of prayer were explained and illustrated almost certainly as an aid in the education of novices during their canonical year of initiation. St. Dominic's behavior, not his speech, was thus held up before the novices as an introduction to what would become a lifelong habit, namely, the imitation of the order's exemplars of Dominican perfection.

De modo orandi, in fact, may have been of special interest in the efforts of the Dominican Observance to renew the fervor of religious life, beginning, of course, with the novices. There is some evidence that Fra Giovanni Dominici, the leader of the Observance, knew the treatise and perceived its usefulness for Dominican imagery.[14] And we are on firm ground in saying that Fra Angelico and his brothers were familiar with it because Antoninus quoted the entire text in his *Chronicon.*[15] In *De modo orandi,* St. Dominic is always shown praying before a crucifix, even though for the most part his prayer, as we might expect, seems to have arisen from meditating on a text rather than from regarding an image. The iconography of the cloister fresco showing St. Dominic with the crucifix, and its twin in the north corridor of the dormitory, would therefore have been instantly intelligible to a Dominican friar, though probably not to anyone else at all. The fresco, in fact, makes completely explicit the general allusions to Dominican customs I have been discussing.

It is in the cell frescoes that *De modo orandi* plays the fullest part in Fra Angelico's inventions for San Marco. Before looking more closely at these, however, we might briefly consider some other char-

Figure 4.4. Biblioteca Vaticana, Cod. Rossianus 3: *De modo orandi*, fol. 6r. Photo Biblioteca Apostolica Vaticana.

acteristics of Dominican life which help us to understand Fra Angelico's work in the dormitory. I have already mentioned that everything connected with the lives of Dominican friars was oriented toward two goals, the vocation to preach and the corollary guarantee that the friar would have all necessary means to prepare himself as a Dominican preacher. This orientation had important consequences for the history of conventual architecture. For example, the library had to be easily accessible, opening directly onto the dormitory, because friars might take volumes to their cells for lengthy consultation. Customs of Dominican study, by the way, assumed that the friar would have several texts before him at once; he therefore needed what we would call a carrel. But since study for preaching involved meditation and prayer, the friar also needed private space. Therefore, as Anselm Hertz has pointed out, the Dominicans seem to have invented the use of private cells and to have concentrated far more important functions in the dormitory than was the custom among monks, whose dormitories were open spaces used for nothing other than sleeping.[16] In Dominic's vision the ideal preacher is what we might call an eloquent contemplative.[17] For Dominic and the other early fathers of the order, effective preaching was the fruit of a transformed life — a life, as it were, refined by the gregarious hazards of community on the one hand, and by the solitude of prayerful study on the other. As the primary method of preparing to preach, study thus became the central domestic activity of a Dominican community. In a Dominican convent, therefore, the dormitory was as important in the lives of the preachers as the refectory or chapter room or even the choir of the church.

It is in this light that the decoration of the dormitory area should be understood. The corridor frescoes in the dormitory at San Marco mark three ritual activities that regularly took place in Dominican dormitories. The first was the "reverencing" or acknowledging an image of the Virgin, always placed opposite the entrance. The *Annunciation* in the north corridor — the image of the Virgin Fra Angelico painted for this function — carries a hortatory inscription across the bottom which reminds us that image and activity were deeply related at San Marco (Figure 4.5). Second, the fresco of St. Dominic before the crucifix, like the one in the cloister below, restates the theme of imitation and perhaps marked the beginning of the community's procession into the choir. And third, the *Madonna delle Ombre,* as the painting in the east corridor is known, would have been the image before which the community gathered for the night office of the Virgin, which the Constitutions specify was to take place in the dormitory.[18] (It seems never to have been pointed out that the *Madonna delle Ombre* is a redaction of the San Marco altarpiece in the choir, and that the two paintings need therefore to be seen as performing precisely the same function in two different places.)

Turning now to the frescos in the cells, in considering their general arrangement it is important to remember that the early community at San Marco, like all Dominican communities of any size, housed

Figure 4.5. Fra Angelico, *Annunciation*. Florence, Museo di San Marco. Gabinetto fotografico, Soprintendenza Beni Artistici e Storici di Firenze.

novices, clerics, and *conversi* or lay brothers. Each of these three sections of the community lived apart from the others, and each had its own function within the community's life and ministry. The frescoes in the novitiate cells (that is, the eight on the south corridor leading to the novices' oratory and classroom) all show St. Dominic with the crucifix. These frescoes are universally ignored both because their execution is far from Fra Angelico's hand and because they are held to be tediously uniform. Setting aside these aesthetic judgments, which in any case have nothing to do with the program, we might say that their uniformity could be as much a function of their purpose as of the unhappy accident of an unimaginative painter. These scenes, in fact, share a fundamental compositional unity with the image of St. Dominic before the crucifix in the north corridor (Figure 4.6). They are all vertical rectangles framed by alternating green and red bands; the figures are set against a flat ground; and there is no suggestion of pictorial space beyond the little horizontal

Figure 4.6. Fra Angelico Workshop, *St. Dominic with the Crucifix*. Florence, San Marco, Cell 20. Gabinetto fotografico, Soprintendenza Beni Artistici e Storici di Firenze.

shelf stretching across the bottom. These cell frescoes likewise share the same iconic subject matter found in the larger paintings in the more public spaces: St. Dominic and the crucifix (not the Crucifixion).

Within this generally uniform arrangement, however, the artist introduced interesting modifications. Each cell painting shows Dominic performing a different gesture or action, eight in all. Each of these eight gestures or actions in turn corresponds with eight of the nine ways of prayer described in *De modo orandi* (Figure 4.7). Here, then, the general theme of imitating the models of Dominican life becomes far more explicit. That is to say, as the novice in his cell studied and meditated on the lessons of the novice master—the history of the order, its rule and Constitutions, its life of discipline and work—the fresco nearby reminded him always that he was preparing himself to become a preacher, a man, like Dominic, sufficiently conformed to the mind of God to speak God's word with wisdom and eloquence and holiness.

After the canonical year of initiation, the novice became a cleric and moved to the east corridor of the dormitory, which was the first built and which contains the best known of the cell frescoes. Here the scenes—their subjects, compositions, and formats—change. With one or two exceptions, each cell in the dormitory contains a fresco with a rounded top and simple frame. Unlike the novices' frescoes, these are based on, but in most cases do not illustrate, a scene from sacred history shown against descriptive backgrounds naturalistically represented. In addition to the full range of characters necessary for the iconography, each painting likewise contains one or two exemplars, usually St. Dominic, St. Peter Martyr, or St. Thomas Aquinas. Similarly, the exemplars are placed outside the space occupied by the actors in the sacred events, not as witnesses but as respondents. We can say that they respond to the event rather than witness it because here, too, each exemplar is shown in one of the modes of prayer found in the treatise *De modo orandi*. The historiated scene is thus a substitute for the crucifix in the novices' cells. For example, in the Cell 3 *Annunciation*, St. Peter Martyr stands outside the loggia where Gabriel and Mary appear. His gesture corresponds to the fifth mode, meditation (Figure 4.8). Or in the Cell 10 *Presentation*, St. Peter Martyr and the Blessed Villana are separated from the rest of the figures by a different plane of space, and they are shown in the fourth mode, compassionate intercession (Figures

Figure 4.7. Biblioteca Vaticana, Cod. Rossianus 3: *De modo orandi*, fol. 7r. Photo Biblioteca Apostolica Vaticana.

4.9, 4.10, 4.11). St. Dominic, by the way, is said to have employed this mode when praying for the brethren and the novices. (It is of interest that this mode appears in the only friar's cell that was originally double, strongly suggesting, as does the iconography of the fresco in the other half of the cell, that this was the first prior's cell.) It thus seems that these oddly ahistorical scenes are not really illustrations of sacred texts; their peculiar character, so empty of narrative force, in combination with the presence of exemplars, makes them pictographs, as it were, of the prayerful study of sacred texts by which a preacher prepared himself to follow in the steps of SS. Dominic, Peter Martyr, and Thomas Aquinas, the model preachers.

The third or north corridor is extremely problematic for a num-

Figure 4.8. Fra Angelico, *Annunciation*. Florence, San Marco, Cell 3. Gabinetto fotografico, Soprintendenza Beni Artistici e Storici di Firenze.

Figure 4.9. Fra Angelico, *Presentation*. Florence, San Marco, Cell 11. Gabinetto fotografico, Soprintendenza Beni Artistici e Storici di Firenze.

Figure 4.10. Biblioteca Vaticana, Cod. Rossianus 3: *De modo orandi*, fol. 9r. Photo Biblioteca Apostolica Vaticana.

ber of reasons, and this is not the place to enter into the maddening complexities of chronology and function that surround the frescoes there. But I may say, if only in passing, that I now believe that the iconographical confusion presented by the frescoes as a whole in this space reflects a change in the nature and composition of the San Marco community following a series of dramatic events between 1445 and 1455. We may observe, however, that the eight cell paintings on the cloister side of this corridor demonstrate yet again an interior cohesion that sets them apart from the two other groups of frescoes in the clerics' and novices' dormitories. Most dramatic is the fact that each of these is a full-scale narrative illustration of a scene from the life of Christ, such as the Sermon on the Mount and the Agony in the Garden. Accordingly, the settings and actions are fully consonant with the stories they depict and

Figure 4.11. Biblioteca Vaticana, Cod. Rossianus 3: *De modo orandi,* fol. 8r. Photo: Biblioteca Apostolica Vaticana.

not with the abstracted pictograms found in the clerics' dormitory. Moreover, the absence of any exemplars, in conjunction with their simplified iconographical content, might suggest that these frescoes were originally made for the cells of lay brothers. There were usually about six conversi at San Marco, and of course they did not have to use their cells as studies. As for the cells on the outside wall, where Cosimo de' Medici's famous double cell is found, we encounter, as I have already suggested, a series of problems that would carry us far beyond the confines of this essay, which is concerned only with the themes that organize the program.

That program was very simple. In typological ways it is well within the limits of what one might expect of any Dominican conventual decoration of the period: Crucifixions in the refectory and chapter room; a painting of the Madonna in the dormitory; other images in the cells. The program departed from tradition, however, in ways that make San Marco worthy of more study than art historians have yet given it. First is the high degree of formal and thematic unity which I mentioned at the beginning, a unity that makes San Marco a fly-in-amber of Christian art in quattrocento Florence. I have tried here to suggest convincingly that three favorite Dominican visual ideas unite all the disparate parts of the decoration as a conceptual ensemble. First is the order's history expressed through commemorative portraits of its most prominent members; second is the role of exemplars, and especially St. Dominic's manners of praying; and third is the use of images as emblems of the liturgy of the Constitutions.

A second departure from tradition arises from the first, though it is one to which I have been able only to allude. So far as I know, no artist since Simone Martini had developed these Dominican themes with the subtlety and iconographical finesse with which Fra Angelico treated them at San Marco. Certainly his experiential familiarity with these notions as a friar prepared him for the task, but I contend that the iconographical inventions, like the monumental St. Dominic before a crucifix, betray the mind of an artist and not that of the designer of a program. This observation brings us to an art historical thorn among all these roses, and it is this: Did it make any difference that the painter of San Marco was also a Dominican of the Observance? I shall perhaps prick my thumb on the question, but I should like to conclude with a straightforward though largely undefended answer: Yes.

As several chapters of this volume make clear, all the major religious orders underwent some sort of reform in the second half of the fourteenth century. These reform movements were usually called the "Observance" because on the moral level their aim was to return each order to the full and unmitigated observance of its primitive rule and customs. The effort to retrieve what was uniquely Dominican or Franciscan or Benedictine is the hallmark of the Observance in each order, and one would not be wide of the mark in saying that the net effect of the various Observant movements was to sharpen differences among them.

This is true of the Dominican Observance, and nowhere more so than at San Dominico in Fiesole, which was the first house of the reform in Tuscany, and at its daughter house, San Marco, which became the leader of the Observant movement in the Order of Preachers. All this rich complex of references to Dominican traditions, the Dominican Constitutions, and even the Dominican liturgy is symptomatic of the resurgence of interest in early Dominican art already evident in the career of Giovanni Dominici, the father of the Dominican Observance. On one level, therefore, Fra Angelico profited from the rise of the Observance in Central Italy, because nearly all of his Dominican commissions — and these constitute the majority of his work before 1445 — were for Observant houses. On another level, too, the almost romantic nostalgia for the historical sources which marks the Observant movement in general meant that Fra Angelico was specially steeped in the traditions of his order. Therefore, I propose that Fra Angelico's having been a Dominican friar of the Observance was a major factor in his formation as an artist.

The other major factor was of course the fact that he came to maturity as a painter in Florence in the 1420s and 1430s. That is to say, he was heir to Masaccio and Ghiberti and passed on that legacy to Piero della Francesca and Domenico Veneziano. Ancient Dominican traditions were thus the primary subjects for an artist who was in every way in the vanguard of what amounts to a revolution in the history of the way we see. A hallmark of the San Marco ensemble as a work of art is its conjunction of conservative content with radically new form. For most of us, that is not an unfamiliar combination. Some of us are preachers; many of us are teachers. Both preachers and teachers know that real eloquence lies in being able to say old things in new ways, and that we have been truly eloquent when our hearers are voluntarily silent. If on occasion we therefore find ourselves standing before these paintings bereft of words, it is because of Fra Angelico's eloquence. Whether it be in the altarpiece that redefined for succeeding generations what a painting of this type might look like and communicate; whether it be in the ineffable pathos of the *Mocking of Christ;* or whether it be in the translation of a theological mystery into a formal mystery as in the exploitation of the white intonaco in the *Transfiguration,* Fra Angelico's voice is everywhere audible. The San Marco ensemble testifies to his gifts as a painter and, as I suspect he would have liked me to say, to his charism as a preacher.[19]

NOTES

1. This chapter presents many points to be argued more fully in my book "Fra Angelico at S. Marco," presently under way. As always, Giorgio Bonsanti, director of the Museo di S. Marco, deserves my special thanks for his kindness, which this time extended even to the last-minute loan of some beautiful slides. For the most recent summary of arguments regarding the dates of Fra Angelico's work at San Marco, see J. Pope-Hennessy, *Fra Angelico,* 2d ed. (London: Phaidon, 1974), 19–28, 199, 202.

2. The convent of S. Marco has never received a careful survey or documentary study; but see G. Marchini, "Il S. Marco di Michelozzo," *Palladio* 6 (1942): 102–14. The history of the church before 1500 may be found in an excellent article by H. Teubner, "S. Marco in Florenz: Umbauten vor 1500: Ein Beitrag zum Werk des Michelozzo," *Mitteilungen des Kunsthistorisch Institutes in Florenz* 23 (1979): 239–72. See also M. Ferrara and F. Quinterio, *Michelozzo di Bartolomeo* (Florence: Salimbeni, 1984), 185–96. Dates for various parts of the conventual buildings were abstracted from the chronicle of S. Marco in R. Morçay, *St. Antonin: Fondateur du couvent de St. Marc. Archeveque de Florence: 1389–1459* (Tours/Paris: Imprimerie Dominicaine, n.d. [1914], 76 n. 1.

3. S. Orlandi, *Beato Angelico* (Florence: Leo S. Olschki, 1954). See also the recent contributions, with further references, of Frs. Alce ("Cataloghi e indici delle opere del Beato Angelico"; "Saggio bibliografico sul Beato Angelico") and Marino ("Beato Angelico: Umanesimo e teologia") in *Beato Angelico: Miscellanea di studi* (Rome: Pontificia commissione centrale per l'arte sacra in Italia, 1984), 351–405, 407–62, and 465–533.

4. The Chapter General of 1254, meeting at Budapest, prescribed that images of SS. Dominic and Peter Martyr be placed in Dominican churches. See *Acta Capitulorum Generalium,* vol. 1 (1220–1303), ed. B. Riechert, in *Monumenta Ordinis Praedicatorum Historica* (Rome, 1898), 3:70 (hereafter MOPH). This chapter general elected Humbert of Romans master general; his *Vitae fratrum* is the first general history of the Order of Preachers.

5. J. Cannon, "Simone Martini, the Dominicans and the Early Sienese Polyptych," *Journal of the Warburg and Courtauld Institutes* 45 (1982): 69–93.

6. Mark 6:1–13.

7. C. Gilbert, "Last Suppers and Their Refectories," in *The Pursuit of Holiness in Late Medieval and Renaissance Religion,* ed. C. Trinkaus with H. A. Oberman (Leiden: E. J. Brill, 1974), 371–402.

8. The evidence is in the chronicle of S. Marco (Biblioteca Laurenziana, Florence, Cod. S. Marco 370, fol. 31), in a passage unnoticed until now, perhaps because it did not appear in R. Morçay's partial transcription in "La Cronaca del convento fiorentino di San Marco: La parte più antica, dettata da Giuliano Lapaccini," *Archivio storico italiano* 71, no. 1 (1913): 1–29. The relevant lines tell us that in 1526 the refectory was enlarged by one-third; i.e., an extra bay was added to the three that already made up the room. It is clear that the addition extended the southern end of the room — thereby necessitating the destruction of Fra Angelico's fresco — because the extra space was taken from the "hospice fratribus S. Domenicus de Fesulani," who were not the least bit pleased.

9. G. Geiger and T. McGonigle, "Fra Angelico's Frescoes in S. Marco" paper delivered at the 19th International Conference on Medieval Studies, Western Michigan University, Kalamazoo, Mich., 19–21 May 1983.

10. The best-known suite of Dominican portraits is of course by Tomaso da Modena, in the chapter room of Sa. Caterina in Treviso. See esp. *Tomaso da Modena,* exh. cat., ed. L. Menegazzi, Treviso, Sa. Caterina, Capitolo dei Domenicani (Treviso: Edizioni Canova, 1979), 115–28.

11. An apposite example is the panel attributed to Andrea di Buonaiuto now in the Pinacoteca Vaticana, no. 118. See R. Offner, *A Corpus of Florentine Painting: A Legacy of Attributions,* ed. H. Maginnis (Locust Valley, N.Y.: J. J. Augustin, 1981), 87–88.

12. The fresco of St. Dominic and the crucifix flanked by the Virgin and St. John, from S. Domenico in Fiesole, is now in the Louvre. See Pope-Hennessy, *Fra Angelico,* 196–97.

13. The discussion of *De modo orandi* which follows (Biblioteca Apostolica Vaticana, Rome, MS. lat. Rossianus 3) is based entirely on my article "St. Dominic's Manners of Praying," *Art Bulletin* 68 (1986): 195–206. A translation of the text, without the accompanying illustrations, may be found in S. Tugwell, ed., *Early Dominicans: Selected Writings* (New York/ Toronto: Paulist Press, 1982), 94–103.

14. The predella of Andrea di Bartolo's polyptych now in the Museo Vetrario in Murano seems clearly to exploit the gestures in *De modo orandi.* It was painted on Giovanni Dominici's instigation for the nuns at Corpus Domini in Venice, one of the very earliest Observant foundations in Italy. See C. Gilbert, "Tuscan Observants and Painters in Venice, c. 1400," in *Interpretazioni veneziane,* ed. D. Rosand (Venice: Editrice Arsenale, 1984), 109–20, fig. 3. I am grateful to Gaudens Freuler for many interesting discussions regarding this painting.

15. Antoninus, *Summa historiale* Nuremberg, 1491), 3:235–36. The third part of the *Summa,* known as the *Chronicon,* was begun about 1456 and finished by the end of 1458. See J. Walker, *The "Chronicles" of St. Antoninus: A Study in Historiography* (Washington, D.C.: Catholic University of America, 1933), 24.

16. A. Hertz, *Fra Angelico* (Rome: Edizioni Paoline, 1983), 69.

17. I am grateful to Salvatore Camporeale, O.P., for his innumerable suggestions and help during the course of my study of Fra Angelico. He kindly pointed out that my characterization of Dominicans as "eloquent contemplatives" is much in the spirit of one of the two mottoes of the Order of Preachers: *Contemplata aliis tradere.*

18. Since the thirteenth century, the Constitutions had specified that the night office (or matins, which is the same thing) of the Virgin be said in the dormitory. In Fra Angelico's day, the custom was reinforced by legislation at no fewer than four Chapters General: Cologne, 1428 (MOPH, 8:202); Lyons, 1431 (MOPH, 8:209); Colmar, 1434 (MOPH, 8:227); Avignon, 1442 (MOPH, 8:245). The suggestion that the *Madonna delle Ombre* was used this way seems to have been made first in I. Strunk, *Fra Angelico aus dem Dominikanerorden* (Gladbach: B. Kühlens Kunstanstalt und Verlag, 1916).

19. Since this essay went to press, two important additions to the literature on this subject have appeared. For an extensive study of the Chapter Room frescoes, see: M. Marek, "Ordenspolitik und Andacht. Fra Angelicos Kreuzigungfresko im Kapitelsaal von San Marco zu Florenz," *Zeitschrift für Kunstgeschichte* 48 (1985): 451–75. A further study of Dominican art in the context of the Observance is to be found in: G. Freuler, "Andrea di Bartolo, Fra Tommaso d'Antonio Caffarini, and Sienese Dominicans in Venice," *Art Bulletin* 69 (1987): 570–86.

5

THE TREE OF LIFE AND THE HOLY CROSS

Franciscan Spirituality in the Trecento and the Quattrocento

RAB HATFIELD

CHRISTIANITY, LIKE JUDAISM, is a "religion of the book," in which the normative spiritual experiences of the group are recorded and transmitted through sacred texts. In this chapter, Rab Hatfield studies the influence of key literary images, derived from the Old and New Testaments and elaborated by later writers, in shaping the spirituality of another of the important preaching orders, the Franciscans. Professor Hatfield's careful analysis of the Franciscan iconography of the Tree of Life in Florence and Arezzo suggests the degree to which pictorial images were tied to biblical, hagiographical, and interpretive texts, and the creative freedom with which artists used texts. His reconstruction of a major theme of Franciscan mysticism as illustrated in painting makes clear that interpenetration of Scripture, Church tradition, monastic usage, and visual imagery characteristic of late medieval and Renaissance Christian life.

RAB HATFIELD teaches the history of art at Syracuse University's Study Center in Florence. His publications include an essay on the Florentine lay confraternity dedicated to the Magi, the Compagnia de' Magi, and a book-length study of Sandro Botticelli's *Adoration of the Magi in the Uffizi Gallery* (1976).

HE FRANCISCANS, more than the Dominicans, elaborately developed several mystical images and legends of and about Christ's cross which might bring them closer in spirit to the fact and lesson of Christ's redeeming death. St. Francis, of course, had been stigmatized; so complete had been his imitation of the Lord, and so perfect his obedience to the Lord's will, that the very wounds of the crucified Lord were manifested in his body. I shall here be discussing pictorial representations in Franciscan convents of the Tree of Life and the story of the Holy Cross. Neither of the two themes was a Franciscan invention, but one is tempted to think of both as having become that order's spiritual property. As I attempt to demonstrate, the two themes are basically elaborations of the same thought, and it seems clear that in Franciscan devotional imagery the one had a decisive influence on the other.

We first read about the Tree of Life in the second chapter of Genesis:

> And the Lord God planted a garden eastward in Eden; and there he put the man whom he had formed.
>
> And out of the ground made the Lord God to grow every tree that is pleasant to the sight, and good for food; the tree of life also in the midst of the garden, and the tree of knowledge of good and evil.
>
> And a river went out of Eden to water the garden; and from thence it was parted, and became into four heads. (Gen. 2:8–10)[1]

In the next chapter we hear more about the tree:

> And the Lord God said, Behold, the man is become as one of us, to know good and evil; and now, lest he put forth his hand, and take also of the tree of life, and eat, and live for ever:
>
> Therefore, the Lord God sent him forth. . . .
>
> So he drove out the man; and he placed at the east of the garden of Eden Cherubims, and a flaming sword which turned every way, to keep the way of the tree of life. (Gen. 3:22–24)

From these brief descriptions we learn a surprising amount. Both mentions of the Tree of Life place it in relationship to the Tree of Knowledge, whose antitype it evidently was. But the Tree of Life was the more important of the two. It was in the middle of Paradise.[2] It is the first specific thing to be mentioned there after man himself, and it is also the last. The reason why God drove out unworthy man, who by eating of the Tree of Knowledge had "become as one of us," was to prevent him from gaining that immortality which would be his if he partook also of the Tree of Life. It was, finally, to bar access to that tree that God placed a guard at the east of Eden.

For further information about the Tree of Life we must turn to the last chapter of Revelation:

> And he shewed me a pure river of water of life, clear as crystal, proceeding out of the throne of God and of the Lamb.
> In the midst of the street of it, and on either side of the river, *was there* the tree of life, which bare twelve *manner of* fruits, *and* yielded her fruit every month: and the leaves of the tree *were* for the healing of the nations. (Rev. 22:1–2)[3]

And finally, but seven verses from the end:

> "Blessed *are* they that do his commandments, that they may have right to the tree of life, and may enter in through the gates into the city" (Rev. 22:14).

The city is the new Jerusalem, coming down from God out of Heaven.

During the Middle Ages, the Tree of Life came to be visualized as the largest tree in Paradise,[4] and as being not only in the middle of the garden but in its highest place as well.[5] It thus made sense to imagine the Water of Life flowing out from a source at its foot and usually—in contradiction to what is stated in Genesis—parting immediately into four separate streams. I am unable to present an exact historical account of the exegetical developments that led to those interpretations of the tree which concern us here. But as the emergence of such interpretations appears in retrospect to have been almost inevitable, it should not be too hard to reconstruct it, at least in its essential lines. Let me try to do so by posing a riddle: What is situated in the middle of Paradise, bears twelve fruits, is a source of perpetual nourishment, and has the power to make us live forever, even if we have sinned? Obvious answer: the Tree of Life. But what is that? Has any of us ever directly experienced this tree? Does our picture of it not convey to us the properties of something more true, more real? What therefore might it signify? Correct solution: Jesus Christ. Convenient scriptural hints are not lacking: on his way to be crucified, Jesus alludes to the world as the green tree when he is in it and as the dry tree when he will be gone.[6] He calls himself the true vine, of which the branches are his disciples.[7] But there is an alternative solution. If it is the fruit of the tree which makes us live forever, then the fruit is Christ and the tree the bearer of that fruit. Please do not, misled by my choice of words, jump to the conclusion that the tree is therefore Mary. The medieval solution, which makes better sense, is that the tree is the cross that Jesus died on. And mystically there can hardly be any doubt that it is.[8] But is it possible that the cross is *literally* the Tree of Life? Was it by any chance the wood of that tree which was turned into the instrument of Christ's redeeming death?

We are now ready to consider the story of the Holy Cross,[9] which is most conveniently available in James of Varagine's *Golden Legend*.[10] According to that work, an angel ordered Seth to plant upon Adam's grave the branch of a tree that grew in Paradise, promising that when this offshoot reached maturity, it would make Adam whole. The tree did grow and was ordered to be cut down by Solomon, whose workmen, angered at being unable to find a place for it during the construction of Solomon's temple, threw it across a nearby river. The sacred wood was thus a footbridge when the Queen of Sheba came before it. Realizing that the Savior of the World was to be put to death upon it, and therefore unable to walk across it, she fell down and adored it, and afterward she told Solomon that to it would be nailed a man by whom the realm of the Jews would be destroyed. Solomon wisely had the wood buried, but in the very spot where the Probatic Pool would later be built. Shortly before Christ's Passion, the wood floated to the pool's surface, and some workmen fashioned it into the cross.

I am interrupting the account at this point in order to take up a vexatious detail. The *Golden Legend* says that it was a branch from the Tree of Knowledge which Seth planted upon Adam's grave.[11] But how can an offshoot of that tree, of all things, have survived God's wrath

during the Flood? What vexes one most, however, is the seeming il-
logic and spiritual inappropriateness of identifying Christ's cross with
the Tree of Knowledge rather than the Tree of Life.[12]

Whatever its ultimate origin, the wood of the cross fulfilled
its destiny when Christ died upon it. However, the story does not end
there. Having been victorious because of it, the emperor Constantine
ordered his mother, Helena, to retrieve the cross, which had been buried
a second time. In order to find it, this no-nonsense lady seized a Jew,
who had been told by his father that Christ was indeed the son of God,
and had him thrown into a well. After six days without food or drink,
the Jew consented to take Helena to the place where the cross had been
buried nearly three centuries before, and she had him hauled out. Having retrieved the cross and borne witness to its power to resuscitate,
Helena took part of it back to Constantine and returned the rest of
it to Jerusalem. But three centuries later the part of the cross in Jerusalem was stolen by a Persian king, blasphemed by him, and finally retrieved a second time by a Christian emperor, Heraclius, after a battle
against the king's son. Heraclius too restored—at least temporarily—
what was left of the cross to Jerusalem.[13] But as he was riding trium-
phantly with it to the gate through which Christ had entered just before his Passion, the stones of the gate closed miraculously, and an angel
explained to Heraclius that when Christ had entered, he had not done
so in royal splendor. Whereupon the emperor, now in tears, removed
his boots, stripped to his shirt, and, bearing the cross himself, restored
it with true humility.

PICTORIAL REPRESENTATIONS OF THE TREE OF LIFE

The earliest picture of the Tree of Life I shall discuss is not Franciscan.
It is the mosaic known as the *Tree of Life* in the apse of the Augustinian
church of San Clemente in Rome, created perhaps in the early thirteenth century (Figure 5.1). This beautiful work is strongly reminiscent
of some of the mosaics at Ravenna; indeed, it contains many Early Christian elements. Its organization, however, is medieval; there is already
a firm identification between the cross of Christ and the great tree, which
is in the form of a vine—a variety of acanthus that harbors a number

Figure 5.1. *The Tree of Life,* mosaic. Rome, San Clemente. Photo Alinari/Art Resource, N.Y.

of religious persons and occasionally sprouts animal heads. It is also noteworthy that the four streams of the Water of Life at the bottom of the tree flow out of a kind of fountain, which is also mentioned in Revelation.[14] The deer who drink have a scriptural basis and are symbols of Christian souls.[15] The upward-facing doves on the cross, probably also symbols of Christian souls,[16] are twelve in number. The twelve lambs beneath it are emerging from the new cities, Jerusalem and Bethlehem, and going to the Lamb of God, which is directly beneath the tree.

The identification of Christ's cross with the Tree of Life is of course apparent in the earliest surviving Franciscan Tree of Life, of major importance. This is the painting by Pacino di Bonaguida, now in the Accademia in Florence, from the early fourteenth century (Figure 5.2).[17] Here scenes of the Creation of Adam and Eve and of their Temp-

Figure 5.2. Pacino di Bonaguida, *The Tree of Life*. Florence, Accademia. Photo Alinari/Art Resource, N.Y.

tation and Expulsion from Paradise, as well as the font from which flow
the four rivers, are seen at the bottom. At the top is the glory of Paradise. What appear at first to be the fruits of the tree are forty-seven
little round scenes from the life of Christ hanging from its twelve
branches (I beg for a moment the patience of those who are baffled
as to why there seem to be thirty-five scenes too many).[18]

The most important of all Franciscan depictions of the Tree
of Life is that by Taddeo Gaddi in the refectory of Santa Croce in Florence, painted during the middle third of the fourteenth century (Figure 5.3).[19] Taddeo's *Tree of Life* is, among other things, the most extraordinary table of contents ever depicted, for the fruits hanging from
the twelve branches give, with far greater clarity than do the real fruits
in the painting by Pacino di Bonaguida—barely discernible at the extremities of the branches—the chapter headings of a little book by St.
Bonaventure, titled, appropriately, *The Tree of Life*.[20] The four inscriptions on each branch, in turn, give the paragraph headings of each respective chapter. They of course correspond to the forty-seven pictures
plus the representation of Paradise in the painting by Pacino and are
here clearly a part of that which sustains the fruits rather than appear-
ing to be the fruits themselves.[21] Bonaventure himself is seen beneath
the tree, writing the first words of a hymn to the cross: "O crux, frutex
salvificus"—"O Cross, health-giving fruit tree"—which also forms part
of the book.[22]

As we learn from Bonaventure, the fruits of this imaginary tree
are Christ's virtues or aspects of his being. They are organized into three
sets of four, corresponding to his origin and life, his Passion, and his
glorification, and they proceed from bottom to top as the tree "grows."[23]
The labels on the branches give four examples of each fruit.[24] In Bonaventure's text, most of the examples are events from Christ's life; the
last are the ultimate manifestations of his glory.

Why, then, are Christ's virtues—or the sum total of his life
and final glory—the fruits of the Tree of Life? The answer is provided
by the prologue to Bonaventure's book, which begins with a verse from
St. Paul: "I am crucified with Christ: nevertheless I live; yet not I, but
Christ liveth in me: and the life which I now live in the flesh I live
by the faith of the son of God, who loved me, and gave himself for
me" (Gal. 2:20).[25] The true disciple of Christ, Bonaventure explains,

Figure 5.3. Taddeo Gaddi, *The Tree of Life*. Florence, Santa Croce, refectory. Photo Alinari/Art Resource, N.Y.

should strive with every effort of his mind to carry Christ's cross continually—not only in his spirit but even in his body.[26] To inspire the reader to do so, Bonaventure has turned to the Gospels.[27] And because the imagination helps the intelligence, he says, he has arranged the few things he has collected from the Gospels into a certain imaginary tree.[28] In all this tree has twelve branches, which bring forth the twelve mysterious fruits of the Tree of Life. But from each fruit the same new plant will grow. Ultimately, then, the fruits are the same.[29]

> Therefore picture in the spiritual faculty of your mind a certain tree, whose root shall be watered by the font of a perpetual spring, which, moreover, shall grow out into a lively and great river, to wit, of four heads, to water the paradise of the whole Church. Next, from the trunk of the tree let there come forth twelve branches adorned with fronds, flowers, and fruits; and let the leaf of the tree be a most effective medication, both preventing and healing, against every kind of disease, because the word of the cross is the virtue of God for the health of every believer. Let the flower, however, which both rewarms and attracts the anxious hearts of the desirous, be beautiful with the loveliness of every color and sprinkled with the sweetness of every scent. Finally, let the fruit, having in itself every delight and the sweetness of every flavor, be twelvefold; and this fruit is thus offered to be tasted to the faithful of God, so that eating they will always be sated by it and yet never tire of it.[30]

These twelve fruits, or rather this twelvefold fruit, correspond to the fruit of the Virgin's womb, ripened on the cross, and ready to be tasted in the garden of Paradise, at the table of God.[31]

All I have said thus far is explicitly stated by Bonaventure. But more is implied. The true disciple of Christ, Bonaventure says, is desirous of perfect conformity with him.[32] He therefore must deny himself, "always bearing about in the body the dying of the Lord Jesus, that the life also of Jesus might be made manifest in our body" (2 Cor. 4:10),[33] as St. Paul had insisted that members of the religious community do. In another book, the *Vitis mystica*,[34] Bonaventure compares Christ, whom he here explicitly calls the Tree of Life, to the vine,[35] of which Christ himself had spoken: "I am the vine, ye *are* the branches: He that abideth in me, and I in him, the same bringeth forth much fruit: for without me ye can do nothing" (John 15:5).[36] Conformity with Christ, then, requires that the disciple become himself a part of the tree. The fruit in these pictures not only provides "consolations,"[37] as Bonaventure calls them, gained through meditation,[38] but also serves as the type or model of the fruit that the disciple must strive to bear — and can bear if he is truly united with Christ.[39]

A perfect program for the spiritual life, but hardly an easy one. There is, however, an aid for the disciple in Gaddi's fresco — a leader for him to follow. It is St. Francis[40] who embraces the tree-cross in the main picture and is seen being stigmatized in the scene at the upper left.[41] As Christ had commanded, "If any *man* will come after me, let him deny himself, and take up his cross, and follow me" (Matt. 16:24).[42] And, in the words of Paul: "But God forbid that I should glory, save in the cross of our Lord Jesus Christ, by whom the world is crucified unto me, and I unto the world. . . . From henceforth let no man trouble me: for I bear in my body the marks of the Lord Jesus" (Gal. 6:14 and 6:17).[43]

In Gaddi's fresco the *Tree of Life* is directly juxtaposed with the *Last Supper* (Figure 5.4). There is evidently a Eucharistic dimension in the work as a whole, as well as a simple thematic connection to the activity — eating — in which the friar was engaged while he contemplated the fresco. Every scene except the *Stigmatization* contains food; indeed, all but that scene and the *Tree of Life* depict meals.[44] One may imagine a friar thinking about his food; directing his thoughts from it to that life-giving food that Christ gave his disciples, or perhaps to the tears that Mary Magdalene shed upon Christ's feet when he dined at the house of Simon; and finally to that food — which is spiritual, not material, as Christ made clear at another meal at which Mary Magdalene was also present[45] — which nourishes us forever. The fresco reads two ways: down, if we follow the direction of the Holy Ghost, whose seven gifts are explicitly prayed for at the end of Bonaventure's little book;[46] up, if we follow the book's order. In other words, it shows us the Lord's sevenfold Grace if we read one way; and the way to him if we read the other.

With Bonaventure's help we have, I hope, succeeded in scratching the surface of this great work.[47] But there is much, much more. I wish only that the reader realize to how many hours of meditation

Figure 5.4. Taddeo Gaddi, *The Tree of Life, Last Supper,* and *Scenes from Life of St. Francis.* Florence, Santa Croce, refectory. Photo Alinari/Art Resource, N.Y.

it invited the friars who took their meals in this refectory,[48] and about how many things it refreshed their memories. I want also to stress the particular quality of spirituality that underlies this fresco. If I may be permitted a bit of high-end audiophile jargon, there is a kind of image shift or wander in this painting, as many of its chief elements are taken now one way, now another. This image wander is fundamentally, if often subtly, different from the more precise focus of much Dominican imagery.

PICTORIAL REPRESENTATIONS OF
THE LEGEND OF THE HOLY CROSS

Probably around 1390, Taddeo's son Agnolo was commissioned to do the cycle of scenes from the story of the Holy Cross which is found in the high chapel of Santa Croce.[49] The subject was evidently suggested by the name of the church. I shall limit my comments to a few observations on the cycle as a whole.[50] Its primary purpose — apart from embellishing the most important part of the church, which it does somewhat restlessly — is evidently to incite devotion toward the cross. It also allegorizes, more or less, the connection between our sinfulness and consequent mortality, on the one hand, and Christ's death and our hope for salvation, on the other. The narration is quite straightforward. But although submerged, a few spiritual cues do seem to be present.

Rather curiously, the cycle starts on the right-hand wall (Figures 5.7 and 5.8), where the protagonists are mostly pre-Christians, and proceeds to the left (Figures 5.5 and 5.6), where they are all post-Christians. We are reminded of Crucifixion and Last Judgment imagery, in which those who are saved are at Christ's right. Agnolo Gaddi's arrangement therefore seems to presuppose an image of Christ in the middle of the chapel — probably on a crucifix or in a Crucifixion scene.[51] Or perhaps Christ's presence was established simply by the sacrifice at the altar. The story of course begins at Paradise, which contains a river (Figure 5.7). There follow two scenes (not illustrated here): one in which the Queen of Sheba worships the sacred wood, and one of the Probatic Pool, made miraculous by the action of the wood. At the bottom is located the scene of the discovery and proof, in which the cross is first itself exhumed and then becomes the cause of a dead man's resurrection (Figure 5.8). In the background are seen a number of hermit monks and also a river. Indeed, there is water in each of the scenes on the first wall as well as in the last two scenes on the second. On the first (right) wall the cross is "discovered" four times: by Seth in Paradise, by the Queen of Sheba near Solomon's temple, by the Jews in the Probatic Pool, and by Helena on Calvary.[52] At the top of the left-hand wall is set the scene of Helena restoring the cross to Jerusalem (Figure 5.5). The second scene thereafter (not illustrated here) is that in which an angel shows the cross to the sleeping Heraclius,[53] just before he is victorious over the son of the Persian king. The cycle then ends with the scene of Heraclius restoring the cross (Figure 5.6). We thus go from Paradise to Jerusalem. Both are seen at the top of their respective walls (Figures 5.7 and 5.5). And on our way to Jerusalem we twice admire the actions of persons who have taken up the cross (Figures 5.5 and 5.6).

Sometime after 1448, Piero della Francesca was called in to complete the decoration of the high chapel of San Francesco in Arezzo, the walls of which had barely been started by Bicci di Lorenzo when illness forced him to abandon work (Figures 5.9 and 5.10). As Creighton Gilbert has shown, it is likely that Bicci was planning little more than an abbreviated copy of the cycle in Santa Croce. It appears that Piero completed the lunette zone utilizing some of Bicci's designs.[54] But the rest of Piero's cycle is completely unlike the one in Santa Croce. One wonders about the reasons for so radical a departure — and why Piero has taken such liberties with both the chronological sequence and the text of the *Golden Legend*[55] — and the more I ponder the matter, the more convinced I become that it was a desire to propagandize the upcoming or current crusade of Pius II which was chiefly responsible for these innovations. What makes the Arezzo cycle so different as a narrative is the inclusion of the *Victory of Constantine* and its placement in the lowest tier of the wall, and the placement of the *Victory of Heraclius* directly across from it (Figures 5.12, 5.11). In this position, though, one would expect to see raisings and miracles, not battles and beheadings. What, then, do these two battles signify? They are, quite literally, both crusades: one a war in which the good army is led by the cross — *in hoc signo vinces* — and one a war in which the good army is fighting for the cross.[56]

Because of the historical circumstances, the Arezzo frescoes have the same left-right reversal that we find in Santa Croce. But here Piero, as Gilbert has pointed out, has neatly managed to keep the arrangement to non-Christians on the first side (Figure 5.10) and Christians on the second (Figure 5.9)[57] — something that Agnolo Gaddi was unable to do. But is there any real input in these works of the kinds of themes I have been discussing? The answer — surprisingly, in view of the apparent propaganda and Piero's great concern for form and natu-

Figure 5.5. Agnolo Gaddi, *Helena Restoring the Cross to Jerusalem.* Florence, Santa Croce, high chapel. Photo Alinari/Art Resource, N.Y.

Figure 5.6. Agnolo Gaddi, *The Beheading of Chosroes; Heraclius Restoring the Cross to Jerusalem.* Florence, Santa Croce, high chapel. Photo Alinari/Art Resource, N.Y.

Figure 5.7. Agnolo Gaddi, *Seth in Paradise; The Burial of Adam*. Florence, Santa Croce, high chapel. Photo Alinari/Art Resource, N.Y.

Figure 5.8. Agnolo Gaddi, *The Discovery and Proof of the Cross*. Florence, Santa Croce, high chapel. Photo Alinari/Art Resource, N.Y.

Figure 5.9. Piero della Francesca, decorations of the high chapel (*left half*). Arezzo, San Francesco. Photo Hatfield.

Figure 5.10. Piero della Francesca, decorations of the high chapel (*right half*). Arezzo, San Francesco. Photo Hatfield.

Figure 5.11. Piero della Francesca, *The Victory of Heraclius*. Arezzo, San Francesco, high chapel. Detail of wall shown in figure 5.9. Photo Alinari/Art Resource, N.Y.

ral appearances— is yes, almost certainly. Indeed, Piero's frescoes bespeak a far stronger spiritual intent than do those of Santa Croce.

This new intent is most conspicuous on the rear wall. The two lowest scenes, both of annunciations, of which one is scriptural, have the shape of the cross built into them (Figures 5.13, 5.14). The Annunciation to Mary (Figure 5.13), the second Eve who reopened the door to Paradise,[58] is explicitly related to the scene of Adam's burial (in Figure 5.10) by means of the branch that Gabriel is holding. The branch should remind us of unity with Christ and may even be meant to suggest his presence, as there is no dove or foetus in this picture. The upper scene on the right-hand side, the *Burial of the Wood* (in Figure 5.10), has long been recognized to be a brilliant visual allusion to Christ bearing the cross. (This does not seem to be the first time that image was punned on in the decorations of a Franciscan church; there is a similar figure carrying a branch at the extreme left in Taddeo Gaddi's *Marriage of the Virgin* in the Baroncelli Chapel in Santa Croce.) The scene op-

Figure 5.12. Piero della Francesca, *The Victory of Constantine*. Arezzo, San Francesco, high chapel. Detail of wall shown in figure 5.10. Photo Alinari/Art Resource, N.Y.

posite, *Raising of the Jew from the Well* (in Figure 5.9), contains an apparent allusion to the three crosses on Calvary. Gilbert believes that this scene also is a deliberate pun, on the descent into Limbo.[59] Perhaps it is. In any case the point is clear: on the "before" side, a burial is taking place; on the "after" side, a man is being raised.

I have sometimes wondered whether or not the last scene, *Heraclius Restoring the Cross to Jerusalem,* seemingly misplaced in the lunette at the top of the left-hand wall (in Figure 5.9), was meant to serve as crusade propaganda by reminding worshipers of their duty to restore the cross, that is, the Christian religion, to Jerusalem. Although the picture does in effect convey such a meaning, I rather doubt that it was intended. For, as the whole cycle works out, we are taken from Paradise (Figure 5.10)—with a great tree spreading its branches above and in the middle, as well as a branch with the power to heal even the dead—down the first side, with its allusion to Christ carrying his cross and a conspicuous image of a woman worshiping the sacred wood.

Figure 5.13. Piero della Francesca, *Annunciation*. Arezzo, San Francesco, high chapel. Detail visible in figure 5.9. Photo Alinari/Art Resource, N.Y.

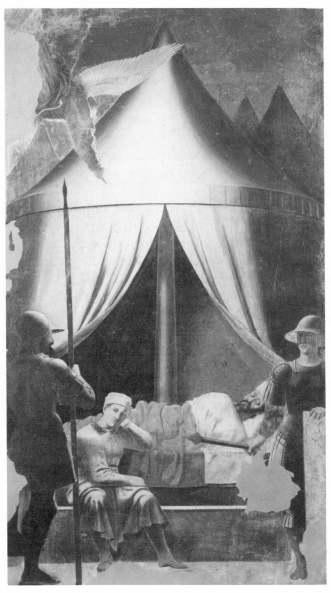

Figure 5.14. Piero della Francesca, *The Annunciation to Constantine in a Dream That He Will Conquer in the Sign of the Cross.* Arezzo, San Francesco, high chapel. Detail visible in figure 5.10. Photo Alinari/Art Resource, N.Y.

Then we go across the chapel and thus past the altar on which Christ is present during the sacrifice—as well as past two cross shapes built into the lowest scenes on the wall and perhaps other Crucifixion imagery that is no longer there—over to the second wall (Figure 5.9). There two exhumations occur and we see a fulfillment of the promise of the branch's power to heal. Then, finally, we ascend the second wall to Jerusalem, where a man who has been reminded of the way a true Christian must bear his cross is restoring the cross to that city—which is set directly across from the Paradise where we began. Now, however, the two imposing trees are green, whereas the great tree in Paradise was dry. I am thus inclined to believe that the intended messages of the last scene—and indeed the principal themes of the whole chapel—are consistent with the ones I have been tracing all along. The scene tells of return and hints in several ways at the promise of salvation and our way to it.[60] And that ultimately is what Piero's frescoes, and the other works I have been discussing, are all about.[61]

CONCLUSION

The synoptic images of the Tree of Life came first, and none of any importance was painted after the Holy Cross cycle was introduced.[62] Perhaps this change is somehow indicative of a general shift in the temper of Franciscan spirituality, or perhaps it is linked to trends in devotion to the Holy Cross. One notices also that the Holy Cross cycles tend to be in places that were more accessible to the laity. Perhaps it was felt that narrative cycles were more suitable for the public than synoptic images were; surely, few laypeople would have had an easy time deciphering the Latin inscriptions in Taddeo Gaddi's *Tree of Life*. Also, cycles were better adapted to situations in which there were two or more walls to decorate; in the high chapels of most churches a Tree of Life simply will not work. Whatever the explanation, I do not think it likely that the cycles were aimed primarily at the public. The spiritual cues they contain must be not only recognized but also understood; that is, recognition must be followed by a "going inside" and afterward by a "rising above." Few laypeople can have been expert at this. We should remember that the high chapels of the great churches of the mendicant orders were mainly for the use of the friars.

One may wonder why the Franciscans did not more fully develop the image of the Water of Life, which theme, as we have seen, is so closely connected to that of the Tree of Life. If Christ is the fruit of the tree, then surely the water that flows beneath it is his redeeming blood. One remembers that Paul had already identified the water that Moses struck from the rock with the blood that flowed from Christ's side when he died for us.[63] The idea that Christ's blood is the Water of Life does, of course, occur often in medieval art and literature. It may be present in the fresco cycle in Santa Croce. But even there, little is made of it. Why such reticence on the Franciscans' part? Perhaps we are dealing with merely one of the more partisan quirks of Franciscan devotion; St. Francis, after all, did not shed any blood when he was stigmatized.[64] Or perhaps it was feared that water imagery would too easily be mistaken for a reference to Baptism. Finally, some Franciscans were worried lest an excessive stress on Christ's blood lead to the erroneous supposition that it was the blood itself that saved us rather than Christ's willingness to die for our sake.[65] Whatever the reason, it remains a disappointment that the Franciscans did not do more with the Water of Life. Still, that disappointment seems a fair price for the spiritual beauty of what they, and some artists who worked in their convents, did with the Tree of Life and the story of the Holy Cross.

NOTES

For their suggestions and help I am especially indebted to Timothy Verdon and Manuel Vega.

1. All biblical citations are from the King James Version; the words in italics were supplied by the translators.

2. Cf. also Rev. 2:7: "To him that overcometh will I give to eat of the tree of life, which is in the midst of the paradise of God."

3. Cf. Ezek 47:12: "And by the river upon the bank thereof, on this side and on that side, shall grow all trees for meat, whose leaf shall not fade, neither shall the fruit thereof be consumed; it shall bring forth new fruit according to his months, because their waters they

issued out of the sanctuary: and the fruit thereof shall be for meat, and the leaf thereof for medicine."

4. Cf. Dan. 4:10–12: "I saw, and behold a tree in the midst of the earth, and the height thereof *was* great. / The tree grew, and was strong, and the height thereof reached unto heaven, and the sight thereof to the end of all the earth: / The leaves thereof *were* fair, and the fruit thereof much, and in it *was* meat for all: the beasts of the field had shadow under it, and the fowls of the heaven dwelt in the boughs thereof, and all flesh was fed of it."

5. For the literature on the Tree of Life, see the *Lexikon der christlichen Ikonographie,* (Rome: Herder, 1968–), 1: cols. 260, 267 f. The tradition that the Tree of Life was the greatest tree in Paradise and that, by implication, it grew in the highest place there is still alive in Milton. See *Paradise Lost,* 4:194 f.: "Thence up he flew, and on the Tree of Life, / The middle Tree and highest there that grew" and 4:216–22:

> Out of the fertil ground he caus'd to grow
> All trees of noblest kind for sight, smell, taste;
> And all amid them stood the Tree of Life,
> High eminent, blooming Ambrosial Fruit
> Of vegetable Gold; and next to Life
> Our Death the Tree of Knowledge grew fast by,
> Knowledge of Good bought dear by knowing ill.

See also 11:366–422, in which the Well of Life is located on the highest hill in Paradise, from which the whole hemisphere of Earth can be seen.

6. Luke 23:31: "For if they do these things in a green tree, what shall be done in the dry?" Cf. Ezek. 20:47.

7. John 15:1–8 (for the text of verse 5, see below). Cf. also Ps. 1:3: "And he shall be like a tree planted by the rivers of water, that bringeth forth his fruit in season; his leaf also shall not wither; and whatsoever he doeth shall prosper."

8. The Tridentine Breviary has the following text for the feasts of both the Invention of the Holy Cross (3 May) and the Exaltation of the Holy Cross (14 September): "Haec est arbor dignissima, in paradisi medio situata, In qua salutis Auctor propria morte, mortem omnium superavit, alleluja, alleluja." And also: "Crux fidelis, inter omnes arbor una nobilis; nulla silva tamen profert, fronde, flore, germine: Dulce lignum, dulces clavos, dulce pondus sustinuit, alleluja." See also the Missal for Good Friday (Adoration of the Cross).

9. For the literature on the legend of the Holy Cross, the *Lexikon der christl. Ikonographie,* 2: cols. 642f., 648; and P. Mazzoni, *La leggenda della croce nell'arte italiana* (Florence: Alfani e Venturi, 1914), 167–79, passim.

10. Jacopo da Varagine, *Leggenda aurea,* ed. A. Levasti, 3 vols. (Florence: Libreria editrice fiorentina, 1925), 2:589–604 (Invention of the Cross), and 3:1144–56 (Exaltation of the Cross).

11. Varagine twice points out that the passage in which the tree is identified as that of the knowledge of good and evil is taken from a source "of the Greeks" which is not trustworthy (ibid., 2:589).

12. In general, the Fathers saw the Tree of Knowledge as the antitype of the cross. The Tridentine Breviary still has: "Per lignum servi facti sumus, et per sanctam Crucem liberati sumus: fructus arboris seduxit nos, Filius Dei redemit nos, alleluja" (14 September). Cf. also

the Missal for Good Friday: "De parentis protoplasti fraude Factor condolens, quando pomi noxialis in necem morsu ruit: ipse lignum tunc notavit, damna ligni ut solveret." The identification of the Tree of Knowledge with the wood of the cross, which underscores the necessary connection between Original Sin and Christ's death, appears to have become common only during the later Middle Ages.

13. According to one version, he afterward took it to Constantinople (Varagine, *Leggenda aurea,* 3:1149f.).

14. Rev. 21:6: "I will give unto him that is athirst of the fountain of the water of life freely." See also Rev. 7:17.

15. Ps. 42:1–2: "As the hart panteth after the water brooks, so panteth my soul after thee, O God. / My soul thirsteth for God, for the living God: when shall I come and appear before God?"

16. See the *Lexikon der christl. Ikonographie,* 4: cols. 241–44.

17. The picture was originally in the convent of Monticelli, which belonged to the Poor Clares. On it see R. Offner, *A Corpus of Florentine Painting, Section* 3, 8 vols. (New York: J. J. Augustin, 1958), 6:122–35.

18. At the top of the tree are Ezekiel and Daniel with scrolls bearing their prophecies (Ezek. 47:12 and Dan. 4:10; texts above, notes 3 and 4). Below it are SS. Francis and Clare, each with scriptural verses on a scroll. That of St. Francis has Gal. 6:14: "But God forbid that I should glory, save in the cross of our Lord Jesus Christ." That of St. Clare has the Song of Sol. 1:13: "A bundle of myrrh *is* my wellbeloved unto me; he shall lie all night betwixt my breasts." On the reason for this verse's inclusion, see note 27 below.

19. For basic information on this fresco, see A. Ladis, *Taddeo Gaddi* (Columbia: Univ. of Missouri Press, 1982), 66–73, 171–82. For an exhaustive interpretation of it, see A. C. Esmeijer, *Lignum vitae* (Assen, Holland: Van Gorcum, 1981).

20. *Lignum vitae,* in Bonaventure, *Decem opuscula,* 5th ed. (Quaracchi: Collegio di S. Bonaventura, 1965), 135–80.

21. For the several fruits and their respective examples, see Ladis, *Taddeo Gaddi,* 171f., and Offner, *Corpus,* 6:124–32.

22. Literally translated, the full hymn goes:

> O Cross, health-giving fruit tree,
> Watered by the living font,
> Whose aromatic flower
> Is the longed-for fruit,
>
> Nourish us with these fruits,
> Enlighten our thoughts,
> Lead us by the right ways,
> Break the enemy's assaults,
>
> Fill us with divine light,
> Breathe devout breaths into us,
> Be to those who fear Christ
> The tranquil condition of life.

(Bonaventure, *Decem opuscula,* 138, 140).

23. A later book on the Tree of Life which is clearly modeled on Bonaventure's, that of Ubertino da Casale (1305), is organized into five parts rather than three. These are: (1) the roots, corresponding to Christ's origin and childhood; (2) the trunk, his public life; (3) the branches, his Passion; (4) the summit, his glorification; (5) the fruits, the Church of the Gentiles. See Ubertino da Casale, *Arbor vitae crucifixae Jesu* (Venice, 1485; Turin: Bottega d'Erasmo, 1961), 7–9.

24. For example, the first fruit, "Preclaritas originis," hangs on a branch having "Ihesus ex Deo genitus, Ihesus prefiguratus, Ihesus emissus celitus, Ihesus Maria natus."

25. Cf. also, 2 Cor. 5:14.

26. Bonaventure, *Decem opuscula,* 137: "ut Christi Iesu crucem circumferat iugiter tam mente quam carne."

27. It is through love that one may truly feel in oneself the experience that Paul describes, with the intensity expressed by the lover in the Song of Solomon: "A bundle of myrrh is my wellbeloved" (1:13; see note 18 above). "So that therefore in us there be ignited the aforesaid affection, there be formed the aforesaid thought, there be impressed the aforesaid memory, I wished to gather this bundle of myrrh . . . from the woods of the holy Gospels" (Bonaventure, *Decem opuscula,* 137).

28. Ibid.: "in imaginaria quadam arbore." Cf. Ubertino da Casale, *Arbor vitae, 9:* "facio tibi unam arborem imaginativam."

29. Bonaventure, *Decem opuscula,* 138: "ex quorum quolibet instar fructus unica pullulatio pendet, ut sic sint quasi duodecim rami afferentes duodecim fructus iuxta mysterium ligni vitae."

30. Ibid.

31. Ibid., 139: "But even though it is one and undivided . . . this fruit nourishes devout souls with manifold consolations that can indeed be reduced to the number of twelve; wherefore this fruit of the tree of life is set forth and described as if to be tasted in twelve flavors on twelve branches, so that on the first branch the devout mind, contemplating the exalted origin and sweet birth of its Savior, may experience a taste of sweetness."

32. Ibid., 137: "qui Salvatori . . . perfecte configurari desiderat."

33. Cf. also Col. 1:24.

34. In Bonaventure, *Decem opuscula,* 365–418.

35. Ibid., 367: "O Jesus, benign vine, come! O Tree of Life, which is in the midst of Paradise, Lord Jesus Christ, whose leaves are for medicine, whose fruits indeed for eternal life; O blessed flower and at the same time fruit of the blessed rod of the most chaste Virgin Mary . . . deign to refresh my weak and arid mind with the bread of intellect and the water of wisdom."

36. Cf. also Deut. 8:17.

37. See note 31 above.

38. *Lignum vitae,* in Bonaventure, *Decem Opuscula,* 139: "I therefore call these fruits, because with their great sweetness they delight and with their virtuousness they comfort the soul that meditates upon them and with great diligence considers them one by one—if it abhors the example of the transgressor Adam, who preferred the Tree of Knowledge of Good and Evil to the Tree of Life."

39. The biblical idea (Matt. 7:15–20, for example) that a tree is known by the fruits

it bears is one that occurs often in Franciscan writings. Trees of course occur frequently as images of religious orders. For an important Franciscan source for such images, see the simile used by Tommaso da Celano in his *First Life of St. Francis,* in *Fonti francescane,* ed. F. Oligiati, 3d ed. (Padua: Messaggero, 1983), 492. See also the extraordinary vision of a Franciscan mystic described in the *Little Flowers of St. Francis* in *Fonti francescane,* 1561–63).

40. The most exhaustive exposition of the identity with Christ achieved by St. Francis is that of 1385–90 by Bartolommeo da Pisa, *De conformitate vitae beati Francisci ad vitam domini Iesu, Analecta franciscana,* ms. 3–4 (Quaracchi: Collegio di S. Bonaventura, 1906–12). This work, too, is "painted" as a "tree" (3:2–3); only here the branches are twenty, each bearing two fruits of St. Francis and two of Christ.

41. According to Bonaventure, the stigmatization occurred around the Feast of the Exaltation of the Cross. See his *Legenda maior* (Quaracchi: Collegio di S. Bonaventura, 1941), chap. 3, no. 3, 107.

42. This verse is the second to be cited (after Matt. 19:21, enjoining strict poverty) at the very outset of the Franciscan *Regula non bullata* of 1221 (Oligiati, *Fonti francescane,* 99 f.).

43. The first half of verse 14 occurs on the scroll held by Francis in the *Tree of Life* by Pacino di Bonaguida.

44. The other three scenes are: *St. Louis of Toulouse Serving a Meal to the Poor* (lower left), *St. Benedict Rescued from Starvation on Easter Day* (upper right), and *The Feast in the House of Simon* (lower right).

45. I am referring to Christ's visit to Martha and Mary; Luke 10:38–42.

46. Bonaventure, *Decem opuscula,* 179 f.: (Prayer to Obtain the Seven Gifts of the Holy Ghost) "Let us therefore pray the most merciful Father, through thee, his only-begotten Son . . . that from among his treasures he send forth into us the spirit of sevenfold Grace . . . that is, I say, the spirit of wisdom, by which we taste the life-giving flavors of the fruit of the Tree of Life, which verily thou art; and also the gift of intellect, by which the perceptions of our mind are illuminated."

47. It should be pointed out that the twelve prophets at the extremities of the branches do not correspond to anything in the *Lignum vitae.* Most, if not all, have prophecies of the Passion on their scrolls. Perhaps they were suggested by some other work based on the *Lignum vitae,* such as the *Arbor vitae crucifixae Jesu* by Ubertino da Casale.

48. Ubertino, *Arbor vitae,* 7–9, describes four ways in which one can be in Christ in one's inmost being. He wrote his book, he says, "so that you may always dwell in Christ."

49. On the iconography of the legend of the Holy Cross, see the excellent article by H. van Os in the *Lexikon der christl. Ikonographie,* 2: cols. 644–47.

50. On the several scenes, see B. Cole, *Agnolo Gaddi* (Oxford: Clarendon Press, 1977), 21–25, 79–81.

51. See the discussion in C. Gilbert, *Change in Piero della Francesca* (Locust Valley, N.Y.: J. J. Augustin, 1968), 76.

52. We thus have four of the five discoveries of the wood of the cross with which James of Varagine introduces the story (*Leggenda aurea,* 2:588). Only Solomon's discovery of the wood in Lebanon is omitted.

53. As Mazzoni points out (*Leggenda della croce,* III), this episode does not occur in the *Golden Legend.*

54. See Gilbert, *Piero della Francesca,* 73–75.

55. Scenes that depart appreciably from James of Varagine's text include the *Dream of Constantine,* the two battles, and *Heraclius Restoring the Cross to Jerusalem.*

56. If this view is correct, Piero's frescoes must have been done circa 1460. Such a date has recently been suspected because of the curiously awkward assortment of classical quotations in the *Death and Burial of Adam.* Piero is most likely to have seen, and become interested in, the models for these poses while he was in Rome in 1459 and 1460. See E. Battisti, *Piero della Francesca* (Milan: Istituto editoriale italiano, 1971), 133 f.

57. Gilbert, *Piero della Francesca,* 77 f.

58. Mary's role as the antitype of Eve is also stressed in the cross allegories of 1421 by Giovanni da Modena in S. Petronio in Bologna (ill.: *Lexikon der christl. Ikonographie,* 2: cols. 597 f.). Mary's inscription reads, "I open up the heavens that Eve had closed to you / Through my son I shall save whoever is guilty," while Eve's reads, "Through my vain eating the human race is ruined / You will die because I closed the door to Heaven."

59. Gilbert, *Piero della Francesca,* 77, 81.

60. For the feasts of the Invention of the Cross and the Exaltation of the Cross there occur often in both the Missal and the Breviary the versicle and response: "Hoc signum Crucis erit in caelo, alleluja / Cum Dominus ad judicandum venerit, alleluja." In fact, the *Last Judgment,* painted by Bicci di Lorenzo, occurs over the archway to the high chapel.

61. How close the thoughts expressed in images of the Tree of Life may come to those expressed—or at least hinted at—in cycles of the Legend of the Cross is demonstrated by a Sienese triptych of about 1400 in the Niedersächsische Landesgalerie in Hanover. See Gilbert, *Piero della Francesca,* 80–82 and fig. 52.

62. See the list of examples in Offner, *Corpus,* 6:132 f. To Offner's list should be added, especially, the important fragment of 1347 in Sta. Maria Maggiore at Bergamo.

63. 1 Cor. 10:4: "And did all drink the same spiritual drink: for they drank of that spiritual Rock that followed them: and that Rock was Christ."

64. He did, however, cause water to turn into wine and also to come forth from a rock. See Bonaventure, *Legenda maior,* 45 and 63 (chap. 5, no. 10, and chap. 7, no. 12).

65. This was the position of Francesco della Rovere, who wrote on this question before becoming Pope Sixtus IV. See L. D. Ettlinger, *The Sistine Chapel before Michelangelo* (Oxford: Clarendon Press, 1965), 9, 83 f.

6

SOME SPECIAL IMAGES FOR CARMELITES,
circa 1330–1430

CREIGHTON GILBERT

T HE DESIRE FOR RELIGIOUS AUTHENTICITY characteristic of late medieval and Renaissance monasticism often entailed reinterpretation of the origins of religious orders and appeals to ancient tradition, as chapter 3 has already suggested. Perhaps the most dramatic instance of this search for identity was the Carmelite order's
claim to be descended from the Old Testament prophet Elijah, discussed here by
Creighton Gilbert. Through his study of works of art created for Tuscan Carmelite
communities over a hundred-year period, Professor Gilbert analyzes the paramount
importance of ancient "roots" and the unique group identity developed by the Carmelites for want of a clearly defined historical founder. Of great interest in Professor
Gilbert's discussion of works by Pietro Lorenzetti, Sassetta, and Masaccio is the mix
of historiography, myth, and contemporary events that he sees in Carmelite iconography.

CREIGHTON GILBERT is professor of the history of art at Yale University and has been
visiting professor at the Hebrew University, Jerusalem, and at the Universities of Rome
and Leiden. For six years he edited *The Art Bulletin;* his own numerous publications
include books on Piero della Francesca and Michelangelo and essays on Renaissance
Last Supper images in monastic refectories and the influence upon art of Antoninus,
the Dominican archbishop of Florence in the mid-quattrocento.

HE FREQUENT REFERENCES in this volume to all sorts of monastic groups make it seem especially important to assign each, on first mention, to the right segment of monasticism. This is fairly easy with the Carmelites; we know that they emerged and grew in Europe along with the Franciscans and Dominicans shortly after 1200, especially in the developing towns. In England, where the Carmelites had exceptional success, their popular name—"Whitefriars"—survives today in names of streets and the like, just as do the "Grayfriars" and "Blackfriars" of the other two. In Central Italian towns, notably Florence and Siena, we still see the Carmelite convent churches of around 1300 on sites then at the edges of the built-up areas, again as were those of the other groups. In Central Italy, however, the Carmelites were a distant third in importance. However memorable to us the Carmine of Florence, it could never compete with Santa Croce or Santa Maria Novella. On the other hand, the Carmelites did greatly exceed in importance such groups as the Servites or Vallombrosans, who never emerged from a local status. This intermediate position will be basic to the discussion that follows.

Good studies have dealt with paintings produced for Carmelite locations. A basic starting point for this, as for so many other topics, is a short chapter by Emile Mâle in his book on art after the Council of Trent.[1] Mâle at once presents the special motif that has remained the most familiar item of Carmelite imagery in art history generally, understandably so because it seems so eccentric. This is their representation of the prophet Elijah as their founder. Their claim to him, as Mâle reports, became during the Counter-Reformation the object of vehement dispute. In particular those high-minded historicists, the Bollandists, refuted the tradition. Eventually a papal ban imposed silence on both sides.

Less often observed, though obvious when mentioned, is the fact that this claim implied similar ones to many other persons between the time of Elijah and the twelfth century. The founder prophet had begun what remained a going concern through that entire period. The list started, naturally, with Elisha, and included most of the figures linked to Eastern desert asceticism. Then, as Mâle rightly summarizes, "when the age of the Gospels began these monks still existed, and John the Baptist was one of them."[2] The Virgin was held to have founded a nunnery under Carmelite rule. Later came the monks of the Thebaid, especially Anthony the Abbot. The order came west when the Crusaders were losing the Holy Land, in the 1230s.

It was in the context of the Counter-Reformation that Mâle offered this account. Most later art historical discussions did the same, for example, the two-volume study by Emond on Flanders[3] and the model article on Dughet's frescoes in Rome by Boase.[4] Dughet's rare image of the emperor Titus visiting a Carmelite prior in the Holy Land is a vivid example of the materials. It would indeed be natural to assume that Counter-Reformation thinking evoked such ideas, and this is the view offered, for example, in the fourteenth edition of the *Encyclopedia Britannica*. The fact that the great Carmelites St. Theresa and St. John of the Cross appeared only then might also support such a view. But in fact, the same claims had been made centuries before, as both Emond and Boase briefly note. The book printed in 1643 which is Mâle's oldest citation for such arguments was a new edition of one printed in 1492 which was in turn compiled from older material. The earliest recorded public dispute in which a Carmelite defended the Elijah claim against doubters took place in 1374.[5]

Why was the claim made, and to what extent did it convince? Some texts that are revealing on these points — Renaissance reports of doubts — seem not to have been noted in this context. Two anecdotes that I would like to cite come from the *facezie* and the *novelle* of the period, its most popular literary types. (Similar comments by Erasmus have of course been noted; they would hardly be unexpected.) My earlier author is the Piovano Arlotto, who was a country priest near Florence around 1475. His stories are a wonderful eye-opener on the way clergy and society interacted on a popular level. The clergy in question (like the majority) knew little or no Latin; they were subject to temptations of sex and quite open about the fact, and they had a most positive rapport with their flock. The human foibles that tended to make them the object of anticlerical novelle by Boccaccio and others are here seen from the inside. These foibles include impatience with other clergy:

> One morning, the vicar Arlotto was in the Carmelite church, listening to the sermon of a friar who was young and more windy than learned. And, preaching on a subject on which he had become rather mixed up (that passage where the messengers from Judea asked St. John the Baptist who he was), the friar turned to the vicar and said: "Who are you? Are you Elijah? Are you Jeremiah?" etc. And the vicar, as these words were repeated innumerable times, lost patience. Unable to hold back his laughter, he answered the friar loudly, "I am neither Elijah nor Jeremiah, but Vicar Arlotto; maybe you don't recognize me!" This riposte made all who were listening to the sermon laugh.[6]

We easily recognize that the text of the sermon was John 1:21, in which the Baptist is asked, "Are you Elijah?" but Jeremiah is not mentioned.[7] This line is added in the facezia; it makes the preacher seem indeed unlearned and windy, and has the effect of diminishing the power of his own argument. For even from the short sketch above of the Carmelite claims and the objections to them, we can readily see why this text was chosen. It helped the Carmelite with his links to ancient history; a text that made Elijah indistinguishable from the Baptist was perfect for the purpose. The chain of hermits would get a good part of the way to 1200, with scriptural authority. But it was an absurd choice for a sermon to a flock, and thus suggests that the topic obsessed the order out of all proportion. And indeed we see the preacher repeating, insisting, and making himself a laughingstock.

The second author is Matteo Bandello, who collected novelle over many years and published them in 1554. In his book he precedes each tale with a preface that purports to describe the circumstances in which the story is told. For one narration, the setting is Milan at the time of the conquest by Louis XII of France. A triumphal procession was being organized, and the local Augustinian canons demanded precedence in the march over the Benedictines, contrary to tradition; why they did so is made clear by Kaspar Elm's essay in this volume. When the Augustinans were refused, they boycotted the entire event. A group of citizens discuss this situation, unfavorably, and one of them recalls a similar earlier case; his account forms the novella.

You should know then that while Galeazzo Sforza reigned as Duke of Milan, there arose in that city a great argument between the Carmelite friars and all the other religious, as to who should have precedence in processions. For the Carmelites wanted to precede not only the mendicant orders but the monks as well. All the others brought forward their customs and usages, approved and confirmed by various Supreme Pontiffs. The Carmelites however said that they had been greatly wronged in the past because of their elders' simple humility, and that this should not prejudice their claims, since they were the most ancient of all religious in the world. This controversy was brought before the privy council of the Duke who, being young, wanted to be present to hear it disputed. Thus one feast day he had all the heads of every kind of religious order assemble in the Castle in Milan, and desired the matter to be argued in the Green Room . . . The excellent Master Gian Andrea Cagnuola, à Doctor of Law, turned to the Carmelite Prior and asked how long it had been since the order began. The Carmelite answered that it began on Mount Carmel, under Elijah. "Then you already existed in the time of the Apostles," observed Cagnuola. "Yes," said the Prior, "as you well know; at that time we were the only friars in existence, since Basil, Benedict, Dominic, Francis, and all the other founders of orders had not yet existed" . . . The Duke had a jester, witty and brave, who—when he heard this fantasy which the Carmelite prior was uttering—leapt between the two and said to Cagnuola, "Master Doctor, the father speaks truly, for at the time of the Apostles there were no other friars beside these. It is of them that St. Paul wrote when he said '*periculum in falsis fratribus.*' They are some of those 'false brothers'." And at this clever joke of the buffoon, everyone started to laugh . . . and the Carmelites left, amid the people's jeers.[8]

In both stories, the Carmelites' insistence on their age is so single-minded that they miss its bad effect in the circumstances, of inducing scorn for them. The second story also shows why they were so powerfully impelled. Their inferiority was due not to their more recent foundation as such, but to their lack of a famous founder, the absence of the Benedict, Francis, or Dominic of whom they spoke. Elijah grandly overcomes this. An art historian is well placed to appreciate the importance of such a lack, recalling how the chief vehicles in the paintings of the other orders are the images and biographies of these founders. Evidently those were the most effective ways for them to approach their public visually. The Carmelites needed an Elijah badly.

CARMELITE IMAGERY: PIETRO LORENZETTI

Turning now to look at Carmelite imagery, it is natural to start with the earliest famous work, the altarpiece of 1329 painted by Pietro Lorenzetti for the order's high altar in Siena.[9] It may be helpful here to approach it through its complex later history. In the sixteenth century, the altarpiece was removed, no doubt as outmoded, and, in a fairly common pattern, its main parts were sent to a country parish church, whose patron was St. Ansano. These main parts—the central panel and its predella—returned to Siena, to the Pinacoteca, in several stages over the nineteenth and early twentieth centuries. The main panel, in the conventional way, shows the Virgin and Child with two saints. The saint on the viewer's left is Nicholas, the patron of the Carmelite church in Siena even before the order acquired it. (We shall see in other Carmelite paintings the inclusion of other cult references.) The saint on the viewer's right appeared to be, when the panel reached the Pinacoteca, St. Anthony: yet an inscription at his feet labeled him as Elijah. On the removal of later paint, Lorenzetti's original figure proved to be Elijah indeed, dressed in a Carmelite robe and holding a long scroll; its text is from 1 Kings 18:19, in which Elijah speaks and calls on all Israel to gather at Mount Carmel. Evidently this figure had been unacceptable in the country church.

The long predella showed scenes, painted in the sixteenth century, of the life of St. Ansano. It was naturally presumed that this narrative was an element added at the date of the transfer. Such an addition was the more plausible because four other small predella panels in the Pinacoteca were reasonable candidates for having been the original predella by Lorenzetti; they show Carmelite stories. Here, too, however, cleaning of the Ansano stories revealed under them another original Lorenzetti scene, likewise of Carmelite subjects, and fitting in its narrative sequence after two of the small ones and before the other two. It followed that the altarpiece must originally have been much wider; since the long middle element of the predella fits under the main central panel of the Virgin and two saints, the four smaller predella panels must have had above them additional panels with saints, left and right. Such a reconstruction (Figure 6.1) has since been handsomely confirmed by the discovery of the panels of saints. The altarpiece form, where a squar-

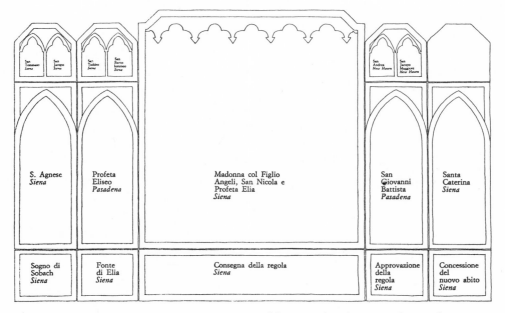

Figure 6.1. Pietro Lorenzetti, reconstruction of the Carmelite altarpiece of 1329 (after Torriti). Siena, Pinacoteca. Foto Soprintendenza B.A.S.

ish main panel is flanked by tall narrow ones, was not uncommon in Siena at this time, as Maginnis has noted. However, all the other examples (all from later than 1329) differ in that the squarish main panel shows a scene, such as the Annunciation in the one by Simone Martini, and thus they require the added narrow panels to show the saints usually placed at the sides of altarpieces. A standard altarpiece with a central Madonna, like this Carmelite one, would not require such additions, which is why at first no such extra panels were presumed to have existed. Hence it differs from all the others having this kind of carpentry in its very rich court of saints, in this respect recalling instead the earlier Maestà type. It is more modern, with its polyptych form, in its carpentry, setting up a formula for the altarpieces with scenes.[10] Thus it is a unique transitional image.

It was early proposed that two saints by Lorenzetti, also in the Pinacoteca, were side panels of the Carmelite altarpiece, and this theory proved to be correct through later evidence, as will be noted. These saints, Agnes and Catherine, again illustrate the presence of a non-Carmelite cult. The final two missing saints emerged in 1973, when the Norton Simon Foundation acquired two unpublished Lorenzetti panels (Figure 6.2). John the Baptist, the figure in one, was noted above as an object of Carmelite interest. The other figure wears Carmelite robes and holds a long scroll whose inscription includes the name Elijah. These figures have the same dimensions as the Agnes and Catherine, assuring that all four saints belong together. The figure in Carmelite robes was identified as Elijah by Meiss, in his initial pamphlet making the works known, on the natural basis of the inscription on the prophet's scroll.[11] As the main panel of our polyptych already includes Elijah, Meiss inevitably deduced that Lorenzetti had painted two large Carmelite altarpieces. Yet it would be strange if two such works—with the same function, not a common one—should each be preserved in just the parts missing from the other. The answer is that there is indeed only one, and the Norton Simon saint is not Elijah but Elisha. The scroll in fact alludes to both prophets, quoting 2 Kings 2:11–12: "And Elijah went up by a whirlwind into Heaven. And Elisha saw it, and he cried, My father, my father, the chariot of Israel." Clearly, it is more understandable that Elisha should hold a text also alluding to Elijah (whose heir Elisha here becomes) than the reverse. The heirship itself is of special Carmelite interest. Elisha reappears in later Carmelite images, as Mâle had reported for the Counter-Reformation. I was able to cite one in another Sienese polyptych (mentioned below) when I wrote to Meiss along these lines in acknowledging his offprint; he passed the suggestion to his student Maginnis, who published the identity as Elisha, with acknowledgment, in 1975, adding the further confirmation that the Norton Simon figure is suitably bald.[12] Zeri published the same conclusions independently in late 1974.[13]

The narrative predella, in a way common with predellas, develops the Carmelite imagery in an even more specific way. The leftmost scene (Figure 6.3) contains an inscribed scroll identifying it as a unique image of the story of Elijah's birth. The text is an incomplete phrase, as signaled by its curling ends and by its syntax: ". . . sleep he saw how, when Elijah was born, men wearing white robes . . ." All commentators reasonably label the scene the story of Elijah's father, Sobach, except Zeri, who oddly reports in his generally valuable article

Figure 6.2. Pietro Lorenzetti, *Elisha,* Pasadena, Norton Simon Foundation (F.73.8.[2].P.).

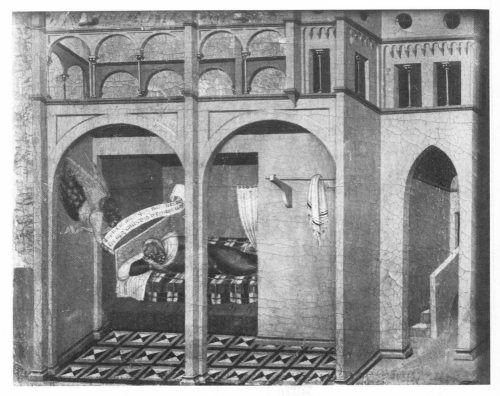

Figure 6.3. Pietro Lorenzetti, *Sobach's Dream*. Siena, Pinacoteca. Foto Soprintendenza B.A.S.

that: "As for the predella stories, they turn on *modern* themes of the order." All others, naming Sobach, nevertheless cite no source for this name or for the legend of Elijah's birth, so that it was reasonably noted as a puzzle by the recent cataloguer of the Siena Pinacoteca that the Bible knows nothing of Elijah's father; the story, "perhaps medieval," probably arose, he suggests, to enhance the "luster of the Carmelites."[14]

The story appears, however, in widely circulated Greek patristic writings from the 4th century A.D. The two earliest tell, in similar phrases, how at the time of Elijah's birth Sobach saw men (or angels) wearing white, greeting the infant and offering him fire to eat.[15] A Western Carmelite around 1337 — that is, just at the time of our predella — is found citing the story, omitting the fire and specifying that Sobach's experience was in a dream, by night.[16] This rendition brings us closer to our image, with the sleeper in the bed, but leaves baffling its omission of what surely is the visual core of the story, the appearance of the men in white. They are relegated to words in the scroll (it is not a matter of a version of the story omitting them). This lacuna is especially odd in view of the fact that for the Carmelite writer these men allude to Elijah's future disciples, the Whitefriars. The formula with the angel might suggest that Pietro, faced with this novel theme, fell back on a known schema, the dream of Joseph, which in Duccio's *Maestà* showed a similar scroll-carrying angel. I will offer below a suggestion of the reason for the omission of the main motif.

The second panel (Figure 6.4) skips past the lives of Elijah and Elisha to their disciples living on Mount Carmel. Here again, writers have correctly named the general theme but not cited the specific text behind it. This is in no less a source than the Constitutions of the Carmelite order, as adopted in 1281 and repeated in the versions of 1294 and 1324, thus certainly most familiar in the Siena convent in 1329:

> Certain brothers, new in the Order, do not know how to reply . . . to those who ask from whom or how our Order took its origin. We wish to indicate to them how to reply, in these terms. We therefore affirm, to witness the truth, that beginning with the prophets Elijah and Elisha, pious dwellers on Mount Carmel, the holy fathers of both the Old and the New Testament, deeply in love with the solitude of the mountain, unquestionably lived there, in a manner deserving praise, near the Spring of Elijah, in holy penitence, continued uninterruptedly in holy succession.[17]

We see the Spring of Elijah, in the mountains, and the brothers at their tasks, "living in a manner deserving praise." Rarely is it possible, in studying church iconography, to point to such a direct illustration of a text that itself articulated the patron's most emphatic beliefs and concerns. The panel speaks to the viewer in just the way the new brother was to reply to outsiders. In this exceptionally clear case of a matching text, it is notable that the message lacks the liturgical or theological symbolism often hypothesized as present in such imagery; its subtext is institutional and political, but it acts entirely through historical narration. It may be contrasted with a Counter-Reformation Carmelite

Figure 6.4. Pietro Lorenzetti, *The Hermits of Mount Carmel*. Siena, Pinacoteca. Foto Soprintendenza B.A.S.

image, an engraving by Abraham van Diepenbecke, in which also the fountain occupies the center and is surrounded by the friars. There, however, the blood of Christ and the milk of Mary flow down from the sky to fill the fountain; it then dispenses its liquid to the friars below.[18] Lorenzetti's scene is a forerunner in that here, too, life-giving water is drawn from the fountain, but the notion of spiritual nourishment—certainly present in other medieval images, and surely part of the ancestry of this one—is entirely reworked into colloquial everyday experience of physical reality.

Among the many striking aspects of the scene is the pattern of striped robes. This uniform was formally adopted by the order in 1281 but was not a success and was rapidly abolished. It was expensive and "excited derision, as if it were the dress of harlequins. It also created suspicion, for diversity of colors in a religious habit was contrary to canonical tradition."[19] Nonetheless, later memories were more positive. From about 1348 the addition appears that when Elijah flew off in his chariot of fire and dropped his mantle to Elisha, he folded it, so that it was scorched in stripes.[20] This implies that it was then so worn by his followers, just as the predella panel shows them.

A more general remarkable quality of this panel may be suggested by noting its analogy to the type of image called Thebaid, seen in paintings from late thirteenth-century Tuscany onward,[21] with the most famous example in the fresco (probably of about 1340) in the Campo Santo at Pisa. In these panoramas of desert crags, hermits are spotted about, some recognizable as specific saints, such as Anthony and Paul, through the events in which they take part, while others are anonymous hermits performing generic actions. Our Carmelites correspond to the latter; in drawing water, saying beads, reading, and traveling, nothing is special enough to identify them as individuals. We can think of them as a detail from the background of a Thebaid, quite like one we might find in a coffee-table book. It has the appeal understood today in such details, partly because it is almost a genre scene. Genre, like some other medieval types of image, such as labors of the months, may be defined as imagery of human action, recognized by us as matching not a specific once-occurring action of a known individual (as history painting does) but our repeated experience of types of anonymous actions. In the predella, however, this image would have to be qualified as genre of a past time and other place. Further, one might have to allow that the fountain is an individual named protagonist, a status confirmed by its central position. Indeed the trecento did produce just one category of paintings without any human beings, and there buildings are the protagonists.[22]

In the third scene, the wide central panel (Figure 6.5), students have rightly recognized the conferring of the Carmelite rule. From familiar Franciscan imagery it is clear what a key event this was for a monastic order. The literature regularly reports that here the patriarch Albert of Jerusalem is giving the rule to Brocardus, prior of Mount Carmel. This description, found in Carmelite lore, has a slighter historical nucleus, as more rigorous recent studies show. This nucleus is

Figure 6.5. Pietro Lorenzetti, *Albert Gives the Rule to Brocardus*. Siena, Pinacoteca.
Foto Soprintendenza B.A.S.

a fatherly letter from Albert, during his incumbency of 1204–16, to a
desert prior who in the early manuscripts is called only "B."; the name
Brocardus emerges in the late fourteenth century. It is the earliest token
of a continuous history of the group later to crystallize as the Carmelites; at this time, they were simply hermits who had come as pilgrims
from the West.[23]

Even if B. had already been called Brocardus when Lorenzetti
painted, it is unlikely that the Carmelites had yet claimed him or Albert
as saints, as they were later to do, and the artist gives neither a halo.
It is hard to be sure which figure Brocardus is. Presumably he is one
of the three monks forming a front row, and the most likely choice
may be the one to the viewer's left, the oldest (or at least the longest-
bearded) and closest to the scroll. In any case, he is part of an almost
undifferentiated mass of similar figures whose heavy robes unite them
and give them a Giottesque bodily weight very comparable to the kneeling
suitors of Mary in the Arena Chapel *Prayer before the Rods*. Thus the
preceding panel's emphasis on the anonymous group of friars seems maintained even when the story has named roles. The second individual
character, Albert, is more distinctive: a bishop flanked by deacons. Yet
he, too, is bound to a crowded procession, of which the curveting horses

at the opposite end are the most emphatic part, and which as a whole seems a counterbalance for the kneeling monks. Modern editorial reflections, at any rate, have been especially attracted to these aspects. The Siena postcard industry offers from this panel only a detail of the monks kneeling, while a detail of the horsemen is the primary reproduction in the gallery catalogue.

The last two panels (Figures 6.6 and 6.7) are oddly similar. The first shows a pope handing a scroll to kneeling Carmelites, again the kind of event emphasized in Franciscan cycles. The panel is always said to depict the confirmation by Honorius III, who indeed was the first pope to provide the Carmelites with a document, in 1226. The Lateran Council of 1215 had forbidden the creation of new orders; Honorius saved the Carmelites from dissolution by ruling that Albert's letter to the hermits had the status of the rule of an order. However, the Carmelites received many papal endorsements, notably from Gregory IX and Innocent IV.[24] The pope in the panel is startlingly replicated by three tiny popes—virtually overlooked in the scholarship—who are upheld by Angels in the air over his head, while they present scrolls with the same gesture as his. Evidently these are souls of previous popes inspiring and approving his action. Beside the pope are two more figures, evidently advisers, whose presence seems to distinguish this papal en-

Figure 6.6. Pietro Lorenzetti, *Innocent IV Approves the Carmelite Rule.* Siena, Pinacoteca. Foto Soprintendenza B.A.S.

dorsement of Carmelites from others. The figures appear to be monks, judging by their black robes, Eastern ones, judging by their long beards; the cross on one robe suggests that its wearer has been on crusade. All this seems to point to the endorsement of the Carmelites by Innocent IV in 1247, to judge from the way in which Antoninus summarizes the establishment of the Carmelites in his survey of all monastic rules (in his *Summa theologica et iuris pontificii,* written about 1450): "All the monks who are Greek or of the Eastern Church act under the rule of Basil, which was the first, and in the West, too, the Carmelite friars were under it for a time, to which Innocent IV in 1247 added some

Figure 6.7. Pietro Lorenzetti, *Honorius IV Approves the White Robe*. Siena, Pinacoteca. Foto Soprintendenza B.A.S.

instructions provided in the manner of a rule by a certain patriarch of Jerusalem called Albert; these were extracted from the rule of Basil, with some additions, dictated by the Dominican Cardinal Hugo."[25]

This provision of a rule by Innocent is indeed treated as the principal one by outside writers, from Antonino to the author of the entry "Monasticism" in the *Encylopedia Britannica*. Antonino, to be sure, reversed the events; the Carmelites had had Albert's instructions long since, and it was the Basilian rule they now added. It too was fundamental to their survival, since, even if it was Eastern, it transformed them from hermits into mendicants, the choice that was viable in the Western world to which they had emigrated. The panel fits this event in all its specifics: in being a papal approbation subsequent to several others, in the assistance of cardinals, and in the presence of Basilians. Lorenzetti knew that the black robes were worn by Basilians; his brother represented Basil in one, in his panel at Massa Marittima. (Other Western orders wear black, but not long beards.)

The fifth scene is a modern event easy to identify. Honorius IV is approving the new white robe in 1286; for some friars in 1329 this was a living memory, and shortly before, Giovanni Villani had taken note of it in writing his chronicle.[26]

The similarity between these two panels works to emphasize the point that popes kept supporting Carmelites; so too does the repetition of popes within the fourth panel. Papal approval, as a familiar recurrence, is again almost like genre. Such repetition had been used to show papal approval of other orders, most strikingly in Ambrogio Lorenzetti's fresco of Boniface VIII with the Franciscan Louis of Toulouse (painted when the event was even more recent). The two long facing benches for the Curia, and the kneeling recipient between, were again copied a century and a half later by Ghirlandaio at Santa Trinita in Florence, as the confirmation of the Franciscan rule. The first of Pietro's two panels illustrates this type very closely. The second modifies it, as if in a self-revision, but also elegantly evokes a difference in the dynamic of the events. The friars had first entered the scene from the left between the cardinals; now they come from the center rear. First they leaned on a cardinal's help; now they are independent, and the mass of friars holding the center is the truest group protagonist. The cardinals, as a result, get pushed to the left side, the Basilians to the right, and the extra popes disappear. Not yet in their new white robes, the friars have already doffed the unpleasant striped ones and wear a neutral brown, more generic than ever.

Both scenes modify the type as seen in Ambrogio's fresco in an extraordinary central detail. In that Franciscan fresco, Louis, the recipient of the papal favor, is naturally the protagonist. Pietro's corresponding figures are played down, the one in the latter scene being literally canceled, behind a post. This device is borrowed from the Arena Chapel, where, in the *Presentation of Mary in the Temple,* the priest receiving the child from Anna is canceled in this way. In that painting, the device is clearly intended to prevent his getting emphasis equal to Anna, but that reason is not applicable in our panels. In the earlier of these, the front Carmelite's whole head can be seen, but he is squeezed between two posts, uniquely near each other, one of which cancels his forearm in the act of accepting the paper. This paradoxical diminution of the chief actor is certainly purposeful. It was probably not known what person had historically played this role, if any. But it is also to be understood in relation to the other scenes, where "Brocardus" is downplayed or where there is no leader at all, as in the well scene.

In the main panel above, the Carmelite problem of a lack of a founder was addressed by offering Elijah,[27] Elisha, and John the Baptist. Yet the usual system of putting stories of their lives in the predella was not adopted; one may think it would have been hard to relate such events to the order. Here the same problem is addressed instead by giving the narrative of the order itself, the members carrying the action *as a group*. Assemblies of equals are the protagonists; it is another analogue of genre. Uniquely for its time, this narrative predella lacks saints and other heroes and does not contain a single halo.[28] The friars move through critical moments en masse; even popes make up a kind of chorus, though with a chorus leader.

Is the initial story of Sobach's dream an exception? The absence of Elijah in the first story of the order he founded is not so odd — other stories of saints' lives begin with their fathers' dreams. But here the oddity, as observed, is that the story of men in white omits them, as if we had a story of Jacob's dream without the ladder of angels. It is not because of a dislike of the supernatural (we have the angel) or the difficulty of many tiny figures in the air (we later see nine such figures, three popes each held by two angels). What is positively emphasized is the architectural space. A large room in the foreground leads to a second measured space behind, the bed alcove, separated by framing and the curtain rod. Such double depths are frequent in the work of Sienese masters. In such notable cases as Duccio's *Judas with the Money,* in the *Maestà,* or Simone's *St. Martin Knighted,* in Assisi, the second room is empty of figures and thus without apparent function from a narrative viewpoint, reinforcing an effect of spatial measure. The Sobach panel seems unique in making the front space the empty one, apart from the angel flying in an upper corner, so that the main human image is in the background. Sobach is then canceled in the way we have seen elsewhere, by a quite unnecessary post that visually slices him at the waist. These unusual devices have in common that they negate or subtract; no doubt that is why they have not been discussed. Such omission, diminution, and suppression may be open to explanation if we inquire what would happen if they were not present. Sobach would be uncanceled, in the foreground, and accompanied by the content of his vision. We would then have a powerful protagonist. Protagonists, we saw, were avoided in all the other scenes, but the method of such avoidance, by grouping equals, was not available in this story where the centrality of one actor seems undeniable. The result here was obtained not with the genre group but by making the field of empty space the foreground image. It is not that the building is the protagonist; when that happens, as with the fountain, it is a solid. Here we see at the left of the interior a bit of open "sky" (of gold) and at the right a separate space leading off, indicating that this is a slice of the world. If the other panels predicted Magnasco's congregations of monks, this one predicts Saenredam's empty interiors of monuments. It seems that the negation of the protagonist is even more urgent than its subcategory, the focus on groups. It also seems that these devices were worked out when the list of themes had already been fixed; otherwise an easier way to the goal would have been to omit the unique Sobach story, only indirectly connected with the order. To be sure, the omitted men in white do foretell the last scene when the order gets white robes, not yet being worn as the cycle ends.

SASSETTA

Again in Siena, about a century later in 1423–26, the wool guild offered the painter Sassetta his first important commission. The Piazza San Pellegrino was the locus of a small church of the same name, and of the wool guild headquarters from as early as there is record, in the fourteenth century. The guild also owned many houses on the square, so that its coat-of-arms was "everywhere."[29] From 1370 the guild was also linked to the Carmine, the place of the chief mass on the annual Feast of Corpus Domini, an event the guild began to support financially.[30] One is not then surprised by a report that on this day the guildsmen went in procession to the Carmine and back;[31] processions among churches were a regular aspect of this feast in other cities. It was out of embarrassment at having annually to borrow an altarpiece to honor the altar on this feast that in 1423 the guildsmen decided to commission the Sassetta; hence its primary theme of the Eucharist and secondary one of Carmelite figures.[32] In 1432 they appear as patrons of the Carmine choir chapel (where the Lorenzetti altarpiece already was)[33] and continued to be so for over a century after the Carmelites had in 1448 lost their Corpus Domini role to the cathedral.[34] The guild maintained their role, and in 1460–63 built an annex chapel beside San Pellegrino, for the annual mass of the feast.[35] It is there that the literary sources report the Sassetta. It was certainly appropriate for this place, but had been painted for somewhere else. This seems not to have been the Carmine, as has been recently proposed.[36] More probably the Sassetta's original location was in the little church of San Pellegrino itself, the home church of the guild,[37] though in a more modest place than the annex chapel. Indeed, as early as 1431 members were debating about moving it elsewhere.[38]

The pleasant implication is of a special relation between two masterpieces of Sienese painting, the altarpieces of Lorenzetti and Sassetta, at the two ends of an annual procession. The link grew more explicit when the guild became the patron of the Carmine choir. The Sassetta commission would have given weight to the near end of the guild procession, as the other end was already splendidly marked, and the older painting was surely in mind when the later one was planned. I know no other case of precisely this relation between two works of art.

When the commission was being planned in 1423, Siena had a further reason for interest in the Eucharist or Corpus Domini. A church general council, mandated by the previous Council of Constance, was about to convene there. The first session was on 17 July. On 1 July, the guild's money-raising plan for the altarpiece had gone into effect. Just as it was to honor Corpus Domini, so the council's discussions of doctrine and heresy certainly turned much on the Eucharist, just as at Constance pressure from the Hussites had led to discussion of communion. The direct connection is documented by the inscription on the altarpiece, whose remarkable phrasing may be translated, "Hence, [that is, starting from the monstrance, the central image shown] O Fathers, Stephanus son of Johannes of Siena constructed the whole work for the altars, acting in detachment from old errors." The strange final phrase was long supposed in scholarship to refer to the artist's youth, as an announcement that he avoided older artists' mistakes. Such explanations are tempting because they seem to give answers to questions interesting to art historians. Thus the recent study by Piero Scapecchi, which first linked the phrase to the Siena council and plausibly identified the "Fathers" as the churchmen present, is most welcome.[39] His related suggestion of a different date for the work is less convincing. The council ended in March 1424, and he proposes that the painting had been finished by then, because the inscription addresses the fathers directly, though he also notes that fund collecting for the painting continued long thereafter. Yet it is not plausible, as he urges, that nine months would have been sufficient for the work. It should be further observed that the council ended unexpectedly, dissipating rather than being brought to a conclusion, so that no one could have aimed for that March as a deadline. Finally, the financial documents counterindicate this proposal and confirm the traditional dating with a completion in 1426.[40]

The altarpiece was scattered and partly lost long ago. Luckily, detailed descriptions made while it was *in situ* allow us to envision its structure and iconography and to identify fragments that have emerged.[41] The main area was a triptych, with a saint on each side. The center showed not the usual Madonna or any other figures, but a large monstrance, an *ostensorium* as an early writer calls it. This image is rare, but does have an interesting later analogue by Botticini.[42] He, like Sassetta, devoted the central predella section to the Last Supper; not only does this refer to the Eucharist, but it retains the general tendency of most images at the centers of predellas to refer to the Passion, or in some way to Christ's work of Redemption. Sassetta showed Thomas Aquinas, who was credited with writing the office of Corpus Domini, at the left. St. Anthony, at the right, is not connected with this cult, but as we have seen, he was important to the Carmelites as one of the major desert hermits. (Pope-Hennessy is puzzling in saying that Anthony was a saint of the wool guild; indeed the altarpiece seems to show very little of their imagery.) In the pinnacles and columns the descriptions report standard saints and images of the Virgin. Two other panels, however, which historians unanimously agree were such pinnacles, even if they are not named, are the surviving little bust figures of Elijah and

Elisha (Figure 6.8) in Carmelite robes with scrolls. They evidently quote the larger figures by Lorenzetti.[43]

But it is again the predella that is most fascinating. Six of the seven panels reported in the descriptions survive. Five are the same size, one referring to Thomas being narrower. This indicates that three were under the central monstrance and two each were under the side saints Thomas and Anthony. The missing scene is one of those under Anthony; the surviving one shows the most famous tale about him, the temptation by devils. He does not resemble his image above and is more like Elisha. One might be tempted to see in this similarity a reference to the interchangeability of holy men in Carmelite prehistory, but that would be speculative.

At the other end, the two stories of Thomas Aquinas both show him kneeling in meditation; his life, to be sure, did not lend itself to drama. In one panel (Figure 6.9) he kneels before the cross; this has been labeled as the occasion when the crucifix spoke the words "Bene scripsisti de me Thoma," and that is indeed the one event that recurs among the (rather few) paintings of incidents in the life of Thomas.[44] Of the second panel where Thomas kneels before an altar (Figure 6.10), the leading specialist reports that the representation "does not seem to refer to any particular episode."[45] One might like to think the saint is shown inspired to compose the office of Corpus Domini.[46] A remarkable clue is provided by a long cloth draped over the crucifix. Its embroidered pattern of crosses, and its proportions, turn out to be identical with those on a cloth draped over the altar in the other panel. Since, then, an altar cloth has been placed over the crucifix here, as over an altar there, the meaning evidently is that the crucifix, or Christ, is also an altar. Though this concept is perhaps not familiar in the iconography of this period, and the image certainly is not, it is nevertheless a central one to the doctrine of altars. It might perhaps be sufficient to quote a brief but authoritative encyclopedia article on the altar, whose section on symbolism reports that the altar is, besides one preceding analogue, "the antitype of the cross of Christ," and then, after citing a medieval source, adds, "symbolically, the altar according to indications of Early Christian and medieval literature, is above all Christ."[47] One might also cite Durandus, whose handbook was the most used by priests in Sassetta's time; he starts his book (after a preface and a

Figure 6.8. Sassetta, *Elisha*. Siena, Pinacoteca. Foto Soprintendenza B.A.S.; courtesy, Frick Art Reference Library.

Figure 6.9. Sassetta, *Thomas Aquinas before the Crucifix,* Vatican, Pinacoteca.

section on the Church as a whole) with a chapter on the altar, in which he tells us that the altar "est ara crucis" (is the altar of the cross) and that it "significat Christum," and again, "significat corpus domini."[48] As Durandus wrote too early to have a special section on the Feast of Corpus Domini, this equation is the more notable. Perhaps best is a citation from a sermon of Thomas himself which is incorporated in the current office of Corpus Christi, telling us that Christ offered his body as a victim on the cross—"Corpus suum . . . in ara crucis hostiam obtulit."[49] Sassetta's two scenes, then, show Thomas once contemplating a literal altar and once the Corpus Domini in its capacity as altar, and thus explicate how the feast of Corpus Domini is a theme for an altar and for this altarpiece. The two scenes, partly repeating or overlapping,

Figure 6.10. Sassetta, *Thomas Aquinas before the Altar,* Budapest Museum of Fine Arts.

and otherwise making a substitution between the literal and its figurative analogue, form a remarkable device of doctrinal explication.

Both scenes show the interior of a convent. (A recent label
"chapel" is far from plausible.) Since the saint is shown in left profile
in one and in right profile in the other, we are allowed to think that
we see the same environment as it stretches out beside him in the two
directions. In both, we are given deep probes, behind the stage of action, into separate empty rooms, the general Sienese device already noted
in connection with the *Sobach.* Just as there, the entry at the left of
the altar, with its open door, opens the edge of the image to a wider
world. But here the notable aspect is the specific, almost anecdotal, marking of the diverse functions of the convent rooms, in both cases through
two long fingerlike corridors extending under arches. In the altar scene
one such corridor shows a library, with five rows of desks in recession,
open and closed books, and light in the window embrasures; the other
goes to the cloister with its well and green growths. Outdoors and in-
doors contrast physical and mental living. In the crucifix scene, one space
has a writing desk with its stool and even a penholder and a lock on

a drawer; the other, outdoors, shows a balcony and its stairs, comprising a pulpit. It is the equipment of a friar who writes and then preaches, the daily tasks of a member of the Order of Preachers explicated solely through objects, in a unique way. All the imagery evokes, as well, loving pride in the convent, highly analogous to the report by a Dominican of the 1440s describing his new convent of San Marco in Florence; among its distinctions, he wrote, the highest place belongs to the library; the second to the "reciprocity and dovetailing arrangements" of the living areas, including the system for catching water; the third to the paintings; the fourth to the garden; and "the fifth distinction is the delightfulness of the dwelling areas."[50] Sassetta did not have this experience; neither did the wool guildsmen. But the Carmelite friars did, and they also had, in the Lorenzetti predella, images of their own living. Thus their influence seems strong here, with the doctrinal iconography perhaps less emphatic than the genre effect of life lived.

The central panel is called, not wrongly but loosely, a Last Supper (Figure 6.11). The table has no supper but only the chalice, and Christ holds up the round communion wafer to show us, as a priest does. It would be difficult to match this with a text from the Gospel that tells the story of the supper, or an exegesis of such a text. Instead, it fits neatly the very opening words of the current office of Corpus Domini: "Sacerdos in aeternum Christus Dominus . . . panem et vinum obtulit." Christ the immortal priest officiates behind an altar. The image also replicates what the people at mass before this altarpiece would see on the feast day.

I regret having omitted this panel from an earlier study in which I was able to show that in this period the more ritual and the more narrative representations of the supper match locations respectively on altars and in nonconsecrated places, the latter being most commonly Passion cycles or Last Suppers in refectories, such as Leonardo's.[51] The power of the difference, and the extreme degree to which this panel exemplifies the former type, is nicely suggested by quoting a comment of Roberto Longhi on a very similar predella panel by Ercole de' Roberti: "the most meditated of all Last Suppers, with the fearfulness of a Mithraic rite . . . the objects on the table severe and discreet . . . in a static composition."[52] Longhi's visual observation is articulate and sensuous, but his excited, unhistorical inference is reduced to a truism when

Figure 6.11. Sassetta, *Last Supper*. Siena, Pinacoteca. Foto Soprintendenza B.A.S.

we insert what he did not: that this panel's difference from a familiar
Last Supper is the result of its having really a different iconographic
theme, perhaps better called the Institution of the Eucharist. The fact
that his description of a Ferrarese picture works for a Sienese one confirms the primacy of the thematic forces in the effects he cites.[53]

The subjects of the two other panels that were under the central image of the monstrance remain unidentifiable, even though their
general category of subject matter is obvious. One (Figure 6.12) shows
an exorcism, as the Eucharist forces a devil to depart from a sinner at
the altar. There are the usual spectators at the left, but the white-robed
Carmelites in the center, who help or observe, are less usual. It is clear
that a story was chosen which allowed two interests, in Corpus Domini
and in Carmelites, to merge in the altarpiece. The other panel (Figure
6.13) was wrongly called a story of St. Anthony in the eighteenth-century
description, a token of its difficulty. Zeri, who recently discovered this
panel, reasonably explained the error, noting that the central figure resembles the Anthony in the adjacent one.[54] Yet even before his find,

Figure 6.12. Sassetta, *Exorcism,* Bowes Museum, Barnard Castle, County Durham, U.K.

analysis of the description allowed the conclusion that it erred, since it required an asymmetry. There would be two Thomas stories beneath the image of Thomas, but three Anthony stories, two beneath the image of Anthony and one beneath the central image.

Once again we have an event involving both Carmelites and the Host. A recent study has proposed that it shows the burning of Jan Hus in 1415, whose heresy indeed involved matters of the Eucharist.[55] The idea may be overtempting, as often happens with suggestions that a painting represents a still-famous person or event of a past age, one of the few recognizable memories from it for nonspecialists. That, to be sure, should not exclude the proposal, but it has other difficulties, in that the accounts of the burning conflict with a number of elements in the painting. (1) No Carmelites were present, which itself would rule out the proposal if the idea suggested here is correct, that, like the exorcism in the corresponding panel, an event was chosen with both Eucharistic and Carmelite significance. (2) No mass was said

Figure 6.13. Sassetta, *Burning a Heretic*. Reproduced by permission of the National Gallery of Victoria, Melbourne.

at the burning. (3) No cardinal was present, but one is shown in the panel, the highest ranking official depicted. (4) Conversely, the chief witness at the burning was the local ruler, Louis of Bavaria, Hus having been turned over "to the secular arm" in the usual way. In this period, it is normal in scenes of execution to see the presiding ruler typically sitting on a throne at the side. Yet here the chief lay figure, the only one in armor, has to hold his own banner—whose arms do not seem to be those of Louis.[56] (5) Hus was made to wear a paper hat, a vivid token of identification which one would not expect to be overlooked; imagery of the period strongly favors hats as identifiers of all kinds of people. Yet in the panel, no such hat is shown. (6) In the panel, the soldiers are shown with shields whose arms, with a ram and a lion, are those of the wool guild of Siena, which, of course, was not present at the burning. (7) The fire is in the wrong place. When Hus's burning was followed by that of Jerome of Prague, Jerome asked that the pyre be specially put in front of him instead of behind. Might this indeed be Jerome?[57]

Scapecchi, in arguing that this is Hus, notes two of these discrepancies and—plausibly—proposes that *contaminatio,* a blending of two moments, could account for them, in that the Carmelites and the wool guild might both have asked to be represented in the picture to show solidarity. To be sure, in the case of the guild shields this seems a weak way of doing so, the sort of thing more likely to occur in making such a hypothesis ("How can these shields be explained in accord with the hypothesis I already believe?") than beforehand ("How can we guildsmen evoke in the painting our concurrence?"). To show two young soldiers with these shields hardly seems a natural or strong choice for that purpose, less so than the common device of putting patrons' coats of arms on frames. The other discrepancies might seem unimportant or unlikely to concern anyone, except that this is an unusual case of a recent event (in the hypothesis) which had actually been viewed by many people in Siena when this panel was planned, some of the very *patres* named in the inscription having been in Constance nine years before. If these patres saw the picture (given Scapecchi's view of its early date) one would think they would quickly complain of the apocryphal cardinal. Similarly, whenever it was painted, its anecdotal elaboration—like that of the other panels—evokes a concern with the specifics; if the picture was meant to show Hus, the painter could have satisfied this concern by asking searching questions of those patres. Moreover, contaminatio is not found in any of the other predella scenes.

If this panel is consistent with the pattern seen in the others, especially the exorcism symmetrical with it, it would show an incident that actually involved both Corpus Domini and Carmelites, and in this case also the wool guild, indicating that it occurred in the city. One would hardly expect to find an event meeting all these conditions. On the other hand, for that very reason, any that did would seem to be one that the patrons would have decidedly wanted to see shown. Surprisingly, a candidate may exist. In the late fourteenth century, a traveling Carmelite friar called Theodosius ab Aquis passed through Siena and there "performed a miracle concerning the Blessed Sacrament."[58] Siena being involved, the connection of its wool guild at least in a spec-

tator capacity is not hard to presume. I have been unable to learn more
about this story, but hope that others may.

In any case, this scene and the exorcism called for ingenuity
of selection. For us it is perhaps most notable that again the Carmelites
are not saints but anonymous. In the exorcism, they occupy the center
in a mass, much as they do in Pietro Lorenzetti's final predella panel.
Zeri finely notes that in the burning scene neither the priest nor the
victim is most prominent; "the true subject is the tumult in which the
event happens, and its interpreters are, just as much as those, the line
of soldiers, the knights, the ecclesiastic or the assistant holding the torch."
It is "realistic narration at this date." But we note that, in Carmelite
contexts, that particular sort of realism is not after all so unusual. Quite
possibly, if there had been important Carmelite saints, stories of them
would have been preferred. But what is interesting is that, in their absence, the positive outcome was to let the rank and file take over that
role.

MASACCIO

Of all artists, Masaccio has the closest association with Carmelites. Writings about him tend to give this connection only passing mention, or
none, yet in his short career his three most complex works were all
for their churches. His Pisa altarpiece of 1426 was for a lay family's chapel
in the Carmine there. The family's choices dominate its imagery, and
Carmelite saints appear only among the small colonnette figures, on
the same scale as Sassetta's Elijah and Elisha. On the other hand, Masaccio's lost *Sagra* fresco was in the cloister of the Carmine of Florence,
within the friars' dwelling area. It seems unlikely that it had any other
patron but the order. Painted no later than 1427 (when Masaccio left
Florence for the last time), it represents an event that had taken place
in 1422, on the piazza just outside the doorway of this very cloister.
No precedent seems to have emerged for its specific theme, despite efforts to find one. It shows the consecration of the church of the Carmine itself in the presence of Pope Martin V, whose stay in the city
at that time no doubt led to the decision to schedule the ceremony.
The descriptions mention him, the officiating bishops, leading citizens,

and the prior of the convent.[59] There obviously were no Carmelite saints, but it is hardly to be doubted that there were other friars of the convent besides their prior, so obvious a set of bystanders that they were not mentioned. Indeed if we think they formed a massed group, while the laity were individuated, silence about them would be all the more natural. In any case, the theme was, from the Carmelite viewpoint, nothing new; once again, as with Lorenzetti and Sassetta, the events in which the friars *as a group* were active became the topic. Masaccio was, among other things, a master of the everyday, of the significance of the man on the street. It is not unlikely that this was his first work for the order, and plausible to think its success led to his further commissions to work in their churches.

The friars who are hypothesized as onlookers in the *Sagra* in any case appear in two scenes in the Brancacci Chapel. The primary theme of stories of Peter of course reflects the interests of the lay family. But once again a secondary input by the friars may be seen, and in two frescoes it takes the same form we have seen several times. The first is Masolino's *Preaching of Peter*. If we agree that in the chapel Masolino's style came closer to Masaccio's than it does elsewhere, it would not be extravagant to suggest that his use here of the pattern under discussion reflects influence from the *Sagra*. Most of those listening to Peter's sermon kneel, but at the far right two Carmelite monks at the back of the crowd are standing up (Figure 6.14). Is this is a realistic observation about people at the very back of a crowd? Is it a compositional device to balance the standing Peter? Is it an assertion by the friars of their own importance? Is it the artist's emphasis on those associated with his patrons? It may be all of the above. But it is also a rather primitive version of what happens in another scene.

This is Masaccio's *Peter in Cathedra*. Among the figures around him are four Carmelites, one kneeling and three standing to our left. They have often been called portraits of the actual friars Masaccio met, a tribute to their vividness. But that does not tell us why they are here and not, say, in the *Tribute Money* or any other scene. Even the question seems shocking, probably because of our sense of the *Tribute Money* as a classic, inevitable composition. Yet iconographically Carmelites would seem no more peculiar there than in the scene where they do appear. The explanation for their presence in the *Cathedra* scene is to be sought

Figure 6.14. Masolino, *Preaching of Peter,* detail, Florence, Carmine, Brancacci Chapel. Gabinetto fotografico, Soprintendenza Beni artistici e storici di Firenze.

in the text that, by universal agreement, was the basis for that representation: the *Leggenda aurea,* specifically its account of the feast of Peter in Cathedra.[60]

Voragine, as usual, not only tells the story but expounds its meaning for us, in this instance indeed giving it most of his space. Near the end of his chapter, some 20 percent of his entire text on the feast is devoted to explaining that we mark this feast in honor of the tonsure (*corona de' cherici*) because according to some authorities it originated on this occasion. When Peter came to Antioch, the pagans shaved his head as a mark of shame, but a shaven crown later became a mark of honor for all clerics. Its symbolic interpretations include purity, the perfection of the circle, and much else. Given the assurance that Masaccio and his clients consulted these pages in connection with the fresco, one cannot deny that this is the reason for conspicuous tonsures in this fresco and in none of the others, though the literature seems not to have remarked this. Indeed, one can perhaps claim this as the explanation of why here, and in no other work, Masaccio shows major foreground figures from the back (Figure 6.15). These three men vary as to tonsure; one has none, the second has one but is not a Carmelite, and the third is a tonsured Carmelite. Similarly, the three standing Carmelites vary in either wearing hoods (Figure 6.16) or revealing the tonsure. This variation doubtless involves the artist's concern to avoid mechanical and didactic repetition, but it also has thematic references. The middle kneeling figure, the layman with no tonsure, is no doubt the king of Antioch. As the story tells, it was after his son's resurrection, shown in the adjacent fresco, that he and all his subjects were converted, thus raising Peter to the Cathedra. To his right and left, the two tonsured figures are presumably two types of clerics, a secular priest and a friar. But why, in the first century A.D., are we being shown a friar? The answer was obvious to any Carmelite, and we have heard it in the novella by Bandello, when the Carmelite explained to the ducal council that his order alone existed "in the time of the Apostles." This statement would mean that when a Carmelite in Florence read Voragine on the Cathedra, and arrived at his mention of clergy in Peter's see, it would for him be a confirmation, even a demand, for the presence of his predecessors. For us it is even more suggestive that once again we see the order as such, a cluster of anonymous members, to mark this point of their history.

Figure 6.15. Masaccio, *Peter in Cathedra,* detail of kneeling figures, Florence, Carmine, Brancacci Chapel. Gabinetto fotografico, Soprintendenza Beni artistici e storici di Firenze.

Building activity was completed in this church around 1400, which explains why paintings were done for it by nearly all the major masters of the next generation, Lorenzo Monaco, Uccello, and Fra Filippo Lippi, as well as Masolino and Masaccio. Fra Filippo was, of course, one of its friars, and what is often called his earliest work is a fresco in the same cloister (Figure 6.17). It may not seem odd now that its theme, showing Whitefriars, has been unclear. When the work was first published in the 1930s after reappearing from under whitewash, its finder suggested that it illustrated a papal bull of 1432.[61] This proposal has been regularly retained in the literature, but seems dubious to me. The bull relaxed the austerity of the rule, allowing more contact among the members, and notably more eating of meat; its bad reputa-

Figure 6.16. Masaccio, *Peter in Cathedra,* detail of Carmelites at side, Florence, Carmine, Brancacci Chapel. Gabinetto fotografico, Soprintendenza Beni artistici e storici di Firenze.

tion within the order as a sign of laxity—noted by Mâle—perhaps did not develop at once. But I know of no paintings celebrating the content of bulls at all, and the imagery here does not match the 1432 bull in the explicit way that would clearly show it had broken that pattern. I fear the hypothesis has benefited too much from art historians' tendency to be less critical when a hypothesis offers them a definite dating, especially when in any case it cannot be far from right. More particularly, the theory that the picture shows the happy results of the bull in allowing the friars more contacts after 1432—the one fairly concrete parallelism—is unsatisfactory, since neither after nor shortly before that

Figure 6.17. Fra Filippo Lippi, *The Hermits on Mount Carmel,* Florence, Carmine, cloister. Gabinetto fotografico, Soprintendenza Beni artistici e storici di Firenze.

date did they live in the sort of little one-room building shown; such structures at this time could be found approximated in the West only among Carthusians. They had, of course, the same sort of monasteries as the other mendicant orders, a fact inescapable to the original viewers of the fresco, not just to the friars themselves but to anybody else, since it was painted inside one. They had lived in this way since they became organized as Western mendicants in the mid-thirteenth century.[62] The fresco thus reflects an image of something earlier and elsewhere. Indeed, once this issue is opened up, it seems obvious enough that we see here the same scene as in Pietro Lorenzetti's image of the Carmelite hermits on Carmel with the spring. Lorenzetti's landscape form, with its bleak rising rock and isolated trees, is in fact closely duplicated. Among these forms we see again the anonymous friars that are now very familiar. To insist on the life of the friars on Carmel in ancient times is, in a general sense, to do the same thing that was done in this very church by the young preacher who annoyed the Piovano Arlotto. They now are shown, to be sure, in white robes, but Masaccio shares that anachronism.

A remarkable series of great masters explored this motif, which seems a unique one in the period, with a group of anonymous people serving as both subject and patron. Prodded into being by an odd self-interest, it yielded an exceptional extension toward modernism. After 1430 this penomenon seems to stop. The Carmelites were beginning to represent the rather ordinary saints of their order in their paintings; St. Albert of Sicily first is found about 1410.[63] In Dughet's seventeenth-century frescoes, where the startling effect of heroic landscapes surrounds us in a Carmelite church, and crowds of tiny figures of holy men fill them, we might seek an echo of these patterns. On inspection, however, the scenes resolve themselves in most cases into specific narratives of Elijah and others.[64]

NOTES

1. E. Mâle, *L'art religieux . . . après le concile de Trente* (Paris: Colin, 1932), 443–54.

2. Ibid., 443–45.

3. C. Emond, *L'iconographie carmelitaine dans les anciens Pays-Bas méridionaux* (Brussels: Palais des Académies, 1961).

4. T. Boase, "A Seventeenth-Century Carmelite Legend Based on Tacitus," *Journal of the Warburg and Courtauld Institutes* 3 (1939–40): 107–18.

5. B. Xiberta, *De scriptoribus scholasticis saeculi XIV ex ordine Carmelitarum* (Louvain: Bureaux de la revue, 1931), 167, cites the unpublished Bodleian manuscript. The dispute had earlier been noted by B. Zimmerman, the classic historian of the order, in his entry "Carmelite Order," in the *Catholic Encyclopedia*, vol. 3 (New York: Appleton, 1908), 354–55. The

entry also offers a list of the real but intermittent earlier eremitical activities around Mount Carmel that the order named in its claims. The *New Catholic Encyclopedia* of 1955 in a similar entry drops that material and puts the beginnings of the order around 1210, in connection with the letter of Albert of Jerusalem to be discussed below; this approach is now standard, Zimmerman, along with most scholars until recently, had put the firm beginnings around 1150.

6. *Facezie, motti e burle del Piovano Arlotto,* ed. C. Amerighi (Florence: Libreria Editrice fiorentina, 1980), 198–99:

> Il Piovano si trovava una mattina nella chiesa del Carmine e ascoltava la predica da un frate che era giovane e più arioso che dotto. E predicando su un argomento su cui si era assai ingarbugliato, riguardo a quel passo in cui gli ambasciatori di Giudea domandavano a San Giovanni Battista chi fosse, il frate si voltava verso il Piovano e diceva: "Chi sei tu? Sei tu Elia? Sei tu Geremia?" ecc. E replicate queste parole infinite volte, venne a noia al Piovano, che non poteva trattenere le risa e che rispose forte al frate: "Io non sono nè Elia, nè Geremia, ma sono il Piovano Arlotto: può darsi che tu non mi riconosca!" Questa risposta fece ridere tutti quelli che stavano ad ascoltare la predica.

7. The insertion of Jeremiah no doubt reflects a conflating memory of the passage in Matt. 16:13–14. When Jesus asks his disciples who the people say he is, they answer, "Some say that thou art John the Baptist, some Elias, and others Jeremias, or one of the prophets."

8. M. Bandello, *Le quattro parti de le novelle del Bandello* (Turin: UTET, n.d. 4:44–46:

> Devete adunque sapere che, regnando Galeazzo Sforza duca di Milano, nacque in questa città una grandissima questione di precedenza nelle processioni tra i frati carmeliti e tutti gli altri religiosi; perciò che essi volevano precedere non solamente gli ordini mendicanti, ma anco tutti i monaci. Tutti gli altri allegavano le loro approvate consuetudini, confermate da diversi sommi pontefici. Ma i carmeliti dicevano che per lo passato gli era stato fatto torto grandissimo, e che la semplice umiltà dei loro maggiori era stata di questo cagione, e che questo non doveva pregiudicare alle loro ragioni, essendo eglino i più antichi di quanti sono al mondo religiosi. Fu dedotta questa controversia al consiglio segreto del Duca: il quale, essendo giovane, volle esser presente a udirla disputare. Un giorno dunque di festa nel castello di Milano fece congregare tutti i capi d'ogni sorte di religiosi, e volle che nella sala verde la cosa si disputasse. . . . L'eccellente messer Giann'Andrea Cagnuola, dottor di leggi . . . al priore dei carmeliti rivolto, domandò lui, quanto era che l'ordine sue aveva cominciato. Il carmelita rispose che sul monte Carmelo sotto Elia cominciò. Dunque eravate voi, soggiunse il Cagnuola, nel tempo degli Apostoli? Ben sapete che si, disse il priore, che noi soli eravamo frati in quel tempo, perciò che ancora non era stato Basilio, Benedetto, Domenico, Francesco, nè altro capo di religiosi . . . Aveva il Duca un buffone molto arguto e galante, il quale, sentendo questa chimera che il priore carmelita diceva, saltò in mezzo, e disse al Cagnuola, Domine doctor, il padre dice il vero, che al tempo degli apostoli non ci erano altri frati che essi; dei quali Paolo scrisse, quando disse: *periculum in falsis fratribus.* Essi sono di quei falsi frati. Ciascuno all'arguto motto del buffone cominciò a ridere . . . ed i carmeliti ne andarono dal popolo beffati.

9. P. Torriti, *La pinacoteca nazionale di Siena: I dipinti dal XII al XV secolo* (Genoa: Sagep, 1977), 97–99, with preceding bibliography.

10. H. Maginnis, "Pietro Lorenzetti: A Chronology," *Art Bulletin* 66 (1984): 187.

He writes that some of the later altarpieces are "polyptychs where standing saints accompany an enthroned Madonna" while others have narratives, but cites cases only of the latter type. The formulation he offers would enhance his view that the altarpiece was influential; his other comment, that it was revolutionary, should perhaps be qualified, in view of its tie to the Maestà form. That tie was noted by E. De Wald in his early basic study of the painting, remarkably so since the evidence for the greater width was not then known ("Pietro Lorenzetti," *Art Studies* 7 [1929]: 9).

11. M. Meiss, *Three Loans from the Norton Simon Foundation, First Public Exhibition, SS. Elijah and John the Baptist by Pietro Lorenzetti* . . . (Princeton, N.J.: Art Museum, Princeton University, May 1973), unpaginated.

12. H. Maginnis, "Pietro Lorenzetti's Carmelite Madonna: A Reconstruction," *Pantheon* 33 (1975): 10–16.

13. F. Zeri, "Pietro Lorenzetti: Quattro pannelli della pala del 1329 al Carmine," *Arte illustrata* 58 (1974): 146–56.

14. Torriti, *Siena,* 99. Only Boase ("Carmelite Legend," 110) had briefly indicated a source.

15. The earliest is a set of prophets' lives traditionally ascribed to St. Epiphanius; J. P. Migne, ed., *Patrologiae cursus completus, series graeca,* 242 vols. (Paris, 1857–67), 23:395. The second, perhaps also of the fourth century and traditionally ascribed to St. Dorotheus of Tyre, is a set of lives of prophets and disciples emphasizing their places of birth and death; our passage is quoted in the exegesis of 1 Kings 17:1 (where Elijah is introduced) in C. a Lapide, *Commentaria in . . . libros regum* (Venice, 1701), 139. Lapide adds that the story appears again in the saints' lives of Simeon Metaphrastes, of the tenth century. This exists in over five-hundred manuscripts, but the one used by Migne lacked the life of Elijah, and as there is no other edition I could not check this version. Lapide's often reprinted and exhaustive commentaries are, incidentally, often helpful in finding patristic references to biblical figures.

16. This version by John of Cheminot is reported by E. Friedman, *The Latin Hermits of Mount Carmel: A Study in Carmelite Origins* (Rome: Institutum Historicum Teresianum, 1979), 202, citing previous scholarship. He suggests that John drew on Epiphanius.

17. Ibid., 200.

18. Reproduced in Emond, *L'iconographie,* fig. 16.

19. Friedman, *Latin Hermits,* 198. Giovanni Villani had already remarked about 1330, in connection with its abolition, that it was "secondo i religiosi molto disonesto." He describes it as having "larghe doghe bianche e bigie, dicendo che quello era l'abito di Santo Elia profeta" (*Croniche,* 7:109).

20. Friedman, *Latin Hermits,* 202; cf. 198.

21. G. Achenbach, "An Early Italian Tabernacle," *Gazette des Beaux-Arts,* 6th ser. 25 (1944): 128–52, esp. 133–43.

22. Notable examples are the Cimabuesque *Fall of Babylon,* in the Apocalypse series in the Upper Church at Assisi, and the visual inventory of the churches founded by St. Martial, in the cycle honoring him at Avignon by Matteo Giovanetti. A useful survey of this type was prepared by Brian Lukacher in a seminar conducted by me at Williams College in 1976.

23. Friedman, *Latin Hermits,* passim. Reviewing this book in the *Israel Exploration Journal* 31 (1981): 258–59, B. Z. Kedar notes that it sums up recent studies proving the name Brocardus to be a later legend and adds: "This summary should be of use to general historians

of the Crusades, still largely unaware of these conclusions." The art historical literature has remained vague about the actual early history of the Carmelites, a part of that topic. I am greatly indebted to Professor Kedar for information on this and other recent publications that have transformed that situation.

24. For Gregory IX's "approbation" of 1229, see Friedman, *Latin Hermits,* 195–96; for Innocent IV's, see E. de la Madre de Dios and O. Steggink, "Carmelite Spirituality," in *New Catholic Encyclopedia,* vol. 3 (New York: McGraw Hill, 1955), 114.

25. Antonino Pirrozzi, *Summa theologica et iuris pontificia* (Venice, 1582), pars 3, tit. 16, cap. 1, sec. 8. Antonino had, to be sure, an ax to grind as a Dominican. Not only does he boast here of a Dominican cardinal's aid, but elsewhere he mocks the "foolish pride" of the Carmelites in claiming Elijah. The fact that they follow the rule of St. Basil proves that they are a later foundation, he argues. See R. Morçay, *St. Antonin* (Paris: Gabalda, 1914), 363. Our panel implies a Carmelite rebuttal, showing the Basilians connected with only a revision of the Carmelite rule, not its inauguration.

26. Villani, *Croniche* (see note 19 above). The date of the pope's approval is some- times given as 1287. Friedman, *Latin Hermits,* 198, records that in 1284 at its chapter general the order called for the change and adopted it at its next meeting in 1287; "the substitution was approved by the Holy See." But evidently this approval preceded the adoption in 1287.

27. A panel painting of similar date inscribed "Sanctus Helyas," showing him wear- ing a Carmelite robe and inscribed "he gathered the prophets at Carmel," has recently been published in H. van Os, "Text and Image: the Case of a Jewish Prophet in Carmelite Disguise," *Non Nova sed Nove: Mélanges de civilisation médiévale dédiés à Willem Noomen* (Groningen: Jaap, 1984), 163–68. Van Os convincingly compares its shape to forms in Florence at the beginning of the century and its style to frescoes at Sta. Maria Donna Regina in Naples, especially those dated c. 1320. But the conclusion that it "must undoubtedly be dated before" Lorenzetti's Elijah may be bold. In Naples, with its dependence on imported forms, a provincial lag in shapes and style may be likely.

28. The literature regularly titles the central predella panel a scene of St. Albert and St. Brocardus. The order, however, assigned saintly status to Albert only in 1504, and the church as a whole never did (A. Staring, s.v. "Albertus," in *Bibliotheca Sanctorum* [Rome: Istituto Giovanni 23, 1961], 1:160); the order assigned it to Brocardus in 1569, and the church in 1609 (K. Kaster, s.v. "Brocardus" in *Lexikon der christlichen Ikonographie,* vol. 5 [Freiburg and Rome: Herder, 1973], 447.) If we try not to think of them as saints, it may be easier not to think of them as protagonists in the image. The habit of calling them saints perhaps reflects what we expect in predellas or an extrapolation back from the Counter-Reformation (which often affects interpretations of earlier church imagery). In 1940, R. Longhi described as "a genre scene" Gentile da Fabriano's predella panel of people visiting the tomb of St. Nicholas, and continued: "If someone could point out to me a sacred story without the protagonist in action and without haloes, of the same years and outside that circle, I would be very glad" (*Opere complete,* 10 vols. [Florence: Sansoni, VIII/1, 1975], 63). His failure to think of the—fairly famous—Lorenzetti panel of the hermits at the well is perhaps due to his notorious conviction that Sienese painting is overrated. To be sure, on a preceding page (61) he had endorsed another scholar's suggestion that Gentile had been schooled by the Lorenzetti, but then added that at this time artists were always formed by the "attuale," not by older models.

29. G. De Nicola, "Sassetta between 1423 and 1433," *Burlington Magazine* 23 (1913): 209; this is the basic study of the documents and reconstruction of the Sassetta.

30. A generally reliable chronicler wrote in 1718 that the guild "dal 1370 al 1448 faceva la festa del Corpus Domini nel . . . Carmine," after which it was transferred to the Cathedral. See G. Moran, "The Original Provenance of the Predella Panel by Stefano di Giovanni (Sassetta) in the National Gallery of Victoria: A Hypothesis," *Art Bulletin of Victoria* (National Gallery, Melbourne) 21 (1980): 36. J. Pope-Hennessy, *Sassetta* (London: Chatto and Windus, 1939), 9, mentioned similar dates. His comment that the feast itself "was adopted in Siena only about 1370" needs to be modified a bit in the light of a document of 11 June 1365, which shows that the Carmelites were then already seeking a subsidy for a tabernacle to show the "corpo" of Christ "nella sua festa" (S. Borghesi and L. Banchi, *Nuovi documenti per la storia dell'arte senese* (Siena, 1898), 29–30.

31. Pope-Hennessy, *Sassetta*, 9, unfortunately with no source given.

32. De Nicola, "Sassetta," n. 19.

33. V. Lusini, *La Chiesa di S. Niccolo del Carmine in Siena* (Siena: Tipografia S. Bernardino, 1907), 33, reports that in that year they began to "renew the apse;" in what way is not known.

34. In 1512 they commissioned decorative painting, stars in a blue field, of the vault of their chapel, "la quale è la capella maggiore" of the Carmine. The contract was signed in the "residentia" of the consuls of the guild, no doubt at Piazza San Pellegrino. See G. Milanesi, *Documenti per la storia dell'arte senese,* 3 vols. (Siena, 1854), 3:57–58. In 1575 the guild paid for an altarcloth, although, it is noted, the altar itself "non est dotatum." Moran, "Provenance," 36, thus seems incorrect in saying that the guild were "patrons of the altare maggiore." Zeri, "Pietro Lorenzetti," 154 wrongly suggests that the guild commissioned Lorenzetti's altarpiece of 1329 on this altar, citing the document of 1512 of their patronage of the chapel (but without its date, and from a later book briefly quoting Milanesi). The documents of 1329 show that the friars had the painting made and, when their funds were insufficient, got *auxilio* from the city government. Zeri was seeking to explain the presence in it of St. Agnes, whose lamb might refer to wool.

35. Earlier scholarship presumed the altarpiece was painted for the annex chapel, but Moran, "Provenance," 36 showed it was built forty years later.

36. Moran, "Provenance," 36. To support his proposal, Moran cites the guild's known patronage of the church and the painting's Carmelite iconography. He does not consider alternative hypotheses where these factors might also be present. The Carmine seems unlikely, in view of a document of 1431, not cited by him, when it is read in the light of the postulate that patrons (here the guild) do not have two chapels (or equivalent) in the same church at the same time. I believe art historical practice takes this notion to be true, from cumulated experience (with allowance for exceptions in extreme situations such as royal families), but its never being presented qua general postulate means it can get lost in judging any particular situation (a common type of deficiency in art history compared with science). In this document, the guild votes not to move their altarpiece. De Nicola, in publishing it ("Sassetta," n. 21) reasonably associated it with the records of 1432, when they are found "renewing" the Carmine choir (see note 33 above) and suggesting it was thither that it had been proposed to move it. But since the vote was to keep it where it was, it would follow, if that site too was in the Carmine (Moran's view) that they would for some time afterwards have two Carmine chapels at the same time. Moran writes (33) that the altarpiece was reconstructed "mainly" in "studies by Zeri" from 1956 and that Scapecchi in 1976 "established" the close ties of the guild, the Carmelites, and Corpus Domini. However, the main reconstruction had been done

by De Nicola in 1913 — Zeri added only four elements, with full acknowledgment of De Nicola's fifteen — and Pope-Hennessey in 1939 had fully described the triple ties. Not referring to their publications, Moran also did not absorb the documents of 1431 and of 1576 (for this, see the next note), fully published only by them, which point to a conclusion different from his. He evidently is a good-faith victim of the procedure in which only the latest literature on a topic is cited, on the presumption that it fully incorporates earlier work; this is a risk when one is offering new hypotheses, since they can be affected by details not recently quoted.

37. S. Pellegrino seems to satisfy both arguments proposed for a location in the Carmine, without the disadvantage of the latter hypothesis noted above. As to its having wool guild patronage, Lusini, *S. Niccolo del Carmine*, 33, wrote that the wool guild's patronage of that church meant "lasciando l'altra di San Pellegrino." While this statement shows he did not know the records of their continuing later at S. Pellegrino, and thus erred, it presumably reflects his awareness of records of the guild's earlier presence there. In any case, that presence would hardly be lacking in the church on their own square. As to Carmelite iconography there in connection with a Corpus Domini altarpiece, in 1576 the guild was continuing (*solet*) to have Carmelites say the masses in their annex chapel at S. Pellegrino, thus evidently before the Sassetta altarpiece with its Corpus Domini theme, generations after the friars had ceased to be involved in that feast (Pope-Hennessy, *Sassetta* 38 n. 7); all the more might the guild have been glad to involve the friars in the imagery in 1423, when that involvement was active and the friars were in charge of the mass for the feast. Further, the known later location in the annex chapel, considered in relation to the proposition that altarpieces in active cult use, when moved to a new place, are moved within one church much more often than to a different church, points the same way. Also, when the guild built the annex chapel in 1460–63, it was arranged to have a Corpus Domini mass held there (Moran, "Provenance," 34); from this we know that the guild's interest in an altar with this function extended outside the church that was the focus of the feast, and to San Pellegrino.

38. See note 36 above. A scenario might then be: well before 1423, while the guild marched annually to the Carmine on Corpus Domini, they also had an altar near the start of their procession at S. Pellegrino. In 1423 they provided it with an altarpiece, by Sassetta, with Corpus Domini and Carmelite themes. In 1431 they discussed moving this altarpiece to the Carmine, where they were acquiring patronage of the choir chapel. In favor of this move would have been that S. Pellegrino was very small — even the annex chapel to which they later did take the altarpiece was called *admodum angustum* (Pope-Hennessy, *Sassetta*, 38). The majority of members were clearly against it, however, perhaps because the starting point of the procession would lose its impressive anchor. The Carmelites may also have been opposed, since their Lorenzetti had suitable iconography for the high altar of a church of St. Nicholas and friars of Marian devotion, and the Sassetta did not. The guild thus became patrons not of the high altar itself, but of its surrounds.

Moran's scenario is that the guild's altarpiece (perhaps not the Sassetta) moved early from the Carmine to the cathedral; though he does not say so, this may be in line with the similar move in 1448 of the locus of the Corpus Domini mass. His basis is a guild vote on 20 July 1507 to move their altarpiece from the "consueto armario della curia" to the S. Pellegrino annex chapel, which was to receive honor suitable to "detta tavola" (Moran, "Provenance," 34). I have not found a basis for his (unexplained) statement defining *curia* as "cathedral." Meanings vouched by dictionaries for the word all involve the meeting places of legal or administrative bodies. These include guilds, and in Florence, two inscriptions of 1308 on the wool guild's building call it their "Domus et Churia." Hence a mention of an unspecified "curia" in these wool guild records would seem naturally to mean their own, and such a reading also fits the situation—transfer from an *armario* there to S. Pellegrino would be easy. Moran further infers that from 1463 or earlier to perhaps 1509, the altarpiece was brought only once a year to the annex chapel for Corpus Domini and was otherwise stored in this cupboard. His basis for this inference is a guild document of 1509 arranging to "fare il tetto" of the annex chapel, which he suggests might refer not to repairs but to building it for the first time. But this seems negated by a 1463 document he refers to, which records a decision to say mass there. The move of 1507 seems more simply explained by the vote for the roof in 1509 (quoted by Moran separately, "Provenance," n. 14); such work, perhaps to patch leaks, would readily suggest storing the picture elsewhere temporarily. The reverse order of the documents would re- flect a not rare variation in the rate of delays in completing jobs. Separately surprising is Moran's view that the altarpiece the guild voted in 1507 to honor in the annex chapel might not have been the Sassetta, which has the right iconography and is the only one recorded in that place. His basis is "that the Armario della curia" of the cathedral "was used to store reliquaries and small portable altarpieces" but nothing this big. No basis is given for thus identifying the cupboard of the 1507 document with any known to have been so used; the cathedral's well-known reliquary cupboard appears in records as the "arliquiera." The cupboard of the 1507 document had held an altarpiece that became the centerpiece of the annex chapel, hence that altarpiece was probably not a portable one and thus probably was not in a little cupboard.

    39. P. Scapecchi, *La pala dell'arte della lana del Sassetta* (Siena: Monte dei Paschi, 1979), pamphlet, 31 pages. In the final phrase, "Agens citra lapsus adultos," Scapecchi translates *citra* as "against," while recognizing that this is not its normal meaning. "In detachment from" is a more usual translation and seems to satisfy the meaning. I am obligated to Dr. Emma Devapriam for making me aware of, and making available, this pamphlet and the article by Moran published in Australia.

    40. The documents are to be read in the light of these postulates: that altarpiece contracts call for a significant down payment, often about 20 percent, and that the balance was to be paid in full on delivery of the finished work. On 1 July 1423 the guild voted that members should fund the future altarpiece by paying eighteen pence for every cloth fulled, for two years. This provision means they could not have contracted immediately with Sassetta, but only after some accumulation in the fund. Lest one imagine an exception in which the guild might have paid him the pennies as they came in, starting at once, the document specifies that the sums are to be "set aside so that they can be accounted for" and not diverted to other purposes. Expecting to have the amount needed only after two years, the guild therefore could ask for delivery only then, in any case a normal span for the completion of an altarpiece. A second vote, however, extended the fee system for another year and a half, to the end of 1426. Clearly the income per month was amounting to hardly more than half what had been expected. If, as is likely, the shortfall was perceptible from the start, or after a short time, the initial contract would have had to be delayed too. Delivery before the end of 1426 would have to presume an initial intent by the guild to deceive Sassetta as to when he could be paid, which the mere fact that many people would know the facts would make implausible. (See documents in Pope-Hennessy, *Sassetta,* 40). Aside from this, even though Scapecchi's idea about the vocative "O fathers"—that there was a desire that the council fathers should physically see the painting—is attractive, it is hardly to be taken for granted that such was the thought.

The inscription could well address them ideally and after they had gone initially, just as it would obviously have had to do eventually.

41. The texts are most conveniently found in Pope-Hennessy, *Sassetta*, 37–38.

42. A chalice in wood relief in the center was flanked by standing saints. The commission was *ad honorem et reverentiam Sanctissimi Corporis Domini;* Giorgio Vasari, *Le vite dei più eccellenti pittori, scultori ed architettori,* ed. Gaetano Milanesi, 7 vols. (Florence: 1878–85), 4:245.

43. Torriti, *Siena,* 240–45, provides a generally up-to-date survey of the surviving panels, with reproductions of the twelve in the Siena Gallery. The standing St. Anthony was acquired by the Monte dei Paschi, Siena, between his first and second editions, though this is not recorded in the latter.

44. G. Kaftal, *Iconography of the Saints in Tuscan Painting.* (Florence: Sansoni, 1952), 981. Kaftal's later volumes on saints in other regions confirm this pattern.

45. Ibid., 984.

46. No such image seems to be recorded, nor one of a legend in which Christ spoke to the saint on a second occasion (saying "Bene de hoc mei Corporis Sacramento scripsisti") during which the saint levitated. A fresco in the Cathedral of Orvieto (a locus of the cult of the Corpus Domini) shows the pope directing Thomas to write this office, the only actual event related to the office cited in early legends of Thomas's life. See G. Kaftal, *Iconography of the Saints in Central and South Italian Painting* (Florence: Sansoni, 1965), 1092.

47. "Altar," an anonymous article in *Lexikon der christlichen Ikonographie,* ed. E. Kirschbaum, vol. 1 (Freiburg and Rome: Herder, 1968), 106.

48. G. Durandus, *Rationale divinorum officiorum,* (n.p.: Vitali, 1519) bk. 1, chap. 2, secs. A and B.

49. *Breviarium romanum,* In Festi Corporis Christi, in 2 Nocturno, Lectio 4, Sermo sancti Thomae Aquinatis (in Opuscolo 57).

50. Quotations from the chronicle of Fra Giuliano Lapaccini, prior in 1444 and 1448–53, translated by C. Gilbert, in *Italian Art 1400–1500: Sources and Documents* (Englewood Cliffs: Prentice-Hall, 1980), 206.

51. C. Gilbert, "Last Suppers and Their Refectories," in *The Pursuit of Holiness in Late Medieval and Renaissance Religion,* ed. Charles Trinkaus with Heiko A. Oberman (Leiden: E. J. Brill, 1974), 371–402.

52. R. Longhi, *Officina ferrarese* (Florence: Sansoni, 1956), 44.

53. Leonardo's *Last Supper* fits this pattern, being an image emphasizing the narrative Gospel drama, painted in a nonconsecrated refectory. It is puzzling that it is persistently called highly eucharistic. Explanations may include (1) that this ultrafamous work has been studied in isolation, not in the context of other images of the Last Supper in its culture. Such study would show that, on a scale, it is remote from the end pointing up eucharistic concerns; this scale was familiar to Leonardo and his patrons, who thus turned away from available eucharistic imagery; (2) that the current emphasis in art history is on liturgical and related ways of reading paintings. Given this emphasis, one can see certainly in Leonardo the basic eucharistic reference any image of the Last Supper has, prior to such choices of emphasis on it or not. By the same token, the most ritualistic Last Suppers retain a reference to the basic Gospel tale of action, but the complementary fallacy of stressing it in a picture like Sassetta's is not a temptation. Thus, in the Leonardo, it is possible to isolate a detail showing Christ's hand in an

expository gesture, with a finger lined up with bread—but not wine. Unlike art historians, theologians currently seem clear that the emphasis is the story of betrayal at the moment shown and that Leonardo's approach does nothing to enhance the eucharistic materials. See most recently C. Pepper, "Saving the Last Supper," *New York Times Magazine,* 13 October 1985, 43–46.

54. F. Zeri, "Ricerche sul Sassetta: La pala dell'arte della lana (1423–26)," *Quaderni di emblema* (Bergamo, Emblema) 2 (1973): 24.

55. Scapecchi, "La pala," 11ff.

56. The banner is not easy to decipher and might even turn out to be again that of the wool guild. Scapecchi, "La pala," remarks that the figures on the shields are the guild's "instead of those of the elector palatine." Since he is explictly observing that his case would be helped if they were the elector's, I permit myself the deduction that he could not suggest the latter's presence anywhere on the panel.

57. For these details about Hus, see M. Creighton, *A History of the Papacy from the Great Schism to the Sack of Rome,* 5 vols. (London, 1899), 2:49–50; for Jerome, see 2:58.

58. B. Zimmerman, the eminent Carmelite historian, reported this in a letter to the editor of the *Burlington Magazine,* published as an appendix to the article of 1913 by De Nicola, mentioned in note 29 above. The editor had asked him to suggest the subject matter of the exorcism panel. Zimmerman replied that the story of Theodosius is "not the one represented" there but "is the nearest approach to an explanation I am able to furnish." Hence his report was not noted anymore. But when we have a second panel, the counterpart to the one he was trying to explain, it seems worth pursuing.

59. These are closely analyzed in C. Gilbert, "The Drawings Now Associated with Masaccio's Sagra," *Storia dell'arte* 1 (1969): 261.

60. J. da Voragine, *Leggenda aurea,* ed. A. Levasti (Florence: Libreria editrice fiorentina, 1924), 358–60.

61. G. Poggi, "Sulla data dell'affresco di Fra Filippo Lippi," *Rivista d'arte* 18 (1936): 45–76.

62. The confirmation in 1247 by Innocent IV, noted above as assimilating them to mendicants, specifically provided for having all the cells in one building (De la Madre de Dios and Steggink, "Carmelite Spirituality"). The "mitigation" of 1432 permitted walking in the cloister as its main aspect having anything to do with buildings.

63. Kaftal, *Saints in Tuscan Painting,* 13.

64. Two recent studies propose identities other than Hus' death for Sassetta's *Burning a Heretic:* L. Mencaraglia, "L'indovinella del Sassetta," *Bullettino senese di storia patria* 88 (1982): 41–53, and K. Christiansen, *Painting in Renaissance Siena* (New York: Abrams, 1988), 77. Both improve on the previous one by locating the event in Siena, but neither accounts for the Carmelites or other specific persons present.

7

CIVIC PREACHING IN THE EARLY RENAISSANCE
Giovanni Dominici's Florentine Sermons

DANIEL R. LESNICK

T HE RELATIONSHIP OF THE MONASTIC WORLD to the world of lay men and women arose from parallel social aspirations: both "worlds" were comprised of human communities with interlocking ideal and pragmatic components. In this closing chapter of Part One, Daniel R. Lesnick focuses on the point of intersection of these related social visions. Professor Lesnick analyzes how Florentine Dominicans, as members of an ecclesial "community," undertook the task of translating monastic ideals into terms accessible to the civil community, and how members of the main Dominican house in Florence articulated these ideals in public preaching. He traces the tradition of Dominican involvement in Florentine political life from the late Dugento through the fifteenth century; his principal figure is Giovanni Dominici, who was prior of Santa Maria Novella before going on to become head of the Observant community at Fiesole and, later, a cardinal of the Roman Church. Using Dominici's preaching, Professor Lesnick illustrates the classical humanist values and biblical and prophetic cast of Dominican social teaching in Florence, which paved the way for Savonarola's success at century's end.

DANIEL R. LESNICK is associate professor of history at the University of Alabama at Birmingham. He has published on Franciscan and Dominican preaching and the creation of capitalist ideology in late medieval Florence.

CCORDING TO THE EARLY FIFTEENTH-CENTURY FLOR-
ENTINE DIARIST Bartolomeo di Michele del Co-
razza, "In the evening of 4 May [1406] the venerable poet Messer Coluccio [Salutati], counselor
of the magnificent *Signori* of Florence passed from
this life; he was their notary. And the fifth day
of the said month . . . the distinguished Messer Coluccio was crowned
poet with the laurel crown . . . in Piazza de' Peruzi. The same morning
Friar Giovanni Dominici preached in that piazza; and he enumerated
and named many of [Messer Coluccio's] great virtues. . . ."[1]

This account hardly accords with what we know of Dominici
as an adversary of Salutati, the outstanding contemporary Florentine
exponent of the new classicism.[2] Indeed, Dominici fought a valiant
rearguard action against what he regarded as the dangerous effects of
the humanist educational program. In treatises—especially his *Lucula
noctis* of 1405[3]—and his vernacular sermons,[4] the Dominican friar criticized the new learning, with its focus on classical pagan authors, the
world of nature, and rhetorical eloquence. According to Dominici, the
classical authors—Cicero and Plato, of course, but the Dominican Thomas
Aquinas's beloved Aristotle as well—use the art of poetry and their eloquence to make white appear black and black appear white. The books
of fables, of philosophy, of wisdom are used to gain worldly pomp and
to learn to lie and deceive your "compagno." Writings of the poets and
writings about nature are dangerous; they lead you into the pit; they
are the smoke of darkness and of stinking manure. Studying worldly
writings and learning about the beasts of nature, we become like the
beasts. But studying sacred Scripture, we discover our own sacred nature.[5]

Dominici's attack on the new learning is based not on a mind-
less anti-intellectualism but on the conviction that the intellect must
be directed toward that which we should love, and we should try to
know only that which is beneficial to our health; the rest is vanity. Man
has an insatiable desire to know, and it is therefore most important to
our spiritual health that all knowledge and inquiry be founded in God,

the Gospels, and Scripture.[6] This Dominican's educational program was obviously incompatible with that of the humanists.[7] Nothing less than salvation was in the balance. Nevertheless, Dominici preached at Salutati's funeral, at which the poet was posthumously awarded the laurel crown. How can we explain Dominici's apparent inconsistency?

The answer lies in Dominici's civicism, which forms part of a tradition going back to the early establishment of the Dominican order in Florence and which would stretch forward at least to the time of Savonarola. Commitment to the civic world was by no means the exclusive preserve of the Renaissance humanists. Indeed, the Dominicans participated fully in Florentine civic life from the early years of the thirteenth century, even well before the establishment of the republic in the 1290s. From the Florentine civil war between Black and White Guelfs in the very first years of the fourteenth century to the civic crisis precipitated by the Milanese threat exactly a century later, the Dominicans served the fragile republic as ideologues and concerned critics. And toward the final years of the fifteenth century, the Florentine Dominican tradition of civicism culminated in the historical establishment of a New Jerusalem.

THE DOMINICAN PREACHERS' CIVIC TRADITION

The Dominicans established themselves in Florence at a very early date. Shortly after the 1216 confirmation of the Dominican order by Pope Honorius III, Dominic sent his disciple Giovanni da Salerno to establish a Dominican seat in the Arno commune in 1219, and in 1221 the small band of Florentine Dominicans was given possession of the early church of Santa Maria Novella.[8]

Early mendicant participation in Florentine civic life was deeply colored by partisan politics, but by the 1280s civic harmony was what the preachers advocated. The Dominican preacher Peter of Verona, known as "malleus hereticorum" ("the hammer of the heretics") and Peter Martyr to his admirers, came to assist the Florentine inquisitor Ruggiero Calcagni during the years 1244–45.[9] They seem to have confounded the terms *heretic* and *Ghibelline;* most often, those they condemned as heretics were proimperialists.[10] These *domini canes* (hounds of the Lord) were also *guelforum canes* (Guelf hounds). When the Dominican cardinal Latino Malabranca came to Florence in 1279, though, he came as a conciliator to bring civil peace between warring Guelfs and Ghibellines. Even though Rome wanted Florence stabilized in order that it might be a more effective ally in achieving the papacy's north Italian political dominance,[11] nonetheless, it was more than papal schemes alone that brought the Dominican *cardinale paciere* (peace-making cardinal) to the city. At least in the eyes of contemporary Florentines, it was the Florentines themselves, hungry for peace, who initiated the project. The contemporary chronicler Dino Compagni claims it was the Guelfs, wishing to avoid an outbreak of war with the Ghibellines, who came up with the idea of joining with the Ghibellines to request the pope to send the Dominican Cardinal Latino to impose peace.[12] The chronicler Ricordano Malaspini claims that it was both the Guelfs and Ghibellines, independently of one another (the Guelfs fearful of fighting among themselves, the Ghibellines wanting to be restored to power), who requested intervention.[13] Whichever the case, the Florentines asked the pope to send the Dominican cardinal to their troubled city to heal division and discord and to bring stability to the commercial commune. On 18 November 1280, Cardinal Latino summoned a general *parlamento* of the *popolo fiorentino* to the *piazza vecchia* of Santa Maria Novella, where he preached on the subject of peace (Figure 7.1). He asked for full dictatorial powers to reorganize the Florentine government and impose peace on the warring parties; in response the gathered populace cried out three times, "So be it!"[14]

During the 1290s and the first two decades of the fourteenth century, the Dominican preacher Remigio de' Girolami became one of the most prominent voices in Florence calling for civil peace. The brother of Salvi del Chairo de' Girolami and uncle of the Chiaro di Salvi, Girolamo di Salvi, and Monpuccio di Salvi de' Girolami—among the most frequent members of the governing priorate from the 1280s to the early 1300s[15]—Friar Remigio was a great patriot and civic booster. His sermons to the city's priors, like his treatises, show him wedding Thomistic Aristotelianism with Florentine *campanilismo* (patriotism).[16] An early disciple of Aquinas well before his teachings became officially those of the Dominican order in 1313, Remigio held that man is by nature a sociopolitical creature.[17] Thus in his *De bono communi* (written

Figure 7.1. Santa Maria Novella, Florence, in an old view. The Piazza Vecchia, not shown, is to the east of the wing of the transept visible here. The north/eastward expansion of the nave was inaugurated by Cardinal Latino Malabranca on the occasion of the *parlamento* of 1280. Photo Alinari/Art Resource, N.Y.

shortly after the Black Guelf coup d'etat of 1301–2, while White Guelfs and Ghibellines were struggling to retake the city), Remigio warned his fellow citizens that if "you destroy the city, O Florentines, you destroy yourselves. If Florence disappears, there are no more Florentines. Then you will be able to weep over how you will have ended, for you will have ceased to be men. If you are not a citizen, you are not a man, because man is 'by nature a civil animal.'"[18]

Because man has a natural and rational need for the community and because the purpose of the community is to be an area of self-sufficiency in which individual virtue can be more easily attained, it follows that the well-being of the community is more important than that of the individual. Without the community the individual could not exist, and the Christian could not spiritually aid others and earn salvation.[19] In sermons delivered before the priors of Florence in 1295, Remigio urges them to proceed toward the common good, justice, and peace. And in his *Speculum,* written in the first years of the fourteenth century, he decries the current fighting between White and Black Guelfs. Despite the fact that his own kinsmen were staunch White Guelfs, who suffered banishment in the wake of the Black Guelf coup, Remigio is against all factionalism; he declares both sides guilty of the sins of pride, avarice, luxury, and obstinacy. Their wills, he says, are alienated from God, from reason, and from each other. He concludes that to bind their political community together, the citizens must join their hearts and their wills for peace, the *summum bonum* (highest good) of the state.[20]

Remigio's Dominican contemporary Giordano da Pisa preached in Florence between 1302 and 1307 and displayed intense sympathy for the problems that Florence's merchants and bankers encountered in trying to create a stable sociopolitical community.[21] Giordano preached consistently against particularism and family vendetta, both characteristics of earlier semifeudal communal society. He, like the Florentine merchant-capitalists themselves, saw the particularist tendencies of the great families and the vendetta as composing a major social and religious problem. To the older semifeudal corporate mentality, personal ties, honors, and pride were respected badges necessary to success in communal life. In the early years of the Florentine republic, however, the man or family choosing to stand above the rest or indulging in prideful and interminable vendetta was labeled a threat to the *bene comune* (general well-being).

Heading Giordano's list of crimes and sins in Florence is homicide, or vendetta. Nowhere in his sermons does he concern himself with the crimes or sins of workers and the poor. The murder that interests him is clearly a facet of the great families' affairs of revenge or retribution. As often as not, the murderer that Giordano describes has received no direct offense himself but acts instead on behalf of his *consorteria* (extended family). In a sermon delivered on 6 October 1303, Giordano chastens his audience: "So in this way you will choose hate and warfare on behalf of your father and your relatives. How are you so blind and mad that for a creature from whom you receive no hate or ill will, you will kill your own soul?"[22] The vendetta is understood by Giordano to be an act of revenge and, as such, part of a never ending spiral of disruptive social behavior that has no place in the new Florentine republic. The preacher seeks to cut the prideful, civicly dangerous families down to size—just as the early fourteenth-century Statute of the *Podestà,* "De turribus exquadrandis," was intended to stem a major threat to the republic, excessive consorterial pride, by limiting the height of family towers.[23]

DOMINICI'S CIVIC PREACHING

We can now see that for at least a century and a half before Giovanni Dominici preached in Florence other Dominican preachers there were deeply involved in civic life and in helping the Florentine citizenry to resolve the tensions generated by the collision between private interest and public well-being.[24] Born in late 1355 or early 1356, Dominici himself was a native Florentine, the son of a Florentine silk merchant and a noble Venetian woman. In his youth he knew Catherine of Siena, and at the age of sixteen he took the Dominican habit at Santa Maria Novella. He rose within the order and under Master General Raymond of Capua served as vicar to the new Observant friaries of Italy. In 1388 Dominici was appointed lector at the friary of Santi Giovanni e Paolo in Venice, and his activities remained focused on Venice until 1399. Here he established and guided the Dominican nuns of Corpus Christi. In 1399 he was expelled from Venice for his support of the wandering penitential bands of Bianchi, whom the Venetian authorities considered subversive. Dominici returned to Florence at the end of 1399, where he immediately began preaching a series of Advent sermons. His preaching in Florence, mostly during the seasons of Lent and Advent, continued until 1406. In 1405 the Florentine republic sent the Dominican friar to Rome as ambassador to Pope Innocent VII, and a year later, when Innocent had died, they sent him again to try to help heal the Schism. Pope Gregory XII took Dominici into his service as adviser, envoy, and major penitentiary of the Church, and in 1408 elevated him to the archbishopric of Ragusa and the cardinalate.[25]

Dominici's best-known vernacular works, *Il libro dell'amore di carità* and *La regola del governo di cura familiare,* were both originally composed for rather limited audiences of women—the former for the Dominican sisters of Corpus Christi in Venice and the latter for Bartolomea degli Alberti. In his vernacular sermons of 1399–1406, however, we see him addressing a far broader Florentine audience.

Dominici had close ties to that archetypal nouveau riche Francesco di Marco Datini, Iris Origo's Merchant of Prato, and his notary friend Ser Lapo Mazzei. Upon first hearing Dominici preach, Ser Lapo wrote to his friend Datini describing the event: "I tell you that I have never heard such a sermon, nor such preaching. It really looks as though the friends of God are on the rise again, to reform clerics and laity. And he's supposed to preach here at Lent; he's coming from Venice, where everyone follows him about. You'll think you're hearing a disciple of St. Francis reborn. All of us either wept or stood stupified at the clear truth he showed us."[26] Mazzei's enthusiasm for the Dominican preacher apparently was contagious; in a short time Dominici had become Datini's spiritual adviser. In a letter of 1403, Dominici admonishes the merchant Datini, in a rather familiar tone, to "remember the time appointed for your debt with God, for you did not pay it at Easter. And do not fail, for the Creditor would demand of you an interest too heavy to bear."[27]

Dominici also preached at moments of great civic celebration. In October 1406, shortly before the *signoria* was to send him again on an official embassy to Rome, Dominici preached at the citywide festivities celebrating the capture of Pisa, once a linchpin in Milanese aspirations in Tuscany and a seaport long coveted by the Florentines. The conquest of Pisa provided Florence's citizenry with arguably the most immediately gratifying political event in the city's history. Civic joy in the acquisition of Pisa was manifest in three days and nights of public celebration,[28] described by the diarist Bartolomeo del Corazza:

> The first infantry came into Florence at 21 hours; the second came at 23 hours with an enormous olive branch. There was great celebration and rejoicing; and by and by the shops were locked up. There were so many people that you almost could not go through the streets on horse. . . . That evening they made large fires; and the same evening it was publicized that Sunday morning everyone should go to San Giovanni to hear a solemn and devout mass. The Signori and Colleges and

Captains of the Guelf Party went there. And the same evening it was
ordered that Monday, and Tuesday, and Wednesday no one should have
his shop open and that everyone should go to the solemn and devout
processions that had been ordered. And the third morning all the religious, parading and with relics, brought along the panel of Our Lady
Santa Maria of Impruneta. The companies brought their standards. . . .
It was the richest and most beautiful procession that I ever saw. Mass
was said in Santa Reparata with great solemnity, and Friar Giovanni
Dominici preached.[29]

Usually this Dominican preached to his audience on unsurpris-
ing religious themes, such as confession, penance, the Apocalypse, and
clerical autonomy. There are five things necessary to know about holy
confession, Dominici explains: first, you must recognize and acknowledge that when you confess to a priest, you are confessing to Christ's
representative; second, you must feel the guilt of a bad conscience; third,
when you are in mortal sin no work you perform is valid; fourth, the
sinner's voice may loudly proclaim his faith in the Lord, but his powers,
his memory, his intellect, and his will proclaim "No!"; and fifth, because when in mortal sin you cannot perform any valid spiritual action,
you must confess fully every sin to the priest, without any reserve whatsoever.[30] In an Ash Wednesday sermon, Dominici explains appropriately enough that heading the list of reasons for fasting is making penance for your sins; elsewhere, he fulminates against those who dance
and sing, inebriate and gorge themselves, dress lavishly and adorn their
faces rather than recall Christ's sufferings on their behalf. He uses an
Advent sermon to talk about the Second Coming of Christ on the Day
of Judgment and gives a doctrinal description of the Apocalypse. Here
Dominici takes advantage of the occasion to speak about a dark cloud
over the Church and to warn against modern learning. And in an Ash
Wednesday sermon delivered on 24 February 1406, the Dominican argues that just as the laity want religious to stay out of temporal affairs,
so too the laity should stay out of religious affairs and not try to control
the clergy.[31]

This conservative attention to spiritual and ecclesiastical matters should not, however, obscure Dominici's fundamental sensitivity
to the social concerns of the Florentine laity. In typical mendicant fashion, he likens the profit to be gained from Scripture and the words of

the saints to the profit from commercial trading investments.[32] And he speaks of Christ's gifts as commercial merchandise: "Birth, work, death: These are the merchandise of our country. . . . And just as every merchant gives and takes—he gives what he has and takes what he doesn't have—Christ the celestial merchant . . . takes what abounds here (that is, birth, work, and death) and gives resurrection and eternal reign; He takes shame from us and gives honor; He endures death and gives us life; He takes dishonor and gives glory."[33] Thus Dominici links Christ and the merchant through metaphor and thereby validates the lay condition of a major portion of his audience.

Dominici also shows sympathy for contemporary society in his treatment of violence and vengeance. Consorterial vendetta appears to have been far less a problem in the early fifteenth century than it had been during the late thirteenth and early fourteenth centuries, but violence and vengeance continued to characterize Florentine society even in the Renaissance. A focal sermon *topos* in the age of Dante,[34] the vendetta held little interest for the early Renaissance preacher; the great consorterie, with their habitual recourse to passionate vengeance had to a large degree given way to less formal networks of "parenti, amici e vicini" concerned with the calculable promotion of their mutual material well-being.[35] Nonetheless, as physical violence (what we today might term criminal physical violence) among members of the upper social classes continued, Dominici dealt with this in a most sympathetic manner. Certainly the preacher inveighs against murder and vendetta, calling the Florentines knaves and, worse, assassins, but he also understands quite well how difficult it is actually to forgo vengeance.[36] Preaching a Lenten sermon on the theme "Love your enemies," Dominici explains why it is indeed hard to live up to the injunction to love and pardon your enemy or one who has injured you. It is difficult to forgive an injury committed in front of many people or given to you in the face. (Here the preacher shows great understanding that a public injury causes a person to "lose face.") Another type of injury Dominici concedes as difficult to pardon is one committed by a person inferior in either "forza" or "parentado."[37] Thus, as morally reprehensible and spiritually dangerous as vengeance is, loss of face or injury by a social inferior (also bringing a loss of face) constitutes reasonable, if not pardonable, grounds for vengeance. In another, undated sermon, Dominici gives tacit approval to principles of family vengeance when he likens the vices to family enemies. In either case, one should not easily come to peace.

> And thus when we are in these holy days invited by Christ, we must chase away all these vices and not make peace with them. And for an example of this, let us recite a little story of a woman who had three sons and a husband . . . who had died. He being dead she took his shirt and put it to rest, thus all bloody, in the house. The boys, growing up, were requested by their friends to make peace with their enemies; and agreeing with this, they wanted to ask their mother for permission. So she took the bloodied shirt of their father and said, "When this shirt is washed and clean, then make your peace with your enemies." And because of this, they decided not to make peace. For this woman, let us understand the Holy Church. For the husband, let us understand our Lord Jesus Christ crucified. For the sons, let us understand ourselves. For the enemies, that is those who killed our father, the vices. Those who called us to peace, the demons, with whom we hold such friendship that we let them advise and guide us into their ways without thinking that they lead us to the blind pit of the wretched inferno. Therefore, when we are asked to make peace with these accursed vices that have murdered our father, we should take council with this Holy Mother Church of ours, the Wife of Jesus. And she, as you see, places before you this bloodied shirt, that is, the holy gospel of the Passion. And what does she tell you? When this shirt is washed, then make peace with them. Thus, seeing yourself mirrored in this most holy blood of Christ, never again will you make peace with these wretched vices.[38]

Obviously, Dominici intends to make a moral point about relentlessly refusing to come to peaceful terms with vice, but at the same time he implicitly sanctions the mentality that will not allow the sons to forsake vengeance.

Dominici's concerns extend as well to the realm of politics and government. He criticizes ambition and pride in those who seek office for personal gain.[39] And in a Palm Sunday sermon he explains a type of theft which occurs through negligence in government; here he uses a characteristic medieval theme of the powerful hurting the weak, and God's punishment is war.

> I say that the first manner in which one can steal is to steal through negligence. And this pertains to all those who occupy governmental and

ruling positions, those who have the wand, the beans, to render judgments, to watch over and take care of the people, their subjects; and
because of negligence, they let the poor be robbed. The less powerful
are robbed. . . . See how your princes are made, those who are put to
govern others. Just think how faithful they are to the Republic: they're
accompanied by thieves to steal. And they're supposed to protect, but
they say, "Go steal; don't be afraid, because I'll stay by your side and
I'll help you so I can fill up my purse." O, Florence has so much to weep
for, for the ones you put in ruling positions to protect the others, the
less powerful, the "poveretti" from thieves, go along with the thieves
to steal. And you want to see what God says: "See to it that the less
powerful, the widow, children, orphans, the poor, the weak, the prelates
are cared for and defended. . . ." And thus God says to such states, re-
gimes, and princes, "Don't be amazed if I cast war upon you, if I make
you persecuted, if I make you quake. For as you are a thief and increase
in evil-doing, I shall castigate you."[40]

However, as much as political critic, the preacher is also the
conscience of his society. As a Dominican preacher in the civic tradition, Giovanni Dominici left no doubt that he was speaking to his fellow Florentines about their salvation. On Ash Wednesday, 1406, he
explicitly linked being a man, being a Christian, and being a Florentine. It is through behaving as a good Florentine that one is a good
Christian; and it is the preacher's hard, thankless duty to castigate his
fellow citizens.

> Remember . . . that you are a Florentine! And if you don't want to be
> a hypocrite, look at your origin; etymology teaches it. If you look at
> your origin, you'll see that you've descended from higher to lower. O,
> thinking of this, how much you would humble yourself! Descended from
> the Romans, so noble, so flourishing [fioriti] in virtue! If you are Floren-
> tine, then make sure that you blossom [fiorischa] and that everything
> doesn't spoil. Think where flowers are. And know that one of the reasons
> Florence got its name was because this land was superabundant with
> flowers and lilies. Where are your blossomed [fiorite] works? Everything
> [is] spoiled.
>   If someone wants to kill me for telling the truth, he's welcome!
> It has been said that I am stooping to find fault with our citizens by
> talking about these vices, and that I could preach about their virtues
> as easily as about their vices. Please excuse me for this; if I chose to preach
> about the virtues of the Florentines, I just wouldn't know where to start.

But I think I know where their vices are since they stink so! So I'm telling you: You're a hypocrite; you're not a Florentine; you don't blossom [*fiorischi*]. If you're a Florentine, you must fight for the *patria,* not steal from the commune, not practice usury, not sodomize. . . .

Now you have understood what hypocricy is and if you fit that name. And if you do not feel yourself a true man, a true Christian, a true Florentine, return, return! Listen: Tonight Christ in Glory will teach you. . . . Be truly faithful, good men, good Christians, good Florentines.[41]

Dominici can be even more explicit in his civic instruction of a specifically Florentine audience. He devotes a major portion of a sermon to how the city of Florence should be counseled and governed, enumerating ways in which bad counsel occurs. "It is important for those who want good counsel to choose wise men. And those who do not feel knowledgeable and experienced — not like those children who put themselves in the council in Florence — should not let themselves be called there, or at least should not go seeking office. In the councils you need men who are older, mature, knowledgeable, and for the common good. These men would counsel well."[42] Another path to bad governance is violence against members of the council. Dominici notes that "the outcome of every council of Florence today is determined by and with this sin." And the sermon ends with this traditional civic admonition: "Therefore, whoever wants to counsel well in all things must forget himself and place all his concern with the common good."[43] A clear, ringing echo of Remigio de' Girolami a century before.

Keeping in mind the connection Dominici makes between being a Christian and being a Florentine, we can understand the importance of the preacher's characterization of Jerusalem. Yes, Florence is the New Jerusalem, but citizenship is not enough for salvation; in addition, one must belong to the Church within that city. His Palm Sunday sermon makes that point.

"Sanna filio Davit beneditti qui venit in nomine domini." The crowd cried out these words at the top of their voices. "Health to you, son of blessed David, and may he who comes in the name of the Lord be well." And as events turned out, it appears it wasn't enough to cry out with these voices to be saved; this good thought wasn't enough, for shortly

you could hear these same ones cry, "Crucify him, crucify him." And
you should note that this shouting of the people occurred in three places:
first, outside Jerusalem; second, inside Jerusalem; third, inside the temple. Neither those who cried out outside Jerusalem nor those who cried
out inside were saved. But only those who cry out inside the temple
can be saved. Jerusalem is a vision of peace. Christians cry out within
the vision of peace. But the temple of grace is necessary, for without
that you would cry out in vain.[44]

How dear must have been this vision of peace to the Florentines in the
first years of the fifteenth century, after so many years of war with the
Milanese. Dominici criticized his fellow Florentines so lavishly because
he wanted Florence to be a New Jerusalem and his fellow citizens to
cry out from within the temple and be saved.[45]

CONCLUSION

Giovanni Dominici criticized his fellow citizens as a Christian and a
Florentine. The civic tradition was quite strong and well established
within Florence's Dominican order, from Ruggiero Calcagni and Peter
Martyr in the mid-thirteenth century; to Latino Malabranca, Remigio
de' Girolami, and Giordano da Pisa in the late thirteenth and early fourteenth centuries; to Giovanni Dominici in the early fifteenth century.
Dominican civicism drew heavily on Thomistic-Aristotelian notions of
the secular bene comune as the foundation of the Christian community.
By the early fifteenth century, Dominican civicism was further enhanced
conceptually by the notion of Florence as the New Jerusalem.

Almost a century after Giovanni Dominici preached in Florence,
this vision reached its ultimate, catastrophic realization in the establishment of the New Jerusalem in Florence by the Dominican friar Girolamo
Savonarola. Savonarola himself was fully aware and proud of the Dominican civic tradition. In a sermon of 20 January 1494, he reminded
his confrères,

> You of the Order of St. Dominic who say that we ought not to busy
> ourselves with the state, you have not done your reading. Go, read in
> the chronicles of the Order of St. Dominic what he did in politics in
> Lombardy, and likewise what St. Peter Martyr did here in Florence, how

he intervened to settle and pacify this state. . . . The Cardinal Messer Latino of our order was the one who made peace between the Guelfs and the Ghibellines. St. Catherine of Siena [a great inspiration to Dominici] arranged for the peace of this state at the time of [the war with] Pope Gregory. Archbishop Antoninus, how often did he go to the palace to prevent the making of bad laws![46]

Savonarola's preaching reminds us of the longstanding marriage between Dominicanism and civicism. Of course, whereas Dominici's civicism was only lightly colored by visions of the New Jerusalem, Savonarola's was radically millenarian. Hence, he justified his peace-keeping intervention in the Florentine political crisis of 1494 by referring to the examples of his own Dominican predecessors. But from this he went further, soon identifying the goal of civic peace with the ideals of good government, constitutional reform, and revolution.[47]

By the end of the fifteenth century in Florence there was nothing new about a Dominican preaching the causes of civic peace and good government. Even the notion of the New Jerusalem, a new order, was not new. Conceptually, Savonarola simply took the next small *passo avanti*, for Giovanni Dominici and his Dominican predecessors had paved the ideological road for Savonarola's Christian-civic revolution.

NOTES

1. "Diario fiorentino di Bartolomeo di Michele. Anni 1405–1438," ed. G. O. Corazzini, in *Archivio storico italiano*, 5th Ser. 14 (1894): 241.

2. On the polemic between Salutati and Dominici, see Lidia Santamaria, "Il concetto di educazione e di cultura nel Beato Giovanni Dominici," *Memorie domenicane* 47 (1930): 14–27, 97–106, 340–52, 392–400, and 481–515; H. Dehove, "Jean Dominici," in *Dictionnaire de théologie catholique* (Paris: Librairie Letouzey et Ané, 1924), 4: cols. 1661–67; Alfredo Galletti, *L'eloquenza dalle origini al XVI secolo* (Milan: Vallardi editore, 1938); and B. L. Ullman, *The Humanism of Coluccio Salutati* (Padua: Antenore editore, 1963).

3. Giovanni Dominici, *Lucula noctis,* ed. E. Hunt (Notre Dame, Ind.: University of Notre Dame Press, 1940).

4. Some of Dominici's vernacular sermons delivered in Florence between 1400 and 1406 are extant in MS. 1301 of the Biblioteca Riccardiana in Florence (hereafter BRF 1301). These sermons were first brought to light and discussed by Alfredo Galletti in "Una raccolta di prediche volgari inedite del Cardinale Giovanni Dominici," in *Miscellanea di studi critici pubblicati in onore di Guido Mazzoni dai suoi discepoli*, ed. A. Della Torre and P. M. Rambaldi (Florence: Tipografia Galileiana, 1907), 253–78.

5. BRF 1301, fols. 42r; 20v; 22r; 23r–v and 21v.

6. Ibid., fols. 35r–v, 60r, and 94r.

7. For a full account of Dominici's educational program, see his *Regola del governo di cura familiare,* ed. Piero Bargellini (Florence: Edizione Fiorentina, 1927).

8. Robert Davidsohn, *Storia di Firenze,* 8 vols., trans. Giovanni Battista Klein and Eugenio Dupré-Theseider (Florence: Sansoni editore, 1972–73), 2:192; Archivio di Stato di Firenze (hereafter ASF), Diplomatico, Sta. Maria Novella, 8 November 1221, and 12 November 1221.

9. Stefano Orlandi, *Il VII centenario della predicazione e ricordi di S. Pietro Martire in Firenze (1245–1945)* (Florence: Edizioni Il Rosario, 1946), 3. Galletti, *L'eloquenza,* 98.

10. Davidsohn, *Storia di Firenze,* 2:407–9 and 417–28. See also ASF, Diplomatico, Sta. Maria Novella, 24 August 1245; Orlandi, *VII centenario,* 25; and idem, ed., *"Necrologio" di Sta. Maria Novella. Testo integrale dall'inizio (MCCXXXV) al MDVI,* 2 vols. (Florence: Leo S. Olschki, 1955), 1:218.

11. Marvin B. Becker, "A Study in Political Failure: The Florentine Magnates: 1280–1343," *Medieval Studies* 27 (1965): 247.

12. *La Cronica di Dino Compagni,* ed. I. del Lungo, *Rerum italicarum scriptores,* n.s. 9, no. 2 (Città di Castello: S. Lapi, 1913–16), bk. 1, chap. 3.

13. Ricordano Malaspini, *Storia fiorentina dalla edificazione di Firenze sino all'anno 1286* (Florence, 1816; anastatic reprint, Rome: Multigrafica editrice, 1976), 179.

14. Ibid., 179–80; Paolino Pieri, *Cronica di Paolino Pieri delle cose d'Italia dall'anno 1080 all'anno 1305* (Rome, 1755; anastatic reprint, Rome: Multigrafica editrice, n.d.), 43; *Cronica di Compagni,* bk. 1, chap. 3; Giovanni Villani, *Cronica,* 8 vols., ed. F. Dragomanni (Florence, 1844–46), 6:57; Davidsohn, *Storia di Firenze,* 3:214–34.

15. The Girolami had extraordinarily high representation on Florence's supreme governing body, the priorate. From the institution of the government of the Guild Priors in 1282 to 1311, the Girolami sat on the priorate twenty-one times. ASF, Manoscritti, 248 (Priorista Mariani, 1), fol. 7r; Marchionne di Coppo Stefani, *Cronaca fiorentina,* ed. Niccolò Rodolico, in *Rerum italicarum scriptores* (Città di Castello: S. Lapi, 1903), 75; Bernardino Barbadoro, ed., *Consigli della repubblica fiorentina* (Bologna: Casa editrice Zanichelli, 1920–30; anastatic reprint, Bologna: Forni, 1970–71), 696.

16. Ovidio Capitani, "L'incompiuto 'tractatus de iustitia' di fra' Remigio de' Girolami (d. 1319)," *Bulletino dell'Istituto storico italiano per il medioevo* 72 (1960): 91–134; Charles T. Davis, "An Early Florentine Political Theorist: Fra Remigio de' Girolami," *Proceedings of the American Philosophical Society* 104 (1960): 662–76; Giuseppe Briacca, "La Respublica Christiana nel pensiero di Remigio de' Girolami," *Laurentianum* 19 (1978): 199–221; G. Salvadori and V. Federici, "I sermoni d'occasione, le sequenze e i ritmi di Remigio Girolami fiorentino," in *Scritti vari di filologia a E. Monaci* (Rome: Forzani e compagnia tipografia, 1901), 455–508; Biblioteca nazionale centrale di Firenze (hereafter BNF), Conventi Soppressi, G.4.936.

17. Emilio Panella, "Per lo studio di Fra Remigio dei Girolami (d. 1319)," *Memorie domenicane,* n.s. 10 (1979): 191–92; William A. Hinnebusch, *The History of the Dominican Order,* vol. 2, *Intellectual and Cultural Life to 1500* (New York: Alba House, 1973), 165 and 170.

18. Remigio de' Girolami, *De bono communi,* in BNF, Conventi Soppressi, C.4.940, fol. 100v; Antonio Sarubbi, *Chiesa e stato communale nel pensiero di Remigio de' Girolami* (Naples: Morano, 1971), 79–80; Charles T. Davis, "Remigio de' Girolami and Dante: A Comparison of Their Conceptions of Peace," *Studi Danteschi* 36 (1959): 113; idem, "Political Theorist," 668–69.

19. Sarubbi, *Chiesa e stato comunale,* 79; Davis, "Political Theorist," 669; idem, "Remigio de' Girolami and Dante," 113.

20. Capitani, "L'incompiuto 'tractatus de iustitia' di fra' Remigio de' Girolami," 118–19. Remigio de' Girolami, *Speculum,* in BNF, Conventi Soppressi, C.4.940, fols. 146r–54r; Davis, "Political Theorist," 668.

21. On Giordano da Pisa, see Daniel R. Lesnick, "Dominican Preaching and the Creation of Capitalist Ideology in Late Medieval Florence," *Memorie domenicane,* n.s. 8–9 (1977–78): 199–247; Carlo Delcorno, *Giordano da Pisa e l'antica predicazione volgare* (Florence: Leo S. Olschki, 1975).

22. Giordano da Pisa, *Prediche inedite del B. Giordano da Rivalto dell'Ordine de' Predicatori, recitate in Firenze dal 1302 al 1305,* ed. Enrico Narducci (Bologna, 1867), 87. See also sermon delivered 10 February 1306/7 (i.e., 1306 Florentine style, 1307 modern style), in Biblioteca Medicea Laurenziana, Florence, "Acquisiti e Doni," 290:2.

23. "Statuto del Podestà," bk. 4, rub. 41, in *Statuti della repubblica fiorentina,* 2 vols., ed. Romulo Caggese (Florence: Tipografia Galileiana, 1921), 2:338.

24. For another, illuminating perspective on the connections between Christianity and the Florentine commune, see Donald Weinstein, "The Myth of Florence," in *Florentine Studies: Politics and Society in Renaissance Florence,* ed. Nicolai Rubinstein (London and Evanston, Ind.: Faber and Faber, 1968), 15–44, later revised in Weinstein's *Savonarola and Florence: Prophecy and Patriotism in the Renaissance* (Princeton, N.J.: Princeton University Press, 1970).

25. Hinnebusch, *History of the Dominican Order,* 2:369–73; Orlandi, "Necrologio," 1:148–50; 2:77–108; Antonin Mortier, *Histoire des maîtres généraux de l'Ordre des Frères Prêcheurs,* vol. 3 (Paris: Alphonse Picard, 1903), 551–80 and passim, 4:5–21, 60–67, 102–4, and passim.

26. Galletti, "Una raccolta di prediche," 256; from Ser Lapo Mazzei, *Lettere d'un notaro a un mercante del secolo XIV,* 2 vols. (Florence, 1880), 1:227–28.

27. Quoted in Iris Origo, *The Merchant of Prato* (Harmondsworth/Middlesex: Penguin Books, 1963), 280.

28. Gene Brucker, *The Civic World of Early Renaissance Florence* (Princeton, N.J.: Princeton University Press, 1977), 208; for the evolution of the Pisan role in the struggle between Florence and Milan, see 165–225.

29. *Diario fiorentino di Bartolomeo di Michele,* 241–42.

30. BRF 1301, fol. 41r–v.

31. Ibid., fols. 38r and 36r–v; 11v and 16v (for more on Dominici's apocalyptic preaching, see Galletti, "Una raccolta di prediche"; Galletti maintains that millenarianism, influenced by the Joachite tradition, is central to Dominici's preaching); 16r; and 51v.

32. Ibid., fol. 40r–v. On the mendicants' use of merchant language, see Lester K. Little, *Religious Poverty and the Profit Economy in Medieval Europe* (Ithaca, N.Y.: Cornell University Press, 1978), 197–201.

33. BRF 1301, fol. 11r.

34. Lesnick, "Dominican Preaching," 199–247.

35. Brucker, *Civic World,* 29–30.

36. BRF 1301, fols. 61r–63r.

37. Ibid., fol. 43r–v.

38. Ibid., fols. 36v–37r.

39. Ibid., fol. 20r. On the development of pride as the paramount sin in the late-medieval city, see Lester K. Little, "Pride Goes before Avarice: Social Change and the Vices in Latin Christendom," *American Historical Review* 76 (1971): 16–49. On preaching against pride in early fourteenth-century Florence, see Lesnick, "Dominican Preaching," 199–247.

40. BRF 1301, fol. 28r; for more on the misgovernment of Florence, see fols. 89v–92r.

41. Ibid., 50v–51r.

42. Ibid., fol. 90v.

43. Ibid., fols. 91v, 92r.

44. Ibid., fol. 31v.

45. On the development of the myth of Florence as the New Jerusalem, see Weinstein, *Savonarola and Florence,* 27–66.

46. Translated in ibid., 247.

47. Ibid.

Part Two

THE RELIGIOUS WORLD
OF THE LAITY

8 🙦

PENITENCE AND THE LAITY
IN FIFTEENTH-CENTURY FLORENCE

JOHN HENDERSON

As suggested in the introduction, the most characteristic form of lay spirituality in quattrocento Italy was the confraternity. In this opening chapter of
Part Two, John Henderson provides a historical and organizational outline of confraternal life, articulating its relationship to the monastic world treated in the preceding section of our book. Focusing on penitential confraternities, Dr. Henderson
reviews the theology of penitence in the Western Church and the rise of group penitential exercises among layfolk in the thirteenth, fourteenth, and fifteenth centuries.
He illustrates the structural, devotional, and liturgical parallels between confraternal
practices and the usages current in the mendicant orders, discussing as a particular
case the Compagnia di San Girolamo in Florence, dedicated to the early Christian
saint who so strongly appealed to the Renaissance imagination, St. Jerome: at once
a learned classical scholar and a Christian tormented by guilt over his love of pagan
literature.

JOHN HENDERSON is Fellow of Wolfson College, Cambridge, and director of a research
project at the University of London examining plague in early modern Europe. He
is the author of a forthcoming monograph on lay piety and charity in Renaissance
Florence, has edited a volume of essays on charity and the poor in Italy and England,
and is the author of a series of articles on religion, welfare provision for the poor,
and plague in Renaissance Italy.

ENITENCE WAS A HALLMARK of the early Christian ascetic tradition from the Desert Fathers to the Irish monks and hermits of the sixth and seventh centuries. St. Jerome, writing about his life in the wilderness, provided a particularly vivid example of a church father who favored and influenced the adoption of penitential exercises: "The fires of lust kept bubbling up before me when my flesh was as good as dead. Helpless, I cast myself at the feet of Jesus. . . . I remember how often I cried aloud all night until the break of day and ceased not from beating my breast until tranquillity returned at the chiding of the Lord."[1]

Both clergy and laity were fired by his enthusiasm and in the later Middle Ages sought to imitate him by voluntary flagellation. Although Peter Damian had encouraged the practice in his own order, among the Umbrian hermits of Fonte-Avellana, and even beyond the monastic world, it remained largely confined to the clergy until the mid-thirteenth century.[2] The rising importance of the concept of Purgatory, however, with its implicit assumption that atoning for sin in this world was preferable to suffering in the next, and the friars' promotion of the theme of the Passion of Christ, created an atmosphere conducive to the adoption of voluntary flagellation by the laity. The specific occasions were the popular religious movements, beginning with the "Alleluia" of 1233 and ending with the Bianchi of 1399–1400, and Manfredi da Vercelli's processions of 1417.[3] The event most closely associated with the practice was the so-called Movimento dei Disciplinati of 1260, when men, women, and children took to the streets of the cities first in central, and then in northern and southern Italy, bewailing their misdemeanors and doing penance for the sins of mankind.[4]

Participants in these movements, as well as the members of the *disciplinati* companies that emerged subsequently, do not appear to have been accused of taking the discipline as an end in itself, as happened with the German flagellants of 1349,[5] for this exercise was seen by the Italian clergy within the context of the system of penance defined by the contemporary Church. Giovanni dalle Celle, the late fourteenth-century Florentine prior of Santa Trinita, who later became a hermit and was himself an advocate of the spiritual benefits accruing from penitential exercises,[6] provided a fairly standard definition of penitence in the *Summa de casibus conscientiae:* "Penitence consists in mourning for our bad deeds in the past and moreover in not committing further deplorable acts. . . . Thus true penitence has three stages: contrition of the heart, confession with the mouth, and satisfaction for that which has been done."[7]

Penitence is therefore a threefold system in which the last stage—satisfaction—acts as the outward sign of the individual's decision to lead a new life. Normally "satisfaction" was imposed officially by the Church, but in the case of the confraternity, self-mortification of the flesh was voluntary. In this way members could share in the sufferings of Christ and in particular His Passion, an important *topos* of many contemporary sermons.[8] It should also be noted, however, that the central feature of the whole process of penitence was confession and sacramental ablution, which could be administered only by a priest.

It has been suggested that the adoption of voluntary flagellation by Italian confraternities derived specifically from the movement of 1260.[9] Although this may have been true in cities outside Tuscany, such as Venice, Bologna, and Perugia,[10] there is little evidence in Florence that many companies were especially founded to commemorate any of the outbreaks of popular religious fervor, with the exception of the Bianchi.[11] The gradual growth in popularity of flagellant companies in Florence can best be appreciated when seen within the context of the development of all types of devotional confraternity in the city between c. 1250 and c. 1500.[12]

Broadly speaking, there were four main types of lay company in Florence, in addition to the flagellants, and their functions require some explanation before we examine their development.[13] The so-called *laudesi* comprised the earliest type. They were founded predominantly in Central Italy from the middle of the thirteenth century in order to provide a daily evening service, at which the laity sang lauds in honor of Mary and other patron saints. The importance of this practice was that lauds were written and performed in Italian, thus providing the layman with the opportunity to understand and participate in the performance of hymns. This is a point worth emphasizing since it helps to explain the proliferation of most types of religious confraternity in the later Middle Ages. Membership enabled the laity to become involved in services, whereas previously they had been increasingly excluded, both physically—with the building of high rood screens that separated the priest from his flock—and linguistically, because Mass was conducted in Latin and therefore incomprehensible to the majority of the congregation. An indication of the extent to which the laity felt excluded is the strength of the movement that in the late thirteenth century led the friars to create a small opening in the rood screen to allow the laity to see the Elevation of the Host.[14]

In addition to the laudesi there was a second group—the large "charitable" companies—that provided the main poor-relief system in the city.[15] Indeed, charity in most southern European connurbations was provided by private rather than public means, which meant the hospital or fraternity rather than the state. In fourteenth-century Florence, although there were organizations such as the hospitals of Santa Maria Nuova and San Paolo[16] and fraternities such as the Misericordia and Bigallo, the largest philanthropic institution was the Compagnia della Madonna di Orsanmichele.[17] While it could be argued that the very title of the confraternity suggests the artificiality of our categorization—Orsanmichele originated as a laudesi company around the miraculous Madonna—both the public nature of its cult and its extensive poor-relief system served to distinguish it from any other lay society in the city in the fourteenth century.

The two types of confraternity most typical of *quattrocento* Florence were the *fanciulli,* or boys' groups, and the artisan companies. The first were founded in imitation of the adult companies and were linked particularly closely to the "night companies," to which members could graduate when they came of age.[18] The conventual model was obviously not far from the minds of the founders, with the obvious parallels between the passage from the novice to professed friar. The religious associations of artisans,[19] such as the Compagnia di Sant'Andrea of carders and washers of wool, met under the control of the trade guild, and provided devotional and social services for their members.[20] These included the celebration of masses and festivals in local parish churches, and the establishment of hospices and almshouses. This general development can be given sharper definition by examining the numbers of those confraternities known to have been active in Florence between the mid-thirteenth and the mid-fifteenth centuries.[21]

There is very little evidence concerning the existence of Florentine confraternities in the second half of the thirteenth century; only six have been traced as meeting between 1240 and 1260: four laudesi and two charitable. One hundred years later there were thirty-three companies definitely meeting within the city, of which 39 percent were laudesi, 27 percent disciplinati; 15 percent charitable; and the rest either groups of artisans or not identified by the sources as having a specific devotion. By the mid-fifteenth century, however, there had been a considerable increase in the overall number of confraternities, a total of ninety-six are recorded. Moreover, it must be remembered that this figure is only a minimum estimate; other companies may easily have existed but have left no traces. By far the largest number of companies were flagellants. Of all confraternities active in Florence in the mid-quattrocento, 47 percent were either identifiable as flagellants from their statutes or were described as such by Antoninus in his list of companies participating in the procession for the Festival of St. John the Baptist in June 1454.[22] On the other hand, there was no increase in the actual number of laudesi or charitable groups, so that their proportion of the total dropped to 13 percent and 5 percent, respectively. The numbers of the other types had increased, however, with boys' clubs now forming 9 percent of the total, trade groups 13 percent, and the function of the rest was unidentified.

If we take this pattern of foundations as a measure of the appeal of confraternities, we can make two general observations. First, their popularity continued to grow from the second half of the fourteenth century so that by the middle of the *quattrocento* there were at least 100 in Florence. This pattern is contrary to what might be expected from a purely demographic point of view, considering that the population of Florence had shrunk by two-thirds between 1340 and 1440, from more than 100,000 to between 37,000 and 40,000, so that an even higher percentage of Florentines must have become members.[23] Second, and more directly relevant to our theme, one is struck by the large number of flagellant groups existing by the mid-fifteenth century.

The reasons for the popularity of particular types of confraternity in a given period are not easy to explain. For example, one might have expected a sudden proliferation of the *disciplinati* rather than the *laudesi* in Florence after the 1260 movement, but apparently this did not happen. Other popular religious movements as well as wars, floods, and plagues have been held responsible for the growth in the number of confraternities.[24] Millard Meiss, for example, in his *Painting in Florence and Siena after the Black Death* (1951) suggested that the popularity of flagellation was linked to the general feeling of "fear, guilt, and sorrow" following the Black Death.[25] Jacques Chiffoleau also noted an increase in confraternities in Avignon in the second half of the fourteenth century and suggested that they provided some kind of security at a time when society was being disrupted by frequent epidemics.[26] These factors may provide some psychological explanation, but a more prosaic reason may be nearer the truth: namely, that growing numbers of Florentines joined confraternities to ensure themselves honorable burial and guaranteed commemoration of their souls.

While these theories may help to explain in a general way why lay companies multiplied in the second half of the *trecento,* neither accounts for the increased popularity of flagellants in the *quattrocento,* when epidemics became less virulent, society more stable, and there was a general increase in prosperity.[27] Perhaps more directly relevant was the influence that movements within the contemporary Church had on the religious practices of the laity.

The friars were perhaps the single most important influence on lay piety in this period. From the early thirteenth century they had encouraged not only popular religious movements but also the spread of confraternities.[28] Their influence in Florence is attested by the fact that by the mid-*quattrocento* as many as 41 percent of all fraternities in the city met in the five main friaries; equally significant for our theme is the fact that more than half of these groups were flagellants, suggesting that the friars were involved especially in promoting this devotional practice.[29] It is tempting to see the growth of the lay flagellants as parallel to and influenced by the emergence of the Observant movement within the mendicant orders of Florence. It was in the late fourteenth and early fifteenth centuries that these new friaries were established. They included San Francesco di Fiesole (1390), San Domenico di Fiesole (1406), San Hieronimo di Fiesole (1415), and San Marco (1436).[30] The

Snonavola.

lay and the conventual movements both had a common desire for moral reform and a return to a life of greater simplicity based on the direct example of Christ. Obviously one should not push this parallel too far, because confraternity members were very much part-time, but both movements appear to have been influenced by many of the same aspirations and ideals.

A particularly interesting example of the close connection between one of these new orders and a confraternity is afforded by the Hermits of St. Jerome in Fiesole and the lay Compagnia di San Jeronimo.[31] The originator of this order, Carlo da Montegranelli (a patrician like so many initiators of religious reform), distinguished himself by devotion to the penitent Jerome. According to G. M. Brocchi's *Life* of Beato Carlo, he followed the example of Jerome by penitential exercises, "affligendo il suo corpo con cilizi et flagelli",[32] and this became the hallmark of not just Montegranelli's way of life but also of his followers. By 1406 the community had grown sufficiently large for him to request and to obtain papal approbation for the rule; the "Constitutiones S. Hieronymi" were confirmed by Gregory XII in 1415.[33] Significant here is the fact that Carlo, in common with the founders of other Hieronymite orders,[34] had been a Tertiary. Although Carlo did not create a Third Order, he maintained close links with religiously minded members of the laity, in particular those of the Compagnia di San Jeronimo. This confraternity was founded by a group of Florentine merchants who came to the hermitage every Saturday evening for spiritual instruction. The company drew up its statutes in Fiesole in 1410 and then, three years later, moved its main activities to an oratory in the city, on the premises of the Ospedale di San Matteo, near where they meet today.[35]

Taking a leaf out of the Hieronymite's book, the lay *fratelli* practiced a stricter discipline than that adhered to by traditional disciplinati companies. Instead of simply attending mass for a limited part of a morning or evening, members were required to spend every alternate Saturday night together in prayers, orations, and voluntary flagellation. In direct imitation of the Hieronymite's rule, the lay brothers slept in the dormitory on straw mattresses until it was time for their second office.[36] The Compagnia di San Jeronimo was in fact the first of a small group of four or five fifteenth-century foundations—collectively known as the *compagnie della notte*—whose emphasis on a stricter penance may be seen as a lay equivalent of the reforming Observant movement among the friars. Indeed, flagellation appears to have been an activity associated particularly closely with the Hieronymite orders:[37] the founder of the Gesuati, Giovanni Colombini, arranged for himself to be whipped in public to mark his transition from the lay into the religious world,[38] while the rule of Beato Carlo's order prescribed self-mortification every day during Lent and four times a week for the rest of the year.[39] Finally, another devotional theme shared by the Observant movements and the "night companies" was a recognition of the importance of charity toward one's neighbor, a new departure for *disciplinati* groups, which had traditionally supported their own membership, rather than helping outsiders. This association between Jerome, taking the discipline, and almsgiving was taken one stage further later in the century by the Companies of Divine Love. They were founded throughout Italy to promote lay devotion and encourage charity toward the poor and particularly to establish hospitals to tend to those sick with the new "French Disease," syphilis.[40]

St. Jerome is particularly appropriate to our discussion of confraternal devotion in fifteenth-century Florence because it was in Tuscany that the image of the penitent Jerome first originated.[41] Recent studies have emphasized the close connection between the patrons of pictures showing this image and the clerical and lay circles associated with Jerome. The Avignon altarpiece by a follower of Fra Angelico (c. 1460) depicting the *Virgin and Child* accompanied by, among others, SS. Cosmos, Damian, and Jerome, and Francesco Botticini's *Penitent St. Jerome* (c. 1470), have both been linked to the Hieronomite house in Fiesole.[42] Francesco d'Antonio's *Rinieri Altarpiece* (c. 1430), on the other hand, which show the Virgin and Child with SS. John the Baptist and Jerome, has been associated with the Gesuati in Florence. The *predella* of this altarpiece is especially interesting from our point of view, because it not only includes scenes from the life of Jerome, and a representation of the ascetic founder of the Gesuati, Giovanni Colombini, but also shows a man whipping himself, thus underlining the importance of this ascetic exercise to the Hieronomite congregations and, by implication, to the associated lay companies.[43]

Art historians have also postulated connections between particular images of St. Jerome and members of the *compagnia di San Je-ronimo*. Filippino Lippi's *St. Jerome in Penitence* (1485), for example, was commissioned by a member of the Ferranti family, and Francesco di Bartolommeo Ferranti joined the *compagnia* in 1497.[44] Unfortunately, there is no evidence to connect surviving pictures with the company itself, despite the fact that, in common with other lay religious socie-ties, the compagnia di San Jeronimo must have commissioned devo-tional objects to adorn its premises. By the late fifteenth century the company had a two-floored property: an upper story consisting of a chapel with a choir, sacristy, and dormitory, and a lower floor of a room and an entrance area.[45] Each area evidently had some decoration. Thus both the choir and the dormitory had altars, and although the records do not make clear whether or not the altars had pictures associated with them, we know that the dormitory had at least a crucifix as a focus of the brothers' devotion.[46] Other images included a *fighura* of St. Jerome, as well as a panel or fresco in the choir of the Virgin Mary and St. Zenobius.[47] The premises also included a "luogo della limosina"— presumably the place from which alms were distributed—containing an appropriate image of Mary with twelve figures each carrying alms.[48] In common with other flagellant societies such as the *compagnia di San Giovanni Battista detto lo Scalzo*,[49] the compagnia di San Jeronimo also had a small courtyard that was decorated. In 1488 it commissioned for this *corticino* a series of frescoes depicting the lives of Mary Magdalene and St. Jerome, a perpetual reminder to the brothers as they entered their oratory of the need to dedicate their lives to penitence.[50] How-ever, the only surviving image of St. Jerome which can definitely be associated with the company is a miniature in their book of statutes of 1508 (Figure 8.1).[51] The saint is depicted with his usual attributes, a lion and a cardinal's hat, in a traditional posture, kneeling, half naked, with a bloody stone in his right hand with which he beats his chest in front of a crucifix. This reflects faithfully the iconography of one of the images of St. Jerome in penitence with which members of the company would have been most familiar: the Botticini altarpiece in the Hieronymite church in Fiesole.[52]

The increased popularity of the image of St. Jerome from the mid-*trecento*[53] can be attributed partly to the Bolognese canonist Gio-vanni di Andrea, who saw his mission as the promotion of the cult

Figure 8.1. *St. Jerome Penitent.* Initial letter of the 1508 statutes of the Compagnia di San Girolamo. Florence, Biblioteca Medicea Laurenziana, MS. Ashburnham 969, fol. 3r. Photo Sansoni.

of the saint. He achieved this in a number of ways: writing the *De laudibus sancti Hieronymi,* encouraging the foundation of churches and chapels dedicated to Jerome, and commissioning a fresco cycle of the life of the saint on the façade of his house.[54] In tracing the connection between the cult of Jerome and the confraternity, it is significant that Giovanni was not a cleric but a layman. In the early fifteenth century, the saint was adopted by humanists, from Ambrogio Traversari to Lorenzo Valla and Angelo Poliziano,[55] who saw Jerome as leading the way in the rediscovery of ancient patristic texts. Furthermore, just as the confraternity provided the channel through which the cult of the penitent Jerome was popularized among the laity, so these companies provided the means through which his penitential nature was linked to his role as a scholar. The meetings of Florentine companies had long served as occasions for the delivery of sermons by the laity and it was only a short step for confraternities to become, in the fifteenth century, centers in which budding humanists could practice their oratorical skills. In this way, Giovanni Nesi, Alamanno Rinuccini, and Bartolomeo Scala gained early experience in giving orations, and, as Kristeller has pointed out, it was also the confraternity that provided the model for Ficino's Platonic Academy.[56]

The specific connection between St. Jerome the scholar and the world of the devout layman is again provided by those confraternities that took him as their patron saint. In Florence there were two such companies,[57] but the compagnia di San Jeronimo of the Ospedale di San Matteo is the best documented. One member, the humanist Donato Acciauioli, clearly illustrates this connection; as his biographer, Vespasiano da Bisticci, noted, "He gave wonderful exhortations" to the assembled members during their "office" of flagellation.[58] His particular interest in penitence is, moreover, attested by Bartolommeo della Fonte's dialogue "Donato seu de Poenitentia," which may have originated as one of the "exhortations" delivered to the confraternity, and also by Donato's own "Orazione del Corpo di Cristo," delivered before the compagnia de' Magi in 1468.[59] In both these pieces, penance was seen as an individual rather than a collective expression, coming from within rather than being imposed externally by a priest. While this view has been interpreted as an expression of an Italian *devotio moderna,*[60] one should also bear in mind that contemplative, individualistic

devotions had long been encouraged in the practices of traditional confraternities. Statutes do prescribe collective activities but they also reiterate constantly the necessity for each member to undertake a daily
round of religious devotions to develop his or her own spiritual health,
a practice fortified by the emergence of a whole genre of devotional
manuals for the laity. Antoninus's *Opera a ben vivere,* composed for Dianora Tornabuoni, and his confessional *Specchio di scoscientia,* were among
two of the most popular in quattrocento Florence.[61]

Although Donato's view of penance has been represented as
novel because he underlined the importance of the individual's state of
mind and spirit rather than the presence of the priest, it is worth emphasizing that those confraternities to which Donato belonged and to
which he delivered his Eucharistic sermons remained very much under
the shadow of the Church and cannot be seen as part of an independent, lay movement divorced from the clergy. The *compagnia di San
Jeronimo,* for example, not only could boast of archbishops and cardinals
as honorary members, but also employed eight friars and canons, including in 1410 Fra Carlo di Montegranelli, to perform moral, spiritual,
and sacramental functions within the company.[62] Perhaps, though, the
dependence of the confraternity on the ecclesiastical model can be understood best by seeing how clearly the ceremonies of the flagellant companies were based on the liturgy of the Church.[63]

Services were envisaged normally in pairs, either twice every
fortnight or twice a month.[64] At the first service, members disciplined
themselves, and at the second, they sang orations and were then corrected for their misdemeanors. The division underlines the fact that
flagellation was regarded as a stage in their devotion, in the same way
that the liturgical cycle passed from the days of suffering to the days
of joy: the capture, trial, and crucifixion of Christ to His Resurrection
and Ascension. The same pattern is found in the whole of the disciplinati's liturgical calendar, with particular emphasis on the events leading
up to and including Easter Week.

Although there was a basic distinction between the two main
flagellant ceremonies, they also had many similarities because they shared
a common model. They were both based on the Divine Office: the evening service on Compline and the morning on Matins.[65] The former
consisted of a series of orations, psalms, and litanies. It began with a

greeting to the Virgin Mary and was followed by the general confession and the *Oration of St. Raphael*. After invoking the intercession of their patron, the Seven Penitential Psalms led the brothers toward the "office" of flagellation. The governor then delivered a short sermon on penitence to prepare the members for the high point of the service. The candles were now snuffed and the oratory plunged into darkness. This action had both a dramatic and symbolic meaning, for the extinguishing of the lights recalled the darkness which had fallen on earth at the moment of Christ's crucifixion.[66] The brothers were encouraged to share in His suffering by a series of Psalms. The whole service is outlined in some detail in the late fifteenth-century statute of the Compagnia dell'Assumptione:

> The lights are put out and then they say the Stanza of the Passion. And then a few words are said on the brevity of life, accompanied by an exhortation to the brothers to do well. Then a period of silence follows, after which the brothers whip themselves for the space of time it takes to say five Pater Nosters and Ave Marias. Then they say more prayers followed by the psalm *Miserere Mei Deus* or the *De Profundis Clamavi* . . . And then they get dressed again and . . . sing more psalms, lauds, and hymns.[67]

Emphasis was therefore placed upon the misery and brevity of human life and the necessity of doing penance for the good of the members' souls. The "office" of flagellation was relatively brief. It did not continue throughout the service, but occupied a central position around which the rest of the ceremony was organized. This was also true of the organization of their other services on feast days.

The flagellants' liturgical year was not very different from that of the Florentine church itself, just as the services were based very closely on the Mass. In addition to their weekly or fortnightly meetings, members attended ceremonies on all the main feast days associated with Christ, Mary, the Apostles, and locally venerated saints, such as John the Baptist, Lawrence, and Zanobius.[68] Each company also celebrated the festivals of their patrons, many of whom, appropriately, were martyrs. The second most popular feast for many flagellants was Marian, and special emphasis was placed on Purification or Candlemas, which had always been associated with the penitential procession.[69] Holy Week was, how-

ever, the most important period during the year, because it forcibly
reminded the members that their voluntary discipline was undertaken
in commemoration of Christ's crucifixion. They were required to attend services at the company oratory on Holy Thursday as well as on
Wednesday or Friday evening. But Easter Day they all took communion
in their local parish church. In this way the brothers were reminded
that the membership of a confraternity did not exempt them from basic
duties to their parish, duties that had been emphasized by a series of
Church councils and even more recently by Antoninus as archbishop
of Florence.[70]

Holy Week celebrations for many companies began on Wednesday after the office had been completed in church. It was a simple
ceremony, but prepared the members for the days to come by incorporating into their normal evening service both a sermon of penitence
and the "office" of flagellation. A sermon delivered by Giovanni Nesi
in one company during Holy Week demonstrates how the members
were led to dwell on Christ's suffering:

> Behold that true life . . . who [in order] today to destroy our eternal
> death, sustains the most cruel death; considering that He suffered in every
> part [of His body] from His head to His feet. In as much as His most
> holy head was [wounded by] sharp thorns, the brightest eyes by a blind-
> fold, the mellifluous mouth by the bitterest bile, the resplendent face
> by bloody sweat, the weak shoulders by the heaviest weight of the cross,
> the most sacred breast with a sharp lance, and the innocent hands and
> the immaculate feet with pointed nails, and finally all His precious body
> with the sharpest of beatings.[72]

By being asked to contemplate each detail of Christ's Passion,
the brothers were brought gradually to a sense of their own worthless-
ness and the need to atone for their sins by sharing in "the sharpest
of beatings."

Maundy Thursday was the real center of these companies' devotion, for it included the scene from the Last Supper, when Christ had
demonstrated His true humility by debasing Himself before His disciples and washing their feet. Although the service at each company
was essentially the same, there were variations in the order of the parts.
Many of these ceremonies were divided into three sections.[73] The first

established the theme, for as members arrived, one of them recited a passage from the Passion. Although the statutes do not make clear which was selected, it was probably Matthew 27:29–31, the description of Christ's humiliation by the soldiers. Then the office itself was introduced by the penitential psalms, which figured prominently in their regular services. At this point, as in the Tenebrae,[74] candles were blown out gradually, one at the end of each psalm, flagellation followed the Benedictus, and more verses of the Passion were read. After dressing, each member walked around the oratory asking his brother's forgiveness. Preparations were then made for the central feature of the ceremony: the *governatore* knelt down in front of each brother and washed and kissed his feet. Afterward they all sat down to a commemorative meal. Many of the same elements from their normal office are incorporated into this service. The main difference is the literal enactment of the verses from John 13:1–16, which describe the events of the Last Supper. The passage from the Gospel was read aloud during the ceremony and guided members as they went through their imitation of Christ's actions.[75]

Each one of these ceremonies indicated the extent to which the laity had become involved in paraliturgical ceremonies. Even the head of the company, the *governatore,* who acted as Christ in the *lavanda,* was a layman. In this way, members went far beyond their normal, passive role in the Church and participated fully in services. This had been impossible, of course, under normal circumstances, particularly in the mendicant churches with their high rood screens. Voluntary flagellation was, moreover, a very special devotion, for it imitated directly the penitential exercises of the monks and friars themselves. It can indeed be seen as tangible evidence of the effect on the laity of the preoccupation with the Passion of Christ in contemporary theology as reflected particularly in the sermons of the friars.

NOTES

All manuscripts, unless otherwise indicated, are from the Archivio di Stato di Firenze.

1. J. Labourt, ed., *Saint Jérôme. Lettres* (Paris: Société d'edition, Les Belles Lettres, 1949), 1:117–18.

2. In general, see L. Gougaud, *Devotional and Ascetic Practices in the Middle Ages* (London: Burns, Oates, and Washbourne, 1927), 179–204, and J. Leclercq, "La flagellazione volontaria nella tradizione spirituale dell occidente," in *Il Movimento dei Disciplinati nel settimo centenario dal suo inizio (Perugia-1260),* Appendix 9 to *Bollettino della Deputazione di storia patria per l'Umbria* (Spoleto, 1962), 73–83 (hereafter *Il Movimento*).

3. On these movements, see V. Fumagalli, "In margine all' 'Alleluia' del 1233," *Bollettino dell'Istituto storico italiano per il medioevo e archivio muratoriano* (hereafter *BISI*) 80 (1969): 257–72; G. P. Tognetti, "Sul moto dei Bianchi nel 1399," *BISI* 78 (1967): 205–343. On Manfredi da Vercelli, see R. Creytens, "Manfred de Verceil O.P. et son traité contre les fraticelles," *Archivum Fratrum Praedicatorum* (hereafter *AFP*) 2 (1941): 173–208; R. Rusconi, "Fonti e documenti su Manfredi da Vercelli O.P. ed il suo movimento penitenziale," *AFP* 47 (1977): 51–107, and "Note sulla predicazione di Manfredi da Vercelli O.P. e il movimento penitenziale dei terziari manfredini," *AFP* 48 (1978): 93–135.

4. See *Il Movimento; Risultati e prospettive della ricerca sul Movimento dei Disciplinati* (Perugia: Deputazione di storia patria per l'Umbria, 1972); and J. Henderson, "The Flagellant Movement and Flagellant Confraternities in Central Italy, 1260–1400," *Studies in Church History* 15 (1978): 147–60.

5. E. Deprez and G. Mollat, *Clement VI (1342–52): Lettres closes, patentes, et curiales intéressant les pays autres que la France, publiées ou analysées d'après les registres du Vatican* (Paris: E. de Boccard, 1960), 1:291–92; N. Cohn, *The Pursuit of the Millennium* (London: Paladin, 1970), 140.

6. On Giovanni dalle Celle, see P. Cividali, "Il beato Giovanni dalle Celle," *Memorie della R. Accademia dei Lincei, classe di scienze morali,* 5th ser., 12 (1906): 354–477; E. F. Rice, *Saint Jerome in the Renaissance* (Baltimore: Johns Hopkins University Press, 1985), 71–72.

7. This is Giovanni's Italian translation of Bartolomeo da S. Concordio's *Summa de casibus conscientiae* and is quoted in E. Delaruelle, P. Ourilac, and G. Labande, *Storia della Chiesa: Dalle origini ai Nostri Giorni,* trans. G. Alberigo (Turin: Editrice, S.A.I.E., 1971), 14:2, 842.

8. In general, see J. Moorman, *A History of the Franciscan Order from Its Origins to the Year 1517* (Oxford: Clarendon Press, 1968), 399–400; G. Ginzburg, "Folklore, magia e religione," in *Storia d'Italia* (Turin: Einaudi, 1972), 1:621–32.

9. G. G. Meersseman, "Disciplinati e penitenti nel duecento," *Il Movimento,* 59.

10. B. S. Pullan, *Rich and Poor in Renaissance Venice: The Social Institutions of a Catholic State to 1620* (Oxford: Basil Blackwell, 1971), 37–38; A. Gaudenzi, ed., "Statuti delle società del popolo di Bologna," in *Fonti per la storia d'Italia* (Rome: 1896), 4:425; R. Grüeze, "Le confraternite di Sant'Agostino, S. Francesco e S. Domenico di Perugia: origini, profilo storico e attrezature teatrali," *Il Movimento,* 597.

11. R. F. W. Weissman, *Ritual Brotherhood in Renaissance Florence* (New York: Academic Press, 1982), 73–74. The "Bianchi" companies in Florence are listed in J. Henderson, *Piety and Charity in Early Renaissance Florence* (forthcoming), appendix I, nn. 25–28, 50, 51, 58, 84, 86, 93, 109.

12. On confraternities in Florence, see: Weissman, *Ritual Brotherhood,* Henderson, *Religion and Society,* and the many publications of Massimo Papi, including "Confraternite ed ordini mendicanti a Firenze: Aspetti di una ricerca quantitativa," *Mélanges de l'école française de Rome: Moyen âge, temps modernes* (hereafter *Mélanges*) 89 (1977): 723–32. On the Florentine *contado,* see C. de La Roncière, "La place des confréries dans l'encadrement religieux du contado florentin: L'example de la Val d'Elsa," *Mélanges* 85 (1973): 31–77, 633–71.

13. On the Florentine *laudesi,* see Henderson, *Religion and Society,* chap. 2; on their musical performance, see F. A. D'Accone, "Le compagnie dei laudesi in Firenze durante l'Ars Nova," *L'Ars Nova italiana del trecento* (Certaldo: Centro di studi sull'Ars Nova italiana del trecento, 1970), 1:253–80; and idem, "Alcune note sulle compagnie fiorentine dei laudesi durante il Quattrocento," *Rivista italiana di musicologia* 10 (1975): 86–114, as well as Cyrilla Barr's forthcoming monograph.

14. On the choir screen in Florence, see M. B. Hall, *Renovation and Counter-Reformation: Vasari and Duke Cosimo in Sta. Maria Novella and Sta. Croce* (Oxford: Oxford University Press, 1979); Acta Generalia, 1249: *Monumenta Ordinis Fratrum Praedicatorum Historica* (Rome/Louvain, 1896), 3:47.

15. For a survey of charitable institutions in Florence, see Henderson, *Religion and Society,* chaps. 7–9, and studies of specific companies include: R. C. Trexler, "Charity and the Defense of the Urban Elites in the Italian Communes," in F. Jaher, ed., *The Rich, the Well Born, and the Powerful: Elites and Upper Classes in History* (Urbana: University of Illinois Press, 1973), 64–109; A. Spicciani, "The 'Poveri vergognosi' in Fifteenth-Century Florence: The First 30 Years' Activity of the Buonomini di S. Martino," in T. Riis, ed., *Aspects of Poverty in Early Modern Europe* (Stuttgart: Klett-Cotta, 1981), 119–82; and J. Henderson, "The Parish and the Poor in Florence at the Time of the Black Death: The Case of S. Frediano," in Henderson, ed., *Charity and the Poor in Medieval and Renaissance Europe,* in *Continuity and Change* 3 (1988): 247–72.

16. There have been few studies of Florentine hospitals since L. Passerini, *Storia degli stabilmenti di beneficenza ed istruzione elementare gratuita della città di Firenze* (Florence, 1853), though see R. A. Goldthwaite, W. R. Rearick,"Michelozzo and the Ospedale di S. Paolo in Florence," in *Mitteilungen des Kunsthistorischen Institutes in Florenz* 21 (1977): 221–306, and J. Henderson, "The Hospitals of Late-Medieval Florence: A Preliminary Survey," in *The Hospital in History,* ed. L. Granshaw, R. Porter (London: Routledge, 1989): 63–92.

17. S. La Sorsa, *La compagnia d'Orsanmichele ovvero una pagina della beneficenza in Toscana nel secolo XIV* (Trani: V. Vecchi, 1902); Henderson, *Piety and Charity,* chaps. 6–8, and the forthcoming monograph by Diane Zervas on the building of the palace.

18. On the *fanciulli* companies, see R. C. Trexler, "Ritual in Florence: Adolescence and Salvation in the Renaissance," *The Pursuit of Holiness in Late Medieval and Renaissance Religion,* ed. C. Trinkaus with H. A. Oberman (Leiden: E. J. Brill, 1974), 200–264; and idem, *Public Life in Renaissance Florence* (New York, Academic Press, 1980), 370–87. For the compagnie della notte, see C. C. Calzolai, "S. Antonino e le 'Buche'," *S. Antonino* 5 (1958): 9–11, and J. Henderson, "Le confraternite religiose di Firenze del tardo medioveo: patroni spirituali e anche politici?," *Ricerche storiche* 15 (1985): 90–91.

19. Considered briefly by both Trexler, *Public Life,* 408, 411–14; and Weissman, *Ritual Brotherhood,* 63–66, 201–5.

20. The 1454 statutes of the *Compagnia di Sant'Andrea* are in Compagnie Religiose Soppresse (hereafter CRS), Capitoli 854.

21. The statistics that follow are based on Henderson, *Piety and Charity.*

22. Signoria e Balìa, Carte di Corredo 45, fol. 18v.

23. D. Herlihy and C. Klapisch-Zuber, *Les Toscans et leurs familles* (Paris: Presses de la fondation nationale des sciences politiques, 1978), 173–77; available in English as *Tuscans and Their Families: A Study of the Florentine Catasto of 1427* (New Haven, Conn.: Yale University Press, 1985).

24. L. Mehus, *Dell'origine, progresso, abusi e riforma delle confraternite laicali* (Florence, 1785), 125–34; and G. M. Monti, *Le confraternite medioevali dell'alta e media Italia* (Venice: La Nuova Italia, 1927), 1:292.

25. M. Meiss, *Painting in Florence and Siena after the Black Death: The Arts, Religion, and Society in the Mid-Fourteenth Century,* 3rd ed. (New York: Harper and Row, 1973), 80–81.

26. J. Chiffoleau, *La comptabilité de l'au-delà: Les hommes, la mort et la religion dans la region d'Avignon à la fin du Moyen Age (vers 1320–vers 1480)* (Rome: École française de Rome, 1980), 285–86.

27. For an excellent general survey of the development of the Florentine economy in the fifteenth century, see G. A. Goldthwaite, *The Building of Renaissance Florence: An Economic and Social History* (Baltimore: Johns Hopkins University Press, 1980), chap. 1.

28. On this theme, see Henderson, "Flagellant Movement," 147–60, and idem, "Confraternities and the Church in Late Medieval Florence," in *Voluntary Religion,* ed. W. J. Sheils and D. Wood (Oxford: Ecclesiastical History Society/Basil Blackwell, 1986), 69–83.

29. Henderson, *Piety and Charity,* chap. 2, table 2.2.

30. J. Moorman, *A History of the Franciscan Order from Its Origins to the Year 1517* (Oxford: Clarendon Press, 1968), 373; S. Orlandi, *S. Antonino: Arcivescovo di Firenze, dottore della Chiesa* (Florence: Olschki, 1959–60), 373; *Bullarum diplomatum et privilegiorum sanctorum Romanorum Pontificum* (Rome, 1859), 4:653–54; Orlandi, *S. Antonino,* 2:55–56.

31. This connection was noted by M. Meiss, "Scholarship and Penitence in the Early Renaissance: The Image of St. Jerome," *Pantheon* 22 (1974): 137–38, and developed further by B. Ridderbos, *Saint and Symbol: Images of St. Jerome in Early Italian Art* (Groningen: Bouma's Boekhuis, 1984), 75–87; see also E. Rice, "St. Jerome's 'Vision of the Trinity': An Iconographical Note," *Burlington Magazine* 125 (1983): 151–55.

32. G. M. Brocchi, *Vite de' Santi e Beati Fiorentini* (Florence, 1761), 196.

33. Rice, *Saint Jerome in the Renaissance,* 70; Ridderbos, *Saint and Symbol,* 73–74.

34. P. Hélyot, *Dictionnaire des ordres religieux ou histoire des ordres monastiques, religieux et militaires* (Paris, 1849), 2:602.

35. Their early history is outlined in the prologue to their statutes of 1508: Biblioteca Laurenziana, Florence, Ashburnham 969, fol. 4r–v.

36. Their fifteenth-century "office" is described in their 1410 statutes: Biblioteca nazionale centrale di Firenze (hereafter BNCF), Magl. XXXII. 43, chap. 6, fol. 7r–v; the straw mattresses are mentioned in Vespasiano da Bisticci's "Vita di Donato Acciaiuoli," in *Le vite,* ed. E. Greco (Florence: Istituto nazionale di studi sul Rinascimento, 1976), 2:23; and on the rule of the Hieronymites, see Rice, *Saint Jerome in the Renaissance,* 73.

37. On the evolution of the various Hieronymite orders, see Rice, *Saint Jerome in the Renaissance,* 68–83.

38. Meiss, "Scholarship and Penitence," 138.

39. *Codex regulorum monasticorum et canonicarum,* ed. L. Holsten and M. Brockie (Vienna, 1759), 6:89–90; Rice, "St. Jerome's 'Vision of the Trinity'," 151n.1.

40. For the Companies of Divine Love, see P. Paschini, "Le Compagnie del Divino Amore e la beneficenza pubblica nei primi decenni del cinquecento," in *Tre ricerche sulla storia della Chiesa nel cinquecento* (Rome: Edizioni liturgiche, 1945). See also A. Carlino, "L'Arciconfraternità di San Girolomo della Carità: L'origine e l'ideologia assistenziale," *Archivio della società romana di storia patria* 107 (1984): 275–306.

41. Meiss, "Scholarship and Penitence", 134. On this theme, see Ridderbos, *Saint and Symbol,* 63–88; and Rice, *Saint Jerome in the Renaissance,* 75–83.

42. Meiss, "Scholarship and Penitence," 135–36; the author of the first is known as the Master of the Buckingham Palace Madonna; both paintings are in the Musée du Petit Palais, Avignon: see Rice, *Saint Jerome in the Renaissance,* 99–100.

43. Meiss, "Scholarship and Penitence," 137–38, suggested that Girolomo de' Corboli, the patron of Castagno's *St. Jerome* fresco in SS. Annunziata, may have been a member, but Corboli's name does not appear in the company's matriculation list: Archivio della Compagnia di S. Jeronimo, Florence (hereafter ACSJ), Libro della Rassegna, 1445–66. I am grateful to Bernhard Ridderbos for informing me of the whereabouts of this archive and to the brothers for giving me permission to consult their manuscripts. On Colombini see Meiss, *Painting in Florence and Siena,* 86–88.

44. Ridderbos, *Saint and Symbol,* 77–79.

45. ACSJ, Testamenti e codicilli, 1434–1704, no. 4: "l'abitazione di sopra dove al presente è coro, sagrestia, e dormentorio . . . L'abitazione di sotto agguingendono una camera [e] . . . l'entrata di detta compagnia." This is part of the "contratto con il quale fu comprato questo santo luogo," of 6 July 1471, which was drawn up by the notary Anastasio di Ser Amerigo Vespucci, and has come down to us in a copy of 1710.

46. ACSJ, Libro dell'entrata e uscita, 1468–79, fol. 81v: "A festaiuoli . . . per una lanpana nuova chonperossi detto dì [30 September 1469] per l'altare magiore soldi tre"; and fol. 121v: "A Stefano d'Antonio dipintore sono per fare dipigniere l'altare del dormentorio dirietto al chrocifisso e per fare iiii testi de' morti in choro . . . soldi dieci."

47. Ibid., fol. 80r: "A Francesco [di Pagholo Sogliani merciaio] a dì detto [14 August 1469] per uno chandeliere nuovo . . . appie della fighura di Santo Girolomo, soldi 17 denari 8"; ibid., 1479–89, fol. 130v: "Al Antonio di Bartolomeo sargiaio per redipintura d'una Nostra Donna e un San Zanobi nel choro sopra el ghovernatore . . . lire 4"; and fol. 121v: "Spese della compagnia per fare Ia ghocciola nuova di pietra per la Vergine Maria sopralluscio del choro."

48. Ibid., 1468–79", fol. 75r: "A dì 13 di febraio [1469] . . . lire otto e soldi 12 piccioli portò Francesco del Maestro Francesco, sono per dipintura d'una tavola entrovi dipinto Nostra Donna chon 12 fighure colle limosine in mano, la quale tavola si tiene in luogho della limosina in detta compagnia."

49. Andrea del Sarto's fresco cycle of St. John the Baptist is discussed in J. Shearman, "The Chiostro dello Scalzo," *Mitteilungen des Kunsthistorischen Institutes in Florenz* 9 (1960): 206–20.

50. ACSJ, Libro dell' entata e uscita, 1479–89," 16 August 1488: "Spese di nostra chompangnia lire diciotto piccioli per loro a Antonio di Bartolomeo detto marmasso el chonpangnio per dipintura di più storie di santa Maria Maddalena e di San Girolomo, dipinta in freschco nel chorticino di nostra chompangnia." A month before, on 5 July 1488, the choir of the chapel had been whitewashed, possibly to prepare the surface for painting: ibid., fol. 130v: "A Filippo imbianchatore per fare imbianchare tutto el choro della chapella."

51. Biblioteca Laurenziana, Florence, Ashburnham 969, fol. 3r.

52. Now in the National Gallery, London.

53. The most thorough treatment is Rice, *Saint Jerome in the Renaissance,* chaps. 4 and 5, but see also Ridderbos, *Saint and Symbol,* chaps. 2 and 3.

54. Rice, *Saint Jerome in the Renaissance,* 64–68.

55. Ibid., 84–87.

56. O. Kristeller, "Lay Religious Traditions and Florentine Platonism," in *Studies in Renaissance Thought and Letters* (Rome: Edizioni di storia e letteratura, 1956), 108–11. On sermons delivered in confraternities, see the same work, 103–6; R. Hatfield, "The Compagnia de' Magi," *Journal of the Warburg and Courtauld Institutes* 33 (1970): 128–35; Weissman, *Ritual Brotherhood*, 100–104; and his article in this volume. The main collections of sermons given to Florentine confraternities are in: BNCF, Magl., Strozz. XXXV.211, and Biblioteca Riccardiana, Florence (hereafter BRF), Ricc. MS. 2204.

57. In addition to the one that met in S. Matteo there was a *compagnia di S. Girolomo* in S. Giorgio sulla Costa; see their 1491 statutes in CRS, Capitoli 81.

58. Da Bisticci, "Vita," 2:23. On Donato, see E. Garin, "Donato Acciaiuoli cittadino fiorentino," in *Medioevo e rinascimento: Studi e ricerche* (Bari: Laterza, 1954), 211–87; and M. A. Ganz, "Donato Acciaiuoli and the Medici: A Strategy for Survival in '400 Florence," *Rinascimento* 22 (1982): 33–73.

59. Discussed by C. Trinkaus, *In Our Image and Likeness: Humanity and Divinity in Italian Humanist Thought*, 2 vols. (Chicago: University of Chicago Press, 1970), 2:638–47; Garin, "Donato Acciaiuoli," 283; Ridderbos, *Saint and Symbol*, 83–84.

60. Trinkaus, *Image and Likeness*, p. 647; cf. Ginzburg, "Folklore," 631.

61. See R. Morçay, *Saint Antonin, fondateur du couvent de Saint-Marc, archevêque de Florence, 1389–1459* (Tours: A. Mame, Paris: Garibaldi, 1914), 189–93; L. Ferretti, ed., *Opera a ben vivere di S. Antonino* (Florence: Florentina, 1923). There are numerous editions of the confessional manual, e.g., *Specchio di sconscientia* (Bologna, 1472).

62. See ACSJ, "Catalogo de' Fratelli dal 1410 al 1843," and the 1508 statutes, chap. 3, fols. 8v–9r.

63. For further discussion see Henderson, *Piety and Charity*, chap. 4, and C. Barr, "Lauda Singing and the Tradition of the *disciplinati* Mandato: A Reconstruction of Two Texts of the Office of Tenebrae," *L'Ars Nova italiana del trecento* (Certaldo: Centro di studi sull'Ars Nova italiana del trecento, 1978), 4:21–44; and Weissman, *Ritual Brotherhood*, 90–104.

64. See the following: the 1470 statutes of the Compagnia di S. Domenico in Sta. Maria Novella: G. G. Meersseman, *Ordo Fraternitatis: Confraternite e pietà dei laici nel medioevo (Italia sacra: Studi i documenti di storia ecclesiastica, 24–26)* (Rome: Herder, 1977), chap. 7:733; the late fifteenth-century statutes of the Compagnia di Sta. Maria in Sta. Maria Soprarno: BRF, Ricc. MS. 2382, chap. 7, fol. 5r–v; the 1410 statutes of the Compagnia di S. Jeronimo in the Hospital of S. Matteo: BNCF, Magl. XXXII.43, chap. 2, fol. 3r; and the statutes of the Compagnia di S. Jacopo in S. Jacopo Soprarno: Archivio della Compagnia di S. Jacopo, Statuti, chap. 1, fol. 7r.

65. Barr, "Lauda Singing," 24, 26.

66. Description based on the 1456 statutes of the *Compagnia di S. Giovanni Battista detto lo Scalzo:* BRF, Ricc. MS. 2535, chap. 13, fol. 9r–v.

67. BRF, Ricc. MS. 2566, chap. 7, fol. 7v: "Si spenghino e lumi e dichino la *Stanza della Passione*. E di poi si dica alquante parole sulla brevità [della vita], exortando e fratelli a ben fare. Poi si tengha silenzio, facendo disciplina per spazio di dire cinque *Pater Nostri* e *Ave Maria*. Poi si faccino le prece e quelle facte si dicha el psalmo *Miserere mei Deus* overo *De Profundis Clamavi* . . . E di poi si rivesti e facciasi una rachomandigia overamente si chanti psalmi, laude e hymni."

68. Lists of festivals are found in, e.g., the 1454 statutes of the Compagnia di Gesù Pellegrino: P. Ferrato, ed., *I capitoli della Compagnia di Gesù Pellegrino* (Padua, 1871), chap. 30: 27; the early fifteenth-century statutes (undated) of the Compagnia di S. Niccolò in Sta. Maria del Carmine: CRS, Capitoli 439, chap. 4, fol. 2r–v; and the 1470 statutes of the Compagnia di S. Domenico: Meersseman, *Ordo fraternitatis*, chap. 7:735–37.

69. *Butler's Lives of the Saints*, ed. H. Thurston and D. Attwater (London: Burns and Oates, 1956), 1:234.

70. On relations between the Florentine church and confraternities, see Henderson, "Confraternities and the Church," 69–83.

71. Meersseman, *Ordo fraternitatis*, chap. 7:737: "uno sermone esortatorio a penitentia."

72. O. Pugliese, "Two Sermons by Giovanni Nesi and the Language of Spirituality in Late Fifteenth-Century Florence," *Bibliotèque d'humanisme et Renaissance* 42 (1980): 648: "Ecco quella vera vita. . . . che per destrugger oggi la nostra etherna morte, sostenne crudelissima morte, considerato che dal capo a' piedi in lui ciaschuna parte patì. Imperochè il sanctissimo suo capo da pungenti spine, i lucentissimi ochi da obscurante benda, la melliflua boccha da amarissimo fiele, la resplende faccia da sanguigno sudore, le debile spalle del gravissimo peso della croce, il sacratissimo pecto dalla acuta lancia, le innocente mani et gli immaculati piedi da spuntati chiovi et finalmente tutto il suo pretioso corpo da asprissime battiture."

73. Based on the 1476 statutes of the *compagnia di S. Giovanni Battista tra le Arcore:* CRS 1214, chap. 14, fols. 19r–20v.

74. Barr, "Lauda Singing," 28–29.

75. Ibid., 28–31.

9 &

SACRED ELOQUENCE

Humanist Preaching and Lay Piety in Renaissance Florence

RONALD F. E. WEISSMAN

THE EMERGING PICTURE of a reciprocity between Renaissance humanism and the age-old religious matrix here achieves sharp focus. In this chapter, Ronald F. E. Weissman discusses the leading role played by fifteenth-century humanists in Florentine confraternal life, and particularly in lay preaching. He underlines the traditional character of their sermons and the evidence of their heartfelt personal piety, while at the same time pointing toward the shift in meaning which inevitably occurred when men familiar with the original Platonic texts undertook to speak in a Christian theological and devotional idiom itself shot through with late antique Neoplatonism. In the parallel suggested between confraternal association and the academies of classical antiquity, moreover, the flexibility of Renaissance lay spirituality becomes clear. Indeed, the corporate aspects of confraternal life are richly apparent in this chapter. Professor Weissman's descriptions of the liturgical observances of Florentine confraternities complement those in the preceding chapter and, together with the passages from humanist sermons he cites, are a sharp corrective to Burckhardt's view of Renaissance Catholicism as "subjective . . . an affair of the individual and his own conscience."

RONALD F. E. WEISSMAN teaches history at Brown University. His publications include a fundamental work for the study of confraternities, *Ritual Brotherhood in Renaissance Florence* (1982).

INCE WORLD WAR II, scholars of early modern European history have studied religion as behavior to be observed or meanings to be interpreted. The older, ecclesiastically derived dichotomy of *religion* and *superstition*[1] has been replaced by newer contrasts between lay religion and clerical religion, or learned and popular religion. Renaissance historians have followed two distinct traditions in the study of religion, traditions that appear quite similar to the "learned" and "popular" dichotomy. Some historians, following a tradition that has made *humanism* inseparable from *Renaissance,* have sought to locate religion in the formal theology and philosophy of humanist intellectuals. Other historians have located Renaissance religion in lay practice and behavior, particularly in organized rituals and devotional life, charity, and the cult of the saints, many of which have been studied together as components of the spirituality of such groups as confraternities. It is unfortunate that few historians have examined the extent to which confraternal and humanist piety emanated from the same moral and spiritual world. In the discussion that follows, I attempt to interrelate these two central facets of Renaissance Christianity.

At first glance, it appears that middle-class confraternal piety and learned spirituality represented quite distinct modes of religious experience, especially when viewed retrospectively through a familiar Erasmian or Protestant terminology stressing the superiority of "interior" to "exterior" spirituality.[2] Where humanism, especially its late fifteenth-century variety, stressed human dignity and so-called interior piety, the spirituality of confraternities was ceremonially oriented and theocentric, not glorifying man, but instead, in full embrace of a penitential piety, condemning man's sinful and weakened condition.

At the same time, however, important similarities existed. As did middle-class elites, so intellectual elites, too, sought to organize themselves into groups, first informally, around teachers and friendships, and ultimately, by the mid-fifteenth century, more consciously into academies such as that precursor of the Platonic Academy, the Florentine Academy, which, founded by Alamanno Rinuccini, served within a short time of its creation as an Aristotelian gathering place for Giovanni Argyropoulous and his students.[3] In a world in which obligation was as much personal, inhering in relations between real men, as it was intellectual, inhering in vague notions of "mankind" in general, lay religious associations and intellectual circles alike spent much energy cultivating brotherhood, friendship, and *amore* through rites and ceremonies. Both groups made substantial contributions to religious culture, the humanists by producing a large body of moral and theological dialogues, treatises, poems, and letters; confraternal groups by producing *laude*, sacred hymns that, by the fifteenth century, were well on their way to becoming theater.

In addition, both groups delivered sacred orations. Lay sermons recited by an officer, a member, or an invited guest had been a confraternal tradition throughout Italy since the thirteenth century, when Arnold of Brescia delivered sermons to a fraternity of Genoese lawyers and notaries.[4] Like confraternities, both the Florentine and Platonic academies held banquets and were entertained by sacred orations. Marsilio Ficino himself encouraged the development of sacred and secular oratory. He frequently referred to his own moral letters as sermons, with which form they shared much.[5] In 1473, for example, he chose five of his disciples to write orations urging war against the Turks. He delivered moral sermons to the Platonic Academy and to the broader community; in addition to preaching at Santa Maria degli Angeli, there is also evidence that he gave sermons to the Confraternity of the Magi.[6]

Whether or not Ficino preached before the Magi, the sacred oratory of intellectuals was certainly not an unusual occurrence in quattrocento Florence. More than fifty late fifteenth-century confraternity sermons survive, written and recited by intellectuals who were or would soon become Florence's most distinguished men of letters.[7] The sermons discussed here were delivered to at least eight and probably more confraternities of adolescents and adults, including the Magi, Sant'Antonio da Padova, San Niccolò del Ceppo, the Nativity, San Vincenzo, and San Domenico. With the exception of two of Alamanno Rinuccini's brief sermons welcoming new brothers into the Magi, the sermons date from the late 1460s through the mid-1480s—no accident, one supposes, because it was not until this time that restrictions on the participation of the Florentine elite in the city's confraternities were relaxed.[8] One also assumes that Ficino's example of preaching to the academy had no small role to play in the interest and willingness of his friends and students to engage in *oratoria sacra* and to make permanent collections of such oratory, since most of the surviving sermons were given by his students and friends.

Ficino's disciples formed the core group of orators. The surviving sermons include seven by Giovanni Nesi, protégé of another confraternity orator, Donato Acciaiuoli, student of Ficino, follower of Pico, and avid Savonarolian.[9] Poliziano contributed three to a "compagnia di dottrina." Francesco Berlinghieri, student of Argyropoulous, Landino, and Ficino, Platonic Academy member, and Rinuccini's immediate predecessor as one of the four governors of the Florentine *Studio,* wrote three sermons. Other speakers who were also academicians and students of Ficino included Piero di Marco Parenti, Filippo Carducci, Bernardo Canigiani, Giovanni di Donato Cocchi, and Pierfilippo Pandolfini, the last a friend of Rinuccini, Acciaiuoli, and Nesi, and a defender of the hermetic tradition.[10]

Speakers tied to the circle of academicians also included Bernardo d'Alamanno de'Medici, an interlocutor in Nesi's *De Moribus* and a recipient of Nesi's love poetry,[11] and Giorgio Antonio Vespucci, disciple of Ficino and witness to his will, a member of Landino's circle, and a man of deep religious sentiment. In 1497 Vespucci was admitted to San Marco by Savonarola and was personally garbed in his Dominican robes by Fra Girolamo. Another three sermons on penance were delivered by Bartolomeo Scala, a man so respected by Ficino that the Platonist sent him a copy of his translation of the *Symposium,* requesting prepublication comments. While it is unclear which confraternities were addressed by Scala, he was a regular member of Florentine confraternities and an officer of the Company of Sant'Agnese, a group closely allied with the Medici.[12]

The students of Argyropoulous were also well represented among the confraternity orators. Alamanno Rinuccini, who helped bring Argyropoulous to Florence, delivered four sermons to the Magi, a company of which, for a time, he served as governor. His close friend Donato Acciaiuoli,[13] fellow Florentine Academy member, Magi brother, and member of several other Florentine confraternities, contributed one sermon, as did their mutual friend Cristoforo Landino, who had also been a member of the Florentine Academy, and who delivered Donato's funeral oration. Niccolò Machiavelli, an anomaly in this group of orators, wrote a sermon on penance; like those of Poliziano, his was preserved apart from the major manuscript sermon collections.

With the obvious exception of Machiavelli, the principal group of confraternal lay preachers shared an overlapping and multigenerational set of friends, mentors, and teachers (Ficino, Landino, and Argyropoulous), a similar intellectual formation, and common moral and philosophical concerns. Alamanno Rinuccini, Donato Acciaiuoli, Landino, Pierfilippo Pandolfini, and Marco Parenti, father of confraternity orator Piero, were all students of Argyropoulous and members of the Florentine Academy. And as we have seen, many of the orators were protégés of Ficino and members of the Platonic Academy. They formed an important subset of Florence's intellectual elite and have been viewed as a transitional group between civic humanism and cinquecento courtly culture. It is not, therefore, surprising that their sermons have attracted the attention of very eminent scholars, several of whom have made the sermons key documents for the study of late quattrocento culture; others have, on the other hand, dismissed their importance entirely, viewing these sermons as little more than juvenile rhetorical exercises.

About this last point, some clarification is in order. Although frequently associated with boys' confraternities,[14] few of the sermons were, in fact, the work of adolescents. Of the twenty named speakers (many sermons are only partially identified by author, confraternity, and date), four account for all of the sermons delivered to boys' companies, and only one of these, Nesi, is ever explicitly identified as an "adolescent" in the manuscripts. Nesi, the adolescent, was atypical in delivering sermons at the ages of sixteen, eighteen, nineteen, twenty, and twenty-two. The age at which he delivered his last sermon, thirty, was far more typical of confraternal orators. Parenti was twenty-seven when he delivered his sermon, three years older than the traditional age dividing adolescent from adult confraternities. Berlinghieri and Carducci were thirty-six and Acciaiuoli and Vespucci were thirty-nine when their sermons were delivered. Rinuccini was thirty-one when he delivered his first sermon and sixty-one when he delivered his last. By all extant indications, the sermons, for the most part, were delivered by men who were well into their adulthood and professional careers, often well after they had qualified for high communal office. Filippo Carducci, for example, delivered his Magi sermon in the same year that he first served as prior (1485);[15] Francesco Berlinghieri's first dated sermon (1476) was delivered five years after he first served as prior (1471).[16]

Apart from incorrectly considering them to be juvenile oratorical exercises, scholars have, in general, used the sermons to speculate about broader movements in Florentine culture. Paul Oskar Kristeller cited these sermons as precursors of the kind of lay practices found in Ficino's circle, and emphasized the similarity in lay roles found in *compagnia* and the Platonic Academy.[17] Kristeller's general point is one worth repeating and extending, namely, that the culture of brotherhood of Ficino's circle owed as much to traditional confraternal practice as to the example of the *Symposium*.

Cesare Vasoli, in a brilliant study of Nesi's sermons and his prophetic "New Age" opusculum,[18] expanded ideas originally proposed by Garin.[19] Nesi's later sermons and this opusculum represent, for Vasoli, nothing less than the cultural readiness of Florentines for Savonarola's new age of radical religious reform. Nesi's work contains two elements that herald Fra Girolamo: simplicity and prophecy. The sermons, simple, direct, to the heart, emphasize a *devotio moderna*–like interior piety, by inference rejecting Florence's dominant ceremonial and ecclesiastical culture. Nesi's willingness, as revealed in his New Age vision, to entertain seriously the oracular and prophetic traditions of antiquity, coupled with his stylistic insistence on simplicity, reveal a mentality ready to accept Savonarola's message.

Each of these interpretations offers important insights into late quattrocento culture. But none of the interpretations gives much emphasis to what would have been most elementary to a fifteenth-century rhetorician, the importance of interrelating speaker, speech, and audience when analyzing any work of rhetoric. That the content of sermons might have had something to do with their audiences and with the occasions on which they were delivered has escaped the attention of most commentators.[20] Before commenting on the presumed novelty of the sermons of Nesi, Landino, or Acciaiuoli, one ought to place the sermons in their proper ceremonial context. The principal concerns in relating humanism and the culture of confraternal piety involve less the

literary scholar's desire to evaluate the originality of humanist preaching than the historian's understanding of the similarities between humanist oratory and confraternal spirituality. How did the humanist
preachers evaluate confraternal practices? When humanist orators spoke
to confraternal audiences, how did their messages relate to the cultural
world of lay confraternal piety?

Of the sermons contained in the two principal manuscript collections, plus those in print—fifty in all—thirteen treated the Eucharist,
Holy Communion, or the Last Supper, eleven were shorter works, exhortations to penance; seven treated the Passion or the veneration of
the cross; six explored the twin themes of charity and humility; and
the remainder examined more specific moral themes. Nineteen of these
works have explicit or readily inferred festive dates; of these, seventeen
were written for Holy Week, one for Wednesday, fourteen for Holy
Thursday, and two for Good Friday. The thematic similarity between
the dated and undated works makes it all but certain that the great majority of the extant sermons were also for Holy Week.

The Holy Week commemoration of the Passion and Resurrection involved a variety of religious organizations in late medieval
Florence.[21] Easter was a parish affair, but much of the rest of the week
was given over to confraternal celebrations. Holy Thursday was, for
penitential confraternities, one of the chief days of assembly and liturgical significance. On Holy Thursday, confraternities celebrated the rite
of the *lavanda,* Christ's washing of the feet of his disciples. Confraternities commemorated the event with one or more officers washing the
feet of other officers or members. After this rite, the members, having
imitated what confraternities considered was Christ's supreme act of
humility, embraced each other in a ceremony of fraternal forgiveness
and reconciliation. Following the rite of the lavanda, the members shared
a simple meal commemorating the Last Supper, that archetypal example
of fraternity complete with its own betrayal of friendship. Even more,
the meal commemorated the institution of the Eucharist which, for confraternities, was the supreme sign of Christ's charity. On Good Friday
companies celebrated the Passion and crucifixion, commemorated by a
ritual veneration of the cross. On Holy Thursday, the penitential confraternities emphasized charity, humility, and fraternity, and on Good
Friday, lamentation, tears, penance, and the imitation of the Passion.

The themes of Holy Week—sorrow and lamentation, the remembrance of sin, personal penance, reconciliation, charity, and fraternity—were characteristic of the spirituality practiced by penitential
confraternities throughout the year. The imitation of Christ's Passion
through ritual humiliation, flagellation, fasting, and other forms of
mortification, and the generally Christocentric focus of this piety, which
included an emphasis on the veneration of the principal symbol of mortification, the cross, were practices and themes central to flagellant confraternal piety. This, then, is the devotional context of the great majority of extant sermons.[22] While the sermons deal with seemingly
different themes—the Eucharist, humility, charity, the cross, penance,
and the Passion—in reality, most sermons treated several of these topics;
many treated them all.

If one is conscious of the multiple ties linking many of the
humanist orators, particularly the shared associational life of the Platonic Academy, and if one examines the sermons together, as one closely
related body of material undoubtedly shared among friends, borrowed,
copied, and certainly heard live, the commonality of spirituality underlying virtually all of these sacred orations is not surprising.[23] Charles
Trinkaus's admonition, that one should not place too much emphasis
on differing intellectual traditions when examining humanist spirituality, is nowhere more relevant than when one confronts these sermons.
His comment that the humanists revealed "a remarkable degree of ho-
mogeneity in their ideas with a plurality of variations and borrowings
from various schools of ancient and Christian moral philosophy and
theology" summarizes exactly the moral and intellectual coherence of
these sermons.[24]

The Holy Week sermons and exhortation to penance, including that composed by Machiavelli, emphasized these common and complementary themes:

> Man is a fundamentally vile creature, mired in sin;
>
> Spurred on by the contemplation of Christ's Passion, man rec-
> ognizes his sinful condition;
>
> Recognizing his sinful nature, man is led to contrition;
>
> Man's sinful condition is remedied, following Christ's example,
> through mortification and through the twin virtues of charity

and humility, which aid the individual's quest for salvation, and, at the same time, benefit the community as a whole.

This schema, common to most, if not all, of the sermons, is quite recognizable as the process of penance. According to traditional late medieval doctrine, penance begins with sorrow and leads to the recognition of sin and through this awareness to a genuine and deeply felt contrition. Contrition, in turn, leads the sinner to confession and absolution. Though forgiveness be granted by priestly absolution, satisfaction through penances must be performed.[25] This traditional penitential structure provided the organizing theme of many of the humanist sermons. At the same time, a close reading of these sermons reveals that the humanists transformed the theory of penance into something at once in harmony with traditional confraternal practice and with the fashionable currents of late quattrocento Florentine humanist ethics.

"Vermis sum et non homo" ("I'm a worm, not a man"): thus the dignity of man, penitential style, as preached by Cristoforo Landino.[26] The idea that man is vile, steeped in filth, is common to many sermons, including those of Parenti and Nesi. These preachers viewed man as having two natures, one tending toward the the divine, and the other toward the bestial. Tommaso Ginori provided further detail about this common theme, dividing man into an "incorruptible and immortal soul," and a "mortal and fallen body," as, he says, "both the Platonists and Christians affirm."[27] "We are in part corporeal and mortal," preached Bernardo Canigiani, "and part spiritual and eternal. And that part of us which is corporeal is fragile, making us like brutes, corruptible, and full of sin and evil. That part which is spiritual is pure, and simple, and God-like."[28] Our ability to mediate between earthly and divine things is impeded, he says, by our earthly, sensual appetites, and our two natures are in constant battle.[29] So common had the language of Platonic dualism become by the end of the fifteenth century that even Machiavelli conceived of man as poised between rational and animal natures, halfway between angel and devil: lord and servant, man and beast.[30]

For most of those who treated sinfulness, the very corporality of the body that imprisons the soul is responsible for sin. The proper remedy for sin, according to these speakers, begins with self-knowledge. "Let us each, at this holy time," began Francesco Berlinghieri's sermon on penance, "recognize what has been the manner and order of his past life."[31] This true reflection, for Berlinghieri, leads to the recognition that we are, by nature, disposed to carnal pleasures, and are as much like beasts as like men, inclined against virtue.[32] Such self-knowledge leads to penance, which was intellectualized and understood as a kind of illumination. "O most holy penance, O most outstanding virtue, O brilliant sun, illuminator of our minds, you have placed in our hands the keys to the gates of paradise. You are the stairway of eternal life . . . you are the *prima ragione* of human salvation."[33]

Penitential mortifications were considered, according to contemporary theology, as penances, providing satisfaction for sins committed. The very willingness of the sinner to undertake such penances was a sign, in early medieval penitential theology, that absolution had been granted.[34] The humanist sermons, on the other hand, treat penitential mortification in two ways, at one and the same time as satisfaction for sins committed, and as an aid to the intellectual ascent of the soul, that is, as rituals and practices of Neoplatonic purgation. If man's sinful nature owed, as the Platonists affirmed, to a soul/body dualism, then man's spiritual freedom and union with God, his ability to ascend, depended upon the freedom of mind from the body. How does man ascend and return to God? "With the meditation of the soul, the contrition of the heart, and finally, with bodily castigations, we return to Him whole," preached Scala (Figure 9.1).[35] We purge our minds, he said, "with devotion, contrition, and penance."[36] Francesco Berlinghieri was one of many preachers to associate Christian mortification with Platonic purgation: "Inasmuch as we, being rational creatures, are better and more worthy and excellent than all other created things, we ought with every diligence, with zeal, to force ourselves to return to enjoy the infinite and highest good."[37] But we cannot return to enjoy the *sommo bene* because our soul is "jailed in the dark prison of the body, without which we cannot search for the highest good."[38] The remedy is "to castigate, beat, and with whips and fasts to torment the body, turning always to one's maker and creator, omnipotent God, with innocent hands and pure heart, as diligently the prophet David taught, and thus purged and pure, our soul will recognize God."[39] Although the context is Christian, the

Tractato diuoto & tutto fpirituale di frate Hierony,
mo da Ferrara dellordine de frati Predicatori in defen
fione & cõmendatione delloratione mentale
compofto ad inftructione/ confirmatione/
& confolatione delle anime deuote

OPVLVS Hic Labiis.
me honorar: cor autõ
eorum longe eft a me.
Sine caufa autõ colunt
me docõtes doctrinas & mandata
hominum. Matthei. xv. Auẽgha
che fia noto & manifefto a ciafche
duno igegno/ etiam mediocremẽ
te iftructo nella religione chriftia
a i

Figure 9.1. Laypeople at prayer. Woodcut illustration to Savonarola's *Tractato divoto in . . . commendatione dell' oratione mentale.* 1495. Florence, Biblioteca Nazionale Centrale. Photo Artini.

language of his sermon, peppered with references to "divine fervor," "highest good," and "secret mysteries of God," are thoroughly Platonic, drawn as much from Plato, Socrates, and Dionysius the Areopagite as from St. Paul. Our speakers made frequent reference to other sources often cited by Florentine Neoplatonists, including Hermes, Pythagoras, and Sybelline prophecy.

At the same time, although the language is Platonic, the actions demanded by Berlinghieri, Scala, and others were the traditional devotions of flagellant confraternities. Donato Cocchi's list of purgatorial actions was, for example, well within the bounds of traditional confraternal spirituality: prayer, fasts, tears, and charity.[40] The purgatorial practice most frequently mentioned in the sermons, however, is flagellation. "The holy discipline is hard, let us flagellate," preached Pier Antonio Buondelmonti.[41] "Flee every defect and excess," Rinieri Buonafé urged; "put aside pride and arrogance, forget injuries and offenses and your depraved, dissolute desires and vices . . . follow virtue . . . and whip ready, kneel."[42] Francesco Berlinghieri wanted, he said, that tonight, each should "take your whip in your hand and do penance without waiting, do penance" defined, he said, by St. Ambrose as "crying over one's past crimes, remembering your perdition."[43] Or, as Bartolomeo Scala urged, "la disciplina in mano [whip in hand], remedy the injuries of your pus-filled body."[44]

Like the traditional penitential practice of flagellation, the rites of Holy Thursday, for these speakers, were perfect penitential rites, combining man's knowledge of self, truest when man "considers himself vile,"[45] with the contemplation and imitation of Christ. The Christocentric focus of these rites was, for preacher after preacher, major proof of the evils of corporeality, and sermon after sermon recounted Christ's corporeal torments. "I invite you to cry with Him in His bitter pain," preached Poliziano, "to become His disconsolate widow; to see His grieving mother whose heart was pierced with a knife; to cry together with the stones, the sun, with heaven and earth, with all the elements, with the whole world over His incomparable torment. . . . Let us cry tenderly at the death of sweet Jesus. . . . Let us do penance, and with devout contrition let us humiliate ourselves before God."[46] The very fact that God became man and assumed bodily form must have been, argued Landino, the greatest humiliation of all.[47]

Although penance, inner remorse, interior piety, contemplation, and self-knowledge were discussed in the sermons, it is quite incorrect to assume, as several scholars have done, that the sermons of humanists such as Nesi stressed a strictly "personal" and interior or anticeremonial piety. The modern, Erasmian and Protestant distinction between inner spirituality and outer action, the former always somehow more genuine and "religious" than the latter, is for the study of quattrocento Italian Renaissance religion a false and misleading dichotomy imposed on religion by those with little understanding and less sympathy for ceremonial and ritualized behavior. For orators such as Scala, there was, for example, a perfect relation between the interior life of the mind and the ritual practices and mortifications of confraternities. Scala preached that without the "mortifications of our fragile bodies" we cannot return to God.[48] In another sermon, he suggested that through external mortification right reason emerges: "Let us take up the discipline voluntarily, let us give our body conquered by sensuality a beating so that castigated, it is converted to the way of salvation, reconciled with its Creator. Chase away the appetites, exterminate sensuality, and place yourself under the sway of true reason."[49]

We have already seen the frequent and positive evaluation of flagellation and other mortifications. The Holy Thursday rites, *as ceremonies,* were similarly praised as exemplars of spirituality. Indeed, one orator went so far as to suggest that it is precisely because we cannot truly contemplate God while we are imprisoned by the body that it is necessary to celebrate divine offices and rituals.[50]

This spirituality frequently had a civic dimension. During the humiliations of the lavanda rite, Nesi, for example, urged each brother of the Company of the Nativity not simply to think of its own "utility, but that of one's country, one's relatives, and of all those ever born," because humility is the basis of "piety toward family, reverence toward elders, obedience toward those who rightly command you, and not surpassing others in anything . . . the rich man becomes the friend of the poor man, the mighty befriends the powerless, the lord becomes the friend of his servant . . . one does not love one's neighbor less than oneself . . . out of which is born a desire not only not to offend one's neighbor, but, if possible, to defend him."[51] Unlike many modern scholars, Nesi, Rinuccini, and other lay preachers understood the special psychological and social results of rites of charity, humility, and concord.[52] Social peace and harmony, as the flagellants discovered in 1260, throughout the fourteenth century, and in 1399, can be the result of powerful, evocative rituals of abasement. Thus, for humanist preachers, the interior life did not necessarily oppose itself to ceremony but could find fulfillment in such "externals."

Sin was perceived often as social, consisting in such interpersonal actions as lying, betrayal, or hatred. If sin had a high social component, so too did penance, and the fruits of penitential action returned not only to the individual and his quest for salvation, but, in a classically civic fashion, to the community as well. And thus, Piero Parenti addressed the Company of St. Vincent in 1476: "Consider, that if you would all be united in Holy Charity no adversity internal or external would ever be able to offend you. This places perpetual tranquillity in the soul. From her union and concord proceed. From her, finally, every good results. . . . Let us turn with warm hearts to this virtue Charity and her companion Humility. Leave your injuries behind, let each one of us cancel the hatreds that exist between us; extirpate our jealousies, lowering our heads in imitation of Jesus our Lord."[53] In a similar vein, Giovanni Nesi concluded his sermon to the Nativity the same year: "You should want to pardon him who has injured you, because as it is written, "forgive and you shall be forgiven." You should want to convert enmity into amity, hate and dissimulation into love and benevolence, pride into humility."[54] Or, as he concluded his Holy Thursday sermon to the Magi the next year, "Through [charity], beloved brothers, let us cleanse ourselves of hate, lies, and malevolence, and become today one composed of many."[55] Indeed, the interpersonal sins of hate and malevolence are among those most frequently mentioned, using such exemplars as Judas's betrayal of Christ, or (an example used by Ginori) the story of Jacob and Esau to characterize the hate that can exist among brothers.[56]

Once the members had been reconciled and envies and hatreds healed through rites such as Holy Thursday's lavanda, they were to experience the unity and community of communion. And here, again, while the Eucharist was clearly viewed as an act of interior spirituality, the effects of communion were just as clearly seen as producing true love, concord, and fraternity. "Communion," preached one humanist, "is the consummation and perfection of all divine sacraments that collect and conjoin our lives so divided into one and give the individual and the confraternity unity in God the Most High. When commemorating this most solemn supper we are commanded as brothers to live together in the highest peace and concord."[57]

At the beginning of this discussion, I posed a general question concerning the relationship between the learned spirituality of humanists and the ceremonial spirituality of the Renaissance confraternity. What can one conclude about the similarity of "learned" and middle-class spirituality?

First, and most obvious, beneath the neoplatonic idiom of divine love, sommo bene, and sacred mysteries, one finds acceptance of traditional penitential piety and practice. The humanist preachers remained knowledgeable of and faithful (at least when the occasion warranted) to the gestures, rites, and themes of confraternal piety.

At the same time, while approved and accepted, these rites were understood in quite a new way, less as satisfaction for sins committed than as a mechanism to purify the spirit by separating soul from body, thus beginning the ascent of the soul. In traditional theology, mortification was the outcome, the final step in the progress from contrition to satisfaction; for the humanist preacher, on the other hand, mortifications were the beginning of a long process of spiritual purification. Penitential rituals were, in this way, thoroughly assimilated into Platonic concepts of purgation and ascent. While only the first step in a hierarchy of activities which focused in its later stages less on action and more on contemplation, purgation rites, including flagellation, were the first step, enabling the initial purging of the affections and disciplining of the corporeal side of man, a necessary prelude to the return of the purified soul to its creator.[58] It is well known that confraternities served as gathering places for late quattrocento humanists.[59] It is less well known how fully these humanists reconciled confraternal devotional practice to the late quattrocento preoccupation with purgation and purification.

A stress on the contemplative virtues notwithstanding, the evidence hardly suggests, as several commentators believe, that a fifteenth-century humanist-inspired emphasis on a strictly internal piety and simplicity of belief—devotio moderna style—conflicted with or opposed the ceremonial, so-called exterior piety of traditional confraternal culture. As we have observed, confraternal preachers themselves recognized that internal contrition and lamentation were made possible by external acts, through, as Giovanni Nesi preached, "alms, prayers, fasts, and whips."[60] This internal piety—however produced—reinforced and led to new external gestures, which could themselves help to deepen personal piety. And, it should be remembered, if humanists found value in exterior devotions, so, too, the interior piety of conversion and remorse spurred on by the penitential psalms, the contemplation of Christ's Passion, and reflections on human fragility, sin, and death had long been a key element of confraternal culture, having its origins in the very beginnings of the penitential movement in the thirteenth century.

Mary Douglas reminds us, perceptively, that an exaggerated insistence on an interior/exterior dualism (accompanied by the denigration of the latter) is often symptomatic of deep, anti-institutional alienation on the part of intellectuals.[61] As far as lay religion was concerned, Florentine intellectuals did not reject but found acceptable the penitential culture of lay religion in both its internal contemplations and its external rites, and believed that penitential culture itself supported and was supported by the *vita civile*.

If any anti-institutional bias is to be found here, it is against ecclesiastical rather than lay religious institutions. The lay preachers, while frequently claiming and exhibiting great familiarity with confraternal ritual and pious practice, rarely cited the clergy or the formal institutions of the Church as *exempla* to be imitated, as complements of right reason, as sources of illumination, or even as a necessary component of those eucharistic rites about which so many sermons were written. Flagellant confraternities themselves, after their often clerical foundation in the thirteenth or fourteenth centuries, had, by the fifteenth century, only a rather small sacramental role for the clergy to play. Indeed, some confraternities, such as San Paolo, excluded all clergy, save the confraternity's elected chaplain, from membership. And auricular, public confession to the *corpo di compagnia,* the body of the confraternity, its lay members, was one of the central facets of confraternal

rites of penance, as was the practice of having the confraternity's lay
governor impose the penances to be performed for infractions of confraternal discipline, sometimes with and sometimes without the assistance of the company chaplain. As the statutes of the Company of San
Paolo read, the duties of its lay governor, in which post Lorenzo de'
Medici had, on occasion served, were to "propose, correct, and absolve."[62]
While not anticlerical, the city's fifteenth-century flagellant confraternities were lay institutions, celebrating with minimal clerical involvement their own ritual practices in their own private oratories.[63]

While accepting and approving of the devotional life of the
laity, the religion of late Florentine humanism was, viewed in terms
of these sermons, itself rather thoroughly declericalized, stressing the
contrition of the sinner more than the absolution performed by the
priest, and the voluntary actions of the penitent freeing soul from body
more than the sacramental action of the Church. Given a stress on contemplation and spiritual ascent, and the implicit, and not infrequently
explicit, Pelagian message of these sermons,[64] such declericalization is
not surprising. Clearly, within the environment of late quattrocento
lay religious culture, the humanist, expert in the contemplative virtues
and the techniques of ascent, had come close to replacing the priest as
Holy Man.

Finally, just as the participation of humanists in and their positive evaluation of confraternal penitential piety should warn us against
making too strong a distinction between exterior and interior spirituality, so, too, should we avoid distinguishing too sharply the spiritual
impulses of humanist elites from more "popular" movements of Renaissance piety and religion. As Pico suggested:

> Surely our zeal ought to be so turned toward higher things that we seek
> strength for our weakness through holy religion, through sacred rites,
> through vows, and through hymns, prayers, and supplications. . . . it is
> neither ridiculous nor useless nor unworthy of a philosopher to devote
> great and unremitting care to holy prayers, rites, vows, and hymns jointly
> sung to God. If this is helpful and proper for the human race, it is espe-
> cially useful and proper for those who have given themselves up to the
> study of letters and the life of contemplation. For them nothing is more
> necessary than to purify by an upright life those eyes of the mind which
> they turn repeatedly toward the divine.[65]

NOTES

1. On problems of categorization, see Richard C. Trexler, "Reverence and Profanity in the Study of Early Modern Religion," in *Religion and Society in Early Modern Europe, 1500–1800* ed. Kaspar von Greyerz (London: George Allen and Unwin, 1984), 246ff.

2. On the unfortunate effects of such terminology on the serious study of religion and ritual, see Mary Douglas, *Natural Symbols* (New York: Vintage Press, 1979), chap. 1.

3. On the Florentine Academy, see Arnaldo della Torre, *Storia dell'Accademia Platonica* (Florence: G. Carnesecchi, 1902), 354ff.

4. On lay Florentine confraternal sermons, see P. O. Kristeller, "Lay Religious Traditions and Florentine Platonism," in *Studies in Renaissance Thought and Letters* (Rome: Storia e letteratura, 1969), 103–6; Eugenio Garin, "Desideri di riforma nell'oratoria del quattrocento," *Belfagor* (1948), reprinted in Garin, *La cultura filosofica del Rinascimento italiano* (Florence: Sansoni, 1979), 166–82; Rab Hatfield, "The Company of the Magi," *Journal of the Warburg and Courtauld Institutes* 33 (1972): 124ff.; G. M. Monti, *Le confraternite medievali dell'alta e media Italia* (Venice: La Nuova Italia, 1927), 1:187ff., 2:108–9. Charles Trinkaus, *In Our Image and Likeness: Humanity and Divinity in Italian Humanist Thought,* 2 vols. (Chicago: University of Chicago Press, 1970), 638–50, examined two humanist sermons, those by Cristoforo Landino and Donato Acciaiuoli, delivered to the Company of the Magi.

5. Kristeller, "Lay Religious Traditions," 116.

6. A. Chastel, *Art et humanisme à Florence au temps de Laurent le Magnifique* (Paris: Presses universitaires de France, 1961), 198, 246–47.

7. The principal manuscript collections include Biblioteca Riccardiana, Florence, MS. 2204 (hereafter BRF 2204), and Biblioteca nazionale centrale di Firenze (hereafter BNF), Magl. XXV.211. Nesi's sermons have been published by Cesare Vasoli, "Giovanni Nesi tra Donato Acciaiuoli Girolamo Savonarola," *Memorie domenicane* 4 (1973): 103–79. Machiavelli's penitential oration was published in Niccolò Machiavelli, *Tutte le opere* (Florence: Sansoni, 1929), 778–80. Three of four sermons written by Poliziano have been published in I. del Lungo, *Prose volgari inedite e poesie latine e greche edite e inedite di Angelo Ambrogini Poliziano* (Florence, 1867), 3–16. The sermons of Alamanno Rinuccini have been published by Vito Giustiniani, *Alamanno Rinuccini: Lettere ed orazioni* (Florence: Sansoni, 1953), 22–23, 46–47, 145–62, 185–87. The surviving sermons represent a small fraction of the total number likely to have been delivered by lay Florentines to confraternities. The statutes of many confraternities required annual sermons on such occasions as Holy Thursday, but sermons survive for only a few confraternities. On sermon requirements, see, for example, the statutes of the Compagnia di S. Paolo, Archivio di Stato di Firenze, Compagnie Religiose Soppresse (hereafter ASF CRS), Capitoli, 29.

8. See Ronald F. E. Weissman, *Ritual Brotherhood in Renaissance Florence* (New York: Academic Press, 1982), chap. 4, for a description concerning elite participation in confraternities.

9. On Nesi, see Vasoli, "Giovanni Nesi," 103–22.

10. Della Torre, *Storia,* 387–89.

11. Ibid., 723.

12. Weissman, *Ritual Brotherhood,* 171–72.

13. On Donato's membership of the Company of S. Girolamo, a flagellant com-

pagnia di notte, see Vespasiano da Bisticci, *Vite di uomini illustri del secolo XV* (Florence, 1859), 333 (life of Donato Acciaiuoli, sec. 2).

14. On the role of sermons in adolescent confraternities, see Richard C. Trexler, "Ritual in Florence: Adolescence and Salvation in the Renaissance," in *The Pursuit of Holiness in Late Medieval and Renaissance Religion* ed. Charles Trinkaus with Heiko A. Oberman (Leiden: E. J. Brill, 1974), 220.

15. Della Torre, *Storia,* 725.

16. Ibid., 666 n. 7.

17. Kristeller, "Lay Religious Traditions."

18. Vasoli, "Giovanni Nesi."

19. Garin, "Desideri di riforma." There is in Garin's interpretation a strong suggestion that these sermons revealed a deep dissatisfaction with Florentine religious institutions and practices. As I argue below, humanist orators fully appreciated and concurred with many of the traditions of organized lay spirituality in Florence. Many of the humanist orators were themselves members of Florentine confraternities. And far from repudiating the traditions of their contemporaries, many humanist preachers went out of their way to apologize in advance if, because they were laymen, their sermons inadvertently strayed from true doctrine. See, for example, "Oratione del Corpo di Christo di Donato Acciaiuoli et dallui nella Compagnia de'Magi recitata die 13 aprelis 1468," BRF 2204, fol. 180r: "Et se fussi accaduto, amantissimi Padri et frategli, che per mala aduertenza in questio mio sermone hauessi detto cosa alcuna che fussi aliena dalla fede nostra, da hora io la ritracto et in ogni parte mi riferisco alla uerità delle sacre lettere et ad quello che contiene la sacrosancta romana ecclesia." Nevertheless, as I contend below, if dissatisfaction is evident, it is with clerical religion, not contemporary religious practice per se.

20. Hatfield, "Company of the Magi," is virtually alone in noting the importance of Holy Thursday in the oratorical program of flagellant confraternities.

21. On Holy Thursday in Florence, see Weissman, *Ritual Brotherhood,* chap. 2.

22. One should also note that these sermons were all written in Italian. The Latin that does appear is epigrammatic—a short quotation from a patristic, scholastic, classical, or biblical source, cited for authority or effect, and almost always repeated in Italian. In this way the preachers' use of Latin exactly followed that found in confraternal statute books. It is not true, as Trexler has suggested ("Adolescence and Salvation," 220), that the sermons were recited in humanistic Latin and, therefore, would have been incomprehensible to their lay listeners, who might have been impressed by the gravity of the sermons but would not have understood their content.

23. Indeed, some sermons were ghostwritten by orators such as Poliziano; others were recited by other humanists after they had been delivered by their authors. Kristeller, "Lay Religious Traditions," 106.

24. Trinkaus, *Image and Likeness,* 713–14.

25. On penance in late medieval religion, see Thomas N. Tentler, *Sin and Confession on the Eve of the Reformation* (Princeton, N.J.: Princeton University Press, 1977).

26. "Sermone di Messere Christofano Landino fatto in commemoratione del Corpo di Christo et recitato nella Compagnia de' Magi," BRF, Riccardiana MS. 2204.

27. "Exortatione a penitentia di Tommaso di Zanobi Ginori e recitata in sancto uin-

centio 1476," BNF, Magl. XXV.211, fol. 134r: "consideriamo con grande attentione quello che gli antichi philosophi tantamente [h]anno sentito di questa materia, i quali speculati e contemplati la humana natura uidono l'uomo d'animo e corpo hauere el suo essere e l'uno di per essere immortale e incorruptibile, l'altro mortale e caduto; ne mai potere peruenire a noi la felicità se non è dall'animo ma l'animo poi sarà felice, come affermano e platonici oltre a christiani, ritornando lui a quello luogho dal quale è fu creato."

28. "Exortatio ad penitentiam bernardi decanisianis," ibid., fol. 147v.

29. Ibid.

30. Niccolò Machiavelli, "Exortatione alla penitenza," in *Tutte le opere,* 933. Thus, when speaking of the sinful acts man commits, he remarks, "et così l'huomo, mediante queste brutte opere, di animale rationale in animale bruto si transforma. Diventa, pertanto, l'huomo, usando questa ingratitudine contro ad Dio, di angelo diavolo, di signore servo, di huomo bestia."

31. "Exortatio breuis ad penitentiam di Francesco Berlinghieri," BRF, Riccardiana MS. 2204, fol. 160r.

32. Ibid.

33. "Exortatio ad penitentiam," BNF, Magl. XXV.211, fol. 143v: "O santissimo penitentia, o uirtù preclarissima, o fulgentissimo sole illuminator degli intellecti nostri nelle nostre mani s'inposte le chiaui della porta celeste. Tu se la scala dell'eterna vita . . . tu se la prima ragione dell'umana salute."

34. See Tentler, *Sin and Confession.*

35. "Exortatio ad penitentiam bartolomei descalis," ibid., fol. 141r.

36. "Exortatio ad penitentiam bartolomei descalis" (second sermon with this title), ibid., fol. 142r.

37. "Exortatio ad osculum crucis di Francesco Berlinghieri in sancto uincentio," BRF, Riccardiana MS. 2204, fol. 164v: "sono quanto maggiormente noi creature rationali essendo et più degne et più excellente di tutte l'altre cose create con ogni diligentia con sommo studio sforzarci dobiamo per tornare a fruire lo'nfinito e sommo bene della etherna bontà."

38. Ibid. The theme of the soul's imprisonment in the body ran throughout the sermons. See, for example, Filippo Carducci's sermon on penance, delivered to the Magi on 31 April 1485, ibid., fol. 216r: "Ma conciosia che l'anima subito che entra in questo carcere corporale diuenga inferma e per tutta la mortale uita infermità ad infermità miserabilmente aggiunga . . . Adunque, è necessaria sopra ogni altra cosa la penitentia alla salute dell'anima."

39. Ibid. "El quale bene dilectissimi lo immortale nostro animo rinchiuso in questo tenebroso carcere del humano corpo senza epso corpo cercarlo non può, cercarlo adunque, insieme col corpo gastigando, macerando, et con discipline et con digiuni tormentando epsa carne, riuolgendo sempre se medesimo al suo conditore et creatore omnipotente idio con innocentia di mani et monditia di quore come diligentemente insegna Dauid propheta egregio, et così purgato et puro l'animo nostro et non altrimenti ricognosce il suo iddio."

40. "Oratione del corpo di Cristo da Giovanni di messer Donato Cocchi recitata nella Compagnia della Natiuità di Cristo die 23 martij 1474," ibid., fol. 166v: "Et però dice el diuino doctore sancto augustino quanto a noi è possibile colladiutorio di dio ci douiamo sforzare, sudare, et affaticare, dimundare et purgare la conscientia nostra da ogni macula et sorde di peccato; acciochè mediante l'oratione, digiuni, et lagrime interiore et exteriore, et

elemosine, et similiter, mediante tutte le sancte et buone operationi noi possiamo presumere pigliare tale eucaristia cioè buona gratia."

41. "Exortatio ad osculum crucis di Piero Antonio Buondelmonti fatta adì 4 d'aprile 1477 in sancto vincentio," BNF, Magl. XXV.211: "la sancta disciplina in mano, flagelliamo."

42. "Sermo in passione yhu xpi fatto per rinieri buonafé et dallui recitato in sancto domenicho adì 4 d'aprile 1477." ibid., fol. 126r: "dilasciare ogni excesso e difetto, e nel mezo doue la uirtù consiste fermarsi, deponga e fasti l'atti la superbia, pongha giù l'arrogantia, depongha l'engurie, dimentichi l'offese e assioni e depraui e dissoluti desiderij schacci e uitij, e segui la uirtù e in quella forma del corpo proceda che dal nostro degnissimo padre governatore gli sia insegnato non tanto ignudo e condisciplina genuflexo quanto colla boccha spurcissima."

43. "Exortatio ad penitentiam di Francesco Berlinghieri," ibid.: "voglia questa sera la disciplina in mano prendere, e de quegli agli fare sanza più tempo aspettare qualche penitentia la quale non è altro secondo il divino ambrosio che e passati delicti piangere, ricordandosi della perdita."

44. "Exortatio . . . bartolomei descalis" (second sermon): "e colla disciplina in mano rimedichiamo l'engurie che questo misero corpo come puzolente." See also, his first "exortatio ad penitentiam": "e colle discipline in mano al tutto humiliati battendo e percotendo questi nostri corpi cosa terrena."

45. "Oratione del Corpo di Cristo da Giouanni Nesi composta et da lui nella Compagnia di Sancto Antonio da Padua recitata die 7 aprelis 1474," in Vasoli, "Giovanni Nesi," 132.

46. Poliziano, *Prose editi e inediti*, 7.

47. Landino, "Sermone . . . in commemoratione del Corpo di Christo."

48. "Exortatio . . . bartolomei descalis," fol. 141v.

49. Ibid., fol. 146v.

50. "Exortatione quedam fienda ante initium offitiorum," fol. 145v.

51. "Johannis Nesij adolescentis oratio de humilitate habita in fraternitate natiuitatis die 11 aprelis 1476," in Vasoli, "Giovanni Nesi," 142–43: "La terza contemplatione, Padri et Frategli amantissimi, è quando l'huomo considera non solamente a sua utilità, ma della patria, de' parenti et di tutti gl'huomini essere nato, come non solo scriue Platone, Aristotile et Cicerone, ma il sapientissimo Signore in più luoghi cel comanda. Doue cognoscendo l'obbligo grandissimo, col padre intanto s'ahumilia che nulla cosa è benchè difficile et ardua, che per la salute del padre a fare facile non gli paia; et però da questa ha principio pietà inuerso parenti, reuerentia inuerso maggiori, obedientia inuerso di chi giustamente gli comanda; et cognoscendo se in nessuna cosa gli altri superare, conciò sia cosa che d'una medesima massa sieno usciti, il ricco del pouero, il sommo dell'infimo, il potente dell'impotente, il Signore del seruo diuenta amico et, postposti e' fasti e le dignità humane, ciascuno (come è precepto del nostro Signore) non meno il proximo che sé medesimo ama; et quello (come uole Pythagora) un altro sé essere stima; la qual cosa, benché in ogni luogo utile sia, niente di meno in quanto è necessario che tutti siamo d'una medesima uolontà; la quale certamente Pythagora intese quando dixe amicitia essere uno composto di molti, et sappiendo tutte le cose degli amici essere comune, e' ricchi dispensatori e possessori delle loro ricchezza si fanno magnifici e quegli di mediocre facultà diuentono liberali. Di qui nasce uno riguardo non solamente di non offendere el proximo, ma se possibile è difenderlo; per quali duo offici l'huomo ueramente giusto et misericorde si può dire."

52. For a more extensive discussion of Nesi, Rinuccini, and the ritual process in Florentine confraternities, see Weissman, *Ritual Brotherhood*, 52–53, 99–104.

53. "Sermone di Piero di Marco Parenti dell' umiltà et carità dal lui composto et recitato nella Compagnia di Sancto Uincentio l'anno MLXXLVIJ, BRF, Riccardiana MS. 2204, fol. 211v: "Considerate se sarete tutti unitj coniuncolo della santa carità nessuna aduersità nè di fuori nè dentro mai per alcun tempo poteruj offendere. Questa porge tranquilità perpetua alla mente et sicurtà sempiterna alla nostra anima. Dallej la unione et la concordia procede. Dallej finalmente ogni bene risulta. Mediante tutte le cose sono sanza lei ogni cosa è nulla per la qual cosa dilectissimi uoltiamoci con caldo core a questa uirtù di carità et alla sua compagna humiltà, restiamoci le ingiurie l'uno all'altro, cancelliamoci hodi, extirpiamo le inuidie, abassiamo la testa imitando il signore nostro yhu."

54. "Johannis Nesij adolescentis oratio," 146: "Vogliate a chi n'auessi ingiurato perdonare, imperò che gli è scripto: Dimittite et dimittetur uobis. Vogliate le nimicitie in amicitie, l'odio et simultà in amore et beniuolentia, la superbia in humiltà conuertere."

55. "Johannis Nesij oratio de caritate a N.P. habita in sotietate natiuitatis die 25 februarij 1472," in Vasoli, "Giovanni Nesi," 152: "spoglianci d'odio, di simultà et di maliuolentia et diuentiamo oggi uno composto di molti."

56. "Exortatione . . . di Tommaso di Zanobi Ginori, fol. 138v.

57. "Oratio ad comunionem." BRF, Riccardiana MS. 2204, fol. 171v–172r: "È adqunque la comunione una consumatione et perfectione di tutti i sacramenti diuini che collega et congiungne le uite nostri in più parti diuise in un solo unico et perfecto stato et comunicaci et dona la compagnia et individua unita del sommo iddio. Il quale in commemoratione della sua solempnissima cena non ad altro ci comando chellobseruassimo che per che intra noi come frategli insieme alleuati con somma pace et concordia."

58. See, for example, Pico's discussion (*Oration on the Dignity of Man*) of the necessity of purging the soul through moral behavior prior to its enlightenment and perfection through reason and philosophy.

59. Chastel, *Art et humanisme*, 196.

60. "Johannis Nesij adolescentis oratio," 146–47: "Di poi recercare la uostra conscientia, riduceteui alla memoria e' uostri delitti; et di questi ueramente confessi, contriti et pentiti, con elimosine, con orationi, digiuni et discipline dinanzi alla faccia di dio gli rimuouete; et con dolori, sospiri, et lacrime lauate in modo el petto."

61. Douglas, *Natural Symbols*, 194.

62. Weissman, *Ritual Brotherhood*, 130.

63. John Henderson views the clergy as having a significantly more active role in Florentine confraternities than that presented here. He has recently described the claims to oversight of confraternities by Florentine bishops, particularly in the fifteenth century: "Confraternities and the Church in Late Medieval Florence," in *Voluntary Religion* ed. W. J. Sheils and Diana Wood (Oxford: Basil Blackwell, 1986), 78–83. Meeting records of flagellant confraternities such as S. Paolo, suggest, however, that such oversight was largely theoretical and that the actual role of clergy in fifteenth-century flagellant groups was of only minimal importance.

64. On the implicitly Pelagian character of humanist penitential thought, see Trinkaus, *Image and Likeness*, 633.

65. Giovanni Pico della Mirandola, *Heptaplus*, trans. D. Carmichael, (New York: Bobbs-Merrill, 1940), 144.

IO ❧

THE *SCUOLE GRANDI* OF VENICE
Some Further Thoughts

BRIAN PULLAN

I N THIS CHAPTER Brian Pullan returns to the theme of his exhaustive study of nineteen years ago, in light of recent work by John Henderson, Ronald Weissman,
and others. Through selective comparison with Florentine flagellant confraternities,
Professor Pullan brings into sharp focus those aspects of confraternal life unique to
another important Renaissance center, Venice: the distinctive dimensions of social
prestige operative in an aristocratic society; the use made by the state of confraternities as a form of "civic religion;" and the philanthropic activities of Venetian confraternities. Professor Pullan clearly delineates the ceremonial, corporate, and public
activities of the Venetian *scuole,* and contrasts these activities with the more individualistic and introspective spirituality entering Italy from beyond the Alps in the late fifteenth
century. He clarifies the role of the confraternities in the context of the "old" and
"local" Catholicism of the pre-Tridentine period, as distinguished from that sense of
universal brotherhood, transcending city and regional loyalties, on the rise in the late
quattrocento, that was to give its character to the Catholic reform movement of the
sixteenth century.

BRIAN PULLAN is professor of history at the University of Manchester. He is best known
for his monumental and innovative study, *Rich and Poor in Renaissance Venice: The Social Institutions of a Catholic State to 1620,* published in 1971.

EREADING ONE'S OWN WORK is a hard penance, doubly painful to the author who does this nineteen years after publication and twenty-five after starting research, kicking himself for the questions he failed to ask, for the implications and interconnections that he never perceived. When I began work on Venetian social history in 1959, I was excited by Wilbur Jordan's researches on English philanthropy,[1] and much influenced by the doctrine of *il faut compter.* Groping toward an account of the workings of charity and poor relief in a Catholic society of the sixteenth and seventeenth centuries, I was drawn into the history of six great brotherhoods, the Scuole Grandi, through a concern with only one of their activities, charity, which was seemingly the most tangible and measurable. The fascination of their Mariegole or "Mother Rules" lured me almost reluctantly (after all, I was supposed to be a "modern" historian) back into the trecento and quattrocento. Writers on this subject nowadays would be better equipped: they would have at their disposal not only the excellent work of certain Venetian historians on closely related subjects but also a number of imaginative contributions made by scholars interested in other cities, and especially by historians of Florence. These works do not overturn my old, rather cautious, interpretation — nothing so dramatic as that — but they have stimulated new thoughts on the distinctive, or at least unusual, features of the scuole. It is easier now to measure them both against other forms of confraternity that arose in Venice itself and against superficially similar types of brotherhood established in Florence, focusing attention principally on their relationship with society and the state. I should like to share these thoughts, and to start with a brief account of the rise of two new and contrasting cults in Venice, about the year 1480.

From about 1478, a small group of ardent devotees promoted the cult of St. Roch or San Rocco in the city with such vigor and persistence that they could, in 1489, petition the Council of Ten for authority to expand the saint's following to a full five hundred members

and to claim the prestigious rank of a Scuola Grande. The prime movers
were not native Venetians; one of them, no doubt, was Andrea da Bol-
zano, who served as guardian of the brotherhood in 1486.[2] They formed
part of the mass of transient foreigners and recent and seasonal immi-
grants who thronged Venice and far outnumbered the minority of patricians and native-born citizens at the heart of the state: "most of their
people are foreigners," as Commynes would remark a few years later.[3]
But some had settled themselves and their wives and families within
the city, and they were no doubt anxious to win a recognized place
within a society slow to grant standing to newcomers.

The term *Scuole Grandi* had been in use at least since 1467,[4] when
the Council of Ten had applied it to four large confraternities distinguished by the practice of ritual, public self-flagellation — brotherhoods
embodying a tradition rooted in the late thirteenth and early fourteenth
centuries. San Rocco's Venetian followers made no attempt to create
any new forms of worship or organization, and were very likely urged
to imitate older models by members of the older scuole who joined them.[5]
Their chances of winning recognition from the state would surely improve if they adhered to a tried and ancient formula, their chances of
attracting recruits surely be brighter if they were permitted to order
habits of the stuff used by the older brotherhoods.[6]

A Scuola Grande had to be a school of flagellants,[7] but it seems
unlikely that the brothers of San Rocco adopted the practice merely
in order to earn promotion; in Venice it was still a bloody and public —
and not merely a symbolic — nocturnal act.[8] Flagellation was not only
a ritual commemoration of the Passion of Christ, to be performed with
special fervor on Good Friday; it was also an act of placation or expia-
tion, designed to allay the terrible penalties for sin inflicted on a whole
people by the wrath of God. During an epidemic in 1447, barefooted
penitential brotherhoods in Venice had chanted the hymn,

> Alto re della gloria
> Cazze via sta moria
> Per la vostra Passion
> Habiene misericordia.
>
> (High King of Glory,
> Drive away this pestilence;
> By your Cross and Passion,
> Lord, have mercy upon us).[9]

The cult of San Rocco and the rituals of the flagellants were, among much else, a spiritual complement to the long series of highly practical measures against the plague which were set in train a few years later, with the establishment of a permanent magistracy for the care of public health. Over the half century from 1478 to 1528, the pestilence was to recur at intervals of five or six years, and the city had desperate need of the protection afforded by both saints and living persons.[10]

Soon after 1480, the Dominican John of Erfurt, appointed chaplain to the community of German merchants and artisans in Venice, launched from the remote convent of San Domenico di Castello a very different kind of confraternity. This was not to be a specifically Venetian brotherhood, but rather a Venetian branch of a universal fellowship, open (in the words of statutes imported from Germany) to "all Christianity." It would welcome everyone: "clerk and layman, rich and poor, man and woman," and there would be no entrance fee or subscription, "lest on account of poverty or incapacity the poor should be excluded."[11] In principle it would not even need to meet; the sole qualification for membership would be willingness to have one's name inscribed on a register and to perform the essentially private devotion of reciting the Marian Psalter once every week, 150 Hail Marys, punctuated by an Our Father after each decade. Anyone so doing would be entitled to benefit from the entire store of merit accumulated by all members of the confraternity.[12]

This notion of confraternity contrasted squarely with that entertained by the Scuole Grandi, whose religious life focused on public ceremony and collective action, even though not all their members took part in all their rituals and processions. Though reasonably comprehensive in membership, the scuole assigned neither equal rank nor similar obligations to all their brothers, showed no sign of descending socially below the level of craftsmen and shopkeepers, and were accustomed to exact entrance fees and subscriptions. Numbers were limited, firmly in theory and sloppily in practice, by legislation of the Council of Ten.[13]

For centuries the Scuole Grandi had excluded women from membership unless it took the form of spiritual alliances or partnerships formed with communities of nuns. It would have been hard to require women to perform public rituals of self-flagellation, even though some nuns were known to use the discipline with great ardor within their cloisters.[14] True, the difficulty was not insuperable, for the scuole were well acquainted with the practice of exempting certain categories of members — noblemen, clerics, physicians, and others — from the obligation to wield the scourge. But lay women could neither perform professional services nor bring prestige to the scuole. Such things did not matter to the Confraternity of the Rosary. Indeed, statistics from Colmar in Alsace, where women accounted for some three-fifths of the first thousand persons to join this body, suggest the strength of its potential appeal to members of the excluded sex.[15]

It is tempting to see these different species of fraternity, one traditional and one innovative but both pursuing spiritual merit, as manifestations of two differing versions of Catholicism coexisting in Venice. One thinks of William Christian's illuminating distinction between the Catholicism of the Church Universal and the Catholicism which has local roots and is founded on local shrines and local observances.[16] Certainly, Venice was far removed from the agricultural towns and townlike villages of Spain, and the Scuole Grandi were in one respect neither local nor parochial. They promoted ceremonies and observances that cast their net across the entire city, and were concentrated neither on any one of the seventy parish churches nor on any one of the six regions known as the *sestieri*. Though they were not part of a universal fellowship, and were subordinated to no archconfraternity in Rome, their statutes were not peculiar to Venice and did bear a loose resemblance to those of other confraternities in other Italian cities; the influence of the mendicant friars was far-reaching enough to see to that.[17] But their bonds with Venice, the city and the polity, were far more in evidence than were their links with Rome or the diocese or their affiliations to any religious order. One might almost speak of a "Renaissance Catholicism" existing in close partnership with a city-state, striving to bring it prosperity and protection by adding to its store of merit and virtue and helping to curb and cancel its sins.

It is true that, in the fifteenth century, there was not much actual tension between the kind of institution that turned inward toward Venice itself and the kind that, like the Confraternity of the Rosary, looked outward toward the universal Church. Clear contrasts were soon blurred. Before long, the Germans in Venice were demanding a more "visible" School of the Rosary of their own, and in subsequent years a conventional local scuola, dedicated to San Chiereghino in the church of San Simeone Profeta, was to impose on its brethren the task of saying the rosary and so to join the universal fellowship.[18] But the Rosary did stand for a kind of individualistic and introspective piety alien to the Scuole Grandi, and its proponents did represent a kind of austerity easily repelled by Venetian excess. In the late fifteenth century, one Dominican Observant, Felix Faber of Ulm, an affectionate visitor to the religious house in Castello from which the new cult of the Marian Psalter was launched, robustly criticized the kind of opulent and worldly piety represented by the Scuole Grandi in their less penitential moods. "Omniscient God only knows," he wrote after witnessing the splendors of Corpus Christi, "whether the most holy and divine sacrament accepted an honor presented in so worldly a manner."[19]

Though internationally famous, exerting his power over different countries at various times, San Rocco could be called a specifically Venetian saint, in that his Venetian followers acquired his whole body by pious theft and proudly put it on display. It was not that the cult grew up around the relics; rather, it provided the incentive to obtain them, and in 1484 the officers contracted with a Benedictine and offered him 600 ducats for five items, the head, both hands, and both feet, with the possibility of adding the epitaph and other available properties. The Benedictine did even better, and the supposed body of the saint, removed from Voghera in the state of Milan, was certified as genuine in 1485 by the patriarch Maffeo Girardo.[20] Here was a spectacular addition to the vast corpus of relics held in Venetian churches and scuole, which could be expected to earn divine protection for the city. Little boys in Feltre, a subject city, would later be instructed to pray "for our most illustrious overlords in Venice, that the Lord God by virtue of the numerous relics of holy bodies located in that city may uphold them in their gentle and generous power and prosperity, and defend them against all treachery, famine, pestilence and war, and from all adversity."[21] The body of San Rocco would prove a lucrative attraction to pilgrims — whether Jerusalem pilgrims waiting for a ship in May and visiting the churches and relics of Venice to pass the time profitably away, or people who had made a special journey to see it.[22]

Devotion to a healer, and to a "specialist" saint of comparatively recent origin and recognition, was a new departure for the Scuole Grandi; the older ones were dedicated to the Virgin Mary and to saints of the New Testament—perhaps, through them, to all saints. In the early fourteenth century the Scuola della Misericordia had dedicated itself to the Virgin; to John the Baptist; to the apostles Peter, Paul, and Mark; and then to all saints, male and female, with a special obligation to kneel or genuflect when, in public processions, they passed the great door of St. Mark's.[23] As preachers of the Rosary doubtless reminded their hearers, the Virgin was an immensely powerful protector, and to honor her through the recitation of the Marian Psalter would be to win a defense against "the fire of mischief, against lightning and thunder, against brigands, thieves and murderers, and against all the assaults of enemies from Hell;" indeed, the renewal of the devotion, at some unspecified time between the death of the Virgin herself and the coming of St. Dominic, had put an end to a dreadful outbreak of pestilence.[24] But San Rocco had the advantage of a more specific brief. When Master Johannes, the host of a cosy German inn near Rialto, died in 1483, and plague was suspected, his family fled in fear to Padua. But Felix Faber and his fellow-lodgers "went to the church of San Rocco in the city of Venice, and there we invoked the aforesaid saint, who is the special helper of those who fear the pestilence, that they might not be infected."[25] San Rocco, who had himself suffered, had a special power because of his humanity; indeed, he was usually portrayed as having the boil on his thigh, as a symbol of the corruption and vulnerability of the flesh, less elegant but more poignant than the older protector against pestilence, St. Sebastian pierced with arrows. These qualities, and the presence of his bones in the city, may well have made him a fitting patron for a Scuola Grande.

In most other respects, the Scuola di San Rocco was closely modeled on its older sister companies, and the preamble to its statutes echoes those of the Misericordia and San Giovanni Evangelista. There is not much evidence of radical change in the devotional practices of the Scuole Grandi of Venice during the fourteenth and fifteenth centuries. Distrustful of an enthusiastic religious movement, the authorities had dispersed the White Penitents from Venice in the autumn of 1399,[26] and the traditions of the scuole remained, in theory at least, those stemming from the demonstrations of 1260. Changes occurred, rather, in the social and economic structures of the scuole, as they were loaded with responsibility for administering perpetual trusts or *commes-*

sarie di anima, and hence for managing the investments in government stock or house property which yielded those trusts a regular and continuing income.[27] Almost inevitably, this development called for a division of the membership into an order of officeholders — literate, experienced, and sufficiently reputable to undertake these administrative tasks — and an order of social inferiors, who were the most likely beneficiaries from the substantial resources of the confraternity. By the end of the fifteenth century, a kind of contract was being enforced, whereby only the poorer brothers were bound to perform the full range of the more arduous devotional duties, in return for the expectation and enjoyment of the more substantial benefits (which included rent-free housing and regular distributions of alms).[28]

Comparisons with Florentine flagellant brotherhoods may help to identify unusual characteristics of the Venetian scuole. Their Florentine counterparts were more volatile and, in their devotions, more receptive to innovation. According to John Henderson's statistics, between 1240 and 1300, flagellant companies represented a mere 18 percent of the total number of brotherhoods in Florence, but by 1440–60, the proportion had risen to something like 40 percent. Their devotions began to adopt new forms and to focus on private and essentially symbolic rituals performed at night and in near darkness.[29] Individual fraternities could change direction quite abruptly: the Compagnia de' Magi at first devoted itself to magnificent pageantry for the honor of God and the fame of the city but ended its career as a very private and introverted company of flagellants which had turned to the discipline and the hearing of sermons.[30]

Ronald Weissman has interpreted the rituals of the Florentine "night companies" as a means of suspending normal social relationships, of briefly obliterating hierarchy and submerging it (if only overnight) beneath the anonymity of the hooded penitent expiating sin.[31] But the Scuole Grandi, as the state demanded, reflected rather than canceled the social order. Normally deferential enough, they incurred the censure of the Council of Ten on one occasion when they took it upon themselves to define the financial terms on which noblemen might enter their ranks: it was not their business to dictate to the patriciate.[32] Arrangements for exemptions, introduced during the fourteenth century, declared that noblemen were not to "beat themselves;" indeed, certain young patricians were actually sentenced to imprisonment and exile by the Council of Ten for undergoing public flagellation in the church of Santa Maria Zobenigo on Good Friday 1438, an over-zealous act that not only violated public decency but also offended against privilege and threatened to bring their own rank into disrepute.[33]

Certain public ceremonies seemed designed to emphasize the status of noblemen within the great confraternities. Canon Pietro Casola, a Jerusalem pilgrim from Milan, described the splendid Corpus Christi procession of 1494, in which the plebeian members of the Scuole Grandi filed first past the host in its pyx on the high altar of St. Mark's. The friars and clergy of the city followed, and then—clearly separated by these clerics from the rank and file—came a further cohort of sixty patricians. They wore togas, the everyday dress of most Venetians, and not the white overgarments of the ordinary penitents. But they announced their loyalties by carrying *doppieri,* heavy bundles of candles flaming like torches and molded in the different colors favored by the various Scuole Grandi, and the curious spectator was told that they were brethren of these schools.[34] Consciousness of rank, so plainly proclaimed in the procession, may well have reflected the greater rigidity and formality of the Venetian social structure, with its legally defined and castelike patriciate and its secondary privileged order of citizenry.

As mentioned already, social differentiation was almost forced on the brothers by the responsibility of the scuole for large permanent endowments. Here, too, there was a striking contrast, for the more egalitarian flagellants of Florence displayed indifference, even hostility, to possessions. They left the great fortunes to be amassed by the *laudesi* companies; their charity was confined to personal almsgiving, offered first to their own brothers and then, should none prove to be in need, to deserving outsiders.[35] In this the Scuole Grandi came closer to the penitential brotherhoods that later arose in Marseilles in the sixteenth century and, with their large reserves, backed the near dictatorship of the Catholic zealot Charles Casaulx.[36]

Relations between the brotherhoods and the state were more stable, less clouded by suspicion, in Venice than in Florence (Figure 10.1). It was true that the Venetian government's attitude to the penitential movements of 1399 had actually been much more forthright than that of the Florentine communal councils, for the Venetians had first diverted

Figure 10.1. Gentile Bellini, *Procession in Piazza San Marco,* showing members of the Scuola Grande di San Giovanni Evangelista in procession with the doge and other civil authorities. Dated 1496. Venice, Accademia. Photo Alinari/Art Resource, N.Y.

the penitents and then suppressed them and exiled their leaders, while the Florentines had merely displayed an understandable suspicion of the approaching crowds. But Venice came to terms more readily than did Florence with its homegrown fraternities.

In both cities, certainly, the authorities sensed that these organizations could easily harbor conspiracies or become instruments of faction. Hence the early statutes of the Scuole Grandi demand an express undertaking not to engage in plots against the state but to do only things that advanced the well-being of the doge and his subjects.[37] In the 1370s Florentine flagellant companies, involved in peace demonstrations, were dissolved as tools of the Guelf party. In the 1450s at least one Florentine flagellant fraternity tried to extend charity into politics by offering to assist the weaker candidates, the "deboli alo squittino," in the electoral districts or *gonfaloni.*[38]

Both the Venetian and the Florentine states showed anxiety to detach members of their ruling orders from the confraternities or at least to prevent a deep and time-consuming involvement with their administration. Some Italian cities (Arezzo and Milan are examples) charged their patricians with the administration of confraternities and endowed charities.[39] Florence and Venice followed another course, Venice reserving the administration of the Scuole Grandi for its lesser elite of non-noble merchants rather than for its nobility. In 1410 the Council of Ten confined office in the Scuole Grandi either to native citizens or to people who had obtained their citizenship by the issue of a special privilege but had already served at least twenty years in the scuola.[40] And in 1462 they stipulated that notaries of the Ducal Chancery were not to be assigned any duties in the Scuole Grandi.[41] Admittedly, the first decree was probably aimed at foreigners and newcomers as much as against patricians, and the avowed purpose of the second was to save civil servants from distraction by other commitments. There was no open suggestion that either nobles or notaries would make improper use of their positions in the scuole, and no proposal that noblemen be deprived of the spiritual benefits of membership, which they coveted to the extent of making belated attempts to enter them on the point of death. But the effect of these measures was to help consolidate the position of nonnoble merchants and professional men within the social order, and at the same time to stabilize the confraternities by making their social utility clear. One of their functions, henceforth, was to create a more clearly defined role within the state for the middle condition of men and to extend the range of attractive privileges at the disposal of state and society.

In the 1440s the Florentine government passed what Richard Trexler has called a "fundamental law," denying membership in confraternities to members of the city's "political class" of veduti. They may not have enforced the law consistently, but this move was much tougher and displayed a much more uneasy attitude toward confraternities.[42]

Florentines, indeed, were warier than Venetians of confraternities at all social levels. They were more reluctant to permit the development of artisans' brotherhoods, although such institutions became more common in the second half of the fifteenth century,[43] and possibly even earlier. In Venice the scuola, or pious corporation, was closely bound to the arte, which consisted of all persons authorized to ply a particular trade. Despite being founded on different principles, the arte and the scuola normally coincided in membership, although a distinctive cultural or linguistic group within a trade might be allowed (as were the

German journeymen bakers of Venice in 1422) to form a separate scuola of their own for religious and charitable purposes only.

In effect, the overlapping arte and scuola formed the Venetian guild.[44] Guilds in Venice, smaller and more numerous than the Florentine "conglomerates" and forming a cluster of *arti medie* rather than two tiers of greater and lesser guilds, had none of the political significance of their Florentine counterparts. They were not officered by patricians, and membership did not, as in Florence, bestow rights or permit entry to the ruling order.[45] Venetian guilds were important chiefly as administrative links between the state and its subjects, and Venetians were not familiar with the Florentine concept of *sottoposti,* of workers who are subject to a guild but not part of it. Venetian patricians were alert to the ways in which most forms of brotherhood, especially those that dispensed charity, could (if properly controlled by state magistracies) be used in their turn to control ordinary people and remind them of their civic duties. It was not in their interests that artisans should remain outside the professional scuole; if they did, they would be less subject to authority rather than less capable of making trouble.

In dealing with confraternities, the Venetian patriciate tended to rely on constant surveillance, whereas the Florentines uttered at intervals the threat of dissolution and interfered more openly and bluntly. In 1419 their priors had "learned that as a result of the meeting of certain confraternities, the spirits of the citizenry have been perturbed, divisions have arisen, and many other inconveniences have occurred." Hence the threatened dissolution of "every confraternity, whether penitential or dedicated to singing lauds . . . which is accustomed to assemble in the ecclesiastical foundations of the city of Florence."[46] Though not as final or inflexible as they sounded, such measures could cause a hiatus in the activities of confraternities or change the nature of their membership even if they survived the crisis, as did the Compagnia de' Magi after 1419 or the flagellant company of San Paolo after the later ban on confraternities in 1458–64.[47] In Venice the Council of Ten had insisted in 1401 that all statutes be submitted for its approval.[48] During the fifteenth century, it contented itself with regulating the social composition of officeholders, with curbing potentially disorderly activities (from processions to night meetings and public distributions of alms), with asserting proprietorially its own right to introduce into the rank and file of "our Scuole Grandi" persons willing to render service to the state, and with demanding of the scuole expanding contingents of bowmen and boatmen to fight in the republic's wars.[49]

It would have been difficult, in either city, to dissolve brotherhoods that discharged important functions as public trustees. But sudden influxes of excessive wealth could be perilous and might expose a fraternity to very oppressive state interference. In Florence the fraternity of Orsanmichele suffered the imposition of obligations to lend to the commune and had to bear both with the commune's insistence on appointing the fraternity's financial officers and with insinuations that its captains were corrupt.[50] In all probability, the older scuole in Venice advanced toward wealth in step with each other, none being sufficiently prominent to attract a landslide of gifts or legacies.

Given the prestige enjoyed by another board of public trustees, the patrician Procuratori di San Marco, the Scuole Grandi could not claim exclusive control over institutional charity.[51] They retained their separate identities and a certain sense of rivalry, and never submerged them in a unified organization. This probably commended them to the state, for its rulers knew that control over charity is a source of power, and they were reluctant to see too great a concentration of such control; such considerations may explain the state's failure to amalgamate its hospitals and its firm refusal to introduce a Monte di Pietà. True, Venice had at least one miracle-working image to match the famous portrait of the Madonna which showered riches on Orsanmichele. But the chief beneficiaries of the bounty that flowed toward the Madonna dei Miracoli, discovered in a narrow *calle* near the Ca' Amai in 1480, were the nuns of Santa Chiara di Murano and not a lay brotherhood.[52]

Since the state was diverting religious institutions away from investment in house property in the middle and later fourteenth century,[53] and since it was recognized that repairs and maintenance often threatened to soak up income from real estate, there was probably a strong natural incentive to the scuole to turn toward the other readily available safe security appropriate to the sober portfolios of charities: government stock. This undoubtedly provided the foundation for the important dowry fund established by the Scuola di San Giovanni Evangelista in 1422.[54] In Venice the state had less need to insist aggressively on its right to borrow. When bonds began to depreciate and the scuole swung back toward property, the state seemed confident of exacting services from them and thus ensuring that their wealth did not elude the public grasp.[55]

Since the Venetian state could live with and even harness its confraternities, they could the more readily express a form of "civic Catholicism." As one of them proudly announced in 1476, "to the honor of our Lord God, the four Scuole dei Battuti are four pillars of this glorious city."[56] But they did not stand for state worship or for a religion crudely and deliberately employed as an instrument of control and designed to procure submission and obedience to a ruling order. Renaissance states seldom saw themselves merely as manmade constructions designed to meet human needs and seldom found legitimation solely in their origins or descent from Trojans or Romans or other exemplars of human wisdom.

Civic patriotism could well be expressed as belief in a people's special religious mission, in the conviction that the Florentines had been chosen to bring about the rebirth of the Church from its deep corruption, the Venetians to defend Christendom against the Turk, and that both must be pure enough to perform these tasks.[57] The Scuole Grandi set out to secure the intercession of the Virgin and saints on behalf of the city, to keep and show some of its relics, and to enhance the merit it would need in order to win the favor of God, on which depended so much of success in the world. The old statutes of Santa Maria della Misericordia would remind the brothers that the "congregation" was founded "that the aforesaid Virgin Madonna Santa Maria di Valverde, our mother of mercy, may beg Our Lord Jesus Christ to keep our blessed city of Venice in good order and in peace and love, with all the lands of Christendom."[58]

To win divine favor, one must curb sin. As did most confraternities, the Scuole Grandi sought to compose quarrels and to define respectable behavior, by excluding certain kinds of undesirable people and by proscribing certain forms of reprehensible activity, including some that were furtive, hard to trace, and perhaps not actually illegal. In their statutes they observed the conventions widespread throughout Italy pretty closely, deeming it wise to condemn theft, though they did not expressly proscribe either usurious lending or (as in Florence) homosexual practices.[59] "Unnatural" vice perhaps seemed too obviously monstrous for inclusion here. It had always to be a matter for legal action, and not just for fraternal rebuke; a crime to be purged by the ax and the fire, applied by the Council of Ten through its Collegium Sodomitarum.[60] Much of the displeasure of the scuole was directed against blasphemy, gambling, and taking pleasure in taverns—three closely related offenses acknowledged to be of a nature both spiritual and social, since they were said both to impoverish families and to wound Christ. Through their own regulations, with the sanction of fines and expulsion, the Scuole Grandi were imposing on their own members a discipline that was later to be thrust on the whole city by a new magistracy, the Esecutori contro la Bestemmia.[61]

There was nothing unusual in these censorious attitudes, but the Scuole may have contributed to Venice's unusual success in attaching a social stigma to taverns—an achievement handsomely acknowledged even by Felix Faber, whose admiration for Venice was never unstinted.[62] Relatively few Venetian patricians accepted the argument that the dropping of the wind behind the Venetian fleet at a crucial point in a naval battle in 1499 could be traced to divine displeasure at Venice's lack of charity toward poor nobles.[63] But most would have shared the diarist Priuli's more commonplace reflection that "we read in the Bible how often ancient peoples suffered punishment, mortification, ruin and exile on account of their sins and of their refusal to obey the commandments and precepts of God."[64]

In their efforts to correct sin, however, the Scuole Grandi did not go so far as to conduct didactic or evangelical campaigns; they had no particular concern with the moral improvement of youth, although they did offer marriage portions to young women of good reputation; and their objective, seemingly, was to prevent lapses on the part of fundamentally respectable people rather than to reclaim those for whom sinning was a way of life. Such missionary activities were certainly known in fifteenth-century Venice, but they were more appropriate to Brother John of Erfurt, who not only preached the Rosary but also effected the redemption of a number of harlots and the discomfiture of a number of pimps.[65] Didactic campaigns were certainly more prominent in Florence. Richard Trexler has vividly depicted the fifteenth-century youth companies, which sought to control the leisure of adolescents in danger of sin, and he has described the Florentine belief in the redemptive power of innocence.[66]

Are there any Venetian parallels at all? It is certainly true that circa 1500 the Venetian Scuole Grandi liked to include children and young people in their tableaux and ceremonies. Usually they appeared in the guise of angels, as did those who scattered flowers over the doge and ambassadors at the Corpus Christi procession of 1494. Occasionally they took up other roles: a beautiful young woman played Venice itself in 1511, and a child was once assigned the task of "showing San Rocco the pestilence."[67] But they were very much a part of the dramatic ensemble, integrated with other actors, and there is not much evidence that the Venetians were prepared to single them out, much less to abandon their traditional respect for age and experience and see the future of the city reposing in the young. Nothing seems yet to be known of pious youth clubs, as distinct from exclusive festive organizations such as the Compagnie delle Calze, in fifteenth-century Venice. It should be said, however, that by the end of the century such clubs were being promoted by Franciscan preachers of the Observance in certain subject cities on the mainland, and that youth organizations concentrating on imparting Christian knowledge rather than enforcing Christian morality would later appear in the Schools of Christian Doctrine in Venice itself.[68]

The Scuole Grandi represented a civic religion if by *civic* we mean "citywide." In their search for members, they all attempted to embrace the whole city rather than to confine recruitment to particular parishes or quarters. They practiced a kind of ceremonial and administered a species of welfare organization which contributed to the unity of Venice. Some of this was epitomized in the duties of the so-called degani: the older scuole had two for each sestiere, that the whole city might be covered, and they performed the dual function of summoning brothers to processions and of reporting any cases of hardship they encountered among them.[69] There are no systematic analyses of the residence patterns of the brothers of the Scuole Grandi, but from the painstaking researches of Richard Mackenney it is now clear that even minor brotherhoods in Renaissance Venice, though showing a natural bias toward the region in which they stood, could recruit some members from all the sestieri; the more socially exalted the scuola, the more even the distribution was likely to be.[70]

Edward Muir has written of the changes in the public ceremonial life of Venice and of the shift in the late fourteenth and fifteenth centuries towards rituals focusing on the central places of the city and exalting the city's patron, St. Mark, above those of the parish churches. He has made much of the abolition of the Festival of the Twelve Marys, in which the parishes were strongly represented, in favor of a more decorous ceremony involving a solemn procession of the doge and *signoria* from San Marco to Santa Maria Formosa.[71] There is not much detailed evidence to back his suggestion that control of poor relief was then passing from the parishes to the Scuole Grandi[72]—we know too little of the parish accounts to say that with confidence. But it does seem likely that the "parochial age" of Venice lay in the sixteenth century rather than in the fifteenth. It was then that the senate entrusted numerous additional tasks, especially in poor relief and emergency policing, to the parishes and their deputies, and the Catholic church itself had a strong desire to remind the faithful of their duties as parishioners.[73] One symptom of the process was the development, in Venice as elsewhere, of the confraternities of the Blessed Sacrament, which were founded on the parishes and which helped both to enhance their meager revenues and to decorate their churches.[74]

Florentine experience may well have been broadly similar, since some of the flagellant confraternities recruited from all or most parts of the city in the fifteenth century, and the parishes and the smaller subdivisions likewise came into their own during the sixteenth.[75] It is worth remembering, though, that the development of the Scuole Grandi occurred in a city whose political system gave much less weight to the locality than did the Florentine, for there was no Venetian equivalent to the Florentine gonfaloni. Local prominence—the concentration of a family and its friends in a traditional bailiwick—provided no entrée to Venetian politics and officeholding as it did in Florence.[76] The Scuole Grandi were not swimming against a strong tide, although they did perform an impressive role by drawing even humble people into a very broad network of relationships and obligations.

Without doubt, involvement with the state meant the use of the scuole for warlike and diplomatic purposes, and it would be naive to pretend that the sole purpose of the great brotherhoods was to win divine approval for a city and a people devoted to spiritual ends. Their part in recruitment for the armed forces has already been mentioned. Such responsibilities, which seem quite alien to the confraternities of Florence, were to become increasingly burdensome during the sixteenth century, when the enjoyment of much of their charity became conditional on readiness to serve in the galleys.[77] During the wars that began in 1494, the Scuole Grandi moved between sacred celebrations, at which they presented biblical and religious tableaux, and other ceremonies marking the conclusion of new alliances. These were solemnly acted out in civic pageants that depicted Venice itself and the heads of state locked in the struggle for power in the peninsula and included allegorical figures such as Peace and Mercy. Even here, it was customary to proclaim the sacred character of Venice and its peculiar relationship with St. Mark and the Holy Spirit.[78] Occasionally, however (the best example comes from 1526), the procession seemed designed to convey not the piety but the wealth of the city, since its magnificent displays of silver vessels and reliquaries were offered in homage to the power of money to finance war. San Giovanni Evangelista bore the slogans *Venetia plena divitiis* ("Venice filled with riches") and *Hic Venetiis aurum et argentum* ("Here is the gold and silver of the Venetians") (Figure 10.2).[79] In the past, at least one festival had been performed for similar purposes in Florence, as was the Festival of the Magi in a moment of grave domestic crisis during the 1460s.[80] In Venice the intended audience was probably not the Venetian people but rather foreign diplomats, agents, and spies, including those of hostile powers. Ambassadors of friendly states might join the pageant; others watched it. Commynes was invited to witness the processions celebrating the Holy League of 1495, which was directed partly against the too-rapid successes of the king of France; so was the Turkish envoy, "hidden at a window; he had been dismissed, but they wanted him to see this festival."[81] For many Venetians, no doubt, the point was not to watch but to take part and so to feel some identity with the city and its friends abroad.

Such talk of a civic religion inevitably conjures up those ominous terms *secularization* and *laicization*. They imply different things. *Secularization* suggests a move toward worldly concerns: perhaps toward a pompous and materialistic piety, perhaps toward activities whose avowed

Figure 10.2. Detail of figure 10.1, showing members of the Scuola Grande di San Giovanni Evangelista carrying the richly adorned reliquary of the true cross. Venice, Accademia. Photo Alinari/Art Resource, N.Y.

purpose was to benefit society rather than the soul. *Laicization* may well refer to something almost opposite, that is, to a fuller participation of the laity in religious life, and the breaking down of barriers between the world and those who are out of it. One may well suspect that by the late fifteenth century the brotherhoods had come to represent a formalistic, mechanical version of religious experience, unduly concerned with outward things, and badly in need of the reinvigorating hands of the devotion of the Rosary and of the Companies or Oratories of Divine Love.

Italian brotherhoods in general had long promoted the role of the laity in the ceremonies of the Church, through processions and the singing of lauds, and had encouraged their better understanding, by means of specially provided sermons.[82] They had laid heavy stress on those things that laypeople could and did do without the intervention of a priest, such as the recitation of prayers, the distribution of charity, and the acting of sacred characters in pageants or mystery plays.[83] Possibly the companies did worse than that. Gilles-Gerard Meersseman, the historian of Dominican brotherhoods, noted with regret a number of (to him) ominous secularizing developments that occurred within the fifteenth century: emancipation from the influence of spiritual directors, nepotism in the form of bequests made conditional on the admission of relatives to the brotherhood, roistering on the feast days of patron saints, and above all a tendency on the part of brotherhoods devoted to works of mercy (as at Arezzo and Imola) to abandon liturgical duties in favor of social administration.[84] Judiciously, however, he cheered himself with other, more hopeful, signs, of a readiness to look beyond the formal and external. An extensive commentary on the statutes of a flagellant company in Bologna, written in 1443, seemed clearly intended to explain the spiritual meaning of ritual, to diminish the value of physical acts, such as extravagant gesture in prayer, and to represent prayer itself as an act of the mind.[85]

Venetian evidence suggests that the Scuole Grandi had long been unlikely to submit in any formal or official manner to the direction of clerics. There seems to be no obvious trace of their having chosen, or asked a local convent to choose for them, a preeminent spiritual director, as did the *disciplinati* of Siena and Prato in the fourteenth century.[86] They were, however, eager to foster good relations and pool good works with Venetian clergy and nuns, and they undoubtedly walked with them (or rather, before them) in the great public processions. At the close of the fifteenth century, the Scuola di San Rocco could refer without hesitation to its priestly and clerical brothers.[87] Once, in 1345, another scuola had doubted the propriety of giving them any such name, since laymen could not compel clerics to observe a rule, and therefore the officers would not have full power to command them.[88] No such scruples appeared to trouble the devotees of San Rocco. The scuole were not content with chapels in mendicant churches or with meeting-places in their convents: they wanted premises of their own, and the Scuola di San Rocco aspired from the beginning to have a church for itself. But the Franciscan Conventuals of the great church of the Frari became its landlords, and it built nearby. For half a century, from 1489 to 1540, their relations were governed by an unduly complicated agreement, which not merely entailed the payment of rents and dues to the friars but also imposed on both parties an obligation to attend each other's festivals and funerals. The friars could certainly have exerted great influence on the brothers through the pulpit, since the contract bound the scuola to invite the Franciscans to preach at all the monthly assemblies.[89] But it would no doubt have been unwise, and unacceptable to the Council of Ten, to offer any of them a position that could imply that the scuole were clerically dominated and therefore entitled to claim fiscal or other privileges as ecclesiastical institutions. Their entitlement to receive and administer extensive properties depended in part upon their recognition as lay organizations. In Florence, formal clerical control is easier to detect. The statutes of confraternities seem to have been willingly submitted to the energetic archbishop Antonino Pierozzi, and he was not the first to receive them. Friars were included among the captains of at least one brotherhood and probably more.[90] It is true that in Venice the patriarch had to be consulted where a scuola wished to build a church or to remove it from one site to another, that he might be called upon to authenticate relics, and that he could add to the indulgences available to members of a confraternity.[91] But the approval of statutes fell to the Council of Ten, and subjection to the state was far more in evidence than was any formal deference to the judgment of the Church.

The Venetian scuole were remarkable not only for their freedom from formal clerical control (they may have received clerical advice more often than they admitted) but also for their conservatism in devotion. To judge by statutes alone, in the absence of information about actual practices, the Scuole Grandi of the late fifteenth century adopted a traditional attitude toward the sacraments and were not inclined to insist on the value of frequent communion and confession. "It is customary for men of the world to shave their beards and wash their shirts at least once a month," declared the mentor of the disciplinati of Bologna, exhorting his readers to a spiritual cleansing in the form of confessions made at similar intervals.[92] But the Scuola di San Rocco seemed unwilling to urge its brothers beyond the legal minimum of annual communion, with some encouragement to confession, and it reserved much of its rhetorical power for extolling daily attendance at the Mass, as the reenactment of the Passion of Christ.[93]

Without doubt, to take up another of Meersseman's points, officers of the Scuole Grandi did involve themselves in charitable activities which, being elaborate and systematic, threatened to divert time from devotional to administrative pursuits. Conservative in their devotional regime, they were quite enterprising in the practice of mercy and charity. Like the Buonomini di San Martino in Florence, they dealt with the problems of those loosely called *poveri vergognosi,* who had to be sought out and assisted in their own homes. Venice had no confraternity solely and expressly devoted to these people until the 1530s, when — acknowledging their debt to Florence — they established the fraternity of Sant'Antonino. In effect, however, the Scuole Grandi were dealing with vergognosi long before that time and using the word in their records. This term could be used with a strict meaning to refer to persons who had fallen from good fortune and could no longer maintain their noble or civil condition: some were merely in reduced circumstances, others actually in a state of destitution. But the words could be stretched to denote almost any kind of respectable house poor, as distinct from street beggars or persons shamelessly pursuing charity: the poveri vergognosi were the "shamefaced poor," who would struggle to conceal rather than advertise their distress.[94] The Scuole Grandi were aware of both kinds of poor, and when they wrote of the decayed gentlefolk and citizens they sometimes used the participle *mensuegnudi.* In 1506 the Scuola della Carità announced that it was "at present heavily burdened and weighted with poor persons, and especially with our own good citizens, who on account of their own ill fortune and for no other reasons have been brought low and have descended into the greatest poverty and wretchedness, so that they not only lack the means to maintain their lives and those of their families, but even require assistance in order to cover their bodies and conceal some part of their need."[95]

The scuole resembled the Buonomini di San Martino of Florence in that they concentrated chiefly on the problems of poor families rather than on those of solitary individuals. But they differed from the Buonomini in concerning themselves principally with their own membership, with persons who had contributed to the common pool of merit. And the Scuole Grandi were far more than almsgiving societies. Their resources came to include both extensive dowry funds and a number of almshouses, as well as some tiny hospitals similar in dimensions to the many small private foundations distributed throughout the city.[96]

Administering charities certainly implied much concern with the practical and the material, both on the part of the officers and on that of potential beneficiaries. Some of the entrants were driven by questionable motives, and seemed eager only to scheme for and bargain with the benefits the scuole offered.[97] But the wording of their records does not suggest any glaring contradiction or unresolved tension between charity performed as a spiritual action and charity addressed to practical and worldly concerns. Resolving to build a new block of almshouses in 1511, for the benefit of poor brothers with numerous children and indebted for rent, the officials of San Rocco reminded themselves that "works of charity lie chiefly in assisting the poor and needy, and since our blessed confraternity was founded in the love of God we must with all diligence assist our poor brothers, of whom we must have care no less than of ourselves, according to the divine precept, which says, 'Love your neighbor as yourself.'"[98]

In the late fifteenth century, friars of the Dominican Observance, visiting the city, believed in detaching the worldly from the sacred and in divorcing pagan from Christian culture. They were sometimes unfavorably impressed by the Venetian tendency to confuse the two. John of Erfurt self-consciously resisted the temptation to base his sermons on Cicero or Virgil or "the fantastic dogma of the philosophers and the pretty fictions of the poets."[99] Felix Faber, censorious of the Dominicans of Santi Giovanni e Paolo, referred with distaste to the presence of pagan images in their great church, including the figures of naked gladiators and boys embellishing the doges' tombs. But he noted that the Venetian people took them for saints or biblical figures, supposing that Hercules must be Sampson and Venus the Magdalen.[100] Perhaps it was true of the Scuole Grandi that they, too, were capable of absorbing worldly paraphernalia, material resources, and even a smattering of classical culture into a conservative Christian devotional regime. In the 1460s, the Scuola della Carità enjoyed quoting Seneca and citing Cicero and other ancient authors in evidence of the need to be grateful to benefactors;[101] this was an agreeable literary flourish imparting elegance to normally austere registers, and was hardly a surrender to the values of the ancient world.

In general, the Scuole Grandi were expressions of a form of civic Catholicism, and they could become so in Venice because of the state's capacity for coming to terms with them, and for harnessing fraternities more effectively than did the rulers of the Florentine commune. Though not militantly anticlerical, they stood for a species of religious organization that had developed, through the Council of Ten, far stronger links with the state than with the parish, the diocese, or the pope. They promoted the cohesion of Venetian society by stressing the mutual obligations of rich and poor, by defining the limits of respectability, by proscribing antisocial behavior, and by enticing their members away from essentially local concerns. Yet the state they served was a sacred corpus, and one of their purposes was to add to its virtue, to beg for it the intercession of the saints, and to make it worthier of the favor of God. In the next century, their importance would scarcely be challenged. True, they would be increasingly affected by the state's obsessive concern to raise oarsmen for its reserve fleet; they would face stronger rivalry from the parishes; and new kinds of charity, redemptive as well as supportive, would arise to deal with the obtrusive problem of the unrespectable poor. But on dramatic occasions, especially during Paul V's Interdict, they and the Conventual Friars would still stand publicly for an old Catholicism that had forged strong links with the state, against a new Catholicism linked through the newer religious orders to the pope in Rome.[102] During the Counter-Reformation, the tension between the Venetian state and the Society of Jesus, between the Catholicism of St. Mark and that of St. Peter, had become much more formidable than the mild but unmistakable contrast between the civic and the universal brotherhoods of the late fifteenth century— between the Scuole Grandi of Venice and the Confraternity of the Rosary in the convent of Dominican friars.

NOTES

My thanks are due to John Henderson, Richard Mackenney, Richard Palmer, and William Wurthmann for their kind permission to consult and to cite material of theirs not yet in print.

The following abbreviations are used in citing archival material:

ASV   Archivio di Stato, Venice
IRSG   Inquisitori et Revisori sopra le Scuole Grandi
SDRM   Sala Diplomatica Regina Margherita
SG   Scuole Grandi
SR   Archivio della Scuola Grande di S. Rocco, Venice

1. I was especially excited by Wilbur Jordan's first volume, *Philanthropy in England, 1480–1660* (London: Allen and Unwin, 1959).

2. SR, Mariegola, fols. 11r–16r. See also W. B. Wurthmann, "The Scuole Grandi and Venetian Art, 1260–c. 1500" (Ph.D. diss., University of Chicago, 1975), 118–25.

3. *The Memoirs of Philippe de Commynes*, ed. S. Kinser, trans. I. Cazeaux, 2 vols. (Columbia: University of South Carolina Press, 1969), 2:493.

4. L. Sbriziolo, "Per la storia delle confraternite veneziane: Dalle deliberazioni miste (1310–1476) del Consiglio dei Dieci. Le scuole dei battuti," in *Miscellanea Gilles Gerard Meersseman*, 2 vols. *Italia Sacra: Studi e documenti de storia ecclesiastica*, 16 (Padua: Antenore, 1970), 2:737.

5. Cf. SR, Mariegola, fols. 8v–9r.

6. Ibid., fol. 14, 16 May 1487.

7. Sbriziolo, "Per la storia," 761–62.

8. F. Faber, *Evagatorium in Terrae Sanctae, Arabiae et Egypti peregrinationem*, ed. C. D. Hassler, 3 vols. (Stuttgart, 1843–49), 3:428–29.

9. Quoted in A. Niero, "Pietà ufficiale e pietà popolare in tempo di peste," in *Venezia e la peste, 1348–1797* (Venice: Marsilio, 1979), 287.

10. See esp. R. J. Palmer, "The Control of Plague in Venice and Northern Italy, 1348–1600" (Ph.D. diss., University of Kent, 1978), 57 ff., particularly his excellent chapter, "Religion and the Plague," 280–314; see also E. Rodenwaldt, *Pest in Venedig 1575–77. Ein Beitrag zur Frage der Infektkette bei den Pestepidemien West-Europas* (Heidelberg: Sitzungsberichte der Heidelberger Akademie der Wissenschaften, Math.-naturw. Klasse, 1953), 66 n. 1.

11. G. G. Meersseman, "Le origini della Confraternità del Rosario e della sua iconografia in Italia," in his *Ordo fraternitatis: Confraternite e pietà dei laici del Medioevo*, 3 vols., *Italia sacra*, 24–26 (Rome: Herder, 1977), 3:1170–1232; for the statutes, see 1215–18.

12. Cf. J. C. Schmitt, "Apostolat mendiant et société: Une confrérie dominicaine à la veille de la réforme," *Annales: Économies, sociétés, civilisations* 26 (1971): 103–4, and idem, "La Confrérie du Rosaire de Colmar (1485): Textes de fondation, 'Exempla' en allemand d'Alain de la Roche, listes des prêcheurs et des soeurs dominicaines," *Archivum Fratrum Predicatorum* 40 (1970): 97–124.

13. Sbriziolo, "Per la storia," 7–8; B. Pullan, *Rich and Poor in Renaissance Venice: The Social Institutions of a Catholic State to 1620* (Oxford: Basil Blackwell, 1971), 86–87.

14. Note the statute of Sta. Maria della Carità (probably of the second half of the thirteenth century): "Item volumus et ordinamus quod non liceat aliquibus nostris officialibus huius fraternitatis recipere aliquam mulierem in fraternitate ista, nisi esset conventus integer monacharum" (SG, Sta. Maria della Carità, 233); see also that of S. Giovanni Evangelista in March 1327: "fuit ordinatum et placuit omnibus quod aliqua domina mundana deinceps non

possit nec debeat recipi in istis nostris scolis ullo modo seu ingenio" (SG, S. Giovanni Evangelista, 7: fol. 17r–v). On the ascetic practices of the nuns of Corpus Christi, see L. Sbriziolo, "Note su Giovanni Dominici," *Rivista di storia della Chiesa in Italia* 24 (1970): 26–27.

15. Schmitt, "Apostolat mendiant," 100.

16. See W. A. Christian, *Local Religion in Sixteenth-Century Spain* (Princeton, N.J.: Princeton University Press, 1981).

17. For several examples, see Meersseman, *Ordo fraternitatis,* vol. 2.

18. A. Niero, "La mariegola della più antica Scuola del Rosario di Venezia," *Rivista di storia della Chiesa in Italia* 15 (1961): 324–36; idem, "Ancora sull' origine del Rosario a Venezia e sulla sua iconografia," *Rivista di storia della Chiesa in Italia* 28 (1974): 465–78; Meersseman, "Le origini," 1199–1201, 1206–14.

19. Faber, *Evagatorium,* 1:106.

20. SG, SR/2, 7, 12 October 1484; SR, Mariegola, fol. 13.

21. See V. Meneghin, "Due compagnie sul modello di quelle del 'Divino Amore' fondate da Francescani a Feltre e a Verona (1499, 1503)," *Archivum Franciscanum Historicum* 62 (1969): 549.

22. SG, SR/2, fol. 6, 18 May 1516; Pullan, *Rich and Poor,* 157–58.

23. SDRM, 76:11.

24. The words are taken from an important piece of propaganda, launched by enthusiasts for the cult of the Marian Psalter, summarizing the sermons which its proponent, the Breton Alain de la Roche, delivered at Douai in 1475. Very likely, this would be used by John of Erfurt. See G. G. Meersseman, "Alano della Rupe e le origini della Confraternità del Rosario," in *Ordo fraternitatis,* 3:1158–59, 1164–65, 1167.

25. Faber, *Evagatorium,* 1:101. On the cult of S. Rocco and its iconography in Venice, see S. Mason Rinaldi, "La peste e le sue immagini nella cultura figurativa veneziana," in *Venezia e la peste,* 209–24.

26. See E. Delaruelle, "Les grandes processions de pénitents de 1349 et 1399," in *Il Movimento dei Disciplinati nel vii centenario del suo inizio (Perugia–1260),* Appendix 9 to *Bollettino della Deputazione di storia patria per l'Umbria* (Spoleto, 1962), 109–45; G. P. Tognetti, "Sul moto dei Bianchi nel 1399," *Bullettino dell' Istituto storico italiano per il medioevo e archivio muratoriano* 78 (1967): 205–343; Sbriziolo, "Note," 9–19.

27. On the development of trusts in Venice and their range of investments, see R. C. Mueller, *The Procuratori di San Marco and the Venetian Credit Market: A Study of the Development of Credit and Banking in the Trecento* (New York: Arno Press, 1977), 47–48, 58–60, 65–71, 114–19.

28. Pullan, *Rich and Poor,* 63–83.

29. See J. S. Henderson, "Piety and Charity in Late Medieval Florence: Religious Confraternities from the Middle of the Thirteenth to the Late Fifteenth Century" (Ph.D. diss., University of London, 1983), 28, 31–32, 77–88. See also G. G. Meersseman, "I Disciplinati di S. Domenico a Firenze," in *Ordo fraternitatis,* vol. 2, esp. 733–39.

30. R. Hatfield, "The Compagnia de' Magi," *Journal of the Warburg and Courtauld Institutes* 32 (1970): 107–61.

31. R. F. E. Weissman, *Ritual Brotherhood in Renaissance Florence* (New York: Academic Press, 1982), 52–53, 91–104.

32. IRSG, 1: fols. 2v–3r, 6 March 1409.

33. Pullan, *Rich and Poor,* 72; G. Ruggiero, *The Boundaries of Eros: Sex Crime and Sexuality in Renaissance Venice* (New York: Oxford University Press, 1985), 141.

34. *Canon Pietro Casola's Pilgrimage to Jerusalem in the Year 1494,* ed. M. M. Newett (Manchester: Manchester University Press, 1907), 148–52.

35. Henderson, "Piety and Charity," 118, 137, 315–17; Weissman, *Ritual Brotherhood,* 130–31.

36. R. R. Harding, "The Mobilization of Confraternities against the Reformation in France," *Sixteenth-Century Journal* 11 (1980): 92–98.

37. For example, SDRM, 76:11; SG, S. Giovanni Evangelista, 3, fol. 13v and 7, fols. 11v–12r. For Florence, Venice, and the Bianchi, see esp. Tognetti, "Sul moto," 256–57, 313–23.

38. See G. A. Brucker, *Florentine Politics and Society, 1343–78* (Princeton, N.J.: Princeton University Press, 1962), 320–21; N. Rodolico, *I Ciompi: Una pagina della storia del proletariato operaio* (Florence: Sansoni, 1945), 54–55; Weissman, *Ritual Brotherhood,* 164–68; J. S. Henderson, "Le confraternite religiose nella Firenze del tardo medioevo: Patroni spirituali e anche politici?," *Ricerche storiche* 15 (1985): 77–94.

39. G. G. Meersseman, "Le Congregazioni della Vergine," in *Ordo fraternitatis,* 2:998; A. Noto, *Gli amici dei poveri di Milano, 1305–1964* (Milan: Giuffré, 1966), 24–25.

40. IRSG, fol. 3r–v, 12 February 1409 (Venetian style).

41. Ibid., fol. 12, 31 March 1462. On the notaries of the chancery, see M. Neff, "A Citizen in the Service of the Patrician State: the Career of Zaccaria de' Freschi," *Studi veneziani,* n.s. 5 (1981): 33–61.

42. R. C. Trexler, *Public Life in Renaissance Florence* (London: Academic Press, 1980), 408; Weissman, *Ritual Brotherhood,* 164–72.

43. Trexler, *Public Life,* 404, 411–12, 414; Weissman, *Ritual Brotherhood,* 64–65.

44. On Venetian guilds, see R. S. Mackenney, "Trade Guilds and Devotional Confraternities in the State and Society of Venice to 1620" (Ph.D. diss., University of Cambridge, 1982), and idem, "Arti e stato a Venezia tra tardo medioevo e '600," *Studi veneziani,* n.s. 5 (1981): 127–43. See also B. Pullan, "Natura e carattere delle scuole," in *Le scuole di Venezia,* ed. T. Pignatti (Milan: Electa, 1981), 9–26.

45. Cf. R. A. Goldthwaite, *The Building of Renaissance Florence: An Economic and Social History* (Baltimore: Johns Hopkins University Press, 1980), 242 ff.

46. Text in G. Brucker, ed., *The Society of Renaissance Florence: A Documentary Study* (New York: Harper and Row, 1971), 83–84; see also idem, *Renaissance Florence* (New York: Wiley, 1969), 208.

47. Hatfield, "Compagnia," 110–11; Weissman, *Ritual Brotherhood,* 117–18, 173–74. See Henderson, "Le confraternite," 86, for examples of the different effects on various confraternities of the law of 1458.

48. IRSG, fol. 2r–v; Sbriziolo, "Per la storia," 724.

49. Sbriziolo, "Per la storia," 724, passim; IRSG, fols. 2r–20v; Wurthmann, "Scuole Grandi," 104–11.

50. See R. C. Trexler, "Florence, by the Grace of the Lord Pope . . . ," *Studies in Medieval and Renaissance History* 9 (1972): 164–69; and, for an extensive and detailed discussion of the fortunes of Orsanmichele, see Henderson, "Piety and Charity," 146 ff.

51. See Mueller, *Procuratori,* passim.

52. D. Malipiero, *Annali veneti dall' anno 1457 al 1500,* ed. A. Sagredo, in *Archivio Storico Italiano* 7 (1843–44): 672.

53. Mueller, *Procuratori,* 125 ff.

54. SG, S. Giovanni Evangelista, 2: fols. 38r–39r.

55. Mueller, *Procuratori,* 140–41; Wurthmann, "Scuole Grandi," 68–69, 84–87.

56. SG, Sta. Maria della Carità, 236; fol. 10v, 1 December 1476.

57. Cf. D. Weinstein, "The Myth of Florence," in *Florentine Studies: Politics and Society in Renaissance Florence,* ed. N. Rubinstein (London: Faber and Faber, 1968), 15–44, and idem, *Savonarola and Florence: Prophecy and Patriotism in the Renaissance* (Princeton, N.J.: Princeton University Press, 1970).

58. SDRM, 76:11.

59. See Trexler, *Public Life,* 379–82; Weissman, *Ritual Brotherhood,* 88.

60. See E. Pavan, "Police des moeurs, société et politique à Venise à la fin du Moyen Age," *Revue historique* 264 (1980): 276 ff.; P. H. Labalme, "Sodomy and Venetian Justice in the Renaissance," *Legal History Review* 52 (1984): 217–54; Ruggiero, *Boundaries of Eros,* 109–45.

61. See R. Derosas, "Moralità e giustizia a Venezia nel '500–'600: gli Esecutori contro la Bestemmia," in *Stato, società e giustizia nella repubblica veneta (sec. 15–18),* ed. G. Cozzi (Rome: Jouvence, 1980), 431–528.

62. Faber, *Evagatorium,* 3:407–8.

63. R. Finlay, *Politics in Renaissance Venice* (London: Ernest Benn, 1980), 77–78.

64. G. Priuli, *I diarii,* 4, ed. R. Cessi (Bologna: Nicola Zanichelli, *Rerum Italicarum Scriptores,* vol. 24, pt. 3, 1938), 29–30.

65. From the *Historia mirabilis* concerning John of Erfurt, printed in Meersseman, *Ordo fraternitatis,* 3:1227.

66. R. C. Trexler, "Ritual in Florence: Adolescence and Salvation in the Renaissance," in *The Pursuit of Holiness in Late Medieval and Renaissance Religion,* ed. C. Trinkaus, with H. A. Oberman (Leiden: E. J. Brill, 1974), 200–64, and Trexler, *Public Life,* 367 ff., 473 ff.

67. *Canon Pietro Casola's Pilgrimage,* 149; M. Sanuto, *I diarii,* ed. R. Fulin et al., 58 vols. (Venice, 1879–1903), 13: cols. 132 ff., 20: cols. 274–75, 21: cols. 46–7, 42: col. 65.

68. See Meneghin, "Due compagnie," on the foundations inspired by Fra Timoteo da Lucca; see also Pullan, *Rich and Poor,* 401–4.

69. For example, SG, S. Giovanni Evangelista, 2: fols. 4v, 46v–47v.

70. Mackenney, "Trade Guilds," 107–24.

71. E. Muir, *Civic Ritual in Renaissance Venice* (Princeton, N.J.: Princeton University Press, 1981), 135–56, 299–300.

72. Ibid., 153.

73. See Pullan, *Rich and Poor,* 253–54, 297–301; J. Bossy, "The Counter Reformation and the People of Catholic Europe," *Past and Present* 47 (May 1970): 51–70.

74. Pullan, "Natura," 12–13; see now P. Hills, "Piety and Patronage in Cinquecento Venice: Tintoretto and the Scuole del Sacramento," *Art History* 6 (1983): 30–43; and N. S. Davidson, "The Clergy of Venice in the Sixteenth Century," *Bulletin of the Society for Renaissance Studies* 2 (1984): 19–31.

75. Weissman, *Ritual Brotherhood,* 66–74; 206 ff.

76. Cf. F. W. Kent, *Household and Lineage in Renaissance Florence: The Family Life of the Capponi, Ginori, and Rucellai* (Princeton, N.J.: Princeton University Press, 1977), 171–73, 179–80, 186–88, 195–96; D. V. Kent and F. W. Kent, *Neighbours and Neighbourhood in Renaissance Florence: The District of the Red Lion in the Fifteenth Century* (Locust Valley, N.Y.: J. J. Augustin, for Villa I Tatti, 1982), 17–19.

77. Pullan, *Rich and Poor,* 143–56.

78. Sanuto, *I diarii,* 13: cols. 132–41, 20 October 1511.

79. Ibid., 42: cols. 62–78, 8 July 1526.

80. Hatfield, "Compagnia," 114–18.

81. Commynes, *Memoirs,* 2:500–501.

82. Meersseman, "Le Congregazioni della Vergine," *Odo fraternitatis,* 2:949 ff.

83. Cf. Hatfield, "Compagnia," 124–25; M. B. Becker, "Aspects of Lay Piety in Renaissance Florence," in Trinkaus and Oberman, *Pursuit of Holiness,* 177–99.

84. Meersseman, *Ordo fraternitatis,* 2:618–21, 743–45, 997–98, 1001–3.

85. Ibid., 612–27, 669–89, 692–97.

86. Ibid., 599, 635–36, 650.

87. SR, Mariegola, fol. 9v.

88. SG, S. Giovanni Evangelista, 3: fols. 20v–21v.

89. SR, Mariegola, fols. 37r–39r, 46v–48v.

90. Henderson, "Piety and Charity," 35–36, 333, 342–43.

91. SR, Mariegola, fol. 13; Meersseman, *Ordo fraternitatis,* 3:1217.

92. Meersseman, *Ordo fraternitatis,* 2:673.

93. SR, Mariegola, fol. 7v.

94. Cf. Pullan, *Rich and Poor,* 267–68; R. C. Trexler, "Charity and the Defense of Urban Elites in the Italian Communes," in *The Rich, the Well Born, and the Powerful: Elites and Upper Classes in History,* ed. F. C. Jaher (Urbana: University of Illinois Press, 1973), 64–109; A. Spicciani, "The 'Poveri Vergognosi' in Fifteenth-Century Florence," in *Aspects of Poverty in Early Modern Europe,* ed. T. Riis, Publications of the European University Institute 10 (Stuttgart: Klett-Cotta, 1981), 119–82.

95. SG, Sta. Maria della Carità, 236: fol. 30v, 28 August 1506: "questa nostra benedeta scuola se atrova al presente esser molto carga et agravada de poveri et maxime de nostri boni citadini, i quali per la loro mala fortuna e non per altra causa sono mensuegnudi e venuti in grandissima calamità e miseria, ita che i non hanno solamente bisogno de substentar la loro vita et de quelli de caxa sua, ma etiam hanno bisogno de qualche suffragio de coprir le carne sue et nasconder qualche parte della sua inopia."

96. On these, see F. Semi, *Gli "ospizi" di Venezia* (Venice: Helvetia, 1983).

97. SG, Sta. Maria della Carità, 236: fol. 24r–v, 8 July 1492.

98. SG, SR/2, 44: fol. 78, 6 January 1511 (Venetian style): "le opere della charità consistono prezipuamente in subvegnir li poveri bixognosi et essendo questa benedetta confratternità fondata in charità del signor dio dovemo eziam chon ogni studio e diligenzia atender a la subvenzion delli nostri poveri fradelli, de li qual dovemo aver chura non mancho che de nui medeximi sechondo il prezetto divino che dize 'dilige prossimum sichut te ipsum'."

99. Meersseman, *Ordo fraternitatis,* 3:1227–28.

100. Faber, *Evagatorium,* 3:425.

101. SG, Sta. Maria della Carità, 236: fols. IV, 5, 8 February 1460 (Venetian style), 18 March 1466.

102. Pullan, *Rich and Poor,* 58–61.

II ❧

DEATH AND CHRISTIAN CHARITY
IN THE CONFRATERNITIES
OF THE UPPER TIBER VALLEY

JAMES R. BANKER

STANDING BACK from the special circumstances of confraternal life in major centers like Florence and Venice, James R. Banker suggests other preoccupations of Renaissance brotherhoods: decorous funeral rites and commemoration for members and the disposition of the property of the deceased. Professor Banker analyzes lay associations in Borgo Sansepolcro, on the border between Tuscany and Umbria, through their philanthropic and funerary activities. He stresses the spontaneous initiative of the lay founders independent of clerical and monastic advisers, even while affirming the profound influence of monastic practices upon the ideals and organization of lay confraternities. Professor Banker illustrates the enormous spiritual prestige enjoyed by the lay confraternities he studies and traces their gradual shift in function to something like that of a modern charitable entity, administering the bequests of numerous lay testators.

JAMES R. BANKER is associate professor of history at North Carolina State University, at Raleigh.

N ANALYSIS OF THE PLACE OF CHRISTIANITY in the Italian Renaissance would be incomplete without an examination of practices surrounding death. Discussions of the meaning of death, reduction of the fear of dying, the consolation of survivors, the disposal of the body, the supervision of the deceased's property, and the transcendence of death through some form of immortality have been among the concerns of the world's religions. To concede an essential role to death in the Christianity of the Italian Renaissance, one need not accept the view, popularized by Tylor and Frazer in the late nineteenth and early twentieth centuries, that religion has its origins in the individual's fear of the dead, or the view, asserted by Roman pagans in the late empire, that the ignorant were drawn to Christianity because of the promise of bodily resurrection.[1] Alberto Tenenti has shown that a novel awareness of death in the Renaissance derived from an appreciation of the value of the things of this world and of an immortality based on earthly fame.[2] Despite the value of Tenenti's work, our understanding of death in Western civilization has been derived from French experience. Only the French historians Ariès and Vovelle have written general histories of death, and their data is overwhelmingly drawn from French history. Italy in the Renaissance is not attributed an innovative role by Ariès and given only a minor role by Vovelle.[3]

But were there substantial changes in attitudes and practices surrounding death in the Italian Renaissance? I believe there were. Tenenti explored death as a topic in the intellectual history of the Renaissance. In this chapter I argue that the pattern of social practices surrounding death in the Renaissance changed radically in the course of the fourteenth century, resulting in an enlarged sphere of responsibility over death for the laity, primarily through the confraternity. With a minimum of conflict with the clergy, the laity assumed several practices of the monks and the mendicants which enhanced their ability to gain merit before God, and which endowed them with a charisma sufficient to act on the boundary between life and death.

The laymen of Italy founded several hundred, perhaps a thousand, confraternities from the thirteenth to the sixteenth century.[4] The lay confraternities served many purposes but common to all was the forging of a nexus between a social or liturgical act and a reward at death and in the afterlife. The confraternal leaders maintained the accounts of those members who served the purposes of the brotherhood and thereby merited fraternal aid at funerals and remembrance thereafter. The officers became experts in addressing problems that accompany death: the provision of a pall, candles, a monklike cowl, and mourners at interment, the saying of masses and prayers for the deceased's soul, and the administration of the deceased's property. Through such a provision of remembrance and administration of the property of the dead, the confraternal officers became the mediators between the dead and the living, thereby displacing to a degree the family and the clergy. The type of confraternity predominant in the thirteenth century took in hundreds or thousands of members in town or citywide recruitment; such groups exhibited optimism about serving the poor through their distribution of charity and about serving all members through confraternal remembrance. By the middle of the fourteenth century, however, membership in these charitable confraternities was inconsequential; they survived through their acceptance of testamentary bequests and their administration of property and charity. In the fourteenth and fifteenth centuries, the majority of the laity turned to brotherhoods that were smaller, and more localized than the earlier type, requiring an individual contribution to achieve merit for the afterlife. These smaller brotherhoods concerned themselves with flagellation, singing praises, administering hospitals, dispensing charity to members, and providing remembrance for members alone. The restrictive nature of these flagellant and *laudesi* confraternities points to a conception of individual labor leading to individual reward and a narrowing of the charitable impulse.

For a closer analysis of the pattern of death practices in the religion of the Italian Renaissance, I am taking evidence from the upper Tiber valley, particularly San Sepolcro.[5] This town, on the border of Tuscany and Umbria, has been chosen because of its ample documentation of confraternal activities and the analysis of lay confraternities made by Francesco de Largi. In the fifteenth century Largi served for thirty years as notary for one confraternity and on three occasions headed another confraternity, that of San Bartolomeo, which Piero della Francesca likewise headed later in the century. The sources from San Sepolcro are lay, not clerical, in origin and in character. Though I trust my conclusions will prove to have relevance beyond San Sepolcro, these lay sources provide a unique opportunity to analyze religion from a lay perspective, one that returns time and again to problems of death, remembrance, and the deceased's property. This chapter in the social history of religion is not social in the sense that religion is seen as a reflex of more a fundamental social reality and is not religious in the sense that individuals or groups accept religious teaching without re-engaging the social and intellectual problems that originally prompted the founding of the religion. Nor does this study view religion as simply an affair of theologians and clergy. Despite the available lay sources, the study of the confraternities has suffered from a historiographical subordination of the initiatives of the laity to those of the clergy. Nowhere is this more evident and troublesome than in the conventional notion that the confraternities were a consequence of the desire of the mendicants to combat heretical movements and to heal divisions in the Church. This interpretation reduces the participation of the laity in the confraternities to the purposes of the mendicants; the laity are neutered and lack motivation. In my view, the mendicants played an important but not an essential role in the Italian confraternities. The rise of the *popolo* to authority in the communes and the activities of the artisans and merchants required an institution, modeled on the monastery but not inimical to lay activities, to memorialize the laity's achievements. The confraternity served this purpose. Through an examination of how the particular existential problems surrounding death reconstituted traditional acts and beliefs, and how the laity generated the merit to perform sacred acts, we come to a better understanding of lay confraternities and thereby of the religion of the Renaissance.[6]

The Fraternity of San Bartolomeo, founded before 1244, supervised charity to the poor and burial of the dead in San Sepolcro. The statutes of 1269 describe the activities of the corporation. Each Saturday morning, its executives, three rectors, walked "through the land, especially through the streets and paths where the artisans and good men and those of the Fraternity are, asking for the pennies of God. And one of them carries the bag and then all who promised to give pennies every Saturday, and even many who are not of the Fraternity, place their pennies in the bag." These "pennies of God" are the dues that members promise to pay in varying sums, usually one penny (*denaro*) a week, though if a member preferred, he could pay "according to his choice." On the first Sunday of the month, the fraternity congregated in the church of San Bartolomeo, officiated by the secular clergy, and the rectors solicited another penny from those attending for every member who had died in the previous month.[7]

Every Thursday and the first Sunday of each month, the rectors distributed the accumulated contributions. They gave out the pennies they had collected, along with cooked food and boxes of meats, to the poor and to religious houses of the town and countryside. At the same time, they accepted bread and eggs from the housewives; Largi, writing in the mid-fifteenth century, informs us that the women would give large loaves of bread to the rectors, who would return to them small "pane di Dio."[8] The rectors also distributed cloth to the poor: wool each November and linen each spring. These practices were institutionalized by 1269 when the communal government made the fraternity the "General Administrators of the Poor." The commune granted to the rectors the responsibility of assisting the poor and defending their rights. The bishop of Città di Castello also recognized the substantial labor of the rectors by granting them a plenary remission of sins for their distribution of charity.[9]

Members of the fraternity received small indulgences for their donations and for attendance at the confraternal meetings.[10] In these activities the Fraternity of San Bartolomeo and other contemporary confraternities are remarkably similar. The documentation on the service of remembrance of this fraternity is unique in its detail, however. The rectors led the first phase of this remembrance of the dead; they circulated through the congregation announcing the names of those who had died in the past month and collecting the one denaro that members could choose to pay for the dead of the corporation. A second phase of remembrance was led by a priest who was selected yearly by the fraternity and was to hold no other office. This priest, given the title of prior by the fraternity, again recalled to the minds of the members the recently deceased by intoning their names. The assembled members be-

seeched God's mercy for the dead man or woman, requesting the safety
of each soul, one by one. Then any nonmember who had bequeathed
a gift to the fraternity would receive the same remembrance, including
the statement that the benefactor belonged to the fraternity. The fraternity possessed confidence in its ability to gain divine favor for all
categories of persons, whether they had membership or not, property
or not. The corporate virtue was so grand and the beseeching of the
members so eloquent that the fraternity permitted the name of any deceased individual to be announced by the prior, with the soul receiving
remembrance identical to that of a member or benefactor.[11]

The faith of the people of San Sepolcro in the corporate virtue
of the Fraternity of San Bartolomeo was doubtless built on its charitable work. By 1269 the number of members must also have persuaded
contemporaries of the fraternity's ability to arrest the mind of God. From
the fraternity's *matricola* (membership list) and a "Book of the Dead"
for the years 1269 to 1309, we can gain a clear idea of the size and social
composition of the fraternity. In 1269 there were 694 female members and approximately 570 male members, and over the following forty
years the number of entrants averaged 920 per decade. We may conclude that the fraternity was made up of about 1260 members in 1269,
and that thereafter until 1309, and perhaps beyond, its corporate presence derived from at least 1,000 members.[12] The fraternity integrated
nearly all the social groups from towns and villages in the upper Tiber
valley and recruited some members from beyond the valley. From the
ecclesiastical hierarchy, the fraternity recruited the abbot of the Camaldolese monastery in San Sepolcro, who had ecclesiastical jurisdiction
within the town, the bishop of Città di Castello, who had jurisdiction
outside the walls, various priests, *frati,* and monks. Among the laity
who entered the fraternity were counts, knights, judges, notaries, and
merchants, but the largest number of members were drawn from those
of lower status: local shopkeepers, artisans, and agricultural landowners
and renters; especially numerous were tailors, shoemakers, bakers, and
blacksmiths. And the rectors were as likely to come from the latter
groups as from the former.[13]

The members of the Fraternity of San Bartolomeo possessed
a confidence in their ability to confer social honor in this world and
call forth the assistance of God in the next. Any individual could receive

memorialization: lay or cleric, male or female, of whatever social status or occupation, however inclined to commit to or hold off from a specific rate of dues-paying, of whatever ethical life; a person could even enter the fraternity after death. Members sought association with the fraternity for its corporate virtue. There is no sense of necessary individual input of money or labor and resulting individual merit. The fraternity's aid to the poor and the size of its membership acquired sufficient merit for the corporate body to honor its dead within the earthly community and to place a claim on divine mercy. Salvation remained under the clergy and a question of the sacraments, but in a Christianized Europe the problematical aspect of religion centered on how individuals could reduce their punishment in the afterlife and, increasingly after 1300, how they could purify their character or take part in some act that would gain them individual merit. After 1300 the older corporate virtue of the fraternity no longer attracted as many members as before. Membership lists for the fraternity are not extant for the period after 1309, but the features of the decade 1299–1309 signal fundamental changes. In that decade females constituted fully 66 percent of the recruitment of new members, while in the period from 1279 to 1299 females made up only 48 percent of the new members.[14]

Despite the fall in male recruitment, the Fraternity of San Bartolomeo continued to be the chief institution supervising death in the town. By the middle of the fourteenth century, recruitment was no longer of importance, and dues were either not collected or were so inconsequential that the notaries of the fraternity chose not to record them. Males continued to lead the fraternity, and increasingly sons of the leading families took the position of rector, by 1350 one of the most prestigious offices of the commune.[15] Family status or some form of social honor became important in choosing a rector because the confraternal officials exercised new and different roles, particularly the administration of the property of the dead. In 1437 Largi searched through eighty-seven registers of the fraternity because, he said, it had declined from the prosperity of its earlier years and could only be revived if its executives were instructed in its ancient practices and sources of wealth. To accomplish these ends he noted the 1,033 bequests made to the fraternity in the preceding two hundred years. Arranging these bequests by quarter-century and analyzing their character enable us to determine the fraternity's new role in the mortuary behavior of the people of San Sepolcro into the fifteenth century. From the year of the first bequest — 1247 — until 1300, there were 58 gifts to the fraternity, whereas in the first quarter of the fourteenth century, 530 individuals bestowed gifts on it. Between 1326 and 1350, 324 individuals, or 61 percent of the previous quarter, made gifts to the fraternity, despite the great mortality of 1348. And in the period from 1351 to 1375 there were only 52 bequests, followed by an equal number in the last quarter of the fourteenth century. Conclusive evidence of the fall from citizen favor is the minuscule 16 bequests given between 1401 and 1425, which constituted only 3 percent of the bequests of the quarter-century one hundred years earlier.[16]

A fundamental and significant change also occurred in the nature of the bequests. In the first half of the fourteenth century, the vast majority of bequests were small grants of money or grain and were free in that the confraternal officers were not held to perform any reciprocal act. The money went into the corporate treasury and the grain was distributed to the poor or sold from the fraternity's granary-oratory, from circa 1320 located on the town's chief *piazza*. After 1350 the few bequests were often of substantial value, frequently being property requiring administration by confraternal officials. Fully one-third of the properties came to the fraternity after life-use by one of the testator's family members, and often the fraternity had to share ownership with other ecclesiastical corporations, or supervise the construction of a chapel, monument, or house, or grapple with conflicting legal claims over the property. Many of the substantial bequests were contingent on the deaths without family heirs of several men and required supervision of payments to clerics for prayers and masses in perpetuity. The officers of the fraternity increasingly became administrators of the property of the dead, agents of the well-being of the dead souls and the fruitfulness of their property.[17]

The responsibilities of administering the bequests of hundreds of testators diminished the importance of the individual members and redirected the pious corporation into an administrative-charitable entity. In the *Specchio* written to reform the administrative practices of the Fraternity of San Bartoloemo and in his writings as notary for the Confraternity of Santa Maria della Notte, Largi attempted to elevate administrative labor to a moral-spiritual plane. He formulated an administrative piety, which has at its core the idea that the supervision of charity to the poor and the control of bequests for the well-being of departed souls constitutes religious activity. The unparalled expansion in the number of individuals making wills in the course of the fourteenth century necessitated a large corps of notaries and confraternal officers to record and administer pious bequests. This is not to say that confraternities came into existence for that purpose, but the early ones, with their pious activity of caring for the poor and burying the dead with memorialization, brought them to the minds of the dying as they made their testaments. In a century of reoccurring plagues and truncated families, the confraternities appeared as sempiternal institutions with a tradition of supervising property and death. To many, these corporations constituted the surest trump against the vagaries of fortune, the surest means of securing one's patrimony for the well-being of one's children and one's own soul.

In the course of the fourteenth century, the lay confraternal officers gained authority over a large proportion of bequests for the benefit of deceased souls, and over bequests for those whose family, for whatever reason, could not adequately or equitably supervise the administration and dispersal of the testators' property. Largi perceived that the confraternity's paramount responsibility was to the dead and to the provisions of the testaments that provided wealth to the brotherhood. These activities required the brothers' careful and sustained attention. When he wrote the statutes of the Confraternity of Santa Maria della Notte in 1441, he had spent twenty-eight years as the notary of the company, and had not failed to notice the primary place of testamentary income and resulting confraternal labor. In these statutes, Largi stated the central tenet of the administrative piety of the fifteenth century.[18] After recounting the various charities the legacies were to support, Largi exhorted future priors that "above everything the Priors are held quickly to satisfy the particular bequests and the annual bequests. And upon this they are admonished and pressed by the *Preposto* in every way, and if the said Priors in this will be negligent and will not pay the legacies they will be written into the Book of Debtors and [their names] will not be placed in the sacks" for the next selection for the office of the priorate.[19] He termed "pious works" the accumulation of charity and its distribution to the poor and the administration of the property of the dead.[20]

COMMUNITIES OF PRAISE AND PENITENCE

In the years that the Fraternity of San Bartolomeo failed to recruit as many new male members, two diverse types of confraternities with radically different means of acquiring merit and preparing for death appeared in San Sepolcro. Members of the *laudesi* confraternities sang praises to Christ and Mary, while the *disciplinati* confraternities flagellated themselves in their private oratories and public processions. Both demanded of their members a more intense pious life through participation in the liturgical activities of the parish and a more scrutinized form of social behavior. Although women became the majority of the membership of the Fraternity of San Bartolomeo, they could not contribute to these more active brotherhoods. In a sorting out of pious activity appropriate for males and females which occurred around 1300, women were accorded the passive role of membership and attendance at church services; men led the charitable Fraternity of San Bartolomeo or joined the new laudesi or disciplinati companies, where they actively contributed to their own spiritual well-being and that of the corporation. This sexual division of pious activity may have been more accentuated in San Sepolcro than elsewhere, but I believe the exclusively male acquisition of merit in the confraternities to be generally characteristic of the Italian Renaissance. More was required of men than in the thirteenth century, and less of women; the latter were denied the opportunity to contribute to their merit or that of the confraternity through action. The appearance of both types of confraternities in Sansepolcro, as in many other Italian towns and cities, coincided with the grasping of power by the popolo. In 1301 the abbot of the Camaldolese abbey sold his political jurisdiction over San Sepolcro to a communal council representing the people of the town.[21] Within two decades, the citizens formed six laudesi and four flagellant confraternities, and by 1348 an additional one and three respectively.

The laudesi companies took Mary as their patron and employed her name as the confraternal name. The first, founded circa 1300, was associated with the Franciscans.[22] The second, the aforementioned Santa Maria della Notte, took its name from the practice of singing processionally at night. These brothers had no specific clerical sponsors; their processions through the town and their oratory in the center of the town apparently identified this confraternity in the minds of the citizens as its preeminent laudesi company. The group received 485 free bequests in the four decades after the Fraternity of San Bartolomeo lost its ability to attract large numbers. But after this forty-year period ending in 1380, the Confraternity of Santa Maria della Notte, in an evolution similar to that of the fraternity, received a few bequests of valuable property, often with entangling provisions, that required administrative skill on the part of the confraternal officers.[23] The third laudesi company met in or near the Augustinian convent by 1317.[24] At approximately the same time the laudesi confraternity of San Bartolomeo received a bequest that implies it had been in existence for some years. This church was officiated by the secular clergy and also housed the Fraternity of San Bartolomeo.[25] By 1318 another group of laudesi had congregated at the Camaldolese priory of San Niccolò.[26] The Camaldolese also sponsored a laudesi confraternity in their abbey in the center of San Sepolcro by the year 1320. Finally, a seventh confraternity, dedicated to Mary, was formed sometime before 1348 around the tower in the central *piazza* of San Sepolcro.[27] These laudesi confraternities divided the town, with three in its center and two each in the southwest and northeast corners. Affiliation with clerical corporations was also relatively dispersed; two brotherhoods were associated with the Camaldolese, two with the mendicants, one with the secular clergy, and two had no apparent clerical identifications. Only two of the laudesi brotherhoods survived the demographic crises of the mid-fourteenth century, the most active, Santa Maria della Notte, maintaining its existence by becoming less a chanting brotherhood than an administrative unit of a few members who received and oversaw the property of the wealthy dead.

In the same years that the men of San Sepolcro founded these seven laudesi confraternities, they also formed seven brotherhoods of flagellation. According to tradition, the Confraternity of Santa Maria della Misericordia was founded in the first decade of the fourteenth century. It is best-known today as the patron of Piero della Francesca's *Ma-*

Figure 11.1. Piero della Francesca (with assistant?), *The Deposition in the Sepulchre of Christ*. Central panel of predella of the altarpiece commissioned in 1445 by the Confraternity of Santa Maria della Misericordia for their hospital. San Sepolcro, Pinacoteca, Photo Alinari/Art Resource, N.Y.

donna della Misericordia (Figure 11.1).[28] In the fourteenth century the citizens of San Sepolcro valued the brotherhood for its charity to the poor of the town through its administration of a hospital of the same name and the honors it bestowed upon its members at death. In 1348 the Confraternity of Santa Maria della Misericordia was remembered in approximately one-half of the ninety-seven testaments extant from that year, frequently by bequests exchanging a gift of property or money for burial under the protection of the brotherhood and with its cloak.[29] Bequests to the disciplinati of San Bartolomeo and of San Niccolò in 1318 reveal that the two companies were founded some time before that year.[30] Another brotherhood, the Flagellants of Santa Croce, was founded at this time and practiced flagellation from its oratory in the southwest corner of San Sepolcro.[31] It had no apparent clerical affiliation. Three other flagellant confraternities were founded in the 1330s: the brotherhood of Sant'Antonio built a church and hospital by 1350, and in several bequests their burial of the dead was the focus of the testator's waning mind. The second disciplinati brotherhood of the 1330s built an oratory near the female Camaldolese convent of Santa Caterina, while another group of flagellants built an oratory near the convent of the reformed Benedictine nuns of Santa Maria Maddalena.[32]

Of the seven groups of flagellants, two were associated with the Camaldolese, one with the secular priests, one with a reformed

Benedictine female order, and three possessed no close clerical affiliation. Thus of the fifteen confraternities in existence in the 1340s, six had no clerical affiliation and only two had an association with the mendicants. Not one of the two confraternities with a mendicant association survived the Black Plague. The laudesi companies located in the convents of the Franciscans and the Augustinians failed to stir support from the diminished number of citizens after 1348. This evidence places into question the suggestion of Meersseman that the mendicants played the preeminent role in stimulating the founding and growth of the confraternities of the thirteenth and subsequent centuries. Doubtless there were cities and towns where the mendicants sponsored a majority of the brotherhoods, but for general interpretation the link between mendicants and confraternities obscures more than clarifies our understanding of the latter.[33]

The documentation from San Sepolcro serves to demonstrate that the laudesi and disciplinati confraternities replaced the Fraternity of San Bartolomeo as the chief expression of lay piety in the town. I shall not discuss further the laudesi but rather concentrate on the disciplinati, which protray more vividly than the laudesi the new connection between death and confraternal activity. I shall discuss two basic points concerning the flagellant confraternities: their attempt to construct a sacred community beyond that required by the church, and their capacity to recruit a high percentage of the men of the town.

Within the secular world of labor, family, and political participation, the disciplinati attempted to construct a sacred community by ensuring that members would periodically undergo priestly confession and its penance as well as the scrutiny and punishments of the officers and brothers of the confraternity. The flagellants purged from their social behavior acts that blemished their purity and undertook a positive molding of their spiritual lives stimulated by a participation in the Passion of Christ. In San Sepolcro the survival of the 1364 statutes of the Confraternity of Santa Croce enables us to examine closely this twin process.[34] These statutes reveal a narrowing of aspirations on the part of the disciplinati of San Sepolcro when compared with those of Padua and Bologna of the thirteenth century. The early flagellants believed their processional penance served to pacify Christendom and lessen the factional conflict of the communes. Their flagellation would persuade others to attenuate their violent behavior.[35]

By the second half of the fourteenth century, the disciplinati of San Sepolcro satisfied themselves with the project of constructing a microsociety that was sacred in itself. Conflicts between nonmembers were beyond the scope of the Confraternity of Santa Croce. Nor did substantial charity to the poor of Sansepolcro concern these flagellants. As the statutes inform us, the purpose of the confraternity was to aid "the health of the souls of the members."[36]

To construct the sacred community, only men of exemplary character were recruited. A candidate was admitted to the brotherhood only after a long process that included initial nomination by a member (who presumably would screen out any man with unsuitable behavior), a period of eight days within which members could report and discuss any moral or character defect of the candidate, and a vote on his candidacy by the members. In describing this process, the statute writers addressed two particular objections to a candidate: that he had a conflict with an existing member and that he had extracted usurious profit or fraudulently dispossessed anyone. If either applied, he was rejected. Acceptance did not exhaust the effort to preserve the purity of the disciplinati. The new member had to purge his being of contamination by receiving confession immediately before entering the brotherhood. And after entering, the new member, and indeed all members, had to confess each month.[37]

Supplementing the thirteen confessions in his parish church, each member also permitted himself to be scrutinized by the confraternal officials and brothers. The prior examined the flagellants' behavior and could punish the brothers for a number of acts, including usury, sodomy, and playing games of dice. The prior could send any member failing to conform to the confraternal statutes to punitive flagellation. For example, a member who lent his cloak to a nonmember or who failed to resolve amicably his conflict with a fellow member was sent to discipline. For eight lesser infractions — note, not sins — the prior punished according to his discretion; one assumes the offending member could be sent to private or public flagellation, or simply chastised. These infractions included failure to confess before taking a confraternal office, bringing nonmembers to meetings of the brotherhood, and failure to be present at the mass in honor of the Holy Cross. For sixteen more serious errors of commission or omission—failure to pay dues, for example—the member could be thrown out of the brotherhood.[38]

In constructing their sacred community, the Confraternity of Santa Croce required more than a purging of behaviors reprehensible to the Church and to the brotherhood. The statutes required members to demonstrate their love of God. Private prayers at rising, before going to bed, at meals, on each Friday in honor of the Passion, and on one other weekday were required. Members' devotion was to be exhibited by attendance at weekly Friday meetings as well as at the confraternal oratory on several feast days.[39]

There is little evidence to prove that the flagellants of the Renaissance suffered some overwhelming isolation or feared the approach of death, as Philippe Ariès would have us believe. The confraternal member in fact performed his flagellation within the brotherhood and his acts contributed to the group's sacred character. Moreover, the confraternity existed to serve the member in his moments of peril. The members exchanged concern and aid at these extreme moments, thereby enveloping each other within the security of the social group. This principle of reciprocity is evident in the confraternity's fundamental service for members, the exchange of care in sickness and at death. Two officials served as supervisors of charity to the sick; they were to watch solicitously the health of members and when a brother fell ill, they were to attend to his needs, including calling out the other brothers for around-the-clock care and giving him up to 30 soldi on each occasion.[40]

The death of a member aroused the brothers to a series of acts that brought them to the center of the mortuary rituals in San Sepolcro and thereby supplemented or replaced a portion of the family's responsibilities. Upon the death of a member, the prior sent six men to his home dressed in the confraternal white mantle (*vesta*) with its insignia of a green cross.[41] They took with them the deceased's vesta and his *disciplina*, his whip of reeds or rope. The six brothers dressed the corpse and then carried it in the procession to the burial church. The confraternity also sent two candles to flank the body in the procession; if the deceased was an officer he was entitled to four candles for the procession and the mass. In addition, the cross of the confraternity could be sent to head the procession.[42] These provisions for the deceased brother were recognized by communal statutes that limited the honor accorded other citizens of San Sepolcro at funerals. These communal laws permitted the deceased to have the confraternal *gonfalone* or banner in the processions. Also, in times of high mortality, while the average individual was limited to one candle, the priors of the confraternities of the town could have their customary four candles (Figure 11.2).[43]

The sacred community at these moments of death fulfilled their reason for being. Their individual and corporate voices, raised in prayer, came to the assistance of the deceased in order to aid his passage to the next world, to help him through the purging fires.[44] The prior would inform each man of the death of their fellow member to assure that all would meet their obligation and attend the funeral. This presence of members at burial constituted an honor one member could give to another. The statutes also obligated each member to say one hundred Our Fathers and one hundred Hail Marys for the deceased's soul, and, within fifteen days, the prior and the members were required to go in procession to his burial church, where an office for the dead was said. Within a month of the death, the prior would pay six denari for another mass and three candles and arrange for ninety-nine more masses at churches of his choice in the town.[45] Finally, in the week after All Saints' day, the prior would arrange for a mass in honor of the brotherhood, with all members attending this memorial service and offering some contribution for their deceased brothers.[46] In constructing the sacred community, the brothers accumulated material wealth sufficient to honor and commemorate their dead. More important, the sacredness of the individuals and of the corporation claimed a merit that endowed their prayers for their brother's soul with a vast authority.

Each member, when serving as an officer, sentenced to discipline other members and was in turn required to accept the next officer's discipline. Members chose to burden themselves with an enlarged sphere of scrutinized behavior to the honor of God and Christ's cross, as well as for the salvation of their souls.[47] The intense discipline, replete with punishments and expulsions, did not work outward for the well-being of the poor of San Sepolcro. The introductory invocation of the statutes speaks of the members working for the "peaceful state" of Sansepolcro, but the benefit to its citizenry could only be the presence in the town

Figure 11.2. Unknown artist, *The Chaplain and Brothers of the Company of the Crucifix of San Sepolcro Bury a Citizen Deceased in the Plague of 1523*. San Sepolcro, Pinacoteca. Photo Artini.

of a group of men who obeyed the laws. The only charity the disciplinati of Santa Croce performed in the fourteenth century was to give some undefined gift to the poor of the town on the Festival of Santa Croce, celebrated in early May.[48]

Monastic practices of charity and commemoration profoundly influenced lay devotion. At the center of monasticism was the rejection of the values and practices of the laity, especially those of urban society, though the monks served the laity through their penitential acts and prayers. Such a sacred community could persuasively appeal to the divine for the souls of the dead. The Fraternity of San Bartolomeo gained a similar sacred character through their charity, so that they, as a corporate entity, could beseech God in the interests of the dead. When the Fraternity of San Bartolomeo and the Confraternity of Santa Maria della Notte abandoned or lost their membership, and the vast majority of the laity had no effective way of gaining merit or commemoration in these two corporations, the laymen sought alternative means of gaining merit from the divine and remembrance at death. For many, the confraternities of flagellation served this purpose. But how is the flagellant movement to be understood? Should the flagellants of San Sepolcro be viewed as a few who withdrew from society as a means of redeeming the many, as monks had done for centuries and as the flagellants had in 1260, when Fra Fasani stirred them to frenetic processions? Did a few men reject and hope to redeem urban society and its values by constructing a purged personal character and a sacred community? Or, despite their rejection of the more exploitative practices of urban society, did the flagellants represent an even more radical religious idea: that a large number of laypeople could constitute a sacred community, with sufficient merit to promise remembrance after death for their members alone, while yet maintaining intimate contact and participation in the earthly pursuits of urban society?

The evidence from San Sepolcro demonstrates that the flagellants (1) voted in the communal council; (2) represented the middle social groups that participated most fully in the commercial activities of this market town;[49] and (3) rather than being a remnant, constituted a substantial proportion of the male adults of the town. I want now to take up this third point and discuss the extent of membership in the disci-

plinati confraternities. Five of the seven flagellant confraternities survived the Black Death. Drawing from membership lists of the decades
after 1348, particularly those lists of members attending business meetings,
I estimate that approximately 169 male adults actively participated in
the life of the flagellant confraternities in the third quarter of the fourteenth century.[50] The number of flagellants had, however, increased dramatically by the 1420s. Although it is, again, impossible to determine
the exact number of men in the companies, I have made an estimate
of flagellants in San Sepolcro for this decade. Of the two confraternities for which membership lists are extant, the disciplinati of Sant'Antonio in the 1420s was the larger group, with 252 men. Not all these
men necessarily participated continuously in all the confraternal activities. But when in 1420 the brothers debated whether or not to permit
three confessed murderers to enter the confraternity, 120 men voted.[51]

In this same period thirty-four men attended a meeting of the
Confraternity of Santa Maria della Misericordia.[52] Evidence on the
number of members of the other three discipline confraternities is not
extant. If we were to consider all 252 men as members of the Confraternity of Sant'Antonio and estimate that the three confraternities lacking data each had a membership equal to that of Santa Maria della
Misericordia, surely a modest estimate, the number of flagellants in San
Sepolcro would have been approximately 488 in the 1420s. In the 1440s
the population of the town was 4,397 individuals; we assume it was
approximately the same in the 1420s.[53] Through a comparison with
another Tuscan town of the same size, we may estimate that approximately 1,319 male adults lived in San Sepolcro.[54] From these calculations
it is conservative to assert that at least 40 percent of the male adults
of the town were members of the flagellant confraternities.

What, then, does this examination of the confraternities of this
upper Tiber valley town inform us concerning the general pattern of
death in the fifteenth century? First, throughout life and at the approach
of death, the individual possessed the consolation of the sacraments and
specifically the aid of the *viaticum*. I have not here analyzed problems
of the individual in confronting his own mortality. The documents of
San Sepolcro do not permit this type of analysis. There were, however,
several social behaviors through which the laity could acquire merit or,

more pertinently, through which they could mitigate the time they had to suffer the burning and freezing of their souls in Purgatory. Confraternal members performed acts of social utility which also possessed eternal significance. Administration of hospitals, burial of the poor, fulfillment of the bequests of the dead, sale or refining of grain from properties donated by testators, and distribution of bread and pennies to the poor were religious acts roughly equal to flagellation or the singing of praises to Christ and Mary. Owing to the nature of the sources from San Sepolcro and the fact that administrative labor has largely been ignored in discussions of confraternities, I have emphasized the importance of confraternal administrative labor as a means of achieving merit. Certainly part of this merit derived from the plenary indulgence granted to confraternal officers, but the instrumental acts of these officers brought them great esteem, enabling them to mediate between the living and the dead. The reconstituted mortuary system of the fifteenth century can be seen as composed of several institutions, with each contributing essential services to the laity. The Fraternity of San Bartolomeo provided its officers social prestige here and merit hereafter for their labor in supervising the patrimony of wealthy testators, distributing charity to the poor, and assuring each citizen that should he die destitute, the fraternity would provide elementary honor at his burial. Though no longer memorializing members in monthly services, the fraternity recorded each person of the town in their "Books of the Dead" and took from each a small mortuary tax. The flagellant confraternities addressed the needs of their members exclusively, providing each other with sickness insurance, often a confraternal doctor, and honors at death which surpassed those most families could provide. Because of costs, communal prohibitions seen in the sumptuary laws, or the desire of the dying to have greater honor, the family was supplemented or surpassed in importance by the confraternities in the acts surrounding death. In these acts, Renaissance men expressed neither the individualism seen by Burckhardt nor the awareness of "one's own death" seen by Philippe Ariès. Rather, most Renaissance men sought, beyond the sacraments and their family's concern, the assistance of other men who generated merit by exchanging prayers and being present at burial, as well as by sharing the benefits of their sacred communities and their disciplined selves.

NOTES

1. Edward B. Tylor, *Researches into the Early History of Mankind and the Development of Civilization* (London: Murray, 1865); James G. Frazer, *The Fear of the Dead in Primitive Religion,* 3 vols. (London: Macmillan, 1933–36); Pierre Courcelle, "Anti-Christian Arguments and Christian Platonism: From Arnobius to St. Ambrose," in *The Conflict between Paganism and Christianity in the Fourth Century,* ed. Arnaldo Momigliano (Oxford: Clarendon Press, 1963), 161.

2. Alberto Tenenti, *Il senso della morte e l'amore della vita nel Rinascimento* (Turin: Giulio Einaudi, 1957), chaps. 1 and 2.

3. Philippe Ariès, *The Hour of Our Death,* trans. Helen Weaver (New York: Alfred A. Knopf, 1981), 95–201 and esp. 128–29; Michel Vovelle, *La mort et l'occident de 1300 à nos jours* (Paris: Gallimard, 1983), 119–25.

4. The literature on Italian confraternities has become too extensive to cite completely; I here cite only the most valuable. Gennaro Maria Monti, *Le confraternite medievali dell'alta e media Italia,* 2 vols. (Venice: La Nuova Italia, 1927); Gilles Gerard Meersseman with the collaboration of Gian Piero Pacini, *Ordo fraternitatis: Confraternite e pietà dei laici nel medioevo,* 3 vols., *Italia sacra: Studi e documenti di storia ecclesiastica,* 24 (Rome: Herder, 1977); *Il Movimento dei Disciplinati nel VII centenario del suo inizio,* Appendix 9 to *Bollettino della Deputazione di storia patria per l'Umbria* (Spoleto, 1962); *Risultati e prospettive della ricerca sul movimento dei disciplinati* (Perugia: Deputazione di storia patria per l'Umbria, 1972); Brian Pullan, *Rich and Poor in Renaissance Venice: The Social Institutions of a Catholic State, to 1620* (Cambridge, Mass.: Harvard University Press, 1971); Charles de la Roncière, "La place des confréries dans l'encadrement religieux du contado Florentin au XVIe siècle: L'exemple de la Val d'Elsa," *Mélanges de l'Ecole française de Rome: Moyen âge, temps modernes* 85 (1973): 31–77, 633–71; John Henderson, "The Flagellant Movement and Flagellant Confraternities in Central Italy, 1260–1400," *Studies in Church History* 15 (1978): 147–60; Ronald Weissman, *Ritual Brotherhood in Renaissance Florence* (New York: Academic Press, 1982).

5. The basic sources on the history of San Sepolcro include Pietro Farulli, *Annali e memorie dell'antica città di S. Sepolcro* (Foligno, 1713); Lorenzo Coleschi, *Storia della città di Sansepolcro* (Città di Castello: Tipografia S. Lapi, 1886); Guistiniano Degli Azzi, "Inventario degli archivi di Sansepolcro," *Archivi della storia d'Italia,* 4th ser. 4 (1914): 77–194; and the several volumes of Ercole Agnoletti, esp. *Sansepolcro nel periodo degli abati (1012–1521)* (San Sepolcro: n.p., 1976).

6. This interpretation is an extension of the idea that the mendicants played the fundamental role in restoring the laity's adherence to the medieval Church following the problems associated with Gregorian reforms and the heretical movements. See esp. Meersseman, *Ordo fraternitatis,* 2:744, 920–32.

7. Biblioteca comunale, San Sepolcro (hereafter BC) ser. 32, reg. 159, fol. 1r. The date of the statutes is derived from the accompanying list of incoming members begun in 1269. "Perceptio et exactio helemosinarum fit per dictos Rectores hoc modo: Ipsi omni quolibet die sabati post tertiam vadunt per terram specialiter per stratas et vicos ubi morantur artifices et boni homines et illi qui sunt de Fraternitate petendo denarios dei et unus eorum portat thefamam, et tunc omnis qui promiserunt se daturos denarios quolibet die sabati offerunt denarios in thefama, et etiam multi alii qui non sunt de Fraternitate. Item die dominica prima cuiuslibet mensis, omnes de Fraternitate et multi allii qui non sunt de Fraternitate congregantur apud

ecclesiam Sancti Bartholomei voce preconia et sonitu campane post tertiam sumpto prandio, et interim dum gens in ipsa ecclesia congregat, predicti Rectores quilibet cum sua thefama vadunt per ecclesiam dicendo tot sunt mortium precedentis mensis, et tunc illi qui promiserunt pro quolibet mortuo 1 denarium, offerunt tot denarios quot sunt mortui illius precendentis mensis, et aliqui offerunt secundum promissionem eorum et aliqui secundum eorum voluntatem, et etiam mulieres offerunt panem, ova et denarios."

8. Ibid. "Et congregata gente in ipsa ecclesia, antequam surgat predicator qui debet predicare, surgit quidam presbyter qui est Prior Fraternitatis qui eligitur quando eliguntur dicti Rectores per eos de Rectoribus precedentes et permanet in offitio priorati similiter uno anno; et hic Prior in ipsa congregatione adnuntiat, et dicit mortuos Fraternitatis et alios qui non sunt de Fraternitate qui Fraternitati aliquid relinquerunt dicendo talis erat de Fraternitate et obiit et reliquit Fraternitati tamen rogate deum pro ipsius anima et sic de ceteris. Postea talis non erat de Fraternitate, tamen reliquid Fraternitati tamen rogate deum pro ipsius anima. Et hic Prior non habet aliud offitium exercere; de inde surgit predicator et adnuntiat verbum dei. Item dicti Rectores simul et separatim et die qualibet recipiunt helemosinas ab offerentibus, et exigunt legata et relicta et omnes proventus Fraternitatis. Distributio helemosinarum et proventuum Fraternitatis fit per dictos Rectores hoc modo: Ipsi omes habent quolibet die iovis certam quantitatem primis [?] cocti paratum et carnes, porcinas, fruttanti [?], meisas, et quilibet Rectorum cum sua maletta cum pane et quidam puer cum eis cum cista carnium simul vadant per omnos vicos terre exibendo pauperibus et locis religiosis et incarceratis helemosinam panis et carnium tribuendo cuilibet ut inspiciunt convenire, et aliquibus pauperibus exibent helemosinam per interpositam personarum, et ipso die a multis dominabis panem et ova recipiunt quem et quae distribuunt simul cum pane quem portant." Largi's comments are found in his *Specchio;* see BC, ser. 32, reg. 182, fol. 6r and published by Degli Azzi, "Inventario degli archivi," 146.

9. BC, ser. 32, reg. 159, fol. 1r. "Item dant pauperibus vestimenta lanea et linea, lanea videlicet in inceptione iemis circa festum omnium sanctorum et linea tempore estatis." In these same statutes the communal law is recounted: "Item dicti Rectores ex lege municipali dicuntur generales administrationes pauperium et possunt et debent eos defendere et iuvare in curia et extra et iura eorum manutenere. Item ex lege municipali commune Burgi debet ipsum Fraternitatem et Rectores manutenere et defendere." For the rectors' plenary remission, see Largi's comments, *Specchio,* fols. 6v–7r. "Nel 1266 a dì 12 de genaio Messer Nicolò Vescovo de Castello conferma tucto como de sopra et—7r—ai rectori che potaranno una anno la maletta confesati che siranno di loro pecchati habbino plenaria remissione di tucti i loro peccati."

10. Largi, *Specchio,* fols. 6v–7r and summarized in Degli Azzi, "Inventario degli archivi," 146.

11. See note 8 above.

12. BC, ser. 32, reg. 159. For a short description of the MS., see Degli Azzi, "Inventario degli archivi," 141. The MS contains (1) the 1269 statutes, (2) names of women but without a date, (3) male entrants to the fraternity from 1279 to 1309, (4) female entrants to the fraternity from 1269 to 1309, (5) lists of the dead of the fraternity organized by month and year from 1269 to 1309. Along with the yearly entries of new members and of deaths the rectors for each year are recorded. The quote from 1269 reads: "In nomine domini amen. Iste sunt persone qui intraverunt in Fraternitate Sancti Bartholomei de Burgo, tempore rectorie Kimbu et Ciacio et Forti, Rectores Fraternititatis predicte sub anno domini a navitatem eius millesimo ducentesimo sexagesimo nono, in primis de mense agusti."

I reached my totals for 1269 by counting the names of listed females for whom on paleographic grounds I ascribe a date of 1269 and add in an estimate for males. My estimate for males is based on the ratio of females to males in the first decade for which there are extant lists of male entrants, 1279–89. For the total entrants for the years 1269 to 1309, I have simply counted the females from 1269 to 1309 and the males from 1279 to 1309. For entries from 1269 to 1279 in which the names of males are not extant, I have followed the same procedure as in the estimates for male membership in 1269, that is, taken the male entrants of 1269 to 1279 to be of the same ratio to female entrants as in the period 1279 to 1289 when the data is extant.

13. BC, ser. 32, reg. 159. This MS. is unpaginated; my comments are based on an analysis of female recruitment in the year July 1274 to June 1275 and male recruitment from 1285 to 1289. For the social positions of the rectors I have examined all the names from 1269 to 1309.

14. Ibid., to the years.

15. My conclusion that dues no longer were of significance in the fraternity is based on an analysis of a financial account register of the fraternity for the years 1313 to 1323: BC, ser. 32, reg. 202, and on the fact that when Largi listed all the extant fraternal registers in 1437, not one of them was set aside for dues; see *Specchio*, fols. 18r–21v. My comments on the status of the various rectors by 1350 — in fact called priors from c. 1320 — is based on an analysis of the priors' names; see Farulli, *Annali e memorie*, 89–90.

16. Largi, *Specchio*, fols. 25r–69v. My total of 1,033 bequests from Largi is less than Amintore Fanfani's total in "La beneficenza in un comune toscana dal XIII al XV secolo," in his *Saggi di storia economia italiana* (Milan: Società editrice "Vità e pensiero," 1936), 43. I have subtracted Largi's cases of misnumbering and repeating of bequests and their testators.

17. Largi, *Specchio*, fols. 25r–69v.

18. Largi's notarial activities for the Confraternity of Sta. Maria della Notte have survived throughout that brotherhood's records, now in Florence; Archivio di Stato di Firenze (hereafter ASF], Compagnie Religiose Soppresse, San Sepolcro (hereafter CRS), L. XX. See, for example, L. XX., reg. 2.

19. Ibid., fol. 8r: "E sopra omni cosa sieno tenuti i Priori subito satisfare i legati particulari e così i legati annuali. E sopra ciò dal Preposto sieno per tucti i modi amoniti et sollicitta, et se i detti Priori in ciò negligenti sirano et non pagaranno i detti legati sieno scripti nel Libro di debitori et non possino essere in saccati in l'officio del priorato in la proxima futura inborsationi."

20. ASF, CRS L. XX., reg. 145, fol. 1r. Largi's phrase is "pietose opere."

21. See a copy of the act of acquisition, purchased with wealth from the Fraternity of S. Bartolomeo, in Degli Azzi, "Inventari degli archivi," 171–74; see also Farulli, *Annali e memorie,* 20; Agnoletti, *Abati,* 81.

22. Largi, *Specchio,* fol. 26r.

23. As he did with the records of the Fraternity of S. Bartolomeo, Largi abstracted from the registers of the Confraternity of Sta. Maria della Notte all the bequests made to the laudesi brotherhood. See these abstracts in ASF, CRS, L. XX. 8.

24. ASF, Notarile Antecosimiano [hereafter NA], F. 123 (Notarial acts of Fedele de Ruzzalo), not foliated but in the 1317 testament of Domina Palia, wife of Borgensio.

25. Ibid., in the 1319 testament of Domina Clara, widow of Salvuccio d'Orlandino.

26. Ibid., in the 1318 testament of Grazia di Piganello.

27. For the confraternity of laudesi gathering in the Camaldolese abbey, ASF, NA, C. 713 (Notarial acts of Cristoforo de Fedele), filza 1 (1318–28), fol. 21v. The first notice of the laudesi who gathered near the Torre di Berta is in NA, P. 121 (Notarial acts of Paolo di Ciuccio), fols. 43v–44r.

28. For the first known citation of this confraternity in a testament, see ASF, NA, C. 714 (Notarial acts of Cristoforo de Fedele), in the testament of Gnoglo(?) di Guido, 22 June 1338. The date of this testament suggests that the confraternity was later than the years following the 1301 sale, but Agnoletti (*Abati*, 83) states that tradition holds that the confraternity was founded soon after 1300. Moreover, already in a will of 1300, Bonavere de Raynieri del Ghiotto had made a bequest to the "Spedale de Sancta Maria de la Misericordia"; see Largi, *Specchio*, fol. 26r. The founding dates of the Hospital and the Confraternity of the Misericordia are not known; neither is it known which one preceded the other.

29. These statistics are taken from testaments redacted by Paolo di Ciuccio in 1348; see ASF, NA, P. 121, fols. 4v–83r, 125 bis r–v.

30. For the disciplinati of S. Bartolomeo, see ASF, NA, C. 713 (Notarial acts of Cristoforo de Fedele), filza 1316–18, in the testament of Vanni di Pietro Gualrade; and NA, F. 123 (Notarial acts of Fedele de Ruzzalo), in the testament of Clara, widow of Salvuccio d'Orlandino, August 1319. For the disciplinati of S. Niccolò, see NA, F. 123 (Notarial acts of Fedele de Ruzzalo), in the testament of Tratia di Pagnaello, March 1319.

31. Agnoletti, *Abati*, 83–85, claims that the disciplinati of Sta. Croce were founded in the first decade of the fourteenth century. The confraternity appears in the extant historical record in 1339; ASF, NA, C. 714 (Notarial acts of Cristoforo de Fedele), see the testament of Neri di Raniero Giancanello, February 1339.

32. For the disciplinati of Sta. Caterina, see ASF, NA, F. 132, filza 1, fol. 157v. The disciplinati of Sta. Maria Maddalena are mentioned in a notarial act of this same notary, filza 3, fol. 271r.

33. See note 6 above.

34. The manuscript containing these statutes of the Confraternity of Sta. Croce is now displayed in the Pinacoteca Comunale of Sansepolcro, but cataloged as ser. 32, reg. 152. The statutes have several additions in the centuries after their redaction of 1364. Inasmuch as the foliation is not consistent, I shall cite the material by the numbering of the Capitoli (statutes).

35. See Roberto Morghen, "Raniero Fasani e il Movimento dei Disciplinati del 1260," in *Il Movimento*, 29–42; Piero Meloni, "Per la storia della confraternite disciplinate in Umbria nel secolo XIV," in *Storia e arte in Umbria nell'età comunale. Atti del Convegno di studi Umbria* (Perugia: Deputazione di storia patria per l'Umbria, 1971), 2:535–37.

36. BC, ser. 32, reg. 152, cap. 1.

37. Ibid., cap. 9, 10, 36.

38. Ibid., cap. 14, 23, 26, 27, 36, 39, 44. For the eight offenses which the prior punished at his discretion, see cap. 9, 29, 38, 40, 41, 47, 60. For examples of the sixteen errors of commission, see cap. 14, 15, 21, 24, 43, 44, 45, 53, 55, 56, 58, 59, 60.

39. Ibid., cap. 34, 35.

40. Ibid., cap. 34.

41. Ibid., cap. 33, 55.

42. Ibid., cap. 80.

43. BC, ser. 2, reg. 1, fols. 38r–39v. The document with these laws enacted for the onslaught of the plague carries the date 24 July 1417, but it is evident that the legislation was created earlier. This redaction was written by Largi in that terrible plague year as provided by the statutes themselves. The statutes may have been enacted in 1377 when the fraternity began to record all the burials in the "terra" of San Sepolcro; see BC, ser. 32, reg. 143, fol. 15r.

44. Jacques Le Goff, *La naissance du Purgatoire* (Paris: Gallimard, 1981), 481–84; Jacques Chiffoleau, *La compatabilité de l'au-delà: Les hommes, la mort et la religion dans la region d'Avignon à la fin du Moyen âge (vers 1320–vers 1480)*, Collection de l'Ecole française de Rome, 47 (Rome: Ecole française de Rome, 1980), 389–425.

45. BC, ser. 32, reg. 152, cap. 33.

46. Ibid., cap. 42.

47. Ibid., cap. 1.

48. Ibid., cap. 40.

49. These two statements are based on an evaluation of the twenty-two names of members of the Confraternity of Sta. Croce that appear in the statutes of 1364 and subsequent additions through 1408; see BC, ser. 32, reg. 152, cap. 1, 48, 63, 71, 75, 81. To guage political participation of the confraternal members, I have compared the twenty-two members of the confraternity with the 353 names of members of the New Council of San Sepolcro of the 1390s; see BC, ser. 2, reg. 1, fols. 7r–10v. The New Council was the chief legislative body of the town in the 1390s.

50. In the years from 1349 to 1374 there are extant records on membership for four of the five flagellant confraternities. The exact number of members in the confraternities is never stated. In three cases, the type of evidence yielded by the documents is the number of members attending confraternal meetings. I take the number of members attending as the minimum membership and calculate a maximum by assuming that the number of members attending is the two-thirds of the membership necessary for a quorum. In a 1349 meeting of the Confraternity of Sta. Maria Maddalena, 29 members attended, so we may assume a membership of 29 to 44 members; see ASF, NA, P. 114, filza for 1347–49, fol. 144r. In 1357, the Confraternity of Sta. Maria della Misericordia had 20 members in attendance at a business meeting, which implies a maximum of 30 members; see NA, P. 119, register of 1352–77, fols. 151r–v. In 1359, 25 men attended a meeting of the disciplinati of Sta. Caterina, from which we may assume a maximum of 38 members; see NA, B. 1257, unfoliated, act of 3 February 1359. For the fourth group of flagellants, that of S. Antonio, more evidence is available. In the period from 1354 to 1374, the Confraternity of Sant'Antonio had at least 45 members. See the list ASF, CRS, A. 343, reg. 5, fols. 3r–50r. If we take the middle number of the range of minimum to maximum for the three confraternities with minimums and maximums, we arrive at the average of 31 active members. For the Confraternity of Sta. Croce, for which there are no membership data in this period, this average of 31 is taken as its membership. Adding the 45 members of the Confraternity of S. Antonio to the four others with an average of 31 members, we arrive at the total of 169 flagellants in the town of San Sepolcro in the third quarter of the fourteenth century.

51. ASF, CRS, A. 343, reg. 35, fols. 1r–27v.

52. ASF, NA, M. 516, reg. of 1425–30, fol. 21v.

53. In the 1440s, an individual, possibly Francesco de Largi, placed a slip of paper with a count of the population of San Sepolcro in a register of the Confraternity of Sta. Maria della Laude; see ASF, CRS, L. 20, 27, fol. 28r bis.

54. I have compared San Sepolcro with the town of Prato, which in 1427 possessed a population of 3488. In Prato 57.5 percent of the population were above the age of nineteen. I do not have a breakdown of males and females in Prato for that year, but for all of Tuscany males made up 52 percent of the population. Therefore, we may estimate that adult males made up 30 percent of a small town in Tuscany in the early fifteenth century. These estimates are taken from David Herlihy and Christiane Klapisch-Zuber, *Tuscans and Their Families: A Study of the Florentine Catasto of 1427* (New Haven: Yale University Press, 1985), 184 and 186.

I2 ❧

THE FLORENTINE CONFRATERNITES TODAY

NERI CAPPONI

I N HISTORICAL STUDIES GENERALLY, "translation" of past realities into contemporary language often clarifies the character and objectives of the institutions under consideration. In this chapter Neri Capponi reviews the current status of the surviving confraternities in Florence and examines their philanthropic and social-service activities. His analysis of the problems facing this kind of religious association in a secularized social context casts light upon the reasons for the success of lay confraternities in a former age.

NERI CAPPONI lectures in church history and canon law at the University of Florence and is a practicing canon lawyer: advocate of the Holy Roman Rota and of the Apostolic Signatura. Head of a Florentine family prominent since the Middle Ages, Count Capponi is himself a member of several of the confraternities that he discusses here.

F THE MANY CONFRATERNITIES that existed in fifteenth- and sixteenth-century Florence, very few remain. Most were suppressed by Grand Duke Peter Leopold at the end of the eighteenth century; others have died a natural death. Only nine or ten have survived.

Confraternities existing in Florence today can be roughly divided into two main categories: those that, besides liturgical activities, have a charitable purpose, and those whose activities are mainly liturgical. To the first category belong two of the most famous confraternities: l'Arciconfraternita della Misericordia and the Procuratori dei Poveri Vergognosi, known as the "Buonomini di San Martino." The more important of the two is the Archconfraternity of the Misericordia. Founded by the Dominican St. Peter the Martyr in 1244 as the "Compagnia della fede," to defend Catholics from the attacks of the heretic Patarini, the Misericordia later devoted itself to the care of the sick and the burial of the dead. It was "nationalized" in 1425 and united with the Bigallo, regaining its independence in 1490. In 1891, the Misericordia was again put under state supervision, but this time it managed to save its autonomy and it has flourished ever since. The members of the Misericordia today number about 12,500, of whom 2,500 are active.

The main activities of the Misericordia are: (1) The provision of an ambulance service. As this is the main activity of the archconfraternity, every active member of the Misericordia is bound to dedicate one hour or more to it a week (Figure 12.1). It comprises a day service, supplemented by night duties of the same kind and by a first-aid service that operates during big football matches. (2) Washing and attending to the sick who have no other assistance. (3) The operation of an old people's home. (4) The operation of a first-aid and medical center. (5) The provision of aid to those needy members of the archconfraternity who have a five-year seniority. (6) The provision of burial for its members in the cemetery of the Misericordia (Figure 12.2).

These activities make the Misericordia the most popular and

329

Figure 12.1. Vehicles of the Misericordia volunteer ambulance service on call in front of the confraternity Oratory. Photo T. Verdon/E. Epis.

influential of all of Florence's confraternities and similar bodies. It is also the largest of these groups. It is governed by a self-co-opting body of seventy-two members, divided into four classes: prelates, nobles, priests, and "aprons" (an old guild reminiscence), the last having the real control of the confraternity. The "constitutions" of the Misericordia, which are still based on those of 1501, strongly reflect those of the Florentine republic in their controls, balances of power, short terms of office, and random selection (by lot) of names for office (except for that of the *provveditore,* or purveyor, who leads the executive and is elected by the seventy-two). The small gifts that the Misericordia gives to its officeholders (except the purveyor) at the end of their terms are reminiscent of past ages: a tiny bag of pepper or a candle. Its members wear a black habit with a hood, and a rosary.

The oratory of the Misericordia is still a center of Florentine spirituality (inasmuch as modern secularization will allow). Most of the

Figure 12.2. Late nineteenth-century photograph showing members of the Misericordia in their habits, bearing the coffin of a deceased brother from the confraternity Oratory. Photo Alinari/Art Resource, N.Y.

ceremonies of the Misericordia take place in the oratory; the "clothing" of new members, however, today occurs more and more often in the cathedral, owing to the large number of candidates involved. One of the principal feasts, known to all Florentines, is that of St. Sebastian, patron saint of the Misericordia; on this occasion, the "brothers" distribute to large crowds rolls of bread which have been blessed for the occasion. Conscious of the need for spiritual renewal in a secularized age, the Misericordia is taking steps to emphasize the supernatural character of Christian charity, an approach that distinguishes it from similar associations.

The other confraternity whose main activity is social work is that of the Procuratori dei Poveri Vergognosi, the "Buonomini di San Martino." This group was instituted with the blessing of Sant'Antonino,

prior of the reformed Dominican convent of San Marco and later archbishop of Florence, to help those poor who were ashamed to beg. Many
great families had been reduced to a state of poverty and destitution
as enemies of the Medici faction and because of their status could not
join common beggars. According to a legend (unsupported by known
historical sources), twelve "good men" (*buonomini*) were summoned by
Antonino to his cell at San Marco in 1442, and so the confraternity
was born (Figure 12.3).

This group, today numbering eighteen members (twelve Procuratori plus six Aiuti), still continues its work from the church of San
Martino, its premises since 1478. For organizational purposes, the city
is divided into six wards (on the lines of the old medieval wards). All
the activities of the confraternity are surrounded by silence and discretion, even co-option is announced privately to the surprised and flat-
tered nominee! All help is given in secrecy, as it is supposed that the
recipient, being ashamed to beg, would not like it to be known publicly
that he is being helped. The recipient is required to maintain a certain
standard of external dignity, and the help provided is chiefly to maintain
that dignity. The Buonomini were enjoined by Sant'Antonino never to
amass capital, and to this ideal they have remained faithful, for donations never fail them. When they are down to their last penny, the
Buonomini have mass said and a candle put on the doorstep of the church;
this call is always answered. The Buonomini appear in public, as a body,
only on the annual Feast of Sant'Antonino in San Marco.

After World War II, the decline of Florence's confraternities
was accelerated by several factors, among them increasing secularization; an ill-advised liturgical revolution, ruthlessly imposed, which has
caused church attendance everywhere to fall sharply and has dealt a death
blow to the confraternities; and the terrible flood of the Arno in 1966,
which destroyed the premises of several groups. Today, even if members
of a confraternity number in the hundreds, very few attend the weekly
or monthly liturgical celebrations, and most of those who do are el-
derly. Few new members are made and practically no young people join.
Curiously enough, the confraternities that have survived best, and in
some cases taken a new lease on life, are those acting as hosts to the
activities of other bodies—like those shells found on beaches that serve
as receptacles for little crabs.

Figure 12.3. Domenico Ghirlandaio, *Members of the Confraternity of San Martino Visiting the Sick and Bringing Food to the Poor.* Florence, San Martino dei Buonomini. Photo Brogi, Alinari/Art Resrouce, N.Y.

One such host group is the Confraternita di San Girolamo e San Francesco Poverino in San Filippo Benizzi. Founded in 1410 as the Confraternita di Santa Maria della Pietà e di San Girolamo, it was merged in 1911 with the Confraternity of San Francesco Poverino, by which name it is commonly known today. San Francesco gained a new vitality after it began to give hospitality to the youth group of the Florentine section of the Order of Malta: young men and women who go as nurses and stretcher-bearers to the pilgrimages of the sick to Lourdes and Loreto. Other groups also gravitate toward San Francesco, including the Florentine section of the Italian Latin Mass society with its weekly mass. Together, these groups have infused rich new life into the old confraternity.

A similar process of revival, although on a smaller scale, has occurred in the venerable confraternity known as the "Buca di Sant'Antonio Abbate." It houses the Society of St. Vincent De Paul, an old but flourishing Catholic charitable organization.

Two confraternities are still closed owing to the flood of 1966. One is the Confraternita del Santissimo Nome di Gesù e San Francesco Saverio, in the oratory of San Tommasino. Known as "La Disciplina dei Nobili," it was founded at the end of the sixteenth century. The other is the Compagnia di Santa Maria della Croce al Tempio, known as the "Neri." Founded between 1327 and 1360, it was suppressed by Grand Duke Peter Leopold at the end of the eighteenth century and revived in 1912. This group, in past ages, used to assist those sentenced to death on their last journey. Both these confraternities still exist, but their membership is by now nominal.

Four other Florentine confraternities also still exist:

1. The Archconfraternity of San Francesco known as the "Vanchetoni." Founded by the Blessed Ippolito Galantini in 1602 for the teaching of Christian doctrine, this confraternity no longer fulfills its original teaching purpose, nor does it continue to organize the sumptuous yearly repast for which it became famous. Its activities are limited to a weekly mass which is sparsely attended.

2. The Compagnia di San Niccolò del Ceppo. Founded in 1417 and for centuries closely associated with the Confraternity of San Girolamo della Notte (now suppressed) the activity of this group is now reduced to a monthly mass, which, again, is sparsely attended.

3. The Confraternity of San Jacopo Sopr'Arno. This group merged with that of San Sebastiano dei Fanciulli and was known in the past as the "Compagnia della Notte." According to tradition, it was founded circa 1300 primarily for the formation of children's choirs. Its activities are reduced to the celebration of a monthly mass and some other liturgical ceremonies. Once a year it raises a collection for the poor.

4. The Confraternita dei Librai e dei Cartai. This group exists only on paper.

It is clear from this account that the confraternities of Florence, while still existing, are slowly disappearing in the face of modern influences and problems. Although some of these confraternities remain very well off financially, the number of their members and activities continues to dwindle. Only the special cases of the Misericordia and the Buonomini di San Martino retain a spark of the spirit that informed the confraternities of quattrocento Florence.

13 ❧

CULT OBJECTS AND ARTISTIC PATRONAGE OF THE FOURTEENTH-CENTURY FLAGELLANT CONFRATERNITY OF GESÙ PELLEGRINO

KATHLEEN GILES ARTHUR

S EVERAL ESSAYS IN THIS SECTION suggest the role of lay confraternities in commissioning works of art for liturgical use and for the embellishment of their meeting places; the splendid pictorial cycles that adorn the Venetian *scuole* are the most prestigious examples. In this chapter, Kathleen Giles Arthur analyses the nature and function of cult objects owned by a Florentine confraternity in the fourteenth and early fifteenth centuries. The detailed inventory that forms the basis of Professor Arthur's reflections suggests the full range of "artistic" expression fostered by confraternity life: above all, the essentially creative character of confraternal liturgical and devotional activities, for which painting and sculpture, along with vestments and altar furnishings, were necessary functional components.

KATHLEEN GILES ARTHUR teaches the history of art at James Madison University in Virginia.

HE ROLE OF ARTWORKS in the worship rituals of the flagellant confraternities is a little-known aspect of their history. While there have been substantial investigations into the origins of their theatrical presentations, the artistic cult objects of such groups remain largely unexplored.[1] Art historians have tended to identify the lay confraternities as artistic patrons without recognizing the differences between the *laudesi* and flagellant confraternities.[2] Whereas a laudesi or devotional image is intended to reflect the image of the saint being venerated, the flagellant artwork has a more active role: that of stimulating the viewer's identification with the suffering and sacrifice of Christ. Thus the images commissioned by the flagellants have a distinctive purpose and character not yet documented through specific models in fourteenth-century art.[3]

Cult images are often mentioned in the statutes of various Florentine trecento religious confraternities, but usually with the barest of descriptions. A passage in the statutes of the laudesi Company of San Zanobi, which met in Santa Reparata, describes the ritual candlelit procession of laud singing every Saturday, but states only that members carried "the painting of the Madonna" to the altar in the upper church.[4] Even this type of notice is often lacking in statutes of Florentine flagellant companies. The statutes of the Company of Gesù of Santa Croce mention an image of Christ crucified, but few if any trecento or quattrocento pictures attributed to the flagellant confraternities have been rediscovered.[5]

In the case of the flagellant confraternity of Gesù Pellegrino, founded as the Company of the Misericordia di San Salvatore in January 1334 (n.s.) at Santa Maria Novella in Florence, its statutes make no mention of the company's cult images.[6] However, at least one early panel with a definitely established provenance from this company, a *Man of Sorrows* (Figure 13.1) attributed to Niccolò di Pietro Gerini, is preserved.[7] It appears from the recently rediscovered inventories of the confraternity's chapel in 1341 and 1350 that the statutes are unreliable sources of

Figure 13.1. Niccolò di Pietro Gerini (?), *Man of Sorrows*. Florence, Accademia. Gabinetto fotografico, Soprintendenza Beni artistici e storici di Firenze.

information about a company's cult images and objects. The Gesù Pellegrino inventories not only list the confraternity's possessions but also often allude to their purpose or placement in the chapel (see Appendix I).[8] Thus they permit us to reconstruct the decoration of the chapel of Saints Simon and Thaddeus in the Chiostro dei Morti in Santa Maria

Novella, and to trace changes in the religious imagery of the company in the fourteenth and fifteenth centuries. In this chapter I concentrate on the early development of the confraternity's images and decorative art objects associated with funeral rites.

The inventories demonstrate that after initially using as their cult image an archaic type of crucifix with the Virgin and St. John flanking Christ, confraternity members commissioned a large, ornate altarpiece, the *Madonna and Child with Saints,* in 1346. The patrons of this piece, its subjects, and the identity of the saints in it can be determined from the original text of a confraternity meeting in January 1347 (n.s.), which was previously known only from an inaccurate eighteenth-century copy.[9] By 1350–51, the company had added a banner painted with Christ's flagellation as an altar hanging "in front of the altarpiece" ("dinanzi la tavola d'altare") thus creating a sophisticated dual-level imagery. This *Flagellation* was seen at first view with the *Madonna and Child with Saints* revealed afterward, or only on feast days. Given the *Flagellation* banner and other objects, including a miniature column, it seems that the penitential focus of the company strengthened in the early 1350s, during the turbulent period after the Black Death. In addition, from the 1340s on, great emphasis was placed on the confraternity's practice of publicly honoring deceased members with elaborate funerals. In 1345 the company's account book records a payment to the major mid-fourteenth century painter Andrea Orcagna for decorating their funeral torches. Finally, based on the concrete evidence of the flagellant company's art objects and chapel environment, we may gain some insight into the spiritual tenor of religious experience in the mid-fourteenth century.

The Company of Gesù Pellegrino was one of four flagellant confraternities we know to have been founded in Florence in the first half of the fourteenth century.[10] According to Dei's copy of the company's statutes of 1354, it was formed in 1334 following the "terrifying and horrendous" flood of 4 November 1333, the motive for its foundation being "to placate God's wrath," for which its members performed penitence, and, "with other good works and to separate themselves in a certain way and at certain times from worldly affairs and give themselves to the service of God, they withdrew behind the church of Santa Maria Novella."[11] The manifest desire of the confraternity to achieve a kind of temporary monastic withdrawal from the world is thus an early quintessential part of the group, despite its lay character.

At first the congregation did not have a place solely its own for meetings. Members were known as the "Disciplinati della cappella di San Niccolò" because they met in the Chapel of San Niccolò, which had been built around 1333 as a burial chapel by Dardano Acciaiuoli.[12] It was situated in the southwest corner of the convent next to the dispensary, an uncomfortably public, accessible location for a confraternity whose statutes stressed privacy and secrecy. The earliest preserved membership list of 1336 records 62 men in the company;[13] by 1341, however, membership had risen to about 150, judging from the 148 white and 5 black confraternity robes listed among its possessions. If membership had more than doubled in five years, a larger space for the semimonthly meetings must have been required. The treasurers maintained long lists of small donations "for the new chapel," and one document states that it was built with their own funds.[14] Sometime before 1345 they moved to an oratory located beyond the north end of the east wing of the Chiostro dei Morti, today completely destroyed.[15]

In this early period, the image of Christ on the cross was both the confraternity's public symbol and the focal point of its services. Since the thirteenth century, Christ on the cross had been adopted by the flagellant companies for their banners and seals.[16] According to the first inventory of 1341, the company owned "a carved wooden crucifix which we carry outside with a white linen drape with a red and blue cross" (inv. no. 39). Just such a combination of banner and crucifix is represented in an illustration of the Bianchi in the later fourteenth-century Lucchese chronicle of Sercambi (Figure 13.2).[17] In 1341 the company also possessed "the crucifix that is above the altar with Our Lady and with St. John at the sides" (inv. no. 38). The crucifix hanging above the altar in the Chapel of San Niccolò must have served to inspire the members with the example of Christ's suffering. The Gesù Pellegrino company was, in all likelihood, simply copying the usual decoration in mendicant churches, for instance the crucifix hanging above the choir screen in Santa Maria Novella. In their choice of the crucifix, the lay confraternity not only expressed the penitential character of their service but also legitimized their identity in a social and religious sense by creating a "paramonastic" environment. This interpretation of their artistic im-

Figure 13.2. *Confraternity Members in Procession with Crucifix: Cronica di Sercambi*, fol. 618. Biblioteca Capitolare, Lucca. Photo Arthur.

agery complements the "paraliturgical" character of the flagellant companies' worship services suggested by historians.[18] As befitted its devotion to Jesus, the company also owned several other small crucifixion panels: one double-sized panel with two flagellants on the reverse (inv. no. 48) and another showing the crucifixion and twelve Apostles (inv. no. 45).

Based on the inventory's description of the cross, it can be argued that the confraternity exhibited conservative taste for the period circa 1335, choosing a type of crucifix which was iconographically archaic. The terminology "colla donna nostra e con san Giovanni da lato" could perhaps refer to bust-length images of the Virgin Mary and St. John placed on the terminals of the cross, but "da lato" more probably meant full-length figures flanking the body of Christ on the apron of the cross, as on the Bigallo Crucifix dating from the 1280s (Figure 13.3).[19]

Figure 13.3. Unknown artist, painted cross. Florence, Bigallo. Photo Alinari/Art Resource, N.Y.

Full-length figures in close proximity to the body of Christ would have a much greater emotive power to stimulate the members' identification with Christ's pain, and could give the members a sense of spiritual communion with the Virgin Mary and St. John, who were also mourning Christ's suffering. Thus they were too important to be reduced to symbolic ciphers distanced from Christ on the arms of the cross. The archaic type of crucifix was selected not for the sake of tradition, but because it ideally suited the confraternity's spiritual needs.

One surviving early trecento Florentine cross corresponds to the same type and may be connected with a flagellant confraternity. The Academy Cross (Figure 13.4), attributed to "Assistant of Daddi" by Richard Offner, shows the Virgin Mary and John the Evangelist beside Christ; in addition it has narrative scenes of the Flagellation, Mocking of Christ, Via Crucis, and Last Judgment in the four terminal quattrofoils. Offner explains its iconographic peculiarity by suggesting that it might have been painted to replicate some older miracle-working image.[20] While this is always a possibility in this period, the emphasis on the Passion and especially the central placement of the Flagellation scene suggests that it, too, was commissioned by one of the Florentine flagellant confraternities. Since the Gesù Pellegrino inventory of 1341 presumably would have mentioned the presence of the narrative scenes, I suggest that the Academy Crucifix belonged to another flagellant company, and that, on the basis of these two examples, one might begin to look for a "flagellant type" of crucifix.

The Gesù Pellegrino inventories also document the chapel's furnishings, which indirectly reflect confraternal religious customs and give clues about cult images. The whips used for the ritual act of flagellation are described as "fuscelli," straw sticks (inv. nos. 46, 69), indicating that the flagellation was more symbolic than actual. An allusion to the candelabra in front of the boards where the straw sticks are placed (inv. no. 69) conjures up a picture of whips laid out ceremonially with candles lighted before them. The thirty cushions to kneel upon (inv. no. 82) represent another, somewhat ironic, concession to comfort. Six large benches and a desk with a stool "dove si sta a scrivere" (inv. nos. 53, 55) are significant because the statutes stress the maintenance of written records of deceased brothers, of officials, of members fined or dismissed from the company, and of members' pious donations. In fact, the inventory

Figure 13.4. Daddi assistant (?), painted cross. Florence, Accademia. Photo Alinari/ Art Resource, N.Y.

of 1341 shows that in six years two copies of the statutes had already been written: the red-covered book of "Capitoli" (inv. no. 24) and the green-covered "Libro di Capitoli nuovi" (inv. no. 25). The inventory books themselves were special objects. An extant volume of successive inventories dating from 1420 to 1600 is decorated on its vellum cover with a miniature of Gesù Pellegrino (Figure 13.5). This small painting probably was modeled on a major cult image, such as the "tabernaculo col pellegrino," which appears in later fifteenth century inventories.[21] In this manner, an unusual iconographic type of Christ is preserved.

The authors of the 1341 inventory began their survey of the chapel with the altar itself, and thus we find that the company did not possess a monumental altarpiece. The first item was an "archa" or tabernacle, listed in 1341 but crossed out in 1350 with the notation that it had been sold to one of the confraternity members. The third item, a painted predella upon which a cloth is placed, must have served as the main decorative element. Further accouterments of the company's altar included a box containing the equipment for the altar (inv. no. 4), a blessed relic covered with a cloth three *braccie* long (inv. nos. 5, 7), the missal (inv. no. 23), the container for the Host (inv. no. 26), a gold chalice (inv. no. 27), and a book of lauds (inv. no. 28). Finally, there was a small angel (inv. no. 64) to be placed above the altar.

By 1350 a most important artistic change in the chapel's decoration had taken place: a large altarpiece equipped with columns, colonettes, and a predella had been acquired (inv. no. 105). Unfortunately, this and later inventories do not clearly specify the imagery of this altarpiece.[22] One version of its commission has been known since 1893, when the "Memoria della tavola dell'altare della Compagnia di Gesù Pellegrino" was published by Milanesi; he interpreted the subject as "nel mezzo Nostra Donna col Divin figliuolo e dalle bande Santi Filippo e Zanobi."[23] His text, based on Dei's copy, was incomplete but the original still survives and can be used as a basis for determining the patronage and subject (see Appendix 2). The Gesù Pellegrino document is not in fact a contract between the company and the artist but constitutes a unique early example of collective discussion of a projected commission, a particular type of document which has no extant parallel until a century later, when the Society of the Most Holy Trinity in Pistoia met in 1455 to discuss its new altarpiece.[24]

Figure 13.5. *Christ as Gesù Pellegrino,* cover of MS. Compagnie religiose soppresse 918 (no. 34), Archivio di Stato, Florence. Photo Arthur.

The original text consists of notes from an informal meeting in January 1347 (n.s.). Three of the four men named at the head of the page—Ser Ciuto Cecchi, Piero Rinaldi, and Lapo di Cione—were long-standing confraternity members who had regularly held various offices since 1338–39.[25] The last, Filippo Niccoli, who was mentioned as first serving as a confraternity official between July 1342 and March 1343,[26] was the newest member of the four but was also the most important on a practical level, since he had already paid for the wooden panel and offered sixteen gold florins toward the general cost of the painting and the depiction of his patron saints San Filippo and San Zanobi. A fifth person, Neri Guiducci, was also involved; his comments at the end of the second page were omitted from Milanesi's transcription. The lists of company officials show that in November 1346 Neri Guiducci had been elected captain, while Piero Rinaldi (a *rigattiere*), Lapo di Cione (a *lanaiuolo*), and Ser Ciuto Cecchi (a *notaio*) were *consiglieri*.[27] Thus the patronage constellation is clear: the altarpiece was to be commissioned by the confraternity's top officials and by a relatively new and presumably wealthy member who would bear most of its cost. No mention is made of any ecclesiastical adviser or of Piero di Francesco, their "visitatore," and thus the theme appears to have been entirely a lay decision.

Apparently each member (or two members jointly) took responsibility for a single compartment, "uno conpasso," of the polyptych and pledged payment of one or two gold florins for each figure of a saint.[28] Ser Ciuto Cecchi and Piero Rinaldi ask for "the compartment in the middle of the altarpiece and to have it painted at their expense [with] our Lady with Her Son." Lapo di Cione asks for another compartment with Santo Simone, and Neri Guiducci completes the altarpiece with Saint Taddeo. Although the original altarpiece by Pietro di Civillari has not been traced, its subject and format, a five-part polyptych with the Madonna and Child flanked by saints Filippo, Zanobi, Simon, and Taddeo, can be reconstructed.[29] The choice of the new cult image shows us the strength of the cult of the Virgin Mary even in a flagellant confraternity.[30] A contemporary parallel of this phenomenon is the *Madonna of Humility* painted by the Pisan artist Bartolomeo (Pellerano) da Camogli in 1346 for the flagellant confraternity of St. Anthony in Palermo.[31] There, traditional Mariolatry is interwoven with flagellant imagery by the predella's illustration of kneeling confraternity members worshiping the cross, column, and other symbols of the Passion (Figure 13.6). Unfortunately, the decoration of the predella of the Gesù Pellegrino altarpiece is not described.

The addition of an image of the Flagellation of Christ, "a green-colored cloth [on which] is painted Christ at the column, to keep in front of the altarpiece" (inv. no. 108), indicates that the Company of Gesù Pellegrino felt the need for a more penitential theme than the Madonna and Child for their everyday use. This Flagellation banner supplied a direct narrative example to inspire members before they flagellated themselves in their meetings. Since the banner is first recorded in the inventory revision of 1351, it may be compared with a later trecento miniature illustrating Villani's text on the flagellants which shows them carrying a Flagellation banner (Figure 13.7).[32] One large banner from the later trecento, also painted in *terra verde* but displaying the Crucifixion with small-scale kneeling flagellants of the Company of St. Anthony of Genoa, is preserved in the Victoria and Albert Museum in London.[33]

Figure 13.6. Bartolommeo (Pellerano) da Camogli, *Madonna of Humility.* Palermo, Pinacoteca. Photo Alinari/Art Resource, N.Y.

Figure 13.7. *A Flagellant Confraternity in Procession*, from the *Cronica di Giovanni Villani*, Cod. L.V. III. 296, fol. 197v. Biblioteca Apostolica Vaticana.

Perhaps painted images were not quite enough in the captains' view to inspire true compassion with Christ. A miniaturized but actual symbol of the Passion was introduced into the confraternity meeting place: a small column with an iron candlestick placed before the crucifix (inv. no. 98). This was more than a convenient candlestand because the later Gesù Pellegrino inventory of 1421 describes one item as "in front of the altar with the column."[34] Thus the confraternity apparently had an altar with a column in the early fifteenth century. The use of the column as a cult object is illustrated in an image in the *Madonna of Humility* showing the flagellant company worshiping the cross and the column (Figure 13.6). Both cross and column have been interpreted in the past as abstract conceptions rather than literal images of worship practices. The Gesù Pellegrino company's fifteenth-century liturgy calls for candles to be snuffed out during a series of prayers at the beginning of the members' flagellation, and lighted upon its conclusion.[35] The column before the crucifix could have been the last object seen before the ritual flagellation and the first seen afterward. This dramatic symbolic effect in the flagellant service may have been created from as early as 1350.

For the Company of Gesù Pellegrino in Santa Maria Novella, the commemoration and burial of its deceased brothers was one of its most sacred duties and also a practical social service that attracted membership.[36] The statutes of 1354 repeatedly emphasize the importance of paying respect to the dead, by perpetuating their memory with masses (inv. no. 85) and by maintaining lists of dead members.[37] The statutes describe the elaborate funeral ritual accorded confraternity brothers: sixteen members dressed in the company's white robes and hoods would go in procession to collect the corpse at the house of the deceased. While half the group knelt praying in a circle in the street in front of the house, the other eight would enter and carry the body out to the waiting bier. After draping the corpse with the company shroud, they would solemnly return to the church, their way lighted by the processional torches.[38] The recently reassembled Gesù Pellegrino *Man of Sorrows,* which the inscription calls a "tavola dei morti," illustrates in the predella a synthesized view of the funeral ritual (Figure 13.8).

The mid-fourteenth-century inventories record a number of

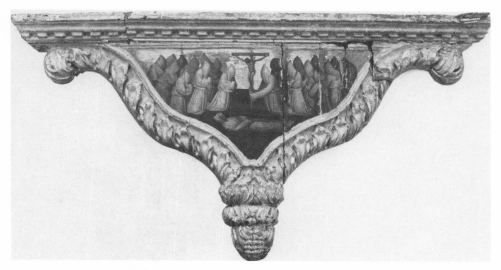

Figure 13.8. Niccolò di Pietro Gerini (?), *Funeral Rite for a Confraternity Member.* Predella of the *Man of Sorrows* shown in figure 13.1. Florence, Accademia. Gabinetto Fotografico, Soprintendenza Beni artistici e storici di Firenze.

decorative arts items used for confraternity funerals, including two embroidered shrouds with a matching pillow for the funeral bier (inv. no. 78), and decorated portable candelabra or torches (inv. no. 96). In 1350 "due torchi grandi forniti di giunte di ferri da portare a'morti della compagnia" were added to the previous inventory of 1341. The torches were probably the same as those mentioned in the account book entry for 26 June 1345, where it is stated that Andrea di Cione, painter, was paid for painting *torchi*.[39] This is interesting in view of the fact that Andrea di Cione, nicknamed Orcagna, had been expelled from the company of Gesù Pellegrino two years earlier.[40]

Although Orcagna's torches have not survived, a general idea of such ceremonial torches may be gathered from miniatures and from one outstanding example of the trecento decorative arts in Pisa. In a late fourteenth-century Paduan illuminated manuscript in the British Museum, one scene shows two artists in the process of carving a large standing candelabra.[41] Of similar design is the painted and gilded wooden candelabra in the Museo di San Matteo of Pisa, currently attributed to

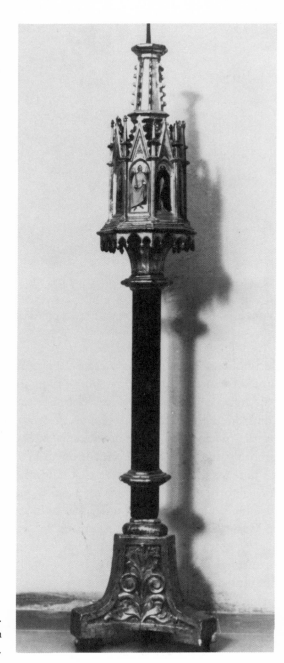

Figure 13.9. Painted torciera.
Pisa, Museo Nazionale di San
Matteo. Photo Amendola.

Cecco di Pietro (Figure 13.9).[42] This piece stands almost five feet high on a three-legged base that appears to be dated somewhat later than the upper gilded tabernacle. Around the top is placed a gabled screen of eight niches with a painted cycle of seven saints and the "Noli me tangere" scene. Orcagna's painted processional torches were probably not as elaborate, judging from his payment, but they certainly seem to have been important decorative objects for the confraternity.

The 1341 and 1350 inventories of the Company of Gesù Pellegrino convey a sense of the increasing aesthetic sophistication of the altar decoration and diversity of images and cult objects assembled in their chapel of Sts. Simon and Thaddeus. While the cult increased its private penitential focus around 1350, a social dimension was added which might be considered antithetical to the company's original paramonastic goal of "withdrawal from the things of this world." Elaborate public funeral ceremonies are not the only symptom of this social element; the rapid accumulation of decorative objects and the careful documentation of the company's material possessions are further proof. Consciousness of status and material concerns are also betrayed in chapters 33 and 35 of their statutes, which advised members that "they should not pray to be elected to office," and adjured brothers "to remember the Confraternity in their wills."[43] Altogether, the evidence suggests that members were caught between the simple, original goal of withdrawal from the world and greater, more diverse needs resulting from the growth of the confraternity as a lay religious institution. Ascetic, pietistic, and penitential impulses seem to have warred with social/confraternal ones in the hearts of members of Confraternity of Gesù Pellegrino during the period 1335–50.

APPENDIX 1

Inventory of the Company of Gesù Pellegrino's Possessions, 1341 and 1350: Compagnie Religiose Suppressi 910, no. 6

Items are numbered according to position in original list; utilitarian objects and linens are condensed or omitted. Revisions of 1350 are found in parentheses on fols. 91v–92v and fol. 93r, nos. 93ff. Thanks and acknowledgment are due to John Henderson and Gino Corti for reviewing the transcription of the documents.

fol. 91v

"In the name of God, amen, the year 1341 . . ."

"In the name of God, the Holy Mother and Virgin Mary, and all the saints of Paradise, amen. Here below we will write all the possessions, robes, and objects of the company and all the things which are registered by the old custodians, that is Gianchello the armorer, Giusto Chelli, Pierozo di Ser Bonaguida and the new custodians Jacopo di Bonsi, Giovanni del Fede, Cambino di Baldino.

1. a small tabernacle (was sold to Lapo di Cione, the company received 3 lire)
2. predella [wooden platform] that stands at the foot of the altar
3. a painted predella that stands on the altar, and thereupon a linen towel
4. a chest that holds the altar furnishings
5. a holy relic that stays upon the altar
6. an altar cloth of four braccie that lies on the altar, and attached to it a checkered cloth that hangs in front of the altar
7. a cloth of three braccie that rests above the holy relic
8–12. [linens]
13. a checkered red and white pillow with a St. Nofrio dressed in linen
14. a handkerchief where the priest rubs his hands
15. a cloth that rests on the lectern with a red cross
16. a linen tunic that the priest wears
17. an amice of multicolored cloth
18. an alb in which the priest preaches
19. a belt with which one ties around the waist
20. a stole with two maniples
21. a red chasuble . . .
22. a piece of linen towel . . .
23. a missal for the altar (Frate Ubertino had it)
24. a book of chapter rules with a red cover
25. a book of new chapter rules with a green cover

fol. 92r

26. a dish with the white cloth
27. a gilded chalice
28. a book with the office of the lauds, with a white cover
29 a book with a red cover to receive the novitiates
30. a book with a cover on which is the Savior, which is carried when the obsequies of the dead are done
31. a large box in which is kept the *forlige* [?]
32. a large box in which is kept the seal of the company
33. a box inside which are the four privileges
34. a box inside which are the oblations [?]
35. a box to carry to those who are given punishments

36. two wooden candleholders that stand on the altar
37. two iron candleholders where the candles are placed
38. a crucifix that is kept above the altar with Our Lady and St. John on the sides
39. a carved wooden crucifix that we carry outside, with a drape of white linen with a red and blue cross
40. a lectern with two iron hooks and a weight with red leather ties
41. a blue cloth [?] which stays on the altar (it is torn and to be thrown away)
42. two small colonettes where the candles are attached above the altar
43. two torches with handles which are lighted at the altar when God is praised
44. a gessoed panel that is in the church where the dead of the company are recorded ([it] was carried into the place [i.e., their oratory])
45. a painted panel with the crucifixion and twelve Apostles
46. a pouch where the straw sticks are kept
47. a panel where the gifts of *roma* [?] and gowns are written [canceled]
48. a panel with a cross and inside two flagellants
49. four small gessoed panels
50–51. [chests]
52. a low chest to enclose possessions
53. six large benches where the men sit
54. a table with two trestles [canceled]
55. a desk where one writes, with a small bench to sit upon
56. 153 black robes for men [canceled . . . 5 black robes]
57. 149 men's robes of white

fol. 92v

58. 16 pieces of wood which are around the walls where the gowns are hung
59. two tin cups one for wine and the other for water to place on the altar [canceled]
60. a small copper basin to collect the offerings
61. a copper cup to heat wine
62. an iron brazier for charcoal
63. two red boxes painted for elections
64. a small angel to place on the altar
65. a painted wooden "tasseria" [?]
66. a chest with two keys where the money for the poor is placed
67. a small chest to hold candles, with a cover
68. a box to keep candles
69. a small iron candleholder that stands in front of the boards where we place the sticks of straw
70. three wooden candleholders for candles of animal fat
71. two writing stands, one of lead, the other of wood
72. a small box of paint
73. a large *temperatoia* [candlesnuffer?] [canceled]
74. two small wooden boxes for dust
75. two pairs of small scissors

76. a little cap which stands under the lighted lamp
77. two pieces of wood to hold the books with weights
78. a large pouch inside of which is a linen pillow with two shrouds, on one the Savior in rough linen cloth and this is the equipment that is carried to the dead of the Company (there is no pillow . . . lost because of the plague)
79. a small bell
80. a glass dish with casing in which stays the sacrificial wine
81. a cloak with narrow sleeves
82. thirty cushions to kneel upon (they are very tattered . . . good for nothing)
83. a book in which is written the men of the Company, that is, their names
84. a little book in which are written the initiates
85. a book of the company of the masses
86. a book where the inventory and officials of the Company are written
87. four old books with vellum covers
88. three black veils, two of linen cloth [canceled]
89. a bottle of ink
90. a light robe of Carmenese cloth (sold)
91. a black chasuble, a stole, and a maniple
92. two bags which we tie around to carry the crucifix
93. a chest where the [names of the] new captains are placed with three keys

Fol. 93r

"the year 1350, first of July . . ." [right column]

94. two linen cloths that are kept beside the altar
95. a black covering for the lectern
96. two large torches equipped with iron handles to carry to the dead of the Company
97. a large covering made in the manner of an altar cloth of four braccie, offered by Niccolò di Fredi to the Company [this is found written twice]
98. a small colonette, on which is an iron candleholder in front of the crucifix
99. a "farfetta" [beret?] that belonged to Frate Bernardo [canceled]
100. a candelabra with five lights in front of the altar
101. a desk with built-in bench with two keys, one around the side of the altar
102. a tall *predella* [platform?] to light the candles at the altar
103. eight pieces that are to keep under the feet
104. a panel that is in the Saint where the dead of the Company are written [canceled]
105. a large altarpiece, furnished with columns and colonettes and a predella
106. a small panel to give the blessing
107. two wooden crucifixes to carry outside
108. a green-colored cloth [on which] is painted Christ at the column, to keep in front of the altarpiece
109. a tabernacle in which there is a crucifix that belonged to Ser Matteo Becchi
110. 99 white robes that we have from the old custodians
111. a gessoed panel where the captains sign

APPENDIX 2

Minutes from the meeting of the Company of Gesù Pellegrino for the new altarpiece, January 1347 (n.s.)

Compagnie Religiose Soppressi 910, no. 6, fol. 90v

"January 1346/7

In the name of God and of His blessed mother, Amen.

Here and *following* we make a record of the altarpiece which is to be placed above the altar and who will pay for it and the painter who will make it and how much it will cost.

The wood for the altarpiece with the predella and with the columns cost five gold florins. Filippo himself paid Niccholi for the love of God.
And the said Piero painter had from the said Piero Rinaldi three gold florins.
Also the said Piero had from the said Piero [Rinaldi] two gold florins.
It [the commission] to paint the said picture was given to Piero di Civiliari known as Chiozzo [and] Filippo Nicholi and Piero Rinaldi made an agreement with him concerning the said picture and predella and columns [for which] he asked twenty gold florins and it all [is to be] made with fine gold, that is the picture and the predella, and the columns other gold and not fine. . . ."

fol. 91r

"[In] memory of those of the company who will contribute to the said picture to have it painted . . .

Filippo Nicholi has requested to have painted for him in the said picture two saints, that is St. Philip and St. Zanobius. He gave [to Piero] and Piero Rinaldi received [from him] four gold florins.
Ser Ciuto Ciechi and Piero Rinaldi have requested to have painted for them the section in the middle of the altarpiece . . . Our Lady with [Her] Son. Ser Ciuto and Piero gave one gold florin . . .
Lapo di Cione has requested to have painted a section in the said picture and to have painted St. Simon. Neri Guiducci requested [and] wants to have placed in the other section St. Taddeus . . . Neri gave and Piero Rinaldi had one gold florin."

NOTES

1. The only general studies on artistic images of flagellant confraternities are Adriano Prandi, "Intorno all'iconografia dei Disciplinati," in *Il Movimento dei Disciplinati nel settimo centenario dal suo inizio (Perugia 1260)*, Appendix 9 to *Bollettino della Deputazione di storia patria per l'Umbria* (Spoleto, 1962), 496–508 (hereafter *Il Movimento*), and idem, "Arte figurative per le Confraternite dei Disciplinati," in *Risultati e prospettive della ricerca sul Movimenti dei Disciplinati: Convegno internazionale di studio, Perugia 1969* (Perugia: Arti Grafiche, 1972), 266–90. Inventories of art objects used as scenery, props, or costumes in festival plays have attracted the

attention of scholars of drama, for example, Angela Maria Terrugia, "In quale momento i Disciplineti hanno dato origine al loro teatro?," *Il Movimento,* 451–53. Much important material is found within general historical studies; see, for example, Luigi Passerini, *Storia degli stabilimenti di beneficenza e d'istruzione elementare gratuita della città di Firenze* (Florence, 1853); G. M. Monti, *Le confraternite medievali dell' alta e media Italia* (Venice: La Nuova Italia, 1927); and John Henderson, "The Flagellant Movement and Flagellant Confraternities in Central Italy 1260–1400," *Studies in Church History* 15 (1978): 147–60. For Sicilian flagellant confraternities and art, see Carmelina Naselli, "Notizie sui Disciplinati in Sicilia," *Il Movimento* 317–27; and Geneviève Bresc-Bautier, *Artistes, patriciens et confrèries* (Rome: Ecole française de Rome, 1979); Ronald Weissman, *Ritual Brotherhood in Renaissance Florence* (New York: Academic Press, 1982); Henderson, "Piety and Charity in Late Medieval Florence: Religious Confraternities from the Middle of the Thirteenth to the Late Fifteenth Century" (Ph.D. diss., University of London, 1983).

2. Confraternity artworks are often discussed as a subcategory of guild patronage; see Martin Wackernagel, *The World of the Florentine Renaissance Artist,* trans. Alison Luchs (Princeton, N.J.: Princeton University Press, 1981), 219. More attention has been paid to the artworks of the Florentine laudesi companies; see, for example, G. Poggi, "La Pala di San Zanobi," *L'arte* 2 (1901): 1–12; I. B. Supino, "Le sculture del Bigallo," *Rivista d'arte* 2 (1904): 210–14; Rab Hatfield, "The Compagnia de' Magi," *Journal of the Warburg and Courtauld Institutes* 33 (1970): 125–35; Hanna Kiel, *Il Museo del Bigallo* (Milan: Electra, 1977); Ugo Procacci, "L'affresco dell'oratorio del Bigallo ed il suo maestro," *Mitteilungen des Kunsthistorisches Institutes in Florenz* 17 (1973): 307–24 (including also Mariotto di Nardo's triptych of 1415 for the original hall of the Bigallo); Nancy Rash Fabbri and Nina Rutenburg, "The Tabernacle of Orsanmichele in Context," *Art Bulletin* 63 (1981): 385–405. In contrast, only the portable crucifixes of the flagellants have been studied in depth; see Magrit Lisner, *Holzkruzifixe in Florenz und der Toskana 1300–1500* (Munich: Bruckmann, 1970).

3. Prandi attempted to trace a development within flagellant art from the literal scenes of flagellation to the more iconic or emblematic representation of flagellant symbols (Prandi, "Intorno all'iconografia," 497–98).

4. Monti, *Le Confraternite Medievali,* 163. For a more detailed description of their double-sided standard, see the "Libro dei inventari e testamenti," in Archivio di Stato di Firenze (hereafer ASF) Compagnie Religiose Soppresse (hereafter CRS), 2170, Z.1, vol. 4. Cf. Weissman, *Ritual Brotherhood,* 84.

5. Henderson, "Piety and Charity," 82 n.21, 104.

6. Pietro Ferrato, ed., *Misericordia del Salvatore: I Capitoli della Compagnia di Gesù Pellegrino* (Padua, 1871). The original statutes were extant until the flood of 1966; see ASF, CRS, Capitoli 867.

7. Luisa Marcucci, *Gallerie nazionali di Firenze,* vol. 1, *Catalogo dei dipinti del secolo XIV* (Rome: Istituto poligrafico dello stato, 1965). For another work on art from the Company of Gesù Pellegrino, published in 1978, see Ulrich Middledorf, "Gesù Pellegrino: A Quattrocento Sculpture Rediscovered," in *Raccolta di scritti* (Firenze: SPES, 1980), 3:217–20.

8. For published excerpts of inventories from 1421 to 1520, see Jacques Mesnil, "La Compagnia di Gesù Pellegrino," *L'arte* 2 (1904): 64–73.

9. Gaetano Milanesi, *Nuovi documenti per la storia dell'arte toscana dal XII al XV secolo* (Rome, 1893) 2:42–43.

10. Other flagellant companies were S. Giovanni Decollato in Sta. Maria in Verzaia (founded 1314–17), Gesù Maggiore in Sta. Croce (founded 1332), and S. Niccolò di Bari in Sta. Maria del Carmine (founded ca. 1334). Cf. Henderson, "Piety and Charity," 80.

11. ASF, Gianbattista Dei, MS. 173, fol. 147r.

12. Rev. James Wood-Brown, *The Dominican Church of Sta. Maria Novella* (Edinburgh: O. Schulze, 1902), 107–8; Walter Paatz and Elisabeth Paatz, *Die Kirchen von Florenz,* 6 vols. (Frankfurt am Main: V. Klostermann, 1940–54) 3:752.

13. ASF, CRS, 910, fol. 93.

14. ASF, Gianbattista Dei, MS. 173, fols. 43v, 126r–137v.

15. Comparison of the present plan of the Chiostro dei Morti with the eighteenth-century plan of the cloisters of Sta. Maria Novella (ASF, CRS, 102, 107, fol. 29) suggests that some structural elements of the northwest corner of the oratory could be preserved.

16. Giacomo Bascapé, "I Sigilli delle confraternite," in *Il Movimento,* 591–96.

17. Giovanni Sercambi, *Le Chroniche di Giovanni Sercambi Lucchese,* ed. Salvatore Bongi (Lucca, 1892); *Le illustrazioni delle Croniche nel Codice Lucchese di Giovanni Sercambi,* ed. Ottavio Banti and M. L. Testi Cristiani (Lucca: Archivio di Stato, 1978), fig. 445.

18. Henderson, "Piety and Charity," 82–86.

19. Evelyn Sandberg-Vavalà, *La croce dipinta italiana* (Verona: Casa editrice Apollo, 1929), 903.

20. Richard Offner, *A Critical and Historical Corpus of Florentine Trecento Painting* (New York: New York University, 1960), sec. 3:5, 131.

21. ASF, CRS, 918 and 903:6. See also note 4 above.

22. Ibid. In the 1444 inventory, fol. 4v., the first item is "una tavola d'altare cho molti sainti dove si dice la messa," which is not specific enough to be identified with the altarpiece of 1346. The first reference to a painting of the Madonna and Child with SS. Simon, Thaddeus, Filippo, and Zanobi is in the inventory of 1520 (Mesnil, "La Compagnia," 65 n. 2); this reference is repeated in 1591, fol. 21v.

23. Milanesi, *Nuovi documenti,* 42 n. 2.

24. Creighton Gilbert, *Italian Art 1400–1500, Sources and Documents* (Englewood Cliffs, N.J.: Prentice-Hall, 1980), 114–16. To my knowledge, no other trecento artistic document is quite like this one. Regarding the separate, prior purchase of the wooden panel, see idem, "Peintres et menusiers au debut de la Renaissance en Italie," *Revue de l'art* 37 (1977): 14–15. For other lay confraternity patronage, cf. David S. Chambers, *Patrons and Artists in the Italian Renaissance* (London: Macmillan, 1970), 52–55; John White, *Duccio, Tuscan Art, and the Medieval Workshop* (London: Thames and Hudson, 1979), 185–87; and Stephen Orgel and Guy Fitch Lytle, *Patronage in the Renaissance* (Princeton, N.J.: Princeton University Press, 1981).

25. ASF, CRS, 910:6, Lapo di Cione: fols. 2r, 3r, 6v, 12r, 13v, 14r, 15r–v; Ser Ciuto: fols. 3r–v, 6v, 10r, 11v, 13v, 15v, 16r; Piero Rinaldi: fols. 7r, 9r, 10v, 11v, 12r, 13r, 14r–v, 15r, 16v.

26. Ibid., fols. 7v, 9r–v.

27. Ibid., fol. 14r (November 1346).

28. For the term *conpasso,* see Niccolò Tommaseo and Bernardo Bellini, eds., *Dizionario della lingua italiana* (Torino, 1895), 1545; and *Vocabolario degli Accademici della Crusca* (Firenze, 1729–38), 3, 249. Although at first the text seemed to suggest that *conpasso* was a

decadent form of the Latin *compassio*, the term appears more commonly in trecento documents to refer to any compartment or framed field for painting or sculpture. My thanks to Profs. Creighton Gilbert and Charles Hope for mentioning to me other examples of this usage.

29. Milanesi quotes the name of the artist from Dei as "Pietro di Culliari," but the original text definitely calls him "Pietro di Civiliari chiamato Chiozzo" (fol. 90v). The painter still cannot be identified among the lists of Florentine painters (cf. I. Hueck, "Matricoli dei pittori fiorentini dopo 1320," *Bollettino d'arte* 57 (1972): 114–21). According to Carlo Battisti and Giovanni Alessio (*Dizionario etimologia italiana* [Firenze: G. Barbera, 1957], 2:908), *chiozzo* or *chiozzola* is Venetian dialect meaning "from the City of Chioggia" or "from the plain," so it possible that Pietro was a foreigner, not a member of the Florentine guild.

30. Other flagellant altarpieces with the Madonna and Child as a central image include the Venetian polyptych by Simon da Cusighe dated 1394 (Venice, Academy) and a fifteenth-century Sienese panel in the Musée de Cherbourg, France; both are Madonnas of Misericordia. Cf. Paul Perdrizet, *La Vierge de Misericorde* (Paris: A. Fontemoing, 1908). Concerning the *Madonna and Child with Flagellants* by Vitale da Bologna in the Vatican Pinacoteca, see Prandi, "Intorno all'iconografia," 506.

31. For bibliography, see John White, *Art and Architecture in Italy, 1250–1400* (Baltimore: Penguin, 1966), 242; Ferdinando Bologna, *Pittori alla corte angioina di Napoli, 1266–1414* (Rome: U. Bozzi, 1969), 7, 34; and Bresc-Bautier, *Artistes, patriciens,* 78.

32. Luigi Magnani, *La Cronica figurata di Giovanni Villani* (Vatican: Città del Vaticano, 1936).

33. Victoria and Albert Museum, London, 781–1894.

34. Mesnil, "La Compagnia," 65.

35. Bibilioteca nazionale centrale di Firenze (hereafter BNF), Cod. Magl. VIII.1282, 58–73.

36. Henderson, "Piety and Charity," 113–14.

37. Ferrato, *I capitoli*, 30. Lists of dead members starting from the mid-fourteenth century are found in BNF, Cod. Magl. VIII.1282, fols. 115–19. Painted panels of the dead are preserved from the flagellant confraternities of St. Simon and Thaddeus, and from San Niccolò Reale in Sicily (see Bresc-Bautier, *Artistes patriciens,* figs. 2–4).

38. Ferrato, *I capitoli*, 13–14.

39. ASF, CRS, 918, fol. 55r. The document and Orcagna's early work for the confraternity will be published elsewhere.

40. ASF, CRS, 910, fol. 73r.

41. British Museum, London, Add. MS. 15.277, fol. 277. See Gianfranco Folena and GianLorenzo Mellini, *Bibbia istoriata padovana della fine del trecento* (Venice: N. Pozza, 1962), 36 and plate 107.

42. Enzo Carli, *La pittura pisana del trecento* (Milan: A. Martello, 1958), 87–95.

43. Ferrato, *I capitoli*, 30.

14 ❧

THE WORD MADE FLESH

The *Rappresentazioni* of Mysteries and Miracles in Fifteenth-Century Florence

NERIDA NEWBIGIN

T HE MOST ELABORATE FORM of artistic expression to which Renaissance confraternities dedicated their resources were public theatrical displays incarnating the mysteries of religious faith. In this chapter, Nerida Newbigin reconstructs in rich detail the physical properties used in the production of Florentine *sacre rappresentazioni* in the fifteenth century. Her analysis of surviving confraternity records makes it clear that virtually all the visual media available in the quattrocento came together in the staging of religious plays: not only ritual, with its splendid costumes, but also scenographic painting and sculpture, stage architecture, and the advanced technology of stage machinery needed for special effects. Dr. Newbigin's vivid evocation of the backstage activity involved in producing Renaissance religious plays, moreover, suggests the role such spectacles had in shaping contemporary audiences' mental images of the great events of Christian history.

NERIDA NEWBIGIN is a Senior Lecturer in Italian at the University of Sydney, Australia. She has published widely on the subject of Renaissance religious theater and has edited publications of Renaissance theater texts.

N MY EXPLORATION OF THE FUNCTION AND MEANING of the Florentine *sacre rappresentazioni,* the play texts most interesting to me are those that circulated in roughly the third quarter of the fifteenth century, and the performances that I have been able to document, of these plays or of others bearing the same names (and there is seldom any way of differentiating the one from the other), belong to the years 1430–78. The plays are by no means homogeneous, for they are conceived for performance in at least four different contexts. Moreover, collectively they are quite different in their use of space, narrative, language, and spirituality from those sacre rappresentazioni printed from 1490 onward and constituting the corpus which Alessandro D'Ancona published in 1872.[1] While we can still turn to D'Ancona's *Origini del teatro drammatico italiano* for an extraordinary amount of documentary evidence on performances,[2] we must look beyond his anthology for texts, and we must verify every piece of evidence he adduces against the evidence provided by plays in manuscript, by confraternal and government records, and by chronicles and descriptions of performances.

Confraternal records, and in particular the records of the Compagnia della Purificazione in San Marco, the laudesi Compagnia di Sant'Agnese in the Carmine, and the Compagnia di Santa Maria delle Laude e dello Spirito Santo, detta del Pippione ("pigeon") which met in Santo Spirito, have yielded a considerable amount of information. It is primarily on the basis of two of these companies, the Purificazione and the Pippione, that I attempt to answer some basic questions. How and why did the companies put on plays? How did they justify the expense and effort? Did the plays have a spiritual purpose or are they simply an extension of mimetic ritual? Are they games, or are they possibly an attempt to realize, to transform into momentary but tangible images, that which is both more and less real than present "reality": the Word that inspires them.

In order to ensure that the problem of uncertain correlation

between text and performance would not invalidate my hypotheses even
before I began, I chose to look first in the records of the Compagnia
della Purificazione, a boys' company founded in 1427, for possible details of a performance of the first Florentine Prodigal Son play, the *Festa
del vitello sagginato* (Play of the Fatted Calf), which we know was written by the company's leader, Piero di Mariano Muzi, *borsaiuolo* ("purse-
maker").[3] Fortunately, the Florentine State Archive's holdings of the
Purification company's records are almost continuous in the period that
interests me, and the company's statutes are preserved in the Maglia-
bechi collection of the National Library in Florence. A search has revealed records not only of performances of a Prodigal Son play, but also
of an annual Purification play and other plays, and also details of expenditure on feste generally. According to their surviving statutes, the
members of the Purification company were mostly young tradesmen,
committed to living "in fiori di virginità e castità" ("in the flower of
virginity and chastity").[4] They entered between the ages of thirteen and
twenty-one, and were required to leave on the Feast of St. Peter and
St. Paul following their twenty-fourth birthday.[5] From the age of eighteen they could hold office, and the offices rotated every four months.
After paying an entrance fee of ten soldi, each member contributed dues
of one *denaro* (or alternatively three *paternosters*) at each weekly meeting,
and paid a special levy of two soldi in January to cover the costs of
the Candlemas festa of 2 February. The number of new members in-
ducted annually may have been as many as sixty (making this a very
large company) and the income from the entrance fees and weekly contributions was then spent on the running of their oratory (candles and
oils), on the blankets that they provided for the Ospedale dell'Elmo,
and on their principal festa.[6]

In exceptional years, levies were imposed for extraordinary expenses, as in 1461 when Benozzo Gozzoli was commissioned to paint
an altarpiece for their oratory, and in 1469 when a new *segno* ("emblem")
was constructed for the company to carry in the St. John the Baptist
procession.[7] But even in ordinary years, the bulk of the company's income was spent not on alms for outsiders, or even on alms for members
and the families of deceased members, but on *magnificentia*: a particularly public interpretation of the biblical injunction to let their light
shine before men. This must also have suited Cosimo de' Medici, patron

of San Marco and the man whose personal munificence had provided the company of Piero di Mariano with an oratory of its own within the walls of the new San Marco in 1444.[8]

Chapter 23 of the company's statutes, approved by Archbishop Antonino four years later in 1448, sets out the procedures for organizing the company's feste:[9]

> In praise and honor of the glorious Virgin Mary, Mother of Jesus and our advocate and guide, we order that every year on the day of her Purification, a most solemn and devout festa should be held, and organized in the following way. Let our leader choose an appropriate number of brethren as festaiuoli to organize the festa, and let them be diligent in decorating our oratory with laurel or myrtle and bench drapes and such other honest and devout things as are necessary. And if it is possible for there to be enough priests for a choral mass, let it be done in the name of God. Otherwise, let mass be said as our company leader sees fit. Then our leader should have bread rolls made, enough for the brethren to have one each, and let them be blessed by the priest, and handed out by the priest who says mass in person, and given to the brethren one by one. And if it is feasible to give a blessed candle with the bread, let our leader buy them. And in order to be able to save our confraternity money and give away bread on this morning, we wish that in January of every year each of the brethren should be bound to pay two soldi, and the treasurers will collect this money and keep account of it in a register called the *Subscription Register*, and this money is to be spent on making the said bread and buying wax or other things as appropriate for the festa, and let each bread roll weigh from two to three ounces, and no more, and on the said day of the Purification of Our Lady, and after they have eaten, let the brethren sing most solemn lauds.
>
> Then they should do the Representation of the Purification of Our Lady, that is, when she took our Lord Jesus Christ to the temple, with her humble offering.

The first record of such a Purification play, as distinct from a celebration of the festa, comes only in November 1449. From the earliest records of 1434, there had been regular expenditure for the various feste on string, nails, bench drapes (*pancali*), for erecting wall hangings (*spalliere* and *sarge*), laurel and myrtle branches, candles, and food. But from November 1449 to February 1450, we find extraordinary expenses for stage properties and costumes ordered on behalf of the company by Mariotto di Giovanni, the doublet maker.[10] These details of the

Purification play are gratifying in themselves, but remarkable confirmation that this confraternity is the same one assumed to have performed Piero di Mariano Muzi's Prodigal Son play, the *Festa del vitello sagginato,* comes on the same page of the records: "At the expense of the company, on 19 February, to Giovanni the customs clerk, 2 soldi for a pass for the heifer for the Play of the Fatted Calf." "At the expense of the company, on 21 February, to Bartolomeo d'Antonio, butcher, for the flour for the carnival doughnuts that were made for the Play of the Fatted Calf."[11]

The Purification play, judging by the stage properties bought by the company, contained angels in colored taffeta tunics, a Jonah's whale of paper (and wickerwork?) decorated with gold stars, Simeon in an ornate hat, three other people in hats or headpieces (probably Mary, Joseph, and Anna), and a gilded temple. Of these, it is the whale that is most intriguing; it caused considerable distress to the company's treasurer, whose grudging words suggest that he regarded at least some of the expenses as unwarranted.

Two Florentine Purification plays are known, the earlier of which was copied in 1464.[12] Although no documents specifically link this play to the performance for which we have expenses, it may help to examine it in conjuction with the Compagnia della Purificazione's account books.

The older Purification play begins, like almost all Florentine *sacre rappresentazioni,* with the angel's prologue. A second angel announces to Simeon that he is soon to see God. A third angel then places himself next to Simeon at the altar of the temple and calls forth twenty-one prophets and three sibyls to prophesy the coming of the Messiah. Only at line 360, well into the play, does the angel call Mary and Joseph, signaling the start of the second and narrative part of the play. Mary offers her Son, and two doves and two turtledoves; Simeon rejoices with his "Nunc dimittis servum tuum, Domine"; and Joseph makes his offering of five pence, one for each of Christ's wounds, in fulfillment of the prophecy of Exodus 13:2. An angel returns to excuse the actors and invite the audience to take its leave. The action is thus taken from at least four different sources, and is an excellent example of the hybrid origins of the *sacra rappresentazione,* and of the way in which the Florentine mystery play attempts to create real space somewhere between the unreal-because-intangible world of God and the unreal-because-imperfect human world.

There are, as I have said, twenty-one prophets, including Anna and Simeon, and three sibyls whose prophecies are lifted from Belcari's *Annunciazione*.[13] Each is summoned by an angel to sing his foreknowledge of Christ, and this is done in terms of light and heat, as we hear in Jacob's concluding words: "Make the shadows be consumed / and illuminated with your holy splendor."[14] Illumination, the simplest stage effect available to the festaiuoli, was thus integrated with the spiritual imagery of light in darkness: *lumen gentilium*. The result is justified in the letter and the metaphor of the Scriptures, and the splendor is enhanced through the symmetry of the prophecy and fulfillment. The references to light are presumably given physical expression in candles, lanterns, and maybe even fireworks like those used in the 1439 Annunciation.[15]

Jonah's whale as a stage property is less easy to explain, but a close examination of the prophets' words in the *Rappresentazione della Purificazione* may provide the answers. The prophets appear in chronological order (Abraham, Isaac, Jacob, Moses, and so on) and utter prophecies based to varying degrees on the Bible. They speak as if emerging in real time and from the real space and darkness of Limbo (where they must still have been at the moment of the Virgin's Purification) into the presence of the Light of the World. Limbo is implicitly associated with the whale in Jonah's own words:

> Three days I remained in that sea-fish,
> a symbol of forgiveness of sins,
> for that's how long Christ remained in his tomb
> and then triumphed with his human nature.[16]

Since Jonah's sojourn in the belly of the whale foreshadows Christ's descent into Limbo between the Crucifixion and the Resurrection, it seems possible that the whale ordered by Mariotto the doublet maker underlined that whale-Limbo link scenographically. And to parallel contemporary scenes of Christ's Harrowing of Hell,[17] the prophets of the Purificazione may well have been summoned forth from a capacious paper whale decorated with gold. Since the text specifies no scenic element beyond the "altare dov'è Simione" (the altar where Simeon is), a leviathan would have served well as wings.

But why did the festaiuoli make constant reference to Limbo? In the authentic Belcari *Annunciazione,* Christ sends Gabriel to announce his incarnation first to Adam in Limbo and only second to the Virgin in Galilee. In the *Rappresentazione di San Giovanni Battisita quando fu decollato* (Play of the beheading of St. John the Baptist),[18] Christ visits the Baptist secretly in his cell and sends a message by him to the Old Testament Righteous. Then, when the time comes for his beheading, the stage direction tells us:

> *St. John bowed his head and it was cut off as the Seneschal waits with the basin and put the head in, and the Soul departed from the body and went to Limbo and said to the Holy Fathers who are in Limbo as follows:*
>
>> Celestial joy and infinite happiness
>> I announce to you, first father Adam.[19]

The reason for this constant return to Limbo lies, I believe, in the early Renaissance concern with the purpose of Christ's Incarnation, namely the redemption of the Old Testament Righteous from Limbo, and with the moment in which that purpose was fulfilled. As John O'Malley points out, Renaissance preachers emphasize the preeminence of Christ's Incarnation over his death on the cross as the redemptive act, and they view all the subsequent events of Christ's life as "articulations of what was already inchoately accomplished in the initial moment of man's restoration, which was the Incarnation in the Virgin's womb."[20] And in the transformation from Scripture to dramatic representation, the Word undergoes a further incarnation, a fleshing-out, as the event is made real.

The Purification play was only one of the ways in which the company sought to transform Scripture into action. In all the confraternities, *colezioni*—suppers in imitation (on the conventual model) of the Last Supper—are extremely important, but in the Compagnia della Purificazione the imitation is taken a step further in their Prodigal Son play where the homecoming feast requires not only a live heifer (the woodcuts that illustrated the early editions show the fatted calf alive and well at the feast) and but also *berlingozzi* (carnival cakes) for the members.[21] Since feasting occurs in a large number of plays, and is usually interpreted as deliberate prefiguring of the Last Supper, it is likely that in some of the plays at least the dramatic feast is combined with the communal meal that ends in singing and sometimes even in dignified dancing.[22]

The Compagnia della Purificazione performed at least three other plays, of which only the titles appear in their records: a *Sant'Alesso* in 1471/2, a *Barlaam [e Josafat]* in 1474, and a *Santo Stagio* (St. Eustace) in carnival 1476/77,[23] but their plays were small in comparison with the huge productions mounted by the three laudesi confraternities attached to the great conventual churches across the Arno, to which I now turn.

Each year, in the period after Easter, three great spectacles were mounted in honor of the Virgin: the Annunciation in San Felice in Piazza, on the Tuesday after Easter (or later on the octave of Easter);[24] the Ascension in the Carmine; and Pentecost in Santo Spirito. All three seem to have been well established by the 1430s and have much in common. All are performed by adult laudesi companies; all require elaborate machinery that communicates between heaven and earth (Figure 14.1); and all make extensive use of lights, fireworks, and special effects as well as of choral elements to capture the attention of the audience. And whereas the Purification plays in San Marco seem to have been relatively private affairs (in 1450 men were placed on the door to guard it), at least two of the plays across the Arno were publicly funded and mounted with the intention of honoring the entire city.

Since Cyrilla Barr has dealt extensively with the Sant'Agnese company's Ascension play in the Carmine[25] (and I have found no trace as yet of the Annunciation company's records), I have focused on the Pentecost play performed annually in Santo Spirito by the Compagnia di Santa Maria delle Laudi e dello Spirito Santo, detta del Pippione, in particular comparing the description of the play given by Richa[26] to the company's inventories for 1444 and 1463, and to their account books for 1427–71,[27] the year in which they burned the old church down.[28] Richa describes the play as follows:

> I should like here to relate what I have managed to assemble
> about these Representations from numerous manuscript Diaries.
> In the middle of the church above the choir, or rather the rood

Figure 14.1. Filippo Brunelleschi's sets and stage machinery for the Annunciation play in San Felice in Piazza, as reconstructed by Cesare Lisi for the 1975 exhibition "Il luogo teatrale a Firenze." A rear view showing Mary's house, the upper platform representing heaven, and the machinery for the Angel Gabriel's descent and return. Photo Raffaele Bencini, courtesy of the Amministrazione Provinciale della Toscana. Documentation in *Il luogo teatrale a Firenze* (catalog of exhibition), ed. M. Fabbri, E. Garbero Zorzi and A. M. Petrioli Tofani, intro. Ludovico Zorzi (Milan: Electa, 1975), scheda 1.24.

screen, there was a Heaven set up full of angels, which moved mechanically, and there was an infinite array of lights that looked like stars, which could be uncovered and then concealed again in a flash. The angels were boys of twelve, appropriately dressed and fastened to special bases, so that in spite of the swift movement of the contraption they could not have fallen if they had tried. And besides moving [with the wheel], when the time came they took one another by the hand and as they swung their arms they seemed to dance. By means of a turning hemispherical dome, in which there were three garlands of lights which couldn't tip up, and all around ingenious clouds of cotton wool, stage clouds were created, on the highest point of which the Eternal Father sat, and on one side Christ, both surrounded by angels who were likewise little boys of eight years old. In the middle a shining white dove, symbolising the Divine Spirit, spread its wings and sent down a shower of fire. And the Eternal Father, Christ, the Holy Spirit, the angels, the infinite number of lights and the sweetest music truly represented Paradise. And below was added a *cenacolo,* a room illuminated by the tongues of fire shining above the heads of the Apostles, who sat with the Mother of God, making the most natural gestures that changed frequently. And finally, right below on a stage, the festa was performed by fine actors, but it ended in a most terrible tragedy, as has been mentioned: through the carelessness of the attendants who were meant to put out vast number of lamps, one was left alight within a wooden tube, and in the early hours of the night it caught alight and was the spark of that terrible fire from which only the wooden Crucifix of the Bianchi survived unharmed, as we shall see in the description of the new church.

From the account for building and rebuilding each item, and from the inventories, we can deduce even more. The mechanical heaven machine consisted of the *stella* ("star") and the *rocca degli angioli* ("angels' fortress"). On the stella were mounted 24 gold angels, each two *braccia* (116 cm) tall (the evidence for live angels is inconclusive); 24 serafim; 48 doves; and 528 lanterns. The whole contraption was lowered from Heaven, in which sat God the Father and Son, who were masked. On a lower level, but still on a raised platform, above the chapel of San Giovanni delle Donne, was the *castello* ("castle"), representing the upper room of Pentecost. There, dressed wooden figures of the Virgin and the Apostles were arranged around a wooden table. All thirteen had crowns *con canoni* ("with cannons") or *per acciendere* ("for lighting"), which apparently exploded when the rocket-powered dove flew down from Heaven on a cord running the length of the church. Two texts of a Pentecost play which the actors might have recited while the spectacle went on above their heads survive: one in three stanzas by Feo Belcari; the other in thirty-three stanzas, unknown in the manuscript corpus, but printed by Bartolomeo de' Libri in the 1490s and probably dating from quite late.[29] Whatever the text, however, it is clear that here, in contrast to the Purification company's plays, it is the spectacle and not the text which matters.

Why did the confraternities put on plays? The Santo Spirito company spent well over half its annual income on its festa, and since it did not apply for communal funds, we do not know how its members justified the expense. Probably they used the same terms as the Annunziata and Sant'Agnese companies: "to increase devotion and for the honor of the city"; "to honor God and increase the glory of this city"; or "in honor and reverence of God and of his blessed Mother the Virgin Mary."[30] The Pippione company may even have been inspired by friendly rivalry with the other two churches to invest its time and effort as well as money in the festa. In 1471, however, it put itself out of the race, and for ten years the company does not appear to have met. When the new church was dedicated in 1481, and the company resumed activity, there is no trace of theatrical activity.[31] But it does not seem sufficient to attribute the plays of the Compagnia della Purificazione and of the *laudesi* companies across the Arno just to that elaborate ritual transaction between city and patrons which Richard Trexler has delineated so well.[32] The enthusiasm for plays rather than other forms of group activity seems to lie in the very nature of the plays: they seem to bring together in a single activity a great many of the disparate activities of the confraternities.

These activities should perhaps be seen within the context of theories of play evolved since Johan Huizinga's *Homo Ludens* of 1938. Huizinga defined play as:

> a free activity standing quite consciously outside "ordinary" life as being "not serious", but at the same time absorbing the player intensely and utterly. It is an activity connected with no material interest, and no profit can be gained by it. It proceeds within its own proper boundaries of time and space according to fixed rules and in an orderly manner. It promotes the formation of social groupings which tend to surround themselves with secrecy and to stress their difference from the common world by disguise or other means.[33]

The confraternities of fifteenth-century Florence lie somewhere in this field of meaning. They constitute a separate existence, circumscribed in time and space, but they adopt a structure that mimics the spiritual and ritual life of the convent. Their activities have an element of make-believe which goes beyond the business of mounting plays: there is a specific awareness of a second reality inside the broader reality of the outside world. Two elements normally associated with play may however be lacking: the faith of the *confratelli* renders their activities neither uncertain nor unproductive, for faith makes certain that penitent sinners will be saved, and ritual has evolved for the purpose of reinforcing that faith. But as Huizinga and others have pointed out, many of the features held to be characteristic of play are present in ritual: liturgy, one of its highest examples, may be seen as pointless yet significant.[34]

Plays belong both to the fun-world of make-believe and to the business of making people believe: the alternative designation of the confraternities as "scuole" reminds us that *ludus,* at the root of "illusion," is not just play but also the space that contains "class," school," "instruction." In creating physical images of mysteries, the confraternities were playing with complex "realities" of Word-made-flesh. But I have no doubt that in their plays they, as well as their public and their patrons, also enjoyed themselves immensely.

NOTES

1. Alessandro D'Ancona, ed., *Sacre rappresentazioni dei secoli XIV, XV e XVI,* 3 vols. (Florence, 1872).

2. Idem, *Origini del teatro drammatico italiano,* 2d ed. (Turin, 1891; reprint, Rome: Bardi, 1971), esp. 1:217–76.

3. The play can be found in Nerida Newbigin, ed., *Nuovo Corpus di sacre rappresentazioni fiorentine del Quattrocento* (Bologna: Commissione per i Testi di Lingua, 1983), 29–55. On Piero di Mariano Muzi, see also xxix n. 29.

4. Capitoli della Compagnia della Purificazione, Biblioteca Nazionale Centrale, Florence (hereafter BNCF), Magl. VIII.1500.II, fol. 3r.

5. Ibid., fol. 14r.

6. This information is derived from their registers of Entrata and Uscita, Archivio di Stato, Florence (hereafter ASF), Compagnie Religiose Soppresse (hereafter CRS), 1654 (P.XXX.29).

7. Ibid., (P.XXX.30), fols. 108v and 117r–v.

8. BNF, Capitoli, fols. 4r–5v.

9. Ibid., fol. 17r–v.

10. ASF, CRS, 1654 (P.XXX.30), 90v–91v, November 1449 to February 1450.

11. Ibid., fol. 91v.

12. See Newbigin, ed., *Nuovo Corpus,* 79–106. The *Purificazione,* in D'Ancona, *Sacre rappresentazioni,* 1:211–22, dates to the first quarter of the sixteenth century.

13. A critical edition of the text is Feo Belcari, *La rappresentazione quando la Nostra Donna Vergine Maria fu annunziata dall'angelo Gabriello,* ed. Nerida Newbigin (Sydney: University of Sydney, 1983). See also my discussion of Belcari's *Annunciazione* in *Nuovo Corpus,* 81–85, and in "Between Prophecy and Redemption: The *Disputa delle Virtù* and Florentine Plays of the Annunciation," in *Atti del IV Colloquio della Société Internationale pour l'Etude du Théâtre Médiéval (Viterbo 10–15 giugno 1983)* (Viterbo: Centro Studi sul Teatro Medioevale e Rinascimentale, 1984), 261–73.

14. "Fa che le tenebre sien consumate / e del tuo sprender santo illuminate" (*Purificazione,* ll. 143–44, in Newbigin, ed., *Nuovo Corpus,* 93).

15. The description is in D'Ancona, *Origini,* 1:251–52.

16. "Tre giorni stetti in quel pesce marino, / figura d'indulgenza degli vizi, / ché tanto stette Cristo in sepultura, / poi trionfò coll'umana natura" (*Purificazione,* ll. 177–80, in Newbigin, ed., *Nuovo Corpus,* 95.)

17. Thomas F. Worthen observes, however, that the representation of the entrance to Hell as a leviathan's mouth, while common in Northern Europe, is almost never imitated in Italy. See his "Harrowinig of Hell in the Art of the Italian Renaissance" (Ph.D. diss., University of Iowa, 1981), 51.

18. Newbigin, ed., *Nuovo Corpus,* 107–33.

19. "*San Giovanni chinò el capo e fugli tagliato e il Siniscalco aspetta col bacino e drento vi messe la testa, e dipartissi l'Anima dal corpo e andonne al Limbo e disse così a' Santi Padri che sono nel Limbo:* Celeste gaudio e letizia infinita / annunzio a te, principal padre Adamo" (*San Giovanni Battista quando fu decollato,* ll. 561–67).

20. John W. O'Malley, *Praise and Blame in Renaissance Rome: Rhetoric, Doctrine, and Reform in the Sacred Orators of the Papal Court, c. 1450–1521* (Durham, N.C.: Duke, 1979), 138–39.

21. The Prodigal Son play was performed again in Carnival 1461/2: "For the Play of the Purification and for the Play of the Fatted Calf . . . L1/8/8" (ASF, CRS, 1654 [P.XXX.30], fol. 109r, 14 March 1461/2); and in 1468: "To Mome di Giovanni di Miniato, stationer . . . for expenses incurred in the *Play of the Fatted Calf* that was done in the cloister of San Marco, that is for the heifer and for the hire of *quarteruoli* [small barrels?], porters, and other things L1/5/–" (fol. 115v, 3 August 1465).

22. The final stage direction of the contemporary manuscripts of Belcari's *Abramo e Isac* reads: "Everybody in the household dances in a ring and sings this song, each one accompanied by an angel." In the *Vitello sagginato,* the guests are invited to dance at the homecoming feast for the Prodigal Son.

23. For *Sant'Alesso:* "To Domenico di Stefano our company leader, on this same day [25 February], L2/6/–, paid in cash, for various expenses for the representation of the Play of St. Alexis" (ASF, CRS, 1654 [P.XXX.30], fol. 120v, 25 February 1471/2); *Barlaam [e Josafat]:* "At the expense of the company, 3 lire that [Antonio di Piero dell'Avveduto] had beforehand

for part of the Play of Barlaam" (ASF, CRS, 1654 [P.XXX.30], fol. 126v, September [?] 1474); and by chance there is record of a possible Saint Eustace play:"To Giovanni del Raggio, mender, L1/2/–, for the mending of a woolen velvet cloth that was torn in the garden of Lorenzo for the Play of St. Eustace, done on 22 February 1476[/7]" (ASF, CRS, fol. 130r).

24. The play apparently was not performed on 25 March, which often fell in Lent. In 1470 it was moved from Easter Tuesday to the Sunday after Easter so that "the noise and banging that goes on continuously in those days" should not disturb the Holy Week devotions of the faithful (see ASF, Provvisioni Registri (hereafter Provv. Reg.) 161, fol. 14r–v, 16 April 1470).

25. See chapter 15 in this volume.

26. Giuseppe Richa, Notizie istoriche delle Chiese fiorentine (Florence: Viviani, 1754–62), 9:15–16.

27. ASF, Compagnia di Santa Maria delle Laudi e dello Spirito Santo detta del Piccione, 57 (D e C, E e U, 1427–34, 1501–12); 58 (E e U, Dare e Avere, Obblighi, 1435–38); 59 (D e C, E e U, 1441–43); 60 (E e I, 1455–57); 61 (E e U, D e C, 1461–68); 62 (E e U, 1481–152[?]; 78 (Inventario, Ricordi); 79 (D e C, Nomi di fratelli, 1451–1522). I hope to publish extracts relating to festive performances and inventories in the near future.

28. Some of the accounts are summarized in d'Ancona, Origini, 1:272–73. The anonymous chronicler of BNCF, MS. II.I.239, records: "To honor [Galeazzo Maria Sforza, duke of Milan] there was more celebration than was necessary in Lent. That is, on 20 March in San Felice in Piazza there was the representation of the Annunciation of Our Lady; on 21 March in the Carmine, Christ's Ascension into Heaven; on 22 March in Santo Spirito, God sending the Holy Spirit to the Apostles. And that night, when lights that had been lit in the church fell on timber, around eleven o'clock, it caught alight and burned the church completely. The roof fell in and nothing was left in the church except the external walls and they were all cracked and blackened by the fire, and it was a great loss. On 24 March the said duke departed" (ad diem).

29. The Rappresentazione dello avvenimento dello Spirito Santo il dì della Pentecoste was edited by A. G. Galletti from BNCF, Magl. VII.690, in Feo Belcari, Le rappresentazioni (Florence, 1833), 113–14. La festa del miracolo dello Spirito Santo [Florence, c. 1490] has not been reprinted since the seventeenth century.

30. These words are found respectively in the Sant'Agnese company's request for communal funds in 1435 (ASF, Provv. Reg. 126, fols. 195v–196v, 28 August 1435) and 1445 (Provv. Reg. 136, fols. 212v–213v); and in the request of the Societatis Annuntiate et ecclesie Sancti Felicis in Piaza pro oblatione sex Capitudinis recorded in ASF, Provv. Reg. 135, fol. 162v, 22 March 1444/5.

31. The Santo Spirito festa was revived briefly in the Carmine in 1489: "Having considered that the house of Lorenzo di Piero di Cosimo de' Medici is a benefactor of our company, and seeing that Piero di Lorenzo de' Medici wishes to stage the festa of the Holy Spirit in the church of Santa Maria del Carmine, the captains [of the Company of St. Agnes], in the hope and intention of making available all means at their and their company's command to stage this festa, by their vote and four black beans gave and conceded to the said Piero de' Medici full authority and power to make use of the said Company of St. Agnes and of all its properties and belongings to stage the said Festa of the Holy Spirit and any other festa that he

might wish to do at his pleasure" (ASF, *Compagnia di Santa Maria delle Laudi detta di Sant'Agnese* 4, fol. 27v).

32. Richard C. Trexler, *Public Life in Renaissance Florence* (New York: Academic Press, 1980), 1–8.

33. Johan Huizinga, *Homo Ludens: A Study of the Play Element in Culture* (London: Paladin, 1970), 32.

34. Huizinga, *Homo Ludens,* 37–38. The question is considered further in Emile Benveniste, "Le jeu comme structure," *Deucalion* 2 (1947): 159–67; Roger Caillois, *L'homme et le sacré,* 3d ed. (Paris: Gallimard, 1950); Jacques Ehrmann, "*Homo Ludens* Revisited," in *Game, Play, Literature,* ed. Jacques Ehrmann, *Yale French Studies* 41 (New Haven: Yale French Studies, 1968), 31–57; and Richard Schechner, "From Ritual to Theatre and Back: The Structure/Process of the Efficacy-Entertainment Dyad," in his *Essays on Performance Theory 1970–1976* (New York: Drama Book Specialists, 1977), 63–98.

15 ❧

MUSIC AND SPECTACLE IN CONFRATERNITY DRAMA OF FIFTEENTH-CENTURY FLORENCE

The Reconstruction of a Theatrical Event

CYRILLA BARR

D EVELOPING THEMES introduced in the preceding essay, this chapter reconstructs the stage action and musical accompaniment of the Ascension play staged regularly in the Carmelite church of Florence, Santa Maria del Carmine. Using confraternity inventories, manuscript miniatures and mechanical drawings, and accounts of performances written by a visiting Russian bishop in 1439, Cyrilla Barr illustrates the creative world of the pious laity producing religious spectacle in mid-quattrocento Florence. Reflecting on the music that must have given Renaissance plays some of the character of later oratorios or opera, Professor Barr vividly re-creates the sounds as well as visual effects associated with the Renaissance stage: from the pounding of nails and creaking of capstans backstage to the poetry and music presented to the public.

CYRILLA BARR is a Professor of Musicology at the Benjamin T. Rome School of Music, Catholic University of America, Washington, D.C.

N EYEWITNESS DESCRIPTION from the remote past, whether of people or events, communicates a sense of immediacy to its subject as if it were momentarily suspended in the present to be experienced by the reader here and now. Consider Egeria's vivid account of the liturgy as celebrated in Jerusalem circa 400, or Joinville's description of the pious king Louis IX. It must be acknowledged, however, that the narrators of such events may have embellished the topic to their own ends, either deliberately to emphasize a point or involuntarily out of enthusiasm for the subject. Only when such descriptions are supported by verifiable documents can their accuracy be established.

One singularly detailed eyewitness account that can be so documented is the well-known description of the Ascension play presented regularly in Florence throughout the fifteenth century in the church of Santa Maria del Carmine. It comes from the pen of Abraham of Souzdal, a Russian bishop who attended the Ecumenical Council held in Florence in 1439.[1] Until recently it was believed that, except for a few fragments published by Alessandro d'Ancona, the sources documenting the play had been lost in the flood of 1966.[2]

Although Abraham at no time mentions the agent responsible for mounting the spectacle, it can now be substantiated beyond doubt that the play was the work—and indeed the pride—of the Compagnia di Santa Maria delle laude in Sancta Maria del Carmine, detta di Sant'Agnese, founded in 1248. The ardent devotion of this company both to the mystery of Christ's Ascension and to St. Agnes can be traced back as far as 1280, through its primitive Ordinances of that year, a document that also underscores the importance of the *lauda* in the company's ritual.[3]

The earliest extant primary source to describe the Ascension play is a brief account given by the prior Paolo di Pietribuoni in 1422;[4] as early as 1425 the account books of the Compagnia di Sant'Agnese begin to reflect expenses for the plays.[5] There is, however, evidence to indicate that the Ascension was being re-enacted already in the trecento in a form similar to that outlined by Abraham, for Sacchetti (d. 1399/1400) tells a tale of a friar who preached that Christ went to heaven so swiftly that he made a loud noise, whereas, in the Ascension play at the Carmine the Lord was drawn up very slowly to the roof by means of a rope.[6] Unfortunately, no documents of the sponsoring company have survived from the fourteenth century to provide any information concerning the mechanism used to accomplish that feat.

Unlike certain more modest plays of the quattrocento, produced in private primarily for the edification of the members of a given confraternity, the St. Agnes Ascension play was mounted for the larger audience of the general public and supported in part by government subsidies.[7] It is undoubtedly this very public disposition of the play and its increasingly spectacular effects that account for its character as what might be called "sacred entertainment," which, although calculated to inspire devotion, sought to do so by means of the spectacle.

While my purpose here is to document the scenographic and musical components of the play, I must emphasize that the very elements comprising the spectacle — the *cose da fare stupire* — were in fact the literal incarnation of images derived from Scripture, liturgical practices, and the exegesis of certain of the post-Nicene church fathers.[8] It is important to realize that dogma in the abstract — without a certain amount of graphic representation — was simply not to be comprehended by this audience; while we can presume its members had accepted the Incarnation in "the Word made flesh," they nonetheless longed to experience "the flesh in the word" as well.

In still another sense, however, the "word" is lacking, since to date no *rappresentazione* of the Ascension is known to exist save a very brief fragment of one by Feo Belcari.[9] There is no way of establishing if it may have served as the text for the Ascension play produced in the Carmine or, for that matter, if Belcari ever completed it. Neither Abraham's description nor the records of the Company of St. Agnes contain anything to suggest the kind of rhetorical devices, interpolated scenes, and explications used in some of Belcari's other rappresentazione (such as Abraham and Isaac) to generate the conflict and supply the moralizing interludes.

An examination of the confraternity records together with Abraham's account of the Ascension spectacle illuminates the play as a kind of visual exegesis, sketching on a broad temporal canvas not only details from various New Testament accounts of the Ascension, but also those of certain passages from the Messianic Psalms, in which Judeo-Christian writers saw a prefiguring of the Ascension. Those very aspects of the play described with the greatest enthusiasm by the Russian bishop — "truly nothing like it has ever been seen" — are the levitation of Jesus, the cloud mechanism, and the lighting effects.

Although the didactic intent of these efforts to translate symbols into actual corporeal images may have been the primary motivation for mounting the spectacles, there were other considerations that tended to adulterate the purity of that intention. In choosing to solemnize the Feast of the Ascension with a religious-theatrical event, the Carmine was completing the celebration of the paschal cycle, which in earlier times had always been comprehended as one mystery. In fifteenth-century Florence, Easter was already celebrated with the *scoppio del carro* and in the nearby church of Santo Spirito the Pentecost play was being performed.[10] It is possible that the choice of the Carmine as the site of the Ascension play may have been conditioned by the dimensions of the church, which Abraham points out at the beginning of his account.[11] That the Carmine was large and well-suited for the spectacle is confirmed by Giuseppe Richa and others, who emphasize not only its height but especially its large rood screen, which could provide the necessary elevation to function as a stage.[12]

Beyond the obvious physical suitability of the church, however, is it not possible that the choice of the Carmine may have been influenced by its affiliation with the Carmelites, who claim Elias as their founder? The text of the septuagint translation of the "ascension" of Elias has long been seen as a type prefiguring Christ's ascent. The description in the Acts of the Apostles (1:9–11) manifests an almost literal dependence upon the Old Testament account of the prophet's leave-taking from this earth (2 Kings 2:11–12) and the return of Elias has become a classic prefiguring of the Second Coming of Christ. The festive and celebratory nature of the Ascension play might readily have served as a device of Carmelite propaganda at this time, when the association of the order with the Old Testament prophets Elias and Eliseus was a vigorously contested theory.[13]

Whatever the motivation, it is obvious from biblical exegesis of the church fathers that the theme of the two ascensions was well known. Medieval iconography as well as legend helped to popularize the parallel between the two—though not without clearly stressing a crucial difference: while Christ rose through his own power, Elias was "taken up" in the fiery chariot by the efficacy of the Almighty.[14]

In the liturgy of Ascension day, after the reading of the Gospel, the paschal candle, which has been lit since the Easter vigil as a visible reminder of Christ's physical presence among mortals, is extinguished. There is a striking parallel between this liturgical action and the climax of the play when Abraham observes that as Christ is enveloped in the cloud "The music ceases and all becomes dark."[15]

Any such conscious hermeneutical intent probably originated with the ecclesiastical guardians of the company. But for the members themselves the play—from preparation to aftermath—must have been as socially beneficial as it was uplifting and entertaining to its audience, for a decided sense of community and cooperative effort is communicated by the confraternity records. One cannot but be struck by the camaraderie implied in the frequent expenditures for food and the abundance of wine consumed by both workers and actors and usually entered under such designations as "food for the angels" and "breakfast for the apostles on the morning of the Ascension."[16] In 1471 particularly, the festaiuoli dined very well, consuming "sixteen pounds of veal, a kid goat and a whole liver for the midday meal."[17]

Although the documents granting the subsidies for the Ascension play state plainly that it was presented every year (Vasari says "quasi ogni anno") there are no records for some years.[18] Those that have survived, however, provide abundant information to define the playing areas more precisely, to document advances in the technology of stagecraft and special effects, to clarify the manner in which living actors participated, to trace the ongoing process of renovation and refurbishing of the play, and finally to provide some understanding of the spoken dialogue and music to which Abraham refers.

The Russian bishop clearly outlines separate acting areas, speaking specifically of the mountain, the cloud, and the castle. These are even more clearly delineated in later disbursements; it appears that each locus was administered by its own festaiuolo[19] and that monies paid for materials, sets, properties, and costumes are entered under these headings, thus providing a more exact picture of the *messa in scena* as well as of the placement of the actors at the beginning of the play.

One might conceivably interpret *cielo* and *paradiso* to be one and the same locus, and indeed the records before 1471 seem to use the terms interchangeably, but for the play of that year debits entered separately under these two headings indicate that they were then distinct entities. Perhaps this is what Vasari alludes to when he remarks, "In addition to the part that supported Christ, another heaven was sometimes erected, according as it was thought advisable, over the chief tribune."[20] This distinction between cielo and paradiso becomes especially evident in those payments that mention both in one entry, such as that of 11 May 1471 for "nine ounces of cotton-wool yarn for wicks for the lamps of the heaven and of paradise."[21]

There are no documents to describe the mechanism used in the trecento to draw Christ up to heaven so slowly that Sacchetti's friar was prompted to say, "If he went any more slowly he would still be on his way."[22] The first known designer of the stage machinery was Brunelleschi, whom Vasari credits with the invention of the device used to raise and lower the cloud.[23] Since the earliest primary record of the play is dated 1422, just when he was working on the cupola of the Duomo, it seems possible that the mechanism for the play was a by-product of the hoists designed by Brunelleschi for the work on the cathedral. But three years later some refurbishing must have been necessary, for the account books record payments to Masolino for "painting the angels that go around the cloud" and to other craftsmen for repairing the machines.[24] Still later improvements were made by the Florentine engineer Cecca (1447–88).[25]

In his discussion of the additional heaven just mentioned, Vasari explains the system of cables, pulleys, braces, and counterweights of lead by which means, he says, the "angels, when a little rope was unwound from the heaven above, came down the two larger ropes on to the said *tramezzo* [rood screen] where the representation took place, and announced to Christ that He was to ascend into heaven. . . . And since the iron to which they were bound by the girdle was fixed to the platform on which they stood, in such a way that they could turn round and round, . . . [In reascending] they turned toward the heaven,

and were then drawn up again as they had come down."[26] The descent
of the angels described here appears to be a later invention, for in
Abraham's account they are already stationed on the stage at the opening of the play.[27]

Of all the surviving documents of the company, one of the most
illuminating with regard to the play is the inventory made by the artist
Neri di Bicci, a member and sometime office holder of the company.
As *sindaco,* Neri compiled in 1466 a detailed list of belongings which
not only enumerates items needed for the play, but often describes their
function, how they were made, and by what nicknames they were known.
In section 8 of the inventory, for example, he lists "2 irons to which
the angels in the cloud are fastened when the feast is kept, . . . [and]
1 large iron called 'seste' upon which the two angels go down to accompany Christ and then return upward and are joined with the cloud."[28]
This account confirms Vasari's mention of the angels descending first,
and is likewise in accord with Abraham's remark that "from heaven above
where God the Father is found, a very beautiful cloud descends. . . .
He [Christ], with the help of the seven ropes, rises in the direction
of the cloud . . . and the person representing Christ seems actually to
go up on his own power." Clearly, the descent of the cloud and the
ascent of Christ are simultaneous until that moment when they meet
in midair in a burst of light.[29]

Neri's inventory also contains further clarification of the mechanism, enumerating "1 iron named 'el palo' to which Christ is fixed when
he goes in the cloud . . . [and] 2 irons, one new and one old, which
are used as supports attached behind the shoulders of Christ by means
of leather straps when he is pulled up on the cloud."[30] The function
of the seven ropes mentioned by Abraham becomes clearer in the next
entry, which lists "1 large rope which pulls up the cloud, 1 large rope
which pulls the iron called 'seste,' 1 small rope used to pull up Christ,[31]
1 rope which acts as a guide [rudder] to Christ and the 'seste,' 1 separate guide line for the cloud, 'seste,' and Christ, all three, 1 slender rope
which guides the star behind the cloud and 1 iron rod called 'el ti,'"
which appears to have been part of the steering device.[32] In addition,
part 11 of the inventory mentions many "little halters of reinforced rope,
which are used to secure the angels in the heaven and in the cloud."[33]
These, along with the guide lines, steering devices, and counterweights

mentioned very likely account for Abraham's astonishment that the man being pulled up on the rope "appeared to ascend by his own power without swaying." In addition, the rope halters may explain the references in the account books to the angels dancing around God the Father.

But the aspect of the illusion which seems to have most impressed the Russian bishop was the lighting. Here again the disbursements as well as the inventory help to identify several types of light source. The general illumination of the playing area was accomplished by burning oil lamps arranged in clouds fashioned from cotton wool. That this obvious fire hazard was a matter of concern to the company is reflected in a payment of 1447 "to Donato the cooper in Piazza de' Nerli for the loan of a tub that is placed in the heaven full of water."[34] Payments for vessels to use as lamps, cotton-wool yarn to make wicks, and oil to burn are too numerous to list here, but it should be sufficient to recall that Neri's inventory places the count at "500 clay lamps which burn for the feast."[35]

There were other light sources as well which could be classified as special effects. These are referred to as *pianeti:* color mediums used to diffuse light by means of filling glass receptacles with water into which the desired pigment was infused. In 1438, an amber light must have been produced for there is a payment recorded in that year "for five ounces of saffron . . . to yellow the water in the pianeti."[36] Some later accounts, as well as Neri's inventory, make it clear that pianeti were also fashioned by other means: dyed parchment was fixed into wooden frames inside of which were placed oil lamps or candles.[37]

One such device deserves special mention: that used to create the aureole around Christ. Neri describes it as "a star of wood which is called 'il sole,' which goes behind Christ when he ascends and which is attached to the iron called 'seste' with a pianeto of parchment dyed red, with a lamp inside (Figure 15.1).[38] But by far the most astonishing of the lighting devices was the *stella nuova,* described by Neri as "a large wooden star standing above the cloud in an edifice made of cloth and decorated with painted angels, in which structure is hidden the said star of wood which has many rays and at each ray is a square copper lantern with much fireworks which is lit when Christ enters the cloud and not before."[39] The contrivance was similar to that illustrated in the *Zibaldone* of Bonaccorso Ghiberti (Figure 15.2) where the accompany-

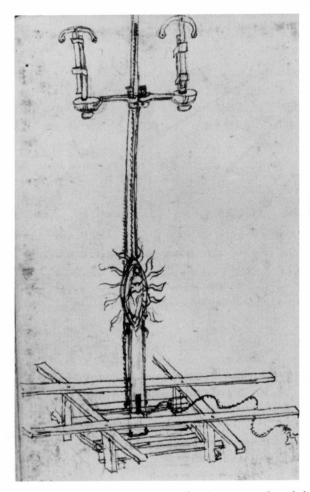

Figure 15.1. The "iron called *seste*," with braces for the two angels and the mandorla for Christ. From the *Zibaldone* of Buonaccorso Ghiberti, MS. B.R. 228. Florence, Biblioteca Nazionale Centrale, fol. 115v. Photo Pineider.

ing inscription explains its function thus: "The tube is [made] of leaded [soldered?] iron fixed on a 'throne'; inside it has a copper lantern and an iron wire is below. When a cord, as is shown on the drawing, is pulled it sends lights out of the tube. One cord sends out six or eight of them, so that when it is time [to do so] they all come out simultaneously."[40] This explains the splendid light emanating from the cloud of which Abraham speaks.

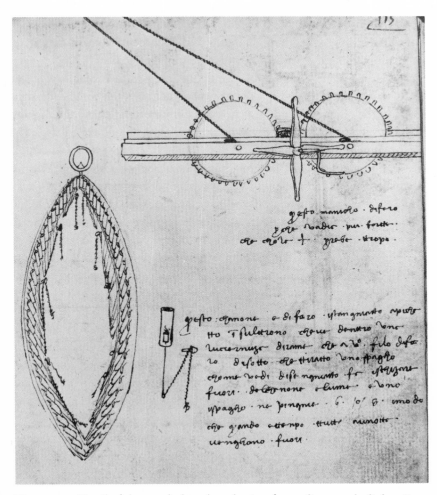

Figure 15.2. Detail of the mandorla and mechanism for sending out the lights. From the *Zibaldone* of Buonaccorso Ghiberti, MS. B.R. 228. Florence, Biblioteca Nazionale Centrale, fol. 115r. Photo Pineider.

It is obvious from the Russian bishop, Vasari, and from the confraternity records that painted representations were used in conjunction with living actors:[41] life-sized painted angels, which were set in motion by gears and thus "appeared to be alive," were placed at the highest elevation, near the roof, perhaps because it was less cumbersome than raising human beings to that height and was certainly less dangerous. In his study of the Carmine, Santi Mattei speaks of an accident in 1485 in which two people were killed, a tragedy in consequence of which the church had to be reconsecrated.[42] No documentation for this statement, for which the author unfortunately gives no source, has yet been found. But an entry just three years later lends some credibility to the allegation. It is recorded in 1488 that the *capitani* voted to celebrate the Feast of the Ascension, adding the special injunction "begging God and the Blessed Virgin Mary that it be done without scandal and with the well-being of soul and body."[43]

Evidence in the account books indicates that the refurbishing of costumes and renovation of sets was an on-going process. Obviously such expendable items as oil and candles were needed every year and minor repairs and replacements were also routine. But from time to time more extensive restoration was necessary. In 1453 the artist Piero del Massaio was paid for making a new cloud.[44] And in 1503, more than 350 lire were spent to build "a new heaven opposite where the old one was."[45]

Payments for such renovation often provide fresh details of sets and costumes through descriptions, for example, of the various ornaments of the set dressing and other embellishments. Vasari's mention of brightly colored angel gowns and Abraham's description of gold wings are well supported by the accounts, which contain many payments for pigments used to dye costumes — ocher, indigo, saffron, and cinnabar — as well as disbursements for red and blue shoes for the little angels on the cloud, who figure so prominently in the description.[46] The angels' wings were sometimes made of painted paper and were decorated with a variety of ornaments, including colored ostrich plumes, beaten brass, and peacock feathers.[47] Garlands of flowers decked the cloud and the mountain, and petals rained down from above where God the Father was stationed, clad in an old red dalmatic and wearing a mask.[48]

Since the actors were young boys, wigs and beards were a necessity. Payments indicate that those provided for the Apostles were made from horse tails, oxtails, and pigtails of straw, while the wig for Mary Magdalene was fashioned from two pounds of hemp rope.[49]

It is significant that the most thorough renovations for the play occurred in those years marked by the visit of some important dignitary to the city of Florence, such as Galleazzo Maria Sforza in 1471 and the ambassador of the king of Spain in 1486.[50] This no doubt reflects the close association of the Medici with the Company of St. Agnes and their use of the Ascension spectacle to promote their reputation for munificence. Lorenzo and Piero were both members of the company and held office at various times. Giuliano was granted special dispensation to enter the company at the age of sixteen, and there is mention of a "monsignore" de' Medici—probably Giovanni.[51]

Regarding the perception of the Ascension play as a matter of civic pride and a vehicle of Medici propaganda, it is well to remember the wording of the documents granting the subsidy: "for the honor of God and the magnificence of the city." Giuseppe Bacchi suggests that since so many artists were at one time or another associated with the St. Agnes company, the play may have reached a higher artistic standard than that of a merely popular festival.[52] Among the artists mentioned are Brunelleschi, Masolino, Bicci di Lorenzo, Neri di Bicci, Piero del Massaio, Filippo Lippi, Giovanni di Francesco, Iacopo di Cristofano, Bonaiuto di Giovanni, and a certain Simone identified as an engraver and disciple of Donatello.

The spoken dialogue to which Abraham refers is never mentioned in either the accounts of the company or the inventory. However, several entries from 1471 indicate payments to actors, some of whom are identified only as angels, while others are mentioned by name.[53] It seems unlikely that these payments indicate professional status, however. They appear rather to suggest that these individuals were paid because of the risk involved, for in each case the remuneration is followed by the phrase, "which he had to have because he went up on the cloud into heaven."[54]

Music also plays an important part in Abraham's account of the play: he mentions specifically the angels arranged around the throne of the Father, holding bells, lyres, and flutes. It is not possible to ascertain whether the instruments were actually played by these angels or if this was a tableau with music supplied from some other source. Abraham does say that "the children who represent the angels move around him [God the Father], while harmonious music and sweet song resound from afar." The exact significance of "from afar" is not clear, but the difficulty of playing and singing while dancing, especially at that height, suggests that the music was being produced by singers and instrumentalists hidden from view. Company records also mention pay-

ments to *pifferi*,[55] and, by the latter half of the century, to salaried singers as well, while in 1488 a festaiuolo "alla boce" was appointed.[56]

The absence of references to paid singers in the earlier records
of the company undoubtedly indicates that the members of the confraternity did the singing themselves, much as they did at their prayer
meetings. This was after all a company of *laudesi*.

An especially noteworthy feature of the payments recorded later
is the consistent reference to singers by voice types, *soprani* or *tenori*,
and the further distinction made between laudesi (*laudisti, laudieri*) and
tenoristi — designations that strongly suggest polyphonic rendition of the
laude.[57] These designations also indicate that the St. Agnes company
had begun to follow the lead of other more wealthy laudesi, such as
those of Orsanmichele and San Pier Martire, in employing "professional"
singers to discharge their duties. Although the names of certain singers
recur consistently enough to show that their services were rendered continuously over a period of years, these musicians were certainly not professionals in the modern sense. The records substantiate that they were
daily laborers, supporting themselves primarily as weavers, cobblers,
cabinet makers, and tanners, for example. Their fees for singing, moreover, were significantly lower than those of singers employed by the
wealthier companies mentioned above.

The very paucity of musical sources for the quattrocento lauda
may suggest that these polyphonic renditions were vocal improvisations,
perhaps based upon the older monophonic lauda. Without the evidence
of surviving music it is simply not possible to know exactly how this
was done. It is quite clear, however, from the testimony of the Florentine poet-composer-singer Andrea Stefano that the singing of laude in
parts need not have been an exclusively improvisatory practice. A manuscript preserved in the Biblioteca Marucelliana (C 152) dating from ca.
1400 contains some of Stefano's lauda texts, with the composer's own
comment that "all of these laude have been harmonized in three parts
and notated in my own hand along with the words."[58] Unfortunately,
the music has been lost.

Polyphonic performance by the laudesi of the Carmine is confirmed in the company's records. They indicate that on feast days the
singers of the St. Agnes confraternity joined with the *fanciulli* of
Sant'Alberto, a company of young boys (trebles) also affiliated with the

Carmine. An entry in 1506 records that "although the boys sing with
pleasure they are lacking a tenor. And since the Company of St. Agnes
deems it a praiseworthy thing to sing laude thus [presumably in parts]
on feast days" one of their own members, Lorenzo d'Antonio di Lucha,
was appointed to hold the tenor ("tenere il tenore") and to teach the
laude to the boys. It is clear from the context that this was a much
older custom, which had apparently declined by the turn of the century, for the document identifies such polyphonic performances as an
"ancient" practice.[59]

The lauda had achieved a high degree of popularity by the time
these religious representations were being performed in Florence. And
given the very a-liturgical nature of the plays, it is quite certain that
the music employed would not have been Latin ecclesiastical chant, but
rather these popular religious songs in the vernacular. Furthermore, some
of the rappresentazioni of Feo Belcari (1410–84), who was active in
Florence at this time, indicate that laude were introduced at climactic
moments in the action. Hence the use of laude to heighten the dramatic
impact of the Ascension play would have been entirely in keeping with
local tradition.[60]

This at once raises the obvious problem of identifying the musical sources. It should be remembered that the same laudesi from nearby
Santo Spirito with whom the St. Agnes company enjoyed friendly relations, owned a splendid, richly illuminated *laudario* — one of only two
containing musical notation that have survived from the Middle Ages
intact.[61] But the lauda repertoire that was passed on by oral tradition
was widely known, and the mere possession of a laudario manuscript
by a particular company in no way indicates that the music in it was
peculiar to that company.[62] Hence it is likely that the singers from the
Carmine would have been thoroughly familiar with the music of their
fellow company located in such close physical proximity in the Oltrarno.

It is known for certain that some of the other laudesi of Florence also owned manuscripts of laude; because of their beautiful miniatures, however, these manuscripts were unscrupulously dismembered
and sold folio by folio.[63] These fragments, which are scattered among
various libraries of Europe and America, are well known to art historians, but Fernando Liuzzi was the first musicologist to pay attention
to them: several are reproduced in his publication of 1935.[64] In a more

recent study Agostino Ziino has advanced the theory that some of these
are from a "presumed" laudario of the Company of St. Agnes.[65] The
validity of Ziino's hypothesis is confirmed by Neri di Bicci's inventory.
In part 2 it lists the books belonging to the company—seven in all.
Of these, five are books of laude, four of which he describes as richly
illuminated, and one in particular he singles out because it contains musical notation below the illuminations.[66]

Of the surviving fragments examined, the one most obviously
suggesting affiliation with the laudesi of the Carmine is the lauda "Fac-
ciamo laude a tutti santi," at the National Gallery of Art, Washington,
D.C. The Florentine origin of the manuscript is attested by the lauda
to San Miniato contained on the recto, while the verso is richly illuminated with a representation of Christ and Mary enthroned with forty
saints (Figure 15.3).[67] Many of the figures in the painting are easily identifiable, but more important even than the Apostles, martyrs, and virgins
portrayed are two figures garbed in the Carmelite habit, prominently
placed at either side of the cross. Their portrayal as old men suggests
that they are the two Old Testament prophets Elias and Eliseus, the
founder of the Carmelite order and his immediate successor. The large
scrolls that the figures hold are reminiscent of the Lorenzetti panel paintings that depict Elias and Eliseus similarly.[68] The emphasis upon these
two figures argues for Carmelite provenance, and the appearance of St.
Agnes in the second roundel from the top in the left-hand mar-
gin may suggest association with the company bearing her name.

A second miniature, formerly in the Lehman Collection of the
Metropolitan Museum in New York depicts the familiar scene of the
Apostles and Mary kneeling at the foot of the mountain, gazing up
to the already partially ascended Christ.[69] The musical intonation of
the lauda proper to the feast, as contained within the frame beneath
the picture, is identical to the version of the melody found in its en-
tirety in the laudario of the fellow confraternity of Santo Spirito, and
may well have been the "sweet song" to which Abraham refers (Figure 15.4).

The illumination perhaps most convincingly linked with the
laudesi from the Carmine is a miniature in the British Library, *Sancta
Agnesa da Dio amata,* which in the large frame at the top portrays the
saint in glory and in the smaller ones beneath depicts scenes from her

Figure 15.3. *Christ and the Virgin Enthroned with Forty Saints.* Master of the Dominican Effigies, National Gallery of Art, Washington, D.C., Rosenwald Collection.

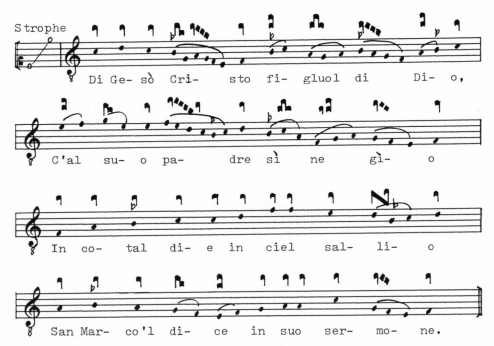

Figure 15.4. Lauda 25, fols. 36v–37v, *Laudario* of Santo Spirito, Florence, Biblioteca Nazionale Centrale MS. Magl. II, i, 122 [B.R. 18], as transcribed by Barr, text only from Luizzi, XXII.

life as related in the *Golden Legend* (Figure 15.5).[70] The painting is particularly significant since *laudari* of this period rarely contain such large and sumptuous illuminations of a saint: most illustrations of this dimension are reserved for major mysteries of the life of Christ and the Blessed Virgin. To so honor a saint is strong evidence that he/she was either the patron of the company or of the church in question. The laudario from Santo Spirito offers contemporary and analogous evidence to support this argument. The frontispiece of the manuscript (Figure 15.6) clearly establishes the confraternity's ties to the church of Santo Spirito in the large illustration of the descent of the Holy Ghost upon the Apostles, while the Augustinian affiliation of the church is reflected in the only slightly smaller illumination of St. Augustine in glory, surrounded by members of the company below in secular dress and tonsured friars above wearing the habit of the order (Figure 15.7).[71] Many other saints are depicted in this manuscript but all without exception are confined to the small space within the initial letter of the text. The artist's intent here is reflected not only in the dimensions of the miniature, but also in the ornate nature of the music which accompanies it, for it is one of the most melismatic laude in the entire collection.

In attempting to trace the provenance of these illuminations, the two most suggestive of Carmelite/Agnesian origin are the *Forty Saints* now in Washington, D.C., and the *St. Agnes in Glory* in the British Library, which Ziino believes to be sister miniatures.[72] In view of Neri's inventory, however, which lists four illuminated books of laude, the assumption that these fragments are from one and the same laudario is no longer critical to establishing their ties to the Company of St. Agnes.

One consideration remains, however. Musicologists and art historians agree that these miniatures are all from the trecento. Is it then reasonable to assume that the manuscripts would still be used throughout the quattrocento, which was a period of considerable stylistic change in music? Once again the answer may be sought in the company's documents. Although the manuscripts are listed in the inventory of 1466, that alone does not necessarily imply that they were still in use. But in 1475 the company made a payment of s.12 and d.8 "for repairing the lectern for the laudi."[73] This indicates that some sort of book was still being used. Even more convincing are the payments to singers, which in the last quarter of the century become more numerous. Whether these singers performed the laude as they are notated in the manuscripts or whether the music served as a basis for improvised embellishments of the melodic line or extemporaneous harmonizations resulting in po-

Figure 15.5. *St. Agnes in Glory,* The British Library, MS. Add. 18196.

Figure 15.6. *The Descent of the Holy Ghost upon the Apostles.* MS. Magl. II, i 122, (B.R. 18). Florence, Biblioteca Nazionale Centrale, fol. 2v. Photo Pineaider.

Figure 15.7. *St. Augustine in Glory.* MS. Magl. II, i 122 (B.R. 18) fol. 96v. Florence, Biblioteca Nazionale Centrale. Photo Pineider.

lyphony is an issue probably destined to remain unresolved, its answer forever lost in the unrecorded history of oral transmission.

Attempting to document the oral traditions of a popular cultural phenomenon is an exercise fraught with difficulties. But despite the danger of arriving at conclusions based upon prejudicial misconceptions, it is a useful exercise, allowing one a glimpse into the existence of a segment of society—at work, at play, and at prayer—which is traditionally poorly recorded. The names of a few luminaries may be found here, but for the most part the men who pounded the nails, manned the capstans, carted the lumber and formed the angelic choir belong to that class which enters this world unheralded and leaves it unchronicled except for a few artifacts that remain.

And while the study of documents such as these many produce more questions than answers, it does most assuredly impress upon the reader that the people of Florence who witnessed the Ascension play in the Carmine might well have identified with the Apostles. St. Luke tells us that after the Ascension "they went back full of joy." (24:52) And so also the *cittadini* must have done, for truly they had seen the flesh in the psalmist's words "God has ascended with jubilation" (Ps. 47 [46], v. 5).

NOTES

Research for this study was made possible in part through a Travel-to-Collections Grant from the National Endowment for the Humanities, summer 1984.

The following abbreviations are used in citing lauda manuscripts:

Aret.	Arezzo, Biblioteca Consorziale, MS. 180
Ars.	Paris, Bibliothèque de l'Arsenal, MS. 8521
Cort.	Cortona, Pubblica Biblioteca del Comune e dell' Accademia etrusca, Cortena Laudario, MS. 91
Fior.	Florence, Archivio della Curia Arcivescovile (no number assigned)
Luc.	Lucca, Archivio di Stato, MS. 93
Mgl[1]	Florence, Biblioteca Nazionale Centrale, MS. Magliabechiano II I 122 (Banco Rari 18)
Mgl[2]	Florence, Biblioteca Nazionale Centrale, MS. Magliabechiano II I 212 (Banco Rari 19)

Pis.   Pisa, Archivio di Stato, Comune di Pisa Div. A, n. 11

Triv.   Milan, Biblioteca Trivulziana, MS. 525

1. The description is contained in manuscript fragments, first published by Andrea Popov in *Obzor*, 11–15b (Moscow, 1875) and was then translated into German by Alexander Wesselofsky in "Italienische Mysterien in einem russischen Reisebericht des 15 Jahrhunderts," *Russische Revue* 10 (1877): 425–41. It is best known through Alessandro d'Ancona's Italian translation in *Origini del teatro italiano*, 2 vols., 2d ed. (Turin, 1891), 1:251–53. All translations of quoted material are mine, made from d'Ancona's text.

2. *Il luogo teatrale a Firenze*, eds. M. Fabbri, E. Garbero-Zorzi, and A. M. Petrioli Tofani (Florence: Electa, 1975), 58.

3. Giulio Piccini, ed., *Libro degli ordinamenti de la Compagnia di Sta. Maria del Carmino scritte nel 1280* (Bologna, 1867), 29, 37, and 47.

4. Quoted in Götz Pochat, "Brunelleschi and the 'Ascension' of 1422," *Art Bulletin* 60 (1978): 232–34.

5. Unless otherwise stated, all documents quoted are from the Archivio di Stato di Firenze (hereafter ASF) Compagnie Religiose Soppresse (hereafter CRS), *filze* of the Compagnia di Sta. Maria delle laudi in Sancta Maria del Carmine, detta di Sant'Agnese.

6. Franco Sacchetti, *Il trecentonovelle*, ed. Emilio Faccioli (Turin: Einaudi, 1970), 188. I am indebted to Prof. Creighton Gilbert for calling my attention to the Sacchetti reference.

7. ASF, Provvisioni Registri (hereafter Provv. Reg.) 126, 1435, fols. 195v–196v; 136, 1445, fols. 212v–213v; and 146s, fols. 255v–256v.

8. See Cyrillus Hieros., *Catechesis* 14:25; Jacques Paul Migne, ed., *Patrologiae cursus completus, series graecae*, 166 vols. (Paris: 1857–87), 33:858–59; and Johannis Chrysostom, *Homiliam de Ascensione* 5, in *Patrologiae graecae*, 30: 450 ff.

9. Biblioteca nazionale centrale di Firenze (hereafter BNCF) Mgl VII.690. The text has been edited by A. G. Galetti in *Le rappresentazioni de Feo Belcari ed altri di lui poesie* (Florence: Moutier, 1833), 107–12.

10. See Nerida Newbigin's chapter in this volume.

11. Abraham in: A. d'Ancona, *Origini*, 1:251: "The church measures 560 feet in length and 140 feet in width. . . . it has a rood screen 140 feet long erected upon columns 28 feet high."

12. Giuseppe Richa, *Notizie istoriche delle chiese fiorentine*, 10 vols. (Florence, 1762), 10:16–17. Richa estimates the height at 50 braccia (a Florentine braccia = 1.9324 feet). For contradictory figures, see Ugo Procacci, "L'incendio delle chiesa del Carmine de' 1771," *Rivista d'arte* 14 (1932): 140–232.

13. See Robert A. Koch, "Elijah the Prophet, Founder of the Carmelite Order," *Speculum* 34 (1959): 547–48.

14. An example is the central portal of the church of St. Maurice, Vienne (Dauphiné) c. 1480, which was probably influenced by the blockbook edition of the *Biblia Pauperum*. See Koch, "Elijah the Prophet"; see also Koch, "Elie et Elisée," in *Iconographie de l'art chrétien* (Paris: Presses universitaires de France, 1956), 2:347 ff. An example of the legend may be found in *A Stanzaic Life of Christ*, compiled from Higden's *Polychronicon* and the *Legenda aurea*, edited from the MS. Harley 3909 by Frances Foster (London: Oxford University Press, 1926), 298 ff.

15. The symbolism of light/darkness permeates the "Exultet," the blessing of the paschal candle sung at the Easter vigil, and is expounded extensively in Augustine. See W. H. Marrevee, S.C.J., *The Ascension of Christ in the Works of St. Augustine* (Ottawa: Ottawa Press, 1967), esp. chap. 2. See also P. Benoit, "L'Ascension," *Revue biblique* 56 (1959): 161–203.

16. CRS 24, Entrate e Uscite, 1447, fol. 9r: "A Antonio da Bachereto adì XVIII di maggio, s. uno, d. quatro, sono per pennuti chonperò per dare mangiare agli angioli;" and fol. 9v: "A Domenicho para gl'asini, adì IIII di giugno, lire una, s. uno, sono per . . . chollezione degli apostoli la mattina dell'As[c]ensione."

17. CRS 125, Entrate e Uscite, 1471, fol. 53r: "A' festaiouli di cielo adì 23 di mag[i]o. L. tre, s. quindici piccioli, portò Leonardo fabro e paghò a Lapo di Santi, bechaio, disse per libre 16 di vitella e un chaveretto e un feghato, per disinare la mattina dell'As[c]ensione."

18. A question is rasied by a curious entry in Part 4 of the Inventory of Neri di Bicci, which lists "the things needed for the star in the church many times a year for the feast." A large star with rays of wood was placed in the church and various devotional items could be hung from it, depending upon the feast. Among those mentioned by Neri is the following entry, which might suggest that in some years the play was not mounted for the feast day, but the feast day was kept in a less spectacular manner: "22 little clouds upon which are painted an image of Christ rising to heaven simply."

19. CRS 4, Partite e Ricordi, 1483–1509, fol. 18v: "Item e prefati capitani per loro solenne partito, oggi, questo dì XI di maggio 1488, ottennono che gl'infrascripti huomini in questo modo sortiti s'intendino essere quegli che hanno a ffare la festa nostra dell' Ascensione: Al cielo / Paradiso / Monte / [fol. 19r] Castello alla boce."

20. Vasari, *Lives of the Most Eminent Painters, Sculptors, and Architects,* 3 vols., trans. Gaston Du C. de Vere, intro. Kenneth Clark (New York: Abrams, 1979), 1:625.

21. CRS 125, 1471, fol. 51r: "A spese per cie[lo] e per paradiso, adì 11 di mag[i]o, lire una, s. uno piccioli, sono per oncie nove di banbag[i]a fine per luscignoli per luminegli."

22. Sacchetti, *Il trecentonovelle,* 160: "Se non andò più ratto, egli è ancor tra via."

23. Vasari, *Lives,* 1:626. See also Arthur R. Blumenthal, "A Newly Identified Drawing of Brunelleschi's Stage Machinery," *Marsyas* 13 (1966–67): 20–32.

24. CRS 98 *Entrate e uscite,* 1424–41, fol. 891v:

"To the painter Masolino of [   ] on the 8th day of July, 2 lire and 4 soldi for painting the cloud and putting on all the blue and fine gold.

To him designated, on the day designated, for painting the angels that revolve around the cloud, 4 lire and 19 soldi.

To Leonardo d'Aricho the pedlar on the said day, for making an iron screw that is fixed behind the cloud, 1 lire and 10 soldi.

To him designated, on the day stated, for making the iron for the lamps above the cloud, 2 lire.

To the same, on the same day, for making the lamps for underneath and to the side of the cloud, 4 lire and 10 soldi.

To Christofano di Michele, on the same day, for an iron rod and tacks, 10 soldi.

To Antonio di Bartoli, to the present day, the 12th of May, and more times, three lire for sheets [of paper] to make the little angels of the cloud, 3 lire."

25. Vasari, *Lives,* 1:623–30. For a chronological table of Cecca's works, see *Le vite de' più eccellenti pittori, scultori ed architertori scritte da Giorgio Vasari* in *Le opere di Giorgio Vasari,* ed. G. Milanesi (Florence: Sansoni, 1906), 3:211–212.

26. Vasari, *Lives,* 1:626.

27. Abraham in: A. d'Ancona, *Origini,* 1:251: "Toward the hour of nine . . . all eyes are turned toward the rood screen to those who are positioned there. Then four boys dressed and adorned as angels make their way to the parapet . . . and then comes one in the likeness of the Son of God."

28. Neri, Inventory, Part 8, CRS 4, 1466, unfoliated: "2 feri in su' quali istanno apichati due agnioli in su detta nughola quando si fa la festa

"1 fero grande, per nome chiamato 'seste' in sul quale istanno 2 ang[i]oli che vanno giuso a fare chompagnia a Christo, e dipoi si ritorna e uniscesi cholla nughola."

29. Abraham in: A. d'Ancona, *Origini,* 1:251: "Then many lights which are also found in the cloud are lit, spreading a splendid light." See also note 39 below.

30. Neri, Inventory, Part 8, CRS 4, 1466, unfoliated: "1 fero per nome chiamato 'el palo' in sul quale è apichato Christo quando va nella nughola.

"2 feri, uno nuovo e uno vechio, e quali s'apichano dirieto alle spalle a Christo quando è tirato suso nella nughola chon choregie di so vatto."

31. Some idea of the quantity of rope required for these functions may be gained from an entry of 1447, which refers to the rope that Neri calls "small." CRS 24, 1447, fol. 5r: "uno chanapo per tirare su Christo pesò libre XIIII."

32. Neri, Inventory, Part 8, CRS 4, 1466, unfoliated: "Uno chanapo grosso el quale tira suso la nughola, uno chanapo grosso el quale tira suso il fero detto le 'seste' co'gli agnioli, uno chanapo minore che tira suso Christo solo in cielo."

33. Ibid., Part II: "Molti chapietti di funicelle rinforzate, le quali s'adoprano a leghare gli agnioli dintorno al ballo di cielo e della nughola e molti altri bisogni."

34. CRS 24, 1447, fol. 9v: "A Donato bottaio alla piaza de' Nerli in dì XVIII di maggio 1447, s. uno d. quatro, sono per prestatura d'una bighoncia, la quale si pose in cielo piena d'acqua" s.1/d.4.

35. Neri, Inventory, Part 9, CRS 4, 1466 unfoliated: "500 lumineglì di tera, e quali s'ascendono quando si fa la festa."

36. CRS 98, 1438, fol. 142r: "A uno speziale s. 2, d. 8, per zafferano per ingialare . . . l'aqua de' pianeti"; and CRS 24, 1447, fol. 6r: "A dì detto [14 maggio] per un pocho di zafferano per pianeti."

37. Neri, Inventory, Part 8, CRS 4, 1466, unfoliated: "For twelve planets [spheres?] made of vellum in wooden circlets, which are attached to the latern in the sky"; Part 9: "Six planets of vellum, fixed in a circlets of painted wood, for use in the paradise, two large and two small." See also CRS 125, 1471, fol. 53r: "Expenses for the heaven, on the said day [24 May] thirteen soldi piccioli, for twelve candle stubs for the planets, weighing one pound, paid to Iachopo di Nucc[i]o, the druggist" s.13.

38. Neri, Inventory, Part 8, CRS 4, 1466, unfoliated: "Una istella di legniame, overo chiamato 'sole' che va dirieto a Christo quando va su, el quale è apichato al fero chiamato le 'seste' chon uno pianeto di charta pechora, tinto di rosso, chon una lucernuza dirieto."

39. Ibid.: "Una istella di legniame la quale si chiama la 'stella nuova' che sta di sopra

alla nughola in uno 'dificio di panno dipinto a Serafini, nel quale 'dificio si naschonde detta istella ed è di legniame cho' molti razi, e a ogni razo una lucernuza di rame quadra, cho' molti artifici la quale aparisce luminata quando Christo entra nella nughola e non prima."

40. Quoted in Pochat, "Brunelleschi and the 'Ascension,'" 234. Vasari describes a similar mandorla made by Brunelleschi for the Annunciation play in S. Felice in Piazza. See Vasari, *Vite,* 1:629.

41. See note 24 above.

42. S. Mattei *Ragionamento intorno all'antica chiesa del Carmine* (Florence, 1869), 16.

43. CRS 4, fol. 18r: "Adì 8 di maggio e prefati capitani . . . vinsono . . . che la festa nostra dell'Ascensione si facci questo anno 1488 e dì consueti, pregando Iddio e la sua gloriosa Vergine Maria ch'ella vengha facta bene et sanza scandalo e con salute dell'anime e del corpo."

44. CRS 114, Debitore e Creditori, fol. 84r: "Piero del Massaio, the painter, who had to be paid, up to this day, 11 November, 7 lire, 6 soldi, and 8 denari, for expenses made for the new cloud constructed for the feast of the Ascension in the year 1453, as they appear in the expense accounts entitled Ricordanze, and marked 'cloud,' p. 3, held by Leonardo Ghualtiere, the sorter."

45. CRS 115, Entrate e Uscite, 1377–1510, fol. 142, left side: "The Company of St. Agnes must give 184 lire and 8 soldi piccioli, for things for the rebuilding of the new heaven constructed in the year 1500 in the church of Maria del Carmine in Florence, opposite where the first old heaven was . . . note how the above mentioned new heaven cost the above mentioned company the above stated sum of 269 lire 1 soldo and 9 denari, for this is found in the account books of the procurator . . . in the year 1501 for celebrating the Feast of the Ascension."

46. CRS 98, 1438, fol. 142r: "To a druggist, 2 soldi and 8 denari for saffron"; and 1425, fol. 80r: "6 soldi for ink and for ocher for the canvas of the round heaven." CRS 99, Entrate e Uscite, 1447–73, fol. 120v: "for 5 ounces of indigo to dye the new canvas of the heaven of Christ." Also CRS 98, 1438, fol. 142r: "To a druggist for cinnebar"; and fol. 142v: "To Zenobi di Nicholò Baldini, hosier, 7 lire and 14 soldi, for four pairs of shoes for the angels of the cloud and on the rope . . . there were three red pairs with soles, and one blue pair for a cleric."

47. CRS 98, 1438, fol. 141v: "To Maringniaso Sasolini, the silk merchant, 1 lire, and 16 soldi . . . for purchase of twenty colored ostrich feathers that were missing from the angels' wings, 1 lire, 16 soldi." See also CRS 99, 1448, fol. 122v: "To Pagholo Chorsellini, up to the 30th day of April, for fifteen ounces of brass leaf, 1 lire, 11 soldi, and 4 denari, paid to decorate the shirts and stoles of the angels and to make feathers for the wings of the angels who go up on the rope"; and CRS 125, 1471, fol. 52v: "Expenses for the paradise, on the said day [20 May], 1 lire, 1 soldo and 4 denari piccioli, paid to Santi di Cino, for . . . 28 peacock feathers."

48. Neri, Inventory, Part 8, CRS 4, 1466, unfoliated: "1 diachano rosso, tristo, tiello indossa Dio Padre quando si fa la festa . . . 1 maschera tiene al viso Dio Padre."

49. CRS 98, 1438, fol. 141v: "A Filipo di Baldo, gio[i]eliere, s. 19, d. 8 . . . sono per chode di chavallo e di bue, e per trecie di paglia per fare i chapeletti delle sàzere degli apostoli"; and fol. 142r: "A Rosso, linaiuolo, s. 11 . . . per due libre di chanapa per sàzere e per la chapeliera di Santa Maria Madalena."

50. Even after the expulsion of the Medici in 1494, the plays continued to be a part of such special occasions as the visit of Margaret of Austria in 1533, the marriage of Joan of Austria to Francesco de' Medici in 1565, and the marriage of Virginia de' Medici to Cesare d'Este in 1586. See John Henderson, "Piety and Charity in Late Medieval Florence: Religious Confraternities from the Middle of the Thirteenth Century to the Late Fifteenth Century" (Ph.D. diss. University of London, 1983), 73 n. 60. I am indebted to Prof. Henderson for allowing me to read the unpublished manuscript.

51. Lorenzo held office in several other Florentine confraternities as well. See Ronald F. E. Weissman, *Ritual Brotherhood in Renaissance Florence* (New York: Academic Press, 1982), 117 n. 4. In addition, CRS 4, Libro di Partiti A, is rich in references to the association of the Medici with the St. Agnes Company.

52. Giuseppe Bacchi, "La Compagnia di Sta. Maria delle laudi e di Sant'Agnese nel Carmine di Firenze," *Rivista storica carmelitana* 2 (1930): 137–51; 3 (1931): 12–39 and 97–122. See esp. 34ff.

53. CRS 125, 1471, fol. 53r: "Expenses for the heaven, to the present day, 10 June, 5 lire, 10 soldi picioli . . . paid to the little boys who go up on the machine."

54. CRS 125, 1471, fol. 53v: "Expenses for the paradise up to the 9th day of June, 2 little lire paid to Francesco Antinori, to give to Domenicho di Dono, that he must have cause he went up on the cloud into heaven.

"Expenses designated up to the said day, 2 lire, 10 soldi piccioli, paid to Bene, the carpenter, and more times, from Francesco Antinori and from me, which he had to have when he went up as Christ into the heaven.

"Expenses for the heaven to the present day, 3 July, 3 lire, 10 soldi piccioli, paid to Francesco Antinori, to give to Agliolo, the tailor, which he had to have because he went up in the cloud of heaven.

"The said expenses up to the present day, 5 July, 1 lire, 13 soldi piccioli, paid to Francesco Antinori, to give to Andr[e]a di Francesco which he had to have because he went up in the cloud of heaven."

55. CRS 98, 1425, fol. 81r: "To the pipers of the Parte [Guelfa] up to the 25th day of May, lire 8, soldi 5, for playing for the feast of the Ascension"; and fol. 91r: "To Parissi di Giovanni and his companions, our pipers for the feast, 7 lire and 10 soldi piccioli, paid to the said Parissi."

57. On the question of polyphonic singing in other companies of Florentine laudesi, see Frank d'Accone, "Alcune note sulle compagnie fiorentine dei laudesi durante il quattrocento," *Rivista musicale italiana* 10 (1975): 86–114.

58. Quoted in Piero Damilano, "Fonti musicali della lauda polifonica intorno alla metà del secolo XV," *Collectanea Historiae Musicae* 3 (1963): 60. See also Bonaccorsi, "Andrea Stefano musicista della ars nova," *Rivista musicale italiana* 21 (1948): 103–5; and Nino Pirrotta, Preface to *Corpus Mensurabilis Musicae* 8, no. 5 (1964): iii.

59. CRS 4, 1506, fol. 116v: "Likewise, on the said day [2 October] the aforesaid captains, together with all their officials, considered that it was a praiseworthy thing to have laude sung on the feast day as it was done in ancient times, but noted that these laude could not be rendered thus without making certain expenditures. And considering that the young boys of the Company of St. Albert sing willingly but do not have a tenor, and understanding

that Lorenzo d'Antonio di Lucha, of the family of our company, is capable of holding the tenor part . . . it is, besides, suitable that he also teach the laude to the said little boys."

60. Luigi Banfi, ed., *Sacre rappresentazioni del quattrocento* (Turin: Unione Tipografia editrice Torinese, 1968), 84–85 and esp. 425. Numerous examples of musical interpolations may be found in Bianca Becherini, "La musica nelle rappresentazioni fiorentine," *Rivista musicale italiana* 53 (1951): 193–241.

61. BNCF, Mgl II.I.122 (Banco Rari 18). The other is the Cortona Laudario, MS. 91, Pubblica Biblioteca del comune e dell' Accademia Etrusca, Cortona (hereafter Cort.).

62. On the phenomenon of oral dissemination of the lauda repertoire, see Giorgio Varanini, *Laude cortonesi dal secolo XIII al XV* (Florence: Olschki, 1981), 1:1, 36–40.

63. One of the most regrettable losses is the laudario belonging to the Umiliati in Ognissanti. The manuscript was very large, containing 160 laude, and was entered into the Magliabechiano catalogue as Cl XXXVI 28. Becherini notes in the modern catalogue that the manuscript has been missing from the library since 1883. It is the same manuscript examined by Charles Burney during his visit to Italy. See C. Burney *The Present State of Music in France and Italy,* 2d ed., corrected (London, 1773), 255.

64. F. Liuzzy, *La lauda e i primordi della melodia italiana,* 2 vols. (Rome: Libreria dello Stato, 1935).

65. A. Ziino, "Laudi e miniature fiorentine del primo trecento," *Studi musicali* 7 (1978): 40–83.

66. Neri, Inventory, Part 1, CRS 4, 1466, unfoliated:

"One large book covered with boards and leather, fastened with large brass tacks, and richly made, in which are written many laude with many beautiful historiated miniatures on vellum.

"A book covered with wood and leather, made of vellum, in which are many ancient laude, with a crucifix painted on it and many other miniatures. Used every day.

"A book of laude covered with boards, made of vellum painted with large illuminations done with paint brush and quill.

"One book of laude on vellum, covered in boards with tacks, in which are many laude that are sol-fa'd [that is set to musical notation], figured below."

67. Rosenwald Collection, B22,128. Concordances (see list of abbreviations of lauda manuscripts): Cort., Aret., Mgl[1], Mgl[2], Fior., Ars., and Triv. See also Gary Vikan, ed., *Medieval and Renaissance Miniatures from the National Gallery of Art* (Washington, D.C.: National Gallery of Art, 1975), 26–28; and Richard Offner, *Corpus of Florentine Painting,* sec. 3, (New York: College of Fine Arts, New York University, 1957), 7: pl. 18.

68. See H. B. J. Maginnis, "Pietro Lorenzetti's Carmelite Madonna: a Reconstruction," *Pantheon* 33 (1975): esp. 12 and 14. See also Federico Zeri, "Pietro Lorenzetti: Quattro pannelli dalla pala del 1329 al Carmine," *Arte illustrata* 58 (1974): 146–56.

69. Concordances: Cort. (different melody), Mgl[1], Mgl[2], Aret., Fior., Ars., and Triv. The illumination has now passed into the hands of a private collector who wishes to remain anonymous and who will not permit the manuscript to be photographed.

70. The lower left-hand frame illustrates the tale of a certain priest who appealed to the pope for permission to marry. The pope instead gave him a ring set with emeralds and

told him to address this plea to the statue of Agnes, which, the story goes, held out its right hand and allowed him to place the ring on its finger. Immediately the temptation left him. The lower right-hand frame depicts the saint accompanied by angels as she appeared to her grieving family after her martyrdom.

71. Concordances: Cort., Mgl[1], Mgl[2], Fior., Ars., Pis., Luc., Triv. For a study of the miniatures of this manuscript and theories concerning the arrangement, see Vincent Moleta, "The Illuminated Laudari Mgl[1] and Mgl[2]," *Scriptorium* 32 (1978) 29–50.

72. Ziino, "Laudi e miniature fiorentine," 66–67.

73. CRS 125, 1475, fol. 61r. "A spese dette (della compagnia) per rachonc[i]are e' legiò delle laude, s. dodici d. otto."

16 🙿

THOUGHTS ON FLORENTINE FIFTEENTH-CENTURY RELIGIOUS SPECTACLE

PAOLA VENTRONE

I N THIS SHORT ESSAY, originally presented as a comment on Nerida Newbigin's paper, Paola Ventrone carefully distinguishes the several kinds of "spectacle-performing groups" operating in Florence in the fifteenth century—including but not limited to lay confraternities. Her observations help situate the *sacra rappresentazione* format in the wider context of Renaissance theater history, in the tradition of her mentor, the late Professor Ludovico Zorzi. Dr. Ventrone calls attention to significant parallels and differences between developments in theater arts and in the visual arts, especially painting, and discusses the methodological problems involved in comparing distinct media.

PAOLA VENTRONE is preparing an extended study of Florentine Renaissance sacre rappresentazioni.

N THE FOLLOWING BRIEF OBSERVATIONS I try to highlight some of the more significant trends in the study of religious spectacle in Florentine society in the fifteenth century. Sparked by Nerida Newbigin's stimulating essay in the present volume, these thoughts are part of my long-term research on the *sacre rappresentazioni,*[1] and constitute an attempt to single out and analyze the features that so clearly distinguish these plays from other theatrical activities that animated social life during the early Renaissance in Florence.

Any inquiry into the sacre rappresentazioni which seeks to explore their cultural milieu—to identify their intended audience, their patrons, and those who commissioned them and to establish their real weight as dramatic plays and the extent of their stagecraft—must pass through several stages. It must identify the social groups that produced these spectacles; it must essay a morphological study of the texts in comparison with coeval literary productions; and it must recognize theatrical "signs" discernible in the figurative arts of the same era. And, in fact, recent English-language studies of Florentine Renaissance spectacle have moved toward just such comprehensive contextual inquiry.[2] Newbigin, for example, in her study of lay confraternities, has shown that some of these groups were assiduously involved in producing religious spectacles.[3] In so broad a context, however, it seems necessary to delve more deeply into the distinctive features of these play-producing companies: to trace their origin, development, and social and dramatic characteristics.

Nineteenth-century historians of religious theater—somewhat too generically and with forced arguments—attributed paternity of the religious spectacles to the *laudesi* and children's confraternities (*compagnie di laudesi, compagnie di fanciulli*).[4] They indiscriminately correlated Florentine reports of performances on sacred themes with available texts of sacre rappresentazioni (a term used here to denote the Florentine eleven-syllable octave plays that have come down to us in numerous manuscript and printed texts). This generalization has been perpetuated in the historical literature, notwithstanding clear indications in contemporary documentary and narrative sources of a wider variety of companies that may be called (referring to one of their functions only) "spectacle-performing groups." Such groups comprised not only members of religious confraternities but also members of guilds and ethnic groups, amateurs, and clerics.[5]

Careful investigation of the sources reveals, moreover, that: (a) throughout the fourteenth century and for the first forty years of the fifteenth century, sacred and secular performances were given exclusively in public places (streets, squares, churches), whether sponsored by the government or by common citizens; (b) they were produced and performed by a variety of groups: including guilds,[6] young men who joined just for the occasion,[7] and adult members of devotional confraternities; (c) performances could be regular and periodic or merely occasional;[8] and (d) performances could consist of competitive and choreographic games, processions, or plays. Above all, the sources show clearly that such performances did not employ accurate dramatic texts. The most distinctive aspect of these spectacles, particularly the religious ones, was, in fact, the preponderance of special stage effects,[9] as the large sums of money spent for them prove.[10] And since no play has yet been found whose performance could plausibly coincide with descriptions of religious spectacles that have come down to us, we are forced to surmise that only simple, uncomplicated texts were used, probably incorporating paraphrases of the Gospel, occasionally in the form of short dialogues.[11]

About the middle of the fifteenth century, however, several related events changed this picture. On the one hand, the dramatic genre of the sacra rappresentazione was born, with a textual tradition that began to take shape in the 1460s.[12] On the other, new social groups (including children's companies) arose, formed for devotional and recreational purposes,[13] and these groups took new subjects for their many sacred spectacles, staging them privately in the children's companies' meeting halls.[14]

The sacra rappresentazione came into being in the middle of the fifteenth century in the learned and devout entourage of Cosimo de' Medici the elder. Foremost among those who waited on Cosimo's "court" were Antonio Pierozzi, the archbishop of Florence (St. Antoninus), a fervent patron of the children's companies; and Feo Belcari, who wrote the earliest sacre rappresentazioni[15] in order to teach the precepts of classical drama to members of the confraternities.[16] These devotional and educational motives in no way diminish the importance of the sacre rappresentazioni in Renaissance theater history, however; such plays were, in fact, the earliest form of Florentine vernacular drama. They had a well-defined textual structure that relied more on the skill of the actors than on the exploitation of stage effects.[17] Moreover, throughout the rest of the fifteenth century, these spectacles remained the sole model for other plays (for example, Politian's *Orfeo*); at the beginning of the sixteenth century they were finally replaced with sterile imitations of classical comedy.

While historical and literary sources furnish ample information about the social and cultural background of Florentine fifteenth-century religious spectacle and of the sacre rappresentazioni, little or nothing is known about their actual staging. No contemporary description of any stage arrangement has been found, and one is left to deduce the missing information from close scrutiny of Renaissance paintings. This approach, however, presents several problems of interpretation. For one thing, it can offer only indirect evidence; for another, we must allow for the fact that pictorial conventions may differ considerably from the conventions that lay behind the staging of plays. Indeed, recent scholarship has given much thought to the relationship between painting and theatrical spectacle;[18] in particular it has stressed that arguments demonstrating a close relationship often proceed by reductive approximations that take full account of neither the pictorial object nor the scenic one.[19] And, obviously, no valuable result can be expected from analysis that compares different forms of expression on the basis of their subject matter only—especially when we consider that occasional similarities in the subjects of religious paintings and plays may be accounted for by a common scriptural or legendary source. Iconographical analysis must, therefore, not only explore external similarities between spectacle and the visual arts, recognizing theatrical "signs" in works of figurative art, but try to explain changes in the cultural climate, in the common ideas and taste lying behind each art form, so as to separate the distinctively scenic components from pictorial elements fashionable at the same time.

One might sum up these reflections by comparing the Florentine sacra rappresentazione of *The Beheading of St. John the Baptist* (*San
Giovanni decollato*),[20] one of the plays of the period richest in scenic
elements, with Filippo Lippi's fresco cycle on the life of the saint in
the cathedral at Prato[21] — even though there is no evidence of their having influenced each other. The fresco cycle and the Florentine play show
a common quest for unity of time, working through the respective narrative structures, this quest establishes the order of the sequences in
the pictorial and in the scenic works. Lippi does not arrange the several scenes of the *Feast of Herod,* for example (Figure 16.1), in chronological order as might the painter of a medieval polyptych, but unifies
them in a single perspective system that focuses on the site of the feast.
In this way, he is able to give a dynamic representation of sequential
action without sacrificing overall unity of time and place in the fresco.
So too, in the text of the play, the various scenes are not treated as
independent units, but follow each other in a close concatenation sustained by stage directions designed carefully to underline all coincidences
in time sequence.[22]

But while these works in different media share the same time
concept, their concepts of space necessarily differ. In the play, the stage
directions show that the scenes were organized in a chronological order
that precluded the unity of space obtained by Lippi through his linear
perspective. Indeed, single-point pictorial perspective is the dominant
element of Lippi's fresco, determining the placement of the principal
scene at the visual center of the composition. Lippi the painter clearly
wanted to unify time and place in his "drama" in a way that would
recall the most advanced contemporary ideas on the dynamics of classical drama.[23] By contrast, the sacra rappresentazione fails to achieve a
scansion of the scenic space comparable to that in Lippi's fresco.

A further difference arising from diverse technical conventions
is that of narrative focus. The spatial configuration of Lippi's fresco,
conceived as a ceremonial hall that looks through an arcade onto a rural
landscape, focuses on the banquet. It thus evokes a form of entertainment which by the mid-fifteenth century was gaining favor with the
gentry and the well-to-do middle classes, whose banquets were in fact
enlivened by song and dance during the *entremets* — elements parallelled
in the fresco by the dance of Salome. This pictorial reference to a spec-

Figure 16.1. Fra Filippo Lippi, *The Feast of Herod*. Prato, Duomo. Photo Alinari/Art Resource, N.Y.

tacle tradition distinct from the sacra rappresentazione—notwithstanding elements of similarity in Lippi's fresco and in the Florentine play— attests to the complex interrelationship of figurative art and dramatic production in the fifteenth century.

NOTES

For my father.

1. The results of this investigation will be presented in the volume *La sacra rappresentazione e lo spettacolo fiorentino del Quattrocento,* now in preparation. The present short essay was translated by Timothy Verdon.

2. I refer to Richard C. Trexler, *Public Life in Renaissance Florence* (New York: Academic Press, 1980), and idem., "Florentine Theatre, 1280–1500: A Checklist of Performances and Institutions," *Forum Italicum* 14 (1980): 454–75.

3. In addition to Newbigin's study in this volume, see her introduction to *Nuovo corpus di sacre rappresentazioni fiorentine del quattrocento* (Bologna: Commissione per i testi di lingua, 1983).

4. Alessandro d'Ancona, *Origini del teatro italiano,* 2 vols. (Turin, 1891) 1:401–12.

5. See the information given in Trexler, '

6. For example, the Company of Sant'Onofrio or of Tintori (dyers) used to organize a *palio* in the streets of the town: see Marchionne di Coppo Stefani, *Cronaca fiorentina*, ed. Niccolò Rodolico, *Rerum italicarum Scriptores*, n.s. 30 (Città di Castello: Lapi, 1903), 495.

7. Such groups of young men were called "brigate di giovani," concerning which ample testimony is given in Bartolomeo Del Corazza, *"Diario fiorentino,"* ed. Odoardo Corazzini, *Archivio storico italiano,* ser. 5, no. 15 (1894), passim; see also Trexler, *Public Life,* 387–99.

8. Periodic spectacles were those organized for patronal feasts of S. Giovanni, or for the district celebrations (arranged in the churches of Sta. Maria Novella, of the Carmine, and of Sto. Spirito). Vasari calls them "solennissime e pubbliche"; see Vasari, *Le vite de' più eccellenti pittori, scultori ed architettori,* ed. Gaetano Milanesi, 7 vols. (Florence: Sansoni, 1906), 3:197. For the Feast of the Magi, set up by the devotional confraternity bearing the same name, see Rab Hatfield, "The 'Compagnia de' Magi'," *Journal of the Warburg and Courtauld Institutes* 33 (1970): 107–61. In particular, the Sto. Spirito Feast of Pentecost has been examined by Newbigin in this volume; and the Feast of the Ascension in the church of Carmine has been analyzed by Susanna Cantore in "Lo spettacolo del cecca al Carmine" (graduation thesis, Facoltà di Lettere e Filosofia, University of Florence, 1977–78), with Ludovico Zorzi as supervisor; and by Cyrilla Barr in this volume. So, too, the Annunciation and the Ascension plays were occasionally performed during the 1439 Ecumenical Council. These spectacles have been studied by Cesare Molinari in *Spettacoli fiorentini del quattrocento* (Venice: Pozza, 1961), 39–54; see also *Il luogo teatrale a Firenze,* a catalogue of the exhibition at the Palazzo Medici-Riccardi, Florence (Milan: Electa, 1975), 55–65; Ludovico Zorzi, *Il teatro e la città: Saggi sulla scena italiana* (Turin: Einaudi, 1977), 71–76 and notes; and idem, "La scenotecnica brunelleschiana: problemi filologici e interpretativi," in *Filippo Brunelleschi: La sua opera e il suo tempo,* 2 vols. (Florence: Centro Di, 1980), 1:161–71; Paola Ventrone, "Avanguardia e tradizione nella rappresentazione fiorentina dell'Annunciazione del 1439," in *L'Annunciazione in Toscana nel rinascimento* (Acts of Conference held in Florence 29–31 October 1986, in press).

9. It suffices to refer to the 1439 *Annunciation* and *Ascension* plays because of the exceptionally rich descriptions of them that survive, documented by d'Ancona, in *Origini,* 1: 246–53.

10. See the studies cited in note 8 above by Newbigin, Cantore (237–373), and Barr.

11. In some scenes, the actors were replaced with dummies or wooden cutouts. This suggests the open structure of the plays, further enriched with music and songs. Whether or not dramatic lays (laudi) were used is unclear. The few Florentine examples that have been transmitted to us are mainly lyrical in character; see Vincenzo De Bartholomaeis, *Le origini della poesia drammatica italiana* (Bologna: Zanichelli, 1942), 443–55. Moreover, no book of dramatic lays from other Italian regions has yet been found in Florence.

12. Newbigin, introduction to *Nuovo corpus,* xi, states that the codex Conventi Soppresi, F.3.488, in the Biblioteca nazionale centrale di Firenze, which was copied between 1464 and 1465, is the oldest collection of sacre rappresentazioni extant. Even the repertory of texts derived from Italian manuscripts (Newbigin, intro. to *Nuovo Corpus,* liv–lv), gives no evidence of the existence of plays composed before the middle of 1400, except the *Contrasto del vivo e del morto* by Jacopone da Todi, which is not a sacra rappresentazione. On the same question, see *Inventario delle sacre rappresentazioni manoscritte e a stampa conservate nella Biblioteca nazionale centrale di Firenze,* ed. Annamaria Testaverde e Annamaria Evangelista, soon to be published.

I am obliged to the authors for their kind permission to examine the typescript of their work. It is worth noting that the oldest reports that are clearly of performances of sacre rappresentazioni concern the *Abramo e Isacco* by Feo Belcari, acted in 1449 (see the *explicit* in the above quoted codex), and the *Rappresentazione della Purificazione,* performed in the same year by a children's company, as Newbigin has proved.

13. On this subject, see Gennaro Maria Monti, *Le confraternite medievali dell'alta e media Italia,* 2 vols. (Venice: La Nuova Italia, 1927), 1:182–84; Richard C. Trexler, "Ritual in Florence: Adolescence and Salvation in the Renaissance," in *The Pursuit of Holiness in Late Medieval and Renaissance Religion,* ed. C. Trinkaus with H. A. Oberman (Leiden: E. J. Brill, 1974), 200–64; and Ronald Weissman, *Ritual Brotherhood in Renaissance Florence* (New York: Academic Press, 1982), 213–14.

14. This qualitative and quantitative change in Florentine religious spectacles is supported by the information in Trexler, "Florentine Theatre."

15. These men were united by common religious and cultural interests, as Fulvio Pezzarossa has shown in *I poemetti sacri di Lucrezia Tornabuoni* (Florence: Olschki, 1978), 48–49.

16. According to classical pedagogy, recovered by the humanists, acting was a fundamental subject in the education of youth. See Eugenio Garin, *Il pensiero pedagogico dell'umanesimo* (Florence: Coedizioni Giuntine-Sansoni, 1958).

17. See my essay, "Per una morfologia della sacra rappresentazione fiorentina," in *Teatro e cultura della rappresentazione. Lo spettacolo in Italia nel quattrocento,* ed. Raimondo Guarino (Bologna: il Mulino, 1988), 195–225.

18. Among many studies, I shall indicate only these: George G. Kernodle, *From Art to Theatre: Form and Convention in the Renaissance* (Chicago: University of Chicago Press, 1970); Pierre Francastel, *La figure et le lieu: L'ordre visuel du quattrocento* (Paris: Gallimard, 1967); Ludovico Zorzi, "Figurazione pittorica e figurazione teatrale," in *Storia dell'arte italiana,* vol. 1: *Questioni e metodi* (Turin: Einaudi, 1979), 421–62; and Eugenio Battisti, "Arti figurative e teatro durante il medioevo e l'umanesimo," *Quaderni di teatro* 14, no. 4 (1981): 7–17; Paola Ventrone, "I sacri monti: un esempio di teatro pietrificato?" in *La "Gerusalemme" di San Vivaldo e i sacri monti in Europa,* edited by Sergio Gensini (Montaione [Florence]: Paccini, 1989, 145–62.

19. Zorzi, "Figurazione pittorica," 432.

20. The text may be found in the codex Conventi Religiosi Soppressi, F.3.488, of the same period as the painting. It has been edited by Newbigin, *Nuovo corpus,* 107–33. This must be referred to for an analysis of the sources.

21. The fresco painted on the choir walls of Prato cathedral was finished about the end of 1464. For the date, see Giuseppe Marchini, *Filippo Lippi,* 2d ed. (Milan: Electa, 1979), 236.

22. Just one significant example: "Hae a parire Gesù e Dio Padre in sul monte e hae a venire Gesù con quattro angeli, due innanzi e due a drieto, e *hae a venire tanto adagio tanto che San Giovanni dica questa istanza innanzi che giunga a lui*" (my italics); taken from Newbigin, *Nuovo corpus,* 116.

23. I am referring to the rediscovery of the pseudo-aristotelian rules of unity of time-space-action which influenced the text structure and the staging of most of Italian dramatic production in the sixteenth century.

17

SACRED MOUNTAINS
IN EUROPE AND AMERICA

GEORGE KUBLER

T HE FINAL CHAPTER in Part Two brings together several of the themes considered in "The Religious World of the Laity": the plastic arts and drama as forms of lay religious expression; the use of lay devotion in the interests of "civic religion"; and the political potential of lay religious associations to act for, or against, the state. Tracing the *sacromonte* format across three centuries, and from Europe to the New World, George Kubler illustrates the vitality and malleability of these architectural/ sculptural/pictorial re-creations of the Via Crucis, introduced into northern Italy in the late quattrocento by the Franciscans as an alternative to the costly and perilous pilgrimage to the Holy Land. Professor Kubler's study of four "sacred mountains" makes clear the relationship of these scenographic tableaux to religious theater; their adaptability to new social needs; and the range of social messages communicable through such dramatic, "kinesthetic" means: in this case a slave rebellion fostered by Brazilian confraternities which at one point involved Thomas Jefferson and the United States government.

GEORGE KUBLER is Sterling Professor emeritus of Yale University, and has been Senior Visiting Kress Professor at the Center for Advanced Study in the Visual Arts, National Gallery of Art, Washington, D.C. He is best known for publications on Spanish Renaissance art and on the art and architecture of ancient Central and South America, and for theoretical works in the tradition of his teacher Henri Focillon.

 HE *monte sacro,* A TYPE OF SHRINE portraying such holy scenes as the Passion at Jerusalem, first appeared at Varallo in the Piemonte of northern Italy in the late fifteenth century. Since its origin there, the monte sacro form has been adapted throughout Europe and America to serve a variety of religious and political purposes and continues to exist today. One of the many monti sacri in the United States is a small replica of the Holy Land at Waterbury, Connecticut; although it was begun only forty years ago, its topographical reduction of Palestine is very similar to that of the first sacred mountain at Varallo, built five hundred years earlier.

In this essay I examine the development of the monte sacro form. Focusing on the sacred mountains at Varallo, Granada in Spain, Braga in Portugal, and Congonhas in Brazil, I have sought to illuminate the variety of interpretations each gives to the underlying theme common to all: the *via sacra* and Calvary at Jerusalem.

NORTHERN ITALY

Before 1486 Bernardino Caimi, a Franciscan friar of the Minorite Observance who had served as patriarch of the Holy Land, chose Varallo in the Piemonte to become what he called the New Jerusalem. Crowning a mountaintop rising five hundred feet above the bridge over the Mastallone River, it still serves as an important site for pilgrimage. Caimi's travels for his order in Palestine had convinced him that the Ottoman empire would soon annex the Holy Land, as it did in 1517. Caimi was among the first to think of expanding the stations of the cross into a series of separately housed stage sets on a hilltop, with life-sized sculptures visible in small chapels, as a monte sacro requiring — and rewarding — the physical exertion of pilgrims with easy access to the hill (Figures 17.1, 17.2).

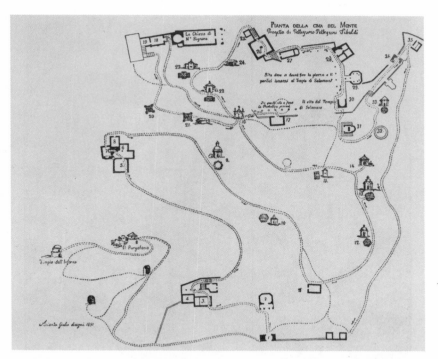

Figure 17.1. Varallo, *Sacro Monte,* plan attributed to Pellegrino Tibaldi, 1570, after S. Butler.

Work began about 1490 with statuary by Gaudenzio Ferrari; nearly one hundred years later, in 1587, the design was enlarged on plans by Galeazzo Alessi, under the patronage of Archbishop Carlo Borromeo in Milan. From the beginning in 1486, Caimi's purpose was to provide an alternative to the increasingly dangerous medieval pilgrimages to the Holy Land. An account in 1686 records extraordinary success at Varallo. The writer is Canon Torrotti on tourism: "Above all, I must praise the Piedmontese who arrive in frequent cavalcades from twenty to five-and-twenty people . . . and they are munificent in the gifts they leave behind them to the holy place. . . . From elsewhere processions arrive daily, even from Switzerland, and there are sometimes as many as ten thousand visitors . . . here in a single day."[1] Caimi's model of a surrogate New Jerusalem prefigures the *Gesamtkunstwerke* of the nineteenth cen-

Figure 17.2. Varallo, *Sacro Monte,* view in 1671, after S. Butler.

tury, as well as the amusement parks of the twentieth. The form spread
rapidly throughout the Piemonte during the seventeenth century, where
variations of it were built on other mountains.[2]

   At Varallo the series of "stations" now begins with the *Original Sin* of Adam and Eve (Figure 17.3), followed by scenes in separate
chapels from the early life of Jesus, in eleven stations from the *Annunciation* to the *Last Supper* and the *Apostles Asleep.* A second series continues

Figure 17.3. Varallo, *Sacro Monte,* tempietto of Adam and Eve, after Trovati.

in seventeen stations from the *Imprisonment* to the *Pietà*. A final series of five stations shows the *Shroud, St. Francis,* the *Entombment,* and *St. Carlo Borromeo.* Thus the Via Crucis takes only five stations from *Calvary* to *Pietà* among forty-three from *Original Sin* to the basilica of the *Assumption.*

The arrangement was never exactly repeated in any other monte sacro, and it is characteristic of the scenario itself that it can be adapted

to widely different serial subjects. Thus the twenty scenes of a monte
sacro at Orta, near Novara (Figure 17.4), built between 1590 and 1616,
are all from the life of St. Francis, whereas at Crea (Alessandria) the
chapels tell of the fourth-century battle by Eusebius against the Arian
predecessors of the Protestants, followed by scenes showing the Mysteries of the Rosary and Paradise. At Varese, the Arian heretics are
evoked again by the actual ruins of their fortifications on the mountain.
Here the stations were reorganized as Mysteries. The five joyous scenes
ended with the *Dispute among the Doctors,* the five sorrowful scenes ended
with *Calvary* and the *Crucifixion,* and the four glorious scenes ended
with the final Mystery of *Paradise.* Arona, on Lago Maggiore, is dedicated to the life of San Carlo Borromeo and to the Mysteries of the
Rosary (Figures 17.5, 17.6). At Oropa, near Vercelli, the Arian heresy
and its defeat are again narrated within the life of St. Eusebius.

In this manner, the seventeenth-century sacred mountains of
northern Italy incorporated the chief themes of Counter-Reformation
strategy. San Carlo Borromeo was the patron and mentor in the building
of these complex shrines, all aimed like mountain fortresses against the
Lutheran invasion from the north.

Their financing is still unstudied, beyond occasional details, such
as that a priest raised a million lire in the bishopric for Varese.[3] Other
support came from the archdiocese in Milan, where Carlo Borromeo
founded several confraternities to support the cults concerned with the
Via Crucis.[4] Before Borromeo, most confraternities were penitential
flagellant societies; afterward, canon law defined a confraternity as having for its purpose only the promotion of public worship.[5] The early
sacri monti, from Varallo on, first answered the need for scenographic
spaces shaped for human motion in sacred history.[6]

GRANADA (SPAIN)

The North Italian concept of the monte sacro became one of many symbols of the return of Christianity to Granada (Figures 17.7, 17.8) after
more than eight centuries under Islamic rule. This return was a slow
process, and the conquest of Granada, begun in 1492, was still unfinished in the late sixteenth century.

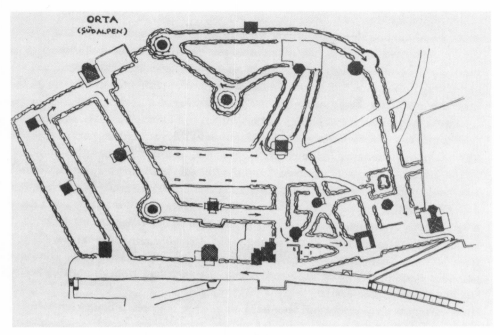

Figure 17.4. Orta, *Sacro Monte,* 1590–1616, after Kramer.

Between 1567 and 1568 the *morisco* majority of Granada held secret meetings on rebellion. Not only was their silk industry being undermined by the produce of Murcia but their children were threatened with deportation to Old Castile, as the moriscos hung between assimilation or expulsion by Spain. This crisis led to an uprising by 50,000 moriscos on Christmas Eve in 1568. After their defeat in battle, 20,000 of them were deported to Africa and to other parts of Spain. By 1598 the government had decided to continue the policy of expulsion; finally, in 1609, at least 170,000 persons were exiled, an act that caused prolonged economic hardship among all those remaining in the peninsula. Most were exiled to Moslem countries such as Turkey and Morocco. But many remained behind in Spanish cities and in the countryside to undergo varying degrees of slavery.[7]

The morisco response took an interesting form. Forged records (Figure 17.9) about Christian martyrs at Granada and on the Sacromonte in the time of the emperor Nero, together with false relics, were

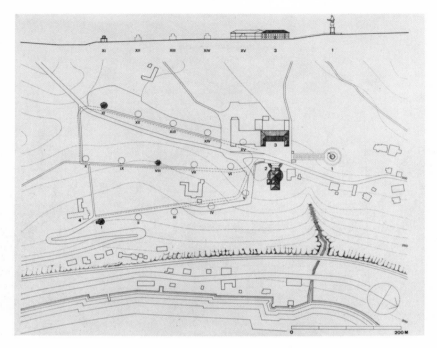

Figure 17.5. Arona, *Sacro Monte,* plan and elevation, after Moser.

revealed by credulous authorities in 1588 and 1596.[8] In 1596 at the Escorial, one of these false relics — said to be a scrap of the veil of the Virgin — was applied to sores on the body of the king; apparently the sores began to heal.[9] The translators of the parchments, Miguel de Luna and Alonso de Castillo, were moriscos; by 1632, they were known to be the forgers. A papal brief declaring the documents to be forgeries (but not exposing the relics, such as the veil) was issued in 1682. Books continued to appear in Spain defending the documents, and new forgeries appeared after 1745. The Jesuit College at the Sacromonte was built on the site of what was alleged to be the graves of early Christian martyrs. Royally protected, it became a place of pilgrimage for penitents. They came bearing crosses to be erected there during acts of contrition and baptisms of morisco converts.

The counterfeiters who had set all this in motion were morisco men of learning. Their aim had been to achieve some reconciliation be-

Figure 17.6. Arona, *Sacro Monte*, view, after Moser.

tween Christians and Moslems in Spain. They manufactured the needed
evidence, proving for the Christians that San Cecilio, the first bishop
of Granada, was a Christianized Arab. They staged the discovery of a
parchment in 1588 written in Latin, Spanish, and Arabic. In 1595–96,
sheets of lead (Figure 17.9) appeared on Monte Valparaiso, as the Sacro
monte then was known. The writing on them was in "Salomonic,"
or ciphered Latin, naming the site Sacro Monte for the first time.

The writing told of the martyrdom by fire of a disciple of Santiago called Hiscio, who was burned with four of his own disciples
in A.D. 56. Another lead sheet explained that Bishop Cecilio was mar-
tyred in Granada and that Jesus was the Word of God. Twenty-two
"books" were found and sent to Rome in 1642. They were condemned
as false in 1682 by Innocent XI, who deemed them "purely human fictions, made to ruin Catholic faith," and taken in part from the Koran.

As to the effect of these revelations before that condemnation,

Figure 17.7. Archbishop Pedro de Castro and the *Sacro Monte* of Granada in 1740, after T. D. Kendrick.

Figure 17.8. Excavating the martyrs of Granada, after T. D. Kendrick.

there is evidence that in 1596 the women of Christian Granada, led by the duchess of Sesa, organized a procession of twelve hundred women (Figure 17.8), bearing crosses to plant on the Sacromonte, "enough to seem a forest." The archbishop sent Ambrosio de Vico, the architect in charge at the cathedral, to survey the site of the martyria. In 1609, when the general Moorish expulsion was ordered, work began on a Jesuit monastery. Pedro Sanchez designed the church, college, and canonry, and Ambrosio de Vico, the adornment of the catacombs. The Way of the Cross was the work of the lay brotherhood of the Third Order of St. Francis and was intended to reconcile the turbulent present with its questionable origins. These actions were part of a syncretistic Jesuit program of cultural assimilation: a "sanctuary of conciliation," in Antonio Bonet's words.[10] Assimilation is what we see today in Granada, much of it owing to the effect of the Sacromonte during the seventeenth century.[11]

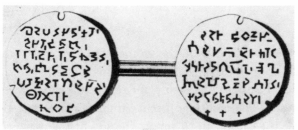

XII (a) The Mesiton inscription: cut on the first 8 in. of a folded lead strip *c*. 2 ft. long. Sacromonte excavations, 1595. See p. 72.

CORPUS USTUM DIVI MESITONIS/MARTIRIS PAS(S)US EST SUB NERO/NIS
IMPERATORIS POTENTAUR (?ATU)

XII (b) Inscription on lead wrapping of the book 'Fundamental Doctrines'.

Sacromonte excavations, 1595. See p. 74.

LIBER FUNDA/MENTI ECLESIAE/SALOMONIS CHA/RACTERIBUS/— — SCRIPTUS

XII (c) Lead disc found in Granada excavations, 1 April 1755.

From MS. 15372, Bib. Lázaro Galdiano. See p. 157.

DEUS PA(TER) FI(LIUS)
SPI(RITUS) SAN(CTUS)
III ET I CHR(ISTU)S
NA(TUS) MARIAE
VIR(GINIS) SINE PE(CCATO)
DIXIT
HOC

EST CORP(US)
MEUM ET HIC
EST SANGUIS
MEUS REMIS(IO)
PECAT(ORUM) AMEN

Figure 17.9. Forged "Salomonic" inscriptions at the Sacro Monte of Granada, after T. D. Kendrick.

At present, the precinct is dilapidated and closed to the public, an institution that has served and outlived its purpose. The steep Way of the Cross is not endowed with figural scenes as are the North Italian examples. The Sacromonte of Granada, surrounded by troglodyte gypsy caves, goats, and fires, is a reminder more of the morisco rebellion of 1568–70 than of the Passion at Golgotha. It asserts the retreat of Islam in Spain before the power of a more ancient Christianity, however fraudulent its documentation was proved to be.

BRAGA (PORTUGAL)

In 1373 the sacred mountain at Braga in northern Portugal existed only as a shrine of the cross on the Monte Espinho ("hill of thorns"), where a steep path drew pilgrims.[12] The name changed in 1629, when a new brotherhood began to collect money for a pilgrimage site dedicated to the Bom-Jesus do Monte (Figure 17.10). The seventeenth-century chapel offered lodging to pilgrims who climbed the winding path adorned with fountains and small chapels housing scenes of the Passion, like those in northern Italy. Today several hotels and a funicular provide a link between ancient pilgrimage and modern tourist jaunt.

The seventeenth-century layfolk also arranged sacred plays on biblical and mythological themes displayed together, using triumphal chariots and allegorical figures. The spirit of such theatrical productions survives in the iconography of the sculptures commissioned for Braga's sacred mountain in the eighteenth century. Christian and pagan themes were combined to illustrate the teachings of a Jesuit humanism in vogue in northern Portugal before the suppression of the Society of Jesus in 1767.[13]

For the new design in 1722,[14] a cascaded stairway was built of eleven reversing and parallel flights, punctuated with fountains dedicated to the Five Senses (Figures 17.11, 17.12), beginning with the Wounds of Christ, and accompanied by statues of Diana, Mercury, Saturn, and Jupiter. In the words of Germain Bazin, this design accorded with the "Christian sensuality" of the court of João V (reigned 1706–50), as well as being a "Jerusalem sancta resaurada et reedificada," as labeled in the gateway inscription of 1723.[15] Flanking the gate are fountains marked

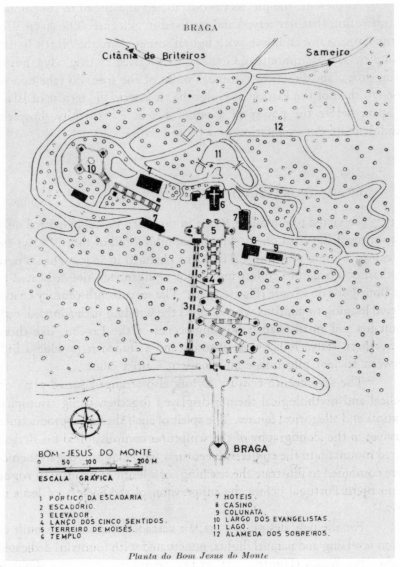

BRAGA

Citânia de Briteiros

Sameiro

12

11

10

7

6

7

5

8

9

4

3

2

BOM-JESUS DO MONTE
0 50 100 ~200 M.
ESCALA GRÁFICA

BRAGA

1 PÓRTICO DA ESCADARIA.
2 ESCADÓRIO.
3 ELEVADOR.
4 LANÇO DOS CINCO SENTIDOS.
5 TERREIRO DE MOISÉS.
6 TEMPLO

7 HOTEIS.
8 CASINO.
9 COLUNATA.
10 LARGO DOS EVANGELISTAS.
11 LAGO.
12 ALAMEDA DOS SOBREIROS.

Planta do Bom Jesus do Monte

Figure 17.10. Braga, *Bom-Jesus do Monte*, plan, after *Guia de Portugal*, Auto Club, Lisbon.

Figure 17.11. Braga, *Bom-Jesus do Monte,* view, 1722, after G. Bazin.

with sun and moon to represent the New and Old Testaments. After 1770 these contrasts were condemned as "indecorous and indecent," and some statues were renamed: Argus became Joseph and Orpheus turned into Solomon. The elliptical Holy Sepulcher of 1725 crowned the stairways, with eight angels bearing the instruments of the Passion on its buttresses (Figure 17.13); between 1784 and 1811, however, it was replaced with the present box-church design by Carlos Amarante, in neoclassical style.[16]

The program at Braga in 1722 produced the most splendid and intricate sacred mountain in Europe. Its bold reconciliation of revealed religion with pagan mythology was unique. But the monumental aspect as a formal cascade of stairs in geometric order was prefigured in the

Figure 17.12. Braga, *Bom-Jesus,* stairway, after G. Bazin.

seventeenth century on the Mont-Valérien at Suresnes (Figure 17.14), in the western suburbs of Paris.[17] In Germany it appeared at Würzburg in the Käppele of 1747 (where the mountaintop Jerusalem of northern Italy became an axial promenade on a hillside park), and in southern Austria, at Kreuzberg near Klagenfurt (Figure 17.15).

CONGONHAS DO CAMPO (BRAZIL)

The gold rush (Figure 17.16) in the Brazilian captaincy of Minas Gerais began in the 1690s to attract many Portuguese men. They worked the mines with black slaves (more than eighty-five thousand in six towns

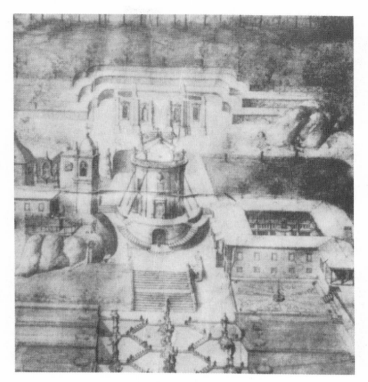

Figure 17.13. Braga, *Bom-Jesus,* Holy Sepulcher, 1725, after G. Bazin.

in 1749). Most of the slaves were of Yoruba-, Twi-, and Bantu-speaking groups. The Portuguese greatly feared conspiracies to massacre whites (as indeed happened in 1724 and 1756).[18] Yet religious brotherhoods that included slaves build splendid churches and chapels and sponsored costly processions.[19]

Because the Portuguese monarchy forbade the presence of any religious order in the remote mining towns, the festival life of the parishes was assumed by the laity, organized into religious brotherhoods, or *cofradias.* Under canon law such sodalities were subject to episcopal authority. Their functions were to support the cult, to perform works of charity, and to assure the spiritual improvement of their members. The three types of cofradias are: sacramental for the adoration of the

Figure 17.14. Suresnes, Mont-Valérien, after G. Bazin.

Eucharist; penitential for the reenactment of the Passion and its stations; and ritual for the veneration of the Trinity, the Virgin, and the saints.[20]

The sacramental and ritual associations were composed of whites, mulattos, and black slaves. Often in mixed groups, these members undertook the building of churches and chapels. The penitential brotherhoods were concerned with processions each year and the public worship they stimulated.[21] Between 1786 and 1823, the slave population dropped from 49.9 percent to 27 percent of the total population; but the mulattos, who made up 49.7 percent of the total in Minas Gerais in 1776, still composed 47.8 percent in 1825.[22]

This same half-century spans the productive life of the sculptor Antônio Francisco Lisboa, nicknamed Aleijadinho ("little cripple"), the

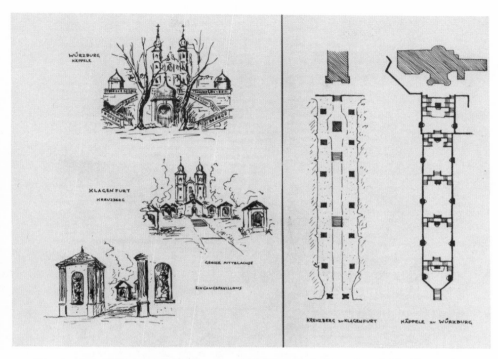

Figure 17.15. Würzburg, Käppele, 1747, and Klagenfurt, Kreuzberg, after Kramer.

mulatto son of a Portuguese builder-architect in Ouro Preto, who was the principal creator of the Santuario at Congonhas do Campo (Figure 17.17). This Santuario includes a church with its atrium (churchyard or *adro*) in front, which is approached uphill by a via sacra of eight chapels containing life-sized statues of the scenes of the Passion (Figure 17.18). The full title of the Santuario is the Bom-Jesus de Matozinhos, and it has the principal characteristics both of a pilgrimage church and of a sacro monte, in receiving pilgrimages and in having a hillside Way of the Cross. The full name honors an image in Portugal at the church of the seaport of Matozinhos north of Oporto. This was also known as a *santuario,* meaning a "votive shrine" dedicated to the cult there.[23] The payments to Aleijadinho for his work at Congonhas were from the Santuario administration. But other accounts record that he was paid at Ouro Preto by the treasurer of a brotherhood of *pretos crioulos*

Figure 17.16. Slaves mining diamonds and gold in minas Gerais, after C. R. Boxer.

(blacks born in Brazil). Among its directors were two women, the prioress (priora) and vice-prioress (vice-priora), who probably represented a large female membership.[24]

During the "age of gold" in Minas Gerais (1695–1750), a social

Figure 17.17. Congonhas do Campo, Santuario do Bom-Jesus de Matozinhos, stairs, prophets, and church, after G. Bazin.

stratification emerged which was based in the parishes and among the brotherhoods in a few parishes called *matrizes* ("motherhouses"). Thus forty-seven brotherhoods, or *irmandades,* in as many towns (including Congonhas) were affiliated with the parish of St. Francis in Ouro Preto, as *paroquias* of the wealthy white colonists. These brotherhoods are comparable in today's terms to cooperatives, clubs, cultural and artistic centers, and labor unions. The rivalry among parishes as well as among matrizes was intense. For example, two matrizes and their paroquias paid for more than half the artistic commissions held by Aleijadinho.[25] Within the lay brotherhoods, blacks, mulattos, and white artisans could win equal prestige by building chapels,[26] and disposed of funds that gave Aleijadinho an *oitavo* of gold daily, or 3.586 grams.[27]

The building history of the Santuario began in 1758 with sixty *cruzados* in gold from a diamond miner who died seven years later. Con-

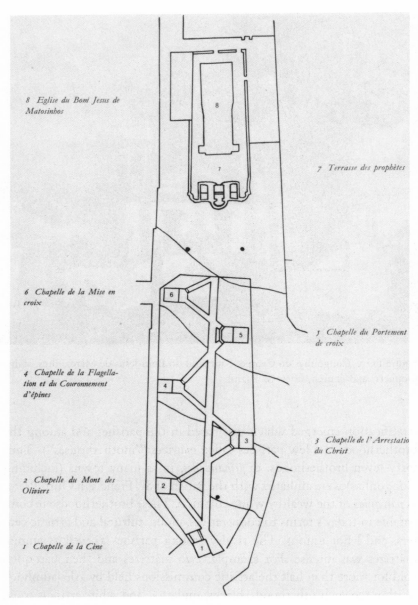

8 *Eglise du Bom Jesus de Matosinhos*

7 *Terrasse des prophètes*

6 *Chapelle de la Mise en croix*

5 *Chapelle du Portement de croix*

4 *Chapelle de la Flagella-tion et du Couronnement d'épines*

3 *Chapelle de l'Arrestatio du Christ*

2 *Chapelle du Mont des Oliviers*

1 *Chapelle de la Cène*

Figure 17.18. Congonhas do Campo, plan of chapels, stairs, and sanctuary, 1758–1805, after G. Bazin.

Figure 17.19. Congonhas do Campo, *Christ Crowned with Thorns,* after 1796, by Aleija-dinho, Antonio Francisco de Lisboa.

Figure 17.20. Aleijadinho, Congonhas do Campo, *The Prophet Amos,* before 1805, after R. C. Smith, Jr.

struction began at the end housing the main altar, which was completed in 1761. The atrium was begun in 1777. Aleijadinho was at work
on the wooden statues (Figure 17.19) in the six chapels on the Way of
the Cross in 1796. The prophets of the atrium stairways (Figures 17.17,
17.20) were begun in 1799 and finished in 1805.

Beginning in 1786, Thomas Jefferson was approached by the
envoy of the United States in France with news of a scheme among
colonists in Rio de Janeiro, Minas Gerais, and Bahia. They were preparing to revolt against Portugal and establish a republican government.
The conspirators were landowners and university students, mostly
Brazilian-born whites in Minas Gerais. These intellectuals were seeking
independence on the model of the North American revolution. In 1788–
89 their conspiracy included mining magnates, magistrates, lawyers, and
clerics. The plan was to assassinate the governor and proclaim a sover-
eign republic, after which a war of three years was planned, financed
by expropriation of the royal fifth on the mines. The leader of this revolt (today a national hero) was an ensign in the Dragoons, Joaquim
José da Silva Xavier, who was dubbed Tiradentes because of his skill
as a toothpuller. He was defeated and hanged in Vila Rica de Ouro
Preto in 1792.[28]

A recent book about Aleijadinho by Orlandino Seitos Fernandez supports a widely shared surmise[29] that the sculptor was among
the conspirators, and that he took refuge between 1789 and 1794 in the
wild country. Although no documents support this belief, Fernandez
thinks that Aleijadinho's statues of the prophets at Congonhas show
sympathy for the rebellion. Fernandez sees the prophets as presages of
freedom for slaves and mulattos in Brazil; "soon he shall come who
will save us" (Baruch), signifies the coming of a mulatto Brazil, and
another prophecy, "Israel shall be saved" (Daniel), is identified again
as meaning Brazil.

Supporting this argument is the long history of slave revolts
in eighteenth-century Brazil and the promises of the leaders of the In-
confidência, which included freedom to native-born slaves and mulattos,[30]
who made up half the population both in Minas Gerais and in Bahia.
In Bahia, mulatto artisans planned a massacre of whites in 1792 inspired
by the slogans of the Terror in Paris, but this conspiracy ended in the

hanging of four of the leaders in 1799.[31] Thus the hopes of blacks and mulattos for freedom were more than empty words.[32]

CONCLUSION

In review, the Piedmontese program of the sacri monti was surprisingly flexible. It allowed Caimi's original scheme of the Way of the Cross as a New Jerusalem to be adopted for a multitude of purposes: at Orta, to warn the faithful of the Protestant danger by substituting the life of St. Francis, and at Crea, to recall the Arian heresy. At Oropa, the life of Mary was the thread, explored through the fifteen Mysteries of the Rosary. At Arona, the scenes from the life of San Carlo Borromeo were included, and at Varallo itself, on the original order by Caimi, a succession of variants was imposed by Gaudenzio Ferrari, Galeazzo Alessi, Pellegrino Tibaldi, and Martino Bassi.

At Granada, the fraudulent but historically correct reminder was made that the Moorish conquest displaced early Christianity, and that a Christian conciliation with Islamic moriscos was to be preferred to the latter's exile or extermination.

In Portugal, the Jesuit-humanist conflation of Scripture and mythology at Braga prefigured a further development at Congonhas in Brazil. There, the traditional parallels of New and Old Testament were surprisingly inverted, with the Passion leading to the prophets, for purposes of a republican revolution demanding freedom and representation in government. The supporting messages spanned the era from Amos to Daniel, through eight centuries all speaking to Jehovah about present evils and the promised release from them.

The prophets of Congonhas displayed once again, and perhaps for the last time, the power of the ancient concordance of new and old law when social justice was at stake. At Congonhas, twelve prophets were inserted between the Way of the Cross and the church of the Bom-Jesus de Matozinhos, as if to remind the pilgrims that the Passion of Christ and his coming again as the Good Shepherd required the intercession of the prophets of the Old Testament, with their messages of doom for the old order of tyranny, from Babylon to Greece and Rome,[33] and, by association, to Portugal. Aleijadinho's versions of their Latin messages (Figure 17.20) state by themselves the argument of the prophecy of liberation.

NOTES

1. Quoted in Samuel Butler, *Ex Voto* (1888; reprint, London: J. Cape, 1928), 21. A convenient guide by P. Angelo Trovati, *The Sacro Monte of Varallo* (Novara: I.G.D.A., 1965), has color photographs of the principal buildings, sculptures, and paintings.

2. Santino Langé, *Sacri Monti piemontesi e lombardi* (Milan: Tamburini, 1967).

3. According to Germain Bazin, *Aleijadinho et la sculpture baroque au Brasil* (Paris: Le Temps, 1963), 199, the priest was Father Giambattista Aguggiari.

4. Aristide Sala, *Documenti circa la vita e le gesta di S. Carlo Borromeo* (Milan, 1857–61), pt. 5, 141. See also Gennaro M. Monti, *Le confraternite medievali dell'alta e media Italia* (Venice: La Nuova Italia, 1927), 1:87; and Andrés Moser, "Arona: ein Sacro-Monte und eine Kolossalstatue für den Heiligen Karl Borromeo," in B. Anderes, *Kunst um Karl Borromeo* (Lucerne: Faksimile-Verlag, 1979). The only Sacromonte in Mesoamerica is at Amecameca, between the volcanoes of Ixtaccihuatl and Popocatepetl (elevation 2570 m). It is likewise dedicated to a revered person, Fray Martin de Valencia, who led the first Franciscan mission to Mexico in 1524. The Sacromonte was founded in 1584. See Fortino Hipólito Vera, *Santuario del Sacromonte* (Amecameca, 1888), 23.

5. F. Lombard, "Confraternity," in *New Catholic Encyclopedia* (New York: McGraw-Hill, 1967), 4:154.

6. Langé, *Sacri Monti*, 7.

7. Ernst Kramer, *Kreuzweg und Kalvarienberg* (Kehl/Strasburg: Heitz, 1957).

8. Antonio Dominguez Ortiz and Bernard Vincent, *Historia de los moriscos* (Madrid: Revista de Occidente, 1978).

9. See T. D. Kendrick, *St. James in Spain* (London: Methuen, 1960); Kendrick reconstructs the history of these forgeries, including those of 1754–61.

10. I. Gómez de Liaño, *Los Juegos del Sacromonte* (Madrid: Editorial Nacional, 1968), 125–26; Kendrick, *St. James*, 70.

11. Antonio Correa Bonet, "Superchería y Fe en Granada," *Historia* 16 (1981): 50; Miguel José Hagerty, *Los libros plumbeos del Sacromonte* (Madrid: Editoria nacional, 1980).

12. Dominguez Ortiz and Vincent, *Moriscos*, 223.

13. João d. Azevedo Coutinho, *Bom Jesus do Monte* (Braga, 1899), 6–10. The title of Bom Jesus probably derives from a confraternity founded at Lisbon during a plague in 1432, for public exercises of piety. See Fortunato de Almeída, *Historia da Igreja em Portugal* (Coimbra/Lisbon: Imprensa accadémica, 1910), 2:490; A. H. de Oliveira Marques, *Daily Life in Portugal in the Late Middle Ages,* trans. S. S. Wyatt (Madison: University of Wisconsin Press, 1971), 225.

14. Bazin, *Aleijadinho*, 207.

15. By Bishop Rodrigo de Moura Teles and a military engineer, Manuel Pinto de Vilalobos: See Bazin, *Aleijadinho*, 207.

16. Bazin, *Aleijadinho,* 205.

17. His drawings (1774) illustrate the remarks by Germain Bazin in ibid., 204–5, 208, 216.

18. Ibid., 201–2.

19. Plans of the Käpelle and the Kreuzberg are in Kramer, *Kreuzweg und Kalvarienberg,* 86–87. For Würzburg, see Martin Wackernagel, *Die Baukunst des 17. und 18. Jahrhunderts* (Berlin: Akademische Verlagsgesellschaft Athenaion, 1915), 198.

20. C. R. Boxer, *The Golden Age of Brazil, 1695–1750* (Berkeley and Los Angeles: University of California Press, 1962), 174.

21. Simão Ferreira Machado, *Triunfo Eucharistico* (Lisbon, 1743). This very rare book is available in a facsimile with commentary by Alfonso Avila. *Residuous Seiscentistas em Minas,* 2 vols. (Belo Horizonte: Centro de estudos mineiros, 1967).

22. Isidoro Moreno Navarro, *Las Hermandades andaluzas* (Sevilla: Universidad del Sevilla, 1974), 15–16.

23. S. Santiago de Montoto, *Cofradias sevillanas* (Sevilla: Universidad del Sevilla, 1976), reviews the history of processions by cofradias arranged according to the days of Holy Week.

24. Kenneth R. Maxwell, *Conflicts and Conspiracies: Brazil and Portugal, 1750–1808* (Cambridge: Cambridge University Press, 1973), 265–66.

25. Robert C. Smith Jr., *Congonhas do Campo* (Rio de Janeiro: AGIR, 1973), 15.

26. Fritz Teixera de Salles, *Associaçoes religiosas no ciclo do Ouro* (Belo Horizonte: Universidade de Minas Gerais, 1963), 19–20, e.g., Cofraria de N.S. das Merces e Perdões in 1775.

27. De Salles, *Associaçoes,* 104, 120. S. Francisco drew the wealthy to its brotherhoods, and the Carmo included merchants. Their rivalry was reflected in a corresponding rivalry between mulatto freemen and black-slave brotherhoods of artisans.

28. Sylvio de Vasconcellos, *Vida e obra de Antonio Francisco Lisboa, o Aleijadinho* (São Paolo: Companhia editora nacional, 1979), 2.

29. Ibid., 139. For all his work at Congonhas, Aleijadinho received in nine years (1796–1805) nearly 1425 cruzados (between 28 and 29 kilos of gold) and for four years' work (between 1790 and 1794) at S. Francisco in Ouro Preto he was paid 1750 cruzados.

30. Bazin, *Aleijadinho,* 1963, 189–276; Smith, Jr., *Congonhas do Campo.* Nineteenth-century additions in the lower chapels are discussed by Orlandino S. Fernandez in his *Aleijadinho: Le chemin de croix de Congonhas do Campo* (Paris: Chène, 1979). The payments to him were published in Andrade, "Contribuiçao," 255–97. The most complete chronology is in Vasconcellos, *Vida e obra,* 119–43 (Aleijadinho's appearances at Congonhas are tabled as of 1764/66, 1796–99, 1800–1805, and 1808).

31. The most complete account of the Inconfidència Mineira is in K. R. Maxwell, *Conflicts,* 84–239.

32. The nature of the cofradia system in western Andalusia has been explained by Moreno Navarro in an anthropological context. Each cofradia was subject under canon law to episcopal authority. Its duties were to help pay the expenses of worship, especially in religious processions, to monitor the spiritual improvement of its members, and to perform works of charity. As in eighteenth-century Brazil, such societies might be of open or closed membership depending on class, property, and ethnicity. Some societies were black, mulatto, *gitano,*

Indian, or "other nations" in Seville. Some societies, as matrilineal groupings, were endogamous. As to worship, the sacramental cofradia might give all attention to adoration of the Eucharist; the penitential to the Passion; others to the veneration of the Virgin or a saint. All cofradias in Spain and Portugal were subject as filial members to the support of a mother-parish and to the duties of mutual help in illness and death. In Andalusia, their history as *cofradias nacionales*, of blacks or mulattos or gypsies or Indians, is of late fourteenth-century origins. Similar organizations existed in Madrid. See Navarro, *Las Hermandades* 34; Antonio Rumeu de Armas, *Historia de la previson social en España* (Madrid: Editorial Revista de derecho privado, 1944), 272.

33. See Maxwell, *Conflicts,* 133, 139: "in itself a startling proposal for 1789." See also Emil G. Kraeling, *The Prophets* (New York: Rand McNally, 1969), 22. In his *Aleijadinho,* 217, Bazin writes that at Congonhas, "le ballet des prophètes . . . administre cette vieille leçon apologétique de la concordance . . . c'est ici pour la dernière fois qu'elle inspirera une ouevre d'art."

Part Three

THE WORLD OF
THE CHRISTIAN HUMANIST

18

HUMANISM AND THE RELIGIOUS CRISIS OF THE LATE QUATTROCENTO
Giovanni Caroli, O.P., and the *Liber dierum lucensium*

SALVATORE CAMPOREALE, O.P.

THE OPENING ESSAY OF PART THREE takes us to the heart of that "troubled marriage" between Christianity and classical humanism alluded to in the introduction. In this chapter, Father Salvatore Camporeale, O.P., analyzes the case of Giovanni Caroli, Dominican friar and humanist historian. Caroli's "crisis" arose from the gradual development in the later quattrocento of precisely that aspect of humanist ideology which Burckhardt would consider primary in Renaissance experience: a heroic vision of the state and of the individual. Camporeale vividly describes the agonizing process by which Caroli was led to sacrifice deep principles of cloistered life in order to preserve what he saw as the innermost spirit of Christian monasticism. The friar's understanding of the moral quandary of his religious community as a microcosm of the problem of Florence, facing slow loss of its civic freedom as Medici influence grew, suggests the same sense of identification between the monastic and secular "cities" discussed in Chapter 7, which also treated Santa Maria Novella. Caroli's ability to exploit antique literary models in arguing his case, and his simultaneous awareness of the inadequacy of ancient history and poetry to express the full character of Christian historical experience, illustrate the poles of this "world of the Christian humanist."

SALVATORE CAMPOREALE is a Dominican friar of the Santa Maria Novella community, and research associate at the Harvard University Center for Italian Renaissance Studies, Villa I Tatti. He also teaches part of each year at the Johns Hopkins University. Father Camporeale's publications include fundamental studies of Caroli's writings and of the thought of Lorenzo Valla.

HE LIFE OF GIOVANNI CAROLI, Dominican friar of Santa Maria Novella (1429–1503), is described in its essentials in the *Cronica fratrum* of this Florentine convent. The *obitus,* or death notice, traces the outlines of Caroli's professional and cultural accomplishments: he was several times elected conventual prior of Santa Maria Novella; he was *magister* in theology and for years was committed to teaching. He also served the monastic community as librarian and copyist, enriching the conventual library with fundamental texts. He wrote, in both Latin and the vernacular, about history and hagiography, theology and liturgy, and biblical exegesis. These writings — still for the most part unpublished — frequently touch on controversies within the political and civil spheres and discuss philosophical and religious problems. Indeed, his literary works are almost always dominated by — and often were provoked by — specific contemporary political or cultural events, and by broader historical trends perceived within both civic and monastic life.[1]

The intimate connection, within the personality of Caroli, between the outward events of his life and his intellectual development, necessitates the utmost precision in dating his writings. For only thus can the specific meaning of the work be grasped and its broader implications accurately assessed. Precisely dated texts are above all necessary in order to define the turning points in his thought: its successive phases of adherence and dissent in regard to the contemporary religious and political situation. And while dating of all of Caroli's works is necessary in order to understand his meaning, correct dating of his works on history and politics is crucial.

In two works, the *Liber dierum lucensium,* and the *Vitae non nullorum fratrum beate Marie Novelle,* Caroli addresses problems of historiography, politics, and religious crisis; that is, the problem of how to write history, the problem of relation between past and present in terms of civic and political life, and the definition of the impact of contemporary humanist culture and religious crisis. The writing of these two books—the first major works by the Dominican—occupied a twenty-year period, from 1460 to 1480. These were years during which Caroli's own life was buffeted by external events; for him, historical research and reflection on the past were the means by which the reality of the present could be confronted. He perceived this reality as a crisis at the core of the religious and civic life of Florentine society and culture. At the end of this first period in his thought, toward 1480, a progressive reversal of his view of the contemporary situation began. The Pazzi conspiracy of April 1478 and its immediate consequences mark a turning point in Caroli's political and historical thought. This change can be detected very clearly in the last pages of the final version of his *Vite fratrum,* finished in 1480.[2]

His next work, written immediately afterward in the early 1480s and titled *Libri de temporibus suis,* is an out-and-out "defensio" of the Medici regime, contesting the criticisms expressed by the humanist Filelfo. And with this begins a second twenty-year period in Caroli's thought and literary production. This second period saw the final consolidation of the Medici regime and, ultimately, its fall with the appearance of Savonarola and the revival of the republic. During these years, Caroli fought against the charismatic Dominican from San Marco and his supporters, criticizing the famous theses of Pico della Mirandola in 1489. But analysis of this second phase of Caroli's thought, ending with his death in 1503, reveals a new set of attitudes and ideas regarding history, politics, and religious crisis. Undoubtedly, this material illuminates much that is interesting about Florentine culture in the last part of the century, but it leads us far beyond the scope of this essay.

RELIGIOUS AND MONASTIC CRISIS

Caroli's historical reflection begins with the *Liber dierum lucensium,* the book of his days in Lucca, written between 1461 and 1462 in the convent of San Romano in Lucca. Here the Dominican had been exiled by the highest authority of the order, Master General Marziale Auribelli of Avignon. What were the events that led to Caroli's removal from Santa Maria Novella?

In April 1460 dissent had arisen between the community of Santa

Maria Novella, of which Caroli was then prior, and Marziale Auribelli, superior general of the order. The conflict concerned the problem of monastic renewal and reform. The clash between the views held by the Florentine community, on the one hand, and the authority of the order, on the other, is but a specific instance of a much more widespread conflict in which divergent opinions on how to carry out this reform were maintained. The issue of the reform, initiated by Cardinal Giovanni Dominici in the early part of the fifteenth century, is one of the key factors determining developments in the Mendicant orders in Italy to the very end of the century.

In the case at hand, these differences of opinion were personified by Auribelli and his Curia on one side and by the prior, Caroli, on the other. Caroli and his community called for reform that would respect the autonomy of the convent and its particular tradition. Auribelli wanted instead to impose reform from above, based on his legal authority as superior general and consequently applied according to criteria alien to the traditions of any individual convent. Despite the support and the interventions on his behalf of the *signoria,* which was in full agreement with the stand taken by the Santa Maria Novella convent, Caroli was deposed as prior and exiled to Lucca. But even after his removal, the resistance of the convent was so unyielding that Auribelli's attempted reform met with complete failure and, as a result, Auribelli was in his turn deposed by Pius II. Such an action, without precedent in the history of the Dominican order, has been explained by some scholars as a political move by the anti-French Pius II against the Avignonese Auribelli.[3]

As the days passed in Lucca, Caroli was to reflect at length on these events. Having fled, together with Fra Giacomo di Pietro, from the "destruction" of the Florentine community just in time to save himself, he was now able to devote his time to what he refers to as "humane studies"—the *studia humanitatis.*[4] But an objective stance was impossible for him; the implications of these events were felt as a personal drama in which life and vocation were in conflict. In carrying out the reform as he understood it, he, Caroli, had led his community to oppose the superior general of the Order. Just as Savonarola was to do a few decades later at his convent at San Marco, Caroli failed in monastic obedience out of a sense of duty. In order to save the religious institution he led, he chose to disobey his monastic vows. Auribelli was the tyrant, against whom it was necessary to rebel in order to defend the *libertas conventus*. But in conceiving of conventual life in such terms as these, previously applied only to civic affairs, the moral dilemma of obedience versus disobedience attained a new dimension, for necessary disobedience affected the very roots and foundations of monastic life. Monasticism as an institution had been traditionally conceived and historically experienced as founded on obedience. Now, however, it seemed possible to save this institution only by denying that fundamental principle. And yet this solution necessarily deepened its crisis, undermining the basis of its existence. The ultimate consequence of this solution would be the complete negation of that institution's own reality.[5]

The *Liber dierum* is written in the form of a dramatic dialogue in three acts, each act corresponding to one of three consecutive days. The drama has a unity of place, all three acts being set in the convent of San Romano, in Lucca. Each spokesman in the dialogue represents a different point of view, thus acting out the internal struggles of Caroli himself.

The first day's dialogue, between a Franciscan and an Augustinian who are both guests of the convent, is a real *quaestio disputata* on the nature of monasticism and the structure of the mendicant orders. The Franciscan maintains the principle of obedience; of obedience even to the point of self-abnegation, as commanded in the Gospels and fundamental to the idea of institutional monasticism. The Augustinian argues against this view, turning the "heroic" obedience of the Franciscan upside down and recasting it as an equally "heroic" disobedience. He rests his argument for the possibility of heroic disobedience on the evangelical message of Christian freedom. As he expounds his thesis, the Augustinian enlarges its scope to include the whole historical experience of mankind. It is not possible to effect a radical transformation of any civil or religious system, he concludes, without breaking equally radically with the past. Human history is based, as are also the evolutionary processes of nature, on the inseparable relationship of decay and new life, *corruptio* and *generatio*. Just as in the physical realm every generation necessarily presupposes a previous corruption, so the historical process results from an annulment of or, better, transcendance of the past. Death and decay are the necessary preconditions for rebirth: renewal is only possible after death.[6]

This flux between life and death reverberated as an inner tension within Caroli. In the face of the present reality, which he felt deeply as the presence of death, the Dominican took refuge in the memory of the past. This is the point of departure for his dialogue with a fellow friar, Giacomo di Pietro, which occupies the second day. The long series of obituaries in the necrology of Santa Maria Novella, the ancient *Cronica fratrum,* is seen by Caroli as the uninterrupted thread of a centuries-long story. It is the story of a community that, since the early thirteenth century, developed as an active and vital organism, reaching the apex of its growth in the early fifteenth century and, having finally matured to full ripeness, rapidly declined toward death. Caroli sought to define the historical periods within this process, yet he was reluctant to accept his own conclusions: it is as if he hoped to save himself and his community from falling over the edge of a precipice; to prevent the present destruction by turning his gaze toward the past.

"When I consider the glory and the virtue of the brothers of old, I am ashamed to have been born in these times in which, within a single generation, I have seen the labor and sweat of those men sink as into the depths of the sea."[7]

At the end of the second day, Caroli collects his thoughts in the quiet of his cell. His reflections continue, now in the form of a monologue. His awareness of a past that no longer exists and of a present devoid of hope becomes anguish. And this mortal anguish, which Caroli would lull with sleep, returns to him in dreams. The third part of the *Liber dierum,* conceived "ad modum Sompnii Scipionis," is an oneiric vision rising from the depths of his soul, like a premonition of the future: the destruction of the architectural complex of Santa Maria Novella.[8]

A vast plain, lit by a huge moonbeam is revealed to the dreaming Caroli. In the middle of the plain, a mountain rises up. Conventual structures on the mountainside cluster around the church of Santa Maria Novella. The moonlight picks out the architectural outlines of the complex: the walls of the buildings, the vaults of the cloisters, the columnar arcades, the marble façade of the church; light reveals their angles and projections, their spatial volumes and their contents (Figure 18.1). While

Figure 18.1. Santa Maria Novella, view of the Chiostro Verde and flank of the church. Photo Alinari/Art Resource, N.Y.

the friar, fascinated, contemplates the splendid nocturnal vision, an immense horde encircles and attacks the monumental complex. The buildings, so harmoniously arranged and joined, collapse one after another as if torn apart stone by stone; nothing remains but an enormous pile of ruins and rubble, a wasteland of stones, broken columns, walls about to fall or already fallen. Now the moonlight penetrates even the most hidden places, picking out the remains of the broken buildings. The vaults of the vast complex have been rent and burst open; the great spaces are exposed, and will find no other closure than the vault of heaven.

The friar looks at the great ruin of what was once a famous artistic monument, erected and enlarged over the course of centuries (see Figure 7.1), and, thinking of Aeneas's exclamation at the sight of the rising Carthage, he recasts Virgil's lines in the negative: "Oh unfortunate those men whose city is in ruins."[9] At this point, three Dominicans appear. He recognizes his beloved master and friend, Antonino Pierozzi, dressed in bishop's robes, and Cardinal Giovanni Dominici, for Caroli, the last of the great men. The cardinal tries to alleviate the pain that weighs down the friar's spirit. But as he speaks, his words take on the character of general reflections about history, about the rise and fall of civic and religious institutions, and the transience of human affairs: "Who has ever seen, in human affairs, anything that has not undergone decadence and death? The curved line is not less real than the straight one. Thus vast and famous dominions of kings and cities, of peoples and dynasties, have bowed over and then become extinct. There can never be stability, for the straight is always accompanied by the curved. Where the moon reigns, there all is changeable and transient."[10]

HISTORIOGRAPHY
Origins and Method

The *Liber dierum lucensium,* as we have seen, becomes a discussion of the crisis of monasticism and, more precisely, of the organization of the mendicant orders. Whereas the antimonastic barbs and criticisms of the humanists were almost always cast in moral, and frequently in moralistic terms, charging the friars with hypocrisy, Caroli's criticism of monastic life is based on very different criteria. For him, the central issue is the loss of the historic role of the mendicants, and of religious orders in general, in the evolution of Florentine society from the commune to the Renaissance city-state. Caroli's criticism of the contemporary monastic institution is based on a decidedly historical view: the religious institution is in a phase of decadence because (as could happen to any institution) it has lost its historical relevance, and therefore its role within the new Renaissance society.

With this realization Caroli, who in the mid-1460s had returned to the convent in Florence, saw no alternative for action except to relive the story of the past in the present. In the 1470s, just a decade after its composition, the *Liber dierum* was rewritten and cast into new dimensions and a new context for his biographies of famous friars of Santa Maria Novella, the *Vite fratrum*. The primary source material for the *Vite* was drawn from the conventual necrology, and in Caroli's hands this necrology, the *Cronica fratrum,* became a tool for historical research. Just as Villani's *Chronicle* was reworked for the *Historia florentini populi* by Bruni, so Caroli subjects an early chronicle to the methods of humanist historiographic thought.[11]

Giovanni Dominici had warned Caroli about the decadent condition of the community of Santa Maria Novella, and the latter found the warning to be accurate. The spirit that had animated its founders was gone. The ancient kingdom of Priam — again a reference to Virgil's poem — had fallen into ruin because Pallas, goddess of wisdom, had abandoned it. The Florentine community, whose members, according to Caroli, were no more than shadows of their ancestors, had lost their love of divine truth and no longer searched for it. Hence the disintegration of their monastic and religious life and the decline of theological research and of that civic and cultural commitment which had been the vital arteries of their existence in past centuries.[12] Caroli compares himself to Aeneas who, having escaped the destruction of Troy, wanders in search of other shores. His wandering brings him to Hades, where he meets those men who had made the ancient city famous, those who had ennobled the now forever lost homeland. "In has describendas vitas descendi" is the opening phrase of Caroli's *Vite fratrum*.[13]

The work is a sylloge of seven biographies of men famous in the history of Santa Maria Novella, from its foundation in the first half of the thirteenth century up to the first decades of the fifteenth. The series is arranged chronologically. The first two biographies concern the "founders" of Santa Maria Novella, Giovanni da Salerno (d. 1242) and Aldobrandino Cavalcanti (d. 1279). These are followed by biographies of Simone Salterelli, bishop of Pisa (d. 1342), and of Angelo Acciaioli, bishop of Florence (d. 1357). The fifth and sixth biographies concern Alessandro Strozzi, master of theology (d. 1383), and Guido da Raggiolo, master of grammar (d. 1394). The seventh and last account is a life of Giovanni Dominici (b. 1355 or 1356 and d. 1419).

The whole collection is preceded by a letter of dedication to Cristoforo Landino; the individual biographies are preceded by prefaces, some of which are dedicated to Florentine humanists who were known to or friends of Caroli: Giorgio Antonio Vespucci, Donato Acciaioli, Roberto Buoninsegni and his son Giovan Battista, Francesco dei Berlinghieri. The series is introduced by a laudatory description — *laudatio domus* — of Santa Maria Novella, which ends with a discussion of the Pazzi conspiracy. The order in which the parts were composed does not correspond to the chronological succession of the lives in the final text. For example, the preface to the whole, the *laudatio domus,* and the sixth biography (of Guido da Raggiolo) were the last pieces to be written, dating from 1479 and early 1480. Composition of the whole work, as inferred from both internal and external evidence, can be dated within a five-year period from 1474 or 1475 to 1480 or 1481.[14]

So much for the overall structure and composition of Caroli's work. It is easy to see, even from these generalities, that, taken together, the *Vite fratrum* constitute a history of Santa Maria Novella from the thirteenth to the fifteenth centuries. This is apparent from the way the lives are correlated one with another and arranged in sequence; from the links traced among the various periods during which the seven individuals were active in the religious, civic, and cultural life of Florence; and from Caroli's interpretation of the architectural complex of Santa Maria Novella as having resulted from the cumulative patronage of these Dominican friars.

The real significance of this collection of lives is that it forms a biography, not so much of individuals, but of the monastic community itself within the context of the city of Florence, as an integral part of Florentine society. Or, to put this in terms that better define its historiographic importance, the *Vite fratrum* is a history of communal Florence from the thirteenth to the fifteenth century as preserved in the "memory" of the mendicant community of Santa Maria Novella and as told within the context of its tradition. It is this perspective that permits Caroli, while looking at the past, to articulate his thoughts about the current crises in the monastic and civic life of Renaissance Florence. This aspect of the *Vite fratrum* is particularly evident in the introductory pages and in the dedications: the *epistola* to Landino; the laudatio domus; and, above all, the prefaces to the individual biographies.

For Caroli, there was a profound difference between the cultural, civic, and political life of pre-Medicean Florence and that of his own late fifteenth-century Florence. The present, from these points of view, is the exact opposite of the past. In the single biographies, Caroli contrasts reality (Medicean Florence) with something approaching myth: the forever vanished past of the commune of Florence.

The boundary between past and present, reality and myth, can be fixed precisely in time: it corresponds to the coming of the Black Death. Caroli strongly emphasizes that the great wave of death which swept through medieval cities in the second half of the fourteenth century also swept away a period in history. Coincident in time with the Black Death was that dissolution of morals and religion which caused the disintegration of an era dedicated, as Caroli writes, to building both the physical and moral "structures" of society—"erigere domus et componere mores."[15] How does Caroli explain this decline that, for us, signifies the end of the Middle Ages? The reasons for it are many. First, there is the destiny of death intrinsic to all natural phenomena, and therefore, in Augustinian terms, intrinsic to the process of history. Next, there was the ecclesiastical schism occurring at the summit of the church hierarchy during the Avignon papacy, which introduced a rift that split open the whole structure of Western Christendom. But above all, according to Caroli, the ending of an epoch can be explained by the demographic devastation of the Black Death iñ 1348 and its recurrences in 1363, 1374, and 1400—this last being, he says, as widespread and lethal as the original 1348 epidemic. The high mortality broke the normal succession of generations, and consequently the cultural and spiritual continuity of civic and religious society. Further, it threatened the very survival of the conventual community which, like the city, had lost a generation of citizens. Both institutions survived, but the interruption of that continuous transmission of their respective cultural traditions entailed the loss of that which had defined them; thus an entire civilization lost its roots and its identity.[16]

The break in history caused by the Black Death meant the end of the communal period in Florence and the twilight of its cultural and civic grandeur. For Caroli, contemporary Florence, oligarchical and Medicean, was a decadent society in which the values that once determined its unique selfhood were no longer operative.

Caroli contrasts the merchant of the communal period with the magnate of the second half of the fifteenth century. The former practiced business according to criteria of austerity (both for himself and his family) and with a view to the good of the commune (in terms of social and civic relationships). The latter, the rich contemporary merchant, on the other hand, was concerned only for profit, political dominance, and social prestige for himself and his family clan. The way in which business affairs were conducted had changed utterly. Commercial transactions had experienced a moral regression, and these factors, acting on the whole spectrum of civic and political life, had resulted in a mutation in lifestyle and taste.

The products of the mechanical arts had also lost their original sobriety and authenticity. Divorced from its function of supplying objects of utility, artistic production had turned to the creation of useless ornaments that were ostentatious rather than splendid. Devoid of "veritas artis et decentia," these works were contrived and affected.[17] Thus, while the modern historian views the development of Renaissance art and architecture as the fruit of the most cultivated patronage, for this contemporary friar they were nothing but a waste of money, revealing petty ambitions for power. Caroli points to the love of the *ornatus,* to the pursuit of this quality in works of art after 1450, as a telling characteristic of contemporary culture. For him, this taste was part and parcel of the general decline in the quality of contemporary life and culture, and constituted further proof that society was regressing in terms of its values.

The Florentine merchant of the late fifteenth century is, then, seen in strong contrast to the austere merchant of the communal age. By the same token, the new rhetorician (the contemporary humanist) is accused of having betrayed the ethical-religious function of a training in letters. He had abandoned the aim of sobriety in linguistic expression, which had been the primary concern of the medieval master of grammar. This contrast between the grammar of Guido da Raggiolo and the rhetoric of the Renaissance humanist acquires the dimension of a paradigm: the new rhetorical training displays the whole spectrum of changes taking place in Florentine society. Caroli uses the same adjectives to describe the break between past and present as to define the difference between the traditional educational system of the *trivium* and *quadrivium* and the new humanist rhetoric.[18]

Coincident with the decline in the quality of civic life was the impoverishment of religious sentiment. Thus membership in a confraternity, which once fostered a serious Christian involvement, became the occasion for that bigotry which makes a mockery of faith. Even the liturgy had lost its profoundly religious and spiritual character, owing to the introduction of *cantus figuratus.* The new vocal polyphony, the complete opposite of the *gravitas urbana, dignitas,* and *devotio* of Gregorian chant, rendered the liturgical text incomprehensible, led to superficiality in terms of piety, and humiliated the solemn simplicity of the liturgy. The new rhetoric and vocal polyphony had thus crumbled the traditional language and ancient harmony of the world of the Florentine commune, the vanished world of the past which Caroli reconstructs as myth.[19]

It was above all in the sphere of political life that the decline of the city was most apparent. The aims of the Florentine aristocracy in public and private life are revealed in their patronage of palaces, intended to exalt the status of the family. Their concern with personal prestige extended to their expenditure on clothes for themselves and their servants, to their efforts to reinforce the network of clients attached to the family group, and to the planning of magnificent parties and receptions. Their ambition resulted in constant discord and factionalism in the citizens' magistracies. The Florentine oligarchy did not govern; it was no longer committed to the glory of the republic and the extension of its dominions. To the Florentine friar, good and bad government, growth or decline of civic life, could best be judged within Florence's most important and characteristic sphere of action: commerce. "It is through commerce that the city is innervated" writes Caroli. Here he repeats the traditional evaluation of *mercatura* which Salutati had already cast in ideal terms. If commerce is not conducive to the wellbeing of the whole social body, that body is weakened, and eventually the political and civic community will disintegrate and fall to pieces. The decadence of the city of Florence is, ultimately, the direct result of corrupt mercantile practices. It is within this context of criticism of the contemporary mercatura that Caroli, in his preface to the life of Alessio Strozzi, introduces the figure of the ideal Florentine citizen, Palla Strozzi. It seems, indeed, that the memory of Palla Strozzi informs all that Caroli says about the decadence of the present and the grandeur of the past. What he writes about Strozzi conforms to the common opinion held of him in Florence (and elsewhere) in the early fifteenth century. But in one particular Caroli's attitude toward Strozzi is unique: he describes the exile of this great Florentine citizen, heir of ancient moral virtue, as emblematic proof of the civic and political crisis of contemporary Florence. In the Dominican's view of history, Palla Strozzi's condemnation to exile represents the immorality of the present and its great rejection of the communal past.[20]

POLITICS AND THE BIOGRAPHIES

I have already touched on Caroli's delineation of Palla Strozzi in the *Vite fratrum*. That passage includes all the essential elements for a biographical account of Strozzi: his motivations, his personal idiosyncrasies, and his outstanding character traits. With Caroli, historical biography becomes the tool by which the past can be recaptured in terms relevant to the present.

The role of the individual and the acts of famous men, writes Caroli, have almost always been recounted by historians as inseparable from the civic and political history of the community. The historian's attention has been focused on the overall development of events. Hence the personal contributions of individual participants have, as it were, been absorbed into the history of the city. By contrast, biography seeks to make the unique quality of each individual as prominent as possible, using contemporary civic and political life as a backdrop for him. What interests the biographer is the path followed by a single person through life, even though that life is inextricably bound to that of the community. In brief, the history recounted by the biographer is not the same as that told by the historian of politics, even though the life of the individual is experienced within the events of the *civitas*.

Having thus defined the aims of biographical narrative, Caroli addresses the specific problem of religious biography. The men whose lives he records had little in common with the kinds of personalities whose deeds were praised in classical and Hellenistic biography. The latter were generals, founders of cities, rulers, or politicians, whose genealogy formed an important part of the account. As historical figures, these men inspired a great body of biographical literature, from Plutarch's *Lives* to accounts by Latin historians of ancient and modern times. But in the lives of the men about whom Caroli writes, what was there, he asks, to celebrate? What great deeds to praise? These men abjured all worldly glory; their actions did not strike their contemporaries as worthy of recording for posterity or, even now, as suitable subjects for rhetoric in the grand style.

Having defined the difference in nature between his subject matter and that of Plutarch's *Lives,* Caroli (urged on by his friend Giorgio Vespucci) composed his work according to criteria different from those that shaped non-Christian biography. The fundamental characteristics of the classical *bios* render it largely irrelevant for Caroli's purposes: it cannot be followed as a model; it cannot be the object of *imitatio* in the humanist mold. The men of the *Vite fratrum* elude attempts to describe them with the "sublime" language of ancient rhetoric; they claim positions as antiheroes. Their lives, their acts, had a totally different inspiration: the Gospels. The strength of these athletes and their ability to conquer were drawn from that *humilitas* which was the unique characteristic of Christ's disciples; here, writes Caroli, Greek eloquence founders. The passage in Paul where Greek wisdom is contrasted with the "folly" of the cross underlies Caroli's whole argument. Religious biography, then, acquires autonomy from classical biography because of its subject matter. It is not only the personages and the acts that change, but, above all, the ways in which these personages and acts are connected, requiring that they be evaluated within an entirely new dimension. Some formal aspects of the classical tradition are retained: for example, the concept of biography as the narration of a past life that serves as a model for the present. But here Caroli recognizes a significant difference between classical and Christian biography. Because of the spiritual unity of the Church, the evocation of the Christian "hero" of the past effects a necessary link between tradition and contemporary Christian practice. Thus the biographer, by recording the hero's life, fulfills its evangelical intent.[21]

These considerations regarding the method and significance of religious biography provide the structure for the *Vita* of Angelo Acciaioli, bishop of Florence from 1342 to 1355.[22] This biography, one of the best and most fully elaborated in the *Vite fratrum,* represents the climax of Caroli's work. The life, which was composed in 1477, is introduced by a long preface and dedicated to Donato Acciaioli, who,

more than other Florentine humanists of his generation, was distinguished by his literary taste and special skill in historical biography. With
this dedication, Caroli intended to return Acciaioli's compliment; in 1466,
the latter had dedicated the Latin version of some of Plutarch's *Lives*
to him.

The unifying theme of this life of Angelo Acciaioli — Florentine
bishop at the time of Walter of Brienne — is, precisely, the bishop and
the city. But this theme serves as more than a unifying element: it is
examined in depth, and in its various aspects.

The *dignitas* of the protagonist, at once citizen and priest, is
a constant point of reference in the narrative. His appearance and his
bearing made the charm of his personality visible to everyone: "In him,
the splendor of his limpid gaze, the decorum of his aspect were remarkable. The tone of his voice was humane, his speech was full of
meekness and devotion and piety. His comportment was gracious and
dignified."[23]

Acciaioli was one of the ringleaders of the rebellion against the
tyrant Walter of Brienne. Thus he acted as a "prince" of freedom —
"princeps libertatis" — says Caroli, borrowing the expression from Bruni.
The restoration of Florentine liberty (6 August 1343) saw the re-emergence
of struggles between magnates and *popolani*. The bishop exhorted both
sides to *concordia,* for the civic and political life of the commune could
not exist without harmony among the various classes. The *oratio* delivered by the bishop on this subject constitutes the most significant
political analysis in the *Vite fratrum*. Acciaioli's discourse provides the
occasion for Caroli's criticism of the oligarchic rule of contemporary
Florence, full of historical references to past and present and citations
from classical and scriptural texts, and thickly woven with political and
theoretical ideas. The oratio failed to bring about concordia between
the opposed factions of fourteenth-century Florence and had no decisive
influence on the communal life of the city. The bishop who championed
Florentine liberty would end his life in exile, far from his city, while
Florence declined in the course of the later fourteenth century toward
that great political and civil crisis, the Ciompi revolt. As a historian,
Caroli realizes that his own criticism of late fifteenth-century Florentine politics would not be heeded and that his native city would again
decline into factionalism and civil crisis.

In composing the life of Bishop Acciaioli, Caroli drew his source material primarily from the chronicles of Giovanni Villani and Marchionne di Coppo Stefani, and from Bruni's *History* of Florence. From Bruni, Caroli drew in particular the thematic material for the biography: the idea of the Dominican bishop as defender of communal liberty and champion of popular government. From Villani, Caroli took the sequence of events concerning the rise and fall of the duke of Athens. But in Caroli's version, more attention is given to the actions of individuals and more emphasis laid on the desires and feelings expressed in political struggles. Stefani's *Cronaca fiorentina,* in which the bishop is described as "a very good, but weak man," stung Caroli into making his biography an apology for Acciaioli. In his political analysis of the Florentine crisis, he attempts to demonstrate that Acciaioli's actions—before, during and after the dictatorship of the duke of Athens—were decisive in the restoration of communal liberty. The actions of the bishop, Caroli concludes, were a turning point in the history of Florence, and for its civic and political institutions. Caroli's analysis brought into prominence a significant aspect, perhaps even the core, of the whole problem of the interpretation of Walter of Brienne's rule and of the events that followed it.

CONCLUSION

As I have said, the biography of Angelo Acciaioli represents the high point of the *Vite fratrum.* And here, in the climax of his work, Caroli seems to resolve his own personal crisis, which had arisen from his opposition to Auribelli. In the rest of the *Lives,* the Dominican progressively reconciles himself to his own choices in life, and changes his stance in relation to the civic and political context of contemporary Florence.

The seventh and last biography, that of Dominici, was written just after the biography of Acciaioli in the last months of 1477.[24] Here Caroli returns to the ideal of the religious and Dominican life as exemplar for a fully authentic life of service to the civic and Christian community. Probably these pages were written for Francesco di Niccolò Berlinghieri, the well-known geographer and Florentine humanist in the circle of Ficino and the Platonic Academy.[25] To Francesco Berlinghieri, committed to cultural values and aspiring to a more intense spiritual life, Caroli proposes the model of the life of Giovanni Dominici. By this time, the author of the *Vite fratrum* had come to see the monastic vocation as a privileged and practically obligatory choice: only within conventual life, and as a member of a mendicant order, was it possible to achieve an ideal synthesis of culture and moral life aimed at the common good of the city. Caroli is not speaking here in terms of an opposition of the active with the contemplative life, or of religious vocation with marriage. On the contrary, the life of the mendicant friar is seen as active in the highest degree: a life in which contemplation is transformed and made concrete through action. In my opinion, Caroli's insistence on this life choice, the reasons for it which he adduces, and certain classical references recall parts of Petrarch's *De vita solitaria*.[26]

Caroli's new point of view is most clearly evident in the *Laudatio domus*, the extended description of the architectural complex of Santa Maria Novella and of the monastic life going on within its walls. Written between 1479 and 1480, and constituting perhaps the most moving passage of the *Vite fratrum*, the *Laudatio domus* is modeled on the *Laudatio florentine urbis* by Leonardo Bruni, although it possesses a strongly original character of its own.[27] This eulogy of the "dignitas domus" opens (once again) with a reference to the *Aeneid*: to those same verses of Virgil's poem which Caroli had pronounced in his dream of the destruction of Santa Maria Novella, recorded in the *Liber dierum*. But this time, Aeneas's words in front of the rising Carthage are quoted without reversing their meaning: "Happy those whose walls already rise / cries Aeneas, lifting his eyes to the city roofs."[28] In the *Laudatio domus*, Caroli constantly stresses the relation between the gradual completion of the architectural complex of Santa Maria Novella and the history of Florence over the same centuries. He emphasizes the impact of Dominican culture on the political life of the city. And thus, in these terms, he sees the original function of the Dominican convent as fulfilled in the larger community of the Florentine people. He now declares that this role is still waiting, reversing his earlier pessimism and marking a change in his attitude toward contemporary Florence. Undoubtedly, the decisive event that reversed his stance was the Pazzi conspiracy, occurring as he was completing the *Vite fratrum*. The dramatic events in the cathe-

dral—the assassination of Giuliano and attempt on the life of Lorenzo—
are the subject of the last pages of the *Laudatio domus*.

The priesthood, says Caroli, is guilty at every level of its hierarchy, from the pope to the lowest order of secular clergy, of lese maj-
esty. As the principal catalyst of the anti-Medicean conspiracy, clerical
power was used in violation of every code of law: not only canon and
civic law, but also natural law. This power desecrated the cathedral of
the city in the most solemn moment of the liturgy, and attempted to
eliminate by death those who governed the signoria by legitimate right.
The conspiracy attempted to throw into chaos the peaceful and serene
status of Florence, and to stain the honor of Italy and Christendom:
"pacificum et tranquillum civitatis statum tanta sevitia perturbare ac
totius pene Italie et christiane religionis honorem in dedecus et infamiam
evocare."[29] The antiecclesiastical backlash on the part of the civil
authorities, a consequence of the conspiracy, is considered more than
justified by Caroli who, by the way, had been an eyewitness to the events
in the cathedral.

After the events of April 1478, Caroli identified the legitimate
Florentine government with the Medicean oligarchy, firmly opposing
political interference by the Church or the pope. This turnabout had
a decisive influence on the later writings of Caroli, from the early 1480s
until his death in 1503, altering their content in highly significant ways.

NOTES

For the English version of this essay, and for bibliographical suggestions, the author wishes to thank Professors Christine Smith, Edward Chaney, and William
Hood, friends and colleagues in research at the Harvard Center for Italian Renaissance
Studies, Villa I Tatti, Florence. Particular gratitude is due to Melissa M. Bullard; our
conversations about Caroli have had a determining influence on this paper, as they
have on my other two essays devoted to the Florentine Dominican. The notes to this
essay were put into English by Timothy Verdon.

1. This essay takes up again research and documentation treated fully, with unpublished texts given in appendixes, in S. I. Camporeale, "Giovanni Caroli e le 'Vitae fratrum
S.M. Novellae': Umanesimo e crisi religiosa, 1460–80," *Memorie domenicane*, n.s. 12 (1981): 141–
267 (of which pp. 236–67 form the appendix); and idem, "Giovanni Caroli: Dal 'Liber dierum'
alle 'Vitae fratrum,'" *Memorie domenicane*, n.s. 16 (1985): 199–233; (of which pp. 218–33 form

the appendix). These essays will be referred to henceforth as "Caroli (1981)" and "Caroli (1985)" respectively. Still basic to study of Caroli's life and published and unpublished works is S. Orlandi, O.P., *Necrologio di Sta. Maria Novella: 1235–1504,* 2 vols. (Florence: Olschki, 1955), 1:203–5 (text); 2:353–80 (commentary). Other significant studies include G. Pomaro, "Censimento dei manoscritti della Biblioteca di S.M. Novella: 1. Origini e trecento," *Memorie domenicane,* n.s. 11 (1980): 325–470; and idem, "Censimento dei manoscritti della Biblioteca di S.M. Novella: 2. Secoli XV–XVI," *Memorie domenicane, n.s. 13* (1982): 203–353. These two articles are hereafter referred to as "Censimento 1" and "Censimento 2" respectively; in both, see the onomastic indexes *s.v.* "Johannes Caroli."

2. The autograph version of Caroli's *Liber dierum lucensium* is contained in a manuscript originally from the convent of Sta. Maria Novella and now in the Biblioteca nazionale centrale of Florence (hereafter BNF), Conventi Religiosi Soppressi, C.8.279, fols. 1r–56v. There also exists an autograph version (incomplete) of the *Vite nonnullorum fratrum beate Marie Novelle,* in a manuscript in the Biblioteca Laurenziana, Florence: Plut. 89, inf. 21. Missing from the Laurentian MS, however, are two of the seven biographies that make up the complete *Vitae fratrum:* the *Vita Angeli Acciaioli* and the *Vita Johannis Dominici.* These two Lives can be found in manuscripts in the Vatican Library: the fifteenth-century MS. Cod. Vat. Lat. 8808 (with the Life of Angelo Acciaioli, fols. 95 ff.), and the sixteenth-century MS. Cod. Vat. Lat. 6329 (with the Life of Giovanni Dominici, fols. 280 ff.). In addition, there is a copy of the *Vitae fratrum* made from the autograph version and checked by Caroli himself, containing all seven biographies, in a manuscript in the Archive of Sta. Maria Novella, in Florence: Cod. SMN, Fifteenth Century. On the manuscript tradition and history of the editions of these two works, see Camporeale, "Caroli (1981)," 148 ff., 161 ff.; and Pomaro, "Censimento 2," 239 f., 307 f., 309 f. References in this essay to Caroli's two works are, for the *Liber dierum,* to the BNF, Conventi Soppressi, C.8.279; and for the *Vite fratrum,* to the Convent MS., Cod. SMN. These will be referred to henceforth as "Caroli, *Liber,*" and "Caroli, *Vite*" respectively, with modern or Renaissance pagination or foliation indicated.

3. R. Creytens, "La déposition de Maître Martial Auribelli, O.P., par Pie II (1462)," *Archivium Fratrum Praedicatorum* 45 (1975): 147–200. Cf. Enea Silvio Piccolomini (Pius II), *I Commentari,* ed. L. Totaro (Milan: Adelphi, 1984), 659 and esp. 1941–45.

4. "Cum memorabilis illa flebilisque domus et familie nostre ruina mihi, urbe excluso, Luce exilium detulisset, unaque mecum Jacobus Petri ex eodem vix excidio liberatus venisset, comiter et perhumane a fratribus excepti, in studiis humanitatis tempus hyemale transegimus." Caroli, *Liber,* fol. 4v; Camporeale, "Caroli(1981)," 144, 147–50.

5. Caroli, *Liber,* fols. 1r–4v; Camporeale, "Caroli(1981)," 148, 150–52.

6. Caroli, *Liber,* fols. 4v–34v; Camporeale, "Caroli(1981)," 149, 152–56.

7. Caroli, *Liber,* fols. 34v–42v; Camporeale, "Caroli(1981)," 149, 156–60.

8. Caroli, *Liber,* fols. 42v–56v; Camporeale, "Caroli(1981)," 149–50, 159–61. Caroli titles this "third part" of the *Liber dierum* "liber tertius dierum lucensium . . . Continet autem presentium temporum conditionem: Ad modum Sompnij Scipionis" (fol. 42v). It is published in my "Caroli (1985)," and all future references to the third part of the *Liber dierum* will be to my edition of it there.

9. Cf. *Aeneid* 1:423–38. The English translation given below is from the Loeb Classical Library edition: *Virgil,* 2 vols., trans. H. Rushton Fairclough (London: Heinemann, 1916). Virgil's verse 1:437, "O fortunati quorum iam menia surgunt," is given a new sense by Caroli:

"Maronis illud carmen, diversa tamen sententia, sese animo ingerebat 'O *in*fortunati, quorum iam menia *ruunt*'," *Liber (tertius) dierum,* fol. 45v; Camporeale, "Caroli (1985)," 203 f., 219–221.

10. Caroli, *Liber (tertius) dierum,* fols. 47v–48r; Camporeale, "Caroli (1985)," 206, 224.

11. Camporeale, "Caroli (1981)," 156–59, 160–61, 176–78.

12. Caroli, *Liber (tertius) dierum,* fols. 46v–48r; Camporeale, "Caroli (1985)," 205, 222–24.

13. Here is Caroli's own text: "Cum sepenumero et corpore et animo perturbarer, eo libentius in has describendas vitas descendi, quo et nostrorum causam facto isto aliqua ex parte tueri viderer et conceptum animi languorem mestitiamque adimere, vel certe hac honesta oblectatione lenire." Caroli, *Vite,* 13–14; Camporeale, "Caroli (1981)," 190, 244.

14. Camporeale, "Caroli (1981)," 161–78; the appendix on pp. 236–67 publishes from the *Vite fratrum:* (1) the dedicatory epistle to Landino, (2) the laudatio domus, (3) the *prefationes* to the seven individual biographies that make up Caroli's whole work.

15. "Periit quidem pene omnis illa priscorum patrum sancta devotio, qua ad erigendas domos et componendos mores ardentissime ferebantur." See Caroli, *Vite,* 11; Camporeale, "Caroli (1981)," 189, 243.

16. Camporeale, "Caroli (1981)," 192–97.

17. "Artes quoque, quas mechanicas vocant, summa fide et integritate quondam homines exercebant; nunc autem fucata omnia ac ficta, et ad ostentationem magis quam ad veritatem artisque decentiam facta. Quis ergo iniuria dixerit hanc nostram inter et superiorem etatem distare plurimum, quando quidem tam varie tam insulse tamque perdite omnia cernimus immutata?" See Caroli, *Vite,* 213; Camporeale, "Caroli (1981)," 221, 258.

18. Camporeale, "Caroli (1981)," 224–28.

19. "Qua in re non satis etiam probo id quod in non nullis nostre civitatis hominibus abunde observari ingenti multorum concursu videmus, ubi figuratis—ut aiunt—melodiis et consonantiis vel propheticos psalmos vel divinos hymnos decantare consuescunt: auribus hominum blandientes et multitudinem inani illo allicientes cibo. . . . At multo melius certe fuerat, sanctorum patrum vestigiis inherentes, cantu illo—ut dicunt—firmo ac proinde gravi ac solido laudibus divinis devote insistere, ne per insolentiam aut levitatem noster animus evagetur, quam figurato illo, levi atque infirmo, effluere atque labi ac tandem nihil spiritualis fructus secum afferre. Neque vero hoc ideo dixerim, quo decantantes Divinitati hymnos ac Deo psallentes vituperem; sed velim ista, cum gravitate atque devotione cumque cordis fervore, cum reverentia et Divinitatis honore, cantari. Cum enim hiis vel Deo gratias agamus vel ipsum magnificis laudibus prosequamur, quemadmodum ista hominibus nequaquam leviter exhibenda censemus, at loca et tempora observamus, cumque hiis utimur, urbana quadam gravitate verborum id agimus, ita Deo et longe magis quam hominibus exhibenda profecto sunt." Caroli, *Vite,* fols. 251v–52r; Camporeale, "Caroli (1981)," 228–29, 261.

20. Camporeale, "Caroli (1981)," 216–23.

21. Ibid., 199–207, 249–51.

22. Orlandi, *Necrologio,* 1:89 f. (death notice), 1:472–91 (biography). See also "Angelo Acciaioli," in *Dizionario biografico italiano,* 31 vols. (Rome: Istituto dell'Enciclopedia italiana, 1960–85), 1:75 f. (article ed. A. d'Addario, 1960).

23. I have already given ample treatment to Caroli's biography of Angelo Acciaioli,

discussed here, in Camporeale, "Caroli (1981)," 171–72, 207–16, 251–55. The Latin text cited above is in Caroli, *Vite*, 146–47.

24. Camporeale, "Caroli (1981)," 229–32, 262–67.

25. See "Francesco di Niccolò Berlinghieri," ed. A. Codazzi, 1967, in the *Dizionario biografico italiano*, 9:121–24.

26. See T. O. Calhoun, "*De vita solitaria, Alieniloquium*, and Petrarch's *Canzoniere*," *Italian Quarterly* 23, 87 (1982): 21–32.

27. The text of the laudatio domus is taken from Caroli, *Vite*, 5–14. See Camporeale, "Caroli (1981)," 239–44, and my analysis, 178–91.

28. See note 9 above.

29. Caroli, *Vite*, 12–13; Camporeale, "Caroli (1981)," 243–44.

19

MARSILIO FICINO AND THE MEDICI
The Inner Dimensions of Patronage

MELISSA MERIAM BULLARD

T HE SENSE OF SOCIAL TRAUMA resulting from the new understanding and use of power in late quattrocento Florence discussed in the preceding essay had private as well as public repercussions. In this chapter, Mellissa Meriam Bullard analyzes the changing relationship between a foremost humanist of the age, Marsilio Ficino — priest, classical scholar, and philosopher — and Lorenzo de' Medici, grandson of Ficino's first patron. From the fine detail and sensitive reflection of Professor Bullard's pages emerges a picture of the ethical quandary of the "subsidized scholar" in an era passing rapidly from egalitarian to princely standards. At a still deeper level, this chapter articulates the dynamics of a human friendship based on Christian and humanist ideals, in which each participant holds true to what he perceives as the moral imperatives of his state in life.

MELISSA MERIAM BULLARD is associate professor of history at the University of North Carolina at Chapel Hill. In 1980, Cambridge University Press published her study, *Filippo Strozzi and the Medici: Favor and Finance in Sixteenth-Century Florence and Rome.*

 OVERS OF WISDOM cannot achieve much without good princes, nor again can those princes govern the state without wise men." Giovanni Corsi used this paraphrase from Plato's *Republic* in his biography of Marsilio Ficino in 1506 to describe Ficino's long and fecund relationship with the Medici family, which had begun when Cosimo had selected the young son of his personal physician to become a master of Plato in Florence, and which continued through three generations of his descendants, until Ficino's death in 1499.[1] Corsi's description seems particularly suited to Ficino's relationship with the young Lorenzo de' Medici in the 1460s and 1470s, during the period in which the young Medici "prince" and the Platonic philosopher, sixteen years his senior, developed a close friendship. Lorenzo participated in the informal gatherings known as the Platonic Academy, and he had perhaps been an inspiration behind the famous banquet of 1468, celebrating Plato's birth and death.[2] He must have been among the devoted group of young men with whom Ficino held discussions about love in the Socratic manner, described by Corsi in his biography, for in his own *Altercazione,* set in dialogue script, Lorenzo placed a lengthy discourse on love in the mouth of Ficino.[3] He also saw to Ficino's material needs, securing for him two modest benefices following his ordination as a priest in 1473.[4] During 1474 the intensity of their letters reached a new peak, and it seemed as though Lorenzo had indeed found his perfect Platonic philosopher-guide in Ficino. Equally touching is Ficino's almost paternal affection for the young Medici, who, since the death of his father Piero in 1469, had been left at only twenty-one years of age to direct his family's affairs and to assume political leadership of Florence.

But something changed. After 1474 Lorenzo ceased to write to Ficino. Ficino wrote several brief letters to Lorenzo between then and 1482; then he too fell silent. There is no record in the registers of Lorenzo's letters that he ever wrote Ficino again. The trauma of the Pazzi Conspiracy and war with the papacy had intervened, and scholars

468

speculate that the silence between them indicated a growing estrangement, especially after some of Ficino's friends were implicated in the Conspiracy. Ficino's own political sympathies may have lain on the side of those who were critical of Lorenzo's growing hegemony over the city.[5] Ficino no longer appears among Lorenzo's innermost circle of friends, and the fact that Filippo Valori, not Lorenzo, financed the publication of Ficino's writings seems to indicate that Lorenzo was showing much less interest in being his patron, in studied contrast to the encouragement and active support given Ficino by Lorenzo's grandfather Cosimo, or even his father Piero. That Ficino, in his public statements, in prefaces, and in letters to others, remained outwardly loyal to the Medici family has been taken as a sign of his continuing dependency upon them, a dependency inclined toward obsequiousness, that common affliction among late fifteenth-century humanists forced to rely upon their patrons for positions and for their livelihood.[6]

Too little is known about Ficino's relationship with Lorenzo in later years. Research in the Medici family archives, however, has recently turned up new material relative to Lorenzo's patronage of Ficino in late 1487, indicating that their relationship had continued but in a more puzzling and complex manner than the preceding narrative would imply. The information, contained in part in a previously unidentified letter of Lorenzo to the Florentine ambassador in Rome, concerns his attempts to secure an additional benefice for Ficino from the pope. In October 1487, Lorenzo wrote to Giovanni Lanfredini, directing him to request the pope as a personal favor to grant a special dispensation allowing Ficino to hold a third curacy. He mentioned the bishopric of Cortona which might soon be vacated. "Bear in mind that this idea is entirely my own. I have not discussed it with him [Ficino], and I want the matter taken care of before he or anyone else learns of it."[7]

The hush surrounding the matter and the way Lorenzo pursued it is unusual, since he normally handled his requests for papal favor in a much more public manner. Successful petitions helped bolster his reputation and visibility. Even if a particular supplication or dispensation should be denied, public knowledge that Lorenzo had written a letter of recommendation was marketable proof of a person's good standing. In fact, after Lorenzo's daughter Maddalena became engaged to Innocent VIII's son, Franceschetto Cibo, everyone from the king of France to a prospective general of the Augustinian order who needed a favor at the Vatican sought it through Lorenzo's mediation. Anything Lorenzo could get for the king of France, as he did not hesitate to remind the ambassador on more than one occasion, would make him look good and bring him increased public honor.[8] In the same letter in which he privately requested the dispensation for Ficino, he instructed Lanfredini to screen the other recommendations he sent so as not to trouble the pope excessively. Given his position, and the reputation as power broker he sought to maintain, he could not refuse to write the many letters people requested, but he clearly did not expect that all should actually be pursued with the pope.[9] In the following weeks, he wrote Lanfredini about Ficino's dispensation twice more, reminding the ambassador how highly he esteemed messer Marsilio and recommending his doctrine and exemplary way of life to the pope. He also reaffirmed his desire to give Ficino a "beneficietto," a "little benefice" about to be vacated.[10] Lanfredini wrote back, "It is going to require some effort, but I hope to be able to get it [the dispensation]."

According to canon law, a cleric could not simultaneously hold three benefices involving the care of souls. To begin the appeal for special dispensation, Lanfredini needed a list of the titles and value of Ficino's other two benefices and the name of the third if Lorenzo could divulge it.[11] Lorenzo sent the information immediately by return post, and six days later, on 16 November, the ambassador announced success, reporting that he hoped to arrange the expedition of the dispensation the following week.[12] Ficino's new benefice was not a bishopric, but that of canon of the cathedral of Florence, a position previously held by Lorenzo's son Giovanni, who vacated it for Ficino.[13]

The benefice and the way Lorenzo procured it, together with other information about their post-1487 relationship, seems to indicate that he and Ficino were hardly estranged. After 1487, Ficino was frequenting the Medici palace (Figure 19.1), for there is record of him among the small number of honored guests invited to dine with Ermolao Barbaro on his way to Rome in 1490.[14] When the German scholar Martin Prenninger asked him to name his friends, Ficino unhesitatingly placed the Medici in the very top category of those closest to him, and when Lorenzo died in 1492 Ficino openly expressed his personal grief and sorrow at Florence's loss of so great a man.[15]

Figure 19.1. Michelozzo, courtyard of Palazzo Medici in the Via Larga, designed for Cosimo the Elder. View from the garden toward Via Cavour. Photo Alinari/Art Resource, N.Y.

It is tempting to assume that the documents of 1487 signaled a healing of the old rift between them and that Lorenzo's desire to provide for Ficino, notably by giving him a prebend that had been in the

Medici family for generations, rose more out of genuine loyalty to his old friend than from the largesse of the powerful *signore* of Florence in response to the financial plight of a dependent client. Still the quiet manner in which Lorenzo went about it is curious, especially in that he did not want Ficino to know anything beforehand. We are led to wonder whether there was not still some awkwardness in their relationship and whether Ficino might have felt uncomfortable accepting Lorenzo's gift had it been handled in a more public manner. We can only speculate about what kind of pas de deux they were engaged in in 1487, but a broader examination of Ficino's long association with the Medici family might at least lend perspective to the complex nature of patron/client relationships during the second half of the fifteenth century.

Private patronage provided the structure within which most Renaissance humanists like Ficino lived and wrote. In the fifteenth century in particular, men of letters and artists found new avenues of protection and support in their personal patrons; this in turn helped stimulate that efflorescence of culture we call the Renaissance. A Maecenas could permit them to study and work outside the older ecclesiastical and university structures and urban chancelleries where many intellectuals found employment. There were few men like Count Pico della Mirandola who had the private resources to study independently. The majority, people like Ficino, the Pulci brothers, Poliziano, and Landino, had to find a Maecenas. The development of Christian Neoplatonism in the fifteenth century in particular was tied to private patronage. Since the new interest in Platonic studies had not yet found a place in the universities, where the Aristotelian tradition had flourished from the thirteenth century on, for someone like Ficino to be able to study Plato in depth, he had to place himself under the protection of rich persons who professed a special interest in the new humanist culture. Ficino owed his studies of Plato to Cosimo de' Medici, something he never forgot. At various times he made references to the fact that he had two fathers, his natural father, Ficino the physician, from whom he was born, and Cosimo de' Medici, from whom he was reborn when Cosimo gave him the means to dedicate himself to the study of Plato.[16] In this sense, private patronage is indissolubly linked to Florentine Neoplatonism, creating the ambience within which the new humanism developed.

Ficino's own connection with his Medici patrons lasted nearly fifty years and covered the entire development of his thought and writing.

The new creative space offered by private patronage has very complex and subtle dimensions that merit further discussion, especially since, unfortunately, they are usually treated in a reductive manner by historians, who are more interested in the cultural products of patronage and in its outward social and economic forms than in the personal dynamics of a rapport between two individuals. It is a temptation, for example, among some art historians whose major concern is the product, the work of art, to consider the relationship between the artist and his benefactor not in itself, but primarily as a specific and characteristic factor of production. Typical of this approach is the analysis of artists' contracts with the purpose of determining precisely how much the patron participated in defining the program and materials needed for the work of art. In this way, the rapport between artist and Maecenas is considered not for its own sake but in relation to those material aspects that facilitated artistic productivity.[17]

A second approach to patronage and culture is more characteristic of historians of literature and ideas. It resembles the first insofar as attention is focused upon the cultural product, in this case the thought of a particular humanist, which is studied by itself, divorced from the particular historical and personal context out of which it was born. Often the circumstances under which the humanist wrote, such as his relationship with his benefactor, are not considered as impinging upon the process of conceptualization or the composition of a particular literary piece. There have been many valuable analyses of Ficino's thought of this genre,[18] but few attempts to explore the connections between how he wrote and the patronage system within which he lived.

Even though the contribution of private patronage to Renaissance culture has been recognized since the era of the humanists themselves, the way in which it functioned as the basis, or underlying structure, of the Renaissance world, and how it penetrated not only culture but almost every other aspect of that society, needs greater emphasis. Recently, a number of historians have studied the patronage relationship from the standpoint of its social and political roles, emphasizing particularly its hierarchical structure. This approach has even led one historian to argue that the variety of sometimes conflicting political views expressed by humanists can be understood to derive essentially from their dependency upon their patrons.[19] Another has studied the social role of patronage of the visual arts in a provincial court to show how it reflected and reinforced the exclusive, precious, and despotic style of the duke.[20] As valuable as these studies are in broadening our appreciation of the many varieties of patronage, their exclusive attention to the external forms and products of the relationship does not help us understand how patronage actually functioned from the inside any more than a study of a finished painting can tell us everything about the vital process of its formation. To give an example, in earlier researches on finance and banking under the Medici popes in the sixteenth century, I discovered that Renaissance economics, like Renaissance culture, could not have existed or functioned apart from the favor of powerful patrons. But beyond that, the key to understanding papal high finance, the meteoric careers and enormous wealth of some papal bankers, lay precisely in the highly subjective nature of the personal bonds that they established with various popes. A modern economic analysis of banking or of the Florentine and Roman economies of the period based upon the supposition that market forces operate almost independently of other factors in society, would not have been able to explain the economic power at the papal court of such a person as Filippo Strozzi. Contemporary documents, particularly his private letters, clearly show that Strozzi owed his position and opportunities for financial investments to his intimate, personal ties of friendship with the family of Leo X.[21] The crucial, dynamic element lying at the heart of a Renaissance patronage relationship, and necessary to our understanding of Ficino's relationship with the Medici, is its essential subjectivity and reciprocity. It is precisely this element that has been overlooked in recent analyses of patronage, which focus simply on its external, structural, and materialistic aspects.[22]

Inasmuch as patronage provided a foundation for the new humanistic culture in fifteenth-century Florence, it lent a distinctive stamp to Ficino's and other humanists' writings. The kinds of classical models, especially from epideictic rhetoric and history, which the humanists chose to emulate were not unrelated to the inner requirements of their relationships with their patrons. That relationship often required the humanist to praise and glorify his benefactor and establish an identification between the Maecenas and the new humanist culture. On the other side, it required the patron's active interest and support for the humanist's studies.

The letters and laudatory dedications that compare the patron to a god or to the sun sound extreme or overly fawning to our ears, but they constitute part of a rhetorical language that reflected the very nature of the patronage relationship. In 1477, when Ficino was suffering from cataracts, he wrote to Lorenzo lamenting the diminution of his vision. He compared Lorenzo to a fountain of restorative light and to Ananias, who had cured Paul of his blindness. Ficino took the occasion of his illness to solicit Lorenzo's sympathy and favor, but not so much to obtain material assistance for himself. Through the allegory of blindness and by virtue of their friendship, he wanted to evoke Lorenzo's more active participation in favoring with his "light" the pursuit of philosophical studies and culture in general.[23]

In his analysis of Ficino's philosophy, Kristeller has rightly stressed Ficino's metaphorical, poetical language as the philosophical medium which he used to express his metaphysics of interiority, or spiritual consciousness, and his understanding of the problem of the soul.[24] The same style of symbolic language in his letters must likewise be considered as more than just a pleasing literary device. As in the example given here, the metaphor functions on two levels. On the surface it mirrors the hierarchical structure of the patronage system within which Ficino lived, but at the same time, on a deeper level, it conveys the content of his ethical position in regard to Lorenzo. The inner, symbolic dimension of his language provides the key to how Ficino chose to orient himself morally and spiritually in relation to his patrons.

Patronage relationships in the Renaissance also characteristically required the full participation and reciprocity of both benefactor and client. This is an aspect of the relationship which Ficino's biographer Giovanni Corsi took for granted but which modern society has lost sight of. Renaissance patronage operated very differently from the modern system, where support for the arts and culture has been transformed by its passage into the hands of the state and large foundations. Even though these institutions exercise control through their choice of who is worthy of support, there is no longer direct participation and personal interest on the part of the patrons in the individuals whom they sponsor. In the Renaissance, by contrast, patronage did not flow in just one direction—that is, from the patron toward his client—but also from the beneficiary toward the benefactor. In the case of Ficino, it would be misleading to restrict our gaze to the material support the Medici gave him. Ficino received impressive gifts from Cosimo—a villa on Medici property at Careggi and a house in Florence—which enabled him to carry out his translations of Greek philosophers; but in addition Cosimo shared a fascination in Plato with Ficino and supported his studies for that reason as well. For his part Ficino reciprocated by giving Cosimo his friendship and instruction and by engaging him in philosophical discussions, which he himself tells us lasted over a period of a dozen years.[25] Cosimo was not just a patron to Ficino in the limited sense; he was also a friend.

The lasting friendship between them, with all the personal commitment and mutual respect the word implies, constitutes the larger context of Renaissance patronage which I want to emphasize. To Ficino, Cosimo was a true Maecenas in the sense that the first Maecenas of Rome, also rich and powerful, had helped such men of letters as Horace out of friendship for them.[26] How else can we explain the moving eulogies that Horace wrote about Maecenas or Ficino about Cosimo? When Ficino told Cosimo's grandson Lorenzo that he had never had a person closer or more dear to him than Cosimo, he was being sincere, not simply adulatory.[27] The experience of friendship which Ficino had with Cosimo, and with others, helps to explain why in his letters and treatises and in his very way of life he placed so much emphasis on being a good friend, and why, in general, humanists, most of them in close and intimate relationships with their patron/friends, stressed the theme of friendship in their writings. They would not have picked up the subject from classical antiquity simply for an empty intellectual exercise or to be obsequious and to please their benefactors; friendship was a theme from classical literature which corresponded to their own experience. Ficino devoted numerous letters to it, and he was fond of saying that whereas reading Plato had once taught him about the concept of virtue, only through the personal experience of knowing Cosimo had he truly understood what a life lived virtuously day by day entailed.[28] Ficino's conscious recognition of the educational value of the subjective, personal experience of friendship was a characteristic attitude of Renaissance humanists.

Ficino's relationship with Cosimo had had its beginnings in their mutual interest in Plato. For Ficino, the informal encounters with friends at Careggi, the so-called Platonic Academy, and Cosimo were inseparable, and he imagined the academy to be a temple of contemplation in which to celebrate the spirit of Plato together with that of Cosimo.[29] Ficino dedicated his first translations of the *Dialogues* of Plato to Cosimo, and Vespasiano da Bisticci tells us that when Cosimo fell ill toward the end of his life and was spending most of his time at his villas at Careggi and Caffagiolo, his friends, among them Ficino, used to visit him and discuss philosophy.[30] In a letter of 1464, Cosimo specifically requested that Ficino read to him from Plato, "because," he wrote, "I want nothing more than to learn the path to true happiness."[31]

The experience of close personal friendship with Cosimo, despite the difference in their ages, made a deep impression on Ficino and left him in anguish when Cosimo died in 1464. There are intimations of how much Ficino suffered at the loss of his friend in the dedication to his translation of Xenocrates' treatise on death. Ficino had read portions of his translation to Cosimo shortly before he died. When he finished the work, Ficino dedicated it to Piero de' Medici. In the dedication, Ficino placed in Piero all his hopes for finding a new Cosimo. He wished him a long life filled with prudence and piety for the good of Florence and of the academy at Careggi, "so that," he wrote, "we will feel that Cosimo has never left us."[32]

No patronage relationship, especially one like Ficino's, spreading over four generations of Cosimo's family, was without its vicissitudes. Ficino could hardly have expected to find another Cosimo. But his attempts to work out a *modus vivendi* with each of Cosimo's heirs allows us a unique opportunity to observe changes in his attitudes toward his benefactors, changes that were partly personal, partly indicative of subtle mutations in the general practice of patronage in the late fifteenth century in the direction of the more institutionalized forms of the court.

To start with, Ficino was sensitive to the moral and material problems implicit in his relationship with his benefactors. He had to consider the ethical implications that his need to live within a patronage system, with all its obvious pitfalls of dependency and obsequious-ness, could have for his life and work. He could not avoid a series of personal crises regarding his patrons, which were painful to confront. To resolve them, he would have to change his posture toward the Medici, and in the process choose those personal values most important to him. The ideas on love and friendship which he expressed so eloquently in his *Commentary on Plato's "Symposium"* often came into conflict with his relationship with his patrons. After Cosimo's death, Ficino's personal drama was to try to combine two conflicting values, one arising from his need of the material support for his existence that he derived from the Medici and the other being the value of true friendship, the fount of inspiration for his work, which, after the death of Cosimo, he found increasingly outside the Medici palace. Living out the drama in full, he had to ask himself what a true patron was and what kind of rela-tionship he should have with such a person. After 1464 the real ques-tion for Ficino became, who was his true Maecenas: what person or persons stimulated and sustained his thinking? Men such as his dear friends Giovanni Cavalcanti and Bernardo del Nero or his official Me-dici patrons?

Piero did not turn out to be that new Cosimo Ficino desired. He listened to the philosopher's discourses and encouraged his trans-lations and commentaries on Plato, even his public lectures, but Ficino never found in Piero that intimate rapport that he had experienced with his father.[33] Nor was Piero a particularly generous benefactor, and Fi-cino turned more and more to other friends, such as Filippo Valori, for help in the publication of his works. Four years later, in 1469, Piero died, and Ficino placed his renewed hopes in the young Lorenzo. Ini-tially there was a great sympathy between them, heightened by shared philosophical interests, especially in the mid-1470s when their corre-spondence was so intense. Lorenzo seems to have been captivated by Ficino's conversations on love and frequently sought his company; his letters to Ficino testify to this attachment. "All that comes from you is good. Everything you think is just, and therefore everything you write is of value and delight to me."[34] "You belong not to Marsilio, but to your Lorenzo, who is no less yours than you are yours. So that if you want to be restored to yourself, you must understand that however much you regard yourself, you must equally regard me at the same time, because that which immortal God has brought together, he lets no man cast apart."[35]

Ficino reciprocated with letters full of affection and wise counsel, such as one gently admonishing Lorenzo not to waste time, which evoked a gush of gratitude from the young man:

> Often you have revealed your mind to me, but in this letter you have gone beyond every sign of friendship in your benevolence toward me. Perhaps because you are first in love and go beyond all others in friendship toward me. Perhaps because you can give me in abundance the gifts of friendship that others cannot. Others who surround us can give riches, honor, or pleasure. But those gifts belong in the hands of Fortune such that we have no surety of them other than their lack of surety, and nothing more constant than their inconstancy. You have often taught me this lesson, and I have experienced it myself many times. You are such a fount of instruction, and you show me such friendship that for this you are the first among my friends in virtue and before everyone in love. You are this way out of your native goodness. You know that these virtues have been given to man by immortal God on one condition, namely that they be used to benefit as many as possible. You certainly will not abuse this divine generosity.[36]

From this letter of 1474 it is apparent that Lorenzo understood the man Ficino had become: someone who placed greater value on friendship and love than he did on power, position, and the glitter of court life. Perhaps for this very reason, more than for any gap between their ages, Ficino's relationship with Lorenzo turned out to be very different from the one he had enjoyed with Cosimo. Their rapport, though intimate, remained that of a master with his pupil. In his letters and dedications to Lorenzo, Ficino always exhorted him to seek virtue before wealth, power, or honor, and he praised the Magnificent with the sole purpose of instructing him and encouraging him.[37] In one letter, he reminded Lorenzo that he had loved him more than he had praised him and that he had formed an opinion of him before he had ever loved him.[38]

Ficino's greatest hope was to see Cosimo's qualities blossom in Lorenzo, as he expressed in a letter of 1473 to Niccolò Michelozzi, Lorenzo's secretary: "I see the phoenix rising from its ashes, the light in the rays of the sun. The splendor of Cosimo shines every day in Lorenzo

in a hundred ways, bringing illumination to the Latin peoples and glory
to the Republic of Florence."[39] He repeated this desire in another letter
to Lorenzo: "Just as God shaped Cosimo according to the idea of the
cosmos, make Cosimo your model, as you have already begun to do."[40]

But the master does not seem to have been always very pleased
with his student. If in Ficino's mind the image of Cosimo as a model
of virtue and father of his country continued to grow brighter with
the passage of time, it is in part a result of the fact that Lorenzo's methods of running the Florentine state were very different from those of
his grandfather. The break in their correspondence after 1474, which
scholars have interpreted as a rift between them over politics at the time
of the Pazzi conspiracy, was in reality a much more fundamental di-
vergence over basic values, the seeds of which were already present in
Ficino's gentle admonishments to Lorenzo and in his attempts to use
praise for edificatory purposes.

Behind Ficino's didactic posture with Lorenzo, the historian
must recognize his personal crisis, which was deepening during the 1470s
in the midst of a political situation in Florence, in which the *vita civile,*
or civic traditions, were being increasingly sacrificed to Lorenzo's personal power. Ficino and others of his contemporaries, notwithstanding
their affection for Lorenzo, felt themselves estranged from the new way
of life, where patriotism was coming to mean loyalty to the Medici
faction. From the death of Cosimo up through the Pazzi Conspiracy
and War, opposition to Lorenzo was growing among various prominent Florentines, and Ficino was not the only humanist upset by the
changes in the vita civile under the Medici in this period. Others, including Cristoforo Landino, Alamanno Rinuccini, and Giovanni Caroli,
began to express a symptomatic nostalgia for past times and a growing
criticism of their own era. Leon Battista Alberti had earlier given intimations of this kind of disquiet in his *Della famiglia,* in which he exalted the family over the state because the one was founded on love,
the other on treachery.[41] The *Disputationes Camaldulenses* of Landino reveal a certain disaffection from the Florentine way of life in the 1470s
in their emphasis on retreat into contemplation, and Rinuccini, in his
De libertate, written soon after the Pazzi Conspiracy, clearly expressed
his disillusionment with life in Florence under Lorenzo.[42] Giovanni Caroli launched a bitter criticism against all aspects — political, social, and

moral — of the new Florentine society under the Medici.[43] During this period, Ficino found himself in a situation where his loyalty to Cosimo's descendants came into conflict with his loyalty to other friends, such as Francesco Salviati, who were opposed to the Medici.[44] He could not choose the side of the Medici for purely political reasons; neither could he renounce his friends in favor of the Medici just because the Medici were his patrons.

Ficino's biographers all point to the decade stretching from the late 1460s to the late 1470s as one of particular difficulty for him, but they have interpreted it variously. His first biographer, Giovanni Corsi, writing seven years after Ficino's death, made no mention of a crisis over political issues but said that Marsilio had been seized by a bitterness of spirit similar to that felt by St. Jerome when he anguished over his intense love of Cicero.[45] Corsi, and later Della Torre, interpreted the crisis as a classic conflict between Ficino's fascination with pagan philosophy and his Christian faith, a crisis that was resolved only when Ficino renewed his commitment to Christianity, a rededication supported by his ordination into the priesthood in 1473 and his composition of the De christiana religione.[46] More recently, Kristeller has dismissed Corsi's account as a literary fiction and attributed the so-called crisis to periodic states of depression rising out of Ficino's melancholy nature.[47] Raymond Marcel, too, has suggested that Ficino's ordination was not just a clear-cut case of a conversion from paganism to Christianity and argues that in his fascination with Plato, Ficino never lost sight of his Christian faith; his decision to become a priest was valid in and of itself and was not a rejection of Plato.[48] And recently, Riccardo Fubini has stressed the ideological side of Ficino's crisis and interpreted the possible break with Lorenzo as being basically over political questions.[49]

Undoubtedly, during the decade from the late 1460s to the late 1470s, Ficino had to confront a variety of problems that included both his decision to take holy orders and his displeasure over the changing character of Florentine politics under Lorenzo. But his outer responses to those particular situations were the result, not the causes, of his crisis. What appears on the surface to be a doctrinal or political crisis probably masks a much more deep-seated, personal one, which was "Platonic" in the sense that it led him to rethink his whole system of personal values. Modern psychologists would call this a "mid-life crisis," one that requires the search for new values and a new life perspective.[50] Such an existential crisis could not help but have repercussions on everything from Ficino's religious and political preferences to the way in which he chose to live out his relationship with his Medici patrons. It must have begun around 1468, when at age thirty-five Ficino was on the threshold of his maturity. He was already well known for his erudition as the leader in the new Platonic studies, and he had been invited to hold discussions of his findings before a large public.[51] In effect, he was at the top of the ladder of the humanists protected and promoted by the Medici, and he enjoyed the respect and almost adulatory admiration of the young Lorenzo, the new leader of Florence. After having almost finished his translations of Plato, Ficino was beginning to write his own philosophical *Summa*. Just as he had reached the top of his world, he saw the yawning abyss below, and he fell, as Corsi indicated and his letters confirm, into a series of depressions that involved his whole personality and his relations with society. The horizons within which he had lived up to the age of thirty-five could no longer contain him.

Corsi gave us the key to how Ficino confronted his crisis when he said that Ficino found relief from his anguish in writing his *Commentary on Plato's "Symposium,"* his treatise on love, at the suggestion of his most intimate friend, Giovanni Cavalcanti, around the year 1469.[52] In the preface addressed to Cavalcanti, Ficino himself says how important the discovery of love had been in his life. In his studies of the Orphic hymns and in Plato he had encountered the concept of love, but he had not understood its true power and virtue before having experienced it at age thirty-four with Cavalcanti.[53] He was speaking of a genuine Platonic love, which he described in a letter and in the preface to another treatise dedicated to Cavalcanti:

> This constant union in life which is true friendship can not exist except between two people who desire not to accumulate wealth or to satisfy the passions of their bodies, which things are fleeting and transitory, but with a common accord and with all the desire in their souls to acquire and cultivate that unique and constant virtue of the soul that our master and guide, Plato, calls wisdom. And he deemed wisdom to be, more than anything, knowledge of divine things.[54]

Cavalcanti became Ficino's confidant, and he was the person who comforted him during other illnesses and depressions, as their correspondence substantiates. Cavalcanti was probably the inspiration for many of Ficino's writings, among them the *Theologia Platonica,* most of which he wrote while resident at Cavalcanti's villa at Regnano. In his letters to Cavalcanti, and also to many others, Ficino began to develop the theme of friendship and love as the true fountain of life.[55]

Although Ficino's sense of both inner and outer crisis deepened and he was forced to define more clearly his ethical position with respect to his Medici benefactor, he never rejected Lorenzo or his patronage. He never denied the valuable role Cosimo's family had played in his work and life. In response to an inquiry by Jacopo Ammannati, cardinal of Pavia, he wrote that if the cardinal had heard anything about him, it would have been one thing in particular, namely that from the time he was a youth he had grown up in the Medici house.[56] He always gave abundant recognition to the Medici in his dedications and letters, even attributing to Lorenzo the extra push to finish his translations of Plato and his decision to become a priest.[57] If Ficino struggled to preserve his independence while acknowledging his debt to the Medici, he was more the exception than the rule among the humanists and artists who frequented their house. Many did not share the same scruples, neither were they willing to pay the price.[58] Alessandro Cortesi, a contemporary of Ficino, was more typical. He already had the mentality of a court humanist and was quite blatant about what he expected from his Medici patron in the form of a benefice: "Having been born and brought up under his [Lorenzo's] protection and having seen how His Excellency elevated the estate of my brother in the secular world, it seems not unreasonable to ask him to elevate me in the ecclesiastical sphere, especially if I go to Naples where benefices abound and where it is customary to distribute them on the recommendations of such *Signori.*"[59]

In contrast, Ficino, when Lorenzo had procured the little church of San Christoforo for him in 1474, waited to thank Lorenzo until he was certain that the benefice came as a true gift, with no other obligations attached.[60] Later on, Ficino rarely asked Lorenzo for favors and seems to have preferred to live modestly on his small income. When he finally did write to Lorenzo in early 1487, he did so on behalf of his orphaned niece and nephew, his brother Cherubino's children, who were in his care. "Indeed, Lorenzo, philosophy bids me to be content to live on that which I once received from you. But the nephews in my house truly cannot be satisfied with so little."[61]

To some, Ficino's attitude toward the Medici might seem inconsistent, even compromising at times. It was certainly complex. But the central point in this whole discussion is not so much that Ficino was willing to accept the patronage of the Medici, but the way in which he chose to accept it. If Ficino managed to preserve his personal integrity, his success was due to the fact that he followed his own moral and ethical path. He never succumbed to total dependency upon his Medici benefactors, as Alessandro Cortesi did, or accepted the kind of clientage of the court which was coming to characterize the cultural ambience of the late Renaissance. He had experienced with Cosimo the value of a life lived virtuously and with Cavalcanti the power of love, and with both of them, friendship. These values reached beyond any social or political structure or patronage system, and by preserving them, Ficino gave himself the chance to maintain his personal and intellectual autonomy. In late 1487, if Lorenzo was particularly delicate in the way he handled the appointment of Ficino as canon, so striking in its contrast to his usual mode of operation with abundant fanfare, it was probably out of respect for and understanding of his old teacher's ways. Even though over the years their paths had diverged and Lorenzo had given up philosophy for politics, perhaps he still remembered what Ficino had taught him about the value of friendship and its true aims even within the framework of patronage.

NOTES

We all build upon foundations laid by others. Anyone who studies Ficino today owes an immense debt to Paul Oskar Kristeller, whose indefatigable scholarship has kept Ficino's thought alive and made the major corpus of his writings accessible in print. Raymond Marcel's sensitive biography of Ficino has been the point of departure for my consideration of the relation between his life and his works. The present article emerged from the conjunction of three additional elements: my archival research for the *Lettere* of Lorenzo de' Medici, which turned up new documents concerning Ficino; a pair of lecture invitations, from the Istituto Nazionale di Studi sul Rinascimento in Florence on the occasion of Ficino's 550th anniversary and from Timothy Verdon for the portion of the Symposium on Christianity in the Renaissance held in Tallahassee, Florida, which provided the occasions to develop an interpretive framework for Ficino's relationship with the Medici; and finally, the friendship and encouragement of Salvatore Camporeale, ever an inspiration to me. In addition, I would like to thank Professor Kristeller for his valuable comments on the final draft of this article.

1. Citations to Giovanni Corsi's *Vita Marsilii Ficini* are to the edition published by Raymond Marcel as Appendix 1 to his *Marsile Ficin (1433–99)* (Paris: Société d'édition "les Belles Lettres," 1958), 680. Marcel's text is based on the sixteenth-century manuscript discovered by Kristeller, which antedates the version published by Bandini and others. References will also be given to the English translation of Marcel's text found in *The Letters of Marsilio Ficino*, ed. The Language Department of the School of Economic Science, London, 3 vols. (London: Shepheard-Walwyn, 1981), 3:136 (hereafter *Letters*).

2. Ficino describes the banquet in Book 1 of his *Commentarium in Convivium Platonis.* See the text and English translation by Sears Reynolds Jayne, titled "Marsilio's *Commentary on Plato's Symposium,*" University of Missouri Studies 19, no. 1 (1944): 1–247. Ficino also mentions it in several letters, *Opera omnia*, 2 vols. (Basel: 1561 and 1576; reprint, Turin: Bottega d'Erasmo, 1962), 1:657 and 782, cited in Marcel, *Marsile Ficin*, 338–39. Recently, Sebastiano Gentile has cast doubt upon Lorenzo's actual role in the banquet, speculating that Ficino added his name to the text *ex post facto*: "Per la storia del testo del 'Commentarium in convivium' di Marsilio Ficino," *Rinascimento* 21 (1981): 3–27. The extent to which Lorenzo had absorbed Ficino's thought, demonstrated in his own letters and in the *Altercazione*, is beyond dispute.

3. Corsi, *Vita*, in Marcel, *Marsile Ficin*, 686, and *Letters*, 3:144. Lorenzo de' Medici, "L'Altercazione," in *Scritti scelti di Lorenzo de' Medici*, ed. Emilio Bigi (Turin: Unione Tipografico–Editrice Torinese, 1965), *capitoli* 2–5, 57–80. See also P. O. Kristeller, "Lorenzo de' Medici platonico," in *Studies in Renaissance Thought and Letters* (Rome: Edizioni di storia e letteratura, 1956; reprinted 1969), 213–19.

4. He was *pievano* of the church of S. Bartolomeo in Pomino and parish priest at S. Cristoforo in Novoli. His letter thanking Lorenzo, dated January 1474, is cited in Marcel, *Marsile Ficino*, 409–10, and published in *Opera omnia* 1:621–22. Lorenzo's reply of 19 January is published in Lorenzo de' Medici, *Lettere*, 4 vols., ed. Riccardo Fubini and Nicolai Rubinstein (Florence: Giunti-Barbèra, 1977–81), 1:502–4.

5. Riccardo Fubini in particular develops this theme in his commentary to the *Lettere*, 1:496–99 and 2:40, 55, and in his "Ficino e i Medici all'avvento di Lorenzo il Magnifico," *Rinascimento,* ser. 2, 24 (1984): 3–52.

6. "Pronto ad ogni adulazione nei riguardi dei suoi potenti protettori"; "la prima grande figura di filosofo cortigiano fin nello stile frondoso e ricercato"; "Con Ficino compare il letterato di corte, neppur maestro d'università, ma al servizio di un signore che se ne vale, non solamente per dar lustro alla propria casa, ma anche, senza dubbio, per sottili scopi di propaganda politica" (E. Garin, "Ritratto di Marsilio Ficino," *Belfagor* 6 (1951): 289–90).

7. "Circa el vescovado di Cortona, quando vacassi per qualunche cagione, harei grande desiderio che Nostro Signore ne provedessi messer Marsilio nostro, la doctrina et qualità del quale sono certo essere nota costi et in molti altri luoghi del mondo, et oltra el piacere che ne riceverei io, Nostro Signore sarebbe assai commendato per le virtù et buona vita sua; advisadovi che questo pensiero è mio sanza haverlo conferito con lui, et vorrei volentieri la cosa fussi facta che lui o altri non ne havessi ad intendere prima" (Lorenzo de' Medici to Giovanni Lanfredini, Florence, 6 October 1487, Archivio di Stato di Firenze [hereafter ASF], Mediceo avanti il Principato [hereafter MAP], 57:117).

8. For examples, see the letters in ASF, MAP 57:5, 10, 91, 149; and my article, "The Magnificent Lorenzo de' Medici, Between Myth and History," in *Politics and Culture in Early Modern Europe: Essays in Honour of H. G. Koenigsberger,* ed. Phyllis Mack and Margaret C. Jacob (Cambridge: Cambridge University Press, 1987): 25–58.

9. "Similemente vi mando quello che chiedete per messer Marsilio, che sarà in una breve poliza. Io vi raccomando molte persone et spetialità d'altri, et non posso fare altramente per la conditione mia et per la coniunctione che ho con Nostro Signore. Parmi vostro officio costì di ponderare le cose et le persone et temporeggiare et favorire secondo che vi pare meglo, che in questo me rimetto a voi, che sapete quello vi ho scripto per altra circa el dare molte brighe a Nostro Signore" (Lorenzo de' Medici to G. Lanfredini, Florence, 10 November 1487, ASF, MAP, 57:143).

10. He wrote on 29 October and 10 November, ASF, MAP 57:131, 143. In the first letter he stated: "Sapete in che opinione io hebbi messer Marsilio Ficino. Et perché potrebbe accadere presto che io li potrei dare un beneficietto curato che è per vacare, sarebbe necessario, havendo come ha due benefitii curati, che fussi dispensato ad tria incompatibilia. Vorrei ne facessi ogni opera in modo che tale dispensa se havessi et presto, benché non si consenta se non a religiosi di qualche qualità. Potete certificare Nostro Signore che si può consentire a messer Marsilio come a qualunche altro."

11. "La informazione di messer Marsilio bixogna sapere li titoli de' benefici tiene con chura e ffarlo dispensare nel terzo, et benché sia faticha, spero farlo. Datemi notitia d'essi e della valuta, e se potete, del terzo che li volete dare, e sarà dispensato" (G. Lanfredini to L. de' Medici, Rome, 3 November 1487, ASF, MAP 58:23).

12. "'O avuto quella di messer Marsilio e spero di questa altra settimana spedirla e avisarvene" (G. Lanfredini to L. de' Medici, Rome, 16 November 1487, ASF, MAP 40:168).

13. Ficino's letter of thanks, addressed to Giovanni de' Medici and dated 18 March 1487 Florentine style (1488 common style) is published in P. O. Kristeller, *Supplementum Ficinianum,* 2 vols. (Florence: L. S. Olschki, 1937), 1:57–58. That Ficino expressed his gratitude to the young cardinal rather than directly to Lorenzo is reminiscent of Horace's indirect way of thanking Maecenas. See J. W. Hewitt, "The Gratitude of Horace to Maecenas," *Classical Journal* 36, no. 8 (1941): 464–72.

14. "Di qui vi fu il Conte della Mirandola, messer Marsilio, messer Agnolo da Montepulciano et . . . Bernardo Rucellai" (Piero de' Medici to L. de' Medici, 10 May 1490, ASF, MAP, 42:59). See also Barbaro's letter to Francesco Gaddi, dated 8 May, expressing his desire to see Ficino among others, published by Kristeller in *Supplementum Ficinianum,* 2:371. In 1491 Lorenzo paid for the publication of Ficino's Plotinus, which appeared in 1492: see Arnaldo Della Torre, *Storia dell'Accademia Platonica di Firenze* (Florence: G. Carnesecchi, 1902), 626–27.

15. "Primum summumque inter amicos locum patroni nostri Medices iure optimo

sibi vendicant": *Opera omnia,* 1:966. Cf. the following passage in the anonymous biography *Vita,* in Marcel, *Marsile Ficin,* 719 (orthography his): "Il che si argomenta dal numero grande che egli hebbi d'amici cari tutti grandi tutti e tutti domestichi e non sono solo de primi della citta di Firenze, ma dell'altre citta d'Italia e d'altre parti piu remote. . . . Tra primi e principali furono Cosimo, Piero, Giuliano e Lorenze de Medici." Ficino wrote a series of letters about Lorenzo's death to his sons, Piero and the young Cardinal Giovanni, as well as to Filippo Valori and Pico della Mirandola: *Opera omnia,* 2:1538; 1:930–32. In the letter to Cardinal Medici, he developed the Platonic idea of portents accompanying the death of a great man. See also Marcel, *Marsile Ficin,* 512–18.

16. "Ego sacerdos minimus, patres habui duos, Ficinum Medicum, Cosmum Medicensem. Ex illo natus sum, ex isto renatus. Ille quidem me Galeno, tum Medico, tum Platonico commendavit: hic autem divino consecravit me Platoni. Et hic similiter atque ille Marsilium Medico destinavit. Galenus quidem corporum Plato vero medicus animorum" (*Opera omnia,* 1:493). Prof. Kristeller dates Ficino's relationship with Cosmio from 1452, before which time he was a student at the University of Florence and tutor to Piero de' Pazzi. See Kristeller, "Per la biografia di Marsilio Ficino," in *Studies in Renaissance Thought and Letters,* 196–98; and Samuel Jones Hough, "An Early Record of Marsilio Ficino," *Renaissance Quarterly* 20, no. 3 (1977): 301–4.

17. See for example Michael Baxandall, *Painting and Experience in Fifteenth-Century Italy: A Primer in the Social History of Pictorial Style* (Oxford: Clarendon Press, 1972), 1–27; and Francis Haskell, *Patrons and Painters: A Study in the Relations between Italian Art and Society in the Age of the Baroque* (New Haven: Yale University Press, 1980), 3–23.

18. Forty years ago the issue to be settled in Ficino studies concerned whether or not he was a syncretist and just a translator and commentator of Plato and Plotinus. As Ernst Cassirer pointed out, one of the most valuable contributions of Kristeller's study of Ficino's philosophy was to establish the originality and intellectual content of Ficino's thought. See E. Cassirer, "Ficino's Place in Intellectual History," *Journal of the History of Ideas* 6, no. 4 (1945): 483–501; and P. O. Kristeller, *The Philosophy of Marsilio Ficino,* trans. Virginia Conant (New York, 1943; reprint, Gloucester, Mass.: Peter Smith, 1964). For other intellectual treatments, see Nesca Robb, *Neoplatonism of the Italian Renaissance* (London: Allen and Unwin, 1935); Giuseppe Saitta, *Marsilio Ficino e la filosofia dell'umanesimo* (Florence: Felice Le Monnier, 1943); and Charles Trinkaus, *In Our Image and Likeness: Humanity and Divinity in Italian Humanist Thought,* 2 vols. (Chicago: University of Chicago Press, 1970), 2:461–504.

19. Benjamin Kohl, "Political Attitudes of North Italian Humanists in the Late Trecento," *Studies in Medieval Culture* 4, no. 3 (1974): 411–27. He has coined the phrase "subdital humanism" to describe this phenomenon. In the same vein, see John F. D'Amico, *Renaissance Humanism in Papal Rome: Humanists and Churchmen on the Eve of the Reformation* (Baltimore: Johns Hopkins University Press, 1983), 3–37; 115–43.

20. Werner L. Gundersheimer, *Ferrara: The Style of a Renaissance Despotism* (Princeton, N.J.: Princeton University Press, 1981).

21. Melissa Meriam Bullard, *Filippo Strozzi and the Medici: Favor and Finance in Sixteenth-Century Florence and Rome* (Cambridge: Cambridge University Press, 1980).

22. The patronage relationship involves many more subtle and complex qualitative dimensions than is implied in the "rule of hierarchies" discussed by W. Gundersheimer in his article "Patronage in the Renaissance: An Exploratory Approach," in *Patronage in the Renais-*

sance, ed. Guy F. Lytle and Stephen Orgel (Princeton, N.J.: Princeton University Press, 1981), 3–23, or than is implied in Peter Burke's five types of patronage systems (the household system, the made-to-measure system, the market system, the academy system, and the subvention system) in his book *Culture and Society in Renaissance Italy, 1420–1540* (London: B. T. Batsford, 1972), chap. 4, 75–111.

23. The title of the letter, dated 14 April 1477, is appropriately, "Pura neque impure quaeras, neque postquam inveneris impuris communia facias," *Opera omnia,* 1:755–56, and *Letters,* 3:14–16.

24. Kristeller, *Philosophy,* 92–99.

25. *Opera omnia,* 1:649, and *Letters,* 1:136.

26. K. Meister, "Die Freundschaft zwischen Horaz und Maecenas," *Gymnasium* 57 (1950): 3–38; K. J. Reckford, "Horace and Maecenas," *Transactions and Proceedings of the American Philological Association* 90 (1959): 195–208; and, in the same issue of *Transactions,* J. W. Hewitt, "The Gratitude of Horace," 464–72. My thanks to Charles Henderson for these references. On the nature of patronage and its code of friendship in Horace's age, see Peter White's excellent article, "*Amicitia* and the Profession of Poetry in Early Imperial Rome," *Journal of Roman Studies* 68 (1978): 74–92; T. P. Wiseman, "*Pete nobiles amicos:* Poets and Patrons in Late Republican Rome," in *Literary and Artistic Patronage in Ancient Rome,* ed. Barbara Gold (Austin: University of Texas Press, 1982), 28–49; and Richard P. Saller, *Personal Patronage under the Early Empire* (Cambridge: Cambridge University Press, 1982).

27. *Opera Omnia,* 1:620, and *Letters,* 1:67.

28. "Multum equidem Platoni nostro debeo, sed Cosmo non minus debere me fateor. Quam enim virtutum ideam Plato semel mihi monstraverat, eam quotidie Cosmus agebat" (*Opera omnia,* 1:649, and *Letters,* 1:136). On Ficino's didactic intent in his letters and the tradition of spiritual letters in the Renaissance, see P. O. Kristeller, "Lay Religious Traditions and Florentine Platonism," in *Studies in Renaissance Thought and Letters,* 99–122; idem, "Marsilio Ficino as a Man of Letters and the Glosses Attributed to Him in the Caetani Codex of Dante," *Renaissance Quarterly* 36, no. 1 (1983): 14–31; Garin, "Ritratto," 292–306; and Leopoldo Galeotti, "Saggio intorno alla vita ed agli scritti di Marsilio Ficino," *Archivio Storico Italiano,* n.s. 10 (1859): 6–7.

29. "Quod tandem pro tantis muneribus referam aliud nihil habeo, nisi ut Platonicis voluminibus que ipse largissime porrexisti sedulus incumbam, Academiam quam nobis in agro Caregio parasti veluti quoddam contemplationis sacellum legitime colam ibique dum spiritus hoc reget corpusculum Platonis pariter ac Cosmi Medicis natalem diem celebrem (Kristeller, *Supplementum Ficinianum,* 2:88, and cited in Marcel, *Marsile Ficin,* 242). He continued to associate the spirit of Cosimo with the banquets at Careggi as late as 1478: *Opera omnia,* 1:728.

30. Vespasiano da Bisticci, *Renaissance Princes, Popes, and Prelates: Lives of Illustrious Men of the Fifteenth Century,* trans. W. George and E. Waters (New York: Harper and Row, 1963), 229–30, 234.

31. "veni ad nos Marsili quamprimum. Fer tecum Platonis in (sic) nostri librum de Summo bono . . . Nihil enim ardentius cupio, quam quae via commodius ad felicitatem ducat cognoscere. Vale et veni non absque Orphica lyra" (*Opera omnia,* 1:608, and *Letters,* 1:32).

32. "Haec igitur lege feliciter, academiae columen ac diu vive, ne Cosmo carere nos aliquando sentiamus" (*Opera omnia,* 2:1965).

33. Corsi, *Vita*, in Marcel, *Marsile Ficin*, 682–83, and *Letters*, 3:139. See also Marcel, *Marsile Ficin*, 300–311, 323–24; Della Torre, *Storia dell'Accademia*, 568–73.

34. "Nihil ex te proficiscitur non bonum, nihil cogitas non rectum: nihil itaque scribi a te potest non nobis utile, non iucundum" (letter of 15 January 1474, Lorenzo de' Medici, *Lettere*, 1:501).

35. "Iam igitur non Marsilii es, sed Laurentii tui, non minus tui quam tu ipsius. Qua in re, si teipsum tibi reddi vis, scito id ea conditione futurum, ut nullam de te habere possis rationem, quin aeque de me ipso eodem tempore habiturus sis. Quos enim immortalis Deus coniunxit, homo non separet" (letter of 19 January 1474, ibid., 1:503–4.

36. "Declaraveras tu quidem saepe mentem erga nos tuam; verum mecum ipsi saepius hanc tuam epistolam volutanti videris omne aliud amicitiae officium superasse, sive quod primas in amore erga nos partes obtineas ac longe caeteris in amicitia praestes, sive quod ea amicitiae munera abunde praestare valeas, quae caeteri nequeant. Caeteri nempe, qui nos benivolentia prosecuntur, aut divitiis iuvare possunt, aut honoribus, aut voluptatibus, quae quidem omnia ita in fortunae potestate constituta sunt, ut nihil firmius habeamus nihilque constantius quam eorum imbecillitatem ac mobilitatem; quod et tu saepe docuisti et nos saepius experti sumus. Tu vero his abundas praeceptis atque eo amicitiae genere nobiscum agis, ut facile appareat, sicut nemini amicorum virtute cedis, ita reliquos in amore superare. Facis hoc tu quidem naturali quadam beneficentia tua; facis insuper, quod te non fugit hac conditione datas esse ab immortali Deo hominibus virtutes, ut quam plurimos iuvent, neque adduci potes ut divina hac liberalitate abutaris" (letter of 22 September 1474, ibid, 2:37–38). Ficino's letter, to which Lorenzo was responding, is in *Opera omnia*, 1:646–47, and *Letters*, 1:130–32.

37. "In epistolis Laurenti, quas ad te scripsi, hactenus semper te ita laudavi, ut admonerem similiter, atque exhortarer. Admonui equidem semper ut a Deo te habere omnia recognosceres, ei gratias ageres, ei te sedulo commendares. Exhortatus sum ut pergeres. Nam principium vel voluntatis est, vel sortis, perseverantia vero virtutis" (letter dated 15 April 1474, *Opera omnia*, 1:655–56, and *Letters*, 1:155). This didactic tone characterizes all of Ficino's correspondence. He clearly intended his letters to provide moral edification, as his giving titles to each one in preparation for publication indicates. On Ficino's role as a spiritual adviser to his friends, see Kristeller, "Lay Religious Traditions," 116–22. His genuine concern for Lorenzo's proper moral instruction helps explain his bitter polemic with Luigi Pulci in the mid-1470s; see Marcel, *Marsile Ficin*, 420–33.

38. "Ego Laurentium magis adhuc amo, quam laudem, et iudicavi antea, quam amarem" (*Opera omnia*, 1:656, and *Letters*, 1:155).

39. "Agnosco nunc in isto adolescente penitus, agnosco totum illum senem, phoenicem video in phoenice, in radio lumen. Emicat iam ex Laurentio nostro foras Cosmianus splendor ille multis quotidie modis, lumen ad revelationem Gentium Latinarum, et Florentiae Reipublicae gloriam" (letter dated 21 January 1474, *Opera omnia*, 1:622, and *Letters*, 1:67).

40. "Vale, et sicut Deus Cosmum ad ideam mundi formavit, ita te ipse quemadmodum coepisti, ad ideam Cosmi figura" (*Opera omnia*, 1:649, and *Letters*, 1:136). This passage comes at the end of a letter wholly dedicated to explaining the power that imitating the lives of illustrious persons has to arouse our own pursuit of virtue, a power superior to that of abstract moral instruction. According to Ficino, more people would be led to virtue by emulating Socrates' way of life than by reading the moral teachings of Aristotle.

41. Leon Battista Alberti, *I libri della famiglia,* ed. Ruggiero Romano and Alberto Tenenti (Turin: G. Einaudi, 1969), especially bk. 3, 228ff.

42. Cristoforo Laudino, *Disputationes Camaldulenses,* ed. Peter Lohe (Florence: Sansoni, 1980); Alamanno Rinuccini, *Dialogus de libertate,* ed. F. Adorno, *Atti e memorie dell'Accademia toscana di scienze e lettere "La Colombaria"* 22, n.s. 8 (1957): 270–303. See also James B. Wadsworth, "Landino's *Disputationes Camaldulenses,* Ficino's *De Felicitate,* and *L'Altercazione* of Lorenzo de' Medici," *Modern Philology* 50 (1952–53): 23–31.

43. Salvatore I. Camporeale, "Giovanni Caroli e le '*Vitae fratrum S. M. Novellae*': Umanesimo e crisi religiosa (1460–80)," *Memorie domenicane,* n.s. 12 (1981): 141–267.

44. Because of Lorenzo de' Medici's opposition to his appointment, Salviati had to wait three years before taking office as archbishop of Pisa in 1477. Ficino wrote him several letters of consolation: *Opera omnia,* 1:649, 667, and Kristeller, *Supplementum Ficinianum,* 1:48. Salviati was executed in 1478 for his part in the Pazzi Conspiracy.

45. ". . . sed divino prorsus miraculo, id quo minus efficeret, in dies magis impediebatur, quadam, ut aiebat, spiritus amaritudine distractus; id quod et divo Hieronymo in Cicerone accidisse memoriae proditum est" (Corsi, *Vita,* in Marcel, *Marsile Ficin,* 683).

46. Ibid.; Della Torre, *Storia dell'Accademia,* 594–95. Corsi states that Ficino's state of health did not improve until his forty-fifth year: Corsi, *Vita,* in Marcel, *Marsile Ficin,* 686.

47. P. O. Kristeller, "Per la biografia di Marsilio Ficino," in *Studies in Renaissance Thought and Letters,* 202–5, and previously Leopoldo Galeotti, "Saggio intorno alla vita," *Archivio storico italiano,* n.s. 9 (1859): 54–58.

48. According to Marcel, the real problem vexing Ficino at this time was a theological and philosophical one, namely, the nature of the soul and its immortality (*Marsile Ficin,* 335–55). On the general problem of religion and philosophy in the Renaissance, and on Ficino's place in it, see E. Garin, "Problemi di religione e filosofia nella cultura fiorentina del quattrocento," *Bibliothèque d'humanisme et Renaissance* 14 (1952): 70–82; see also Galeotti, "Saggio intorno alla vita," 58–76.

49. See note 5 above. Marcel also notes that Ficino was very sensitive to political events and that some of the conspirators of 1478, notably Francesco Salviati, Cardinal Riario, and members of the Pazzi family, were among his good friends. He does not find evidence, however, that Ficino ever turned against Lorenzo; see *Marsile Ficin,* 328ff.

50. Symptomatic of this kind of psychological crisis was Ficino's growing disquiet and his premonitions of impending disaster. He became interested in miracles and turned increasingly to astrology. In 1477 his anxiety led him to advise his friends to retreat to their country villas; see Marcel, *Marsile Ficin,* 441–42. It is worth noting that even though in 1477 Ficino wrote against the misleading judgments of astrologers, his own interest in astrology continued. In fact, he often used his considerable knowledge of the subject in his treatises and personal correspondence. See Kristeller, *The Philosophy of Marsilio Ficino,* 310–14, and Marcel, *Marsile Ficin,* 440–42, 497, 501–3, 538–39. The treatise, *Disputatio contra iudicium astrologorum,* is published in Kristeller, *Supplementum Ficinianum,* 2:11–76.

51. Corsi, *Vita* in Marcel, *Marsile Ficin,* 682–83; Della Torre, *Storia dell'Accademia,* 568–73; Marcel, *Marsile Ficin,* 308–9.

52. "Quo quidem tempore ad levandum hunc, si quomodo posset, animi dolorem, commentaria in amorem scripsit, ad quem librum componendum Joannes Cavalcantes, vir patritius ac Marsilio cumprimis carus, eo quidem consilio adhortatus est, ut eodem tempore dolori

obviam iret, et vanae pulchritudinis amatores ad immortalem pulchritudinem revocaret" (Corsi, *Vita*, in Marcel, *Marsile Ficin*, 683).

53. "Quam vero vim deus hic et potentiam habeat, annos me quatuor et triginta latuerat, donec jam divus quidam heros oculis mihi celestibus annuens, miro quodam nutu, quanta sit amoris potentia demonstraret. Hinc igitur res amatorias abunde ut mihi quidem videbar edoctus, *de amore* librum composui. Quem manu mea scriptum tibi potissimum dedicare constitui, ut quae tua sunt, tibi reddam" (Kristeller, *Supplementum Ficinianum*, 1:87, and quoted in Marcel, *Marsile Ficin*, 341n).

54. "Quamobrem inter illos solum stabilis vitae unio, quae vera est amicitia, esse potest qui neque ad divitias cumulandas, neque ad explendas libidines corporis, quae omnia fluxa et caduca sunt, sed ad unam stabilemque virtutem animi capessendam atque colendam communi quodam inter se studio, et toto mentis ardore proficiscuntur. Animi virtutem Philosophorum ille omnium magister et dux Plato noster sapientiam voluit nuncupari, sapientiam vero esse rerum divinarum cognitionem existimavit" (*Opera omnia*, 1:633–34, 2:1945, and *Letters*, 1:96. See also Marcel's discussion in *Marsile Ficin*, 339–45.

55. The two themes are intertwined in his *Commentary on Plato's "Symposium"* and in numerous letters, such as those in *Opera omnia* 1:633–34, 636, 741, 743, 777–78, and in *Letters*, 1:96–97, 101–2, 2:55–56, 62, 3:65–67. See also Alessandra Canavero Tarabochia,"L'Amicizia nell'epistolario di Marsilio Ficino," *Rivista di filosofia neo-scolastica* 67 (1975): 422–31; P. O. Kristeller, "Volontà e amor divino in Marsilio Ficino," *Giornale critico della filosofia italiana* 19 (1938): 185–214; idem, *The Philosophy of Marsilio Ficino*, 93–114, 278–88; Galeotti, "Saggio intorno alla vita," 32–35.

56. "Proinde si quid ab excelso de infimo hoc homunculo unquam audire potueris, hoc unum, ut arbitror audisti maxime quod in hoc maximum, Marsilium scilicet Ficinum esse antiquissimum Medicae domus alumnum" (letter dated 8 February 1476 [Florentine style], *Opera omnia* 1:745, and *Letters*, 2:68–69).

57. In the dedication of the *De christiana religione* to Lorenzo, he wrote: "Tu nuper volens philosophandi studium in me, quoad posses, sicut in aliis nonnullis consuevisti, cum pietatis officio copulare, Marsilium Ficinum tuum sacerdotio et quidem honorifice, decorasti" (Opera omnia, 1:1–2). In 1490 Ficino planned to dedicate his collected works to Lorenzo, who unfortunately died before they could all be copied; see *Opera omnia* 1:916, and Marcel, *Marsile Ficin*, 506–8.

58. Ficino's position is exceptional by virtue of the personal, moral choices he made in how he lived out his relationship with his Medici patrons. This qualitative distinction is crucial in understanding Ficino's position and is not to be confused with what Grundersheimer defines as the exceptional case, namely those men who were "cultural superstars"—who did not see themselves in the role of clients and felt free to choose or reject offers of patronage because their reputations could do more for the patron than vice versa; see Grundersheimer, "Patronage in the Renaissance," 5–6.

59. ". . . essendo nato et allevato sotto la sua protectione et havendo veduto che Sua Signoria haveva exaltato lo stato del mio fratello in grado seculare, horamai non mi pareva alieno dalla rag[ione] se io piglavo ardire a ricercharlo che mi exaltasssi in grado ecclesiastico maxime andando a Napoli ove è gram copia di beneficii, et facilmente si soleno dare a contemplatione di simili Signori" (ASF, Archivio della Repubblica, Lettere Varie, 16, fol. 363).

60. *Opera omnia*, 1:621, and *Letters*, 1:63.

61. "Me quidem Laurenti philosophia iubet his que olim abs te accepi contentum vivere. Mihi vero domi nepotes contenti paucis esse non possunt" (Kristeller, *Supplementum Ficinianum,* 1:57). Ficino demonstrated the same kind of scruples in recommending others to Lorenzo. When he wrote regarding Gregorio Befani, for example, Ficino emphasized that he recommended him more because of his virtue than out of friendship: "for he is a friend because of his virtue" (*Opera omnia* 1:667, and *Letters,* 1:184). Corsi remarked on Ficino's Spartan existence: *Vita,* in Marcel, *Marsile Ficin,* 686, *Letters,* 3:144.

20 ❧

SAVONAROLA'S PREACHING AND THE PATRONAGE OF ART

MARCIA B. HALL

T HE "TROUBLED MARRIAGE" between traditional Christianity and classical humanism in the late quattrocento and the need for adaptation and change are nowhere more apparent than in the Savonarolan movement and the person of its fiery
leader, the Dominican prior of San Marco, Fra Girolamo Savonarola. In this chapter,
Marcia B. Hall analyzes Savonarola's effort to achieve a balanced statement of the two
coefficients of the cultural "equation," and the influence on the visual arts and on
artistic patronage of this struggle for assimilation and redefinition. In light of Professor Hall's observations, the artistic experimentation dominant in Florence at the
end of the fifteenth and the beginning of the sixteenth centuries takes on deeper meaning, and the new dimension of spiritual grandeur apparent in the style of Leonardo
da Vinci, Michelangelo, and Raphael assumes distinctive character and contemporary
relevance.

MARCIA B. HALL is professor of the history of art at Temple University. Her publications include basic archeological studies of the liturgical space of Florentine churches
before and after the changes dictated by the Council of Trent.

ERTAIN ASPECTS OF SAVONAROLA'S INFLUENCE ON THE ARTS have been studied by modern scholars: the illustrations of his sermons and the alleged conversion of specific artists to his position.[1] A recent publication denies that his influence can be found in any but a few instances of iconography.[2] Some scholars have attempted to define his theory of art. His diatribe against the "Madonna in contemporary dress" has been frequently quoted. But Savonarola, recognizing that his real target had to be the patrons, aimed remarks in his sermons at this group on numerous occasions. The thrust and impact of these comments was surveyed by David Friedman in his article on the Strozzi Chapel in Santa Maria Novella.[3] In the following pages I undertake to enlarge upon Friedman's approach, systematically studying Savonarola's preaching in relation to the major artistic commissions in Florence before, during, and after the friar's rise to political power. I look first at his preaching style and then at the art produced for converts to "the Piagnone"; finally, I outline the most significant results of my survey of patronage between 1494 and 1503.

In reading the sermons I was surprised to find their content to be more humanistic than is usually acknowledged. I found such themes as the dignity of man, the promise of reconciliation and a life freed from the burden of guilt and sin, and the goodness of creation playing a more prominent role than summaries of his preaching had led me to expect. Direct influence from the Florentine humanists is unmistakable. Like the preachers in the papal court studied by John O'Malley,[4] Savonarola knew the humanists, drew upon their writings, and shared their themes. But while he shared the humanist view of human potential, he confronted his listeners with their constant abuse of that potential. Moreover, he did not entirely share the humanists' optimism, which, as Charles Trinkaus has said, is the most affirmative view of human nature in the history of thought and expression. He did not regard human reason as the highest authority, but reserved that place for divine revelation.[5]

Here we have both sides of Savonarola: the contemporary pertinence of his vision displayed, as Donald Weinstein has brilliantly demonstrated, in his adaptation of the Myth of Florence to his political message,[6] and at the same time his insistence upon "baptizing" these secular sources in the service of his theocratic vision. Certainly Savonarola is a complex and many-faceted figure: we cannot fail to see his puritanical legalism but the positive side of his message — what he shared with the humanists — tends to be overlooked. Despite our new appreciation for his political acumen, we have still tended to characterize his religion as neomedieval pietism.

His articulation of the classic message of reconciliation is far removed from the apocalyptic thundering we usually associate with Savonarola. The explanation for the disparity between what he actually said and what he is remembered as saying may lie in his failure to find the appropriate form for his content. Unlike preachers of the Renaissance papal court, who in reviving the epideic style of antique rhetoric found a form in which they could express their humanism — a form meant to lay before the listener, for his appreciation and contemplation, what should be praised and what blamed — Savonarola never shed the didactic framework of traditional preaching. His style drove him all too often to a scolding, admonitory tone that is not fully consonant with his intended message. Typically, he exhorted his listeners by presenting two opposing situations, describing, for example, their present, unholy condition and then enjoining them to abandon it for the rewards of life in the light of the Holy Spirit. Effective as this style was, its confrontational character led Savonarola away from moderation and conciliation to a shrill articulation of extremes (Figure 20.1). It is this extremism that is remembered and not his moderating exclusions, which become, instead of points that refine his meaning, forgotten parenthetical remarks.[7]

Savonarola's comments on art in his sermons were addressed to the patrons who were in his congregation, and those who were conspicuous by their absence, as well. He opposed the rich spending lavishly on their own comfort while refusing to give to the poor. He comments that the palaces of Rome and Florence are built with the blood of the poor.[8] There is always present the note of contrast: it is not luxury itself that he attacks but the fact that it represents a diversion of needed resources. He lamented the patrons' willingness to spend a hun-

Figure 20.1. Woodcut illustration showing Savonarola preaching in the Florence Cathedral. From the *Compendio di Revelatione dello inutile servo di Iesu Cristo Frate Hieronymo da Ferrara,* printed in Florence 23 April 1496, for Piero Pacini da Pescia. Florence, Biblioteca Nazionale Centrale, Sav. 146. Photo Artini.

dred florins for a chapel, but not ten florins for the poor, particularly when their purpose, he asserted, was to display their coats of arms for their own honor, not to honor God.[9]

He deplored such self-vaunting on the part of the patrons on several occasions. In November 1494, he declared that only the saints should be buried in churches. The rich who have themselves buried under the altars where the Holy Sacrament is celebrated daily are in the flames of the inferno, while the saints who endured tribulations, poverty, martyrdom enjoy eternal tranquility.[10] In March 1496, he again denounced the pretension of placing coats of arms all over the convent. One is awed by the audacity of the Strozzi heirs, who dared to continue construction of the family chapel in Santa Maria Novella when subjected to such public ridicule!

Savonarola's populist spirit flared in the face of good works "purchased" by the rich: The lukewarm think, he declared, that building a chapel or altar is the only sacrifice to the honor of God that is required. They do not realize that God looks at the heart not the hands.[11] Note, however, that he does not oppose the building of a chapel or altar per se, only the misguided notion that this will suffice for a ticket to heaven. He called for a reordering of priorities and for a return to simplicity. "Look at the houses of your forebears: they were simple, they did not build palaces of gold and silver."[12] Here again one suspects the preacher is casting an aspersion on the Strozzi, whose vast domicile continued to rise despite widespread economic hardship (Figure 20.2). Paintings and works of art in churches should be simple. In a plea that anticipates the Decrees of the Council of Trent, Savonarola calls for paintings in which nothing gratuitous is added which will distract from the religious content.[13]

Also anticipating Trent, Savonarola urged his listeners to discard lascivious images and books that they had in their houses. The words were turned into ritual enactment during Lent, 1497, and again the following year, with the burning of vanities. Here again it was primarily the patrons, rather than the artists, who were called upon to turn over their obscene books and images. The youth were marshaled to collect the vanities. Richard Trexler has shown how successful Savonarola could be in creating new ritual expressions of his message, as when he organized the boys to march in religious processions ac-

Figure 20.2. Benedetto da Maiano and Il Cronaca, Palazzo Strozzi, Florence. Detail showing costly rustication of exterior masonry and Strozzi armorial bearings carved into *bifore*. Photo Alinari/Art Resource, N.Y.

cording to wards of the city to give force to his concept of the unity of religion and politics.[14] Although it is highly distasteful to us, smacking of the Hitler Youth, the collection of vanities was another ritual invented by Savonarola which brilliantly served his purposes. The corrupt, unregenerate middle-aged citizens, immune to Savonarola's injunctions, found themselves confronted by white-clad "angels" who rebuked them for their self-indulgence, shaming them into contributing their worldly objects to the bonfire.[15] The youth were thus empowered to chastise their elders and betters, a role they would not renounce with Savonarola's passing; neither could it easily be reclaimed from them by their elders without an equally forceful show of moral rectitude on their part. This may have contributed to the unwillingness of patrons to renew their patronage of secular art in the years following Savonarola's death.

As Schnitzer has pointed out, Savonarola was no iconoclast.[16] He recognized the value of images as a spur to devotion and for didactic purposes. In his book *Pictures and Punishment,* Samuel Edgerton has put into a fresh and lively context Savonarola's contribution to the late quattrocento literary genre of the art of dying well. The Piagnone understood well the admonitory function of images, as his precise instructions show. He advised that an image reminding one of the imminence of death be kept in the bedroom for daily contemplation, but not in a place where one would become so accustomed to seeing it that it would lose its efficacy.[17]

Savonarola's belief in the association of physical beauty with spiritual purity enabled him to affirm the painter's practice in another kind of religious image. "Creatures are beautiful in proportion to their participation in the nearness and beauty of God. And the body is more beautiful that houses a beautiful soul."[18] Ideal beauty, then, could represent the spirituality of the Madonna and saints. When he attacked the painters and their patrons for the way in which they represented the saints and deity it was because the image that resulted could in no way be distinguished from ordinary contemporary Florentines. "The young men go about saying, 'This woman is the Magdalen, that fellow is St. John,' because you have the figures in churches painted to the likeness of this woman or that one, . . . This is contemptuous to God." What is lacking, Savonarola is saying, is the spiritual dimension. "Do you imagine that the Virgin Mary would go about dressed as you paint her? I say to you that she was dressed like a poor girl, simply, and covered up so that you could hardly see her face."[19]

His criticisms here are so specific that I have wondered whether some recently exhibited work had drawn Savonarola's fire. None of the few paintings installed in 1495 or early 1496 fits the description. Could he have been looking back to the decorations of the *cappella maggiore* in Santa Maria Novella by Dominico Ghirlandaio and his workshop (Figure 20.3)? These seem likely candidates, not only because of the presence of portraits in a very worldly setting but also because they were commissioned by the Medici in-laws, the Tornabuoni, who were known opponents to Savonarola.[20]

How unique was Savonarola's attitude toward conspicuous consumption? Had the Florentines by and large put the frugality of their forebears behind them? Richard Goldthwaite tells us no, reminding us that although Florentines had become decidedly less inhibited in their spending in the course of the fifteenth century, doubts and fears about wealth lingered on. He characterized the Savonarolan episode as a revival of older notions.[21] It is clear, I think, that Savonarola was exposing to his congregation their own half-concealed guilt, prompted by their memories of the thrift of their ancestors. Thus they were sensitive to his point when Savonarola exhorted them to renounce the empty materialism he saw them substituting for higher, and more fulfilling, spiritual values.

Evidence that attitudes toward conspicuous consumption were slow to die and that Savonarola was probing a still-live nerve is provided by the continuing efforts to enforce sumptuary laws. In Florence such laws were promulgated as late as the rule of Duke Cosimo, first in 1546, again in 1562, and yet again in 1568. Although the latter two efforts were, no doubt, reflections of the Counter-Reformation, the first was not. Similar attempts were made by the government of Rome in 1520 and of Milan in 1498, when it renewed and amplified its legislation of 1396. In 1514 in Venice the *proveditori alle pompe* were directed to examine women's coiffures to see whether they had added jewels, gold or silver cords, or strings of pearls, and to check their cuffs for lace and their buttons for diamonds. In Rome in 1473 such strict sanctions were imposed that Pope Sixtus IV was moved to soften them: in addition to the single cape or coat of velvet or silk that a woman was per-

Figure 20.3. Domenico Ghirlandaio, *Birth of the Virgin*. Florence, Santa Maria Novella, Cappella Maggiore. The group of standing women at left contains several contemporary portraits, and the sumptuous interior reflects contemporary palace decoration. Photo Alinari/Art Resource, N.Y.

mitted to possess (ornamented in front only with a border and costing no more that eighty ducats) the pope magnanimously added a silk dress worth thirty ducats.[22]

In view of his appreciation of the role of ideal beauty in religious art, Savonarola must have been disappointed by the works created under his influence, commissioned by his associates (including Francesco Valori, the leader of his political party) and executed by such artists as Botticelli, who had, in the view of some scholars, been won over to the Piagnone. In these paintings, the urgent, frenetic tone clashes with the message of humanist celebration, joy, and praise of God's creation. Filippino Lippi's *Crucifixion* (now destroyed; formerly in Berlin) and what were apparently the wings for it, representing the ascetics John the Baptist and Mary Magdalen (Florence, Accademia) (Figure 20.4),[23] are backward-looking in style. There is much about this piece that co-

Figure 20.4. Filippino Lippi, *Sts. John the Baptist and Mary Magdalene*. Forence, Accademia. Gabinetto fotografico, Soprintendenza Beni artistici e storici di Firenze.

incides with Savonarola's content, to be sure. The gilded ground recalls a simpler era, the presentation is unadorned and the subject recalls the core of Savonarola's apostolate: Christ's sacrificial death to bring about our redemption through repentance. Nevertheless, there is nothing here of the joy of the Christian proclamation, the reward of repentance. Like Savonarola's hortatory style, the form emphasizes admonition.

Even more of a disappointment must have been Botticelli's renderings of Savonarola's message. Although the Piagnone's vision of Florence —first purged and then, through repentance, redeemed—is graphically represented in the much-damaged Fogg *Crucifixion,* the mood, like that of the Lippi, is frenetic and urgent.[24] The purpose is, again, to urge repentance on the viewer. But the threat of destruction looks more convincing than the promise of reward. Botticelli's *Mystic Nativity* (London, National Gallery), executed after Savonarola's death, recalls his millenarian predictions. Even though its subject offered opportunity for joyful celebration of the incarnation, it becomes another premonitory homily.[25] Lorenzo di Credi's *Adoration of the Shepherds,* which, as F. W. Kent has recently shown, was commissioned by a fervent Savonarolan,[26] is both more successful and less peculiarly Piagnone (Figure 20.5). Like some other works of this period—for example, Perugino's *Pietà* (Florence, Pitti) for the same church of Santa Chiara—it is indistinguishable from other religious paintings except for its more intense and serious piety.

I believe that the failure to find a form appropriate to the content—a form combining admonition with celebration—was both the problem that dogged Savonarola's preaching and the reason for the failure of the art produced under his aegis. The spiritual dimension was present only as a remote and inaccessible reality, disjunctively juxtaposed to the material world. Its immanence in the here-and-now was nowhere indicated. This was a particularly poignant failure in Botticelli's case because he never recovered the magical synthesis of natural and supernatural which had enabled him to represent multiple layers of meanings in his mythological and earlier religious paintings.[27]

Let us turn our attention now to the state of patronage among those who were not particular adherents of Savonarola. The results of this survey can only be outlined here. The works known to have been executed between 1494 and 1504 by the following artists have been traced to determine when they were commissioned and for what destination:

Figure 20.5. Lorenzo di Credi, *Adoration of the Shepherds*. Florence, Uffizi Gallery.
Photo Alinari/Art Resource, N.Y.

Il Cronaca, Antonio da Sangallo, Giuliano da Sangallo, Andrea Sansovino, Michelangelo, Andrea della Robbia, Perugino, Filippino Lippi,
Botticelli, Leonardo da Vinci, Lorenzo di Credi, Piero di Cosimo,
Francesco Granacci, Davide Ghirlandaio, Cosimo Rosselli. (This list
corresponds to the panel called together in January 1504 to decide the
placement of Michelangelo's *David,* excluding those twelve who were
identified as woodcarvers, goldsmiths, engravers, or similar craftsmen.[28]
The group presumably comprised all the major artists working in Florence
at that time.) As a cross-check I have traced Paatz's references to works
in Florentine churches datable to this decade.[29] In many cases, research
since the publication of the Paatz study has enabled us to identify and
date works more precisely,[30] but more remains to be done in some areas,
conspicuously on the chapels of Santo Spirito.[31]

    In light of what was said above, a decline in commissions dur-
ing the Savonarola years (i.e., from late 1494 until June 1498) would
seem likely, along with some revival of artistic activity after Savonarola's removal from the scene. The spectacle of the ritual thrashing of
the San Marco bell, nicknamed La Piagnona, at it was dragged through
the streets of Florence on the order of the *Signoria* in June 1498, suggests that the tide of public opinion had turned.[32] Ficino's denunciation
of Savonarola to the Roman Curia as the antichrist the following year
seems to identify him decisively as the enemy of the humanists.[33] We
might expect, then, that the adherents of humanism and those other
patricians opposed to Savonarola who had been quiescent, delaying commissions for works they wanted until a more favorable moment, would
have emerged after his removal, creating, if not a flood, at least a trickle
of new artistic activity. But though we do find a dramatic dropping-
off of commissions in 1494, the striking fact is that there is no reversal of this trend after Savonarola's death. Quite the contrary: the few
works that were commissioned bore very strongly the stamp of the
Piagnone, suggesting that his influence lingered and was not easily overcome. It is, in fact, worth chronicling the few artistic events that did
occur between 1494 and 1503, when the turnaround finally happened.

    In the years before the expulsion of the Medici in 1494, Flor-
ence was enjoying a flurry of building activity, and other forms of artistic production were at a very high level. Landucci recorded it in 1489:

> At this time all the following buildings were erected: The Osservanza
> di San Miniato de' Frati di San Francesco; the sacristy of Santo Spirito;
> the house of Giulio Gondi; and the church of the Frati di Sant'Agostino,
> outside the Porta a San Gallo. And Lorenzo de' Medici began a palace
> at the Poggio a Caiano, on his property, where so much has been beauti-
> fully ordered, the Cascine and so on. Princely things! At Sarrezana a
> fortress was built; and many other houses were erected in Florence: in
> the street which goes to Santa Caterina, and toward the Porta a Pinti,
> and the Via Nuova de' Servi, at Cestello, and from the Porta a Faenza
> toward San Barnaba, and toward Sant'Ambrogio, and elsewhere. Men
> were crazy about building at this time, so that there was a scarcity of
> master-builders and of materials.[34]

Some of this building no doubt was spurred by the tax exemption that the Signoria granted in May 1489, but it is important for our
purposes to note that although the exemption was renewed in 1494
and extended until 1497, new building projects were not begun with
the frequency recorded by Landucci in 1489, and in fact came to a vir-
tual halt.[35]

In the first years after the collapse of Medici power, many works
already begun or commissioned were completed, so that the actual decline in new commissions is not immediately apparent.[36] In fact, the
only major new commissions from 1494 to 1497, aside from the altarpieces already discussed, were for the building and decoration of the
hall in Palazzo Vecchio needed for the assembly of Savonarola's newly
instituted Great Council.[37] A few works were undertaken, or at least
continued, in an unmistakable spirit of defiance by patrons opposed to
Savonarola. We have already alluded to the most conspicuous examples,
the Strozzi Palace and their chapel in Santa Maria Novella, both undertaken by Filippo Strozzi before his death in 1491, but continued by his
heirs during the Savonarola years.

The situation for artists was bad. Some, like Michelangelo, left
town, or, if they were away, stayed away, like Andrea Sansovino.[38] Others,
like Giuliano do Sangallo[39] and Cronaca,[40] were in and out of town
at frequent intervals, accepting commissions elsewhere. Still others who
were based in Florence received no documented commissions there:
Perugino;[41] Piero di Cosimo;[42] and the Ghirlandaio shop, since
Domenico's death in 1494 headed by Davide.[43]

This situation in no way improved with the death of the friar in May 1498. There was no sudden return to chapel building or the commissioning of portraits, tombs, or mythological pictures; until 1503 there was no decisive change in the pattern. Even in a church such as Cestello which was, in the course of renovation, providing new side-chapels and altars, private patronage all but ceased until 1503.[44]

Economic factors certainly played a part in this. The years between 1494 and 1503 were economically and politically among the most difficult that Florence had to endure in the Renaissance.[45] The Strozzi Palace was the proverbial rule-proving exception. Richard Goldthwaite's study has shown that while construction continued at a steady pace throughout our period, from 1491 to 1506, wages dropped for construction workers in the catastrophic winter of 1494–95. In such an atmosphere of political and economic uncertainty, private investment in construction must have dried up, causing, as Goldthwaite notes, a collapse of demand. The enormous stash of gold florins in Filippo's estate was doubtless what made possible continuation of construction of his palace and chapel, unique in the 1490s. It was not until 1500 that wages began to approach the pre-1494 figure.[46] Actually the situation in Florence only finally improved with the death of the Borgia pope, Alexander VI, and the consequent collapse of Cesare Borgia's threat to the Florentine territory in the summer of 1503.

The works commissioned in 1499 are strongly stamped with the imprint of Savonarola. Bartolomeo della Porta's *Last Judgment* was created to decorate a tomb, but not in a church.[47] In keeping with the Piagnone's directive, it was in the cloister of the dead at Santa Maria Nuova. The scriptural text, carefully designated in the commission, is Luke 21:25–33, which comes from the so-called Little Apocalypse, the most immediately personal version of the final catastrophe. For the frescoes commissioned from Botticelli for Ognissanti a unique iconography must have been created. The commission, discovered by Ronald Lightbown, was given in the will of Giorgio Antonio Vespucci, who had received the Dominican habit from Savonarola's hand in June 1497. Vespucci stipulated that his family chapel be decorated in part with the life of Dionysius the Areopagite, the radical dualist and mystic whose writings appealed to the asectic extremists among the Piagnoni.[48]

San Salvatore al Monte was previously thought to have been

constructed by Cronaca during the decade of the nineties. It has recently been shown, however, that construction of the former church began in 1489, as noted by Landucci. There is evidence in old sources that it was substantially completed by 1490.[49] In 1499 water damage caused collapse of the cloister. Early the following year, a special commission consisting of Leonardo da Vinci, Giuliano da Sangallo, and Cronaca met to discuss the problem. Cronaca then undertook the rebuilding, which consisted of a clever rearrangement of several older structures.[50] Although emergency conditions required that his project be undertaken in the lean opening years of the century, it was not completed until 1504, when the new church was consecrated. It is in keeping with the mood of Florence around 1500 that this project should have been initiated in response to an emergency and that its success was the result of a patch-up effort that turned out better than could have been hoped. Such a history fits with our understanding of Cronaca's talents as well.[51]

The very few commissions of the early cinquecento years are given by either the commune or the Opera del Duomo, and they resound with political overtones. The first recorded installation of a work of art in the new century was on 14 April, when a relief of Christ was placed over the door of the chamber of the Signoria.[52] This is at the same time a forward- and a backward-looking gesture on the part of the commune. Installed soon after the new year and the new half-millennium, it symbolizes the dedication of the Signoria to a new era of government under Christ's guidance. But it also unmistakably recalls Savonarola's oft-reiterated proclamation: "In Florence, we have no other king than Christ."

In the Duomo, virtually no new work had been undertaken since Cronaca was appointed capomaestro on 23 June 1495. After a long period in which only necessary repairs were made, it was decided in January 1501 to use the marble that had been taken from the house of the Medici, stockpiled at the church, for new pavement in the Duomo.[53] There are two things of interest to us in this decision. First, it seems intended to punctuate the end of the Medici era and their hopes, and those of their adherents, for their return. Second, because materials already on hand were to be used, the cost would not be great.

In the spring of 1500, Leonardo returned to Florence after an eighteen-year absence. It is a symptom of the times not usually noted, I believe, that he, too, evidently remained without commissions; a little over a year later he decided to leave again to work for Cesare Borgia, Florence's chief enemy. Certainly the most exciting artistic event of 1501 was Leonardo's exhibition of the cartoon (now lost) for the *Madonna and Child with St. Anne*. Vasari recorded that people crowded into the room to see the new work, attesting to their hunger for new art.[54]

The return of Michelangelo, probably in May 1501, seems to indicate that he, as well as Leonardo, now regarded Florence as holding the promise of commissions. He was more fortunate than his colleagues; despite the nearly desperate political and economic conditions — or perhaps precisely because of them — the Opera del Duomo drafted the contract for the *David* on 16 August. Again, as with the new pavement, they were using materials already on hand so that the only expense was for labor. Nevertheless, in the context of the times it was an extraordinarily bold move. Did the Operai envision that the colossus which would emerge from their botched block would embody the quintessential marriage of the classical and the biblical? Did they stop to think that Michelangelo would undoubtedly create the hero nude? How would Savonarola have resolved the conflict of this "pagan" figure that incarnated antityrannical, republican aspirations he himself had done so much to engender and support? With Cesare Borgia camped five miles outside Florence, with Pisa, Pistoia, and Arezzo all in revolt, with Florence on the brink of political and economic collapse, the improbable shepherd boy–musician who slew the enemy giant was, indeed, the appropriate symbol.[55]

But the *David* stands alone in a desert of artistic inactivity. No other commission is recorded until 28 April 1502, when Andrea Sansovino took the initiative and proposed to the Opera del Duomo that he execute a *Baptism of Christ* for the Baptistry portal and they agreed.[56] The commune followed a couple of months later with the commission for a life-sized marble of Christ as Savior for the Great Council Hall (never executed).[57] Private patronage was still stagnant. The summer of 1502 was perhaps the low point in Florence's fortunes. The internal conflict of the political factions was finally resolved through a compromise, and on 26 August the position of gonfaloniere for life was enacted into law. On 1 November Pietro Soderini took office. The following sum-

mer, when the Borgia threat was removed, Florence's patrons and artists heaved virtually audible sighs of relief and the dam burst.

The double-faced high altarpiece for Santissima Annunziata was
ordered from Filippino Lippi; he died in 1504 before completing it and
the commission was passed in August 1505 to Perugino, breaking at
last his prolonged drought in Florence.[58] Is there any truth to Vasari's
story that Leonardo had asked to do this altarpiece soon after his return
to Florence and that Filippino had gracefully stepped aside?[59] There is
no evidence to support Vasari and the atmosphere in Florence during
these years does not seem to have been conducive to such an action.
If it were true though, it would be another case, like that of Sansovino
in 1502, of the artist taking the initiative. In any event, by 1503 the
mood had decisively changed, and the Servite friars were ready to take
the initiative themselves. Several altarpieces were executed in 1503, the
first in Florence in almost a decade. Albertinelli's *Visitation* (Uffizi) is
dated in this year,[60] as is Ridolfo Ghirlandaio's *Madonna and Child with
Saints Francis and Mary Magdalen*.[61] Piero di Cosimo's *Marriage of St.
Catherine,* though undocumented, has also been convincingly dated to
this year.[62]

The Opera del Duomo, now anxious to hold at bay the rising
competition for Michelangelo's services, contracted with him in April
1503 to execute the series of twelve Apostles for the cathedral (of which
only the unfinished Matthew was ever undertaken), a commission that
would have kept him busy for several years to come. The Pandolfini
procured the services of Benedetto da Rovezzano to create a large chapel
in the atrium of the Badia, modeled along the lines of the old sacristy
of the Medici in San Lorenzo.[63] This substantial undertaking was not
completed until 1511, the same year that Giuliano da Sangallo finished
another major commission begun in 1503, the chapel of the Gondi in
Santa Maria Novella which Giuliano Gondi had provided for in his will
when he died in 1501. Nothing was done in that lean year, or the one
following, but the chapter allocated the chapel site to the Gondi heirs
in 1503.[64]

Commissions for private portraits seem to have come to a halt
in the years of Savonarola. Portraits are, of course, notoriously hard to
date and the rate of loss in this genre is unusually high, so one would
not want to put much weight on this evidence. Nevertheless, one doubts

that it is merely a coincidence that we know of no Florentine portraits between the marble bust of a man in the Bargello, dated 1495,[65] and the *Mona Lisa,* traditionally dated 1503.

The most important new undertaking of the year was the beginning of the Battle Frescoes for the Great Council Hall in Palazzo Vecchio. The walls appear to have been finished and ready for decorating some years earlier, but it was not until 1503 that anything was done. Wilde suggests that the decision to entrust Leonardo with the commission may have been made before his departure in summer 1502, but there is no evidence to support this supposition and it seems highly unlikely to me.[66] Leonardo took possession of the rooms in Santa Maria Novella allocated for his work on this project on 24 October, although the contract was not actually drawn up until spring 1504. Michelangelo, busy with the *David* until March 1504, began his *Battle of Cascina* the following December.

Despite all this artistic activity and the apparent return to normal conditions at last in 1503, there is a notable absence of tomb building in churches and chapels. In this area, at least, Savonarola's influence seems to have lingered long after his death. He had created an atmosphere in which it was difficult for the would-be patron to spend lavishly on frivolous concerns. He had appealed particularly to the newly enfranchised shopkeeper class in his attacks upon conspicuous consumption. This group, whose role in government was not diminished by Savonarola's passing, doubtless continued to exert a braking influence on the potential patron. Furthermore, a whole generation of youth, now no longer adolescents, had been authorized by Savonarola to castigate their elders for their vanities; the patricians under Soderini were perhaps chary of providing them with fresh opportunities. Soderini himself may have intended to break this unspoken ban and lead the way to a return to former practice when he had Benedetto da Rovezzano build his tomb in Santa Maria del Carmine in about 1508.[67] Altoviti, however, was the only patron to follow suit.[68] The other project for a tomb in these years, the ill-fated attempt to move the bones of San Giovanni Gualberto from Vallombrosa to a tomb, again by Benedetto da Rovezzano, in Santa Trinita, would have been applauded by Savonarola because the subject was a saint.[69]

A long period followed—otherwise artistically active—in which no chapels with wall tombs were constructed. In fact, the first I have been able to find is the Medici New Sacristy. New light is cast on this commission if it was intended to bring to an end the last lingering memory of Savonarolan scruples. The scale of the Medici tombs announces unequivocally that aversion to self-aggrandizement is no longer fashionable.[70]

To summarize, then: while we find in Savonarola's preaching many aspects of Renaissance humanism, a preaching style—a form consonant with this content is lacking. This lack in part accounts for the fact that he is so often described as a neomedievalist. I am persuaded that his message had much that was relevant and appropriate to Renaissance Florence. It failed—in part, at least—because he failed to find an appropriate form in which to convey it (Figure 20.6).

The same is true of the art executed under his influence. While it renounced the current mode of shallow naturalism, it also regressed to the manner of a much earlier era. To be sure, there is an aspect of Savonarola's message which is nostalgically recollective of the "good old days," and the subject matter, as well as the style, is in keeping with this emphasis, but this art fails to convey the heartening side of his vision. He failed to inspire artists, or patrons, to fashion an artistic style capable of capturing his theocratic message. He needed propagandists of the skill of those who had served Lorenzo il Magnifico and his circle. Perhaps there was simply insufficient time in his brief hegemony. But— and this is the point—the Savonarolan episode, though an artistic failure, broke the continuity both of style and of patronage. A successful new style had not been forged, but the old one no longer satisfied.

Into this vacuum Leonardo and Michelangelo stepped, introducing the style of the High Renaissance. The wonder and delight that, Vasari records, the Florentine painters expressed over Leonardo's cartoon reflects their recognition that here, at last, was new possibility, a new way out of the stalemate, the dead end they had reached.

Why stalemate? What had the Savonarola years extinguished or destroyed? I believe it was the willingness to be satisfied with representing sheer optical reality at the expense of the spiritual. Perhaps Savonarola's reiterated proclamation that the Christian must live in the light of the Holy Spirit had left an indelible mark. The effort on the part of the quattrocento to "sanctify the secular," in Donald Weinstein's

Figure 20.6. Savonarola writing in his cell at San Marco. Woodcut from his *Libro . . . della semplicita della vita cristiana,* published on 31 October 1496 in Florence by Lorenzo Morgani for Piero Pacini. Florence, Biblioteca Nazionale Centrale. Photo Artini.

well-turned phrase,[71] had wandered astray in the painting of the eighties and early nineties. The secular reality was so successfully represented in religious works that they often failed to suggest the spiritual dimension. The abstractions of the early quattrocento, like Piero della Francesca's geometry or Fra Angelico's absolute color, had been devices to signal the supernatural superstructure; as these gave way to ever greater naturalism, the sanctity of the secular was no longer conveyed. The Flemish device of disguised symbolism, introduced dramatically into Florence with the arrival of the Portinari altarpiece in 1483,[72] was grasped by painters as a way to suggest holiness without disrupting the surface of reality. Allegory, too, was used to imply another level of meaning. But the paintings tended to become no more than a mirror of the secular world and the symbols were esoteric, requiring interpretation in order to be appreciated.

Did Savonarola's direct approach and his call for simplicity make this kind of ratiocination seem elitist, antidemocratic? Certainly one of the hallmarks of the new style of idealization was that it concealed difficulty, striving to make the picture look accessible and not artificial. It is also certain that patrons did not rush to revive the old style of pedestrian realism after Savonarola, and by 1506, when Perugino finished the high altarpiece for Santissima Annunziata in that style, it was derided as hopelessly old-fashioned.[73] And certainly the central achievement of the new style was the marriage of the spiritual with plausible reality.

NOTES

1. In particular, see Gustave Gruyer, *Les illustrations des écrits de J. Savonarole publiés en Italie au XV et XVI siécles et les paroles de Savonarole sur l'art* (Paris, 1879); Joseph Schnitzer, *Savonarola, ein Kulturbild aus der Zeit der Renaissance*, 2 vols. (Munich: Reinhardt, 1924), esp. chap. 35, "Stellung zur Kunst und den Kunstlern"; Mario Ferrara, *Prediche e scritti* (Milan: Hoepli, 1930); Anthony Blunt, *Artistic Theory in Italy, 1450–1600* (Oxford: Clarendon Press, 1940); and André Chastel, *Art et humanisme à Florence au temps de Laurent le magnifique* (Paris: Presse universitaire, 1959, 1982).

2. Ronald Steinberg, *Savonarola, Florentine Art and Renaissance Historiography* (Athens, Ohio: Ohio University Press, 1977).

3. David Friedman, "The Burial Chapel of Filippo Strozzi in Sta. Maria Novella in Florence," *L'arte*, n.s. 3, no. 9 (1970): 109ff. Friedman makes the point that Strozzi had his tomb placed so that it functions as altarpiece behind the altar, an audacious and unprecedented arrangement in fifteenth-century chapels.

4. John W. O'Malley, *Praise and Blame in Renaissance Rome: Rhetoric, Doctrine, and Reform in the Sacred Orators of the Papal Court, c. 1450–1521* (Durham: University of North Carolina Press, 1979).

5. Charles B. Schmidt, "Gianfrancesco Pico's Attitude toward his Uncle," in *L'opera e il pensiero di G. Pico della Mirandola nella storia dell'umanismo*, 2 vols. (Florence: Istituto nazionale di studi sul Rinascimento, 1963) 2:305–13; Schmidt, in making the point that Savonarola has a mistrust of reason as the final authority which runs counter to the humanist philosophers, quotes his sermon of 15 August 1496: "Among the sciences of logic, philosophy, metaphysics and the other sciences, the greatest of all is that of Sacred Scripture."

6. Donald Weinstein, *Savonarola and Florence: Prophesy and Patriotism in the Renaissance* (Princeton, N.J.: Princeton University Press, 1970).

7. An example is provided by his remarks on pagan learning, which illustrate an attitude more complex than it is usually made out to be. First, the impassioned exhortation: "Repent, I say, so that God will have mercy on you. You have many books in your house that you shouldn't have because shameful things are written in them. Burn these books that

are not Christian. If you want to be Christian you need to be annointed by the Holy Spirit, not by shameful pagan things." Then come the modifying remarks, in which he goes on to say that some books are good in themselves and useful because they are moral and that he does not reject the knowledge and doctrine they contain. It is a reordering of priorities he is calling for, a corrective to the substitution of classical learning for scriptural that he sees around him. See his sermon preached on 6 November 1494, text John 12:35, *Prediche italiane ai fiorentini*, ed. Francesco Cognassi (Venice: La Nuova Italia, 1930) 50–51.

8. Sermon preached on 19 June 1496 on Micah 3, *Prediche di F. Girolamo Savonarola*, ed. Giuseppe Bacchini (Florence, 1889) 279: "Udite qua, questo si fa a Roma e a Firenze, che si edificano le case e i belli palazzi col sangue de' poveri."

9. Sermon preached in Lent (no. 17), 1496; cited by Richard Goldthwaite, *The Building of Renaissance Florence: An Economic and Social History* (Baltimore: Johns Hopkins University Press, 1980), 87, who in turn cites Marino Ciardini, *I Banchieri ebrei in Firenze nel secolo XV e il Monte di Pietà fondato da Savonarola* (Borgo S. Lorenzo, 1907), 95–96.

10. Sermon preached on 2 November 1494; the full text and translation is found in Friedman, "Burial Chapel," 123 and n. 34.

11. Sermon on John 15 preached on Ascension Sunday, 15 May 1496; see Baccini, *Prediche*, 80: "Cosi fanno ancora oggi i tepidi, che non vogliono conoscere il culto interiore di Dio, ma solo attendono alle ceremonie di fuori, e credono che il fare una cappella o paramento sia tutto l'onore di Dio, e non conoscere che Dio risguarda il core, non le mani, e pero ogni volta che si scuoprono le loro reti da tirare denari, loro si adirano, e sono i quest' errore per la loro superbia e malignita."

12. Sermon on Ruth 2, preached on 20 May 1496; see Baccini, *Prediche*, 114: "Va vedi le case loro, erano tutte semplici, non facevano palazzi d'oro e d'argento, non era in loro se non semplicita."

13. Sermon on Ps., quoted in Friedman, "Burial Chapel," n. 44.

14. Richard Trexler, "Ritual in Florence: Adolescence and Salvation in the Renaissance," in *The Pursuit of Holiness in Late Medieval and Renaissance Religion*, ed. Charles Trinkaus with Heiko A. Oberman (Leiden: E. J. Brill, 1974), 200–264. See also Pasquale Villari, *La storia di Girolamo Savonarola e di' suoi tempi*, 2 vols. (Florence: Felice Le Monnier, 1930); Villari has pointed out that this ritual was invented as a substitute for a brutal game of stoning traditionally played by the boys at Carnival in which invariably at least one boy each year was killed.

15. George Eliot recreated the scene in *Romola* in an amusing encounter between these children with their baskets and a middle-aged widow who has not been able to bring herself to give up painting her cheeks and covering her graying locks with false hair. The importunate children manage to denude the poor Monna Brigida of her vanities and leave her distraught on the street corner. Romola rebukes them and retrieves the purloined cap and braids, saying that in this they were exceeding in their zeal what even Savonarola would have wished. One suspects that Eliot is correct: it was trivial vanities of this sort, rather than large numbers of paintings and manuscripts, that fueled the flames. (I have not been able to consult André Chastel, "Le bûcher des vanités," *Cahiers du Sud* [May 1956].)

16. Schnitzer, *Savonarola*, 814, 839 ff.

17. Samuel Y. Edgerton, Jr., *Pictures and Punishment: Art and Criminal Prosecution during the Florentine Renaissance* (Ithaca, N.Y.: Cornell University Press, 1985), 175 f.

18. "Tanto sono belle le creature, quanto più participano e sono più appresso alla bellezza di Dio: e ancora più bello è il corpo, quanto è più bella L'anima." He goes on to compare two women who are equally beautiful in body, but of unequal spiritual beauty: "Togli qua due donne che sieno equalmente bello di corpo: l'una sia santa, l'altra sia cattiva; vedrei che quella santa sara più amata da ciascuno che la cattiva, e tutti gli occhi saronno volti in lei, etiam degli uomini carnali" ("Take two women, of equal physical beauty, one holy, the other wicked; you will see that the holy one is more beloved than the wicked woman: that all eyes are turned to the holy one, even the eyes of carnal men"). Quoted in Mario Ferrara, *Prediche*, 386, from the sermon preached on the Friday after the third Sunday of Lent, 1496, in the series on Amos and Zachariah.

19. Ibid., 387: "Le immagini dei vostri dei sono le immagini e similitudini delle figure che voi fate dipingere nella chiese, e i giovani poi vanno dicendo a questa donna ed a quell' altra: Costei é la Maddalena, quello é San Giovanni, ecco la Vergine; perché voi fate dipingere le figure nelle chiese alla similitudine di quella donna o di quell' altra, il che é molto mal fatto e in gran despregio delle cose di Dio. Voi dipintori fate male, ché se voi sapesse lo scandalo che ne segue, e quello che so io, voi non le dipingeresti. Voi mettete tutte le vanità nelle chiese. Credete voi che la Vergine Maria andasse vestita a questo modo come voi la dipingete? Io vi dico che ella andava vestita come una poverella, semplicemente e coperta che appena se gli vedeva il viso. Così, Santa Elisabetta andava vestita semplicemente. Voi fareste un gran bene a scancellarle queste figure che sono dipinte cosi disoneste. Voi fate parere la Vergine Maria vestita come meretrice. Or sì che il culto di Dio é guasto!" ("The images of your gods are the images and likenesses of the figures you have painted in the churches; and youths go about saying of this woman or that one, 'She is the Magdalene, there is St. John, there's the Virgin:' because you have the figures in the churches painted to look like this or that woman, the which is ill done and contemptuous of holy things. You painters do ill: if you knew what spiritual confusion comes of it, as I do, you would not paint these things. You put every vanity in the churches. Do you think the Virgin Mary would go about dressed as you paint her? I say to you that she was dressed like a poor girl, simply, and covered up so that you could hardly see her face. St. Elizabeth too was simply dressed. You would do a very good deed if you erased those figures of yours painted to resemble immoral women. You show the Virgin Mary dressed like a prostitute. Now indeed is the worship of God destroyed!") Quoted in ibid., 387, from the sermon preached in the same series on Saturday after the second Sunday of Lent.

20. Lorenzo Tornabuoni was one of five ringleaders of a conspiracy to restore Piero de' Medici to power who were executed in August 1497; see Weinstein, *Savonarola*, 282.

21. Goldthwaite, *Building of Florence*, 82.

22. Emanuele Rodocanachi, *La femme italienne à l'époque de la Renaissance*, (Paris: Hachette, 1907), 139, 150 ff.

23. A. Scharf "Studien zu einigen Spätwerken des Filippino Lippi," *Jahrbuch der Preussischen Kunstsammlungen* 52 (1931): 20 ff. Scharf connected the Academy wings with the Berlin *Crucifixion*, but Katherine Neilson, *Filippino Lippi* (Cambridge, Mass.: Harvard University Press, 1938), 146 ff. was doubtful. She noted the deliberate stress of their ugliness and suggested that Lippi may have been influenced by Donatello's works in the same vein. R. Steinberg, *Savonarola*, 131 n.9, doubts that the archaism of the gold ground should be associated with Savonarola. Chastel, in the preface to the 1982 edition of *Art et humanisme*, rejected Steinberg's argument.

24. Ronald Lightbown, in his *Sandro Botticelli,* 2 vols. (London: Elek, 1978), 1:133, concluded that this painting must have been created for a follower of Savonarola, probably in 1497. Concerning Botticelli's personal attitude toward Savonarola, there is no proof either that he was, or was not, a *piagone.* He certainly received several commissions from patrons who were, but they may have been attracted by his brother Simone, with whom Sandro lived, whose Savonarolan sympathies were widely known. The case of Filippino Lippi, who worked at the same time for Valori and Strozzi, passionate advocates of opposite sides, indicates that an artist's personal convictions were not what a patron commissioned.

25. Ibid.; "Painted in the last days of the Florentine year 1500," i.e., before 24 March 1501. Lightbown places only two paintings during these years: the small *Judith Leaving the Tent of Holofernes* in Amsterdam, dated between 1498 and 1500, and a lost fresco, discussed below.

26. F. W. Kent, "Lorenzo di Credi, his patron Iacopo Bongianni and Savonarola," *Burlington Magazine* 125 (1983): 539–41. The altarpiece was underway but not completed by mid-1497. It had, in fact, been planned much earlier: Bongianni made his donation for Sta. Chiara in March 1494. His tomb, placed at the foot of the high altar, was already built by July 1497 (Bongianni's will, published by Kent).

27. The discovery of the actual original locations of the *Primavera* and the *Birth of Venus* (John Shearman, "The Collections of the Younger Branch of the Medici," *Burlington Magazine* 117 [1975]: 12–27; W. Smith, "On the Original Location of the *Primavera,*" *Art Bulletin* 57 [1975]: 31–39) has necessitated the rethinking of their iconography, undertaken with practical good sense by Lightbown. In his reading, they are correctly relieved of much of the philosophical and literary baggage with which these pictures had been increasingly burdened. The *Primavera* as a compliment to a new bride is an appealing and persuasive idea. I am still attracted by the association made by Ernst Gombrich, "Botticelli's Mythologies," in *Symbolic Images* (London: Phaidon, 1972), 73, between the Birth of Venus and the Baptism of Christ. The rich fabric of meanings in the Uffizi *Adoration of the Magi* from eucharistic through the Compagnia de' Magi to Medici portraits has been explored by Rab Hatfield in his book, *Botticelli's Uffizi Adoration: A Study in Pictorial Content* (Princeton, N.J.: Princeton University Press, 1976).

28. Those excluded are: Giovanni Cornuola, engraver of hard stones; Attavante, miniature painter; Biagio d'Antonio Tucci, pupil of Cosimo Rosselli; Guasparre di Simone, goldsmith; Michelangelo Bandinelli, goldsmith; Chimenti di Francesco Tassi, wood-carver; Andrea, called il Riccio, goldsmith; Ludovico, goldsmith and master of bronze-casting; Bernardo di Marco della Cecca, wood-carver; Lorenzo dalla Golpaia, clockmaker; Salvestro, worker in precious stones. This list is according to Charles Seymour, *Michelangelo's David: A Search for Identity* (Pittsburgh: University of Pittsburgh, 1967), 141–43.

29. Walter Paatz and Elizabeth Paatz, *Die Kirchen von Florenz: Ein kunstgeschichtliches Handbuch,* 6 vols. (Frankfort am Main: Klostermann, 1940–54).

30. For example, Piero di Cosimo's *Visitation* for one of the Capponi chapels in Sto. Spirito, formerly dated c. 1500 (Washington, D.C., National Gallery), can now be confidently dated a decade earlier on documentary evidence; see Stephanie Craven, "Three Dates for Piero di Cosimo, *Burlington Magazine* 117 (1975): 572–76.

31. At least three chapels in Sto. Spirito have altarpieces of this period not yet firmly dated; see Paatz, *Kirchen,* 5:144–45. It may be that when the documents and sources are studied, the work on these chapels will prove to have been largely finished by c. 1495. For the present, I have had to exclude them from my survey.

518 MARCIA B. HALL

32. The bell that had called Savonarola's supporters to worship at S. Marco and then, on 8 April 1498, to arms, was solemnly sentenced by the signoria in the Decrees of 29 and 30 June. It was to be dragged through the streets and whipped by the public executioner, then exiled for at least fifty years to the hostile convent of S. Salvatore al Monte; Schnitzer, *Savonarola,* 2:432; L. Ferretti, "Per la 'Piagnona' di San Marco," *Memorie domenicane* 25 (1908): 375–78.

33. Chastel, *Art et humanisme,* 400. See also, idem, "L'Antéchrist à la Renaissance," in *Atti di II Congresso internazionale di studi umanistici,* ed. E. Castelli (Rome/Milan, Fratelli Bocce, 1952), 177–86, esp. 182 f.

34. Luca Landucci, *A Florentine Diary from 1450 to 1516,* ed. I. del Badia (New York: Dover, 1969), 48–49.

35. Ibid., editorial note by I. del Badia.

36. For example, Filippino Lippi, *Adoration of the Shepherds* (Uffizi) for S. Donato a Scopeto, signed and dated 1496. The high altarpiece, commissioned in 1485 by Giovanni Tornabuoni for Sta. Maria Novella, was not completed in 1494 when Domenico Ghirlandaio died. The payment to Baccio d'Agnolo in 1496 for the frame has been taken as the date of completion. For the reconstruction of the double-faced altarpiece and discussion, see Christian von Holst, "Domenico Ghirlandaio: L'altare maggiore di Sta. Maria Novella a Firenze ricostruito," *Antichità viva* 8, no. 3 (1969): 36 ff.

37. See Johannes Wilde, "The Hall of the Great Council of Florence," *Journal of the Warburg and Courtauld Institutes* 7 (1944): 65–81. In what is still one of the most useful studies of this period, Wilde reconstructed the remodeling and redecoration of the Sala Grande based upon the documents published without analysis by Karl Frey in 1909. Because of the need of the new government for a large assembly hall to house the newly created Great Council, work proceeded rapidly despite the economic recession. Antonio da Sangallo was nominated architect on 23 May 1495 and on 15 July Cronaca and Monciatto were appointed foreman-builders. The construction was quickly completed—the first meeting was held there on 26 April 1496 (Landucci)—but the furnishing moved at a slower pace. The decoration was delayed until 1503 and the years following (see below), with the exception of the altarpiece, which was assigned to Filippino Lippi shortly before Savonarola's death (Wilde, 76). It was never completed, although Lippi was paid a first installment in 1500 and Baccio d'Agnolo's frame was awarded a high fee when it was completed in June 1502. Fra Bartolomeo was finally given the commission in 1510, but he also never completed it.

38. If Andrea Sansovino was born c. 1467 as Pope-Hennessy estimates *(Italian High Renaissance and Baroque Sculpture* 1, 3 vols. [London: Phaidon, 1963], 3:45), one would expect him to be busy with commissions in Florence in the 1490s. He had already proved his talents with a major work in the tabernacle in Sto. Spirito for the Corbinelli family; he had received this commission by c. 1485 when he was only eighteen. Between this piece and 1502, however, there is no documented work by him in Florence. Vasari was perhaps trying to account for this gap when he said that Sansovino had worked in Portugal in the nineties, an assertion that modern scholarship has found difficult to support. (For bibliography, see Pope-Hennessy.) The important point for our purposes, however, is that he was not working in Florence during the period under study, but was busy with commissions after 1502–3.

39. Giuliano da Sangallo had been the principal architect in Laurentian Florence, so his close association with that group caused him to leave when the Medici were expelled in 1494. Construction on both the Strozzi and Gondi palaces was continued despite his only

intermittent appearances in Florence. He returned to the city at the end of 1500 (G. Marchini, *Giuliano da Sangallo* [Florence: Sansoni, 1943]), but received only minor jobs until 1503, when he was appointed *capomaestro* of the Palazzo della Signoria, replacing Baccio d'Agnolo, and then given the commission for the Gondi chapel in Sta. Maria Novella (see note 64 below). In 1505 Pope Julius II, who as Cardinal della Rovere had been Giuliano's patron in the 1490s, summoned him to Rome. He was dismissed two years later and returned home to Florence. The fact that the renowned and respected Giuliano da Sangallo was not put to work on some major commission in Florence soon after his first return is a further indication that although the artists were returning, the patrons were not yet roused from their lethargy.

40. Cronaca was in a loose sense Giuliano's pupil. It was he who executed Giuliano's design at the Palazzo Strozzi. Cronaca was appointed capomaestro of the Duomo in 1495, was a permanent member of the Strozzi staff from 1491 to 1504, became foreman of the Sala Grande reconstruction in 1495, and was in charge of rebuilding and remodeling S. Salvatore al Monte after 1500. Although involved in virtually every building project in Florence during these years, he accepted numerous outside jobs. He had taken so many leaves of absence that, after being criticized for it, he petitioned to have his salary reduced as capomaestro of the Duomo in 1502. (See Archivio dell'Opera; Deliberazioni dal 1498 al 1507, ac. 188, 8 July 1502, cited in A. Radice, "Il Cronaca: A Fifteenth-Century Florentine Architect," [Ph.D. diss., University of North Carolina, Chapel Hill, 1976], 12.) It is difficult to know whether to interpret this as evidence of his popularity and success or of his need to take additional work during this period.

41. Perugino was very actively engaged in the Florentine artistic scene in the early 1490s. He married at Fiesole in September 1493; although he declared Mantua to be his official residence in 1494, he had bought a house that year in Florence and considered it to be one of his principal residences. See Craig Hugh Smyth, "Venice and the Emergence of the High Renaissance in Florence: Observations and Questions, in *"Florence and Venice: Comparisons and Relations,* 2 vols. (Florence: La Nuova Italia, 1979), 1:230–31. In 1494, Perugino executed the portrait of the Florentine Francesco delle Opere (the date on the back of the painting tells us it was finished in July); probably in that year he painted the *Pietà* now in the Uffizi for S. Giusto. In the following year, he delivered the lovely *Pietà* now in the Pitti to Sta. Chiara, and in April 1496, he completed the *Crucifixion* fresco for Cestello which had been commissioned in 1493. In marked contrast to this pattern, from 1496 on, he busied himself and his shop entirely with commissions for altarpieces outside Florence, in such places as Fano, Senigallia, Pavia, Vallombrosa, and Perugia. He may have even transferred his principal residence to Perugia after 1496. It does not seem likely that he was turning away Florentine commissions in favor of these provincial ones. In fact, he had delayed executing the Fano altarpiece from 1488, when it was commissioned, until 1497, when presumably he took advantage in the lull in Florentine patronage. See F. Battistelli, "Notizie e documenti sull'attivita del Perugina a Fano," *Antichità viva* 13, no. 5 (1974): 65–68. Alternatively, he may have designed it around the time of the commission. See Sylvia Ferino-Pagden, "Pintoricchio, Perugino or the Young Raphael? A Problem of Connoisseurship," *Burlington Magazine* 125 (1983): 87, with further bibliography.

42. The lack of dated works has made Piero di Cosimo's chronology unusually fluid. Current scholarship has shunted most of his paintings to either before 1495 or after 1505. Nothing is securely dated to the decade between. The works that might have been executed within this period are: *The Story of Primitive Humanity* (Oxford, Ashmolean, and New York, Metropolitan), dated by L. Grassi 1490–1500 (*Piero di Cosimo* [Rome: Ateneo, 1963]) and by F. Zeri

1505–7 ("Rivenendo Piero di Cosimo," *Paragone* 115 [1965]: 36–50); the two Vulcan panels (Hartford and Ottawa), again dated by Grassi and M. Bacci 1490–1500 (*L'opera completa di Piero di Cosimo* [Milan: Rizzoli, 1976]) and by Zeri after 1500; and the altarpiece of the Innocenti (Paatz, *Kirchen,* 2:450), dated by Zeri to the beginning of the new century. S. J. Freedberg agrees with Zeri (*Painting of the High Renaissance in Rome and Florence* [Cambridge, Mass.: Harvard University Press, 1963]), but Bacci and others place this work in the nineties.

The Worchester *Discovery of Honey* and the Fogg *Misfortunes of Silenus* were described by Vasari as having been painted for Giovanni Vespucci's palace. E. Fahy, in "Some Later Works of Piero di Cosimo, "*Gazette des Beaux-Arts* 107 (1965): 201–12), associated them with Giovanni's marriage in 1500, although Zeri had dated them 1505–7 and Bacci concurred. If they were executed c. 1500, they would represent a significant exception to the general moratorium, especially because they are nonreligious. Since this branch of the Vespucci family had been leaders of the opposition to Savonarola, one could see a gesture of defiance in this commission.

43. See note 36 above.

44. See Alison Luchs, *Cestello: A Cistercian Church of the Florentine Renaissance* (New York: Garland, 1977). Of the altarpieces for the twelve side chapels, five were produced between 1489 and 1494: one "after 1492." The only work dated between 1494 and 1505 is the statue of St. Sebastian attributed to Lionardo del Tasso for the Riccialbani chapel, although in 1495 six chapels had been founded which lacked altarpieces.

45. See in particular Felix Gilbert, *Macchiavelli and Guicciardini* (Princeton, N.J.: Princeton University Press, 1965); and L. F. Marks, "La crisi finanziaria a Firenze dal 1494 al 1502," *Archivio storico italiano* 112 (1954): 40–72.

46. Richard Goldthwaite, "The Building of the Strozzi Palace: The Construction Industry in Renaissance Florence," *Studies in Medieval and Renaissance History* 10 (1973): 178–79.

47. Christian von Holst, "Fra Bartolomeo und Albertinelli: Beobachtungen zu ihrer Zusammenarbeit am Jungsten Gericht aus Sta. Maria Nuova und in der Werkstatt von S. Marco," *Mitteilungen des Kunsthistorischen Institutes in Florenz* 18 (1974): 273–318.

48. Lightbown, *Botticelli,* doc. 24 and p. 130.

49. See Padre Damiano Neri, "San Salvatore al Monte," *Firenze* 2 (1933): 262. Neri reported that the sources Waddingo and Pulinari both state that the church was begun and finished in 1490. Neri, declaring this impossible, supposed that the work was substantially completed in that year. He noted that the friars began officiating in the church in 1490 and that the Nerli chapel was used for burial in 1496.

50. See Vittorio Vasari, "Il Cronaca al S. Salvatore al Monte," *Antichità viva* 20, no. 4 (1981): 47–50. Vasari takes the date of the transfer of the disgraced bell, La Piagnona, from S. Marco to S. Salvatore (June 1498) as evidence for completion of construction. The peculiar circumstances surrounding this bell (see note 32 above), not mentioned by Vasari, suggest to me that it was not conditions at S. Salvatore which dictated the timing: the bell tower could have been finished and empty for several years. The decision to install it there was a symbolic gesture on the part of the signoria: To punitively remove it from S. Marco and give it to the Franciscan opposition.

51. Goldthwaite ("Strozzi Palace") has noted that Cronaca's role in the Strozzi project was to execute the model made by Giuliano da Sangallo. He made a more detailed model, but he was not honored in the documents with the usual title of capomaestro (or of "architetto") until 1497. He seems in this project and in the Sala Grande renovation to have been more the practical foreman on the site than the conceptual designer.

52. Landucci, *Diary,* 208.

53. Paatz, *Kirchen,* 3:335.

54. The cartoon exhibited in Florence was a successor to the one presently in London's National Gallery, which had been executed in Milan before his departure in December 1499; see Kenneth Clark, *Leonardo da Vinci* (Cambridge: Cambridge University Press, 1952) 107–8. See also Giorgio Vasari, *Le vite dei più eccellenti pittori, scultori ed architettori,* ed. Gaetano Milanesi, 7 vols. (Florence, 1878–85), 4:38.

55. The decision of the Operai to do something about the marble figure called David in the courtyard, "male abbozatum et sculptum," is recorded on 2 July 1501. The commission followed six weeks later. Seymour, *David,* 134 ff., reproduces the documents: nos. 36–37.

56. The group was left unfinished when Sansovino left for Rome in 1505 and was eventually completed by Vincenzo Danti. The angel on the left has been added; see Pope-Hennessy, *Renaissance and Baroque,* 3:46. The previous year he had undertaken a similar commission outside Florence, a *Madonna and Child and John the Baptist* for the Genoa cathedral.

57. The statue was to stand on the gonfaloniere's tribune: "sopra el capo della residentia del gonfaloniere"; see Wilde, "Hall," 77, and the documents published by Poggi, *Rivista d'arte* 6 (1909): 144–46. See also Alison Luchs, "A Relief by Benedetto da Rovezzano in the National Gallery of Art in Washington," *Mitteilungen des Kunsthistorischen Institutes in Florenz* 18 (1974): 363–69.

58. At the time of his death, Vasari tells us (*Le vite,* 4:586), Filippino had completed the upper zone of the *Deposition,* now in the Academy, Florence. Perugino finished this and executed the *Assunta* for the other face (still in the church).

59. Vasari states that although the friars housed Leonardo in the convent, he did not begin work. He connects the cartoon exhibited in Florence in spring 1501 with this commission. Trying to account for the various difficulties raised by Vasari's story, Jack Wasserman has made an interesting suggestion. He argues that Vasari may not have known of Leonardo's return to Florence in 1500–1501 and may therefore have thought that 1503 was the year of his arrival from Milan. The whole episode of Lippi receiving the SS. Annunziata commission, then withdrawing in favor of Leonardo, then being reinstated becasue Leonardo never began work, actually took place in 1503. This interpretation of the documents seems to me to be the most satisfactory yet proposed; see J. Wasserman, "A Re-discovered Cartoon by Leonardo da Vinci," *Burlington Magazine* 112 (1970): 202–3.

60. For a discussion of the high altar of Sta. Elisabetta, see Paatz, *Kirchen,* 2:20. Martin Wackernagel, *The World of the Florentine Renaissance Artist,* trans. Alison Luchs (Princeton, N.J.: Princeton University Press, 1981), 279, states, following Richa, that it came from the Congregation of the Visitation fathers, as the altarpiece for their oratory.

61. Freedberg, *Painting,* 589. The original location of this altarpiece has not been traced.

62. Ibid., 597: c. 1503. It was commissioned by Piero del Pugliese for his chapel in the Innocenti and is now in the Ospedale Museum; see Paatz, *Kirchen* 2:450, "um 1490–1500."

63. Ibid., 1:282.

64. Ibid., 3:711; James Wood Brown, *The Dominican Church of Sta. Maria Novella at Florence* (Edinburgh: Schulze, 1902), 133.

65. Luigi Dami attributes the bust to Pollaiuolo; see his "Il Cosiddetto Macchiavelli del Museo del Bargello," *Dedalo* 6 (1925): 559–69. Dami denied the identification as Macchia-

velli. The attribution was treated skeptically in Pope-Hennessy, *Italian Renaissance Sculpture* (London: Phaidon, 1958), 317, and denied by Leopold D. Ettlinger, *Antonio and Piero Pollaiuolo* (London: Phaidon, 1978), 170–71. The date is inscribed on the inside.

66. Wilde, "Hall," 79.

67. Paatz, *Kirchen*, 4:212. See also Luchs, "Relief."

68. Altoviti died in 1507, but his tomb in SS. Apostoli is not mentioned in Albertinelli, suggesting that it was not yet built. Paatz suggests 1512; see *Kirchen*, 1:238.

69. Luchs, "Relief," 365; Paatz, *Kirchen*, 5:291 and 316.

70. Creighton Gilbert, in what for me is the most useful interpretation of the Medici Chapel iconography to have been proposed ("Texts and Contexts of the Medici Chapel," *Art Quarterly* 34 [1971]: 391–408), emphasizes that its theme glorifies the princes. So, too, do Frederick Hartt ("The Meaning of Michelangelo's Medici Chapel," in *Beitrage für G. Swarzenski* [Berlin: Mann, 1951], 145ff.) and Pope-Hennessy, *Renaissance and Baroque*, 1:22–25. The observation offered here reinforces this view.

71. Donald Weinstein, "Critical Issues in Civic Religion," in Trinkaus and Oberman, *Pursuit of Holiness*, 268.

72. Bianca Hatfield Strens, "L'arrivo del trittico Portinari a Firenze," *Commentari* 19 (1968).

73. Vasari, *Le vite*, 3:586. Vasari reports that when the Florentines took Perugino to task for using figures he had used before, he replied that they had praised them before.

21 ❧

GIAN FRANCESCO PICO DELLA MIRANDOLA

Savonarolan Apologetics and the Critique of Ancient Thought

EUGENIO GARIN

THE HERCULEAN STRUGGLE to reconcile Christian faith with the philosophical principles of classical antiquity reached an impasse in late quattrocento Florence and underwent a decisive reverse. In this chapter, Eugenio Garin shows how Savonarola studied humanist writings only ultimately to reject them, in turn influencing Giovanni Pico della Mirandola's nephew, editor, and biographer — Gian Francesco Pico — to reverse his uncle's most cherished conclusions. From Professor Garin's essay arise both a brilliant picture of the range of historiographic interpretation available to late quattrocento religious thinkers and an astonishing instance of Renaissance Christianity's ability to use humanist thought for its own ends. Of unique interest is the relationship Garin demonstrates existed between the revival of Greek Skeptic thought and conservative Christian apologetics: a paradoxical alliance that would free Western philosophy to explore the natural sciences and in so doing overturn the very foundations of religious faith it was meant to uphold.

EUGENIO GARIN, president of the Italian National Institute for Renaissance Studies and professor at the Scuola Normale, Pisa, is a foremost scholar of Italian Renaissance humanism and the author and editor of many books on Renaissance thought and letters.

HESE BRIEF CONSIDERATIONS arise from long study of the philosophical culture of fifteenth-century Florence in relation to those tensions of religious and political reform that agitated the city in the same period.[1] This relationship extended from the great debates, at the beginning of the century, on ancient poetry and the study of classical literature (involving men like Coluccio Salutati and Cardinal Giovanni Dominici) to the council for the unity and peace of the churches, that exceptional event intertwining Cosimo de' Medici's plans with the utopian prophecies of the Byzantine Platonists. It extended from the Hermetic thought made fashionable by Marsilio Ficino to the scheme for a "Platonic theology" nurtured at the court of Lorenzo the Magnificent; from Giovanni Pico della Mirandola's cabalistic program and dream of the peaceful reconciliation of all religious systems to Savonarola's projects for moral and political renewal. Florence did not merely pass through a splendid season of art and thought; she nourished it with her singularly rich religious life.

The Savonarola affair was the tragic conclusion of all this, almost a symbol of failure. Invited to Florence by that tormented thinker Giovanni Pico della Mirandola, Fra Girolamo Savonarola was soon successful in fascinating those very intellectual groups in which the Neoplatonic renascence had predominated. His influence is clear in the changing relationship between Ficino and Giovanni Pico: Ficino had always tried to present Pico not only as a loyal colleague in Platonic studies but also as an ally in the same cultural struggle. In 1489, when Ficino was in trouble with the church authorities for publishing his *Liber de vita,* he immediately named Pico, invoking him as his "Phoebus" and drawing him into the dispute—even though Giovanni Pico had made little use, and that innocuous, of cabalistic methods in his *Discourse on the Seven Days of Creation,* published in the same period.[2] On his side, Giovanni Pico not only consistently maintained his distance from Ficino but also, as Savonarola's influence on him and his friends grew, increasingly differentiated his position from Ficino's.

524

The question of prophecy is a case in point. Savonarola defended the supernatural character of prophecy against the followers of Avicenna and their theory of a prophetic intellect. In his sermons on the Book of Ezekiel we read that "prophecy, dearly beloved in Christ, is not a natural thing, nor does it proceed from a natural cause." The future cannot be read in the stars, nor is "the gift of prophecy a natural power included in the intellect," as had been suggested by Avicenna, whom Ficino held dear and quoted extensively and who was known in Florence to thinkers outside the field of medical scholarship. A well-known related case is Giovanni Pico's battle against astrology, a part of which Savonarola would sum up in vernacular Italian. Less studied but no less relevant is the battle waged by his nephew, Gian Francesco Pico, against the same opponent but on a wider front and more systematically (here the text to bear in mind is Gian Francesco's *De rerum praenotione*).[3]

Returning to turn-of-the-century Florence, we may say that together with Giovanni Pico, others, some of them important figures, gathered around Savonarola in the meetings at the San Marco library, distancing themselves from Ficino's blazing Neoplatonism. The writings of Pietro Crinito allow us to rediscover the tenor of those discussions — held in Savonarola's presence — in which Pico, with extraordinary enthusiasm, reviewed the theological currents of pagan antiquity which finally culminated in Christian truth. Crinito tells us that Savonarola listened and made comments: indeed, while hardly an original philosophical thinker, Savanarola was not ignorant of philosophy, even if his thought derived from quite different sources, Aristotelian and Thomistic. He had been a *magister* in Ferrara and in Florence, and we have his books (Book II of his *Compendium logicae,* the "hundred questions," is not without interesting passages). Most interesting of all, however, is the effort Savonarola made in Florence to bring himself up to date with fashionable culture.[4]

Years ago, in a manuscript from the conventual library of Santa Maria Novella now in the Biblioteca Nazionale,[5] I found some of the writings mentioned in the old catalogue of Savonarola's works added to the end of his *Vita latina* — writings sought in vain by historians and believed lost. Among these were a *Plato abbreviatus* or *De doctrina platonicorum* and an anthology from Giovanni Pico's concordance of ancient religious systems (*Ex libro Concordia Jo. de Mirand.*). Although this is not

Figure 21.1. Savonarola and an astrologer. Woodcut from Savonarola's *Contra li astrologi*, printed in Florence c. 1497 by Bartolomeo de'Libri. Florence, Biblioteca Nazionale Centrale. Photo Artini.

the place to analyze these texts, they are of great interest. They testify that Savonarola, while never doubting Aristotle's superiority, was willing to concede that Plato, too, was a fine fellow. He qualified his approbation, however: "I do not say their lives were good, or that they were entirely good men—absolutely not."[6] What Savonarola would not in fact concede, even to St. Augustine, was that "by removing certain things from Plato he is in conformity with faith."[7] In his Sermon 22 on the Book of Exodus, Savonarola underlined his position: "And I say this because some people want to make all of Plato Christian. Rather, let Plato be Plato and Aristotle Aristotle; do not make them Christians, because they are not."[8] And in Sermon 25, on Ezekiel, he said, "The smallest Christian child is better off than they [Plato and Aristotle]. They ordained everything to their own honor and glory, not to God's. I remember reading a letter from Plato to Dione, in which he says that in the last analysis all he has done has been done for his own honor. Socrates, he says, followed a demon . . . that never incited him to good deeds. *Ergo,* it was not a good angel."[9]

Savonarola's conclusions with regard to Giovanni Pico's *Concordia* are no more positive. While admiring Pico's moral fervor and enthusiasm, Savonarola makes use only of the humanist's arguments against astrology as a means of divining the future, rejecting both Pico's esteem for Platonic tradition and the basic thesis of a "concordance" among world religions. It is on this very point, however, that a meeting of minds occurs between Savonarola and Gian Francesco Pico, Giovanni's nephew, only five years younger than his uncle and his fervent admirer and indefatigable editor, although not a faithful follower. In Gian Francesco Pico, Savonarola found an acute interpreter who, from his suggestions, drew theoretical and historical conclusions of great importance. These conclusions overthrew the concordist vision of ancient thought delineated by Giovanni Pico and brought to light a critical force that, through a radical skepsis, could rebuild the entire edifice of knowledge: the new encyclopedia of the sciences. Paradoxically, out of this Savonarolan apologetic system, which with tools furnished by Greek Sceptic thought sought to destroy the whole heritage of ancient philosophy in defense of faith in Christ, there arose the foundations of a new system of critical reason.

It was a long and complex process, intermingling a variety of cultural traditions but dominated by the Savonarolan presence. Gian Francesco Pico did not, in fact, arrive at his radical conclusions immediately, implying as they did a clear choice between his uncle's "concord" and Fra Girolamo's refusal to admit the validity of any agreement between ancient pagan and Christian thought. In 1496, not long after his uncle's death and while Savonarola was still living, Gian Francesco dedicated two books to Alberto Pio: two volumes of *De studio divinae et humanae philosophiae* (On the study of divine and human philosophy). These works had their origin in a discussion of contemporary culture in disagreement with the many "pseudo-philosophers" who "adore *humanae literae*" and are "slaves of pagan culture" ("qui se totos gentilium literis mancipiant"). Arguing against such as these, Gian Francesco Pico recalled that "the reign of God is found in the simplicity of faith, not in contentious speech," and that "it did not please God to save his people by logical debate."[10] Still, he recognized a kind of propaedeutic value in classical philosophy: in the ascent toward supreme knowledge, various philosophers have brought individual states of being gradually into focus; their theories are useful as successively integrated "moments" until we pass over into total vision. In this sense, Gian Francesco acknowledged having used his uncle—indeed, several specific works of his uncle's, beginning with chapter 5 of Giovanni Pico's *De ente et uno*. He then names three otherwise unknown treatises, unmentioned by any historian: *De humana hierarchia, De vita perfecta,* and *De perfectae orationis circulo*. It seems that these three works were unfinished products of the period during which Giovanni's religious tensions grew more insistent. Gian Francesco intended to publish them.[11]

Thus, when Giovanni Pico was laid to rest in his tomb at San Marco, Gian Francesco still had some of his uncle's positive view of ancient philosophy and of primitive theology (a view not totally alien even to Savonarola's at a certain point, as we have seen). Later, however, Gian Francesco not only separated himself from such perspectives, but radically overturned this whole way of interpreting the history of human thought. In his major work, *Examen vanitatis doctrinae gentium et veritate Christianae disciplinae* (Examination of the vanity of the doctrines of the pagans and of the truth of Christian discipline), brought out in printed form at Mirandola in 1520 but probably composed between 1502 and 1514, Gian Francesco reverses Giovanni Pico's concept. Phi-

losophy, in its historical unfolding, is not the history of a slow conquest
of truth wherein, on close examination, even marked divergences may
be seen as ultimately semantic rather than substantial. For Giovanni
Pico, if only one employed the right hermeneutical devices, it was possible to grasp the profound harmony that reconciled Plato and Aristotle, Avicenna and Averroes, Thomas Aquinas and Duns Scotus; the
peace of philosophy corresponded to the peace of faith. At some point,
however, Gian Francesco Pico chose a different path — a different vision
of the course of human thought — and declared as much. For him, the
quarrels of the philosophers stand in marked contrast to the peace of
faith. And this was precisely the basic attitude of Savonarola, who, according to Crinito, uttered this warning during a debate in the "academy" at San Marco: "Beware . . . that you do not mistake words for
realities. For those who drag the ancient philosophers into our Academy easily either deceive themselves or cause others to be deceived. For
Plato taught insolence of spirit, and Aristotle, impiety."[12] And between
Giovanni Pico and Savonarola, Gian Francesco chose Savonarola: "To
my mind it seemed more fitting and more useful to recapitulate the
uncertainty of the philosophers' beliefs rather than reconcile them, as
my uncle wanted to do."[13] The more so, he adds, since that is what
the ancient philosophers themselves did: Plato derided and confuted his
predecessors, the Peripatetics did the same with Plato, the Stoics with
the Peripatetics, and so on, without exception (Figure 21.2).

Gian Francesco Pico's *Examen* is really one of the most important philosophical works of the century, coming out in print in the
midst of the Lutheran storm in 1520, defending faith against every pre-
varication of reason. It proceeds systematically, carefully using Greek
thought to argue *against* Greek thought. And in all this, Gian Francesco
was only realizing a wish of Savonarola's, as he himself recalled in a
biography of the friar which he later wrote. It had in fact been Savonarola who pushed Giorgio Antonio Vespucci (who became a Dominican
in 1497) to study the works of Sextus Empiricus, the second-century
Greek physician and Skeptic, follower of Pyrrho, whose works Vespucci
was to have translated into Latin from a manuscript that belonged to
him before passing into the San Marco library.[14]

Sextus Empiricus and Pyrrho were not unknown in Florence,
to be sure. The reading of Cicero had already blazed the trail for this

Figure 21.2. Savonarola discoursing with pagan and Arab philosophers. Over the friar's head hovers the Holy Spirit, while in the background the dome of the Florence Cathedral is visible. Woodcut from Savonarola's *Dialogo della verita profetica*, printed in Florence by Antonio Turbini, Lorenzo d'Alopa, and Andrea Ghirlandi, c. 1498–1500. Florence, Biblioteca Nazionale Centrale. Photo Artini.

Skeptic current of thought. Sextus in particular had been studied and used by Politian, with typical profundity, to give a theoretical basis to that new encyclopedia of the sciences which Politian had in mind and which was to have replaced the medieval encyclopedia.[15] But Gian Francesco's way of using this writer was singularly fruitful: Sextus Empiricus, as is well known, examined critically the premises and procedures of the various disciplines in a theoretical discussion that was both subtle and merciless. Gian Francesco Pico, using the same method, summoned before the tribunal of critical reason the entire system of knowledge: all philosophies, all sciences, all doctrines, every tool of knowledge. Certain parts of his analysis of Aristotle's *Physics,* drawing upon medieval Jewish thinkers as important as they are unknown, are of extraordinary interest. It is true that he does all this in order to juxtapose with the weakness of man's senses and intellect the strength of faith; yet the astuteness of Gian Francesco's reasoning makes his systematic Pyrrhonism a precious resource for the creation of a new encyclopedia of the sciences.

The reawakened interest in Sextus Empiricus in sixteenth-century European culture is well known and need not be dwelt upon here — even if, notwithstanding Charles Schmitt's excellent contributions, more could be said of Gian Francesco Pico. The point of the foregoing discussion is rather to underline that singular paradox by which Fra Girolamo Savonarola's ardent faith was responsible for putting back into circulation the most corrosive heritage of ancient rationalism, with all the radical consequences that Pyrrhonism would have, from the sixteenth century to the eighteenth.

NOTES

1. In addition to the works indicated in the following notes, this essay draws upon my earlier writings on Savonarola, especially in E. Garin, *La cultura filosofica del rinascimento italiano,* 2d ed. (Florence: Sansoni, 1979), and on the reprints of the 1572 Basel editions of the works of both Giovanni and Gian Francesco Pico della Mirandola (*Opera omnia Iohannis Pico,* 2 vols., intro. E. Garin [Turin: Bottega d'Erasmo, 1971]; *Opera omnia Iohanni Francisci Pico* [Turin: Bottega d'Erasmo, 1972]). I intend to develop several of the ideas presented here in a longer article. The present short essay was translated from Italian by Timothy Verdon.

2. An English edition is available in Pico della Mirandola, *Heptaplus, or Discourse on the Seven Days of Creation,* trans. Jessie Brewer McGraw (New York: Philosophical Library, 1977).

3. See note 1 above. On Avicennism in Florence, see A. Cattani, *Opus de intellectu et de causis mirabilium efectuum* (Florence, 1505); see also C. B. Schmitt, *Gian Francesco Pico della Mirandola (1469–1533) and His Critique of Aristotle* (The Hague: Nijhoff, 1969).

4. On Savonarola's intellectual formation, see G. Cattini, *Il primo Savonarola: Poesie e prediche autografe nel codice Borromeo* (Florence: Olschki, 1973). See also Pietro Crinito, *De honesta disciplina*, ed. C. Angeleri (Rome: Bocca, 1955).

5. Biblioteca nazionale centrale di Firenze, Conventi Soppressi, D.8.985.

6. Ibid., "Non dico che . . . siano state buone vite, né che siano stati al tutto buoni, assolutamente."

7. Ibid., "Levate via alcune cose di Platone, lui si conformi alla fede."

8. "E questo dico perché alcuni vogliono fare tutto Platone cristiano. Si vuol fare che Platone sia Platone, Aristotile Aristotile, e non che siano cristiani, perché non sono" (Girolamo Savonarola, *Prediche sopra Esodo,* 2 vols., ed. Pier Giorgio Ricci [Rome: Belardetti, 1955–56], 2:289 ff.).

9. "È migliore il minimo fanciullo delli cristiani che non sono loro. Costoro ordinavano ogni cosa a gloria loro e loro onore, e non a Dio. Io mi ricordo aver letto in una epistola di Platone a Dione, nella quale dice in fine che ogni cosa faceva per onore proprio. Socrate dice che seguitava un demonio . . . che non lo provocava mai al bene, *ergo* non era buon angelo" (*Prediche sopra Ezechiele,* 2 vols., ed. Roberto Ridolfi [Rome: Belardetti, 1955], 1:324 ff.).

10. "Regnum Dei in simplicitate fidei est, non in contentione sermonum," and "non in dialectica placuit Deo salvare populum suum" (*Opera omnia J. F. Pico,* 2:1–39).

11. Ibid., "Quae nos cum reliquis eius operibus perficere, et in publicam dare utilitatem constituimus."

12. "Cave . . . ne verba pro rebus accipias. Nam qui veteres philosophos in academiam pertrahunt, perfacile quidem vel falluntur ipsi, vel alios fallunt. Plato enim ad animi insolentiam, Aristotiles vero ad impietatem instruit" (Crinito, *De honesta disciplina,* p. 1 ff.).

13. "Mihi autem venit in mentem consentaneum magis esse, et magis utile, incerta reddere philosophorum dogmata quam conciliare, ut patruus volebat." See Charles B. Schmitt, "Gian Francesco Pico's Attitude Toward His Uncle," in *L'opera e il pensiero di Giovanni Pico della Mirandola* (Florence: Olschki, 1965), pp. 305–13.

14. Now in the Biblioteca Laurenziana, Florence, pluteo 85, 11, with an inscription indicating that it had been copied on 8 September 1465. On Sextus Empiricus, see W. Cavini, "Appunti sulla prima diffusione in occidente delle opere di Sesto Empirico," *Medioevo* 3 (1977): 1–20.

15. See the preceding note and L. Cesarini Martinelli, "Sesto Empirico e una dispersa enciclopedia delle arti e delle scienze di Angelo Poliziano," *Rinascimento,* n.s. 20 (1980): 327–58.

Part Four

CODA ON METHOD

22 &

ALTARPIECES AND THE REQUIREMENTS OF PATRONS

CHARLES HOPE

IN REACTION to a tendency to "theologize" Renaissance religious art, ascribing erudite iconographical intentions to lay patrons, this chapter presents a more commonsensical approach. Through close analysis of surviving documents, Charles Hope illustrates the normally straightforward devotional concerns of the men and women who ordered altarpieces in the quattrocento and early cinquecento: their interest in images of sacred personages rather than narrative representations of historical events. He proposes a greater degree of interpretive freedom in artists' treatment of religious themes than has sometimes been supposed: an ability to draw upon the repertory of familiar imagery reiterated in prayers, hymns, and other works of art—all known to painter, patron, and public. Dr. Hope's conclusions invite revision of our estimate of the theological learning of the laity and, more generally, of the potential of works of art as bearers of complex doctrinal ideas.

CHARLES HOPE teaches the history of art at the Warburg Institute of the University of London. His publications include essays on Mantegna and Titian.

NTIL QUITE RECENTLY, the iconography of Renaissance altarpieces hardly seemed problematical. But now scholars have begun to ask new kinds of questions about these pictures, often drawing on evidence derived from liturgical practice and devotional texts. The questions are mostly of two kinds: first, about the possible iconographic significance not just of the principal figures, but of virtually every visual element; second, about what exactly is taking place in paintings that we for convenience call "Sacre Conversazioni." It has been suggested, for example, that the saints gathered around the Virgin are celebrating the celestial liturgy, or that the child is held up like the eucharistic host; and, more generally, altarpieces are said to be "about" aspects of doctrine, such as the Incarnation. These are supposedly meanings that would have been known to the artist and to at least a substantial proportion of the faithful, not just the kind of associations that might have been made ex post facto by someone with a sophisticated theological training and a contemplative cast of mind.

In this essay I try, in a very general way, to establish something about the framework in which altarpieces should be understood, to ask what kind of pictures people in the Renaissance thought they were, what kinds of expectation might commonly have been brought to bear on them.[1] Only if we do this, I believe, can we hope to discover what types of interpretation might appropriately be applied to them. I must emphasize that this is very much work in progress; my conclusion, that many of the questions currently being asked about Renaissance altarpieces are based on false premises, may therefore be the result of ignorance.[2]

During the Renaissance in Italy there were no hard and fast rules about the content of altarpieces, merely conventions. When Mass was celebrated, the altar was decorated with a crucifix, or rather with a representation of Christ on the cross, because if this was the principal subject of the altarpiece, then an actual crucifix could be omitted.[3] On

many occasions, too, altarpieces included representations of the saints
in whose honor the associated altar was dedicated, but the principle
laid down at the Synod of Trier in 1310 — that the name of each altar
should be clearly indicated by an inscription or an image — does not seem
to have been widely followed.[4] Carlo Borromeo, for example, merely
recommended that churches be decorated with holy images, without
further specifying what these should represent.[5] In Italy, indeed, clear
indications about the names of the titular saints of altars are often hard
to come by, since inscriptions are by no means always present, while
the altarpieces themselves frequently depict several saints, without necessarily giving special prominence to — or even including — the one in
whose honor the altar was dedicated. It is also important to recognize
that no one said that the content of altarpieces was different in kind
from that of images elsewhere in the church: that it should allude in
some specific way, for example, to the celebrations taking place at the
altar.

 Almost all Catholic discussion of images is of two basic types.
The first is concerned with the question of whether paintings and
sculptures should be shown in churches at all; here the standard text,
repeated on countless occasions, is Gregory the Great's famous dictum
that images are the Bible of the unlettered. The second is concerned
with abuses introduced by artists, such as the undue prominence given
to nude figures or the representation of apocryphal legends or material
likely to mislead the faithful. These issues, of course, became particularly important after the Council of Trent, but they had already been
raised in the fifteenth century, for example by Sant'Antonino.[6] Common to all such discussion was the attitude that the primary function
of art in churches was didactic, and was therefore concerned with narrative. Images of single figures such as saints always raised problems,
simply because they presented an obvious danger of idolatry. But, in
practice, Gregory's remark hardly ever seems to have served during the
Renaissance as a prescription for the selection of subjects represented
in churches generally, let alone on altars. Biblical narrative cycles from
that period do exist — as at San Gimignano, on the doors of the Florentine Baptistry, or the floor of Siena Cathedral — but lives of the saints
were much more common subjects. In altarpieces, moreover, narrative
scenes, whether from the New Testament or from hagiographical texts,

are relatively rare as the principal subject, apart from a very few constantly repeated themes, the most common in Florence being the Adoration of the Magi and the Annunciation. What we find instead, again and again, are representations of the Virgin and Child in the company of two or more saints, or, sometimes, the crucified Christ with saints or the Trinity with saints: in other words, people, not stories.

People, in fact, were exactly what the artists were required to paint. The evidence for this assertion comes above all from contracts, but also from virtually every type of contemporary source in which altarpieces are mentioned, right up to the time of Vasari. It is true that contracts follow standard legal formulas, that they do not tell us anything about informal conversations that may have taken place between artists and patrons and that their emphasis on the figures that a picture should contain might reflect a rule of thumb by which the pricing of paintings was related to the number of figures represented. But the wording of these documents, the specifications included or omitted, nonetheless provide an important guide to the features thought important by patrons when they commissioned altarpieces. Moreover, they exhibit a striking consistency not only in Tuscany but throughout Italy. This is as true of the manner in which the subject matter is described as it is of the clauses about materials and workmanship. I am concerned here principally with the iconographic requirements outlined in contracts, but it is worth emphasizing that patrons were always anxious to ensure that their paintings would be beautiful and well made.[7]

As described in contracts, religious images are divided into two broad categories. On the one hand, there are *storie* — narratives — and on the other, images with one or more figures which are not storie. In practice, before the sixteenth century, the term *storia* was used almost exclusively with reference to predella panels and the components of fresco cycles. On the rare occasions that it was applied to the main panel of a *tavola,* or altarpiece, the names of the principal figures were usually given as well, even though this might seem redundant. So in 1467 we find Neri di Bicci commissioned to paint a panel with "a Nativity of Christ in the middle, with St. Joseph at the left, and with angels and shepherds, as the storia requires, and on the left St. Bernard kneeling and on the right St. Benedict, and in the predella three storie, one of Our Lady, one of St. Benedict, and one of St. Bernard."[8] The 1489 contract with Pinturicchio for a Marriage of the Virgin, the picture subsequently painted by Perugino and now in Caen, specified that the artist should show the "storia and marriage of St. Joseph with the Blessed Virgin Mary."[9] In this case, there was a special reason for choosing this subject: the patrons evidently wanted the altarpiece to allude not only to the Virgin and St. Joseph, after whom the chapel was named, but also to the Holy Ring, which was preserved there.[10] It is difficult to see how they could have done so except by a depiction of the Marriage of the Virgin.

Here the circumstances were exceptional. On other occasions, the requirements of the patrons followed a more stereotyped pattern, as the following examples, chosen from a period of more than two centuries, should demonstrate. The first concerns Pietro Lorenzetti, who agreed in 1320 to paint a standard type of polyptych for the high altar of the Pieve of Arezzo, "a panel of the Blessed Virgin . . . with very beautiful figures, in the middle of which must be the image of the blessed Virgin Mary with her son and with four flanking figures to be chosen by the bishop [i.e., the patron], . . . and in the other spaces around he must paint images of prophets and saints chosen by the bishop."[11] In 1346, the Compagnia of Gesù Pellegrino at Santa Maria Novella decided to commission a new altarpiece, which seems to have been quite similar in design to Lorenzetti's. On this occasion, individual members of the confraternity agreed to pay for the different sections, each of which was to contain an image of a saint of their choice, with the Virgin in the center.[12] More than a century later, in 1461, Benozzo Gozzoli undertook to paint for the Compagnia di San Marco the panel now in the National Gallery, London (Figure 22.1). The contract specified the following:

> The said Benozzo is obliged to conduct himself in the said painting in such a way that the said picture should surpass every good painting executed up till now by the said Benozzo, or at least those with which it can appropriately be compared, and he must represent on the said panel the following images in the form and manner here specified: and first in the middle of the said panel the image of Our Lady with the throne in the manner and form and with ornaments like and similar to the panel of the high altar of San Marco in Florence; and on right side of the panel, beside our Lady, the image of St. John the Baptist in his

Figure 22.1. Benozzo di Lese (called Gozzoli), *The Virgin and Child Enthroned Among Angels and Saints*. Reproduced by courtesy of the Trustees, The National Gallery, London.

usual costume, and near him the image of St. Zenobius with his pontifical ornament, and then the image of St. Jerome kneeling with his accustomed costume, and on the left side the following saints, that is their image, namely first beside Our Lady the image of St. Peter and near him St. Dominic, and then near St. Dominic, kneeling, the image of St. Francis, with every appropriate ornament. And the said Benozzo must with his own hand paint down below, that is to say in the predella of the said altar, the stories of the said saints, each immediately below the saint in question.[13]

Thirty years later, in 1495, Perugino contracted to paint a panel for the chapel of the Magistracy of Perugia, which is now in the Vatican (Figure 22.2). The document specified that he was "to paint and adorn in the said chapel a panel on the altar of the said chapel with the image of the glorious Virgin Mary with her son in her arms and the images of four saints, namely SS. Lawrence, Herculanus, Constantius, and Louis . . . and likewise in the tabernacle above . . . to paint and adorn the image of the Pietà, or another image suited to that place, as the said Master Pietro chooses."[14] The fact that Perugino was permitted the degree of choice indicated in the final clause is all the more striking, given that the contract was drawn up in the presence of a doctor of theology.[15]

A final example is provided by Vasari's account of two altarpieces which he made for the cathedral of Pisa. Following a pattern already established by Sogliani, in the first, he showed the Virgin surrounded by saints — in other words, a conventional Sacra Conversazione. But in the second:

> he showed, as the Operaio wanted, another Madonna with her son at her neck, St. James Intercisus, St. Matthew, St. Silvester the pope and St. Torpes the knight; and so as not to do the same thing in his *invenzioni* as the others had done, even though he had introduced great variation in his other panel, having to represent the Madonna he showed her with the dead Christ in her arms and those saints, as around a Deposition from the cross. And on the crosses, which are high above, shown in the form of tree trunks, are represented two naked thieves, with horses around, and the executioners and Joseph and Nicodemus and the Marys. He did this to please the Operaio, who, in all the said panels, wanted to have represented all the saints who had been shown in the old chapels, to keep alive their memory in the new ones.[16]

The pattern is consistent enough over two and a half centuries. What these commissions reveal is a desire on the part of the patrons to have finely executed images of saints. In other words, they were concerned about who was to be shown in their altarpieces; and very often, as these examples make clear, they also wished to indicate the relative importance of the principal figures by their placing with respect to the Virgin. But the setting, the gestures, and the decorative details were left to the artist. Specifications about such features are extremely rare, and

Figure 22.2. Perugino, *The Virgin and Child with Saints,* Vatican, Pinacoteca. Photo Anderson.

seldom extend beyond the kind of generality that we find in the 1466 commission from the Compagnia della Nunziata in Arezzo to Piero della Francesca for a banner: "in the said *gonfalone* there should be Our Lady Annunciate with the angel, . . . and the heads of Our Lady and the Angel should be 'gentili' and 'belli a visi angelichi.'"[17] Notice here that as well as wanting the heads to be beautiful the patrons were asking for an image of Our Lady Annunciate with the angel, not for an Annunciation. This is standard in the fifteenth century. The patrons do not require a storia, a painting of an event, but an image of a person, Our Lady, who is characterized as the Virgin Annunciate by the inclusion of an attribute, the angel. Even the clause in the Gozzoli commission mentioned above, specifying that there should be "first in the middle of the said panel the image of Our Lady with the throne in the manner and form and with ornaments like and similar to the panel of the high altar of San Marco in Florence," is an instruction to the artist to represent the Virgin in a particular way, rather than to repeat an earlier composition.[18] In fact, Gozzoli diverged from Fra Angelico's painting in various ways: the throne has two steps rather than three; the angels, instead of standing beside the Virgin, replace the architecture behind her; and the Child is standing, not seated (see Figure 4.2). What he took from Angelico were the features that characterized Mary as Queen of Heaven—the throne, the garden setting, and the attendant angels.[19] But in no sense did he make a copy, nor was he required to do so. It is clear, of course, from the later instructions in Gozzoli's contract about the placement of the figures, that the patrons must have had the composition of the San Marco altarpiece in mind, but it is significant that they did not explicitly ask him to follow this model in the arrangement of saints, by placing all of them on ground level, for example. Their primary concern was with the iconography of the altarpiece; had they expected Gozzoli to follow their instructions equally closely in matters of composition, their attitude would have been wholly inconsistent with normal practice as reflected in contracts of this period.[20]

As it is used today, the term *attribute* is associated principally with material objects, such as the keys of St. Peter, or with a costume—for example, the Baptist's camel skin—which serves to identify a particular figure. But this usage, for which there is no real Renaissance equivalent, is unduly restrictive, since in practice other figures, landscape settings, and actions can have just the same function in a painting. Thus, as E. H. Gombrich has pointed out, the attribute of the Archangel Raphael is Tobias.[21] Likewise, the attribute of the Virgin is the Child, as he is also of St. Christopher, and when both are represented in an altarpiece, the Child is often shown twice. Vasari was once asked to paint a picture of this type, but he thought that the repetition of the Child would seem "monstrous," and therefore suggested that the Virgin, seated in the clouds, should place the Child on St. Christopher's shoulder.[22] Some saints, of course, did not have any standard attributes as we would understand the term but could readily be recognized by the context in which they appeared. A case in point is Joseph, who was not regularly shown holding the Child and the flowering rod before the seventeenth century. During the Renaissance, he was most frequently represented as a participant in a scene of the Nativity, as in Francesco Vecellio's altarpiece for the high altar of San Giuseppe in Belluno (now in Houston), for example, in which he is at the center of the composition.[23] Raphael's *Marriage of the Virgin* in the Brera, which came from a chapel of St. Joseph, is another solution to the problem.[24]

In modern English, a painting of Mary holding the infant Christ is usually called a Madonna and Child, but this is misleading in its implication that both figures have equal iconographic weight. In Renaissance documents, as in modern Italian, we read either of just the Madonna, or of the Madonna with the Child; and in paintings of the period inscriptions very frequently underline the fact that it is the Madonna who matters. Because the infant Christ does not appear in this context as a character in his own right but as an attribute of his mother, he is often represented as an adult elsewhere in an altarpiece. Perugino's painting, for example, now in the Vatican was originally surmounted by a panel showing the Man of Sorrows, and many other artists adopted a similar arrangement.[25] The most common location, however, was in the center of the predella, where Christ was regularly shown in a Crucifixion scene or as the Man of Sorrows — and this is arguably the one way in which the imagery of altarpieces might be related to the celebration of Mass on the altar. The faithful in front of such paintings are invited to remember both the Virgin and the Redeemer; but most altarpieces are reflections of devotion to the Virgin and the saints, not to Christ. This is not to say that Christ is never the principal figure in an altarpiece. But when he is, it can generally be assumed that the image reflects a particular cult, such as that of Corpus Domini of San Salvatore, or even of the Bambino; and in such cases one would expect the Virgin to be visually subordinate if she is present at all.[26] Of course, the emphasis on Mary in Renaissance altarpieces need not in itself indicate that she was accorded a more widespread devotion than her son. It could simply be that Christ is in a sense redundant in altarpieces, because he is shown on the crucifix placed on the altar itself.

Just as paintings that we would call Annunciations were described in the fifteenth century as pictures of the Virgin Annunciate with the angel, so, too, in the case of other subjects now given narrative titles, what mattered then was the identity of the protagonists rather than their actions. When the Nativity, for example, was shown as the principal subject of an altarpiece, it seems to have been chosen primarily as a representation of Mary as the mother of Christ. This is clear enough in the case of the painting by Neri di Bicci mentioned above, since here the predella contained stories of the principal figures, namely Bernard, Benedict, and the Virgin.[27] In 1473 Neri di Bicci painted another Nativity in a square panel, which he described in the following terms: "With these images, that is to say in the middle the Nativity of Christ, Our Lady alone, on her knees, and Jesus at her feet, and above God the Father and some little angels; on the right St. John the Baptist, either standing or kneeling as I think best, and likewise St. Michael; on the left St. Nicholas and St. Gregory."[28] That the iconographic focus here was the figure of Mary is indicated not only by the apparent absence of Joseph, but also by the fact that the patrons were members of the Compagnia di Santa Maria of Radda. A third example is provided by a carved wooden altarpiece commissioned in 1473 from Baldino da Surso for the chapel of St. John in San Michele Maggiore, Pavia. The contract specified that this was to show "the image of the glorious Virgin Mary with our Lord Jesus Christ *in presepio* and the ox and ass and also with SS. John the Baptist and John the Evangelist adoring Jesus Christ in presepio and with St. Joseph and with other features and requirements for the adornment of the said presepio and of the said representation, as is the custom."[29] Apart from the two St. Johns, who were presumably at the sides, this undistinguished work still survives; and, as one would expect, the most prominent feature is the figure of the Virgin in the center, kneeling before a diminutive child, with St. Joseph behind her.[30]

The Nativity, in fact, is as often Mariological as Christological, and it regularly appears in cycles of the life of the Virgin.[31] A case in point is Duccio's *Maestà*. It is usually said that the main panel shows the Virgin and Child in glory, and that in the pinnacles above were stories of the life of the Virgin after the Passion, with stories of the early life of Christ, among them the Nativity, in the predella. But Florens Deuchler is right to call the principal picture an image of the Virgin in glory, with Christ as her attribute.[32] And one should add that both the pinnacles and the predella contain stories of her life. She is the patron of Siena, which is why the front of the altarpiece is devoted to her, while the back is given over to stories of the life of Christ. And it is because the Nativity, when shown in the principal section of an altarpiece, is not really a storia but a painting of the Virgin in a particular guise, that there is no incongruity in showing her accompanied by saints who could not have been present at the historical event, and no incongruity either in giving her, as is so often the case, much more prominence than her son. To the best of my knowledge, anachronistic saints are never included in Nativity scenes in predelle, presumably because these are storie.[33]

Unlike paintings of the Nativity, altarpieces whose principal subject is the Adoration of the Magi very rarely include other saints, with the obvious exception of Joseph. At first sight this is unexpected, since both events commonly appear in cycles of the life of the Virgin. The reason, however, is quite simple. Whereas a Nativity scene functions as an attribute of Mary in her role as the mother of the newborn Savior, the Epiphany, traditionally the next episode in the infancy of Christ, does not characterize her in such a distinct way. Instead, altarpieces of this subject are first and foremost representations of the Magi. This is by far the most common context in which the three kings appear, and the context itself is their principal attribute; and it is for this reason that Vasari, for example, so often calls such pictures "tavole dei Magi."[34] As rich men who were among the first to acknowledge Christ and who presented him with lavish gifts, including gold, the Magi had a particular appeal to the wealthy, and above all to the banking families of Florence, an appeal indicated clearly enough in a letter written by

Alessandra Strozzi to her son in 1460, in which she described a *panno dipinto* she had acquired as "the Three Magi, offering gold to our Lord, and they are good figures."[35] It might be argued that devotion to the Magi could have been expressed in just the same way as devotion to saints, by including them in conventional Sacre Conversazioni. But their cult was anomalous, since they are not saints, and it may therefore have been thought slightly indecorous to give them a comparable status in paintings. Indeed, only one conspicuous exception comes in mind: Ghirlandaio's altarpiece for the Innocenti (Figure 22.3). This is generally called an Adoration of the Magi, and it certainly contains the basic elements of the subject: the Holy Family, a stable, and the Magi. But the Virgin, seated in the exact center, dominates the composition, which includes in prominent positions not only the three kings and their attendants, but also St. John the Evangelist, the adult Baptist, and two Holy Innocents.[36] In effect, therefore, Ghirlandaio's altarpiece is a Sacra Conversazione, a painting of the Virgin with saints and the Magi, and certainly not a storia.

There are very few altarpieces produced in Italy before 1500 which cannot be fitted into the scheme I have tried to outline. The surviving documents seem to indicate that the principal concern of the patrons was to have images of saints, especially the Virgin; and even when the subject was one that is now characterized as a narrative subject, a storia, it too can usually be seen as a representation of one or more saints in a setting that acts as a kind of attribute. In the rare instances where the principal panel of an altarpiece was characterized as a storia, we can usually be confident that the subject was chosen not because the patron wanted an illustration of a particular event but because he or she wished to have a representation of a particular person. In this respect, the fourteenth-century altarpieces in Siena Cathedral, showing episodes from the life of the Virgin, are unusual.[37] Here we have a real "Bible of the unlettered."

There is little indication, however, that all—or even some—of the altarpieces in a church would normally have been linked in a coherent iconographic scheme in this way. Rather, they resulted from individual initiatives by different patrons. And what changed between 1300 and 1500 was not the basic content of these pictures, insofar as it mattered to the patrons, but the means adopted by artists to display the

Figure 22.3. Domenico Ghirlandaio, *The Virgin and Child with the Magi and Saints,*
Florence, Ospedale degli Innocenti. Photo Alinari/Art Resource, N.Y.

figures. The iconographic requirements expressed in contracts were fulfilled equally adequately when the saints were shown in individual panels, when they were gathered together in a single picture, or when they were the protagonists in what we would normally consider a narrative subject. Thus even a painting such as the *Baptism of Christ* by Giovanni Bellini is essentially equivalent to a representation of a saint with his attribute, in this case the act of baptizing Christ (Figure 22.4).[38] At first sight, the placement of the three Persons of the Trinity on the central axis might lead one to suppose that the Baptist was not the most important figure to the patron; but this arrangement, which was surely dictated by decorum, was conventional. Christ is similarly located, for example, with the dove above him, in Cima's altarpiece in the Venetian church of San Giovanni in Bragora and in Piero della Francesca's panel in the National Gallery, London, and, without the dove, in the storia of the Baptism in the predella by Bartomeo di Giovanni of Ghirlandaio's Innocenti altarpiece. In all three pictures, St. John is the most significant figure iconographically. This is obvious in the case of the Cima, which was painted for the high altar of a church of which he was the patron saint.[39] The original location of Piero's panel is unknown: but it was the central section of a polyptych by Matteo di Giovanni, which included large figures of St. Peter and St. Paul at the sides, a roundel with an image of God the Father above, and a predella with five storie, four of them about the Baptist and the fifth, in the middle, showing the Crucifixion.[40] As for the Innocenti altarpiece, the contract for the predella specified that the *Baptism* was to be placed below the figure of St. John the Baptist.[41] The subject of Bellini's altarpiece was therefore presumably chosen because the patron, Giovanni Battista Graziano Garzadori, was devoted to the Baptist and wanted a particularly beautiful and impressive image of him.[42] In the same way, St. Sebastian's attribute is the fact that he was shot with arrows; thus Pollaiuolo's famous altarpiece in the National Gallery in London is not primarily a representation of the martyrdom of St. Sebastian, but an image of St. Sebastian.[43] He is there, like all the other saints in other altarpieces, because people wanted to pray to him and honor him; and the Virgin is shown more frequently than anyone else in such pictures because she was their supreme advocate and intercessor.

I would not wish to deny, of course, that these paintings by

Figure 22.4. Giovanni Bellini, *The Baptism of Christ*, Vicenza, Santa Corona. Photo Alinari/Art Resource, N.Y.

Bellini and Pollaiuolo look like storie—narratives; likewise, most Renaissance representations of the Virgin Annunciate with Gabriel are quite
reasonably called Annunciations. The distinction between the principal
panel of an altarpiece and the scenes in the predella is not primarily
a matter of composition, but of function. The former, by convention,
contains a representation of saints, the latter of events. And even though
artists increasingly used similar visual means to fulfill the two functions, these long remained distinct in the minds of the patrons, as the
terminology used in contracts makes clear. Storie, no doubt, would best
fulfill Gregory's prescription for a Bible for the unlettered, but individual patrons presumably did not commission altarpieces primarily to in-
struct the ignorant. They wanted to honor their favorite saints.

One other point also should be mentioned, namely, the presence of kneeling donors. It is often said that such figures are "presented"
to the Virgin, that they see the saints in the picture, or, in the case
of the Masaccio's fresco in Santa Maria Novella, that they see the Trinity. This is inherently implausible, since there is no reason to suppose
that any patron would have presumed to claim access to the beatific
vision before the Last Judgment. The real meaning of such images has
been well explained by Philipp Fehl in connection with Titian's *Pesaro
Madonna* (Figure 22.5).[44] Fehl argues that here Jacopo Pesaro is supposed
to exist on a different plane of reality from the heavenly figures. He
does not see them, but they see him, just as they see all of us. The
picture is first and foremost an invitation to us to honor a particular
group of saints, second, an expression of the donor's devotion to these
saints, and third, an invitation to us to remember him in our prayers
to them. Titian's masterpiece obviously fulfills these requirements particularly well, both because the portrayal of the figures, human as well
as divine, is so vivid, and because its exceptional beauty must always
have attracted the faithful to this altar; but every other image of this
type functions in just the same way. And even though the manner in
which donors were represented might have tempted people in the Renaissance to speak of them loosely as being "presented" to the Virgin,
the actual mechanism of the process seems to have been generally
understood. This is surely in part why a priest is recorded as having
objected to the very unconventional donor portrait of Broccardo Mal-
chiostro in Titian's Treviso *Annunciation* (Figure 22.6). As he put it:

Figure 22.5. Titian, *The Pesaro Madonna*. Venice, Frari. Photo Alinari/Art Resource, N.Y.

Figure 22.6. Titian, *Annunciation,* Treviso, Duomo. Photo Alinari/Art Resource, N.Y.

> When I go to say mass at the altar of the chapel of messer Broccardo
> and I say the Memento, and I see the image of messer Broccardo there,
> I feel thoroughly contaminated, because one is making reverence to that
> figure and not to the image of the Madonna; and when the bishop was
> here he did everything well, apart from the fact that he should have had
> that image of messer Broccardo removed, so that it wasn't in the middle
> of the altarpiece; and anyone who scrubbed it out or dirtied it would
> be doing a good job.[45]

Notice that the priest speaks of making reverence to the image of the
Madonna; he does not say that the portrait of the donor is objection-
able because it is out of place in storia of the Annunciation.

If we think about altarpieces in the terms I have outlined, I
believe that we will recognize that many modern interpretations of these
pictures are irrelevant and inappropriate. The concern of Renaissance
patrons was about which figures were shown; the actions these figures
performed were principally a means of identifying or characterizing them,
though they might also add to the beauty of the painting. There is no
hint in any document of the period, so far as I know, that people wished
to express or sought any deep theological message in altarpieces. At
most, they might have been attuned to note the proximity of individual
saints to the Virgin and would have expected the setting to suit the
status of the persons represented. Mary should sit on a throne because
she is a queen, and if the artist decorates that throne with an image
of the Fall of Man, as Mantegna does in the *Madonna della Vittoria,* she
is thereby further characterized as the new Eve (Figure 22.7). This is
an iconographic refinement, but one that is commonplace and perfectly
straightforward in its meaning. In this instance, moreover, it is very
likely that the fictive relief was added by Mantegna on his own initiative,
simply because he regarded it as suitable decoration. At any rate, this
feature is not mentioned in the correspondence about the picture with
Francesco Gonzaga; neither, for that matter, is Christ or the young Baptist: Francesco was informed only about the principal figures and how
they were to be placed in relation to the Virgin.[46]

In this painting we certainly have symbolism, in the relief of
the Fall of Man; it is almost always in the context of representations
of the Virgin that such symbolic features appear. This is easy enough
to understand. Her cult was particularly highly developed, and it in-

Figure 22.7. Andrea Mantegna, *Madonna della Vittoria,* Paris, Louvre. Service photographiques Musées Nationaux.

volved a repertoire of familiar imagery repeatedly invoked in prayers and hymns to her. More important, devotion to the Virgin was often devotion to her in one of her various guises—as Maria Annunziata, Maria Assunta or Gloriosa, as the Madonna della Misericordia, as Maria sempre Vergine, or as Maria Immacolata. Some of these could be shown, as we have seen, in quite obvious ways, usually by what we could call an Annunciation or an Assumption; though Antonello da Messina, in the paintings now in Palermo and Munich, showed a Maria Annunziata on her own, and Piero di Cosimo included one in a conventional Sacra Conversazione, now in the Uffizi (Figure 22.8).[47] This is unusual, but not really surprising when one recalls that the picture was originally in the church of SS.ma Annunziata.[48] The mechanism by which the angel fulfills the role of attribute to Maria Annunziata is shown particularly clearly by Filippino's altarpiece in the Caraffa Chapel, the entrance to which is surmounted by a prominent inscription proclaiming that it is named after the Virgin Annunciate and St. Thomas Aquinas (Figure 22.9).[49] In the same way, Titian's picture in Treviso was in a chapel used by the "Confraternita e Compagnia della Nuntiata Madre de Jesu Christo Vergene Maria."[50]

Just as Piero di Cosimo and Filippino showed the Virgin Annunciate with other saints, so Pordenone, in his painting in the Duomo at Udine, showed the Madonna of Mercy with St. Christopher and St. Joseph (Figure 22.10). Here, incidentally, the Child appears twice, on the shoulders of Christopher and in the arms of Joseph. As we have seen, at this period the Child alone was not a standard attribute of Joseph, but the latter is further identified here by his proximity to Mary. Presumably, Renaissance viewers would have had no difficulty in understanding such pictures. Problems arose for artists, however, with the newly popular Maria Immacolata because there was no existing iconographic tradition and because the idea of the Virgin's Immaculacy did not lend itself to visual representation in a way that was self-explanatory. Although the famous description in Revelation 12:1 of the woman clothed with the sun, standing on the moon and crowned with stars gradually became canonical in paintings of this subject, around 1500 the passage was not exclusively associated with Mary's Immaculacy.[51] Durer's images of Mary as the woman of Revelation, for example, all include the Child, a feature that would seem to rule out the idea that he intended

Figure 22.8. Piero di Cosimo, *The Virgin Annunciate with Saints,* Florence, Uffizi.
Photo Alinari/Art Resource, N.Y.

Figure 22.9. Filippino Lippi, *The Annunciation with St. Thomas Aquinas and Oliviero Caraffa,* Rome, Santa Maria sopra Minerva. Photo Alinari/Art Resource, N.Y.

an explicit association with the Immaculate Conception. When Italian artists at this time wanted to depict Maria Immacolata, they did not just show her without her son, being singled out by God the Father

Figure 22.10. Pordenone, *Madonna della Misericordia,* Udine, Duomo. Soprintendenza Beni Ambientali del Friuli, Venezia Giulia, Trieste.

with a rod; they literally had to spell out who she was, using inscriptions. Carlo Crivelli did this in his little panel of 1492, while Piero di Cosimo also included saints and doctors who supported the doctrine, holding prominent texts, and Francia and Signorelli added patriarchs for good measure, the latter incorporating the Fall of Man as well, to allude to Mary's freedom from Original Sin (Figures 22.11, 22.12).[52] The public, evidently, was not expected to understand such images without this kind of written assistance. Maria sempre Vergine, a rarer type, was equally problematic. Signorelli, in a painting in Cortona, not surprisingly solved the difficulty by much the same means as in his image of the Immacolata (Figure 22.13). But in this case there is no Fall of Man, God does not have the rod, and Mary herself holds both the Child and the lily of her virginity.[53]

Examples such as these demonstrate the limitations of paintings in the representation of sophisticated doctrinal concepts. And here we may recall what San Bernardino said about his IHS monogram. It should serve as a continual reminder to us,

> like the pictures which recall to you the Blessed Virgin or other saints, which pictures are made only in memory of the said saints. Note therefore that there are four kinds of letters, each better than the other. The first kind are gross letters for rude folk, as, for example, pictures; the next, for men of middle sort, are middle letters, as, for example, written letters; and these are better than the first. The third are vocal letters, invented for those men who desire actively to busy themselves for charity's sake, pleading and discoursing, in order that they may be learned and may teach others; and these excel the first two. Fourthly and lastly come mental letters, ordained by God for those who desire to persevere always in contemplation; and these are more perfect than the others and exceed them all.[54]

Today, many scholars seem reluctant to consider altarpieces merely as "gross letters for rude folk." But nowhere in the early sources do we find clear evidence that the artists were expected to give religious images any kind of elaborate theological content, except by inscriptions; nowhere in the writings of the Catholic apologists for images after the Reformation do we find this justification advanced for them. Indeed, any such justification would have conflicted with the canonical defense of images provided by Gregory. Altarpieces "recall the Virgin or other

Figure 22.11. Francesco Francia, *Immaculate Conception*, Lucca, San Frediano. Photo Alinari/Art Resource, N.Y.

Figure 22.12. Signorelli, *Immaculate Conception*, Cortona, Museo Diocesano. Photo Alinari/Art Resource, N.Y.

Figure 22.13. Signorelli, *Maria sempre Vergine,* Arezzo, Galleria e Museo Medievale e Moderna. Photo Alinari/Art Resource, N.Y.

saints," and it is inappropriate to regard them as comparable to Bernardino's second type of letters. They are not about the doctrine of the Immaculate Conception—though Maria Immacolata, to take one example, obviously could not be depicted without reference to liturgy and doctrine. Their form may change in the course of the Renaissance, but their function does not, both because the aspect of religious practice to which such images were related, the cult of saints and of the Virgin, remained essentially unchanged, and because that function was simple enough to accommodate itself to a variety of types of visual expression, as indeed it was to continue to do long after 1500. During the sixteenth century, there was obviously a certain change in the appearance of altarpieces, as Sacre Conversazioni were increasingly superceded by compositions that look like storie; but the general purpose remained that of "recalling the Virgin and the other saints," and, more specifically, of encouraging the faithful to offer prayers to the divine figures represented in such paintings. These aims could best be achieved by works that would attract the public by their beauty rather than by subtle allusions to theological ideas. Their role is defined with particular clarity in the prayer for the blessing of images contained in the *Rituale Romanum* compiled in 1614 under Paul V:

> Almighty and everlasting God, who does not disapprove that the likenesses of thy saints should be made manifest in painting [or sculpture], so that as often as we behold them with our bodily eyes so often may we resolve in our hearts to imitate their holiness of life, vouchsafe, we beseech thee, to bless and sanctify this image made in honor of thine only-begotten son Jesus Christ Our Lord [or of the Virgin, or of saints]; and grant that whosoever shall venerate and honor thine only-begotten Son [or the Virgin, or saints] in prayer before it, may by his [or her or their] merits and intercession obtain from thee grace in this life and eternal glory in the life to come.[55]

NOTES

1. I am particularly grateful to Elizabeth McGrath for her advice and criticism.

2. The following observations are essentially amplifications of remarks made by E. H. Gombrich in his *Symbolic Images* (London: Phaidon, 1972), esp. 13–17, 26–30; a similar

approach is also implicit in Creighton Gilbert, *Italian Art, 1400–1500* (Englewood Cliffs, N.J.: Prentice-Hall, 1980), esp. xviii–xxii.

3. Joseph Braun, *Das Christliche Altargerät in seinem Sein und in seiner Entwicklung* (Munich: Max Hueber Verlag, 1932), 466–74, esp. 473.

4. It is often said that altars are dedicated to saints, but this is not strictly accurate. All altars are dedicated to God alone, in the honor and memory of certain saints. See Joseph Braun, *Der Christliche Altar in seiner geschichtlichen Entwicklung,* 2 vols. (Munich: Alte Meister Guenther Koch, 1924), 1:725, and 2:281f.

5. Nowhere in the original edition of the Borromeo's *Instructionum fabricae et supellectilis ecclesiasticae libri II* (Milan, 1577) is there a recommendation that images should be placed on altars or that there should be an explicit reference to the titular saint. See Braun, *Altar,* 2:282.

6. Gilbert, *Italian Art,* 148.

7. In quotations from contracts given below I have not attempted to include all the specifications about workmanship and materials, especially in my translations.

8. Neri di Bicci, *Le ricordanze,* ed. Bruno Santini (Pisa: Edizioni Marlin, 1976), 301, no. 570, 20 July 1467: "ò a fare nel quadro una Natività di Xpo nel mezo, e dalla mano sinistra Giuseppo e chon angioli e pastori, chome alla istoria si richiede, e da mano sinistra Santo Bernardo ginochioni monacho e dalla mano destro Santo Benedetto e nella predella da pie' tre istorie, 1ª di Nostra Donna, 1ª di Santo Benedetto, 1ª di Santo Bernardo."

9. Fiorenzo Canuti, *Il Perugino,* 2 vols. (Siena: La Diana, 1931) 2:200: "Mag. Bernardinus Benedicti de Perusia . . . promisit et convenit . . . pingere in capella dictae societatis in Ecclesia S. Laurenti istoriam et sponsalia Santi Joseph cum Beata Virgine Maria . . . cum illis coloribus, et picturis, et aliis ornamentis, prout sibi melius videbitur convenire, habito respectu ad locum ubi est opus, etc."

10. On 31 May 1486, the patrons decided to construct the chapel and commission an altarpiece, explicitly following the recommendation of a famous preacher, friar Bernardino da Feltre, that "construatur quaedam Cappella in nominibus Gloriosissimae Semper Virginis Mariae ac Santissimi ac devotissimi Joseph, viri ipsius Virginis Mariae, et in dicta Capella reponatur Sanctissimum Anulum ipsius Virginis Mariae, ad hoc ut homines . . . possint venerare[?] dictum Anulum, ac altare Gloriosissimae Virginis Mariae ac devotissimi Joseph continue exornare, et ab eis gratias impetrare" (Ibid., 2:199).

11. Gaetano Milanesi, *Nuovi documenti per la storia dell'arte toscana dal XII al XVI secolo* (Florence: G. Dotti, 1901), 22 f., 17 April 1320: "Magister Petrus pictor quondam Lorenzetti, qui fuit de Senis, sollepniter et sponte promisit et convenit . . . pingere tabulam Beate Virginis Marie deputandam in ipsa plebe, de pulcherrimis figuris: in cuius tabule medio debeat esse ymago Virginis Marie cum filio et cum quatuor figuris collateralibus ad voluntatem ipsius domini Episcopi, laborando in campis et spatiis ipsarum figurarum de optimo auro . . . et in aliis circumstantiis circumferentiis et spatiis ipsius tabule pingendo ymagines profetarum et sanctorum ad voluntatem ipsius domini Episcopi de bonis et electis coloribus." I have translated *figura* here as "figure," even though "image" would be more accurate, since I have tried to preserve the distinction in the original document between *figura* and *imago.* The passages quoted below, in notes 13, 14, and 45, show that generally in such documents the most appropriate translation for *figura,* whether in Latin or Italian, is "image." Lorenzetti's painting, which is still in the church, is illustrated by E. T. DeWald, *Pietro Lorenzetti* (Cambridge, Mass.: Harvard University Press, 1930), fig. 1.

12. Milanesi, *Documenti*, 42f: "Memoria di quelli della Compagnia che meteranno nella detta tavola a farla dipignere. Ane chiesto Filippo Niccoli di fare dipingnere di suo nella detta tavola due santi, cioe San Filippo e San Zanobio. Ebbe Piero Rinaldi fiorini iiii d'oro. Ane chiesto ser Ciuto Cecchi et Piero Rinaldi il compasso di mezzo della detta tavola, e farla dipignere da loro e fare la Nostra Donna. A dato . . . Ane chiesto Lapo di Cione a fare dipignere nella detta tavola uno compasso e farvi dipignere Santo Simone." In her essay in this volume, Kathleen Arthur reports that Milanesi's transcription is incomplete. As one would expect, another member of the Compagnia undertook to pay for a further *compasso*, containing the image of another saint. Prof. Arthur has also discovered that those who contributed funds for the new altarpiece were the leading members of the Compagnia.

13. L. Tanfani Centofanti, *Notizie di artisti tratte dai documenti pisani* (Pisa, 1897), 84, 23 October 1461: "il decto Benozo sia tenuto in detto dipignere operarsi in modo che detta dipintura exceda ogni buona dipintura infino a qui facta per detto Benozo, o almeno a quella si possa debitamente equiperare, et debba fare in su la detta tavola le infriscripte fighure nel modo et forma chome apresso si dirà. Et prima nel mezo di detta tavola la fighura di nostra Donna chon la sedia nel modo et forma et chon ornamenti chome et in similitudine della tavola dello altare maggiore di sancto Marcho di Firenze, et dal lato ritto di detta tavola allato a nostra Donna la fighura di sancto Giovanni Batista nel debito usato suo habito, et apresso a llui la fighura di sancto Zanobi chol suo ornamento pontificale, et di poi la fighura di sancto Girolamo ginochioni chol suo debito et usato ornamento, et dal lato sinistro gl'infriscripti sancti, cioè loro fighure, item prima allato a nostra Donna la fighura di santo Piero et apresso a llui quella di santo Domenicho, et dipoi apresso a santo Domenicho ginochioni la fighura di santo Francesco chon ogni ornamento intorno a ciò consueto. Et debba detto Benozo di suo propria mano, chome di sopra è detto, dipignere da piè, cioè nella predella di decto altare, le storie di decti sancti, ciaschuna al dirinchontro del suo sancto."

14. Canuti, *Perugino*, 2:175, 6 March 1495: "Famosissimus in arte pictorum Mag. Petrus q. Vannutii de Castri Plebis, Civis Perusinus, promisit et convenit, praesentibus M[agnificis] D[ominis] P[rioribus] in numero sufficienti, et S. Theologiae Doctori Mag. Andrea Angeli Ordinis S. Mariae Servorum, . . . pingere et ornare in dicta Capella unam tabulam supra altare dictae Cappellae cum figura gloriosae Virginis Mariae, cum filio in eius brachiis et figura quatuor Sanctorum, videlicet S. Laurentii, Erculani, Constantii, et Ludovici . . . et similiter in tabernaculo superiori . . . pingere et ornare figuram Pietatis, aut aliam figuram ibidem correspondentem, ad electionem praefati Mag. Petri." The smaller panel originally at the top of the altarpiece, showing the Man of Sorrows, is now in the Galleria nazionale dell'Umbria, Perugia (Ibid., 1: pl. 62).

15. See note 14 above.

16. Giorgio Vasari, *Le opere di Giorgio Vasari*, ed. Gaetano Milanesi, 9 vols. (Florence, 1878–85), 5:128f.: "Nell'altre fece, come volle l'Operaio, un'altra Nostra Donna col Figliuolo in collo, San Giacopo Interciso, San Matteo, San Silvestro Papa, e San Turpè cavaliere: e per non fare il medesimo nell'invenzioni che gli altri, ancor che in altro avesse variato molto, dovendovi pur far la Madonna, la fece con Cristo morto in braccio, e que'Santi, come intorno a un Deposto di croce. E nelle croci che sono in alto, fatte a guisa di tronchi, sono confitti due ladroni nudi, ed intorno cavalli, i crucifissori, con Giuseppo e Nicodemo e le Marie, per sodisfare all'Operaio, che fra tutte le dette tavole volle che si ponessero tutti i Santi che erano già stati in diverse capelle vecchie disfatte, per rinnovar la memoria loro nelle nuove." Cf. 8:673.

17. Gaetano Milanesi, *Sulla storia dell'arte toscana scritti varj* (Siena, 1873), 299f., 20

December 1466: "in detto ghonfalone sia la Nostra Donna anonziata chon l'Angelo da uno lato et da l'altro di detto ghonfalone . . . e le teste de la Nostra Donna e di l'Angielo siino gentili e beli a visi angielichi."

18. See note 13 above.

19. The significance of showing the Virgin seated is made clear in the contract with Pinturicchio for an altarpiece for Sta. Maria degli Angeli in Perugia, dated 14 February 1495, published in Walter Bombe, *Urkunden zur Geschichte der Peruginer Malerei im 16. Jahrhundert* (Leipzig: Verlag von Klinkhardt und Biermann, 1929), 28: "Nel quadro de mezo de epsa tavola cioè net maiur [*sic*] quadro la imagine de la nostra gloriosa donna cum lo bambino in quello modo che parerà a dicto maestro che serà meglio et in maestà cioè in sedere cum quelli odornamente più convenienti."

20. See Hannelore Glasser, *Artists' Contracts of the Early Renaissance* (Ann Arbor, Mich.: University Microfilms 1975), 31 and 64–70. Glasser has drawn attention to the phenomenon of patrons asking for pictures "in the manner and form" of earlier ones, but she does not clearly distinguish between clauses requiring the artist to follow the design of an earlier panel, a physical object, and those concerned with the picture that was to be painted. In the fifteenth century, the former are much more common. Of the examples from this period cited by Glasser, only the Gozzoli contract could be interpreted as obliging the artist to follow an earlier compositional model for any of the figures. Her principal examples from the early sixteenth century are a group of panels of the Coronation of the Virgin produced for Observant Franciscans in Umbria, all of which are based on a painting in Narni by the Ghirlandaio workshop. Only the one by Lo Spagna in Todi is a close copy of the prototype, and only in this instance do we have a contract that seems to include such a specification, namely that the artist was to "facere picturam de auro cum coloribus et aliis rebus ad speciem et similitudinem tabulae factae in Ecclesia Sancti Jeronymi de Narne." The other surviving contract associated with this group, for Raphael's Monteluce altarpiece, merely called for "una tavola sive cona . . . de quilla perfectione, proportione, qualità et conditione della tavola sive cona existente in nargne nella chiesa de San Girolamo de luoco menore et omne de colore et figure numero et più et ornamenti commo in dicta tavola se contiene et de migliore perfectione si è possibele." Here there can be no doubt that the patrons wanted to have a panel like the one in Narni, and with the same iconography; but it is less clear that they expected Raphael carefully to follow the earlier composition. Glasser's comment that "admiration for a work of art may result in the desire to 'have one like it'" seems therefore to apply more readily to panels and frames than to compositions. For the different versions of the *Coronation of the Virgin*, see Umberto Gnoli, "Raffaello e la 'Incoronazione' di Monteluce," *Bollettino d'arte* 11 (1917): 133–54. See also Christa Gardner von Teuffel, "From Polyptych to Pala: Some Structural Considerations," in *La pittura nel XIV e XV secolo: Il contributo dell'analisi tecnica alla storia dell'arte*, ed. Henk W. van Os and J. R. J. van Asperen de Boer (Bologna: Cooperativa libraria universitaria editrice Bologna, 1983), 323–44.

21. Gombrich, *Symbolic Images*, 26–30.

22. Vasari, *Opere*, 6:302: "essendo quella cappella intitolata in San Iacopo ed in San Cristofano, vi voleva colui [Bernardino di Cristofano da Giuovi] la Nostra Donna col Figliuolo in collo, e poi al San Cristofano gigante un altro Cristo piccolo sopra la spalla, la quale cosa, oltre che parea mostruosa, non si poteva accomodare, nè fare un gigante di sei in una tavola di quattro braccia. Giorgio adunque, disideroso di servire Bernardino, gli fece un disegno di questa maniera. Pose sopra le nuvole la Nostra Donna con un sole dietro le spalle, ed in terra fece San Cristofano ginocchioni con una gamba nell'acqua da uno de' lati della tavola, e l'altra

in atto di moverla per rizzarsi, mentre la Nostra Donna gli pone sopra le spalle Cristo fanciullo con la palla del mondo in mano. Nel resto della tavola poi aveva da essere accomodato in modo San Iacopo e gli altri Santi, che non si sarebbono dati noia." In the event, the picture was never painted because the patron died. A similar solution to the problem of the duplication of the Child was adopted by Paris Bordone in his altarpiece in the Accademia Tadini, Lovere, although in this instance the Virgin is enthroned. For this painting, see *Paris Bordon,* exhibition catalog, Treviso (Milan: Electa, 1984), reproduced on 57.

23. See Fern Rusk Shapley, *Paintings from the Samuel H. Kress Collection, Italian Schools, Fifteenth to Sixteenth Century* (London: Phaidon, 1968), 177 and fig. 423.

24. Georg Gronau, *Raffael: Des Meisters Gemälde,* Klassiker der Kunst (Stuttgart/ Leipzig: Deutsche Verlags-Anstalt, 1909), 15, 222.

25. Cf. note 14 above.

26. Joseph Manca, in his article "An Altarpiece by Ercole de' Roberti Reconstructed," *Burlington Magazine* 127 (1985): 521f., discusses an altarpiece by Roberti which, as he observes, has as its theme the body of Christ. The central panel, preserved in a copy, showed a Pietà with saints, in which the main emphasis, unusually, was very markedly on the dead Christ rather than the grieving Virgin. In the predella was a *Last Supper,* flanked by *Abraham and Melchizedek* and *The Gathering of Manna,* a rare instance of the use of typological imagery in such a context. Manca tentatively suggests that the altarpiece was originally in the church of San Domenico, Ferrara, where it was recorded in the early seventeenth century (p. 522). In 1592, however, the predella panels were mentioned in the inventory of Lucrezia d'Este, Duchess of Urbino, who died in 1590 (p. 521 n.1). The fact that the altarpiece was dismembered could be explained by the hypothesis that it had been moved from its original location before 1590. If so, it is tempting to suppose that it was painted for the church of Corpus Domini. The adjoining convent was much favored by the Este family, and Alfonso I, Ercole II, Alfonso II, and Lucrezia were all buried there: Marc'Antonio Guarini, *Compendio historico ... delle Chiese ... di Ferrara* (Ferrara, 1621), 285f. An example of an altarpiece of S. Salvatore is Titian's *Transfiguration* on the high altar of S. Salvatore in Venice: see Harold E. Wethey, *The Paintings of Titian,* 3 vols. (London: Phaidon, 1969), 1: pl. 124. A rare instance of an altarpiece whose principal figure is the infant Christ is a picture by Francesco and Bernardino da Cotignola in the National Gallery of Ireland, Dublin (no. 106). Here the child is shown seated on a plinth in an impressive architectural setting, flanked by the kneeling figures of the Virgin and St. Francis, with St. Anthony of Padua and another Franciscan saint standing behind.

27. See note 8 above.

28. Neri di Bicci, *Ricordanze,* 413, no. 769, 22 May 1473: "cho queste figure, cioè nel mezo la Natività di Xpo, solo Nostra Donna ginochioni e Giesù a pie' di lei, e di sopra Idio Padre e parechi angiolletti; da mano diritta Santo Giovanni Battista o rito o ginochioni chome a me parà che meglio istia, e Santo Michele al medesimo modo; da mano mancha Santo Nicholò e Santo Ghirighoro."

29. Rodolfo Maiocchi, *Codice diplomatico artistico di Pavia dall'anno 1330 all'anno 1550,* 2 vols., (Pavia: Tipografia già Cooperativa di B. Bianchi, 1937) 1:195f., 8 April 1473: "quod Magister Baldinus faciet . . . himaginem gloriose Virginis Marie cum domino nostro Jesu Christo in presepio ac bove et asino et etiam cum Sanctis Johanne Baptista et Johanne Evangelista adorantibus Jeshum Christum in presepio et cum Sancto Josep ac cum aliis dependenciis et necessariis ad ornamentum dicti presepii ac dicte demonstrationis ut moris est."

30. Adriano Peroni, "Schede per la scultura lignea lombarda," *Arte lombarda* 10 (1965): 48, fig. 7.

31. Thus Vasari, *Opere,* 5:282, reports that Giovan Francesco Caroto painted for the altar of the Fraternita di S. Stefano in Verona, "in tre quadri di figure simili, tre storiette della Nostra Donna, cioè lo Sposalizio, la Natività di Cristo e la storia de' Magi."

32. See Florens Deuchler, *Duccio* (Milan: Electa, 1984), 56 and fig. 46. All scholars today agree that the final scene of the front side of the predella was *Christ among the Doctors,* which includes the figure of Mary (Ibid., 76 f., figs. 78–84).

33. In 1502 Giovanni Bellini declined to include a figure of the Baptist in a *presepio* for Isabella d'Este, on the grounds that "fuse fuore de propoxito ditto Santo a questo 'pre-xepio.'" Presumably he considered that a *Nativity* for a bedroom, as this was to be, fell within the category of storie, especially as he at first assumed that the picture was to be of the size and format of the storie in Isabella's Studiolo; therefore, as an alternative, he proposed to Isabella, "che, piazendo a Vostra Signoria Illustrissima, lo faria la Nostra Donna con el puto, eziam el San Joan Batista et qualche luntani et altra fantaxia che molto più se achomoderia a dito quadro et che molto staria meglio." In the event, however, Isabella settled for a presepio without the Baptist. See Clifford M. Brown, *Isabella d'Este and Lorenzo de Pavia* (Geneva: Droz, 1982), 163–65.

34. E. G. Vasari, *Opere,* 3:323 (Botticelli's Uffizi *Adoration*), 3:596 (Eusebio da S. Giorgio's altarpiece from Sant'Agostino, Perugia, now in the Galleria nazionale dell'Umbria). In a predella, *The Adoration of the Magi* can of course function as a storia of the Virgin, as in Masaccio's Pisa altarpiece.

35. Alessandra Macinghi degli Strozzi, *Lettere di una gentildonna fiorentina del secolo XV ai figliuoli esuli,* ed. Cesare Guasti (Florence, 1877), 230 f.: "l'uno è de'tre Magi che offersono oro al Nostro Signore, e sono buone figure." See also Charles Hope, "Historical Portraits in the 'Lives' and in the Frescoes of Giorgio Vasari," in *Giorgio Vasari: Tra decorazione ambientale e storiografia artistica,* ed. Gian Carlo Garfagnini (Florence: Olschki, 1985), 326 n. 29.

36. St. John the Evangelist must be the kneeling man with the halo at the extreme right. He lacks his familar eagle, but a storia relating to him originally appeared immediately underneath, in the predella. See Paul Erich Küppers, *Die Tafelbilder des Domenico Ghirlandajo* (Strassburg: Heitz und Mündel, 1916), 88, doc. 3.

37. For a detailed discussion, see Henk van Os, *Sienese Altarpieces, 1215–1460: Form, Content, Function,* vol. 1, 1215–1344 (Groningen: Bouma's Boekhuis BV, 1984), 77–89.

38. Thus Neri di Bicci reported on 15 March 1454 that he had undertaken to complete an altarpiece "la quale debo finire in questo modo, cioè nel chorpo di mezo Santo Giovanni quando bateza Xpo" (Neri di Bicci, *Ricordanze,* 12, no. 23).

39. See Peter Humfrey, *Cima da Conegliano* (Cambridge: Cambridge University Press, 1983), pl. 36.

40. Marilyn Aronberg Lavin, in her *Piero della Francesca's "Baptism of Christ"* (New Haven: Yale University Press, 1981), 117–23, has convincingly argued that Piero's panel belonged from the first with Matteo di Giovanni's frame (reproduced on p. 118, fig. 52). She provides documentation concerning the roundel of *God the Father* on pp. 165 f.

41. Küppers, *Ghirlandaio,* 88, doc. 3: "a piè di san Giovanni Batista, el batesimo di Cristo." For this panel, see Luciano Bellosi, *Il Museo dello Spedale degli Innocenti a Firenze* (Milan: Cassa di Risparmio di Firenze, 1977), pl. 61.

42. The Baptism of Christ could also serve later as a representation of the Trinity, but only on rare occasions and in specific contexts. An example is provided by the decoration of the chapel of the Trinity in the Gesù, in Rome, where this episode is shown on a side wall, facing a painting of the Transfiguration, the altarpiece being Francesco Bassano's *Adoration of the Trinity*. It is doubtful, however, that anyone would have chosen the subject for an independent altarpiece of the Trinity, because it was traditionally so much more strongly associated with the Baptist.

43. Leopold D. Ettlinger, *Antonio and Piero Pollaiuolo* (Oxford: Phaidon, 1978), pl. 83. The contract does not survive.

44. Philipp Fehl, "Saints, Donors and Columns in Titian's *Pesaro Madonna,*" in *Renanissance Papers 1974* (Durham, N.C.: Duke University Press, 1975), 75–85.

45. Giuseppe Liberali, *Lotto, Pordenone e Tiziano a Treviso, Istituto veneto di scienze, lettere ed arti. Memorie, classe di scienze morali e lettere* 33, fasc. 33 (Venice, Instituto veneto di scienze lettere ed arti, 1963), 97f.: "quando vado a dir messa al altar de la capella de miser Broccardo et che digo Memento et che vedo la immagine de esso miser Broccardo, e me contamino tuto perche el se fa reverentia a essa figura et non alla immagine de la Madona: et quando el Vescovo fo qua, fece ben ogni cosa, salvo che questa chel doveve far meter da parte dicta imagine de esso miser Broccardo et non far chel stesse in mezzo de la palla, et chi la rassasse zò o imbrattasse, farìa par ben."

46. For the extensive documentation, see Paul Kristeller, *Andrea Mantegna* (Berlin/Leipzig: Cosmos, 1902), 558–62.

47. For Antonello's paintings, see *Antonello da Messina,* exhibition catalog, Messina (Rome: De Luca, 1981), nos. 31, 41.

48. See Mina Bacci, *L'opera completa di Piero di Cosimo* (Milan: Rizzoli, 1976), 92f. Bacci rightly rejects the old theory that this is an Immaculate Conception, an idea devoid of any reasonable basis. She proposes instead that it is "the visualization of the dogma of the Incarnation." To talk in such terms, however, is anachronistic, since Renaissance artists were not asked to represent dogmas, but to paint people and storie; and in this case, appropriately enough, Piero showed a storia of the Annunciation on the plinth below the Virgin, with further storie associated with her—the Nativity and the Flight into Egypt—in the landscape behind.

49. "DIVAE MARIAE VIRGINI ANNVNTIATAE ET DIVO THOME AQVINAT. SACRVM."

50. Liberali, *Lotto,* 93.

51. See Mirella Levi d'Ancona, *The Iconography of the Immaculate Conception in the Middle Ages and Early Renaissance* (New York: College Art Association of America in Conjunction with the *Art Bulletin,* 1957). D'Ancona has argued that allusions to the doctrine were relatively common in art before the establishment of the Feast of the Immaculate Conception by Sixtus IV; but her argument depends on the highly dubious assumption that artists intended to allude to Mary's immaculacy whenever they drew on texts that were given immaculist interpretations by some theologians, even indeed when they chose to show her with the child. See the review by Guy de Tervarent, *Burlington Magazine* 100 (1958): 138.

52. Crivelli's painting, inscribed "VT IN MENTE DEI AB INITIO CONCEPTA FVI ITA ET FACTA," is now in the National Gallery, London (no. 906). For the altarpiece by the so-called Master of the Immaculate Conception in the Museo di Villa Guinigi, Lucca, which is closely related to the one by Francia, and for Piero di Cosimo's picture in S. Francesco at Fiesole, see the still useful study by Montgomery Carmichael, *Francia's Masterpiece: An Essay on the Begin-*

nings of the Immaculate Conception in Art (London: Kegan Paul, Trench, Trübner, 1909), pls. facing 20, 160.

53. See Luitpold Dussler, *Signorelli* (Stuttgart: Deutsche Verlag Antstalt, 1927), pl. 146. The combination of Child and lily was later adopted by Pietro Candido for the same purpose, in a drawing now in the Louvre, helpfully inscribed "Virgo ante partum, virgo in partu, virgo post partum": see Frits Lugt, *Musée du Louvre: Inventaire générale des dessins des écoles du nord publié sous les auspices du Cabinet des Dessins. Maitres des anciens Pays-Bas nés avant 1550* (Paris: Musées nationaux, 1968), 138, no. 673, reproduced in pl. 189.

54. Joannis de la Haye, ed., *S. Bernardini Senensis Opera Omnia* 5 vols. (Venice, 1745), 3:282: "ad instar picturarum raepresentantiam vobis Beatam Virginem, vel alios sanctos, quae picturae solum fiunt ob memoriam ipsorum sanctorum; unde, nota, quod reperiuntur quatuor species litterarum, una melior altera. Primae species sunt litterae grossae pro gente rudi, sicut sunt picturae: secundariae pro hominibus mediocribus reperiuntur litterae mediocres, sicut sunt litterae scriptae, et istae meliores quam primae litterae: tertiae sunt litterae vocales repertae pro illis, qui in activa propter charitatem se volunt exercere petendo et conferendo ut remaneant docti et alios doceant, et istae sunt praestantiores quam aliae duae primae: quarto et ultimo sunt litterae mentales a Dio ordinatae pro illis, qui volunt in contemplationibus semper perseverare, et ista inter alias est perfecta et excedit alias"; quoted in English by G. C. Coulton, *Art and the Reformation* (Oxford: Basil Blackwell, 1928), 248 f. For the very similar remarks of Cardinal Giovanni Dominici, see Gilbert, *Italian Art,* 145 f.

55. *Rituale Romanum Pauli V Pontificis Maximi Jussu Editum* (Padua, 1734), 200 f.: Benedictio imaginum Jesu Christi Domini nostri, Beatae virginis Mariae, & aliorum Sanctorum: "Omnipotens sempiterne Deus, qui Sanctorum tuorum imagines [*sive* effigies] sculpi, aut pingi non reprobas, ut quoties illas oculis corporis intuemur, toties eorum actus, & sanctitatem ad imitandum memoriae oculis meditemur: hanc, quaesumus, imaginem [*seu* sculpturam] in honorem, et memoriam unigeniti Filii tui Domini nostri Jesu Christi [*vel* beatissimae virginis Mariae Matris Domini nostri Jesu Christi, *vel* beati *N.* Apostoli tui, *vel* Martyris, *vel* Confessoris, *aut* Pontificis, *aut* Virginis] adaptatam benedicere, et sanctificare digneris: & praesta, ut quicumque coram illa unigenitum Filium tuum [*vel* beatissimam Virginem, *vel* gloriosum Apostolum, *sive* Martyrem, *sive* Confessorem, *aut* Virginem] suppliciter colere, & honorare studuerit, illius meritis, & obtentu a te gratiam in praesenti, & aeternam gloriam obtineat in futurum. Per eumdem Christum Dominum nostrum. Amen." Carmichael, in his *Immaculate Conception,* xxxiv, rather misleadingly translates the first clause as: "Almighty and everlasting God, who art well pleased that the likenesses of thy saints. . . ."

23 ❧

ART CRITICISM AND ICON-THEOLOGY

EUGENIO MARINO, O.P.

WHILE MEANINGS consciously intended by patrons and artists are necessarily limited, the capacity of an artwork to suggest the full range of meanings operative in the "symbol-system" of which it is a partial manifestation can be virtually limitless. In this chapter, Eugenio Marino reflects upon the aesthetic and intellectual mechanisms involved in experiencing a work of art from within the particular cultural tradition that produced it. Using the theoretical language of German art history writing, along with concepts borrowed from structuralist thought and Christian theology, Father Marino suggests how members of a given cultural group understand artifacts generated by the group's shared experience, and the role of faith in the gestation and interpretation of religious art. Father Marino's challenging essay is perhaps the most detailed analysis ever attempted of how culturally conditioned religious imagination shapes and responds to images.

EUGENIO MARINO is a Dominican friar of Santa Maria Novella, in Florence. The present essay arises as a sequel to his longer "Methodological Essay" on the Trecento fresco in San Domenico, Pistoia, the *Virgin of the Root of Jesse*. He has also published on the history and cultural life of Santa Maria Novella in the Renaissance.

N THE FOLLOWING OBSERVATIONS I seek to clarify the relationship between the criticism of art and the study or activity of iconology. These thoughts expand upon ideas I developed in my earlier "Methodological Essay," which had as its point of departure an undocumented fourteenth-century fresco in the church of St. Dominic in Pistoia. There I attributed the work to Andrea Bonaiuti and gave it a title—"The Virgin of the root of Jesse, tender shoot of St. Anne's plant, fair mother of the flower Jesus."[1] Here I want to analyze in greater detail the method of interpretation appropriate to such works of religious art and to extend the system of iconological study elaborated by Aby Warburg and Erwin Panofsky into what I call "icon-theology." For the sake of clarity, I have divided the present essay into three main sections, dealing respectively with the critic's perception of the artwork, the activity of iconological interpretation, and the role of icon-theology in relation to both.

THE CRITIC AND THE ARTWORK

The critic approaches a work of art through the act of perception which takes place when he stands before a visual form. In this first moment, with a vision of the work based on first sight (i.e., on a simple glance at the work), he takes in the manifest qualities of the object. This optic-contemplative encounter lasts only a moment, however. There immediately follows an intuition based on more sustained observation—what we might call a 'painstaking' or 'careful' intuition—which develops in time and gradually leads to comprehension of the true form of things.[2] It is with this more sustained vision that the critical process of judgment and/or evaluation begins, and the point of departure of the critic's research is thus also the beginning of reflection on the principles and methodology that can best lead to 'truth of vision.'[3]

The process is problematic, however. For one thing, the philological principles applied to visual images are not as concrete as in literary philology, where the standard tools (recension, colation, interpretation) are sufficiently refined—and determining—to allow reconstruction of the original text.[4] By contrast, the description-cum-analysis and interpretation of a visual work implies theoretical presuppositions on several issues: aesthetics, or taste (today a subject of heated debate); the 'cognition' or re-cognition of worlds of meaning not always homogeneous with the critic's own; and the establishment of the cultural world of the artwork in both its synchronic and diachronic dimensions. Description-analysis-interpretation of an artwork presupposes in the critic simultaneous attitudes of objectivity and subjectivity, and of historical and historicistic consciousness, which raise questions about the effective agreement of the critical act with the world of the work of art under consideration.

At a deeper and broader level, moreover, the critic finds himself in difficulty owing to the current skepsis in art historical studies: the "conviction of the uselessness and impossibility of ultimate recourse . . . to an autonomous philosophical authority," as Luigi Grassi put it. The art critic thus finds himself obliged to "judge" without possessing an acknowledged epistemological basis on which to do so. He is forced to establish his research methods and procedures on "an exclusively empirical plane."[5] This is the cultural given, difficult to eliminate in an understanding of research which is not closed in upon itself, which must be borne in mind during the process of critical dialogue, even by those who do not share this gnosiological point of view.

The problem thus becomes how to reduce erudition—knowledge and/or theoretical presuppositions and empirical methodologies—to a unity, and how to raise the multiple and personal, the objective and subjective, to the unified aspect of generally applicable functions. In short, it is a problem of how to put together a unified pluralism that will not be discredited by eclecticism.[6]

Unity of the critical act in the intuition of 'art-intent' (Kunstwollen) in formal-semantic-cultural schemata

I achieved something like this unified pluralism in my *Methodological Essay,* I believe. I did not oppose one critical system to another—

formalism vs. concern for content, technique vs. expression, psychology vs. positivism, and so on; such a procedure is based on the absolutizing of a single critical viewpoint and disregards the complex relationship of 'truth of vision' with the circularity of our processes of perception. (Examples of such oppositions can be found in Konrad Fiedler's work, as Georg Lukács has perspicaciously noted.)[7] My approach involved rather what I called a 'synthetic intuition'—that is, the critic's concrete, working intuition of the meaning of a work of art.

This 'careful' or 'painstaking' intuition, sustained and diligent, begins with description of the formal reality, prior to all iconographic interpretation. Without this preiconographic description, obviously, there is no objective basis for critical activity which can claim a place in art history. Synthetic intuition offers the critic a chance to "work" the raw material implied in the formal and semantic characteristics of the object, using various theoretical points of reference (e.g., Platonism, Aristotelianism, rhetoric, phenomenalism, existentialism, historicism), and various methodologies (e.g., formalism, linguistics, and structuralism). It enables him to move through these, developing a panoramic overview, toward a grasp of the 'signified meaning' (Sinn-Bedeutung) of the work in its totality; a grasp which seizes the interior and exterior ramifications of the work, that is, its iconography. It also allows him a grasp of the context of cultural references in which the artist functioned by action or reaction (Weltanschauung-Gesamtkultur)—that is, the icon-theology of the artwork.[8]

In this way, the critic's concrete, working intuition enters the dimension of historical study, giving further unity to the already attained 'unified pluralism' of disparate elements of erudition mentioned above:[9] the same unity that informed the artist's own personality and constituted his 'will toward art,' or Kunstwollen.[10] Seen in this light, the Kunstwollen is not merely style or formal character, the wie or 'how' of an artwork, as in Alois Riegl's reductive interpretation;[11] it is the subject, the theme, and the content of an artwork: its was or 'what,' determined in a given artistic expression. The Kunstwollen, therefore, is both the focal point of a critic's concrete, working intuition and the fulcrum of the artwork, willed as a cultural whole. The critic is capable of cognition and re-cognition of the artistic intent of a work—of its Kunstwollen—precisely because this intent is stamped upon the work of art as "the artist's distinctive sign" (*das auszeichnende Merkmal des Künstlers*), as Conrad Fiedler, the father of visibilism, affirmed. It is the artist's personal mimesis.[12]

But if the theme-format of an artwork is mimesis of the artist's creative act, the critic in turn can draw from it the stimulus for his anamnesis, that is, his recognition of all its component parts. The critic can ascend, as if on an upward path, from the mimetic form (*Gestalt-Bild*) to the artist's process of invention (*Gestaltung*), the poetic process in which source material is metamorphosed. By his critical anamnesis, he can then ascend further, to the original stimulus (*Ursprung-Urbild*) that left its stamp upon the artist, that first filled him with creative tension and moved him along that downward path from the source (*Gegestand-Urbild*) to a thing having formal being (Gestalt) that was mimesis or imitation of the original source (Urbild). This path passes through the process of generative artistic invention (Gestaltung) by a demiurgic act.   *remembrance of the past*

In this way, a circular gnosiological-critical method takes shape. Along the path of mimesis-anamnesis, this method links critic with artist and artist with critic, joining the re-creative process used by the critic to the creative process of the artist. It also binds together the end of the process (the Kunstwollen concretized as artistic form) with its beginning (the *Urquelle*), and this in turn with the 'end' or goal, the objective toward which both of these point (*operis-operantis*).[13]

Thus, by a concrete, working intuition that unifies the plurality of aesthetic references and methodologies, the critic can move through the work as a cultural totality, weighing it and judging it, while avoiding the liberties and abstractions found in, above all, that *critique créatrice* that goes back to Charles Baudelaire and today enjoys a faithful following.[14]

CRITICISM AND ICONOLOGY
Advantages and deficiencies of Panofsky's methodology

As we have seen, then, the critic can give a certain validity and theoretical and methodological concreteness to his study of a work of art.

But—and this is the second problem, that of iconology—can he overcome "the constant duality in which the artwork appears: its aspect as an original, formal object, and its aspect as a bearer of cultural meaning"?[15]

Panofsky answered this question in the affirmative. He looked at the work of art as a totality (*das Kunstwerk als Ganzes*) with three distinct strata. First, there is the preiconographic level, the world of visual motifs or pure forms. Second comes the iconographic level, that is, the sphere of the subject (themes, concepts), evident in images, narratives, and allegories. Finally, there is the iconological level, that of content or intrinsic significance—of "those internal principles that make manifest the fundamental attitude of a nation, an era, a class; of a religious or philosophical conviction."[16] But Panofsky gave no foundation or theoretical justification for these distinctions, or for the relationship he saw among form, subject, and cultural content. He limited himself to describing an intuition commonly observable in everyday life and applying his conclusions analogically in the context of art. One thinks of his famous example, of an acquaintance greeting him on the street by lifting his hat, and the levels of meaning such an action implies. Panofsky was able to transfer the results of his analysis of everyday life to art, distinguishing the same three levels of meaning.[17]

In Panofsky's analysis, the functioning of a work of art as a cultural totality is asserted rather than explained. Unexplained, too, is why and how the parts become a whole, or how the visual work is formed of style, types, formal content and culture, all of which pervade both the history of style and the history of types. That is to say, preiconography, iconography, and iconology are never really explained! The problem lies in Panofsky's terminology for the working of the methodological circle of preiconography, iconography, iconology. His terms are not pertinent enough to his specific subject to suggest the intrinsic interrelation of each level with the others. In fact, he characterizes formal schemata or pure forms, semantic schemata or themes, and symbolic schemata, as "bearers" (*Traeger*) and/or "means by which" (*durch*), and/or "branches" (*Zweige*), all juxtaposed each with the others (*im Gegensatz*). This loose terminology has allowed the opponents of iconology to interpret Panofsky's three spheres as three separate or separable areas of research—almost "series of free associations," as Carlo Ginzburg would say—rather than as discernible or distinguishable nexes in an indivisible whole.[18]

A clarification of Panofsky's iconology

In the course of writing my methodological essay on the "Virgin of the root of Jesse," I came to see that the objections raised against Panofsky by the anti-iconographers and anti-iconologists, especially on the formalist-visibilist front, were virtually unfounded. At the same time, these objections spurred me to a more systematic articulation of the ideas of this master of the Warburg tradition. Above all, I was able to clarify the correspondence—and thus the unity—among the components discussed above: the critic's concrete, working intuition; the artist's creative-inventive intuition, which results in an artwork; and the visual work itself, made by the art-maker and brought into existence as a "whole made up of parts/parts tending to make a whole" willed by the Kunstwollen. This correspondence is like that between the artist's downward journey from source to artwork and the upward path traced by the penetrating observation of the critic.

Such a view of the artwork as a unified whole is historically standard. We find it in ancient theoretical writers such as Vitruvius, with his concept of symmetry,[19] and in postmedieval writers such as Leon Battista Alberti, with his concept of *pulchritudo-concinnitas,* the beauty of ordered ornament.[20] It is present in Augustine's philosophico-theological aesthetics, where proportional harmony is seen as the basis of beauty,[21] and present, too, in the work of Thomas Aquinas, who characterizes form as "integrity, consonance, and clarity."[22] Panofsky knew such theories well and applied them in his work, without, however, giving them a regulatory interpretive role in the study of iconology.[23]

My own work on Bonaiuti's fresco in Pistoia practically forced me to have recourse to Jean Piaget's theory of method—that is, to structuralism understood as an ideal of intelligibility. With this tool, I was able to arrive at a vision of the artwork that respects the work's self-sufficiency and autonomy but still sees it as the formulation of a cultural totality. Moreover, since this totality is simultaneously formal, semantic, and symbolic, it excludes all forms of associationalism and the breakdown into components. My approach, therefore, makes clear *how*

Panofsky's strata (preiconography, iconography, iconology) are in fact indivisible from one another: articulations at once structured and structuring, transformed in reciprocal relationship with one another, which organize the gestalt of the artwork, itself 'total form' (*Formganzes*), in Heinrich Wölfflin's *lessema*.[24]

This method has also brought me to a clearer understanding of the relationship between Panofsky's three strata and the formalist position. I conclude that it is the formalists, not Panofsky, who have closed themselves up in abstractions when they exercise their critical activity on so-called "pure form," inasmuch as no such thing can really exist.[25] A work of art, which could hardly *not* have properties of formal design, does not exhaust its meaning in such formal characteristics. Rather, it presents itself to intuition simultaneously as thematized form, formalized theme, form employed for symbolic expression, and symbol translated into visible form. In reality, it simply is not true that "iconographic content is entirely different from artistic content," as Riegl maintained. Or, to put it differently, when in a specific case the critic's intuition tells him that the form of a work, its subject and its cultural content, are assembled components rather than a "whole constituted by parts, and parts constituting a whole," then the work is not a "work of art," and iconographic/iconological study cannot take place. Indeed, Riegl himself admitted—although without seeing the internal contradiction— that works of art have "real historic and artistic value" precisely in those cases where, in the work's formal, semantic, and symbolic properties, the critic can show a perfect realization of "that creative will which 'represented' the artistic and figurative form of the work in one way only, and not otherwise."[26]

Finally, my work brought me to the age-old question of the relationship between artistic form and the literary sources that might have stirred the artist's intuition. The tool I chose in order to deal with this problem was structural linguistics, by aid of which I was able to determine the system of relationships in the work of art, similar to—in analogy with—the 'word circuit' in literature. That is, meaning and 'pictorial meaning' in a painting are related in much the same way as meaning and 'literary meaning' in a text. The artist intuits a linguistic message by hearing (and/or, in the case of pictorial art, by sight); he grasps it and welcomes it as an 'acoustical image'; he deciphers it and then encodes it in his own way—that is, he metamorphoses it with his own act of 'meaningful fantasy.' He gives it meaning in terms of a particular Kunstwollen, and impresses-expresses this 'image' as a 'sense referent' (Sinn-Bedeutung) in the form-object/formal mimesis (Figure 23.1).

The critic, whose point of departure is an intuition of the finished form of the artwork, knows/recognizes the artist's process of invention because it was this very process that commanded and guided the artist to produce a given set of formal, semantic, and symbolic properties. And when the artist's fantasy-generated idea denotes or connotes a relationship to written texts in the process of invention, the critic will be stimulated to anamnesis, or recollection of the linguistic referrent that generated the idea, insofar as he enjoys 'familiarity' (*Vertrauheit*) with the same literary culture. In this way, the 'acoustical image,' source of images, narratives, and allegories, and the fantasy-image created by the artist's will, resolve themselves into a figurative unity or 'form.' (If we adapt André Martinet's terminology to the visual world, we might define this as a 'moneiconema,' that is, a double-faceted 'unity-image': signifier and signified; form and theme; form and content.)[27]

Thus, preiconography, iconography, and iconology are three strata that nonetheless 'form' a whole. They are a whole, however, made up of three inseparable parts. They are 'form' in its fullness, the motivating artistic intention of the artist (Kunstwollen). These three levels together constitute the work of art, and are therefore the proper and sufficient object of all art criticism: the recent proclamation of a "post-Panofsky" era seems to me to have been premature.[28]

CRITICISM AND ICON-THEOLOGY
Iconological criticism and visual works with theological-artistic intent

It seemed necessary to reassert in this argumentative fashion the relevance of iconology for art historical study, whether the term 'iconology' is understood as critical intuition or as the formal, thematic, and contentual plenitude of works of visual art. Again, however, the final conclusions of my inductive study go further. Iconology, in fact, has

Figure 23.1. Andrea Pisano, *The Painter at Work in His Bottega* (*Apelles?*). Florence, formerly on the Campanile; today in the Museo dell' Opera del Duomo. Photo Alinari/Art Resource, N.Y.

come to seem inadequate to an understanding of the artistic intent (Kunst-wollen) that one gradually intuits in works of religious art such as the fresco in Pistoia. In practice, formal and historical reconstruction of the process of creation of works of religious art denotes and connotes that the images signified (the 'iconploghema', to use an appropriate syn-thetic term derived from *Bildsprache*) have a relation with the 'context of reference'—that is, an 'organic situation'—at all three levels: in their style (preiconography), in their typology (iconography), and in their cultural reference (iconology).[29] What is more, this relationship tran-scends the "logic" of the Kunstwollen concept and reveals itself as a kind of Kunstwollen-theo-logical activity. Thus the interpretive genre or iconographical category furnished by Panofsky is clearly incommen-surate with the process of description, analysis, and deciphering of a total reality that goes on when we interpret works of religious art.[30]

The 'point of view', or Kunstwollen, that distinguishes the in-tuition of a religious artist—his metamorphosis of the source or origi-nal artistic invention, and the vision of these which he effects in his artwork—is neither the vague "religious genre" mentioned by Antal,[31] nor Gombrich's hardly more precise "dominant meaning."[32] Rather, the 'point of view' of a Christian religious artist is rooted in his 'hear-ing' of the Old and New Testaments. The religious genre of art that he practices is determined by his *faith*. And the dominant meaning— that is, the unifying principle that underlies and explains both the visi-ble product and its intelligible meaning, and which even determines the form that this product will take[33]—is a genre or category pertaining to Christian faith and to theology, the science that seeks an understand-ing of faith.

The category "faith" or "theology" never appears in Aby War-burg's or Erwin Panofsky's interpretive method. Indeed, if one analyzes the physical layout of the library of the Warburg Institute, in its differ-ent temporal and topographical manifestations (Hamburg in the early years of the century, London thereafter), one realizes that it indicates a mental sequence. In both the arrangement of the shelves and the sub-ject division of the different floors, it is obvious that the category of "faith" has been misunderstood, has been fused and confused with the category "religion," in that good-neighbor relationship of books which develops in libraries. But "religion," as distinguished from "faith," is a research category more concerned with human reason than with divine revelation, and this holds true even in the arts.[34]

This cultural arrangement, mirroring intellectual attitudes characteristic of the Enlightenment and of positivism, may be taken both as a symptom and as a cause of the nondevelopment of a theological approach to works of art that clearly depend upon faith as their source and/or stimulus. Panofskian iconological intuition treats the 'revealed content' of religious art (in its character as 'revealed', i.e., in its specific Christian biblical nature) parenthetically, if it does not forget it entirely. Yet it was precisely that world view and cultural whole (*Weltanschauung-Gesamtkultur*) that for centuries gave 'form' to works of art. Such works of art were clearly 'conceived' in faith, in the artist's moment of fantasy-ideation, and 'given birth to' in faith in the demiurgic moment when they were constituted as visual forms. And if the critic who looks at such works does not accept them in terms of their own vision, and does not judge them as icon-theology, it means he has not entered into the intuition from which they arose—probably because he lacks the 'familiarity' (Vertrautheit) and the 'equipment' (*Ausrüstung*) which, as Panofsky himself taught, are the methodological prerequisites for art criticism.[35] One who, like Lukács's "receiver," does not possess in himself the 'transcendental content' that the work of art expresses (i.e., faith) is not capable of icon-theology. For the work of religious art "acts upon us with efficacy thanks to the weight of faith."[36]

Panofsky's iconology and icon-theology

I speak of the inadequacy of Warburg's and Panofsky's iconological method for interpreting works of art which depend on faith or theology or ecclesiastical tradition or on the piety of the faithful, not in order to denigrate that method but to clarify it by defining its limits. To reiterate what I have said earlier, iconological method is a valid and indispensable tool of art criticism; it grasps and establishes the logic of intention and motivation toward art (Kunstwollen) in the artist and in his work, except in those cases—and this constitutes the limit of iconology—where works of art were shaped by theological motivation and express an artistic intention related to transcendent faith. The limit of Warburgian-Panofskian iconology derives from its genesis as a means of discerning the *general* principles of a culture in formal and semantic patterns, rather than as a way of discerning the basic principles of a culture grounded in religious faith.

This observation, which limits the field of application of Panofsky's iconology, is also the theoretical and practical foundation on which Panofsky's methods can be applied fruitfully in icon-theology, with its vast critical and artistic time span. The theologian, and thus also the icon-theologian, has to make use of the wisdom of this world. Thomas Aquinas tells us that "it is commendable that some take on the task of putting profane eloquence and learning at the service of divine wisdom."[37] In fact, theologians and icon-theologians (whether as artists or critics) have, down the centuries, made philology, philosophy, the natural sciences, rhetoric, history, line, color, proportion, perspective, and physical matter itself serve and express the Holy Scriptures. Thus the icon-theologian needs the iconologist; icon-theological method presupposes iconology as a working tool of knowledge to assure that the approach to the figurative work stays inside the parameters of art. At the same time, though, iconology must be elevated and made specific by means of icon-theology, the interpretive-cognitive tool effective in the context of faith.

The relationship between iconology and icon-theology is not extrinsic. Just as preiconography, iconography, and iconology can be understood only as a totality, a synolum, so iconology and icon-theology form a theoretical and methodological unity, rather like theological learning itself, which is unified in character even though it comes about as the result of a reduction of "worldly wisdom" to the terms of the "wisdom of faith." St. Thomas, in fact, noted that the water of human wisdom added to the wine of Holy Scripture does not weaken the wine, because the revealed Word transubstantiates the water totally into itself: "it gives way to the truth of faith . . . and the wine of Sacred Scripture is not diluted but remains pure."[38]

In other words, icon-theology exists not only because the 'content' (in the Panofskian sense) impressed in and expressed by the work of art originates in faith, but also because the very form of the work reveals itself to the 'user' as a theological form, that is, a form mimetic of the process of belief. In the artist's intuition (the downward path toward the artwork), and in the intuition of the critic (the upward path

toward the source), the external exemplar of Scripture becomes an interior exemplar: the acoustical image of the word of Scripture heard
in faith becomes first a fantasy-image in the artist's mind, and then a
concrete image ('*image-chose*') under his skilled hands. Icon-theology not
only does not ask art history and criticism to abdicate their autonomy;
it establishes them as autonomous at its own level, which is that of
the history and criticism of art created in faith—what we might call
historical criticism in light of icon-theology.

In any event, it is historical fact that artists often collaborated
with theologians, as an example will serve to illustrate. On 25 November 1499, the "honorable painter" Luca Signorelli was commissioned
by the officials of the cathedral works in Orvieto to complete the pictorial decoration of the New Chapel, and to do so in a way that would
harmonize with "the design prepared formerly by the venerable Fra Giovanni" of Fiesole, that is, Fra Angelico.[39] And for those portions of
the chapel for which Fra Angelico had left no designs, Signorelli was
instructed to paint "as advised in a series of conversations with local
theologians."[40] A final comment on this passage helps make my point:
when the officials of the cathedral originally decided to bring in Fra
Angelico—on 11 March 1447—they did *not* suggest that theologians
should serve as his advisers. Instead they "deliberated and ordered that
the said master painter should be awaited, and that it was necessary
to listen to him, and once he had been heard they could go on to give
the commission."[41]

This difference of approach suggests that Fra Angelico was understood to unite in his own person—by a kind of hypostatic union,
to use a phrase borrowed from theology (where it is employed in reference to Christ)—two 'natures': the nature of the artist and the nature of the theologian. And never was icon-theology so coherent as in
his case!

NOTES

1. Eugenio Marino, O.P., *L'affresco "La Vergine della radice di Iesse." Andrea Bonaiuti
in S. Domenico di Pistoia: Saggio methodologico su iconografia e teologia* (Pistoia: Memorie domenicane, 1982). This reprint in book form of my article of the same name in *Memorie domenicane*

13 (1982) has two appendixes not contained in the journal: a synopsis of the formal-semantic schemata of the fresco (pp. 203–8), and a dictionary of terms (pp. 209–23). The present article was translated from Italian by Timothy Verdon.

2. The terms 'careful', 'painstaking', or 'sustained' observation here are equivalent to Ptolemy's notion of *aspectus-obtutus*, which, through the Arab thinkers, came down to Witelo and to Thomas Aquinas. See Eva Tea, "Witelo, prospettico del secolo XIII," *L'arte* 30 (1927): 1–28. For an interpretation of perceptual processes consonant with contemporary research into the psychology of form, see R. Arnheim, *Toward a Psychology of Art* (Berkeley and Los Angeles: University of California Press, 1966).

3. I use the term 'truth of vision' in analogy with what literary historians call 'truth of reading'; see A. Asor Rosa, "Lettura, testo, società," in *Letteratura italiana* (Turin: Einaudi, 1982), 5 ff.

4. M. Barbi, *La nuova filologia e l'edizione dei nostri scrittori da Dante al Manzoni* (Florence: Sansoni, 1973).

5. Luigi Grassi, *Teorici e storia della critica d'arte* (Rome: Multigrafica, 1970), 13 ff. On the relationship between the principle of indetermination and the principle of complementarity, see Cesare Brandi, *Teoria generale della critica* (Turin: Einaudi, 1974), 10.

6. It should be remembered that, in Kant's terms, aesthetic judgment belongs not to a priori analytic judgments but to "synthetic judgments" that imply the capacity to judge and the datum of experience. And in fact, the critic cannot avoid assuming either a parameter of general order (even if not strictly necessary) such as 'imitation', 'the beautiful', 'the quality of the artistic', *Grundbegriffe*, and so on, or a sense-intuition, individual and singular in character, such as the 'artistic fact'. Useful, too, is Leibniz's distinction between the 'truth of reason', which is universal, and 'factual truth', which as such is contingent and thus unable to be deduced a priori but only arrived at inductively.

7. See G. Lukács, *Estetica*, 2 vols. (Turin: Einaudi, 1975), 1:38. Lukács notes that in Fiedler's treatment of visibility the means come to be identified with the objectification, and a group of objectifications is put into relationship with a particular, isolated psychic faculty, thus entirely or partially forgetting the dynamics of totality in human psychic life (originally, *Die Eigenart des Ästhetischen*, 2 vols. [Neuwied am Rhein: Luchterhand, 1963]).

8. Marino, *Saggio metodologico*, 183. The iconologist, in the 'in' of the visual work (i.e., in the style and in the theme), 'intuits' (*intus legit*) the 'extra' (and this with only apparent contradiction). In the express form of the work, he seizes the 'universe' that the painter inserted into it, and, as F. Dagonet observed, "discovers its beyond, its richness, a multiplicity of horizons" (*Ecriture et iconographie* [Paris: Vrin, 1973], 48).

9. On historicizing one's own sensibility, see Alessandro Parronchi, *Studi su la dolce prospettiva* (Milan: Martello, 1964), 91. On thinking about a work of art historically see R. Bianchi Bandinelli, *Storicità dell'arte classica* (Florence: Electa, 1950), 5–6: "What does 'historically formed judgment' mean to us? It is not so much comparison of the artwork with others of its time, but understanding and clarifying the work of art as such, in its intimate creative process, in its particular language, in what it has of unique and unrepeatable." And: "The history of art is the internal history of the genesis of a work of art understood as the externalization of the artist's personality—but of his personality in its wholeness, a conditioned result of the context in which he functioned. . . . Tradition, intuition, and expression, however, are

so intimately connected—are so much a single thing—that content and form are no longer separable in those cases where a fully classic style (in the qualitative sense) has been achieved."

10. The first to introduce the term *Kunstwollen* into art criticism was Alois Riegl, in 1893, who proposed it as a criterion without theoretical value but useful for reaffirming the autonomous worth of artistic forms and structures, or as a unitary principle through which the cultural-historical direction of an epoch or of a people is articulated and made manifest. See L. Grassi and M. Pepe, *Dizionario della critica d'arte* (Turin: Unione tipografico torinese, 1978), 271–72. See also Roberto Salvini, *La critica d'arte della pura visibilità e del formalismo* (Milan: Garzanti, 1977), 23. For Panofsky's notion of Kunstwollen, to which I make frequent reference, see Erwin Panofsky, *Il significato nelle arti visive* (Turin: Einaudi, 1962), 61–62; published in English as *Meaning in the Visual Arts* (New York: Doubleday, 1957). In my *Saggio metodologico* I trace Riegl's Kunstwollen back to the artist's 'words', that is, to the act of intuition and will, the specific vision of the painter seen as the "impress" or "stamp" of his character. I also trace it to the 'style-language'—the normative conventions of a given time—and to the artist's synchronic culture (*Gesamtkultur-Grundprinzipien*). This extended interpretation of the meaning of the term seems to correspond to Gombrich's purpose in going through the whole history of art to show why artists worked in a certain way and why they sought certain effects. See Ernst Gombrich, *La storia dell'arte raccontata da E. H. Gombrich* (Turin: Einaudi, 1974), 22. This has been published in English as *The Story of Art* (New York: Phaidon, 1950).

11. Riegl held that "figurative art has nothing to do with the 'what' of a work (the *was*) but with the 'how' (*wie*) of representation. It gets the 'what' from poetry and religion. Iconography therefore shows itself to be not so much the history of the figurative Kunstwollen as the history of poetic and religious will." See A. Riegl, *Industria artistica tardoromana* (Florence: Sansone, 1981), 370 (originally, *Die spätrömische Kunstindustrie nach den Funden in Osterreich-Ungarn* [Vienna: Archaeologische Institut, 1901]). My work on the Pistoia fresco, and my other study, "Iconologia del ciclo 'Via paradisi' di Giovanni di Bartolomeo Cristiani: Penitenza e regno di Dio tra medioevo e umanesimo," *Memorie domenicane*, n.s. 8–9 (1977–78): 249–339, obliged me to distinguish so as to unite the wie-was. In other words, I had to recognize an immanent relationship in the 'how-what', according to which the 'what' (the intuition of the object-theme) leads to the 'how' (style, both as a common characteristic of the given time and place and as a personal statement of the artist). I saw the 'how' as the artistic interpretation of the 'what.' Without that 'what'—a specific intuition on the artist's part—we should not have had that particular 'how', and without the 'how' we would not have had art.

12. Conrad Fiedler, *Schriften über Kunst* (Cologne: DuMont Buchverlag, 1977), 26. My interpretation of the Kunstwollen as the centripetal-centrifugal core of the whole artwork and of the artist's personality, which gives the artwork its existence, is in agreement with L. Payerson, *I problemi dell'estetica* (Milan: Marzorati, 1966), 101–2: "What is it that holds together all the different works of a single author, if not his concrete living personality, which was their point of departure and which in them gradually affirms its own value? . . . Once placed under the sign of art, the persona becomes artistic will and initiative toward art; it assumes an entirely artistic direction, summons an artistic vocation from itself; it becomes charged with formative energy. In the exercise of this activity, one falls into it completely, becoming the act, the very gesture: the whole person becomes the gesture of making, the way of shaping, style."

13. Ibid., 11. I have taken the methodological notion of a double path, going up

and down, from Payerson. Regarding the circular process 'critic-artist/artist-critic', I should note that I am using the notion of mimesis as a unifying element of the entire artistic process. That is to say, mimesis is the *fil conducteur* not only in the relationship 'form-nature' (and/or history), as 'mirroring-mimesis', but also in the relationship 'form-image of artistic invention'. This second relationship subjects the mimesis of the source or 'referent' that takes place in creative invention to a metamorphosis — an 'estangement', or an 'interpretation' — from which the formal mimesis of the work of art is derived and willed. In other words, the critic should take the expressive mimesis that he finds in the finished work of art as a mimesis of the artist's action, which itself was a mimesis of the artist's fantasy-generated invention, which was elaborated mimesis of the source-image.

14. See Y. Florenne, "Critique et création," in Charles Baudelaire, *Ecrits sur l'art,* (Paris: Gallimard et Librairie française, 1971).

15. Grassi, *Teorici e storia,* 9. The problem of form and content should be related to the wider problem of 'classical antinomy', of the relationship of the whole to the parts, and the parts to the whole. Grassi (p. 17) observes that "as early as 1858 Droysen noted the difficulty inherent in historical method, in that 'the particular is to be understood through the whole and the whole through the particulars.'" And in 1910, shortly after Saussure, Benedetto Croce gave an acute definition of the 'classical antinomy' as it confronts the art critic: "To understand a work of art means to understand the whole in the parts and the parts in the whole. Now, if the whole cannot be known except through the parts (and this is the true meaning of the first proposition), the parts cannot be known except through the whole (and this is the true meaning of the second proposition)." I would observe, however, that what at the theoretical level is an antinomy loses its inner contradiction when the critic, with his exercise of analytic judgment, goes into action. Then, in fact, he is in the same situation as someone who simultaneously perceives and intuits. That is, he has in front of him an object in its reality as a whole made up of parts, and parts making up a whole — that is, a 'unity' discernible by means of 'sustained', 'careful', 'painstaking' sight (*obtutus*).

16. Panofsky, *Il significato,* 29. The same general treatment of iconography and iconology can be found in idem, *Studies in Iconology: Humanistic Themes in the Art of the Renaissance,* rev. ed. (New York: Harper and Row Torchbooks, 1962), 3 ff. See also E. Kaemmarling, ed., *Ikonographie und Ikonologie* (Cologne: DuMont Buchverlag, 1979), 207 ff. ("Theorien-Entwicklung-Probleme").

17. Panofsky, *Il significato,* 35. The philosopher Charles S. Pierce was Panofsky's source for determining the meaning of 'content'. For the sense of 'iconology', he based his work on that of Ernst Cassirer. See Marino, *Saggio metodologico,* 182. Eugenio Garin, in his introduction to Fritz Saxl, *La storia delle immagini* (Rome/Bari: Laterza, 1982), discusses and clarifies the contacts that Warburg, Saxl, and Panofsky had with Pierce and Cassirer and also with the cultural world of Burckhardt, Nietzche, and Usener. Eugenio Battisti, in his introduction ("Una rilettura dopo 40 anni") to *Piero della Francesca: De prospectiva pingendi* (Florence: Le Lettere, 1984), xi–xv, called "Cassirer's impact on Panofsky . . . not entirely positive." In fact, if it is true, on the one hand, that Cassirer's thought allowed Panofsky to "move from a concept of art based principally on 'making' or on group psychological motivations . . . to a theory — the symbolic theory — of art as sign, as myth, as metaphor," on the other hand, Cassirer's influence did not prevent Panofsky from putting himself "in a certain sense outside of history" (at least as regards the discussion of perspective construction which Battisti treats) or from regressing into paradox on the level of anthropology.

18. On the *circulus methodologicus,* see Panofsky, *Studies,* 12–13. Among the critics of Panofsky's "layers of meaning," I mention, by way of example, only Brandi, *Teoria generale,* 118–20; P. Francastel, *Studi di sociologia dell'arte* (Milan: Rizzoli, 1976), 19; Carlo Ragghianti, *Arti della visione,* 3 vols. (Turin: Einaudi, 1979), 3:5 ff.; Carlo Ginzburg, *Indagini su Piero* (Turin: Einaudi, 1981), xix.

19. Vitruvius Pollio, *De architectura* 1.2.22 (Pisa: Giardini, 1975). Panofsky, *Il significato,* 73, correctly notes that symmetry, understood as 'harmonious relationship' "is what may be called Vitruvius' aesthetic principle."

20. Leon Battista Alberti, *De re aedificatoria* 6.2 (Milan: Polifilo, 1966).

21. Augustine, *De vera religione* 30 (ed. K. D. Daur [Turnholt: Brepols, 1962], 223). Riegl, *Industria,* 370, cites Augustine's phrase "omnis pulchritudinis forma unitas" ("all beautiful form possesses a unity"), commenting, "The individual closed form has the same value for Augustine as for all his ancient predecessors, both as first condition for all being and as the seat and expressive form of beauty in everything in created nature."

22. Thomas Aquinas, *Summa theologiae* 1, quaest. 39, art. 8 (ed. J. P. Migne, 4 vols. [Paris, 1841], 1:793–98). It should be noted that St. Thomas's concept of *integritas*—a 'wholeness' that he requires if 'the beautiful' is to exist—includes the concept of *totum,* or 'the whole', on which modern Gestalt theory is based.

23. It would be impossible to cite all the relevant passages in Panofsky's work, but see esp. his *Idea: Contributo alla storia dell'estetica* (Florence: La Nuova Italia, 1973), which has been published in English as *Idea: A Concept in Art History* (Columbia: University of South Carolina Press, 1968).

24. Jean Piaget, *Lo strutturalismo* (Milan: Mondadori, 1969). See also Marino, *Saggio metodologico,* 11, 12, 28, 131, 132, 163. I would note that I use structuralism as I use linguistics or any other theory of method, including Warburgian-Panofskian iconology, as a tool. As tools I handle and interpret such theoretical systems according to my own particular 'principle of unity', which, from time to time, I state clearly. Thus, for example (and remaining in the context of structuralism), the concept of 'totality' which shaped my analysis in the *Saggio metodologico* was the Aristotelian-Thomistic idea of a *synolum,* that is, an 'individual unity'.

25. I criticized the abstractionism of the formalists in an explicit way, examining specific works of art, in my *Beato Angelico: Umanesimo e teologia* (Rome: Atena, 1984).

26. Riegl, *Industria,* 212.

27. F. De Saussure, *Corso di linguistica generale* (Bari: Laterza, 1970). See also Marino, *Saggio metodologico,* passim. It has not been sufficiently noted that Riegl, even before Panofsky, had recourse to synchronic literary culture as a corrective principle in order to understand the general Kunstwollen or style of a work of art. See Riegl, *Industria,* 368: "I want to call scholars' attention to a source of art historical knowledge until now considered with the same contempt with which we look at those literary sources that contain merely exterior data of place and date. . . . The judgment of thinkers and writers on a work of art of their own time fully merits the consideration of those who engage in historical and artistic research. It is in fact a sure and convincing way of recognizing whether or not the ideas drawn from our subjective observation about the predominating artistic intentions of a given period were also really the ideas of those who lived at the time the work of art was made."

28. Daniel Arasse, "Après Panofsky: Piero di Cosimo, 'peintre'," in *Cahiers pour un temps,* Centre Georges Pompidou (Paris: Pandora, 1983), 135–50. Basing his argument on Panof-

sky's conclusion with regard to the study of Piero della Francesca, that "the image is irreducible to the text, painting irreducible to the literary discourse it may want to 'translate'," Arasse thinks it possible to set definite limits to "Panofskian iconography." But in my opinion, he has not formulated the question of the relationship between iconography and text correctly. I believe that the 'literary source' should not be understood as a precise text (*ad litteram*), of which the pictorial form is then the translation, but only as the original (Urquelle) stimulus that set the artist's generative-creative process and technical skills in motion. In that way, the 'literary source' can be rediscovered in iconographic form as an expression of the 'person-as-artist/artist-as-person'—an expression mediated by the artist-person's 'intention-fantasy'. In other words, the literary source and, I would add, the circumstances of commission of the artwork stand in a relationship of 'vision' or 'intuition' to the artist. They do not influence the work of art except as 'inspiration', which takes concrete shape in the artist's expressive interpretation of them. They do not influence the artwork by 'formulating the image'; that is the exclusive province of the artist himself. (The distinction between 'formulating the image' and the 'taking of concrete shape' of the image is Cesare Brandi's; see Grassi, *Teorici e storia*, 27 ff.)

29. I refer to Panofsky's methodological orientation; see Panofsky, *Il significato*, 13.

30. I am referring to the 'principle of the primacy of genres' which Gombrich derived from D. E. Hirsch. See E. H. Gombrich, *Symbolic Images: Studies in the Art of the Renaissance* (Edinburgh: Phaidon, 1975), 5 ff. R. Bianchi Bandinelli, in his *Introduzione all'archeologia classica come storia dell'arte antica* (Rome/Bari: Laterza, 1976), 137, correctly specifies the two "moments" in the research process which are the special province of the art historian and which delineate the interpretive "category" of the work of art. First, there is the individuation of "the earlier iconographic schemata from which a given work of art descends, and in what way those schemata are or are not treated in an innovative fashion. Second, there is the definition of the ideological premises that determined the content of the work of art, and whether these were programmatic or not."

31. Frederick Antal, in his *Florentine Painting and Its Social Background* (London: Kegan, 1947), dedicated an entire chapter to "religious sentiment." The Hungarian historian understood that it was not possible to study Florentine fourteenth-century painting art without putting it into relation with religious life. He did not understand, however, that with this category he had failed to achieve specificity, even if one wanted to speak of "sentiment" and not of faith, dogma, doctrine and/or theology—of that "religious sentiment" which is found in evangelical faith. What is more, Antal treated the Florentines' faith (which was certainly open to criticism from many points of view) ideologically, reducing and practically invalidating it as a "social structure" owing to "economic causes." In this way, he lost contact with effective historical reality.

32. Gombrich, *Symbolic Images*, 15–16, says: "This symbolism can only function in support of what I have proposed to call the dominant meaning, the intended meaning or principal purpose of the picture."

33. Panofsky, *Il significato*, 33.

34. S. Settis, "Warburg 'continuatus': Descrizione di una biblioteca," *Quaderni storici*, n.s. 58 (1985): 5–39, esp. 38 n. 31.

35. Panofsky, *Il significato*, 40.

36. Lukács, *Estetica*, 810: "As long as the transcendent content which the allegorical work is called upon to express remains at the base of generally felt religiosity, the work exerts

its efficacy thanks to the weight of this faith, and its artistic qualities offer only accessory support. But if the transcendent content is forgotten, or even if it only undergoes a substantial change, the 'receiver' will find himself before something incomprehensible, because formal and figurative elements in themselves can never become real organs of mediation of concrete transcendent content." The user Lukács speaks of, without the support of faith, in order to overcome the contradiction in which he thus finds himself must culturally reconstruct the cosmos articulated by the 'sign' and the 'thing signified'; this is the prerequisite to any penetration of allegorical art (which is also objective, at least as regards the historical intentions made concrete in it by the artist). And this is the problem that arises every time we use language to articulate the relationship between a cultural referent and its 'sign'. Perhaps it should be noted that interpretation and criticism of art within the category of theology does not require that a critic be himself a man of faith or theologian in the strict sense. It does require, however, that the historian be knowledgeable about the 'faith-context' in which the work of art was generated.

37. Thomas Aquinas, *Contra impugnantes Dei cultum et religionem* 12, in *Opera omnia iussu Leonis XIII P. M. edita,* ed. Fratrum Praedicatorum, 41 vols. (Rome: Istitutum historicum ad Sanctae Sabinae, 1882–1970), 41:135A.

38. Ibid., 41:134A.

39. A. Serafini, *L'epopea cristiana nei dipinti di Beato Angelico* (Orvieto: Marsili, 1911), documents given in appendix, see p. 100.

40. Serafini, *L'epopea cristiana,* p. 101: ". . . quod fiat et pingatur in dicta cappella prout alias oretenus per venerabiles magistros sacre pagine huius civitatis consultum est."

41. Ibid., p. 122: "Et factis inter eos quam pluribus colloquiis deliberaverunt et ordinaverunt fore spectandum dictum magistrum pictorem et ipsum audiendum et deinde audito suo consilio ordinandum."

INDEX

INDEX

CHRISTIANITY AND THE RENAISSANCE

was composed in 10 on 12 Bembo on Digital Compugraphic equipment
by Metricomp;
with display type in Goudy Swash capitals with Bembo capitals and
display initials in Goudy Swash and Cloister;
printed by sheet-fed offset on 50-pound, acid-free Perkins & Squier Offset Smooth,
Smyth-sewn and bound over 88-point binder's boards in Holliston Roxite B,
and Smyth-sewn and bound with paper covers,
with paper covers printed in 2 colors,
by Braun-Brumfield, Inc.;
designed by Sara L. Eddy;
and published by

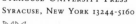

Syracuse, New York 13244-5160

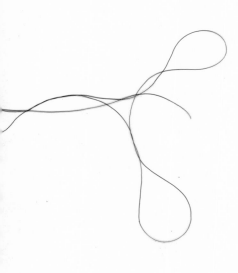